AFRICA DRAWN
one hundred cities

AFRICA DRAWN

one hundred cities

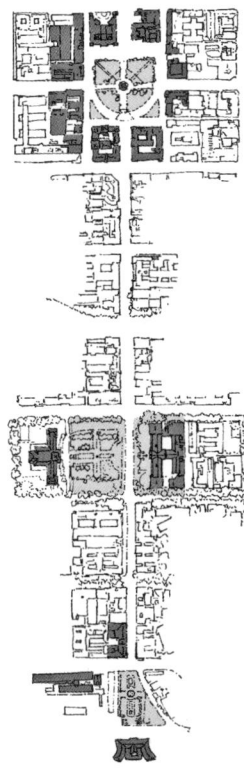

Gary White / Marguerite Pienaar / Bouwer Serfontein
Foreword by Elizabeth Plater-Zyberk

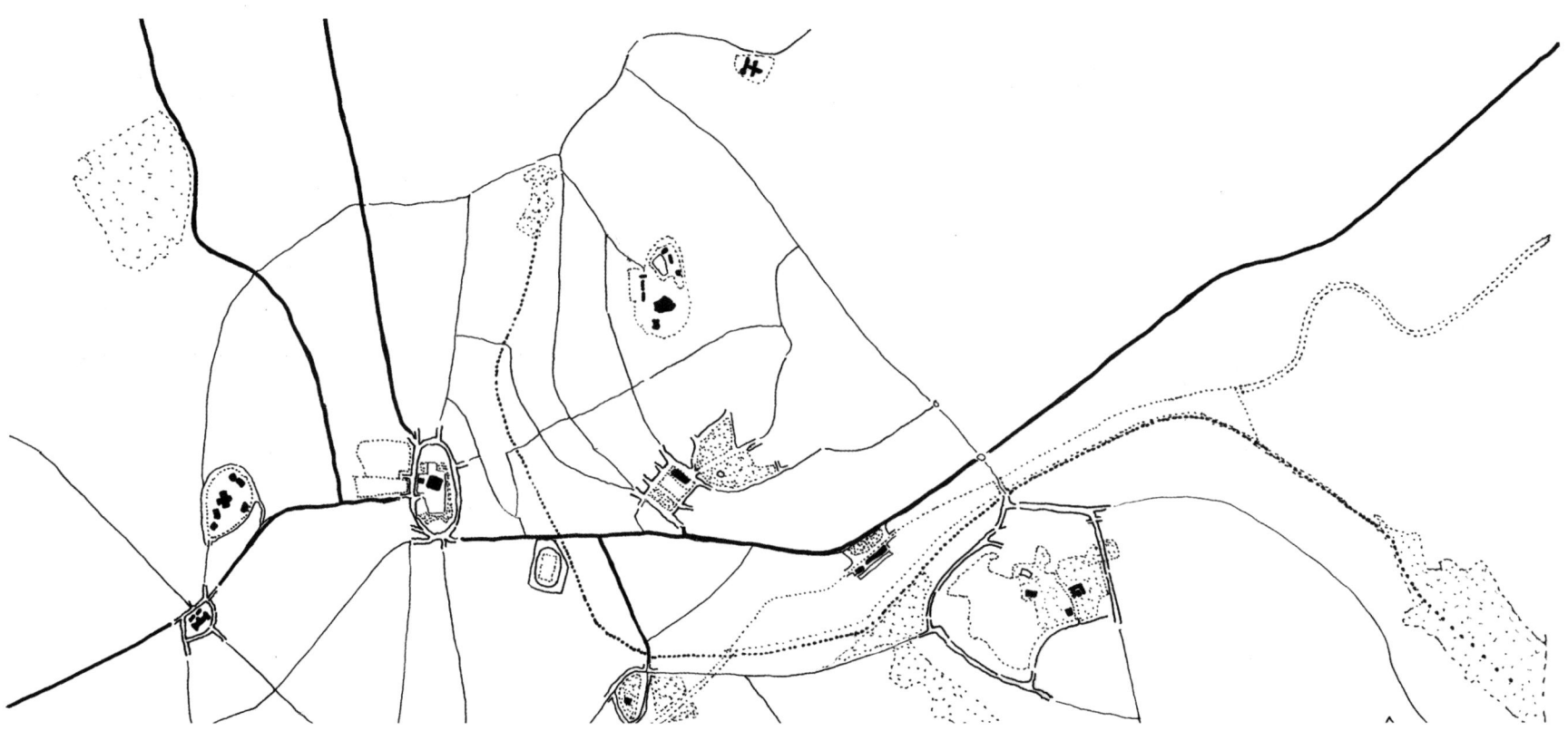

FOREWORD

THE PUBLICATION OF THIS BOOK about urban design in Africa coincides with the new international concern for place-making. The term "place-making" refers to the design and management of public spaces that provide a focus for community activity, identity and well-being.

Cities are the principal destinations or hubs of a global network of mobility. At a smaller scale but in the same manner, each city is made of networks of mobility interspersed with the public spaces that accommodate the activities of commerce, governance, and culture. This duality of public space – corridors of mobility as well as nodes of interaction – evident throughout this book, is the structure of place-making.

The corridors and public spaces of the city support the private aggregations – mixed-use neighborhoods, residential compounds, as well as institutional and business districts – that allow an endless variety of character. Some are culturally singular, others have been layered over time; some are controlled and gated, while others are permeable; some are developed in a top-down process of large-scale design through governmental, institutional or corporate policy, others evolved in a bottom-up sequence of small-scale and informal decisions taken in common; some are organised by geometry, others by informality. Public space mediates the contradictions of private development.

Common to all the cities documented in this book is this structure of place-making, the dispersal of focal places connected by routes. This essential make-up accommodates the centuries-old influences of outsiders overlaying patterns established by indigenous societies.

In most cases, the literature of cities focuses on their problems. The analysis of global economic forces, environmental degradation, infrastructure shortfalls and political volatility sometimes paint a bleak picture of the future well-being of societies with multiplying urban populations. More effective for an urban vision might be a review of the positive characteristics of the place, and its historical form, as a guide for intention and action. The history of a place may be the only shared experience of a diverse society. Graphic documentation reveals this historical layering as a response to the specific conditions of the place.

Africa Drawn: One Hundred Cities presents the historic character of place as a valuable resource for imagining the future of the continent's cities. Its simple and beautiful drawings document the characteristic places of 100 cities in a comparative method. These provide information equivalently for each, across a scale that ranges from its location on the continent and within its country, to its relationship to the greater city, and to the details of the buildings, pavements and landscapes of its special places. This is a catalogue that shows how rich the repertoire is, how endemic to the continent are intentional forms of public space, and how one might call upon the past to envision the evolution of the African city.

Elizabeth Plater-Zyberk, FAIA
Partner, Duany Plater-Zyberk and Company
Malcolm Matheson Distinguished Professor of Architecture
University of Miami School of Architecture

INTRODUCTION

CITIES ARE THE PHYSICAL MANIFESTATIONS of a culture or a combination of cultures, reflecting major influences and development forces. Any attempt to classify or categorise them will be incomplete and based on generalisations. However, it is still a worthwhile attempt to use a comparative method to increase the understanding of an urban phenomenon. The approach of this book is an effort to map the urban form and structure of some African cities, and to describe and illustrate how these different cities and places were formed. Compared to other continents, very few publications exist on urban design for African cities. African history and urban processes are often described in terms of a European point of view, and mostly from a socio-economic or socio-political perspective. Capital city status, along with the extent of infrastructural connectedness, were taken as points of departure in the selection of these cities.

The more connected a city, the more it will be open to outside influences and wider cultural modification during the city-building process. The dominant culture – along with its political and administrative forces – has the most significant impact on the original establishment and development of the urban structure. In the development of the African urbanisation process, colonial or imported cultural influences modified the existing urban structure, but in most cases it created a new colonial city or a city alongside the existing urban structure. This is evident in a number of cities where the urban core consists mainly of a colonial layout based on Western, Roman or Islamic ordering principles. After the handover of political power, these colonial urban cores were either modified by the indigenous cultures or sprawling urban areas clustered around these cores – based on the local subdivision of land. Densification and/or a lack of development control had a major impact on the development of the cities after the colonial era.

SUBDIVISION OF LAND
INDIGENOUS SUBDIVISION

The resultant urban structure and form of a city are primarily guided by typography, cultural-ordering principles, original intent, and the system of land subdivision. In Africa, the subdivision of land is usually based on communal land that is subdivided (claimed or allocated) by the community for private or exclusive use. Land is seldom sold and is usually allocated by means of a common agreement or decree by the ruler (or state). This system of the subdivision of land is not only applicable in rural areas but also in many urban areas. Public or communal land is subdivided, or private land is demarcated out of communal land in order to create allotments. Land is then managed or controlled by either a family or an individual. Access to resources like water or grazing, as well as the respect for certain linkages or paths, modified the definition of allotments.

The result of this land-subdivision process creates a fine-grain pedestrian-based layout. Communal areas that are left unspoilt are respected and used by the community as a whole. The line between private and public space is delineated by agreement and enforced by the community. It is therefore a negotiated boundary. Although these demarcations are respected, they are seldom mapped or described in writing and therefore easily modified. Consequently, the urban structure is often geometrically complex and irregular, and is the result of individual decisions connected only by common agreement rather than by geometric order. Land-use rights and the extent of the allocated area are embedded in the cultural knowledge and communicated verbally to the next generations.

IMPORTED or COLONIAL SUBDIVISION

For a colonial power land subdivision was based on the requirements of the settlers and to enforce administrative control. Therefore, the grid was the most effective way to subdivide and allocate land to people and institutions. Some of the layouts were based on City Beautiful or Garden City principles and the urban structure was developed to erect state buildings and to express the imperial dominance.

European or capitalist (private or state-owned) land was subdivided and sold, or allocated and owned for private use. The land was then allocated with certain land-use rights and the remainder of the land was handed over as public land: be it streets, squares or areas allocated for public institutions. Subdivision was usually geometric and based on the system of land surveying according to certain rules and laws. Land was transferred to and owned by the individual owner and used according to laws and rules that were documented and described in the title deeds. The urban structure that reflected these cultural principles was thereby regular, organised, fixed and enforced.

In the examples explained in this book a clear definition can be seen between the indigenous and colonial way of subdivision of land. In some cases, the regular grid used by the colonial powers was modified due to cultural requirements, urbanisation pressure and/or lack of control. For some institutional planners this is seen as "cadastral vandalism" as it negates the original intent of the controlling forces. Humanisation of the urban structure by the indigenous people is seen as decay and lack of order.

After the withdrawal of the colonial power, the urban order was either maintained or modified while the land was transferred back to communal or state control. In other cases, the land was handed over to the state and the control mechanisms were enforced and maintained. If the land was handed over to the community, the structure was modified over time to accommodate the needs that were not accommodated by the colonial power.

African cities that were developed after the colonial era used a modified colonial system of land subdivision. Cities like Abuja in Nigeria and Nouakchott in Mauritania were developed as new cities and capitals due to the central position required after independence. As these cities were developed based on Modernist or Civic Design principles, a coarse grain and car-based urban structure was employed. These cities have a dispersed and car-based layout with low density and a zoning system to control the land uses.

TYPES OF URBAN FORMS

Anthony O'Connor (1983) developed a number of urban typologies for African cities in his book AFRICAN CITIES. Although the typologies are not exhaustive, it provides a useful way to categorise the complexity of the cities selected. O'Connor's effort led him to establish six possible types in total, which reflect the diverse and heterogeneous nature of African cities. The following descriptions are quoted from this publication:

INDIGENOUS CITIES

The lack of any sharp cultural distinction between the urban and rural population, the cohesion of large kinship units, and the dependence of many town dwellers on farming for their livelihood, have caused some observers to question whether these are truly "urban" settlements at all. However, provided the term is not defined in a narrow ethnocentric way, they surely did represent one form of urbanism, even in the past.

ISLAMIC CITIES

The term "the Islamic city" has been used for some forms of urbanism, for they owe much to Islam and have much in common with the "traditional" cities of the Middle East (Costello: 1977, Blake and Lawless: 1980). There is much debate on how far these cities can be regarded as indigenous to tropical Africa and how far they represent an urban tradition brought across the Sahara. To some extent they vary among themselves in this regard. In many cases the idea of urban life was imported, and some of these cities were founded by invaders from far outside the local area.

COLONIAL CITIES

Europeans created numerous towns for their own purposes of administration and trade, playing a critical role in the process of colonial political domination and in the extraction of profit by colonial business enterprises. Many of those that have prospered are ports developed at the main points of contact between the colonial powers and the local population. In some cases the new town absorbed one or more traditional African settlements, but it was generally immigration that ensured an African majority among the population from the earliest years.

"EUROPEAN" CITIES

The fourth group of cities might be regarded as a special case of the colonial city, but from the point of view of urban traditions they are quite distinct. They might even be regarded as the true "colonial" cities in the original sense of a colony as a place of permanent new settlement. However, the word is not normally used in this sense in writing on tropical Africa – nor in the most notable recent studies. Inevitably there was some interaction with the local population from the start, since they also came under the new territorial administration, and since they offered a source of cheap labour.

DUAL CITIES

Among the most interesting of African cities are those which combined elements of two or more of the types already considered in sectors that can be clearly distinguished in the layout. The two very distinct parts are broadly comparable in their number of residents, although the newer part is considerably larger in extent, and is itself subdivided into what was essentially the European quarter and the zones that were set aside for migrants.

HYBRID CITIES

This final category is reserved for those cities that combine indigenous and alien elements in roughly equal proportions, but which are to a large extent integrated, rather than merely juxtaposed as in the dual city. While various other examples of hybrid cities could have been found at any time during this century, it is probable that up to the time of independence, most of the cities of Africa could appropriately have been fitted into one of the other categories. It is possible that this is no longer the case, and that the urbanisation processes occurring in each type of city over the past twenty years have been making it more of a hybrid.

CITIES IN THE BOOK

The illustrations and descriptions of the selected cities mostly show the urban form, structure and major structuring elements. This is in essence a distillation of the urban complexity and an attempt to describe some of the unique structural elements of the cities. The description is an attempt to explain the origin, reason for being and the main distinguishing features. This book should be seen as an introduction to the understanding of African urbanism from an Urban Design perspective. The study could be expanded to create a series of more detailed volumes to describe each city as a PLACE in more detail. It could also explain the urban processes more comprehensively. With more detailed investigation and study, the unique complexities and sense of place of the cities should be more clearly understood.

Gerrit Jordaan
Director, GWA/HolmJordaan
Member of the international Institute of Urban Design (IfUD) and the Urban Design Institute of South Africa (UDISA)

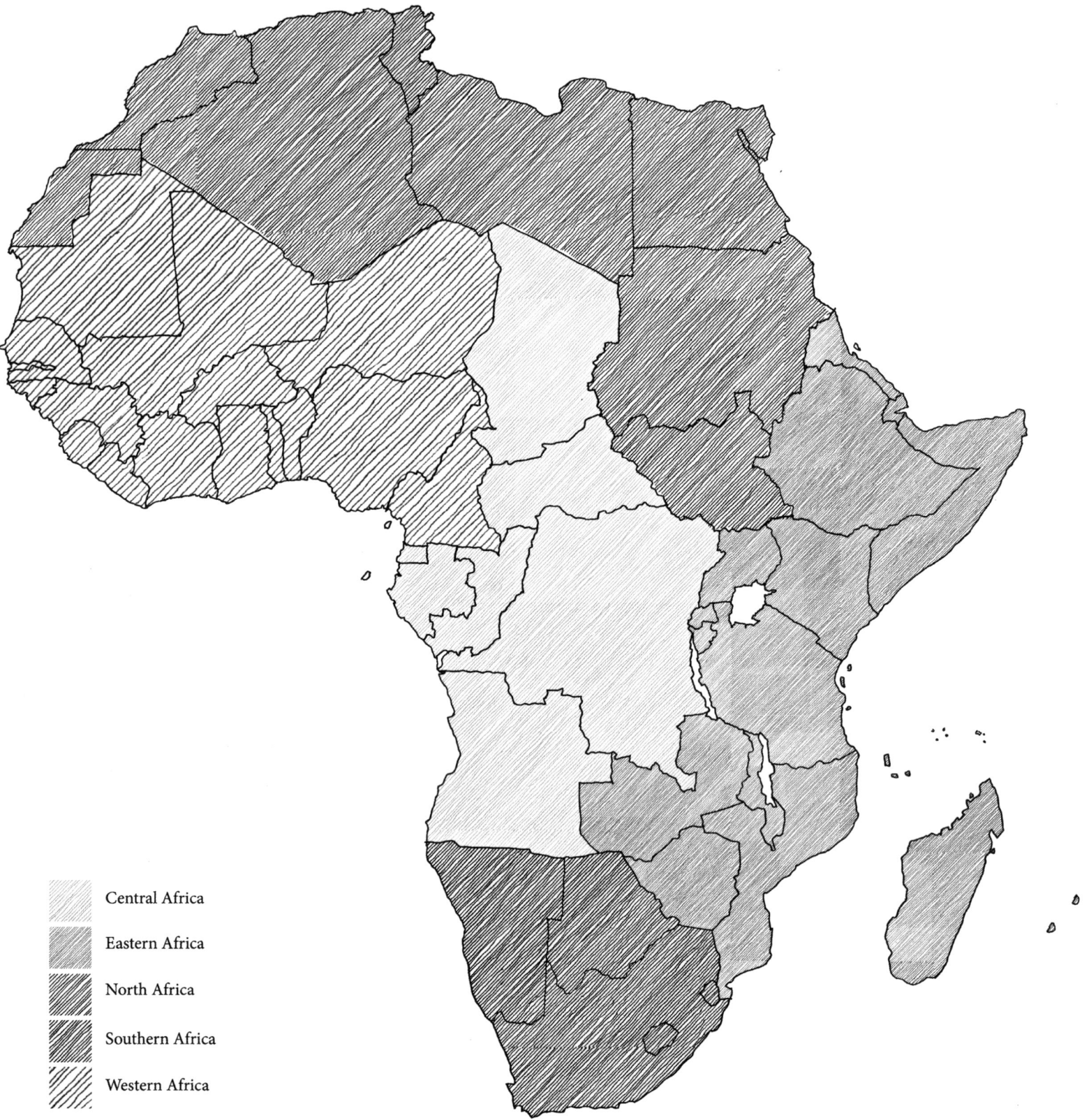

CENTRAL AFRICA

ANGOLA	Huambo	11
	Luanda	13
CAMEROON	Douala	15
	Yaoundé	17
CENTRAL AFRICAN REPUBLIC	Bangui	19
CHAD	N'Djamena	21
DR CONGO	Kinshasa	23
	Lubumbashi	25
EQUATORIAL GUINEA	Bata	27
	Malabo	29
GABON	Libreville	31
REPUBLIC OF THE CONGO	Brazzaville	33
	Pointe-Noire	35
SÃO TOMÉ AND PRINCIPE	São Tomé	37

EASTERN AFRICA

BURUNDI	Bujumbura	39
COMORES	Moroni	41
REPUBLIC OF DJIBOUTI	Djibouti City	43
ERITREA	Asmara	45
	Massawa	47
ETHIOPIA	Addis Aba(e)ba	49
	Aksum (Axum)	51
	Gondar	53
	Harar	55
KENYA	Mombasa	57
	Nairobi	59
MADAGASCAR	Antananarivo	61
	Antsiranana	63
	Toamasina	65
MALAWI	Lilongwe	67
MAURITIUS	Port Louis	69
MOZAMBIQUE	Beira	71
	Ilha	73
	Maputo	75
RWANDA	Kigali	77
SEYCHELLES	Victoria	79
SOMALIA	Mogadishu	81
SOUTH SUDAN	Juba	83
TANZANIA	Dar es Salaam	85
	Dodoma	87
	Zanzibar	89
UGANDA	Kampala	91
ZAMBIA	Lusaka	93
ZIMBABWE	Harare	95

NORTH AFRICA

ALGERIA	Algiers	97
	Annaba	99
	Constantine	101
	Oran	103
EGYPT	Alexandria	105
	Cairo	107
	Luxor	109
	Port Said	111

NORTH AFRICA

LIBYA	Tripoli	113
MOROCCO	Casablanca	115
	Fes (Fez)	117
	Marrakech	119
	Meknes	121
	Rabat	123
SUDAN	Khartoum	125
TUNISIA	Kairouan	127
	Sfax	129
	Tunis	131
WESTERN SAHARA	Laâyoune (El Aaiún)	133

SOUTHERN AFRICA

BOTSWANA	Gabarone	135
NAMIBIA	Windhoek	137
LESOTHO	Maseru	139
SOUTH AFRICA	Cape Town	141
	Durban	143
	Bloemfontein	145
	Johannesburg	147
	Port Elizabeth	149
	Pretoria	151
SWAZILAND	Mbabane	153

WESTERN AFRICA

BENIN	Cotonou	155
	Porto-Novo	157
BURKINA FASO	Bobo-Dioulasso	159
	Ouagadougou	161
CAPE VERDE	Praia	163
	Mindelo	165
	São Filipe	167
CÔTE D'IVOIRE	Abidjan	169
	Yamoussoukro	171
THE GAMBIA	Banjul	173
GHANA	Accra	175
	Kumasi	177
GUINEA-BISSAU	Bissau	179
GUINEA	Conakry	181
LIBERIA	Monrovia	183
MALI	Bamako	185
	Mopti	187
	Timbuktu	189
MAURITANIA	Nouakchott	191
	Rosso	193
NIGER	Niamey	195
NIGERIA	Abuja	197
	Ibadan	199
	Lagos	201
SENEGAL	Dakar	203
	Saint-Louis	205
SIERRA LEONE	Freetown	207
TOGO	Lomé	209

HUAMBO, ANGOLA

FOUNDED: 1912
AREA: 2,609 km²
POPULATION (2008): 325,207
DENSITY: 120/km²
GPS: 12° 46'35.05"S, 15° 44'5.30"E

Huambo, formerly known as Nova Lisboa (New Lisbon), is Angola's second largest city, centrally located in the Angolan highlands and linked to the Atlantic Ocean port of Lobito and the neighbouring Democratic Republic of the Congo and Zambia by the Benguela railway.

Huambo, originally designed by Portuguese General Norton de Matos, was established in 1912. The city was envisioned as the new capital of Angola, and until independence in 1975, was one of the most important urban centres in Angola. Nova Lisboa was renamed Huambo after independence from Portugal in 1975. The Angolan Civil War (1975–2002) halted the development in Angola and Huambo, destroying a great part of its infrastructure.

The city structure resembles Portuguese-influenced spatial organisation, based on the notion of a garden city (a city with a green belt and planned areas for residence, services, industry and agriculture). "Indigenous quarters" were created at a time when all colonial powers promoted racial segregation in residential and social areas. The city environment comprises squares and avenues, with façades and buildings that are representative of Portuguese colonial architecture of this period.

A new plan was ellaborated during 1946–1947 after the intervention of the *Gabinete de Urbanização do Ultramar* ("Overseas Urbanisation Office") whose experts were scandalised by the width of the streets and squares in a city with fewer than 3,500 whites and "civilised" mixed people. Areas designed for hotels and parks were eliminated, residential areas for Europeans were extended and new "indigenous quarters" were planned.

The uniqueness of Huambo's urban design is the theme of the polygonal and radiating plan (with a centred, hexa- or octagonal matrix), replacing the former nineteenth-century grid model. The plan by Carlos Roma Machado was restricted to a single square/roundabout [1] from which eight rectilinear avenues radiated. The simplicity of the design was clear in the street grid and on the definition and size of the land plots. Republican anti-clericalism explains the unusual lack of a church in the original layout with just a chapel "for all kinds of worship" in the cemetery [15].

Huambo was one of the most interesting and complete experiments in Portuguese formal urbanism. The civil war had a detrimental effect on the city's infrastructure and buildings, but these are gradually being renewed as the economy improves and businesses reinvest. Huambo is one of Angola's most rapidly growing cities with a population growth estimated at 6 percent annually between 2010 and 2020.

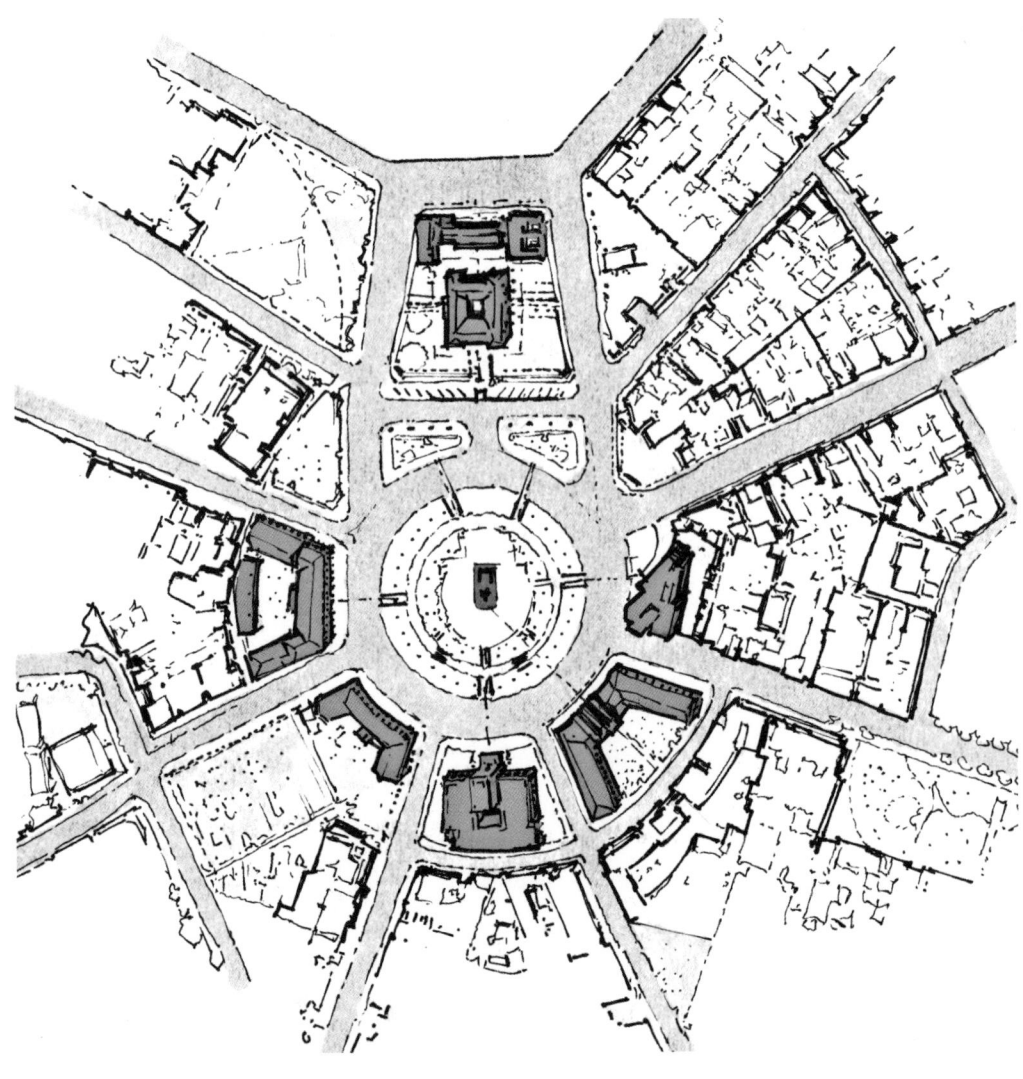

1 September 11th Square
2 Governor's Palace
3 Garden of Culture
4 Regional Library/
  Norton Matos Statues
5 New Huambo Pavilion
6 Greenhouse/Park
7 Municipal Museum
8 Regional Hospital
9 Church of Our Lady of Fatima
10 Cinema Petro
11 Military Hospital
12 Railway Station
13 Cinema Ruacaná
14 St Peter's Church
15 Municipal Cemetery
16 Road towards Benguela
17 Stadium
18 Avenue of the Republic
   leading towards the airport
19 Huambo Cathedral

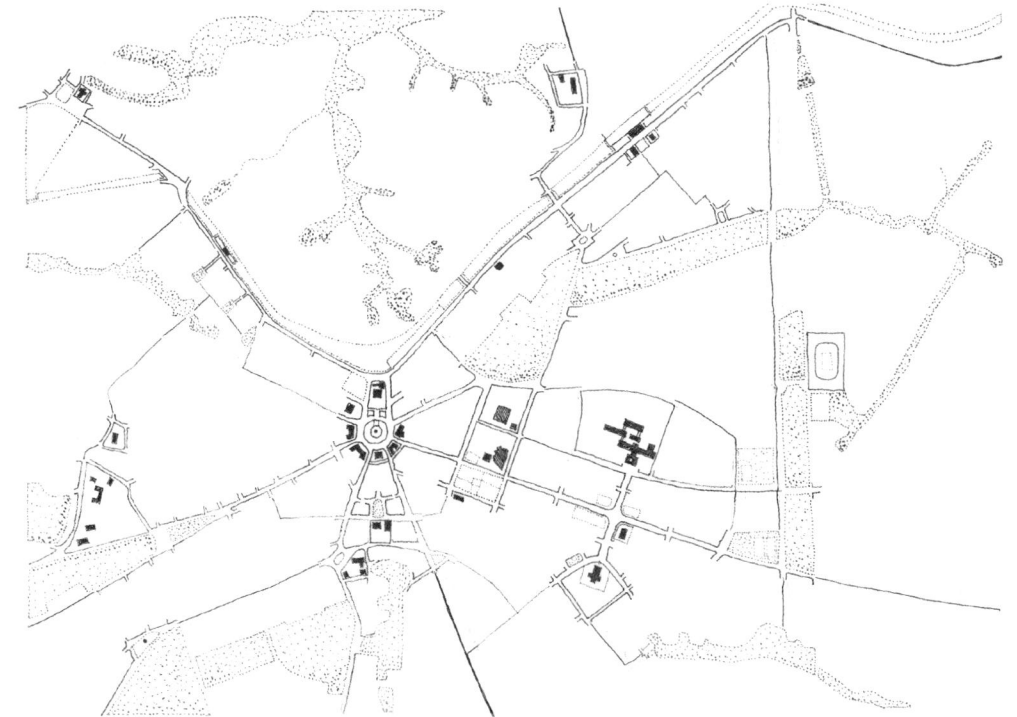

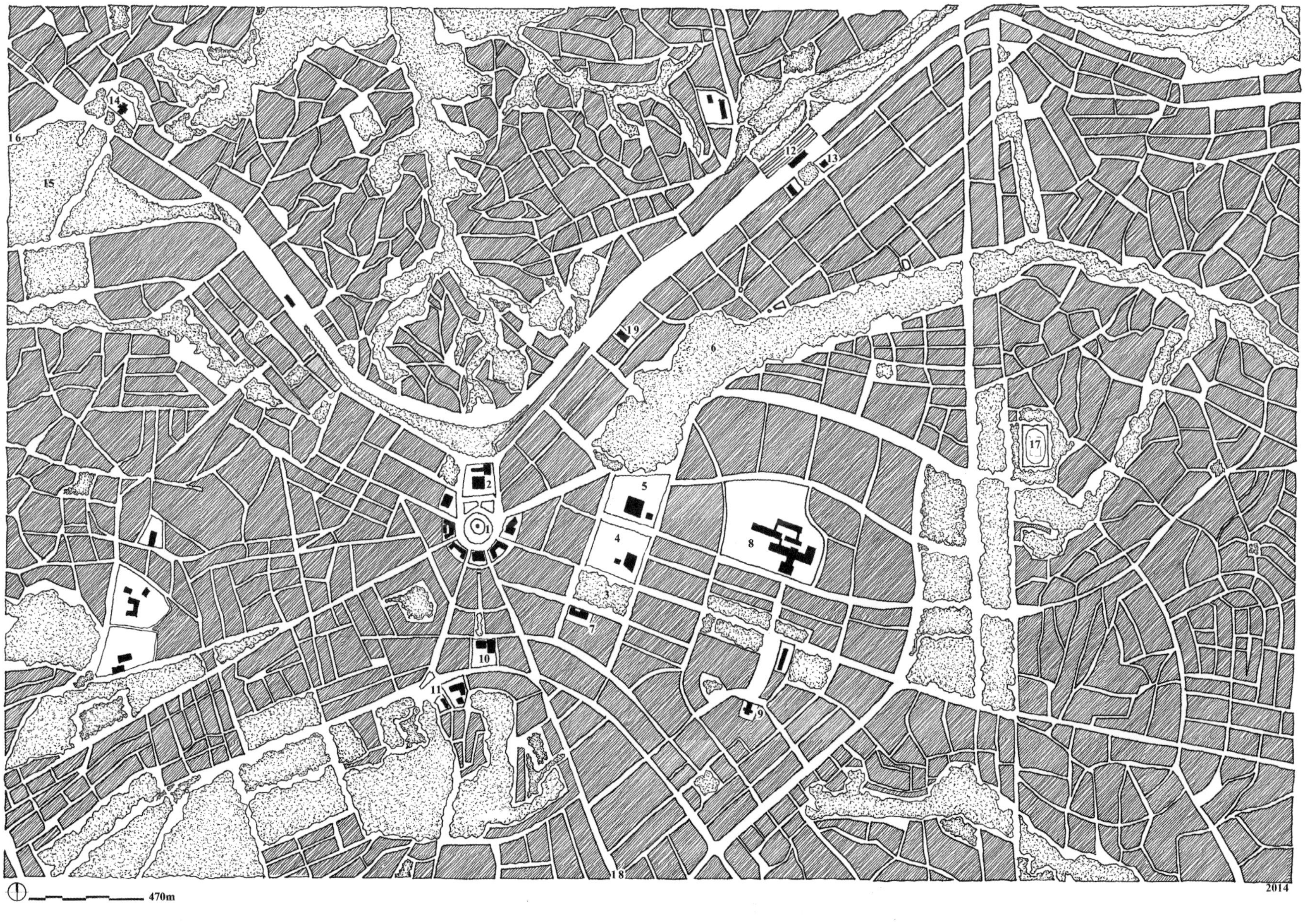

LUANDA, ANGOLA

FOUNDED: 1575
AREA: 113 km²
POPULATION (2011): 2,825,331
DENSITY: 25,000/km²
GPS: 8° 48'9.74"S, 13° 14'31.83"E

Luanda, capital of Angola, formerly known as São Paulo da Assunção de Loanda, is the second largest city in the subregion of central Africa with over five million inhabitants. Located on the coast of the Atlantic Ocean, Luanda is Angola's primary seaport connecting Angola with the rest of the world. Luanda was originally founded by Portuguese explorer Paulo Dias de Novais in 1576. The city was originally designed by the colonial Portuguese planners for approximately 5,000 people, a tenth of its current population. Luanda is rapidly expanding to attempt to deal with the current steep population growth of approximately 5.77 percent per decade. Luanda is presumed to be a megacity in waiting with a projected population of 8.9 million in the year 2025.

The city is infamous for being the world's most expensive city for expatriates, formerly known as the 'Paris of Africa'. Corporate and multinational oil companies are investing in city infrastructure, pushing inner-city costs higher, and consequently, the urban poor to the peripheries of the city. Luanda's slum population was estimated at 86.5 percent in 2005 – these informal settlements are known as musseques.

The fortress, Fortaleza de São Miguel, today known as Museu das Forças Armadas (Museum of the Armed Forces) [1], was built by the Portuguese in 1576 and is Luanda's oldest surviving building. The structure was used as the administrative centre of Luanda during the early part of the Portuguese colonial rule and was a self-contained city for the early military battalion and an important holding place for slaves. The Augostinho Neto Mausoleum, a towering obelisk structure, is dedicated to Augostinho Neto, the first president of Angola who helped in Angola's struggle for independence.

Luanda's city structure is composed of various centres. In the middle (Ingombotas and Maianga) the oldest colonial town is divided into Baixa de Luanda (lower Luanda, from the port to the fortress [1]), Cidade Alta (upper city, where the presidential palace [6] is situated), and Ilha do Cabo (a peninsula surrounding the bay, with beaches and expensive nightclubs, bars and restaurants). Behind and above the historic centre, central bairros include Maianga and Alvalade (mostly residential) and Miramar (with embassies), as well as Kinaxixe and Maculusso, which are characterised by Portuguese apartment blocks. Further outside the centre, the neighbourhoods become more informal (self-construction), dotted with 1970s Cuban apartment blocks and new developments. In the south, luxury gated communities (condominiums) dominate.

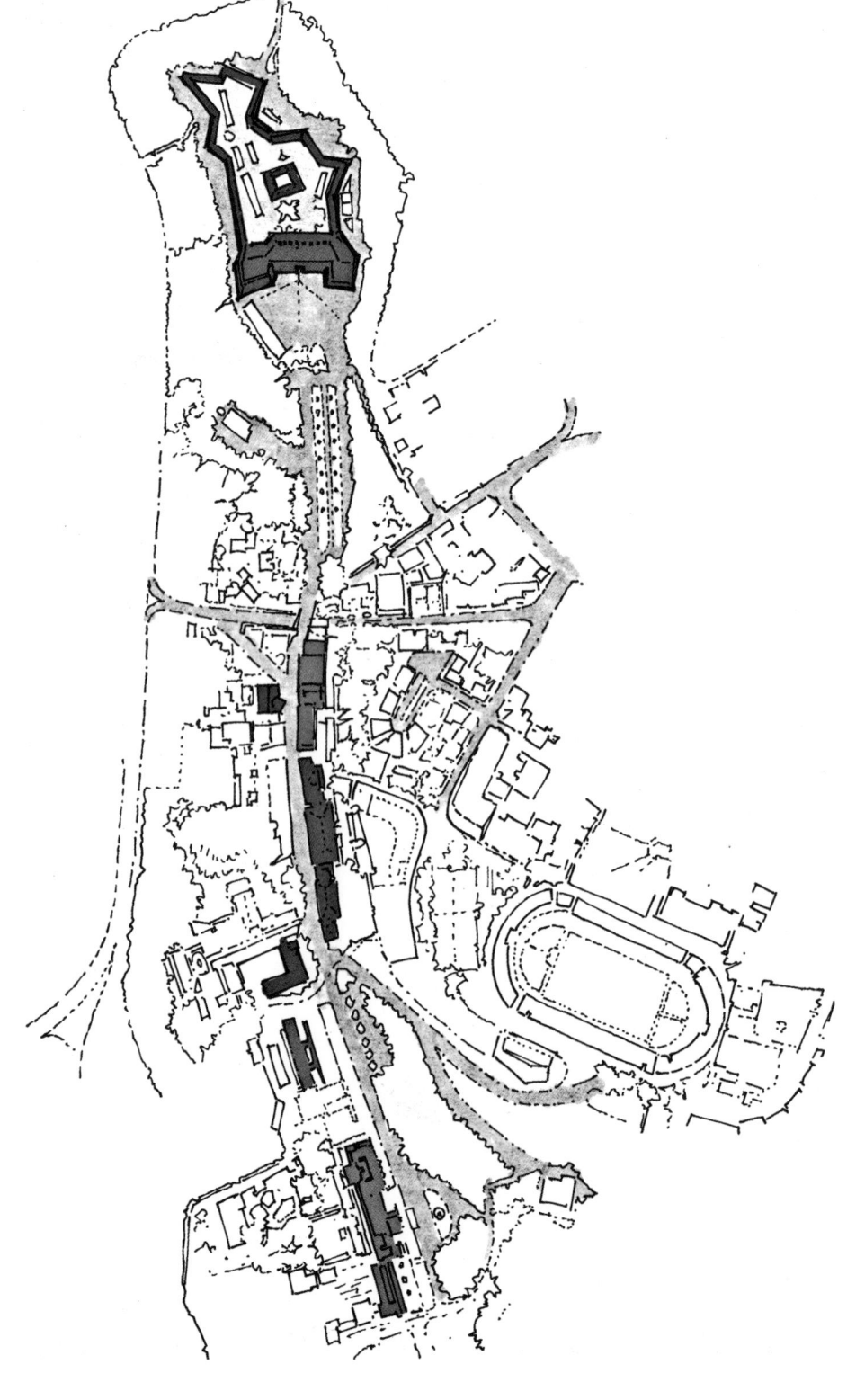

1 Museum of the Armed Forces
2 Ministry of Health
3 Embassy of the United Kingdom
4 Prince Henrique Square
5 National Directorate of Immigration and Borders
6 Government Palace
7 Garden of the High City
8 Church of the Jesuits
9 Ministry of Justice
10 National Press
11 Constitutional Court
12 Church, Our Lady of Remedios
13 National Bank of Angola
14 Iron Palace
15 Museum of Natural History
16 Church of Our Lady of Nazareth 1644
17 Pelourinho Square
18 Mutamba Square
19 Provincial Government, Luanda
20 Irene Cohen Square
21 Carmo Church
22 Amílcar Cabral Square
23 Lumeji Square
24 September 17th Square
25 Ministry of Commerce
26 Port of Luanda
27 Ambiente Square
28 Alto das Cruzes Cemetery
29 Miramar Park
30 Miramar Cinema & Alioune Blondin Beye Park
31 Garden of Urban Oasis
32 Miramar Market
33 Train Station and Port, Luanda
34 Office of the Ombudsman
35 Freedom Park
36 Palace of Congresses
37 Courthouse
38 Ministry of Defence
39 New Government Assembly
40 St Joseph Centre (Ex. Carmelo)
41 Jo-sina Machel Hospital
42 Maianga Square
43 Largo Lenine, Lenine Square
44 Institute of Educational Sciences
45 Sa-grada Familia Church & Military Hospital
46 Avenue of the October Revolution leading towards the airport
47 José Marti Park
48 Agostinho Neto University
49 Rio de Janeiro Square
50 4th February International Airport
51 Independence Square
52 N'jinga M'bande School
53 Medium Industrial Institute of Luanda
54 Soweto Square
55 Cinema Atlantic
56 D. João II Road
57 Estádio Nacional

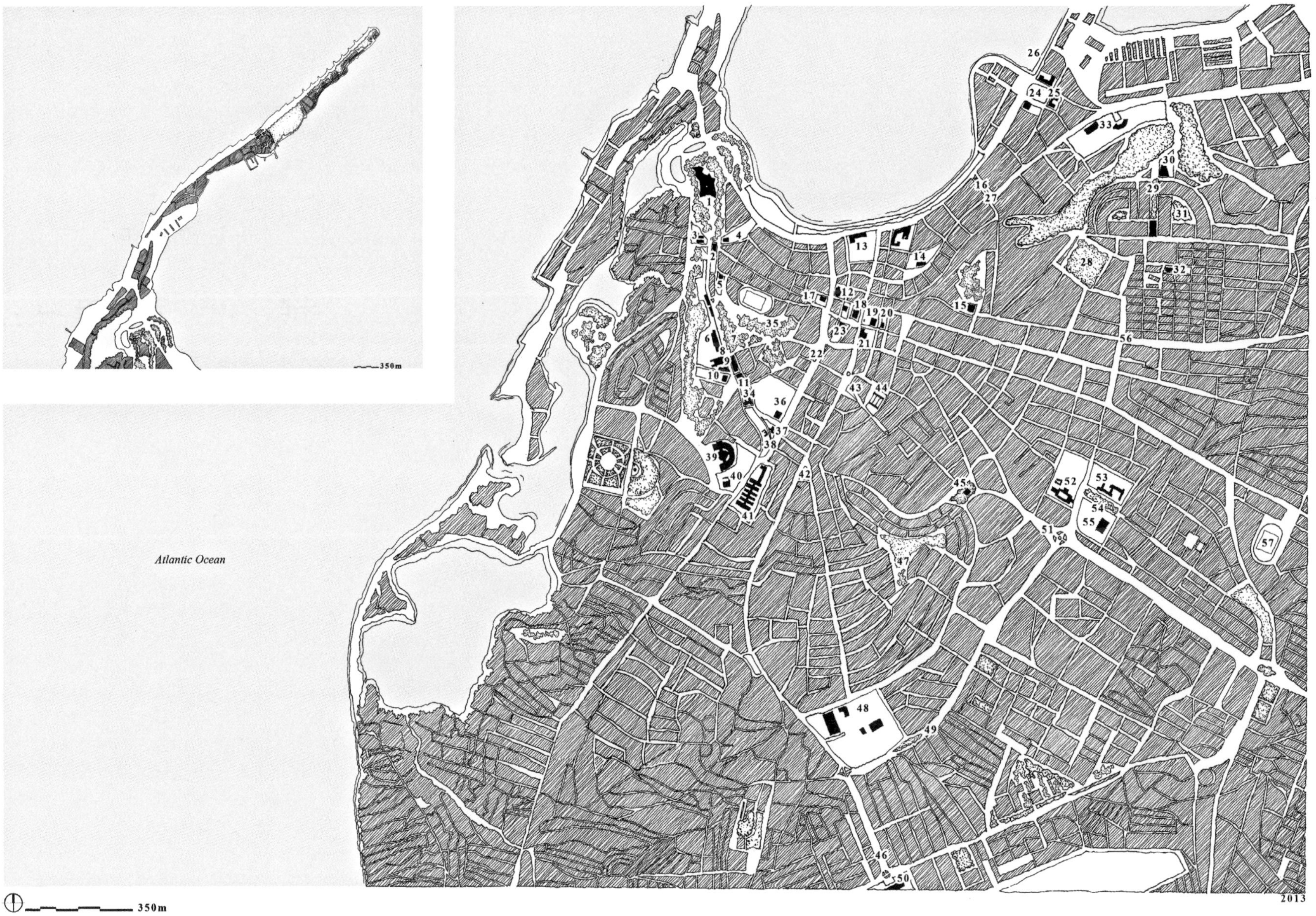

CENTRAL AFRICA 13

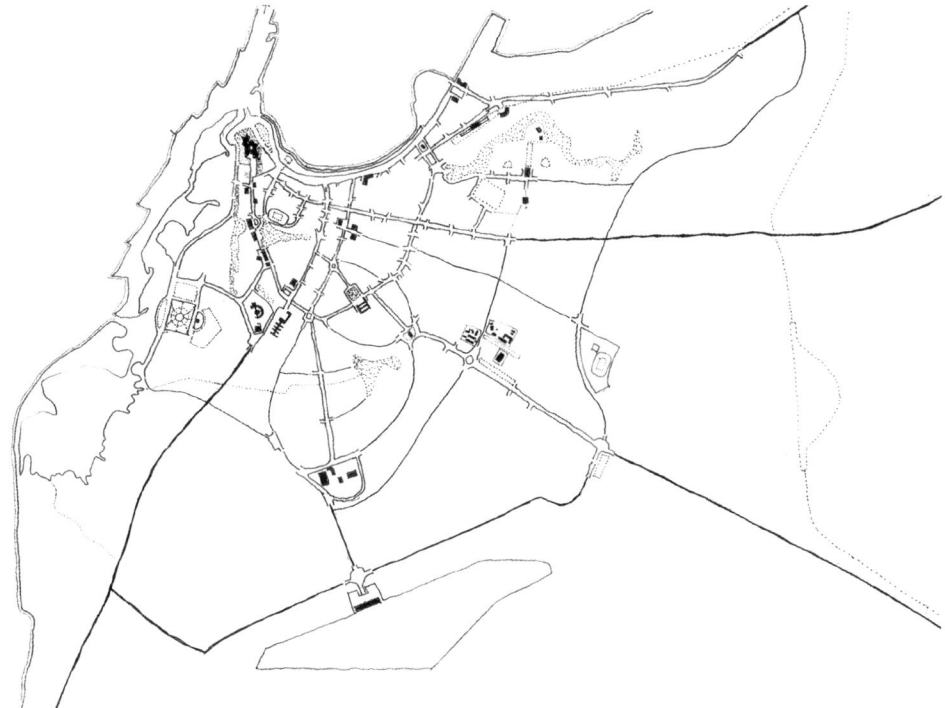

Atlantic Ocean

DOUALA, CAMEROON

FOUNDED: 1900
AREA: 210 km²
POPULATION (2012): 2,446,945
DENSITY: 11,652/km²
GPS: 4° 2'34.54"N, 9° 41'11.89"E

Douala is the largest city in Cameroon and the capital of Cameroon's Littoral Region. Cameroon's largest port and its major international airport, Douala International Airport, is located in Douala, the commercial capital of the country.

This port city is located on the opposing banks of the Wouri River. The two sides are linked by Bonaberi Bridge. The city of Douala originated with four villages, established by Douala families on the banks of the river. Bell (Bonandjo), Akwa and Deido (Bonabela) follow the course of the left bank and face Bonabéri on the other side of the river. These four villages were the origins of the largest neighbourhoods of Douala.

Water was the shaping factor for early settlement in Douala. As Danièle Diwouta-Kotto explains, '[T]he people in Douala are water people'. The river is considered a source of life and wealth, a place for trade and fishing and all the villages were established right up to the shore. Although settlements had already existed before the arrival of the Portuguese, British, and Germans, the city rapidly developed as a commercial and political hub of the German colonial administration during the German colonisation.

Douala is divided into seven districts (Akwa, Bassa, Bonabéri, Bonapriso, Bonanjo, Deïdo and New Bell) with more than 120 neighbourhoods. Akwa, historically referred to as Plateau Joss, is Douala's business district and Bonanjo its administrative district.

Basic plans for the city existed, but were elaborated in 1956 by the architect Danièle Diwouta-Kotto. The Dorian Plan provided Douala with a framework for improvement. The plan was designed for an urban population of 300,000 inhabitants, and primarily focused on the highway, the remodelling of some areas and the creation of new neighbourhoods to enhance the city's use of space and make it more breathable. The plan consisted of the establishment of a network of roads allowing intercommunication between districts, moving the railroad from the southern part, the creation of a major road from east to west between Douala and Bonabéri, and clustering the industries around the port with the creation of a second dock on the right. As with most other African cities, Douala is poorly geared to accommodate the rapidly increasing urban population affecting the city's provision of services and its ability to cope with the rapid growth.

1 Government Place
2 Central Post Office
3 Courthouse
4 Doual'art
5 Douala Museum
6 French Cultural Centre
7 Armed Forces
8 Douala Port
9 Bus Station and Market
10 Cathedral of Saints Peter and Paul
11 Joss School
12 Maritime and Sabena Museum

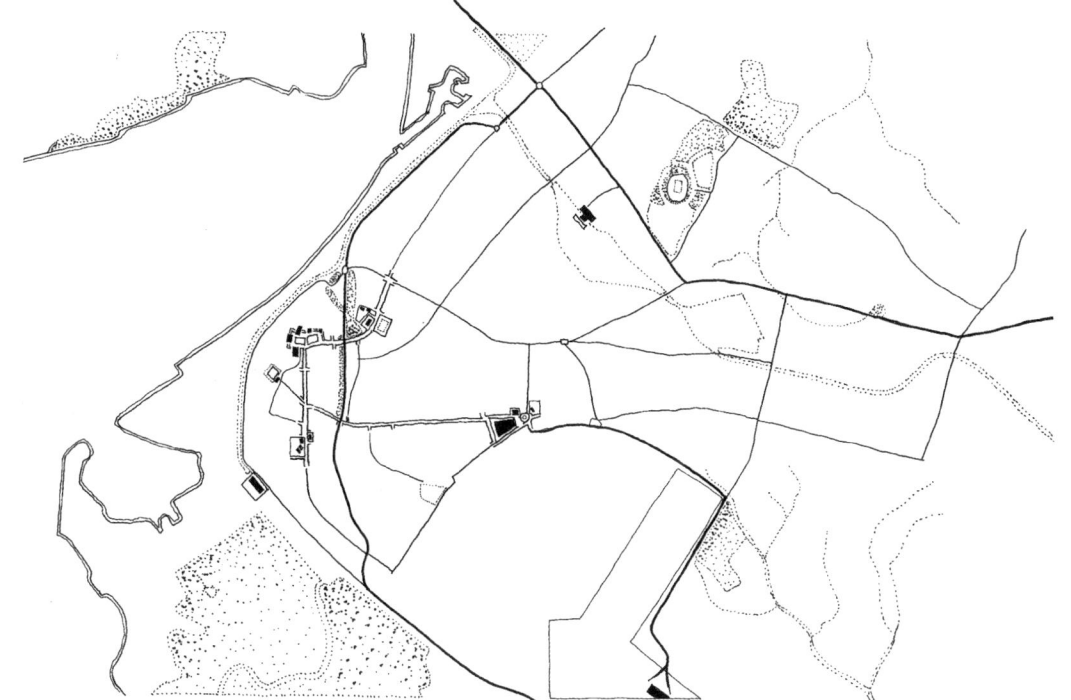

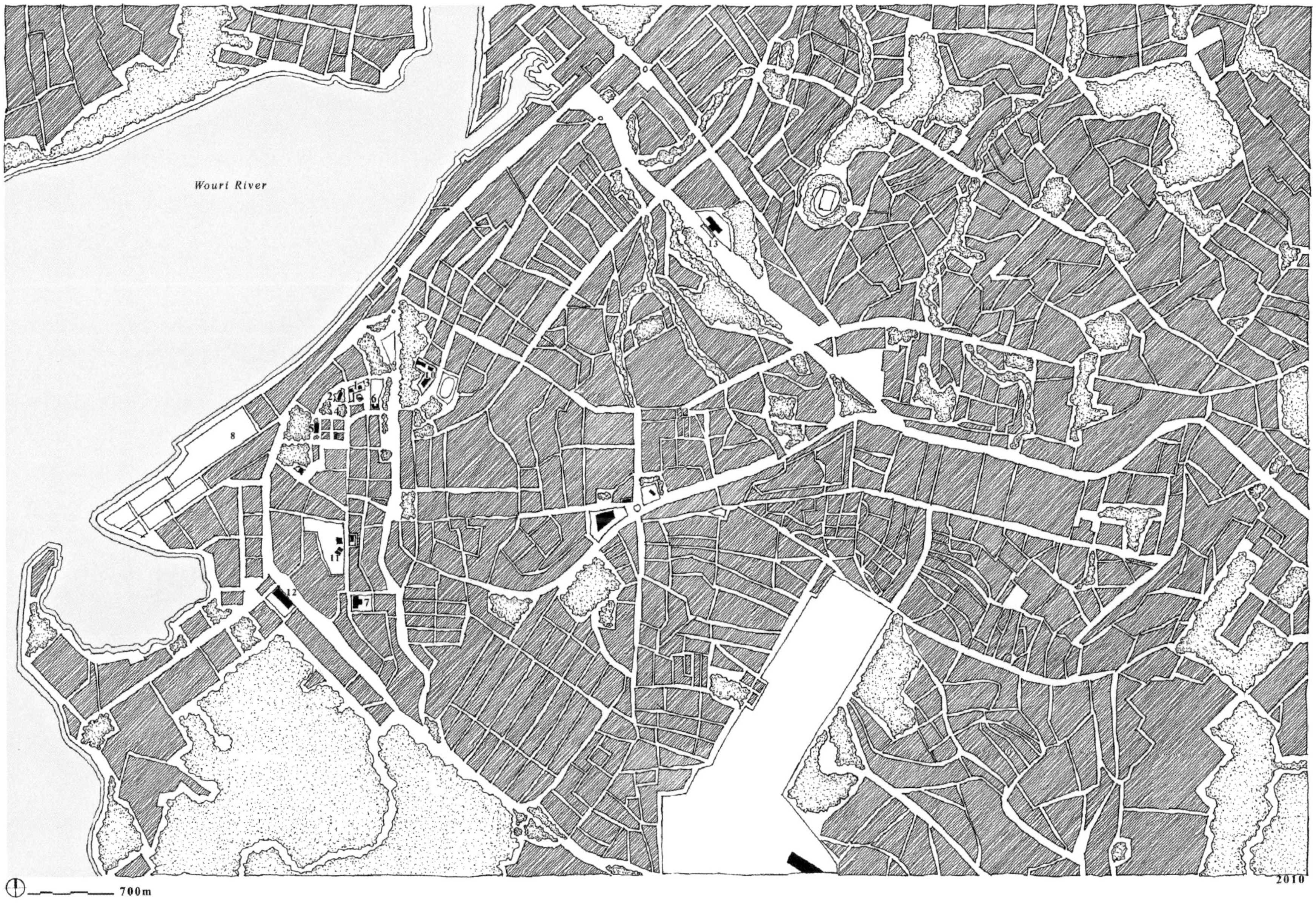

YAOUNDÉ, CAMEROON

FOUNDED: 1888
URBAN AREA: 180 km²
POPULATION (2012): 2,440,462
URBAN AREA DENSITY: 14,000/km²
GPS: 3° 52'22.60"N, 11° 31'2.70"E

Yaoundé is the capital city of Cameroon and unusually situated some distance from the country's coast. It is located in the midst of a rapidly disappearing tropical rainforest, on a hilly plateau, known as the 'town of seven hills', between the Nyong and Sanaga rivers. The city's amorphous urban structure is to a large extent the result of its topography. Its centre is characterised by a number of unusual administrative buildings, arranged along central axes that flow from Independence Square. From there, the nebulous urban form is organically shaped and limited by the natural topography.

Founded in 1888 by the botanist Georg August Zenker, Yaoundè was run during the German period as a military and administrative post. The name Juande, given to the settlement by the Germans, resulted from a linguistic misunderstanding – as the new colonial rulers meant to name the site after a local ethnic group, the Ewondo. The relatively densely populated area soon attracted German merchants, so that by 1895, the first trading post opened. During the First World War, Belgian troops set up their headquarters in the town, which was a favorable location from a military point of view. After Germany's defeat in the war, France became the colonial power in eastern Cameroon. It soon became an important administrative region, and grew rapidly in the post-war period as workers were needed for the completion of public projects launched under the French development scheme. Around the time of independence in 1960, Yaoundé experieced a second growth phase, which is reflected in its rapid present-day increase in population density. The city has grown as an administrative, service, and commercial centre and as a communications hub for road, rail, and air transport. Yaoundé boasts several small manufacturing and processing industries and is also the market for one of the richest agricultural areas in the country.

Following the deep economic crisis of the 1980s, the layering of the informal sector has affected the sprawling urban form. Poverty, growing slums and pollution are dominant features of the modern city and in recent years, ethnic tensions and clashes have increased over access to urban land.

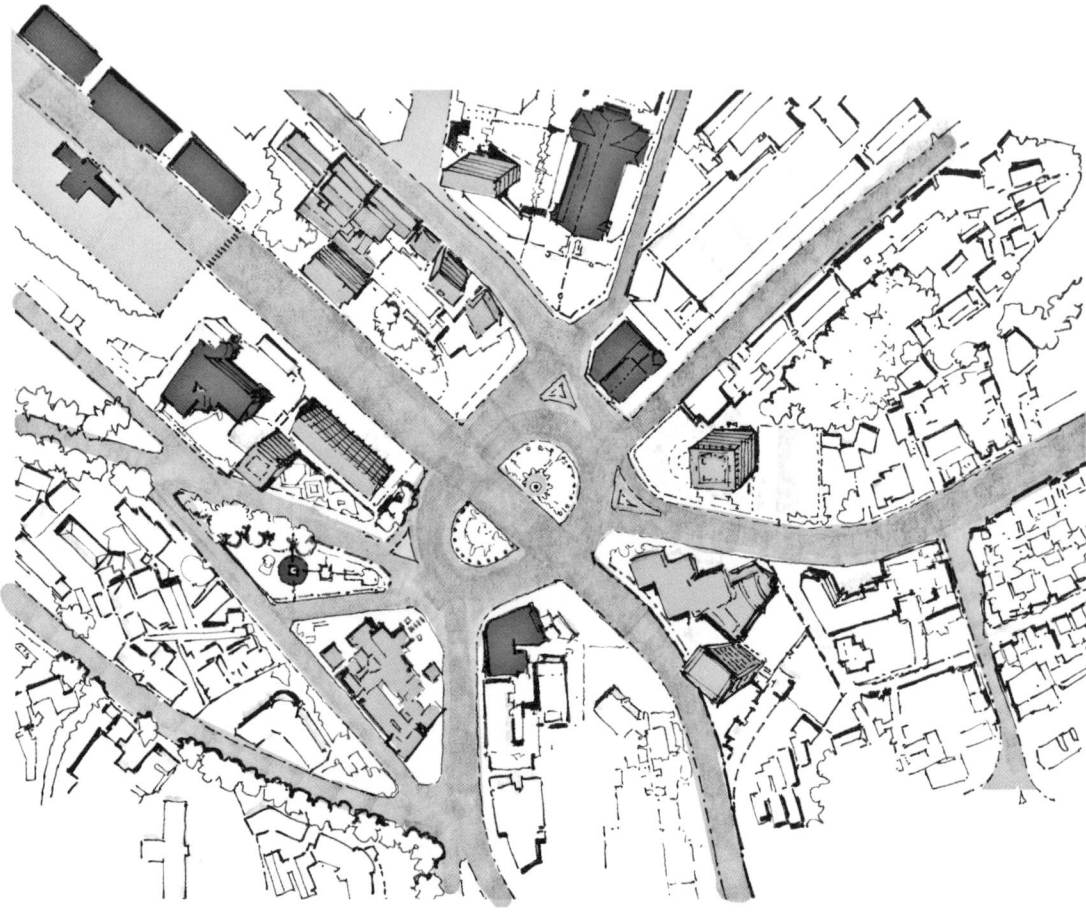

CENTRAL AFRICA **17**

1 Central Post Station
2 May 20th Square
3 Yaoundé Cathedral
4 Ministry of Higher Education
5 Our Lady of Victories Cathedral
6 Independence Square
7 National Social Security Fund
8 National Museum
9 Ministry of Justice & Public Health
10 Forest of Sainte Anastasie
11 Sports Centre
12 Municipal Lake
13 Central Station
14 Statue of Charles Atangana
15 N2 road leading towards the airport
16 Reunification Monument
17 National Assembly
18 Military Stadium
19 Leclerc Stadium

BANGUI, CENTRAL AFRICAN REPUBLIC

FOUNDED: 1889
URBAN AREA: 67 km²
POPULATION: 734,350
URBAN AREA DENSITY: unknown
GPS: 4° 21'43.29"N, 18° 34'58.34"E

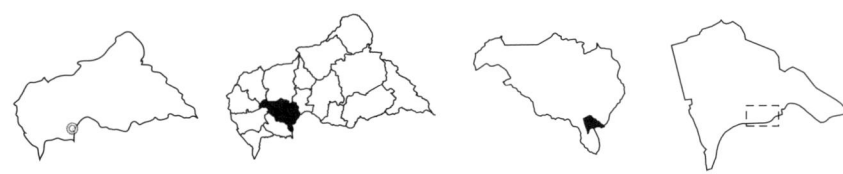

Once described as La Coquette, or the "beautiful city", Bangui has in recent decades become the face of rebel activity and political upheaval. Consequently, it was named one of the most dangerous places in the world in 1996.

Originally established as a French outpost, the city lies on the banks of the Ubangi River, with rolling green hills in the background. In and around the city are Iron Age archaeological sites, some as close as 800 m from Independence Avenue, one of its primary boulevards. Interestingly, the city lies amidst the 700 km x 1,000 km Bangui Magnetic Anomaly, one of the earth's largest crustal anomalies, and the largest in Africa.

As the capital city and administrative, trade, commercial and transport hub of the turbulent Central African Republic, it continues to draw migrants every day. Entry points include the international airport and a river port that handles all international trade. All roads – mostly dirt roads with only toll roads being paved – originate from the Palace de la Republique, connecting the city to urban centres elsewhere.

The colonial city centre features a large arch with wide boulevards, leading to a central market square. Administrative and institutional buildings, mostly from the Modern Movement period, are scattered around the centre of the city. Permanent buildings are generally of cement blocks, while sun-dried brick walls and thatched roofs are reserved for increasingly densely scattered dwelling houses – rendering a strong horizontal character to the expanding city.

Traditionally, village space is completely open, with no enclosures – as concealment is considered a violation to cultural norms by indigenous Central Africans. Similar to village layouts, streets in the city are extensions of communal space where all activities are visible to passers-by. The Muslim religion, having an ever increasing presence in the local, mostly Christian communities, culturally require enclosures.

KM5 neighbourhood, situated roughly 5 km from the physical city centre, is considered by many people to be the real Bangui, with a mixture of ethnic groups and religions. The Church of Fatima and Notre Dame d'Afrique are located in KM5, as well as the city's largest mosque and largest market.

Resources are progressively scarce as urban growth increases, and the intense rebel activity in recent years has led to destruction in the city. Deforestation and loss of agricultural land around the urban periphery, along with lack of infrastructure, sanitation, electricity, running water, access to roads, drainage and lack of housing, all contribute to a desperate situation.

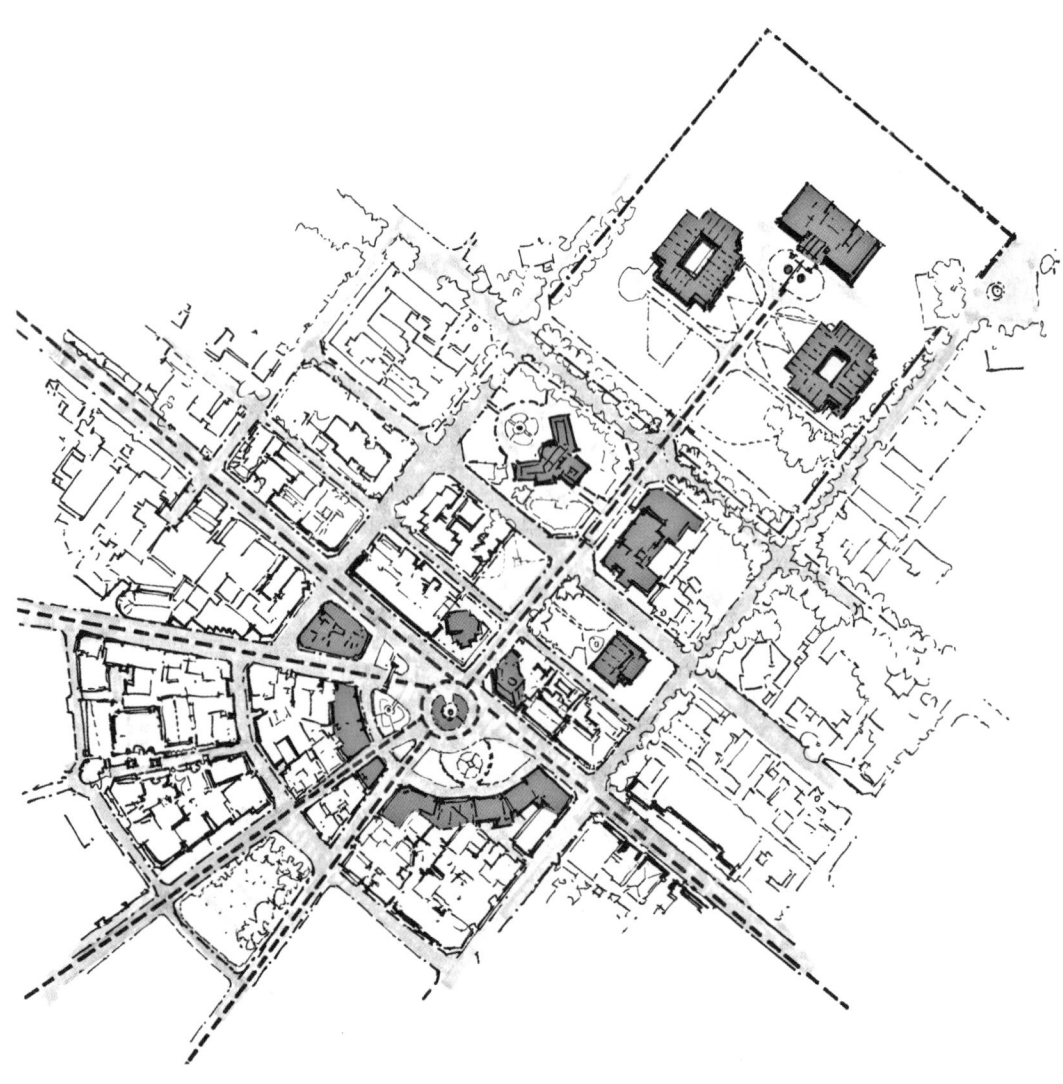

1 Republic Square
2 Presidential Palace
3 Bangui Harbour
4 TGIB
5 African States Bank
6 Bangui Courthouse
7 Court of Cassation
8 Notre Dame Cathedral
9 Public Park

1
2
3
4
5
6
7
8
9
Ubangi River
250m
2013

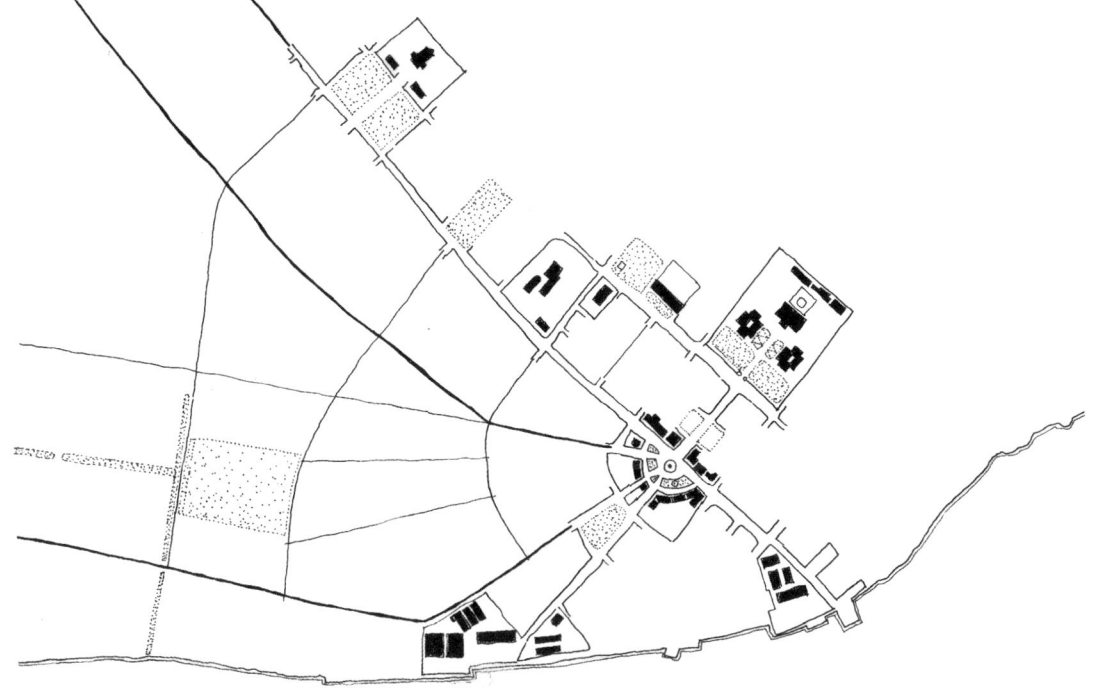

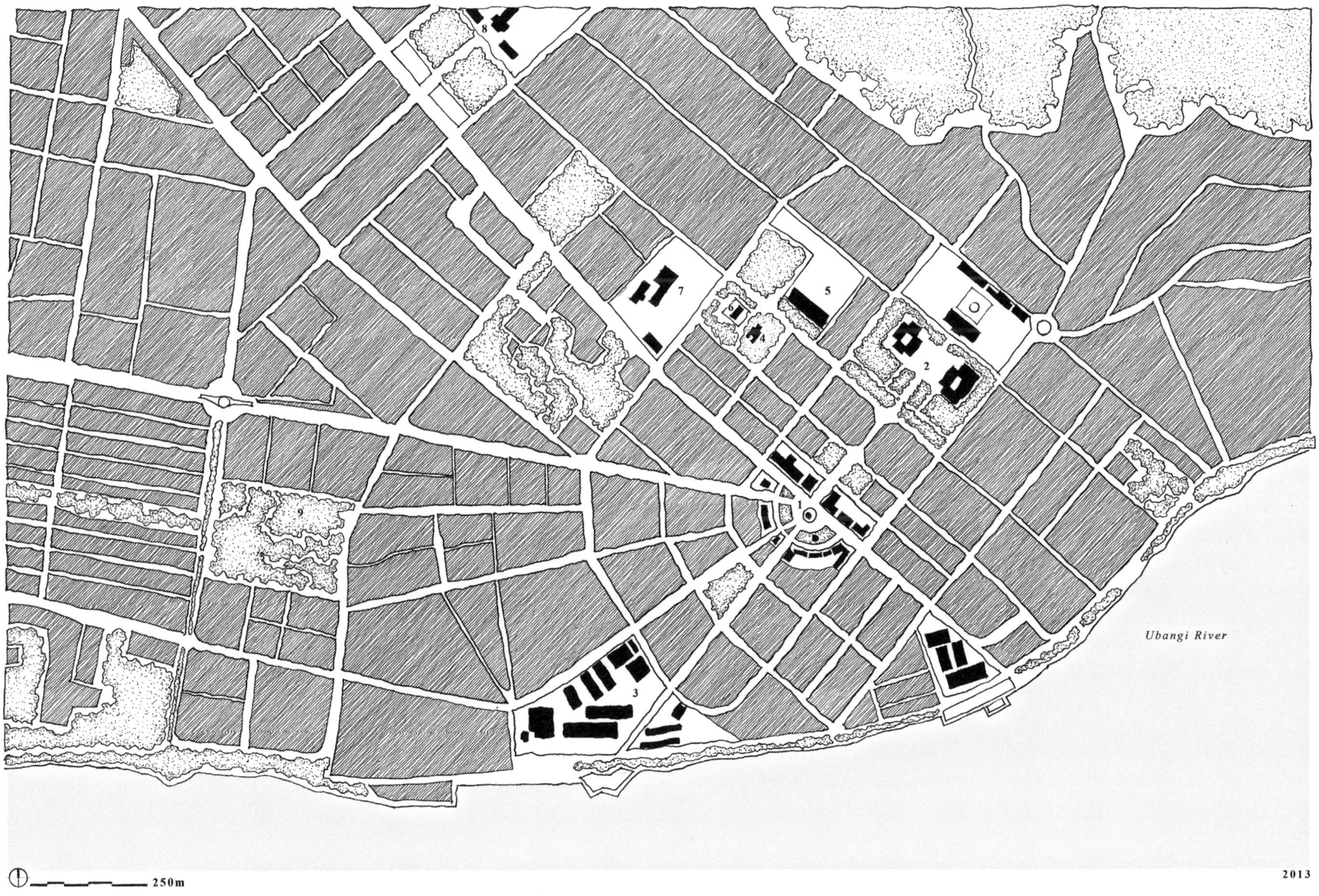

N'DJAMENA, CHAD

FOUNDED: 1900
AREA: 100 km²
POPULATION (2012): 1,092,066
DENSITY: 11,000/km²
GPS: 12° 6′43.42″N, 15° 2′20.56″E

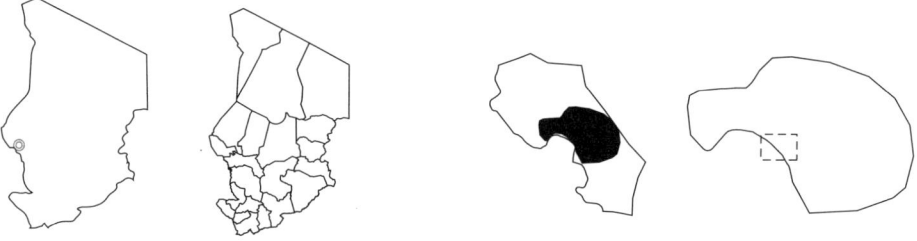

N'Djamena, previously known as Fort Lamy, is the capital and largest city of Chad. The city is located on the Chari River near the confluence with the Logone River, directly facing the Cameroonian town of Kousséri, to which the city is connected by a bridge.

N'Djamena was originally founded as Fort-Lamy by French commander Émile Gentil in 1900, and named after Amédée-François Lamy, an army officer who had been killed in the Battle of Kousséri. The city became the provincial capital, located on the local trading route as a major trading city and established as a market centre. In 1960, the city became the national capital and appropriate governmental institutions were constructed.

The city's structure is bounded by the river edge and resembles a formal French-colonial layout, divided into ten arrondissements. The urban form has a structured street grid and geometric forms, with the classical ideals of symmetry and order, public squares and rectangular plots adhering to urban modernism and colonialism.

The country achieved independence in 1963, after which President François Tombalbaye renamed the city N'Djamena ("the town where one can rest"). The city and country have faced civil unrest for most of its history, leaving the city of N'Djamena with damaged infrastructure and slow growth.

The country has a dual character with the north predominantly Arabic/Islamic while the south is home to people who follow either the traditional religions or Christianity. N'Djamena reflects the country's multicultural character with a commercial and administrative core. Buildings date back to the French period and reflect the particular culture. The Arabic/Islamic section of the city is dominant with an urban sprawl of satellite African suburbs and settlements surrounding the city without any clear borders.

Downtown N'Djamena is located closer to the Chari River where government buildings cluster along Avenue Charles De Gaulle, the main commercial avenue of the city which runs parallel to the river. Buildings along the main avenues include the presidential palace [4], the parliament and the Catholic cathedral [2] dating back to the French colonial period. The principal monument of N'Djamena, a large mosque [5] which was a gift from Saudi Arabia is located further along the avenue across from N'Djamena's main market [6]. The city still serves as the country's economic centre.

The city is the eastern terminus of the Trans-Sahelian Highway and is linked to east Africa by the N'Djamena-Djibouti Highway. The Tripoli-Cape Town Highway also passes through N'Djamena, making it a key Central African location in the Trans-African Highway network.

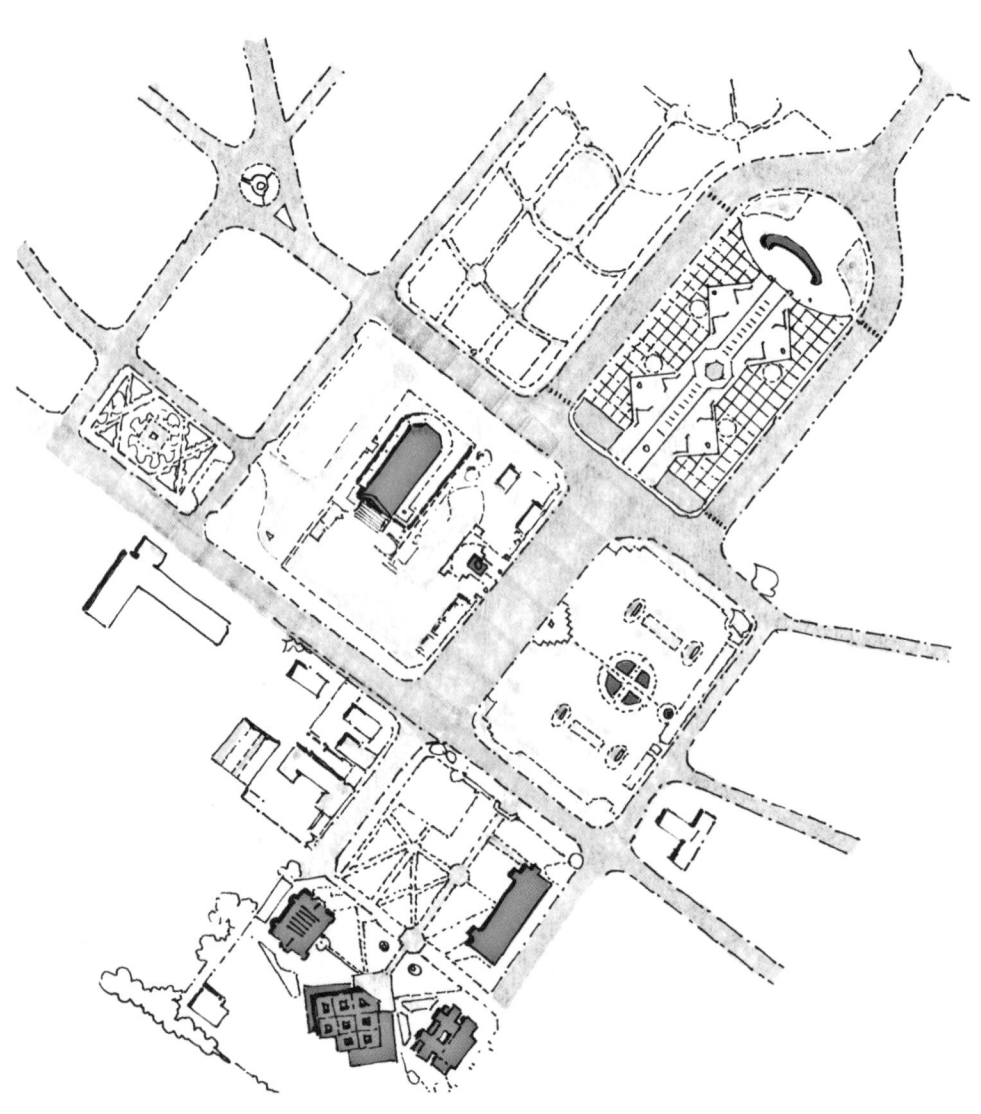

1 Liberation Square
2 N'Djamena Cathedral
3 National Tchadien Museum
4 Presidential Palace
5 Grande Mosque
6 Grande Market
7 Cultural Centre
8 Kabalaye Centre
9 Central Hospital
10 Hôpital de la Mère et de l'Enfant
 (Hospital of the Mother and Child)
 N'Djamena International Airport
11 French Cultural Centre
12 Mahamat Ouya Stadium
13 Centre Medico Social

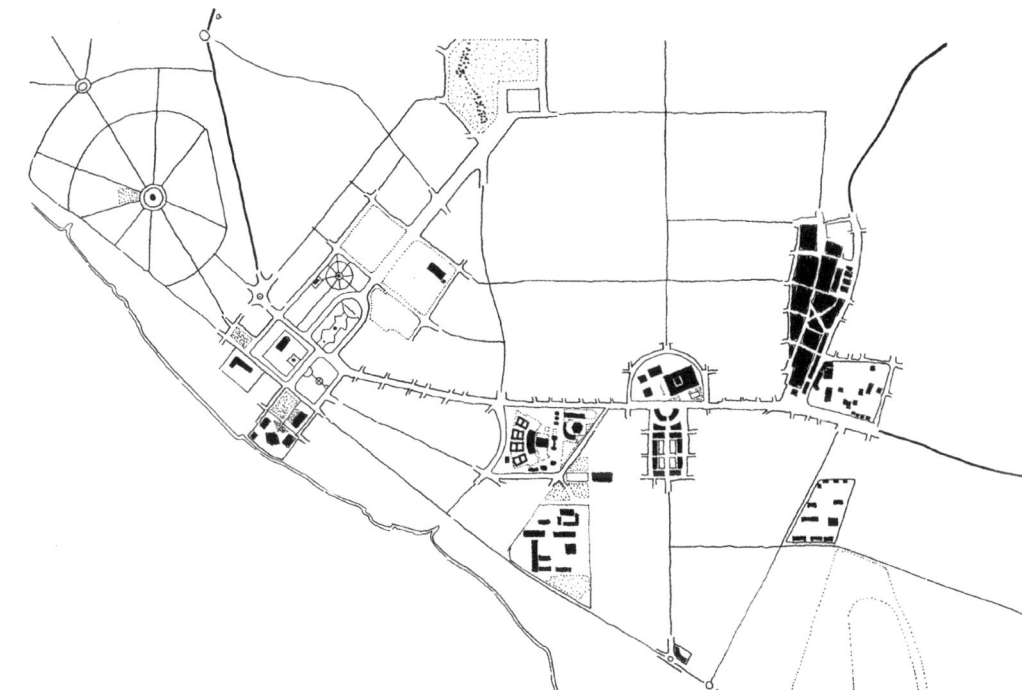

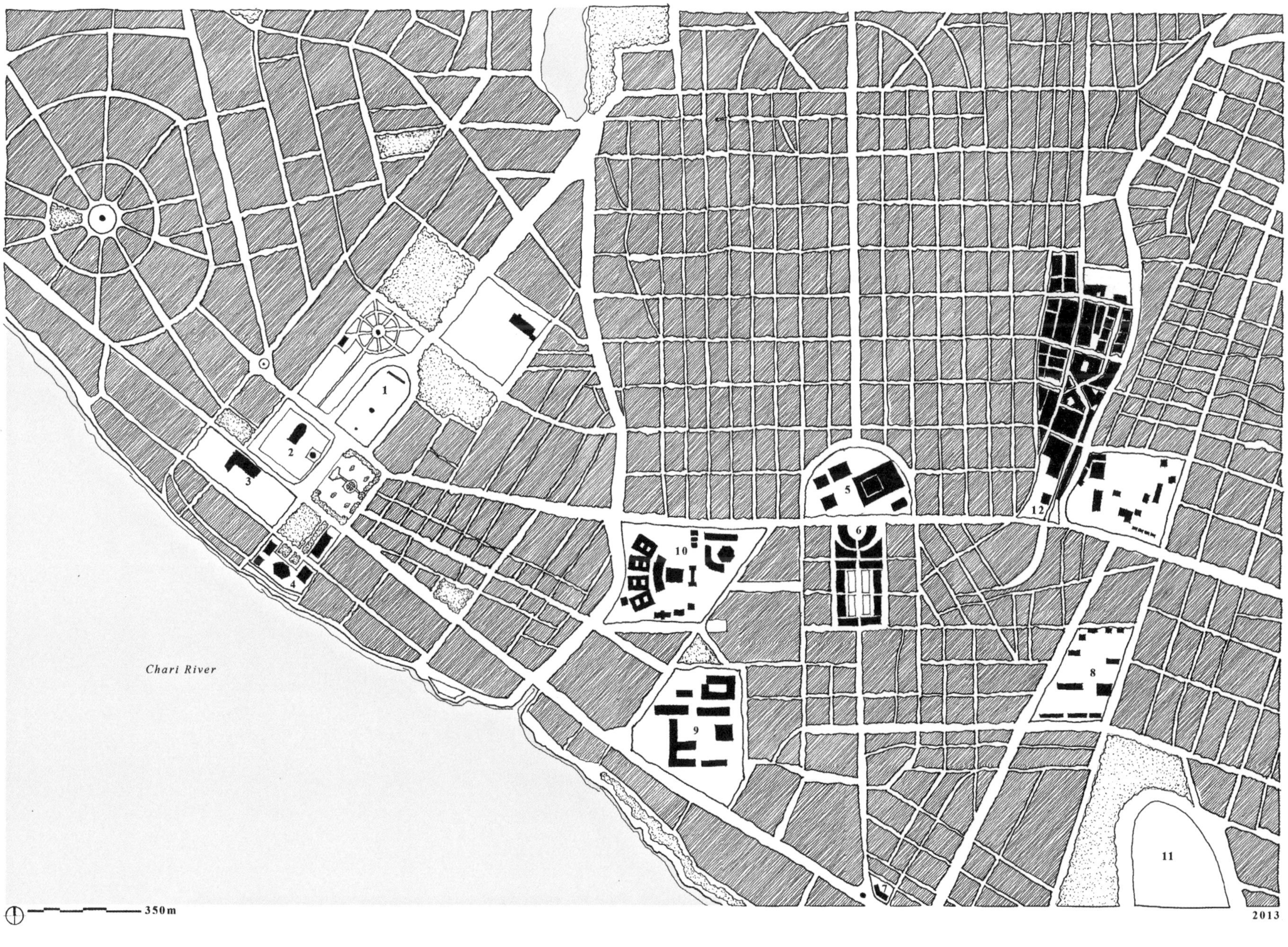

Chari River

KINSHASA, DEMOCRATIC REPUBLIC OF THE CONGO

FOUNDED: 1881
URBAN AREA: 583 km²
POPULATION (2009): Almost 10 million
URBAN AREA DENSITY: 16,000/km²
GPS: 4° 18'3.97"S, 15° 19'2.41"E

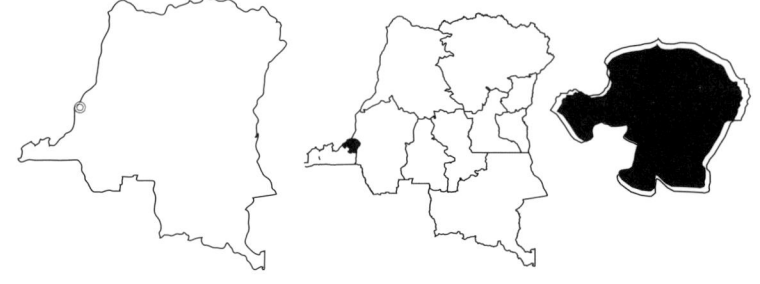

Kinshasa, formerly Léopoldville, developed during one century from a few precolonial settlements into a metropolis of almost ten million people. Now a vast and polycentric city, its origins were in two colonial posts that coincided with two precolonial villages. These were interconnected with a railway, reaching various trading posts along the edge of the Congo River. The city has multiple routes/links to Brazzavillle, the capital city of the Republic of the Congo, which is uniquely situated directly across the river (see *Brazzaville*).

As the colonial capital of the Belgian Congo, ambitious urban and architectural projects were historically developed here, but not all were realised. The colonial boulevard, today Boulevard du 30-Juin, is a major circulation axis that tracks the original railway connection. Various features demonstrating the historical architecture of the city's past can be found on this impressive axis.

Historically, spatial segregation along racial lines resulted in a binary city structure. This is recognisable in the axial boulevard-like urban structure of the European section along the river, and the controlled grid of the native section to its south. Originally a neutral unoccupied zone between these two areas, it was gradually populated as the city expanded. A series of recreational facilities for Europeans were established in the neutral zone such as a zoo, Parc De Bock and the Leo Golf Club.

Together with education, medicine formed one of the spearheads of Belgian colonisation, and as a result, the city boasts several impressive health facilities. These were often situated on prime sites for Europeans along the Congo River, benefiting from the breeze and spectacular views. The main hospital for Africans, Hôpital Mama Yebo, is located in the city centre.

The original public market was located in the European quarter of the city [4], challenging the colonial separation of races. The presence of African tradesmen around the public market was considered unhygenic and inappropriate by many Europeans. As a result, another market was created in the neutral zone in 1943 to remedy the situation [6], where President Mobutu implemented a new, modernist structure during the early 1970s. Today, Kinshasa's central market, designed as a grouping of several concrete shell-shaped pavilions, can be considered one of Africa's largest marketplaces accommodating more than 30,000 merchants. Although the marketplace nowadays has a rather eccentric position in relation to the city, as Kinshasa continues to expand into its periphery, it remains by far the most important confluence of interests, lifestyles and cultures, turning it into a major place of exchange and encounters.

Since the 1990s, public services and administration have collapsed, resulting in the congestion and degradation of the city.

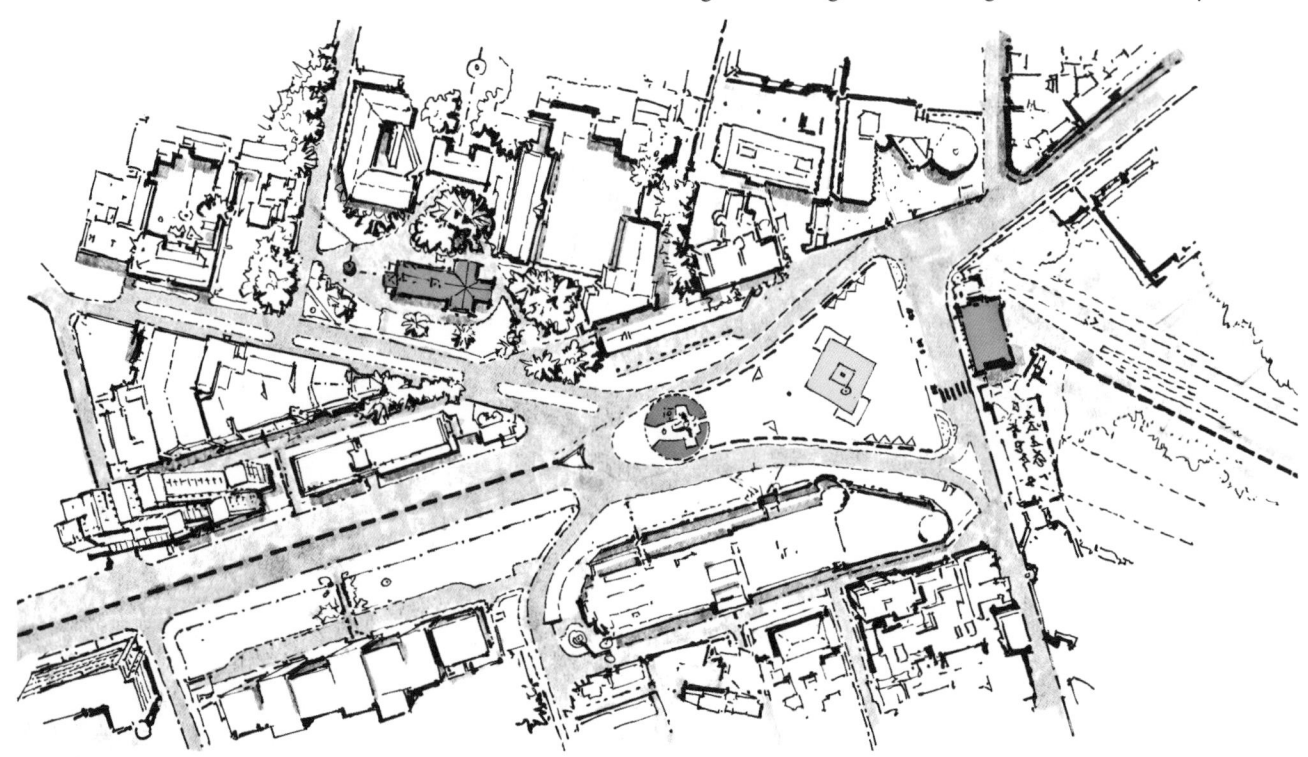

CENTRAL AFRICA

1 June 30th Square
2 St Anne Cathedral
3 Central Train Station
4 Market Square
5 De Boeck Park
6 Central Market
7 Zoological Gardens
8 Grand Port
9 Protestant Temple
10 Supreme Court
11 Nelson Mandela Square
12 Independence Square
13 Mausoleum of Laurent-Désiré Kabila
14 Courthouse
15 Bobota College (Albert College)
16 Gombe Institute (Royal Club)
17 Ngaliema Hospital (Reine Astrid Clinic)
18 Cardinal Malula Staduim
   (Stade Reine Astrid 1937) and St Pierre
19 Kabambare High School
20 Martyrs Staduim
21 Palais du Peuple, People Palace
22 Presidential Park Mont Ngaliema
23 Grand Séminary of Jean XXIII
24 Original Port of Kinshasa
25 Institute of National Museums
26 Old Leopoldville (Ngaliema Town)
27 Aeroport de Ndolo, N'Dolo Airport

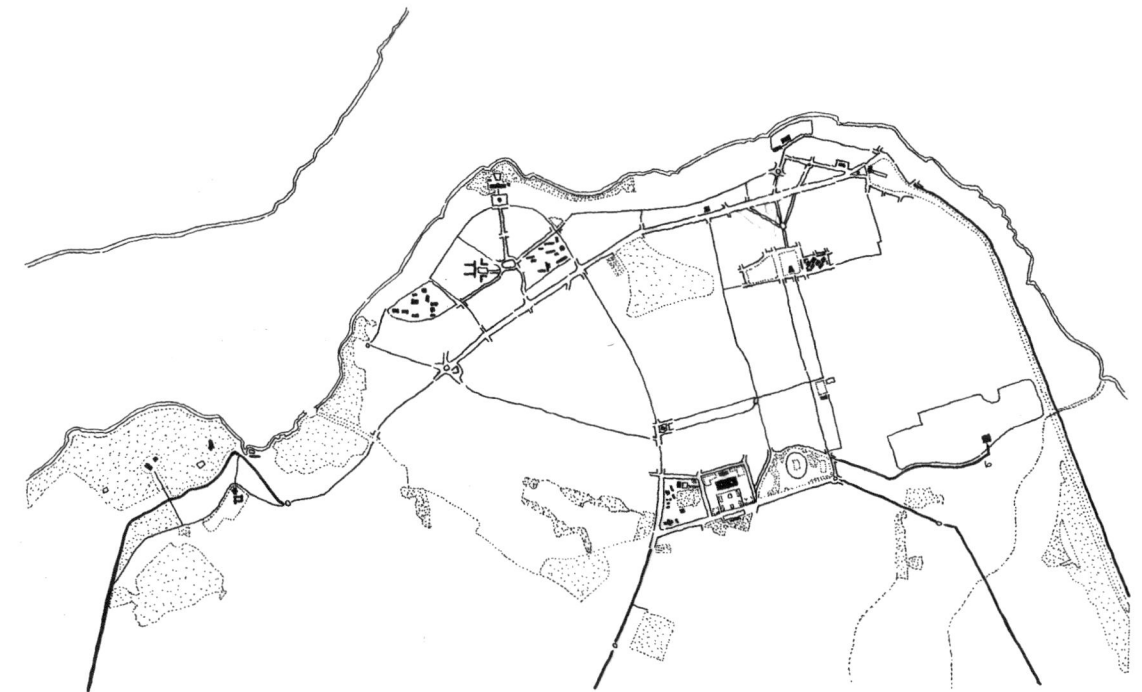

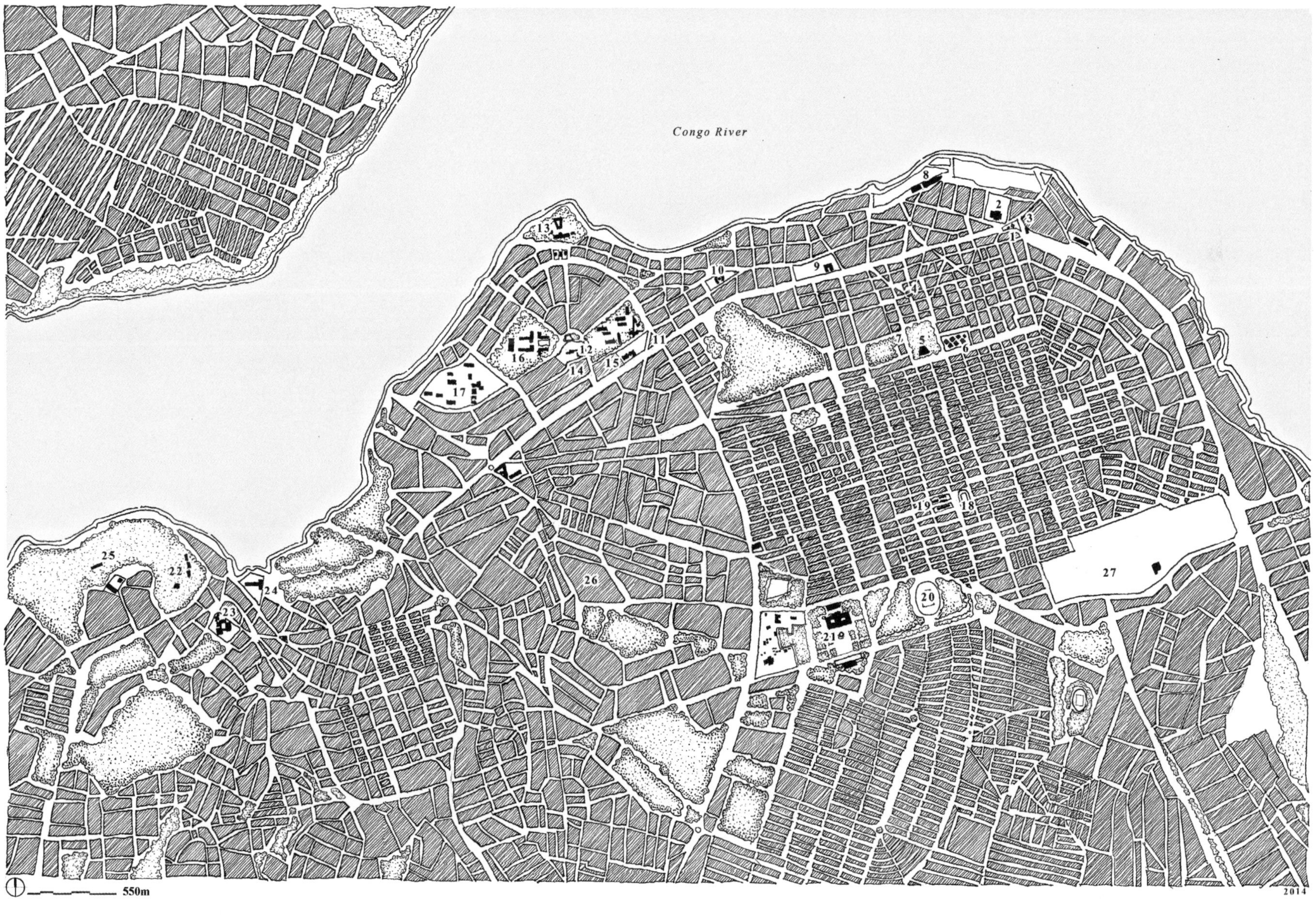

LUBUMBASHI, DEMOCRATIC REPUBLIC OF THE CONGO

FOUNDED: 1910
URBAN AREA: 747 km²
POPULATION (2012): 1,786,397
URBAN AREA DENSITY: 2,400/km²
GPS: 11° 39'6.55"S, 27° 28'32.38"E

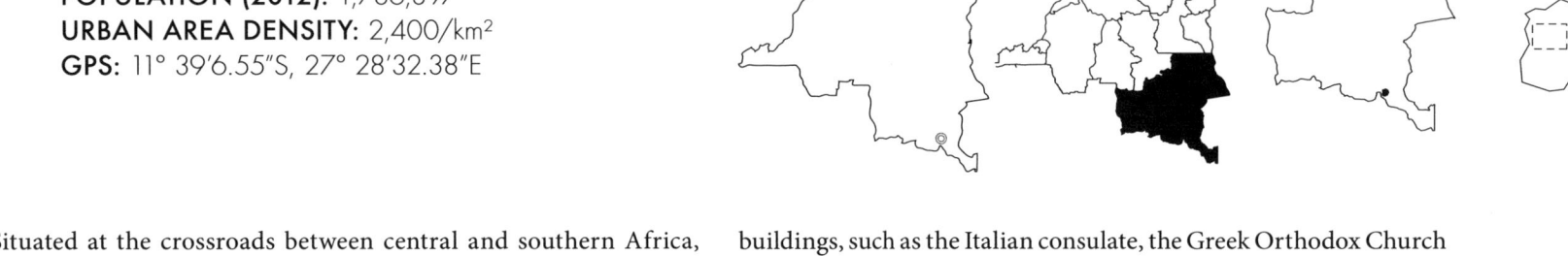

Situated at the crossroads between central and southern Africa, Elisabethville was one of the many cities constructed during the 1900s African colonial period as a mining city in Congo's copper-rich Katanga province. The city was created *ex nihilo* to act as a marker for the Belgian colonial administration. An arid grassland, unsuitable for settlement by African standards, characterised the geographically favourable location. The city developed as a cosmopolitan urban enclave, hosting a diverse European and African population which resulted in a segregated urban organisation. Known since 1967 as Lubumbashi, it was a prominent city in colonial central Africa.

The urban design of the city, influenced by South African and Rhodesian city plans, mostly resembles a prototypical colonial city. The plan was defined by a central station and a rectilinear grid immediately to the west of the station, which was separated by a *zone neutre,* or neutral zone, similar to that of Kinshasa from the indigenous city. The rectilinear grid hosted the European city, while the indigenous city housed the local African workers whose labour supported the mining industry. The grid structure of Lubumbashi's European town was not completely uniform, but differentiated by means of a hierarchy of avenues. Lagae (2013) describes diagonally running boulevards, squares and green spaces that were to be found in residential, commercial, and administrative zones. According to Lagae, in this urban landscape, each group within the white community sought to mark and affirm its identity by erecting distinctive buildings, such as the Italian consulate, the Greek Orthodox Church or the synagogue, one of Lubumbashi's most striking architectural artifacts.

Major landmark buildings, many in the Art Deco style and later buildings hailing the tropical Modern Movement, are associated with the colonial government, missionary congregations, and colonial companies such as the imposing infrastructure of the Union Minière du Haut Katanga (UMHK). The railroad created a quick and efficient means for importing building materials such as cast-iron building parts. According to Lagae, some remarkable constructions date from the 1950s: the monumental classicist Athenée Royal or the cultural centre comprising a theatre, museum and music school being cases in point.

Political instability has marked the country and the city since the 1960s. In the brief period of stability before the most recent ethnic tensions, Lubumbashi witnessed an economic upheaval unprecedented in previous decades. As a result, the city landscape changed at a rapid pace.

CENTRAL AFRICA **25**

1 G.A. Forrest Square
2 Building of June 30th
3 Maadini Institute
4 National Museum of Lubumbashi
5 Imara College & Regina Mundi Church
6 University Hospital
7 Park
8 Lupopo Stadium
9 Park
10 University of Lubumbashi
11 City Council of Lubumbashi
12 Courthouse
13 Cathedral of Saint Pierre and Saint Paul
14 Governorate of Katanga
15 Zoological Garden
16 Synagogue
17 Lubumbashi Railway Station
18 Sendwe University
19 Protestant Church
20 Technical Institute of Salama
21 Institute of the Sacred Heart
22 Kitumaini School
23 Mazembe Staduim
24 Lake Kipopo

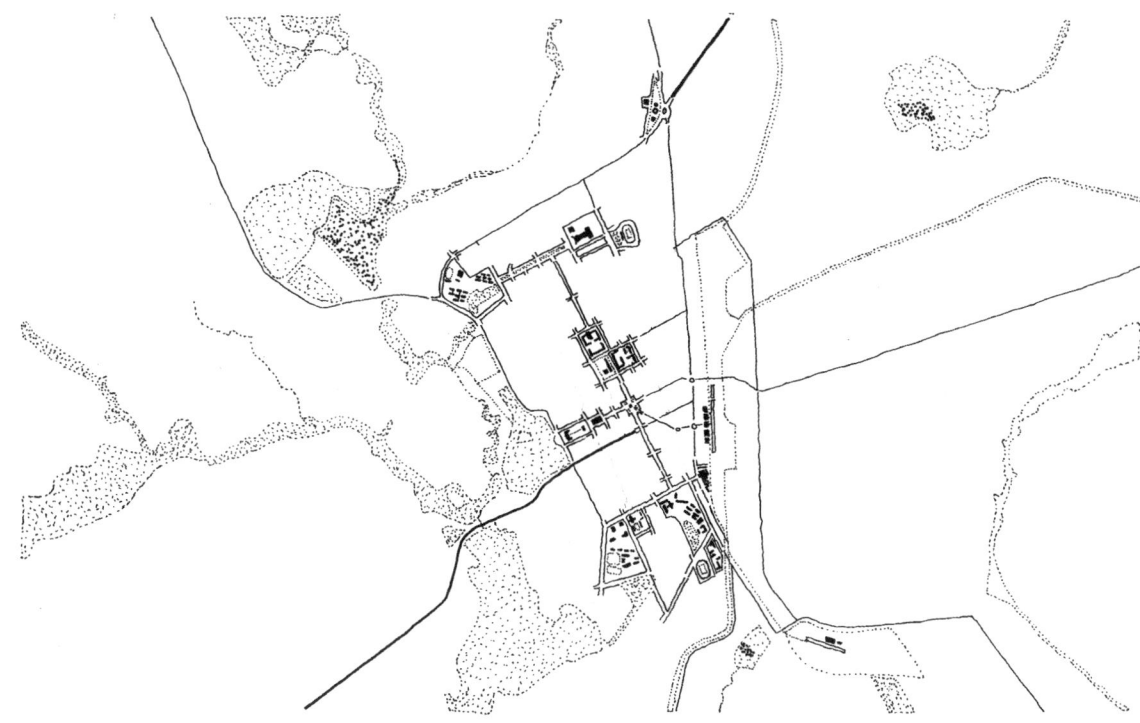

BATA, EQUATORIAL GUINEA

FOUNDED: unknown
URBAN AREA: unknown
POPULATION: 250,770
URBAN AREA DENSITY: unknown
GPS: 1° 51'48.71"N, 9° 45'51.64"E

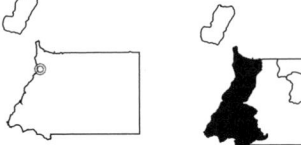  

Bata, a former Spanish colonial city, is said to be the largest city on the mainland of Equatorial Guinea. Even so, it is hardly a vast metropolis, with a small population of 250,770 (2012 census). Operating as a transport hub and port, the urban landscape reflects this small country's tumultuous past with a lack of basic infrastructure, public amenities and urban planning.

Stretched across the Atlantic Ocean, Bata has one of the deepest seaports along the coast. Despite this, it has no natural harbour and a jetty was built to facilitate the offloading of ships' cargoes. The sprawling city takes its form from the coastline, and development continues along its feeder roads from the mainland.

Independence was granted in 1968 and the country became the Republic of Equatorial Guinea with Francisco Macías Nguema elected as first president. Following anti-Spanish riots during 1969, the numbers of the European population dropped, resulting in subsequent severe economic stagnation that affected the city during the 1970s and 1980s.

The Macías regime abolished all government functions, except internal security, which led to widespread terrorism and the death or exile of up to one-third of the country's population. To this day, the vast streets along the coast of the city of Bata seem deserted.

Along with the rest of the country, Bata's infrastructure, electricity, water, roads, transportation, and health fell into ruin. Religion was repressed and education ceased, which explains the lack of landmarks in Bata compared to other cities. All schools were ordered to close in 1975, and the country's churches were closed in 1978.

Following a coup d'état in 1979, Teodoro Obiang Nguema Mbasogo assumed the presidency. He faced the challenge of restoring order in a country that was in shambles. By the end of his dictatorship, the state coffers were empty and the population had been reduced to one-third of what it was at independence. The oil boom of the country in the late 1980s and 1990s boosted its development, with several new infrastructure projects underway in the city of Bata. New buildings, electricity, new roads, streetlights, and a manicured waterfront are all testimony to the fresh influx of monetary sources.

Past the main roads that follow the coast line lies a sprawling urban conglomerate with small markets and small-scale residential development. Beyond the coastal affluent regions, a heterogeneous urban structure represents the majority of the local population.

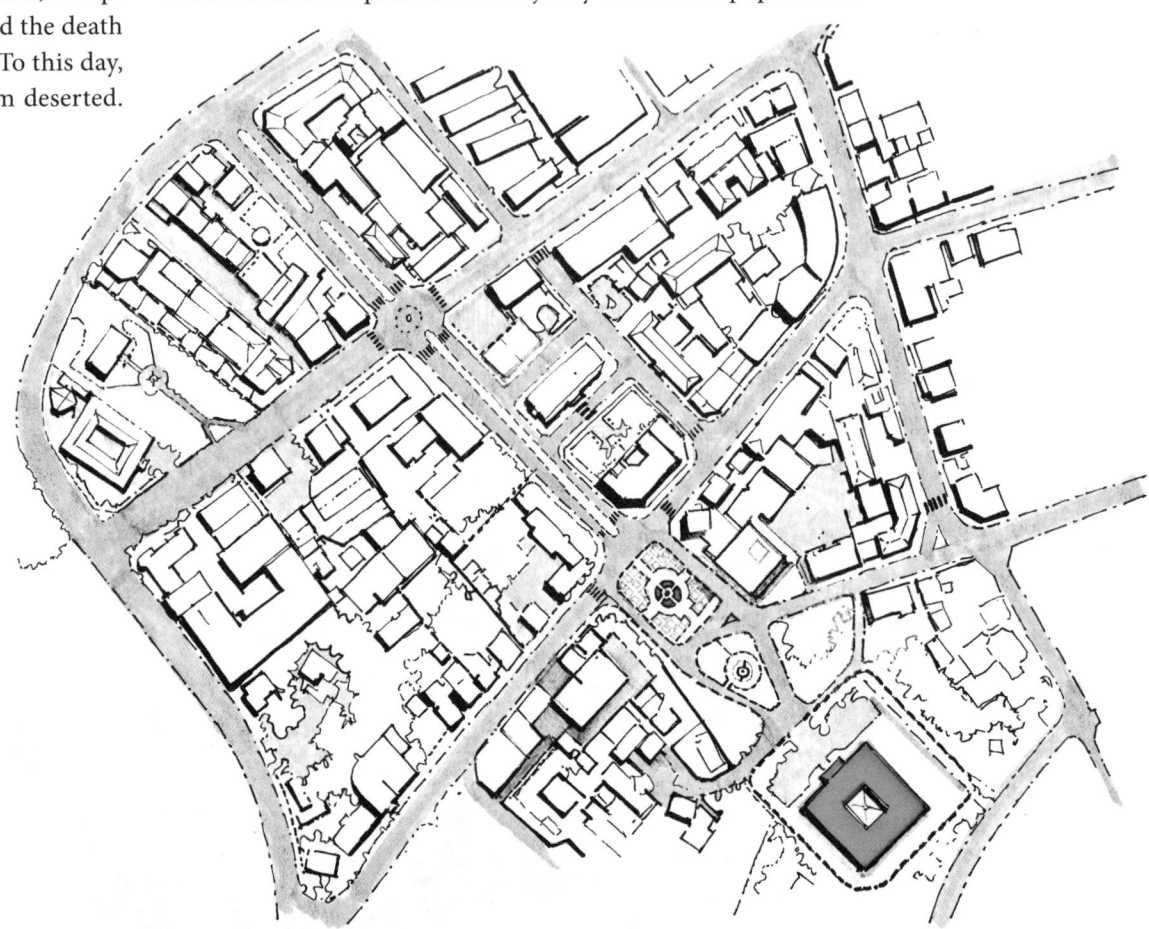

1 Liberty Plaza
2 Promenade & Atlantic Ocean
3 Bata General Hospital
4 Cathedral of the Apostle Santiago and Our Lady of the Pillar
5 Pier and Harbour
6 Cultural Centre of Spain
7 Public Garden / Park
8 Hospital
9 Bata Stadium
10 Market

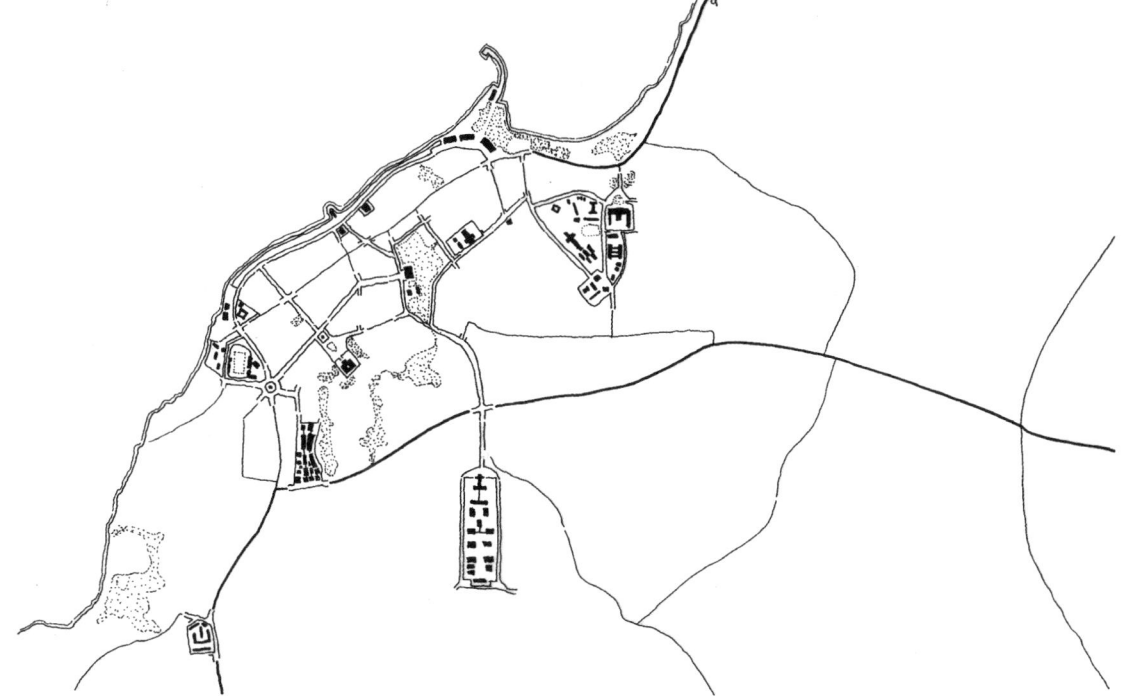

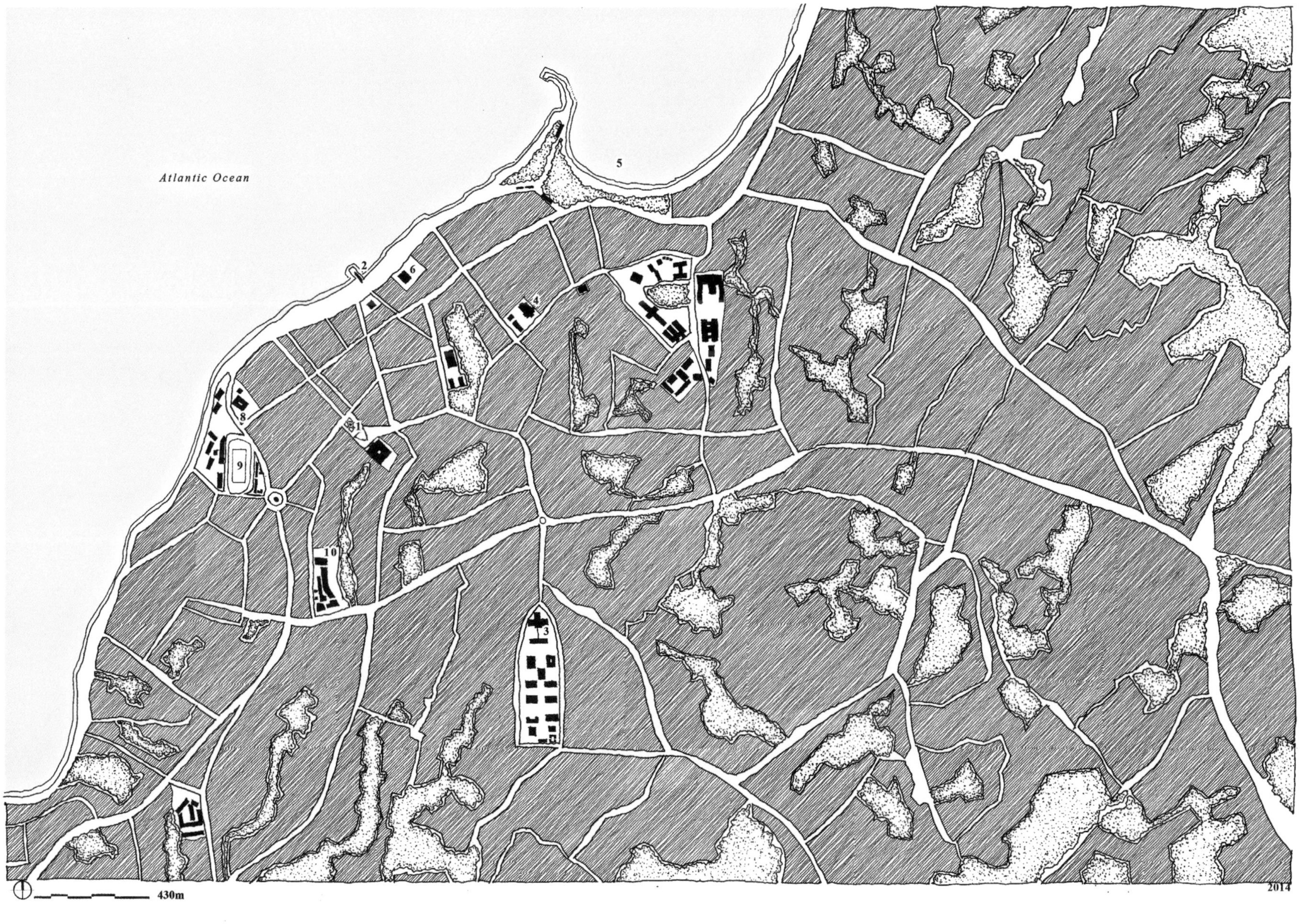

MALABO, EQUATORIAL GUINEA

FOUNDED: 1827
AREA: unknown
POPULATION (2012): 187,302
DENSITY: unknown
GPS: 3° 45'26.63"N, 8° 46'59.02"E

Malabo, Equatorial Guinea's capital and main port, is situated on the northern coast of Bioko island, located in the Atlantic Ocean, south of Nigeria and west of Cameroon. The city, formerly Port Clarence and later Santa Isabel, is located on the rim of a sunken volcano.

The island of Bioko was first discovered by the Portuguese explorer Fernão do Pó, in 1472. The island was named after Fernão and officially colonised by Portugal in 1474. In 1778, the island, adjacent islets, and commercial rights to the mainland between the Niger and Ogoue rivers were ceded to Spain in exchange for territory on the American continent. As an important settlement, Malabo was known as Port Clarence in 1827 after the British leased Bioko island from the Spanish to establish a naval station. This was in order to help fight slavery.

The city became the capital of Equatorial Guinea in 1969 and was renamed Malabo after independence in 1973 as part of President Francisco Macías Nguema's campaign to replace European place names with "authentic" African ones.

Although the city resembles a formal grid, its structure is predominantly influenced by the natural topography of the volcanic rim and Atlantic coast. Malabo's street network is poorly developed with few paved roads leading into the city. The palace [3 & 4], and grounds cover a substantial part of the eastern side of Malabo and have restricted access. The heart of the city is the colonial Cathedral of Santa Isabel [2] at Independence Place [1]. Various buildings in the city reflect the influence of the Spanish colonial era.

The south of Malabo is bordered by the Rio Consul with the hospital to the south-east. Malabo Airport is located towards the west. The coastal northern region of the city is pierced by headlands and bays. The largest peninsula is the crescent-shaped Tip of African Unity [7] behind the Presidential Palace [4]. Malabo is part of a wider bay that represents most of the northern coast of Bioko which stretches from Europe Point in the west, to barren lands in the east. Malabo has an international airport, while ferries sail from its port [8] to Douala and Bata.

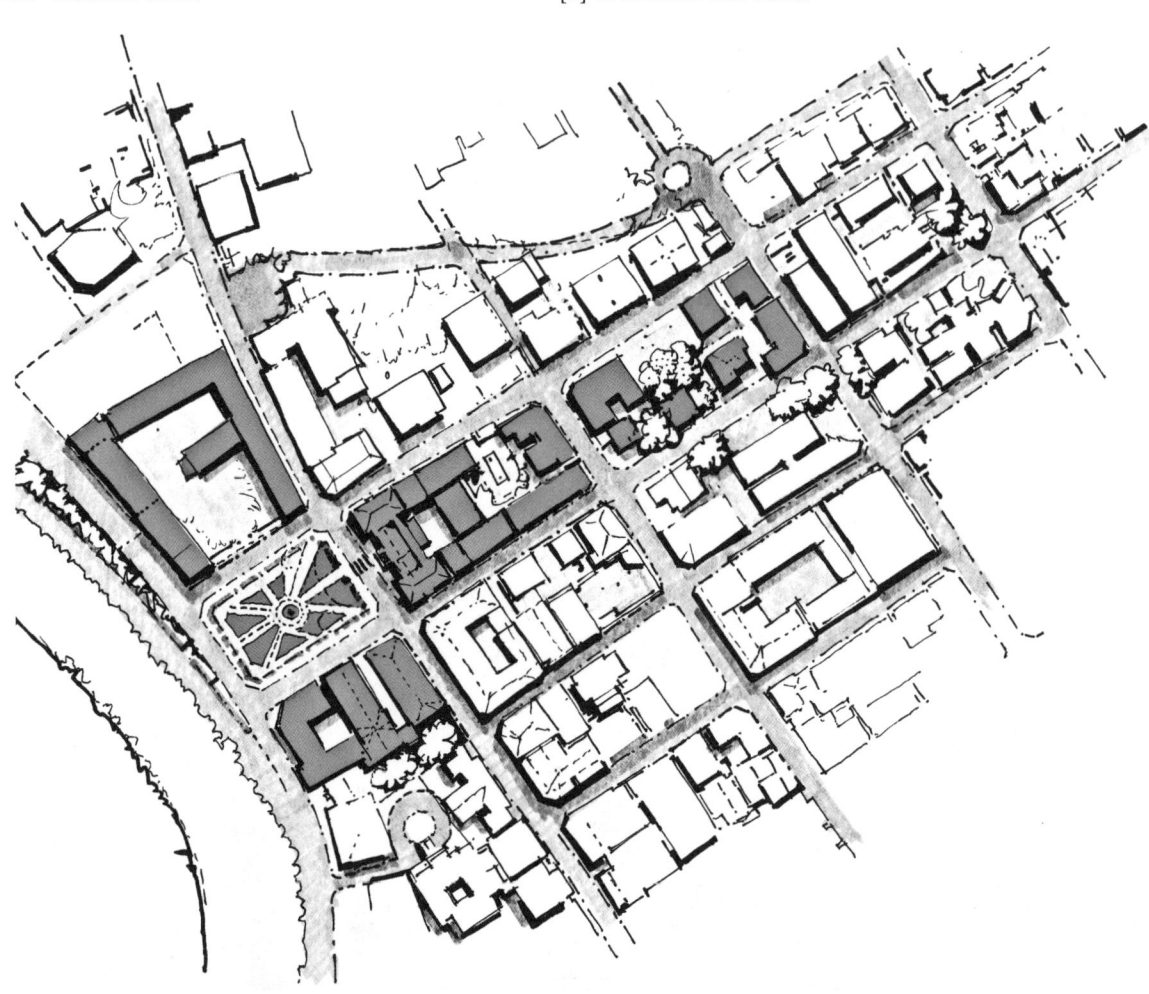

CENTRAL AFRICA **29**

1 Spanish Plaza & Independence Square
2 Cathedral of Santa Isabel
3 People's Palace
4 Presidential Palace
5 Cathedral
6 Former Port
7 Tip Of African Unity
8 Port
9 City Council of Malabo
10 La Paz Municipal Stadium
11 Central Market
12 Hospital
13 Cemetery
14 Spanish College – Salesias
15 National University of Equatorial Guinea

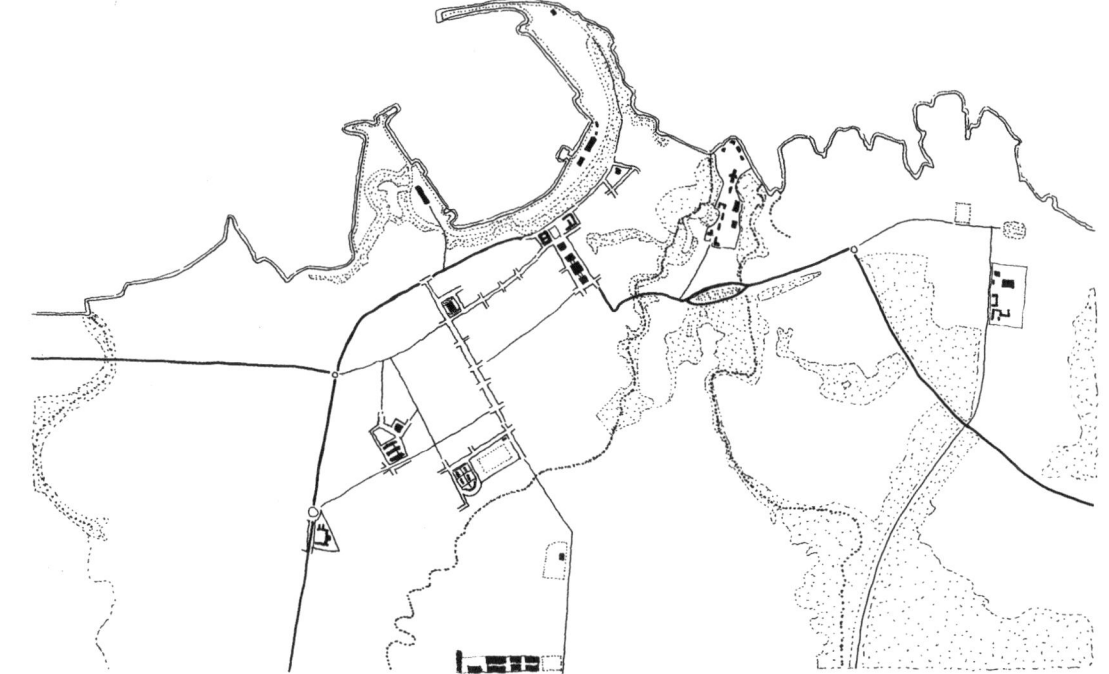

LIBREVILLE, GABON

FOUNDED: 1848
URBAN AREA: 258 km²
POPULATION (2005): 578,156
URBAN AREA DENSITY: unknown
GPS: 0° 23'35.29"N, 9° 26'37.88"E

Libreville is the capital city of Gabon, situated along the tropical west coast of Africa. The city is the trade centre of the small country, with a major railway station and city port along the Komo River, central to the Gabon Estuary. Water ways play a significant role in its urban form and ability to expand, with the port dominating the urban fabric. National parks and dense natural forests surround the city to the east, which has impacted greatly on development, yet promoted growth through the logging industry.

Initial settlement was located around the pier and current "grand" Main Boulevard. The latter is easily recognisable in the urban fabric as a result of the freestanding monuments to religious, political and cultural powers along its boundaries. Various outlying villages were historically settled in the south, with an expansion to the north taking place during the 1940s. The coastal promenade was developed around 1955, along with the upgrade of the main coastal road. The area along the coastline is the most densely populated today, in response to the energy and opportunities offered along the major road networks down the coastline. Rapid urbanisation followed Independence during the 1960s, largely due to public infrastructure programmes implemented by the then new government. The area bordering the Main Street is taken up by commercial properties, with the industrial district, Oloumi, established circa 1930 to the south, displaying warehouses to support the timber industries found here. To the north lie the only planned residential areas. Slums and an informal city fill everything in-between.

The Place of Democracy National Park and heritage district are easily recognisable in the urban form, constituting a large, undeveloped open space. Despite its heritage significance, the increasing pressure on available land in the city has resulted in intensifying informal occupation of the Place of Democracy Park, immediately to the north of the Place de la Paix [5]. Other landmarks that stand out in the low-rise, high-density sprawl of the city are the Omar Bongo Stadium and the Presidential Palace along the promenade. While Libreville is a reflection of a dynamic economy, the discontinuous, organic city form with generous boulevards giving way to shantytowns is also a reflection of the increasing gap between rich and poor.

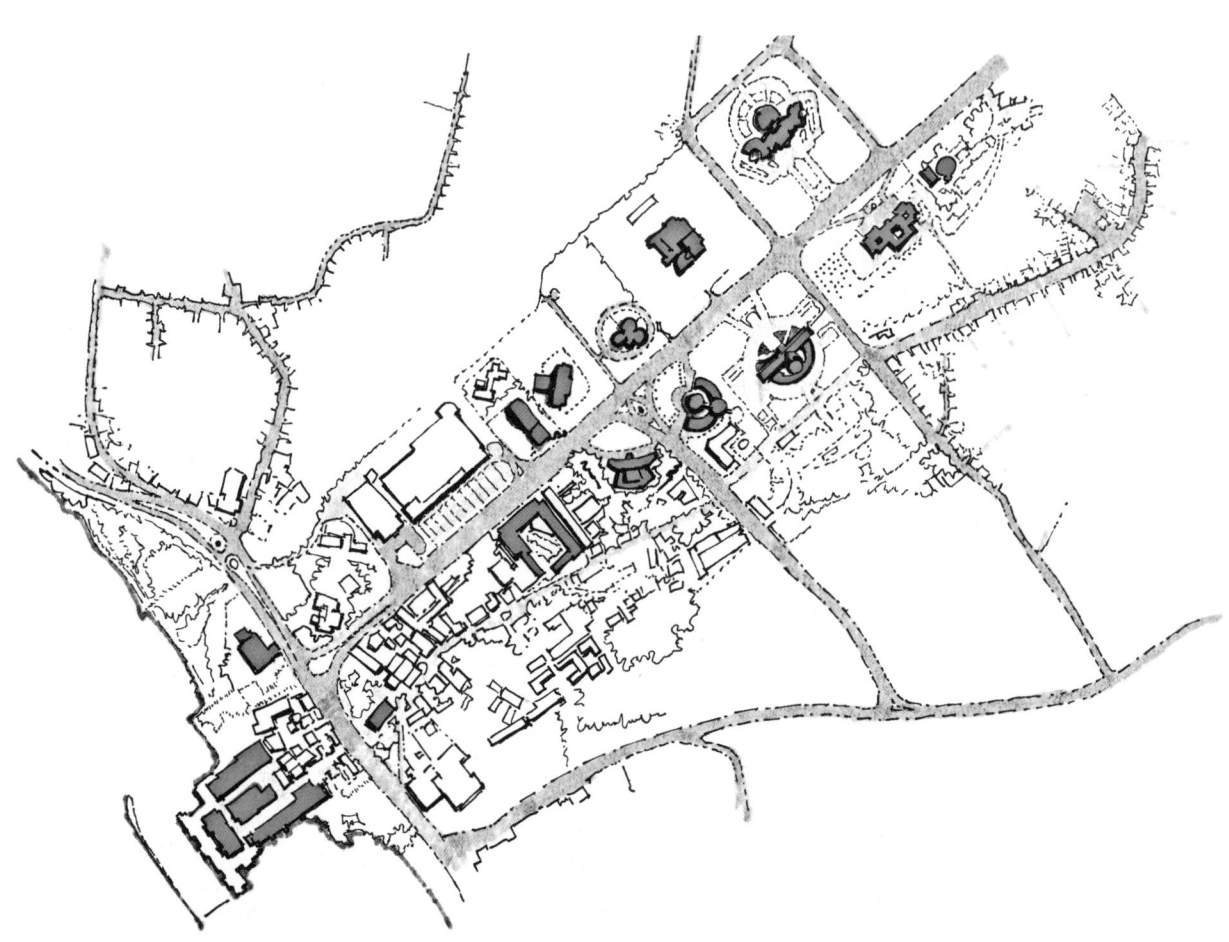

1 Port Mole
2 St Marie Cathedral
3 Mission Catholique, Catholic Mission
4 French Cultural Centre
5 Place de La Paix, Square of Peace
6 Palais Présidentiel, Presidential Palace
7 Hospital
8 Stadium
9 Musée des Arts et Tradition, Museum of Arts and Tradition
10 French Embassy

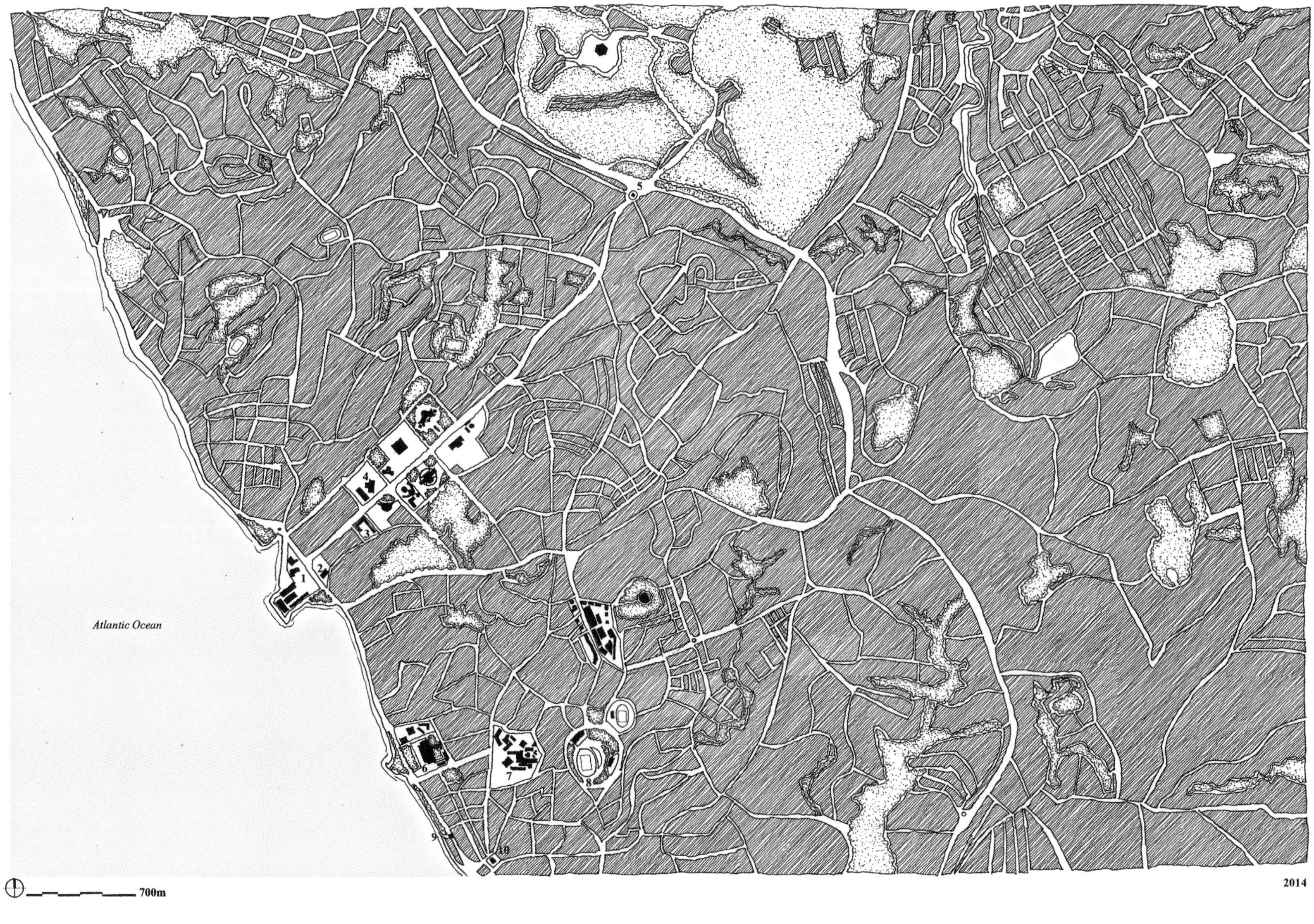

Atlantic Ocean

BRAZZAVILLE, REPUBLIC OF THE CONGO

FOUNDED: 1880 or 1883
URBAN AREA: 100 km²
POPULATION (2007): 1,373,382
URBAN AREA DENSITY: 10,185/km²
GPS: 4° 16'42.49"S, 15° 16'41.95"E

Brazzaville, one of the few African cities that retained its colonial name, is the capital and largest city in the Republic of the Congo. It is set along the northern banks of the Congo River, neighbouring the Democratic Republic of the Congo, of which the metropolis Kinshasa is the capital. Kinshasa is located directly opposite the river to the south. The result is that these two cities have the highest proximity in the world between two capital cities, which historically resulted in a mutual influence and exchange between the two.

The city core of Brazzaville is focused around the new port, close to the railway station. Similar to Kinshasa, Brazzaville was planned with a polynuclear layout with urban centres corresponding to political power. Several ravines divide the urban structure of the city and its operating systems, where small rivers unite with the main river. European establishments historically settled in the upper parts of the city, as these areas were considered healthier than along the river. On both sides of the Congo River, a segregationist system was therefore operated. Traces of the colonial past are visible in buildings of the capital's CBD. The latter was not only an important commercial centre, but also the main colonial residential area, and is known today as the *centre ville*.

The city appears to have expanded, unplanned and sprawling, in concentric semicircles over time. From 1960, the year of the Republic's independence, to the mid–1980s, various attempts were made to plan urban development, but the magnitude of demand far outreached the growth projections calculated in the master plans.

Marxist-Leninist political discourse during the 1970s–1980s was shown in the erection of monuments and public works in the city, followed by widespread physical destruction after multiparty elections and more or less continual violent conflict during the 1990s. By 1999, Brazzaville had lost much of its vitality – yet some years after the war, it became a transformed city.

The reopening of the railway between Brazzaville and Pointe-Noire symbolised the promise of a better quality of life for its residents. Today, the *centre ville* houses specialised tertiary activities related to international trade, information technology, and new services associated with finance, trade and national administration. The city houses the only stadium authorised to host international sports events and a vast array of churches provides new forms of networking and landmarks in the city.

1 Old Harbour
2 Plaine Market
3 Place de la Liberté & Gare de Brazzaville, Freedom Square & Brazzaville Train Station
4 Basilique Sainte Anne & Stade Félix Éboué, Basilique Sainte Anne & Félix Éboué Staduim
5 Mairie de Moungali, Mayor of Moungali
6 Pierre Savorgnan de Brazza Mémorial, Pierre Savorgnan de Brazza Memorial
7 Cathé-drale, Cathedral
8 Post Centrale, Central Post
9 Musée Marien Ngouabi, Museum Marien Ngouabi
10 Parc Marien Ngouabi, Marien Ngouabi Park
11 Collège-Lycée Anne-Marie Javouhey, College Lycée Marie-Anne Javouhey
12 Paroisse Notre-Dame de l'Assomption, Parish of Our Lady of the Assumption
13 Hôpital Central des Armées, Central Hospital of the Armed Forces
14 Cimetière du Centre Ville, Downtown Cemetery
15 Monument en Hommages aux victimes du DC10 de L'UTA, Tributes monument to victims of the UTA DC10
16 Palais de Justice de Brazzaville, Brazzaville Courthouse
17 Centre Cultural de Françoise, Cultural Centre of France
18 Esplanade des Droits de l'Homme, Place of Human Rights
19 Maison Présidentielle, Presidential House
20 Institut Louis Pasteur, Louis Pasteur Institute
21 Parque Zoologique, Zoo Park
22 Assemblée Nationale, National Assembly
23 Stade Massamba-Debat, Massamba-Debat Stadium
24 Stade Marchand, Marchand Stadium
25 Hôpital général de Brazzaville, General Hospital of Brazza-ville
26 L'aéroport international de Maya Maya, International Airport

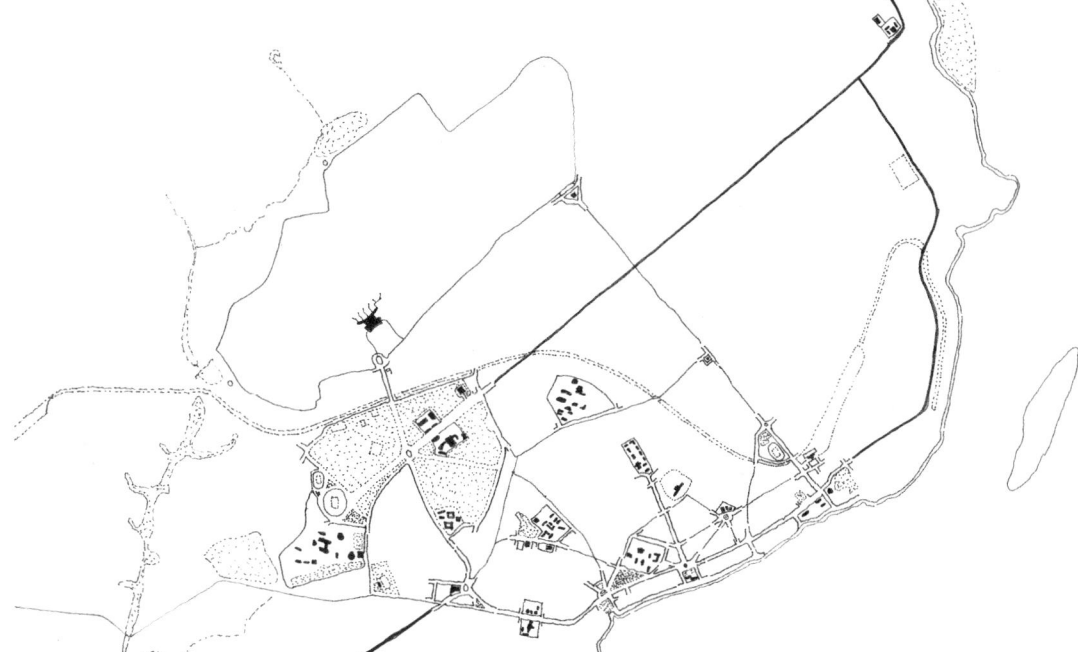

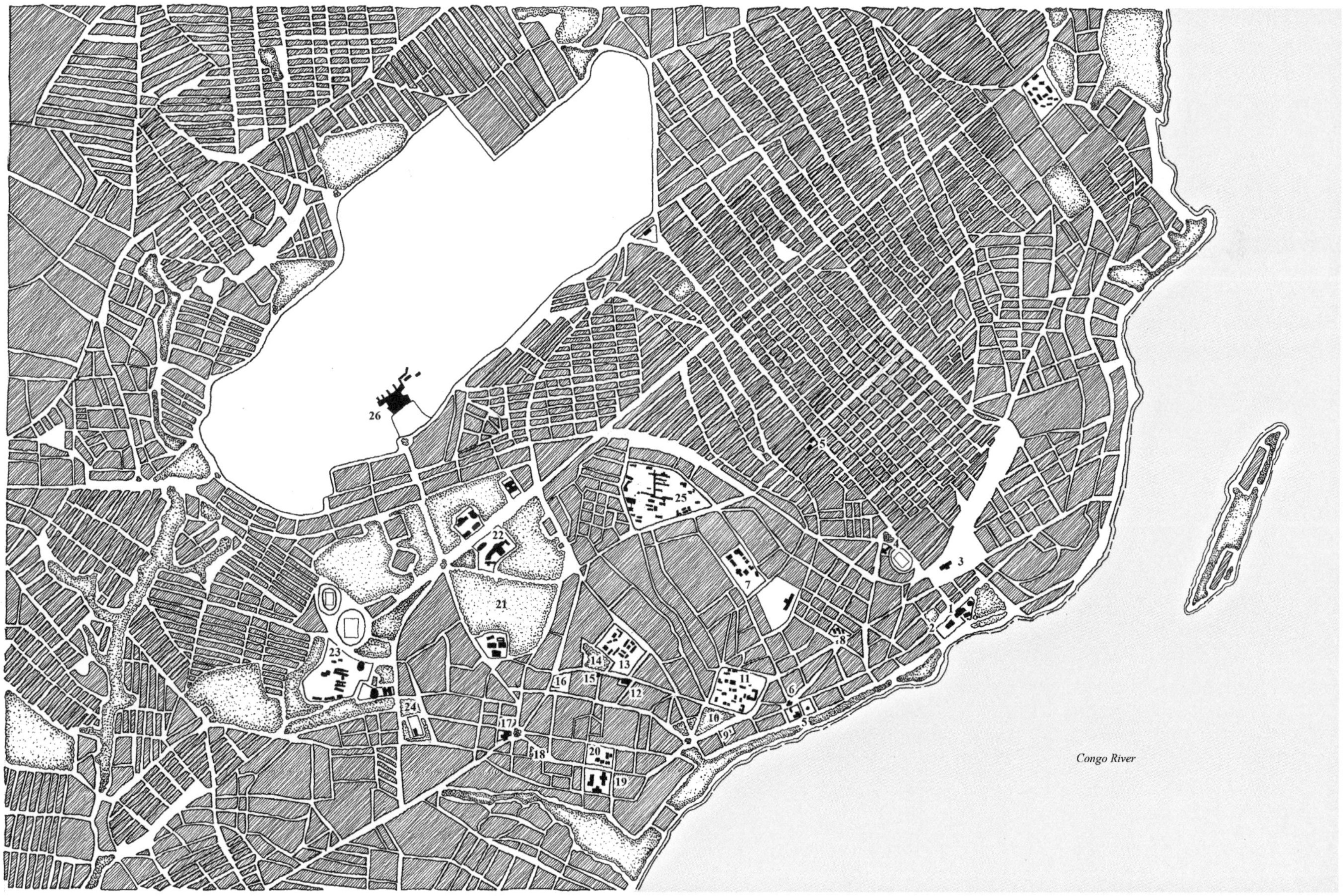

Congo River

700m

POINTE-NOIRE, REPUBLIC OF THE CONGO

FOUNDED: 1883
URBAN AREA: 1,144 km²
POPULATION (2007): 715,334
URBAN AREA DENSITY: 630/km²
GPS: 4° 48'4.31"S, 11° 50'26.57"E

Whereas Brazzaville is the capital of the Republic of the Congo, economic power is located in oil-rich, sprawling Pointe-Noire, the nation's second most important city. Similar to the development of Brazzaville, the development of the city has been greatly influenced by its tumultuous political past.

Located between the Atlantic Ocean and the Mayombe (a geographic area on the western coast of Africa, occupied by low mountains extending from the mouth of the Congo River), Pointe-Noire has open access to markets in Gabon (to the north) and Congo-Kinshasa via Cabinda (in the south).

Pointe-Noire's name (meaning "black point") originated from Portuguese navigators who saw black rocks on the mainland in 1484. It became a maritime reference and then a small fishing village from 1883, after the French signed a treaty with the local people. Forestry, service and fishery industries used to be its most important economic activities, but today the economy of the city is predominantly oil-based.

The Agostinho Neto Airport in Pointe-Noire is one of the most frequented international airports in the country – and highly visible since it is one of the only major open spaces in the sprawling city.

The city also holds the terminus of the Congo-Ocean Railway – the station being an architectural landmark in the city. The railway and maritime port of Pointe-Noire were major infrastructural elements that contributed to the formation of the main urban areas of the city.

The construction of these substantial projects was completed in 1934, and together they symbolised the infrastructural dreams of the then French colonial powers. The railway stations and their associated marketplaces attracted urban migration. By 1958, two years before the Republic of the Congo's independence, there was a noticeable migration of the national population towards the two major cities of Brazzaville and Pointe-Noire. Migration was facilitated by the development of central administrative functions in these cities, designed to accommodate the functional demands of the then new independent state.

The radial pattern from Avenue Moé Kaat Matou converges at the Round Point Lumumba and is highly visible in the urban structure. Beyond this structure, the informal city sprawls boundlessly.

CENTRAL AFRICA

1 Pointe-Noire Station
2 Port Autonome de Pointe-Noire, Port of Pointe-Noire
3 Atlantic Ocean
4 Raphaël Antonetti Square
5 Joseph Pouabou Square
6 Courthouse
7 Jean-Baptiste Missamou Square
8 Place des Amoureux, Lovers Square
9 Grand Market
10 South Mvou-Mvou Primary School
11 Municipal Stadium
12 Kastanis Kassaï Square
13 July 31st Roundabout
14 School St Jean-Baptiste
15 Poaty Bernard Technical School
16 Victor Augagneur School
17 Pointe-Noire Airport

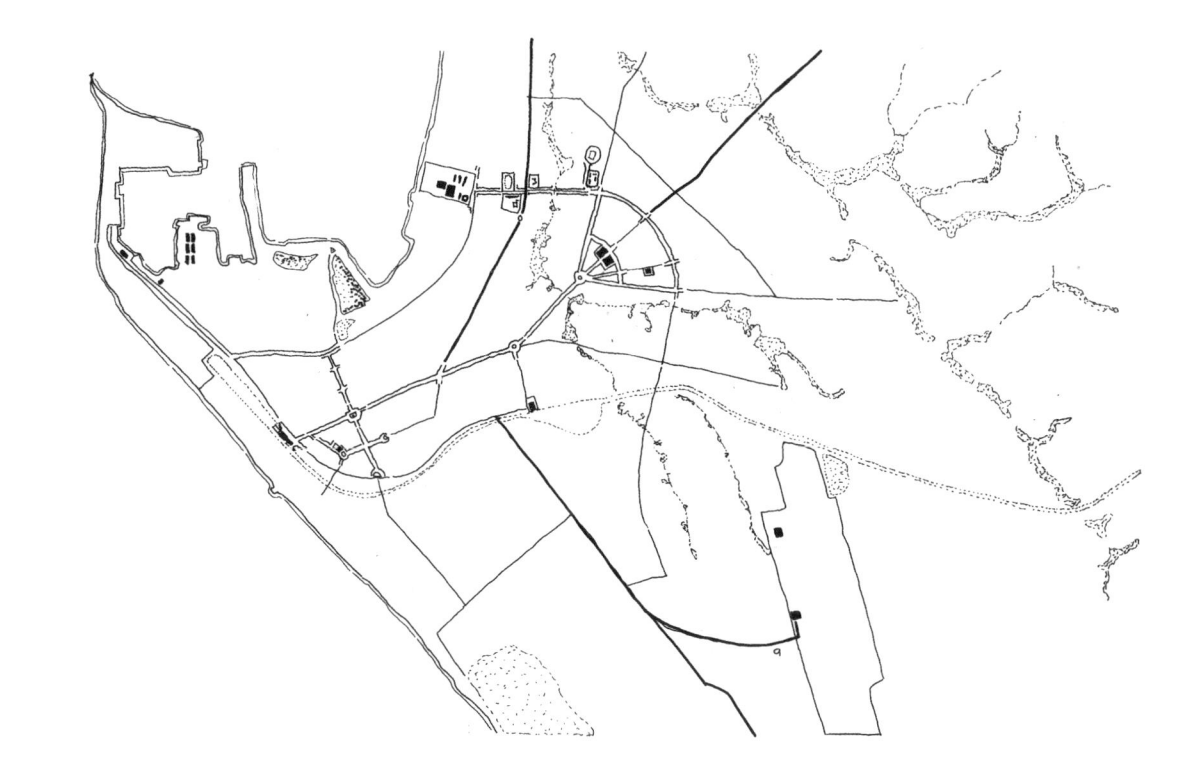

Atlantic Ocean

700m

2014

SÃO TOMÉ, DEMOCRATIC REPUBLIC OF SÃO TOMÉ AND PRINCIPE

FOUNDED: 1493
URBAN AREA: unknown
POPULATION (2005): 56,166
URBAN AREA DENSITY: unknown
GPS: 0° 20'21.79"N, 6° 43'50.44"E

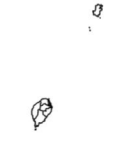

São Tomé is the capital city of the Democratic Republic of São Tomé and Principe. It is located in the Gulf of Guinea, along the eastern coast of Africa, on an archipelago formed by two islands and some islets. The small archipelago became an important colonial outpost of established sea routes and maritime trade.

Tenreiro (1961), as quoted by Fernandes, described the city as having an "ideal location, if not in all aspects, at least in two: a large bay which sheltered the ships and wide open land that, gently and without a rugged terrain, lead to the interior", therefore becoming a "centre of radiation of settlement". The city assumed "a double role of core that attracted settlers to the island's interior and drained products to the exterior".

Uninhabited before the arrival of the Portuguese around 1470, its history is characterised by slave labour, sugar and coffee plantations. The archipelago became one of the world's leaders in cocoa exportation by the twentieth century. According to Fernandes, the buildings are a direct reflection of these enterprises over time, which included the increasing destruction of vegetation, radical changes in land usage, implementation of major infrastructure projects, and the construction of "production estates" which shaped an environment that reflected, and responded to, the specific purposes of its colonial powers. Over time, however, production of cocoa declined. Its devaluation in international markets induced major economic difficulties for the small country and its capital city – resulting in increased poverty.

The colonial inheritance of the city is still visible in its fabric, along with the monuments following its independence during 1975. A waterfront-parallel axis structures the older core of the city. Over time, the city has expanded organically inwards. Urban growth over many centuries was supported by expansion plans during the colonial period, but the provision of infrastructure was unable to keep up with increasing growth in recent years. Today the city is characterised by increasing informal urbanity, creating fragmentation and disparities between planned and unplanned areas. The expansion of the city along the coast and its inward roads form a dispersed, but continuous mass.

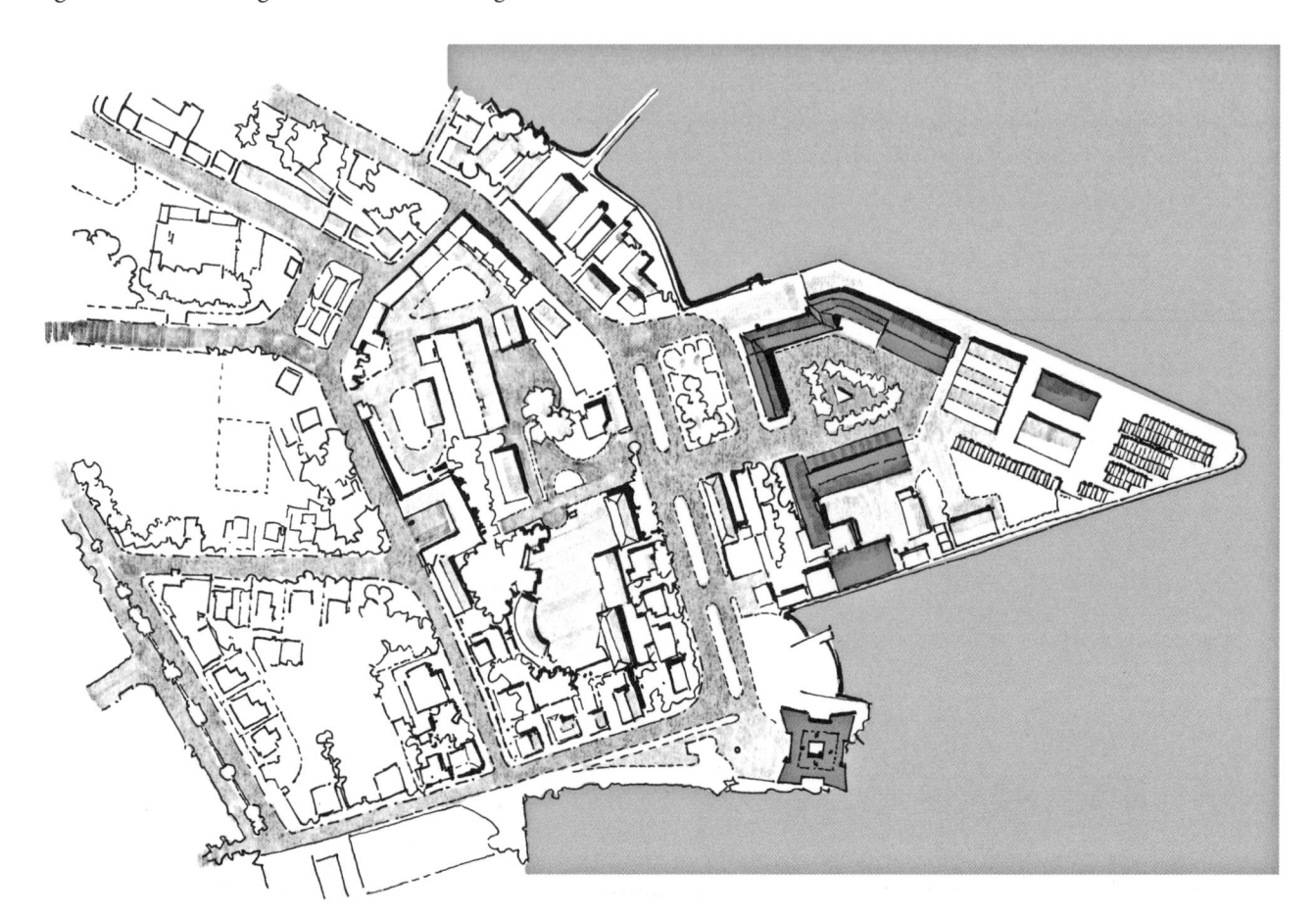

CENTRAL AFRICA

1. St Sebastian Fort
2. Statues of the Portuguese Discoverers
3. Port
4. Church
5. Parque Popular & Parque da U.C.L.A., Popular Park & Park U.C.L.A
6. Marcelo Da Veiga Cinema
7. July 12th National Stadium
8. Cathedral of São Tomé
9. Presidential Palace
10. Monument
11. Independence Square
12. Patrice Lumumba Secondary School
13. Municipal Market
14. Department of Labour
15. Church
16. Bus Station & Market
17. Vitória do Riboque Football Stadium
18. Cemetery
19. Palace of Congress
20. Park
21. Grand Water Channel & Park
22. Central Prison

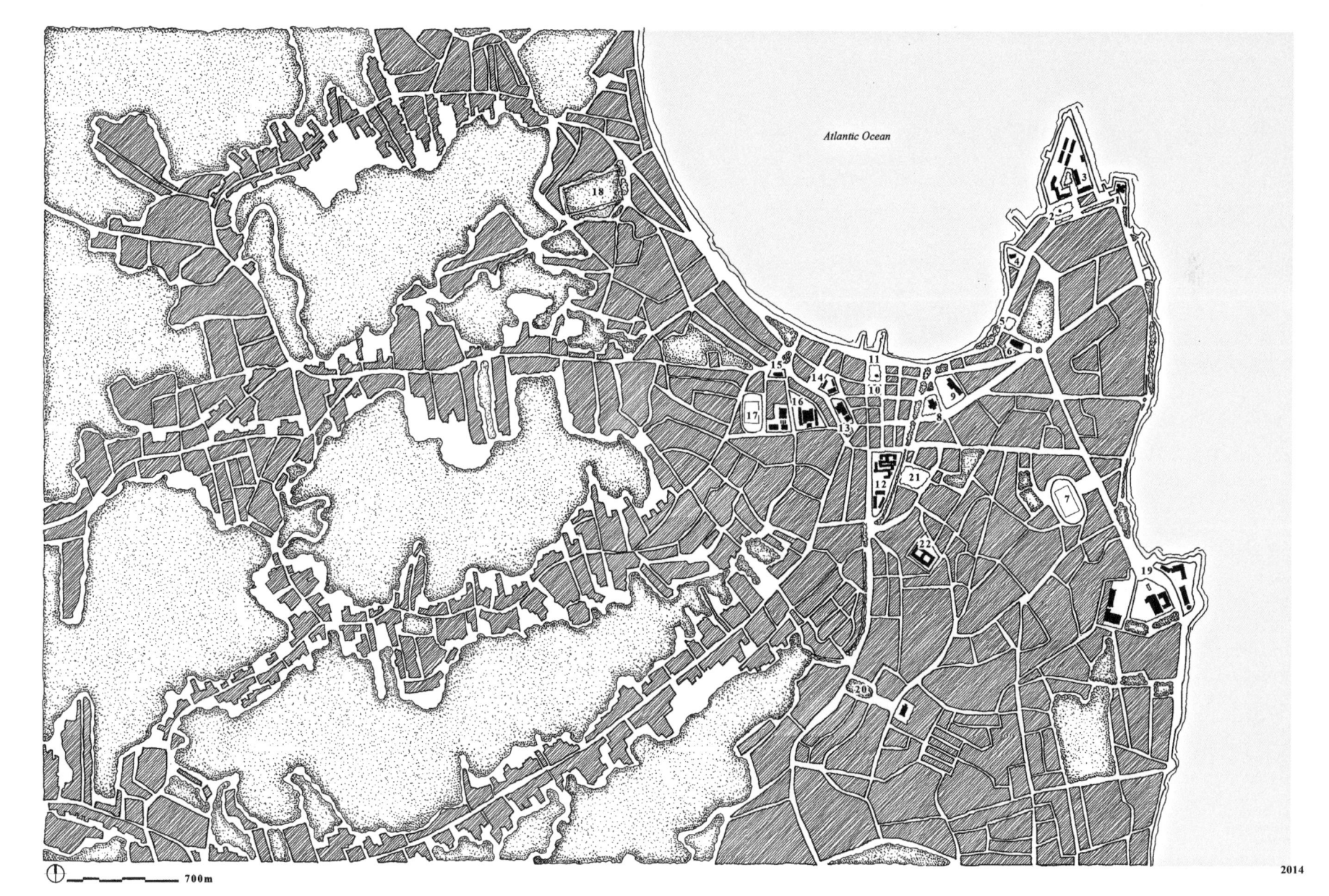

BUJUMBURA, BURUNDI

FOUNDED: 1871
URBAN AREA: 8,652 km²
POPULATION (2008): 497,166
URBAN AREA DENSITY: 2,720/km²
GPS: 3° 23'18.07"S, 29° 21'41.60"E
3° 22'56.56"S, 29° 21'40.93"E

Bujumbura, formerly known as Usumbura, is the capital and largest city in the country, as well as the main port of Burundi. The city, surrounded by hills, is located on the north-eastern shore of Lake Tanganyika. The city centre grew from a small village which developed around a large marketplace known as Mukaza. This is located on the actual site of the current Bujumbura central market – a central gathering place since the 1850s.

Initially, this colonial town was an East African German military post founded in 1889. Bujumbura was made the administrative centre of the Belgian League of Nations mandate of Ruanda-Urundi after the First World War. The city's name was changed from Usumbura to Bujumbura during Burundi's independence in 1962.

The city is divided into thirteen neighbourhoods. These neighbourhoods were originally structured according to their inhabitants' ethnicity (hence the Swahili quarter, Bwiza quarter and Buyenzi quarter for Africans). The German centre was occupied by the Belgians, which kept expanding in residences, administrative offices and trading quarters as the city grew. With the expansion of the city, boundaries were no longer determined along racial lines, but were influenced by economic realities and administrative organisation. The outcome was areas which were very clean and developed quarters inhabited by the rich in contrast with the underdeveloped quarters rented by the poor.

Prominent features of the city include a national stadium [14], a large mosque [11], an international airport, and a cathedral for the Archdiocese of Bujumbura [7]. The Museum of Life or Living Museum [2] was founded in 1977 and was one of the first collections illustrating the rich cultural and artistic diversity of Burundi. The museum is located in a large park area, displaying the cultural heritage of Bujumbura and Burundi, including both natural and human creations. Independence Square [9] is located in the centre of the city as a monument to commemorate Burundi's independence on 1 July 1962. Revolution Square [3], is also commemorative of Burundi's transition from a monarchy to a republic. The Regina Mundi Cathedral [7] is a church established in 1956 by Jesuit priests.

The city is accessible by ferries which sail from Bujumbura to Kigoma in Tanzania as well as through the Bujumbura International Airport. Bujumbura has been affected by frequent fighting between the country's two main ethnic groups, with Hutu militias opposing the Tutsi-dominated Burundi army. Bujumbura is a largely undeveloped city today, but it is still in the process of developing as the country itself develops further.

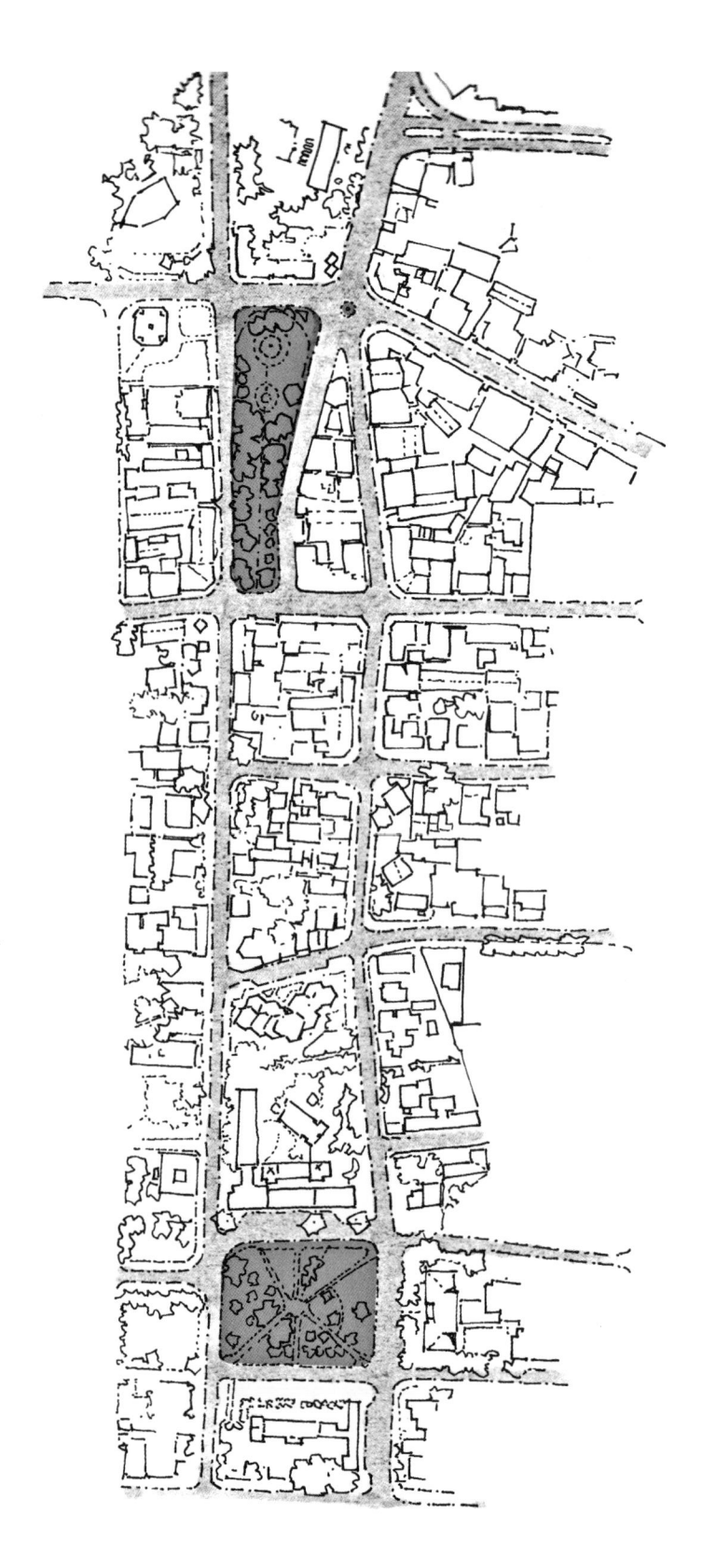

EASTERN AFRICA **39**

1 Lake Tanganyika & Nautical Circle
2 Musée Vivant, Living Museum
3 Revolution Square
4 Department of Justice
5 Department of Foreign Affairs and International Cooperation
6 Department of Finance and Planning Economic Development
7 Regina Mundi Cathedral
8 Memorial to Former Leaders
9 Independence Square
10 Market
11 Mosque
12 Church
13 Grand Cemetery of Bujumbura
14 Prince Rwagasore Stadium
15 Port
16 University of Burundi
17 Congress
18 Bujumbura Bus Station

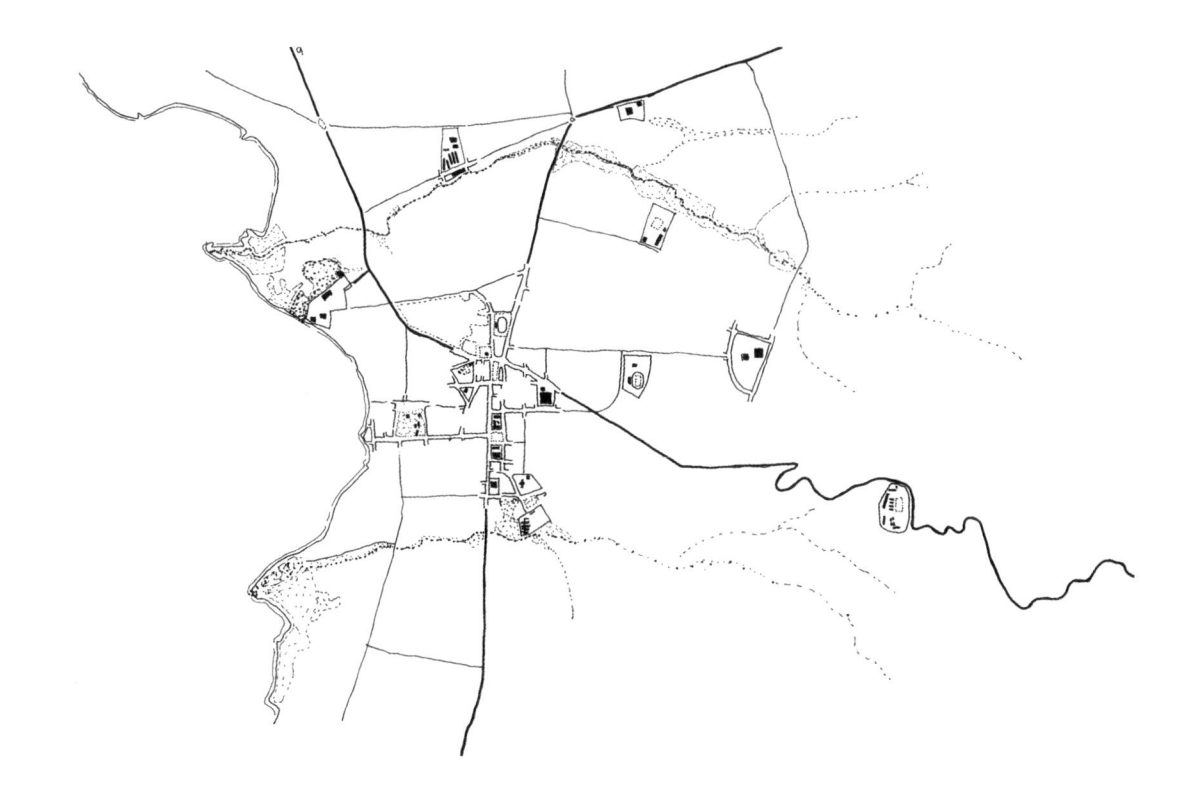

MORONI, COMORES

FOUNDED: 1962
URBAN AREA: 30 km²
POPULATION: 54,000
URBAN AREA DENSITY: 1,800/km²
GPS: 11° 42'14.73"S, 43° 15'6.40"E
11° 42'10.80"S, 43° 15'8.98"E

Moroni is a coastal town and the capital of the Union of the Comoros. This sovereign archipelago in the Indian Ocean comprises three main islands. The capital is located on the south-western Grande Comore (also called Njazidja) island. Moroni was founded by Arabic-speaking settlers, possibly as early as the tenth century AD and became the capital city in 1958 succeeding Dzaoudzi, the original administrative city of the island of Mayotte.

The city is located at the foot of Mount Karthala, 10 km northwest of the active volcano's crater – giving rise to its name 'Moroni', translated as 'in the heart of fire' in Comorian.

Moroni has a port [3] which consists of a small quay in a natural cove. The harbour serves as the connecting point for transport between the other islands in the Comoros archipelago, the African mainland, as well as Madagascar and other Indian Ocean islands. However, the port is not suitable for large ships to enter as coral reefs pose a safety threat. Moroni has a rocky volcanic coastline, mostly without beaches.

This quaint town reflects its Arabic routes with narrow streets lined with traditional shops and cafes. The islands were commercially connected to Zanzibar in Tanzania, explaining the old city centre's layout, a smaller version of Zanzibar's Stone Town. The medina, the historic town centre, resembles a winding maze of narrow alleys and old buildings dating from the Swahili period. The close proximity of the buildings in the medina provides a welcome cool sanctuary with the shaded alleys.

The predominantly Muslim community is represented by the many mosques on the island, including the oldest mosque in the medina – the Badjanani Mosque or Ancienne Mosquée de Vendredi ("old Friday Mosque") [2] originally built in 1427, with a minaret added in 1921. National and international performances are regularly held in the theatre of the Alliance Franco-Comorienne, as well as numerous ceremonies, conferences, film screenings and seminars.

The Zawiyani ya Salmata Hamissi Mosque [6] is one of the older buildings found in Moroni and was named after a wealthy female benefactor who paid for its construction.

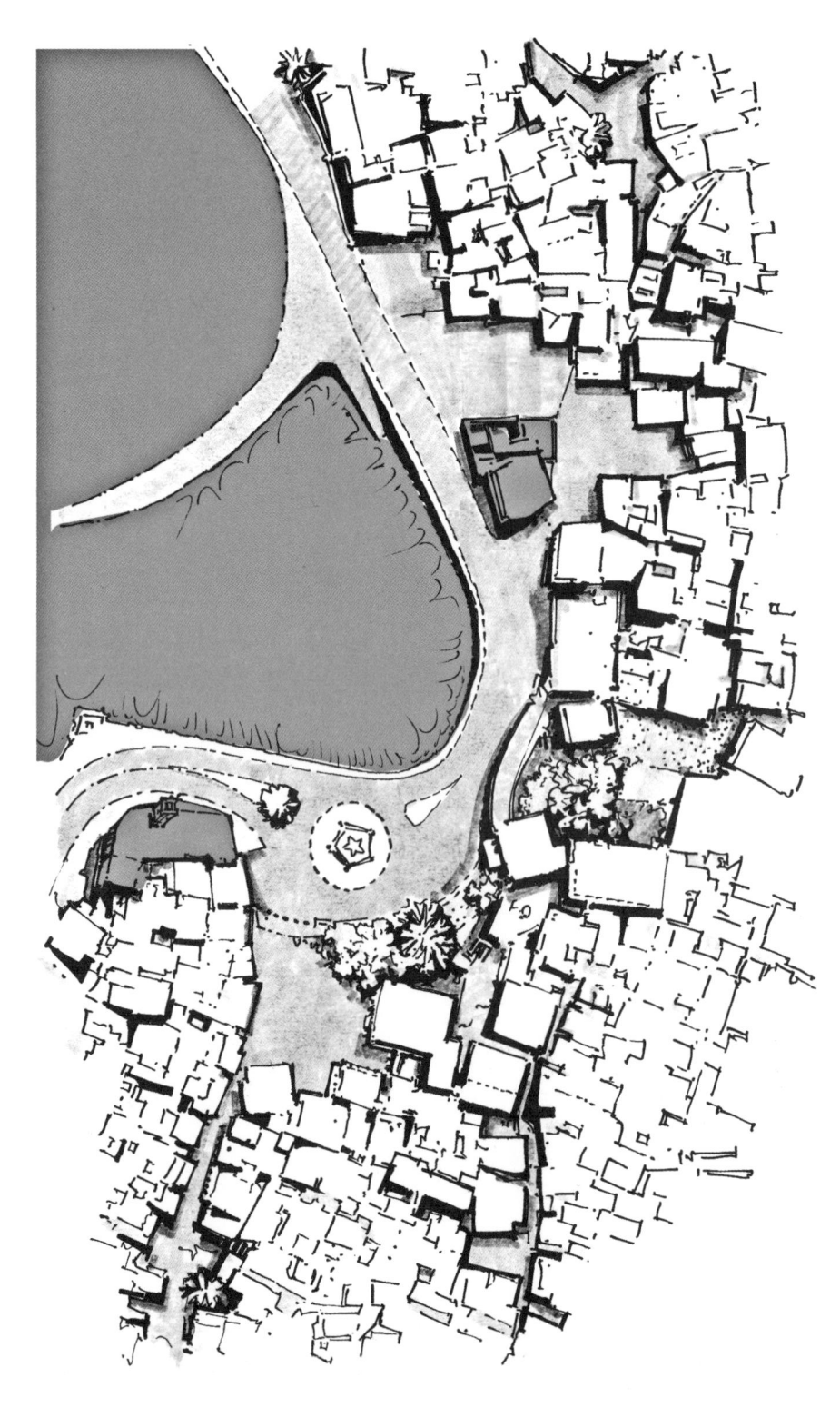

EASTERN AFRICA **41**

1 Mssihiri wa Mtsangani Mosque
2 Old Friday Mosque & Celebration Square
3 Port
4 Mosque
5 Old Market
6 Salmata Hamissi Mosque
7 Adjao Square
8 Courthouse
9 Moriri Stadium
10 Ministry Offices
11 Mosque
12 Centre of Public Works
13 Park
14 Mosque

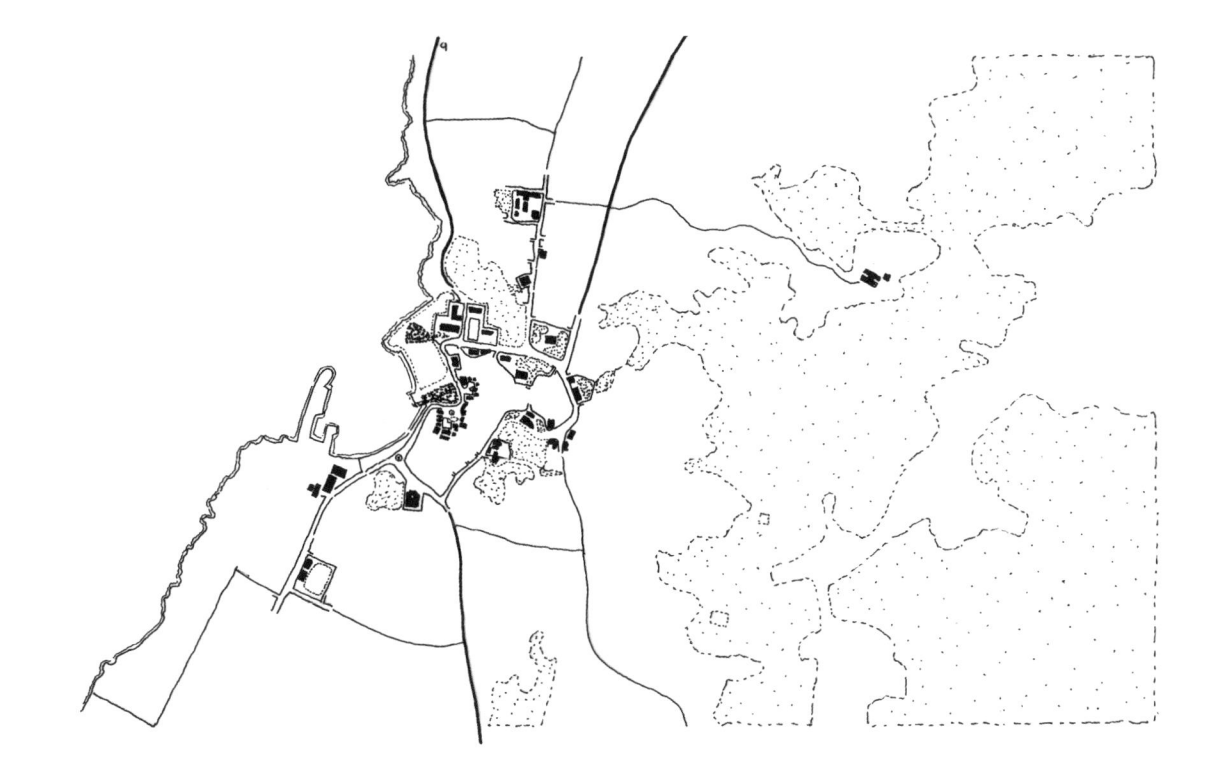

Indian Ocean

2014
500m

DJIBOUTI CITY, REPUBLIC OF DJIBOUTI

FOUNDED: 1888
URBAN AREA: 630 km²
POPULATION (2013): 623,891
URBAN AREA DENSITY: 990/km²
GPS: 11° 35'41.14"N, 43° 8'48.57"E

The seaport city of Djibouti is the capital of the Republic of Djibouti, located in the semi-desert and desert areas along the Horn of Africa. It was officialy inaugurated by the French in 1888 as part of their colonial strategy, and independence was gained in 1977. The city was built from no existing permanent settlement, yet, before colonialism, the territory now called Djibouti was an integral part of the ancient kingdoms and dynasties – its trade network spanning from Arabia to Ethiopia and Sudan.

The city – a cape located in the south of the Gulf of Tadjoura – was linked to several small islands to its north by the processes of infilling and natural shoaling. The islands form the northern boundary of the city, while the port of Djibouti and the railway are the backbone of the national economy.

Under French rule, the primary vocation of the city was as a link to the Horn of Africa region. The first urban plan for the city was developed in 1983, fashioned after the model used in France at the time. A current plan, dating from 1998, was developed during a period that the morphological changes to the city were considerable. These included major social housing projects, residential expansion and port development.

According to Bisaillon and Mohammed (2005), the city has two faces: a modern face and a traditional one. These two faces are reflected in the spatial duality of the urban layout. The European quarter is a well-defined residential and institutional centre. By contrast, the outlying areas of the city – the African quarters – are characterised by organic, colourful and irregular mixed uses. The European residential quarters are located at the extreme north of the city and are the most exclusive in the capital. The European and African cities meet at the city's second main square, Place Rimbaud, where the central market, bus station and Hammoudi Mosque are located. Planned interventions continue to emphasise the major port infrastructure and the French colonial city.

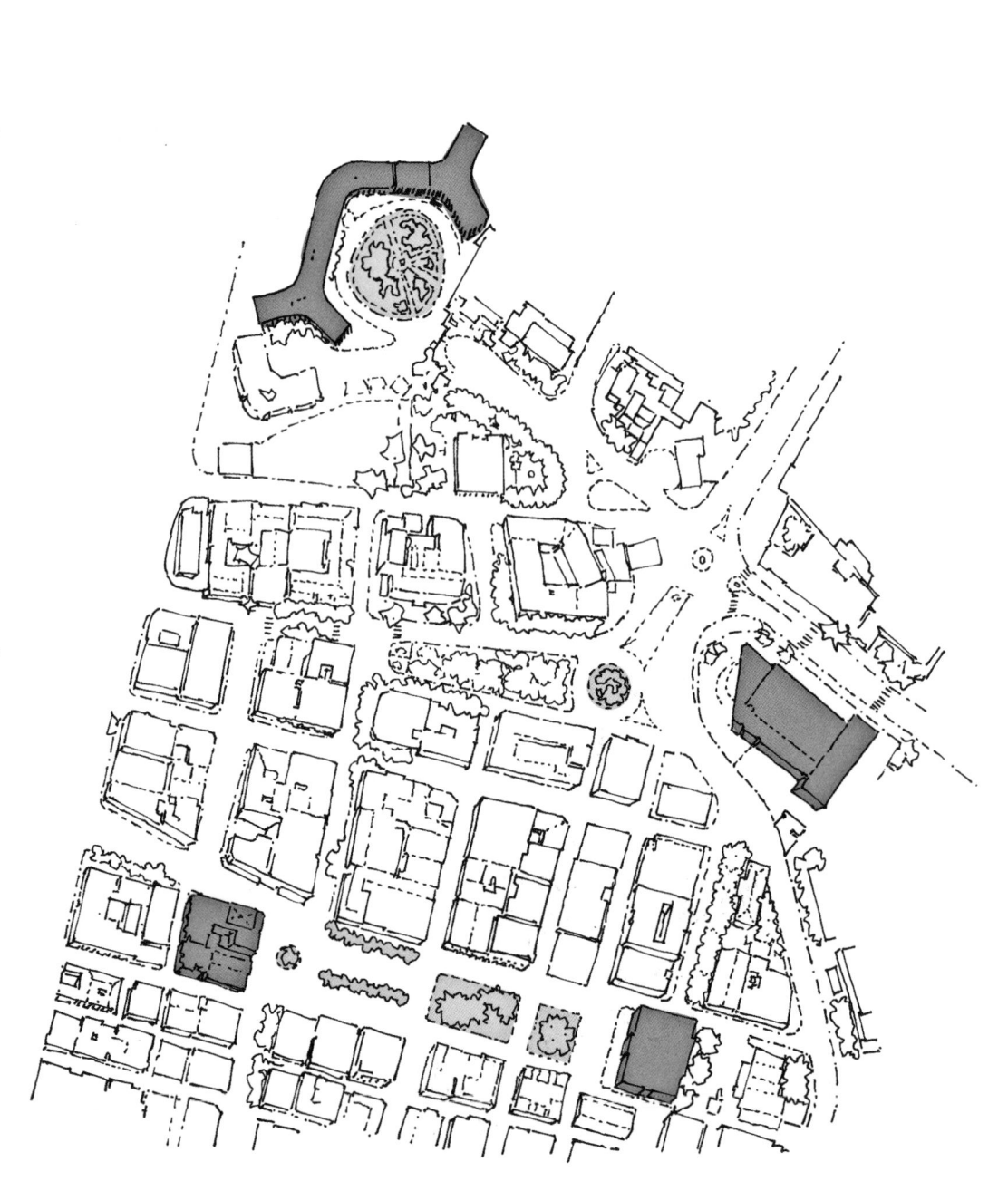

EASTERN AFRICA **43**

1 Independence Square
2 District Office of Djibouti
3 Hamoudi Mosque
4 Great Market
5 Park
6 National Assembly
7 Presidential Palace
8 Port
9 Railway Station
10 Hospital CHA Bouffard
11 Boulaoos College
12 Al Sada Mosque
13 University of Djibouti
14 Cité ministérielle, City Ministry
15 Cathédrale, Cathedral

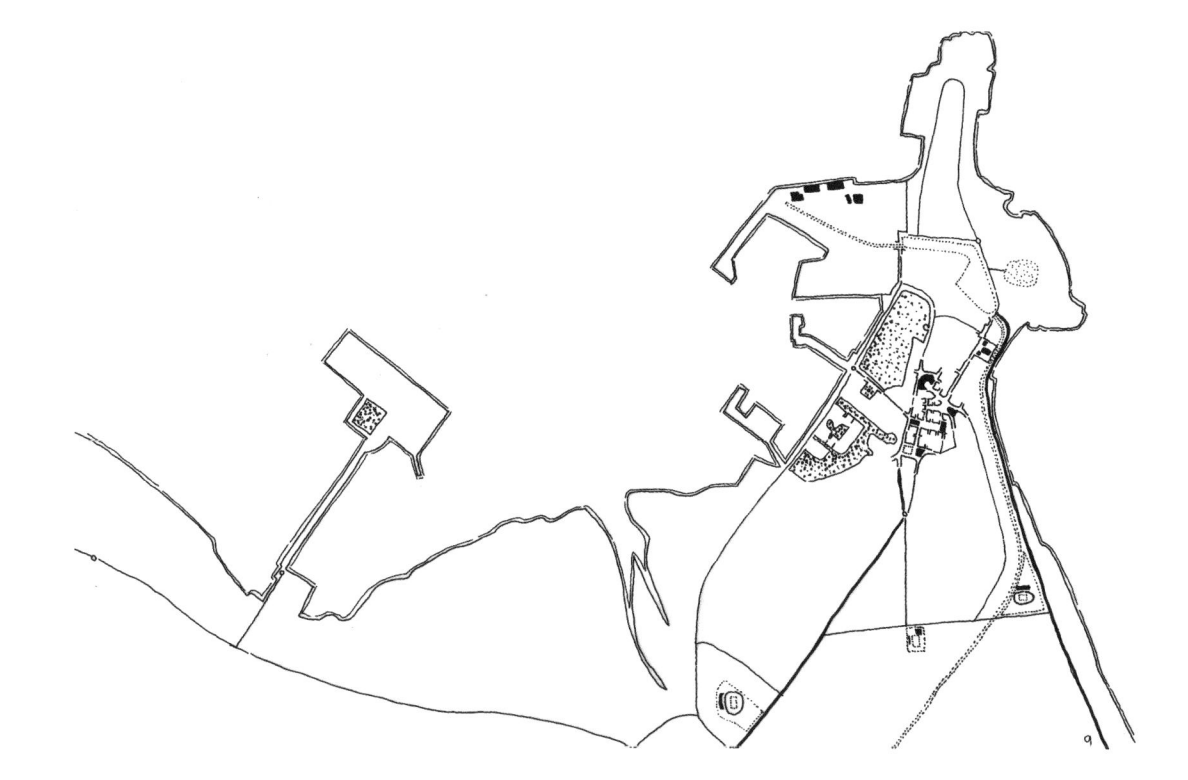

Gulf of Tadjoura

480m

2014

ASMARA, ERITREA

FOUNDED: unknown
URBAN AREA: 1,216 km²
POPULATION: 649,000
URBAN AREA DENSITY: 534/km²
GPS: 15° 33'3.89"N, 37° 53'12.03"E
   15° 20'21.41"N, 38° 56'33.72"E
   15° 20'17.97"N, 38° 56'22.79"E
   15° 20'16.25"N, 38° 56'9.48"E

Asmara, described as 'Africa's Secret Modernist City' is the capital city and largest settlement in Eritrea. Located at an altitude of 2,400 m, it is Africa's highest capital city.

Asmara was occupied by Italy in 1889, and was declared the capital city of Eritrea in 1897 by Governor Martini. A railway line was built leading to the coast in the early twentieth century. The city experienced substantial growth during the 1930s as tens of thousands of Italians moved to the region in preparation for Mussolini's planned invasion of Ethiopia. Consequently, the city became a blank canvas for experimental modern architectural designs resembling Italian architecture as part of the grand city plan.

During the 1939 census, it was established that Asmara was by far Italy's largest centre in Africa with an estimated 55 percent (54,000) of the population being Italian. It was also during this period (1935–1941) that the largest portion of Asmara was established, effectively meaning that the Italians practically built almost an entire city in six years. This period formed part of Mussolini's plan for a second Roman Empire in Africa. Although the war halted his plans, the funding that was contributed by him towards the urban development resulted in the Asmara we see today – an extraordinary modern city. The city was planned for the Italians with separate zoned areas designated for the Eritreans. Typical modern urban planning features include wide tree-lined boulevards and politically dedicated zones and districts.

Today, Asmara is most famous for representing one of the most concentrated and intact assemblages of Modernist architecture anywhere in the world and was recently nominated as a UNESCO World Heritage Site.

The main areas of the city were planned according to an orthogonal grid that was adjusted to suit historic caravan routes and natural features. The more developed city plans indicate spacious European quarters in the southern part laid out according to the garden city planning model, a denser mixed quarter in the vicinity of the main markets and mosque to the north, and an industrial quarter in the north-east corner. Organically developed indigenous quarters were kept outside this planned city.

Although Colonial Asmara was envisaged as a green city, much of its public open space, street planting and other greenery have been absorbed by development in recent decades and there is consequently a shortage of defined public open space.

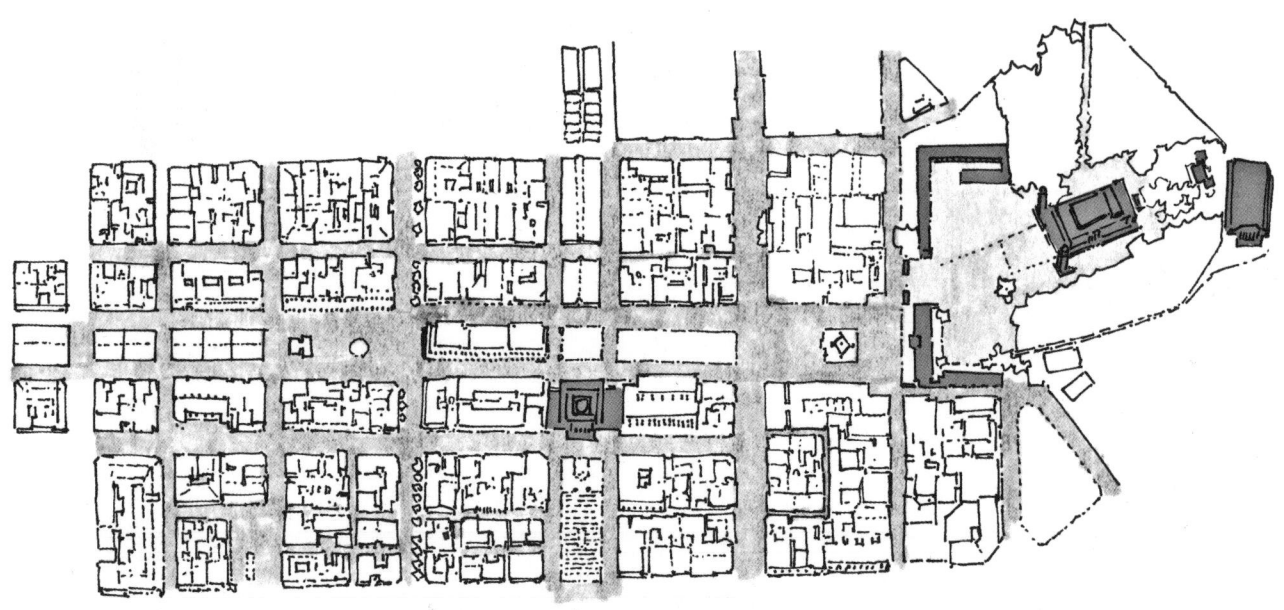

1	Enda Mariam Orthodox Cathedral	16	Park
2	Eritrea Square	17	Opera House
3	Central Market	18	Mai Khan Khan Fountain
4	Greek Orthodox Church	19	Eritrean Evangelical Church
5	Asmara Bathi Meskerem Square & Park	20	Hospital
6	Khulafah Al Rashidan Great Mosque	21	Fort
7	St Joseph Cathedral	22	St Joseph Church
8	Central Post Office & Piazza Roma	23	Stadium
9	Former Governor's Palace	24	Sport Club
10	Presidential Palace	25	National Museum
11	Piazza Italia	26	Tseserat Cemetery
12	Central Train Station	27	Church
13	Central Bus Station	28	Military School
14	Cinema Roma	29	Church
15	Bowling Alley	30	Semaetat High School
		31	Medebar Market
		32	Mak'aaber Cemetery
		33	Cheri
		34	Mosque

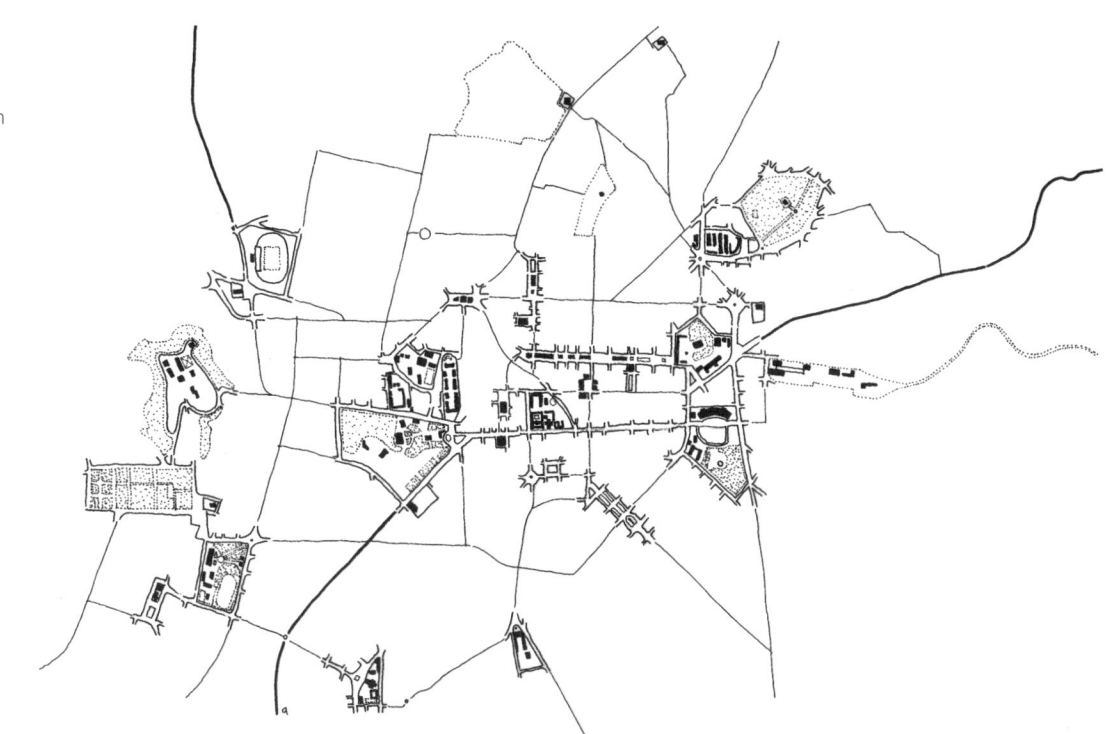

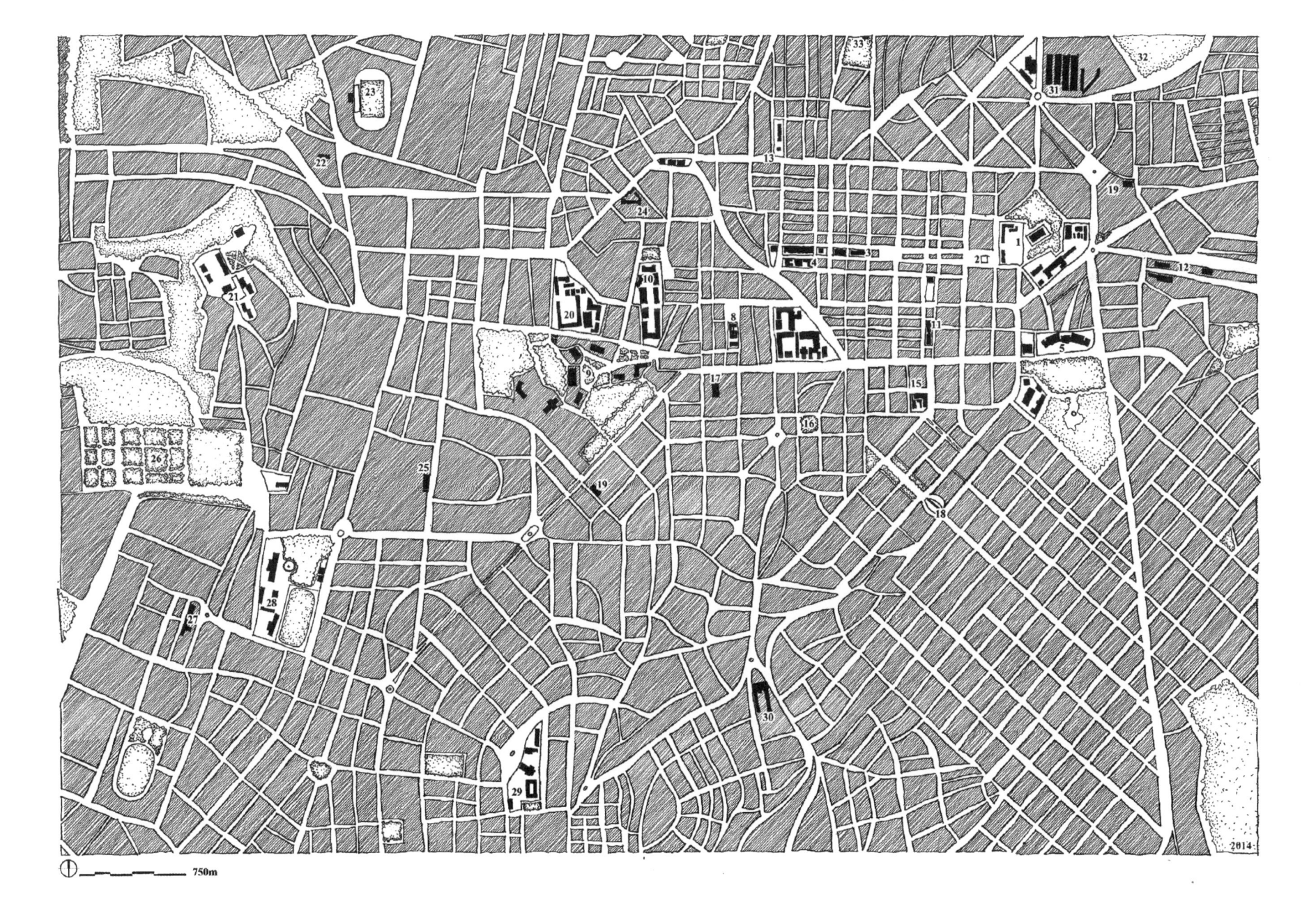

MASSAWA, ERITREA

FOUNDED: unknown
URBAN AREA: 477 km²
POPULATION: 53,090
URBAN AREA DENSITY: 110/km²
GPS: 15° 36'10.35"N, 39° 27'51.26"E
15° 36'28.70"N, 39° 28'31.43"E

Massawa, a city of islands and also known as the "Pearl of the Red Sea", was once the capital of the Italian colony of Eritrea. Originally a small seaside village, this charming city is located on the Red Sea coast of Eritrea. For many centuries, the city was one of the region's most important ports and became East Africa's largest in the 1930s with strong trading links to Europe, the Middle East and India. The island of Massawa remains the largest natural deep-water port on the Red Sea and is now Eritrea's main port and access to the rest of the world.

Massawa is Eritrea's oldest urban settlement with structures dating from as early as the sixteenth century. The city is traditionally built on two coral islands, connected to each other and joined to the mainland by causeways. Old Massawa is a largely residential area and Tiwalet Island is home to some old villas and the administrative buildings. The urban fabric with its low, whitewashed buildings, porticoes and arcades resemble the Arabic influences of the city's age-old connection with Arabia across the Red Sea. The city has an organic street pattern with key public buildings and markets defining the traditional heart of the city.

Massawa's history of occupation by various groups including the Portuguese, Arabs, and Egyptians is evidently reflected in its charming building structures, with the biggest influence coming from the Ottoman Turks who occupied the city for almost 300 years.

With the construction of the railway line between Massawa and Asmara in 1922, new markets were opened for farm produce between other towns. This led to Massawa experiencing unprecedented prosperity – it is said that the city was, up until the 1960s, the largest, safest and most profitable port on the East African coast.

The urban fabric resembles a tapestry of reconstructed buildings, traditionally built with coral stone, and more recently replaced with reinforced concrete in areas destroyed and affected by the 1921 earthquake, the 1988 fire, and the 30-year-long war of independence.

Significant buildings in the city include the fifteenth-century Sheikh Hanafi Mosque [4], one of the oldest surviving structures in the city, as well as numerous Ottoman buildings – including the local bazaar. Later buildings include the Imperial Palace, built from 1872 to 1874, overlooking the harbour; St Mary's Cathedral [2]; and the 1920s Banco d'Italia [6].

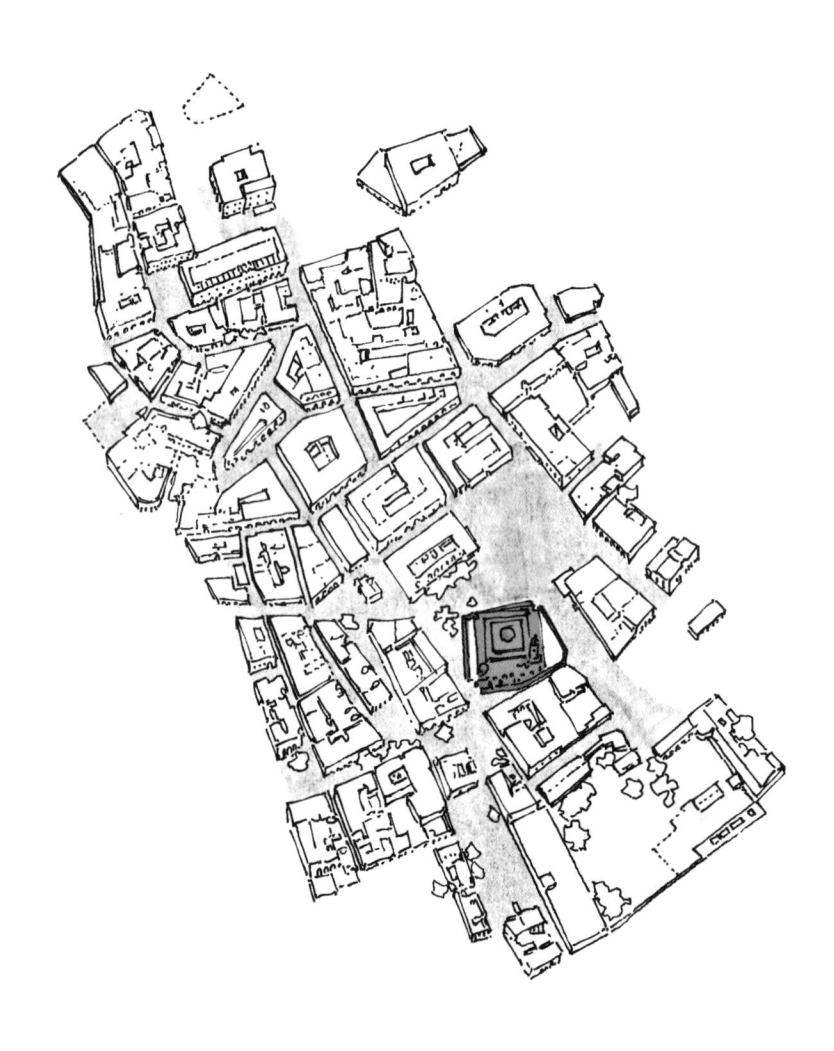

EASTERN AFRICA **47**

1 War Memory Square
2 St Mariam Cathedral
3 Massawa City Administration
4 Sheikh Hanafi Mosque
5 Piazza degli Incendi
6 Former Italian Bank
7 Turkish House
8 Port
9 Old Rail Station

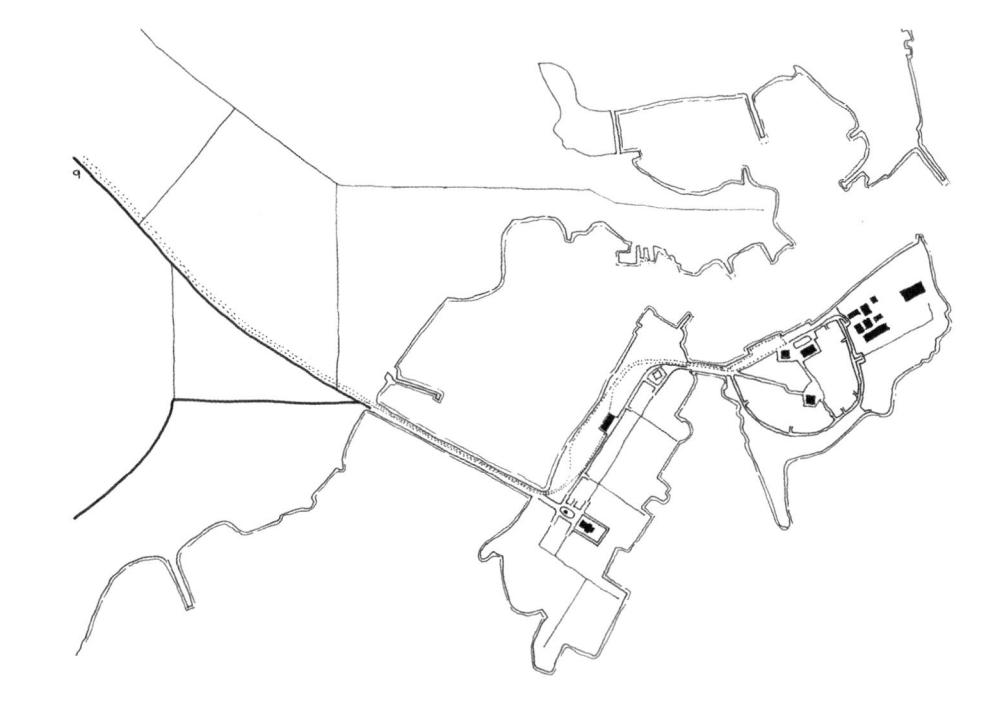

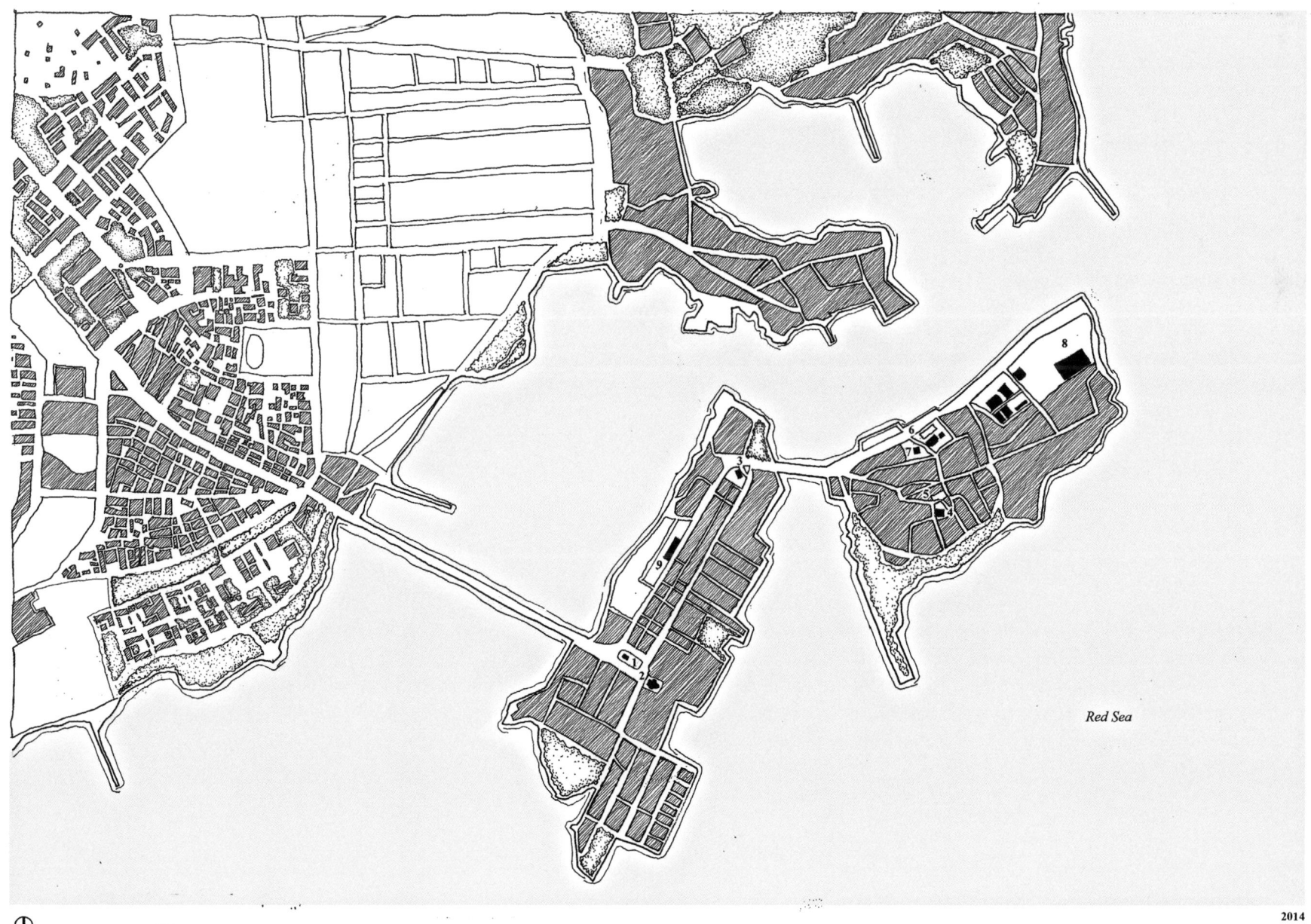

Red Sea

450m

2014

ADDIS ABA(E)BA, ETHIOPIA

FOUNDED: 1886
URBAN AREA: 540 km²
POPULATION (2009): 5 million
URBAN AREA DENSITY: 5000/km²
GPS: 9° 0'36.98"N, 38° 45'40.96"E
9° 2'37.61"N, 38° 45'40.60"E

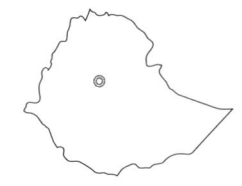

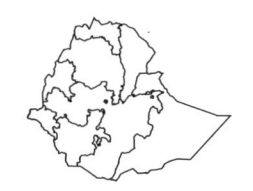

Founded in 1886, Addis Ababa – literally the "new flower" – is the capital city of Ethiopia, which also forms the seat of the African Union. While the city owed its origins to the state and the church, the railway and airline were instrumental over more recent decades in creating new development along its south. With the exception of the brief, still noticeable, intervention of the Italians during the late 1930s, the evolution of the city was shaped by internal forces and has consistently defied planning.

As an indigenous urban settlement formed around hot springs and amidst hills that dotted the landscape, Addis Ababa initially expanded without any formal control as a reflection of its feudal society. According to Baumeister and Knebel (2009), Addis Ababa resisted the western notion of centrality. The earliest settlements developed organically around the king's palace on the highest hill, and the camps of his generals were separated by vacant land from the residences of subordinates. Vacant spaces between camps were gradually inhabited and a residential structure – where the wealthy lived side by side with the poor – emerged.

Infrastructure and streets were not developed as the city was not planned, hence connections between various camps were literally only footpaths. Connecting bridges and streets were only later construed in an organic manner along the hilly urban terrain. According to Baumeister and Knebel (2009) "…with the further growth of the city the dots of the first camps were connected and a net of streets was formed. Here, new and modern urban functions like shops, hotels, cinemas, administration, workshops, etc. emerged. In-between these linear connections with modern features – streetliners – some large areas with mainly traditional building structures developed – in-fills. This pattern of settlement remains characteristic for the urban tissue of Addis Ababa…" They continue by observing that "… the linear space along the large streets in Addis Ababa has a purely functional use as opposed to the Western notion of public space in which streets have particular qualities to invite people to enjoy leisure time outdoors. An example from Addis Ababa: instead of one central building market, many small and specialised building material suppliers are located along one street. The open space is used for display and workshops. Other more general economies like taxis, beggars, etc. are found, too. All other functions, for example for leisure activities, are indoors. In this city structure there are no public squares, often large public events will take place where the street space is widened".

Addis Ababa, distinctive because of its imported eucalyptus trees, is a spontaneous, chaotic city. Often described as a "slum-city", it continues to be overwhelmed by extensive urban poverty, unemployment, inadequate housing, congestion and underdeveloped infrastructure.

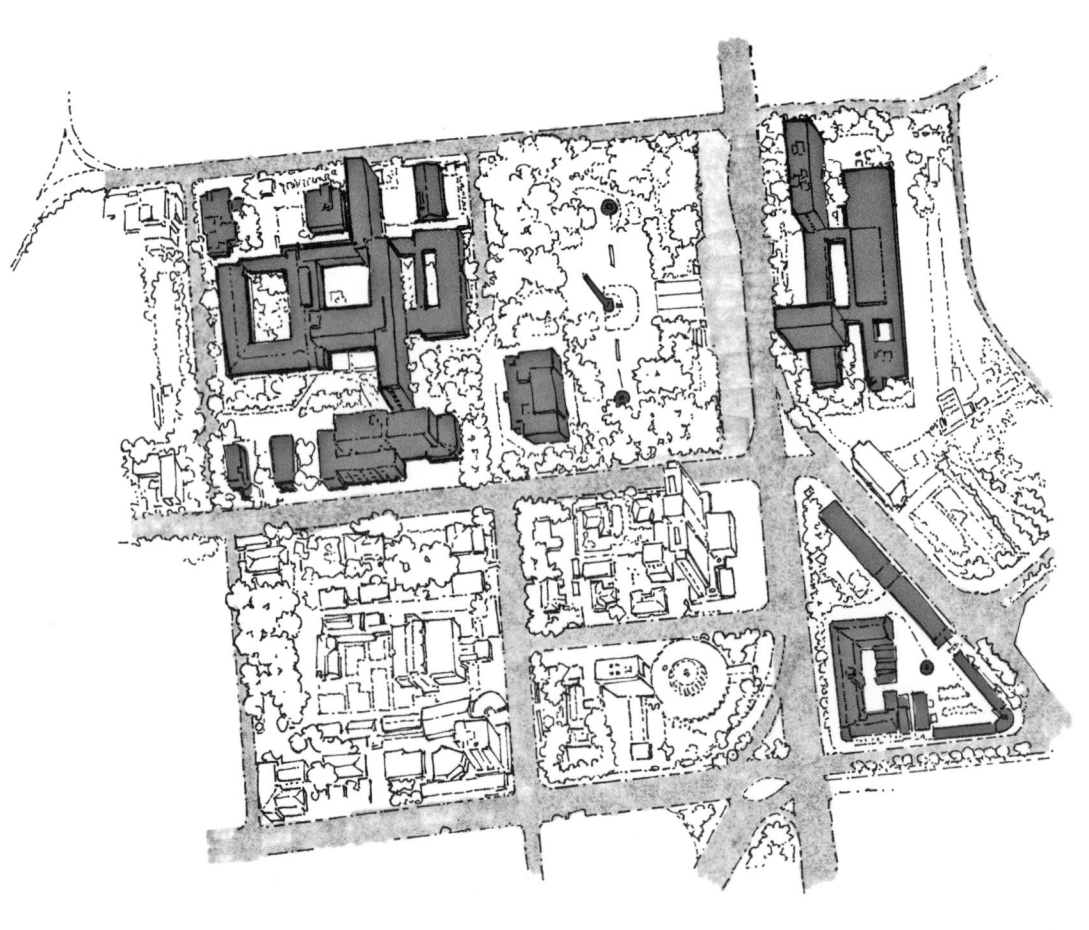

#		#	
1	Railway Station	21	Ministry of Foreign Affairs
2	Lion of Juda	22	Taka Negest Beata Church
3	Ethiopian National Theatre	23	St Gabriel Church
4	Ministry of Defence	24	WRD Congress Hall
5	Ambassador Theatre	25	Prime Minister Office
6	Post Office, Post Museum & Ministry of Communications	26	Zoo Park
7	Mengistu Haile Mariam Revolutionary Memorial	27	Federal Police Commission
8	Black Lion Hospital & Faculty of Medicine	28	Hospital
9	Tewodros Square	29	Lideta Mariam Church
10	St Mikael Church (Gola)	30	Ethiopian School of Architecture, Construction and City Development
11	Addis Ababa City Council & Theatre/Cultural Centre	31	Tekle Haimanot Church
12	Ydnekachew Tesema Stadium	32	Anwar Mosque
13	Oromia Cultural Centre	33	Benin Mosque
14	Meskel Square & Addis Ababa Museum & "Red Terror" Martyrs Memorial	34	Nativity Catholic Cathedral
		35	St George's Cathedral
		36	Yekatit Square
15	Sebastopol Cinema & Exhibition Centre	37	Institute of Technology
		38	St Mary Orthodox Church
16	St Stephen's Church	39	Natural History Museum
17	African Park	40	Holy Trinity Church & World Church
18	Africa Hall & ECA Conference Centre	41	Kidus Raguel Church
		42	Market/Merkato
19	Hilton Hotel	43	AU Parliament
20	National Palace	44	Medhane Alem Cathedral

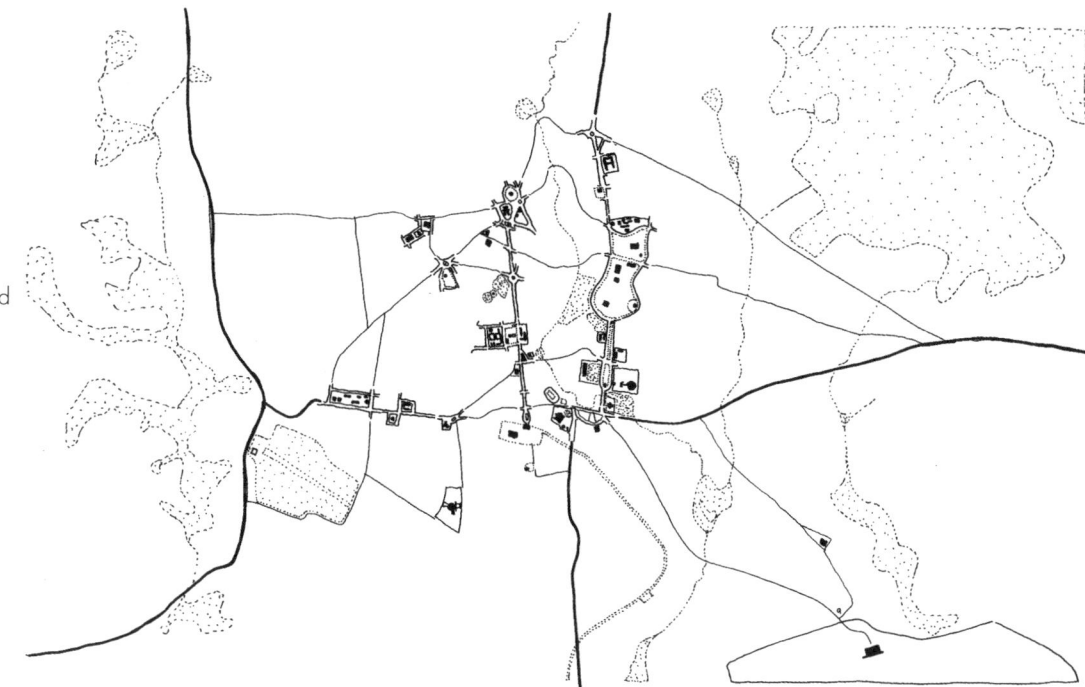

AKSUM (AXUM), ETHIOPIA

FOUNDED: circa 3,000 years ago
URBAN AREA: unknown
POPULATION (2012): 56,500
URBAN AREA DENSITY: unknown
GPS: 14° 7'35.24"N, 38° 43'15.59"E
14° 7'47.89"N, 38° 43'1.01"E
14° 7'53.94"N, 38° 43'9.78"E

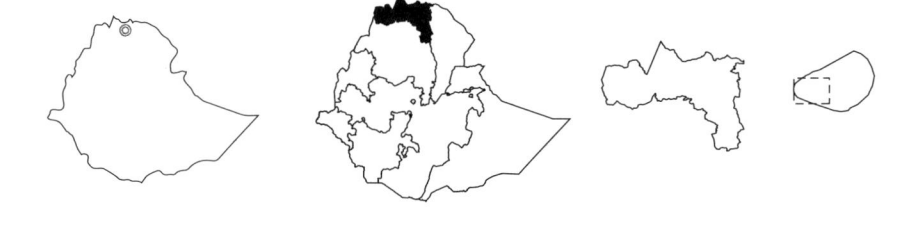

Together with Rome, Persia and China, the Axumite Empire – set in current-day Ethiopia – was one of the great empires of Antiquity, stretching between the Red Sea and Indian Ocean amidst the mountain ranges of northern Africa. Aksum was the original capital city of this majestic kingdom. By today's standards, Aksum is no more than a town – however, it is also a unique place where modern and ancient worlds meet.

According to legend, the story of Aksum begins 3,000 years ago when the Queen of Sheba was said to have ruled the land. During the sixth century BC, hunters and traders began crossing the Red Sea from south-western Arabia. They set up small trading settlements along the Eritrean coast. By the first century CE, farmers and traders had developed their own powerful state – based inland at Aksum and politically independent of Arabia. Soon these rulers were trading in silver, gold, olive oil and wine, along with ivory and slaves.

The original Arabian settlers had introduced the concept of building in stone – a tradition that the early Aksumites developed in a unique way. Aksumite architectural expression was evident in the building of temples, palaces and tombs for the wealthy ruling classes.

Today, the whole area is scattered with the debris of the ancient town. Secular buildings, commonly called 'palaces', are situated near the centre of the old town, and include Enda Semon, Enda Mika'el, Ta'akha Maryam and Dungur.

During the fourth century CE, Christian scholars from Alexandria brought the religion to Aksum. As the first state in the world to adopt Christianity as its official religion, Aksum remains a beacon for the faithful, with pilgrims annually thronging the streets during religious festivals. The religious focal point is the Cathedral of Mary of Zion, founded upon conversion to Christianity. The church imitates the one in Mount Zion in Jerusalem. In fact, Aksum was probably deliberately modelled on and known as the 'New Jerusalem' – and the political ideology was seen to derive from the Jerusalem of the Old Testament. Among the most impressive and unique monuments of the city are the great "stelae" – tall, thin monuments of solid stone placed there to mark the tombs of rulers and which are thought to date back to circa 300 CE.

1 Northern Stelae Field
2 St Mary of Zion Churches
3 Queen of Sheba's Bath
4 Old Palace
5 Dungur Palace/Queen of Sheba's Palace
6 Ezana Park
7 St Mary's Hospital
8 Hotel
9 Main Market
10 Sports Field & School
11 Tomb of Kings Kalep & Gebre Meskel on Gobodura Hill
12 Axum Comprehensive School
13 Ta'akha Maryam

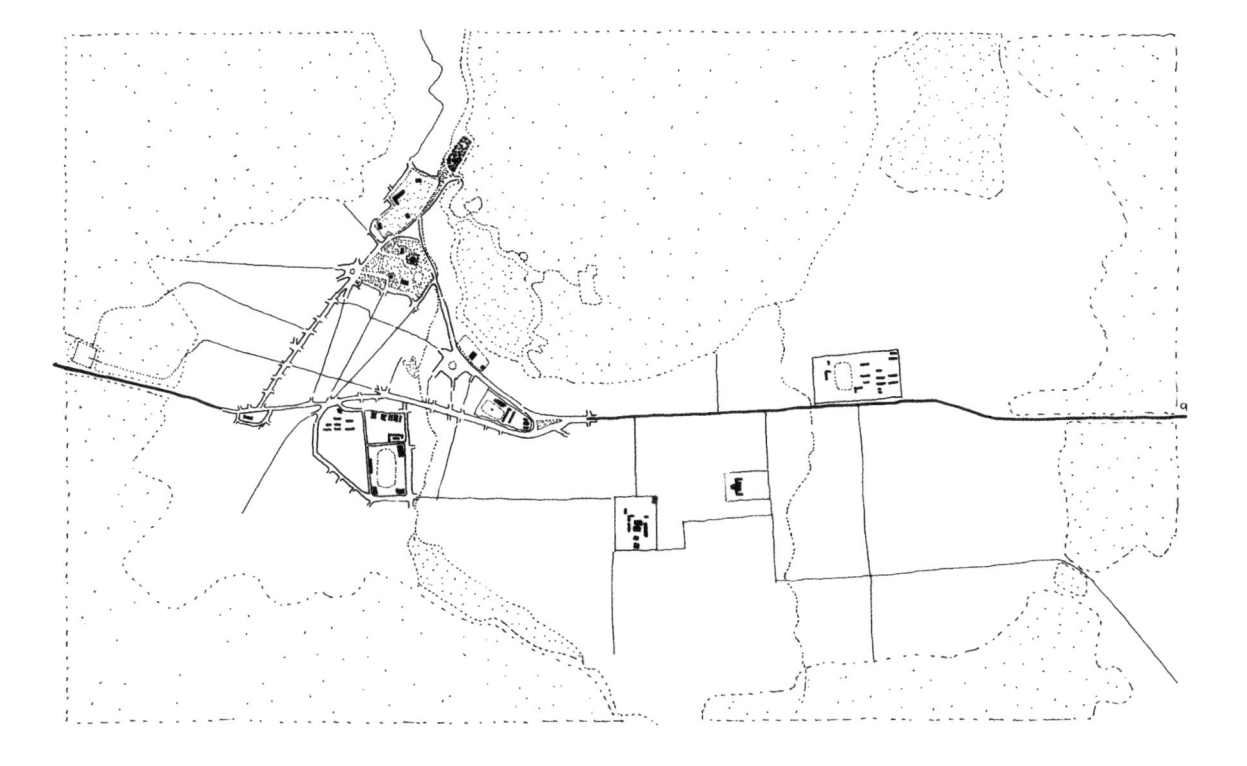

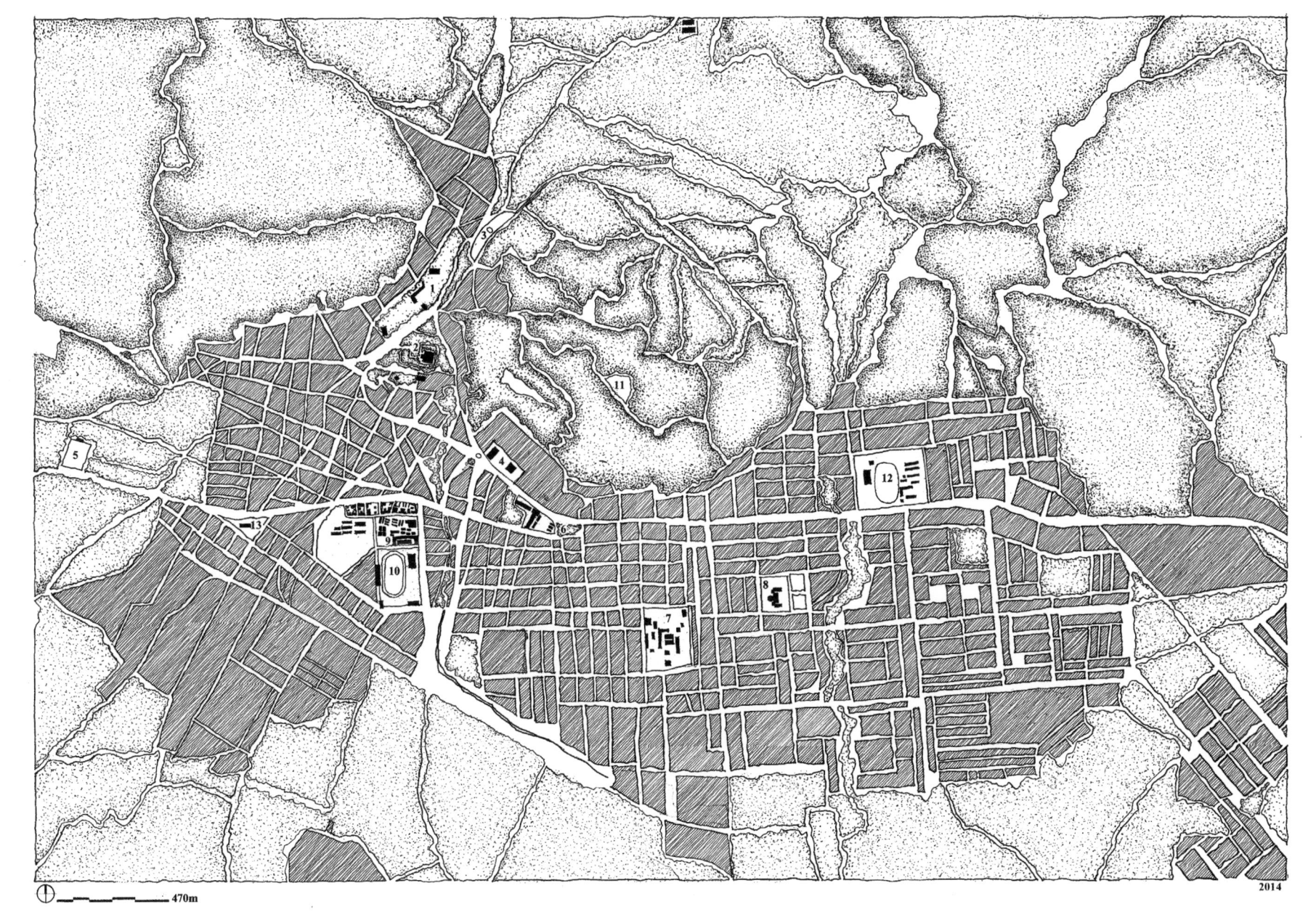

GONDAR, ETHIOPIA

FOUNDED: circa 1635
URBAN AREA: 4,027 km²
POPULATION (2012): 308,257
URBAN AREA DENSITY: 7,700/km²
GPS: 12° 36'43.69"N, 37° 28'11.26"E
12° 36'35.11"N, 37° 28'11.67"E

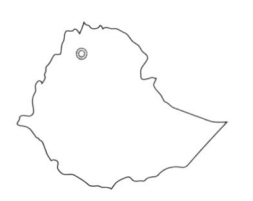

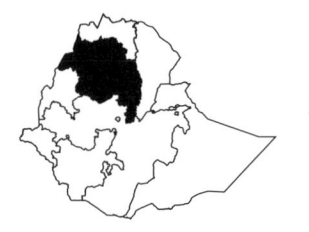

The city of Gondar was founded around the year 1635 as the imperial capital of the then Christian kingdom of Abyssinia, or the so-called Ethiopian Empire. It grew as a market town supported by agriculture. At an elevation of roughly 2,200 meters, it is almost completely surrounded by a range of high mountains. To the south, the landscape opens into a valley with faraway views of Lake Tana – the source of the Blue Nile. The city stretches along a ridge centred on a complex of castles built during the seventeenth and eighteenth centuries. The primary attraction is the "Royal Compound", which was registered by UNESCO as a World Heritage Site during 1979.

Historically, the people of Gondar were segregated by religion and status into different neighbourhoods, still recognisable today. During the occupation by Italy from 1936 to 1943, the Italians used the Royal Enclosure, also called Fasil Ghebbi, as their headquarters. The castle complex divides the ridge in half, serving as barrier between the city's neighbourhoods. The city expanded dramatically after the 1936 conquest, when it served as a colonial administrative centre for Italian East Africa.

According to Rifkind (2011), the city exhibited a "striking sensitivity to topography and historical preservation, yet exploited local conditions to reinforce the colonial authorities' policies of racial and class segregation". Rifkind maintained that the Italians saw great propaganda value in the city's status as a former imperial capital, and they sought to appropriate its symbolic importance in support of its use as a regional capital in their own empire. The Italians concentrated their building activity north of the Fasil Ghebbi on two adjacent levels, separated by a 20-metre change in elevation. The lower level with a wide, tree-lined street running north from the castles to the then new, prominent landmark post office; and a higher area to the east, comprising the government district, centred on monumental military buildings. They exploited the dramatic change in elevation between the two areas of the city to establish a clear hierarchy between commercial and ceremonial functions. The large square to the north of the Castle Compound was arranged so that large crowds could be addressed. At the time, the city grew essentially along the master plan developed by the Italians in 1938.

After its decline in the nineteenth century, the city of Gondar continued to be a commercial and transport hub for north-west Ethiopia. Like all other cities in Ethiopia, Gondar is still growing at a rapid pace.

1 Royal Enclosure / Fasil Ghebbi
2 Meskel Square
3 Gondar Square & Post Office
4 Gondar City Hall & Public Park
5 Sunday Market
6 Debre Berhan Selassi
7 Fasiladas' Bath
8 Tekla Haymanot Church
9 St Johannes Church
10 St Michael Church
11 Kidane Mihret Church
12 Bata Church
13 St Kirkos Church
14 Mariam Church
15 Jami' al-Kabir Mosque
16 St Gabriel Church
17 Stadium
18 Edget Feleg School

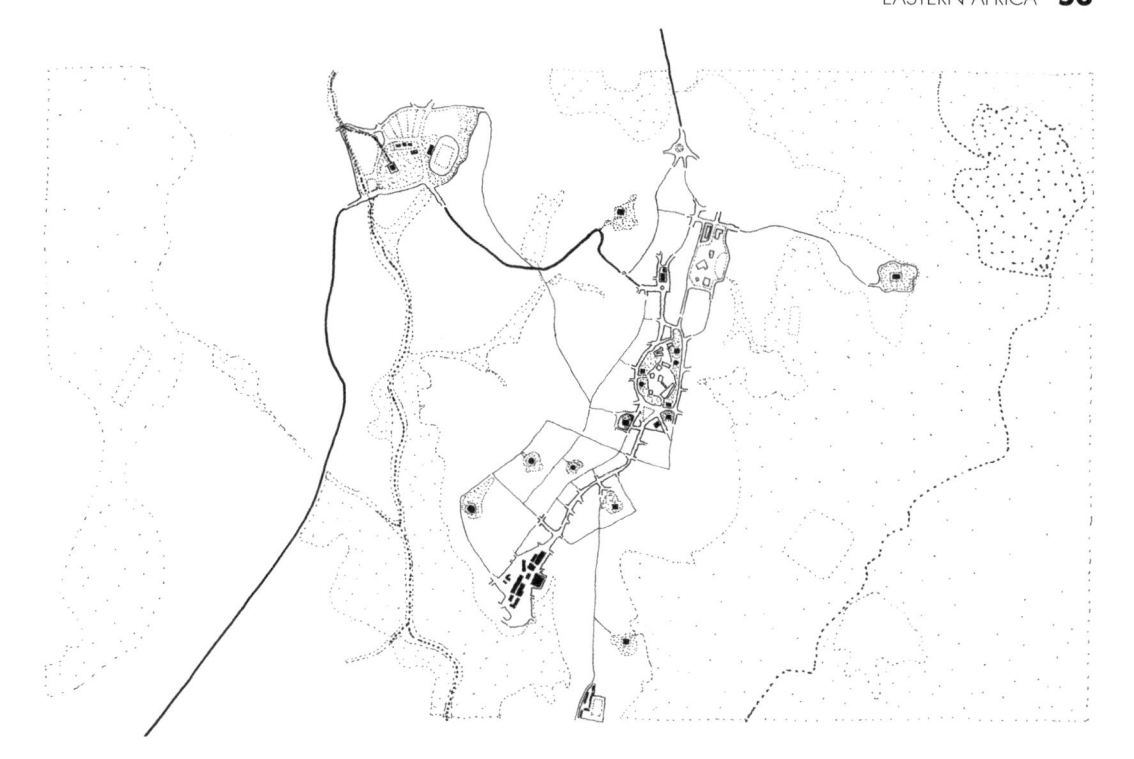

HARAR, ETHIOPIA

FOUNDED: tenth century
URBAN AREA: 20 km²
POPULATION (2012): 151,977
URBAN AREA DENSITY: unknown
GPS: 9° 18'38.57"N, 42° 8'11.11"E
9° 18'43.52"N, 42° 7'34.17"E
9° 18'35.69"N, 42° 7'55.62"E

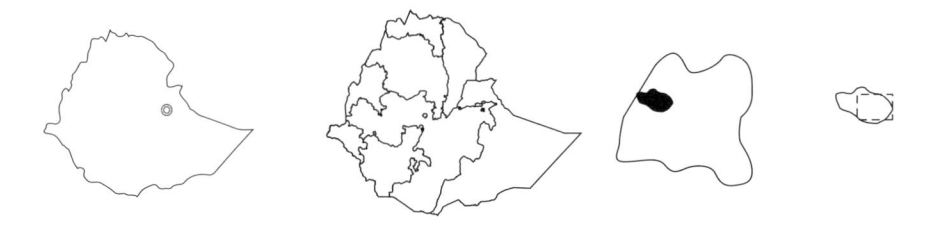

The founding of the walled city of Harar – a UNESCO World Heritage Site in Ethiopia – dates back to the tenth century. One of the oldest cities in the country, it is a former hub of intercontinental trade and Islamic scholarship. The characteristically compact urban form was the result of its added function as a medieval fortification on a plateau 525 km east of the Ethiopian capital of Addis Ababa.

The city, formerly a major commercial centre, is nowadays enthusiastically promoted as a tourist destination by the Harari People National Regional State. The old walled city is called Harar Jugol, surrounded by a 4.5-metre-high protective wall. Beyond that lies a sprawled, substantial and modern centre known as New Town. The two parts of the city are primarily linked by the Harar Gate.

It is in New Town that the majority of Harar citizens live and work, and also where all the government administrative buildings are located. The discontinuity between old and new Harar is visually striking in the form of the physical barrier of the ramparts encircling the medieval city.

New Town was the focus and terrain of Italian colonial urbanism during the 1930s – largely unrealised by the end of Italian occupation in 1941. According to Bisaillon (2010), traces of Italian colonial urbanism in Harar are still visible and coincide with the four predominant ideological concerns of Italian colonial city planners in Ethiopia, which included "racial segregation, road engineering, visibility of colonisers; and manicured landscapes". Perhaps the most visual remnant of this brief interlude in the city's history is the area to the west of Harar Jugol where a monumental city centre was designed similar to an acropolis, holding the military and civic offices intended to dominate the landscape and urban fabric.

According to Bisaillon, there is a complex relationship between Jugol and New Town. The walls impact on mobility and even structure social relationships between the different parts of the city. While Jugol embodies a symbolic soul for the ethnic Harari people, this is not necessarily the case for other population groups represented in the city.

Within Jugol there are 100 mosques and 300 shrines. Islam is visibly reflected in the architectural language and spatial organisation of Jugol, despite the introduction of numerous Christian icons during the Menelik regime, including the levelling of one of the mosques to supplant it with a Christian Orthodox Church, Mehdane Alem.

Bisaillon highlighted that Harar is faced with numerous challenges relating to urban planning and land use because of different interpretations by various local and international role players. Chronic water shortages have adversely affected the quality of life in the city, which according to Bisaillon, will continue to influence prospects of land use and interventions.

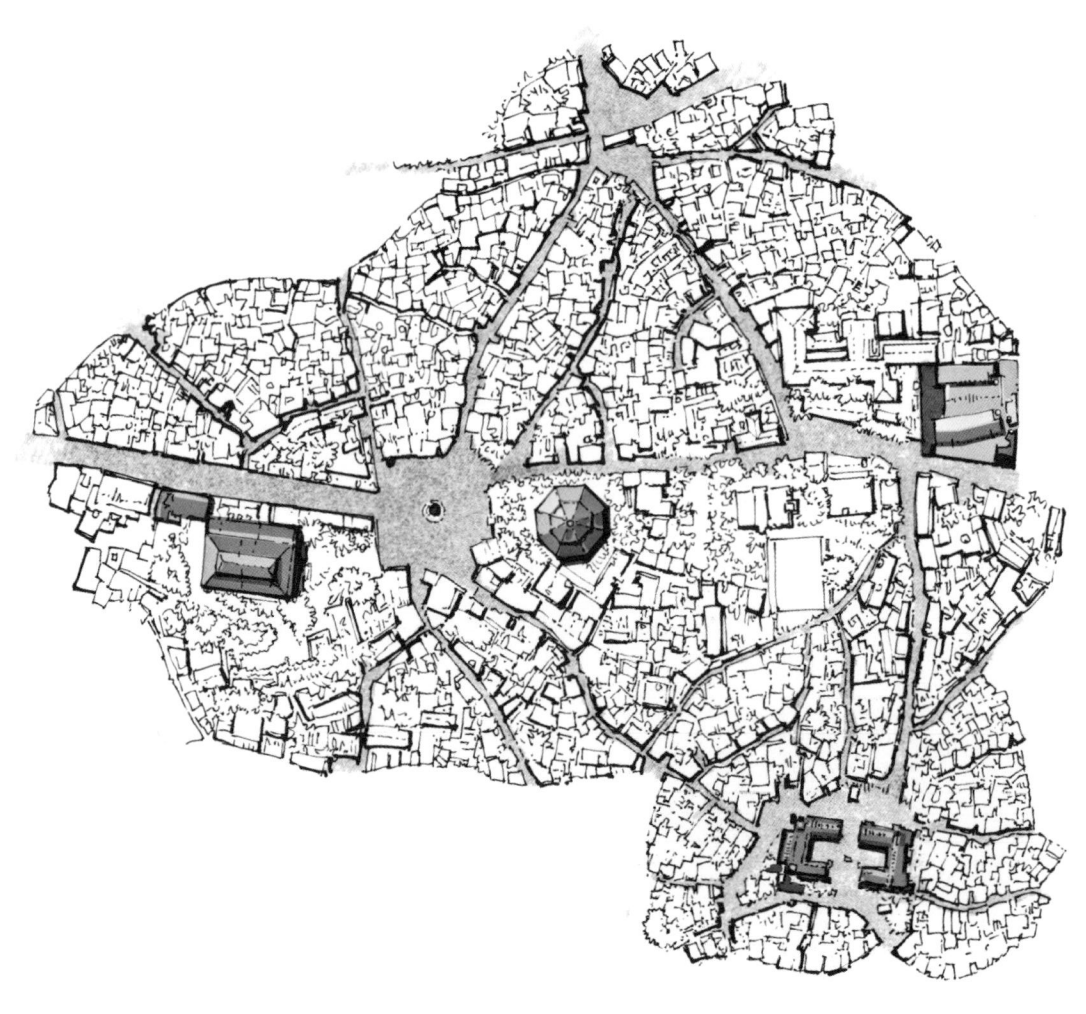

EASTERN AFRICA 55

1 Feres Magala Square
2 Medhane Alem Church
3 Harar Gate/Duke Gate
4 Fallana Gate/Assum Bari
5 Erer Gate/Argob Bari
6 Sanga Gate/Suqutat Bari
7 Buda Gate/Bedri Bari
8 Shoa Gate/Asmaddin Bari
9 Gadir Magdala Market
10 Jamia Mosque
11 Harar Regional Council
12 Ras Makonnen Statue
13 Selassi Church
14 Former Seat of Government
15 Harar Stadium
16 Ras Makonnen School

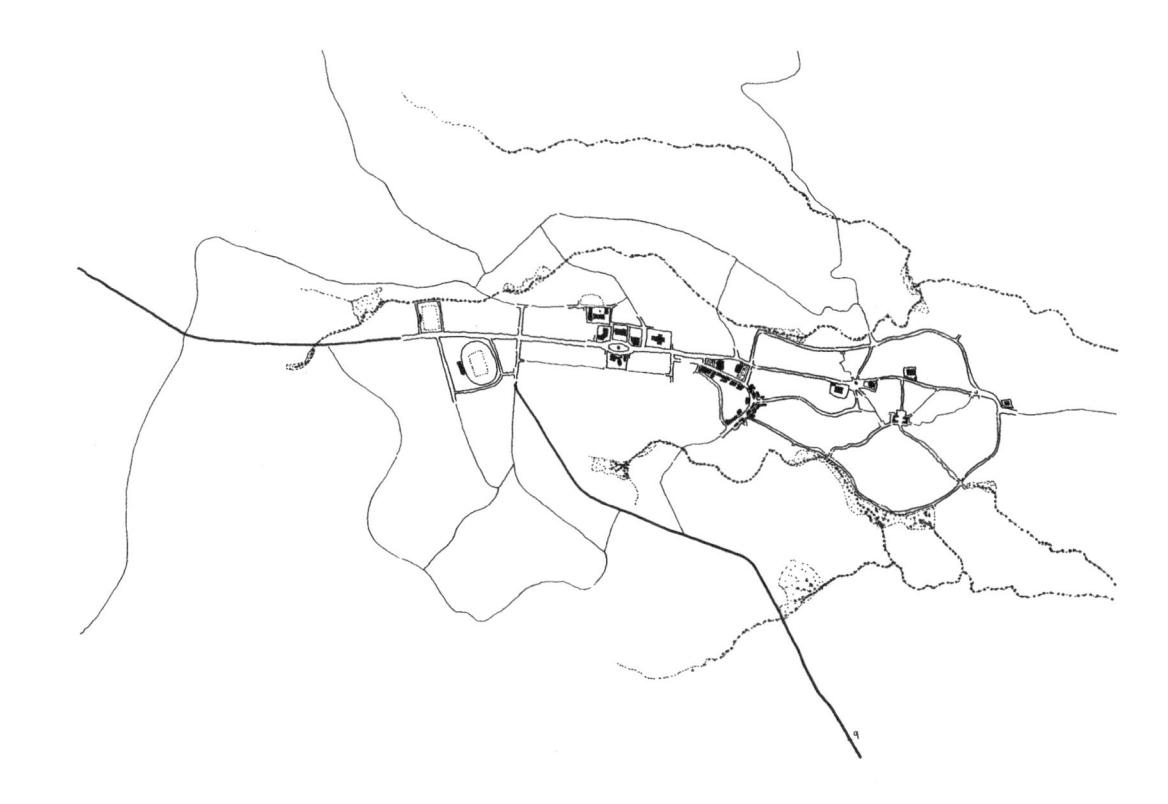

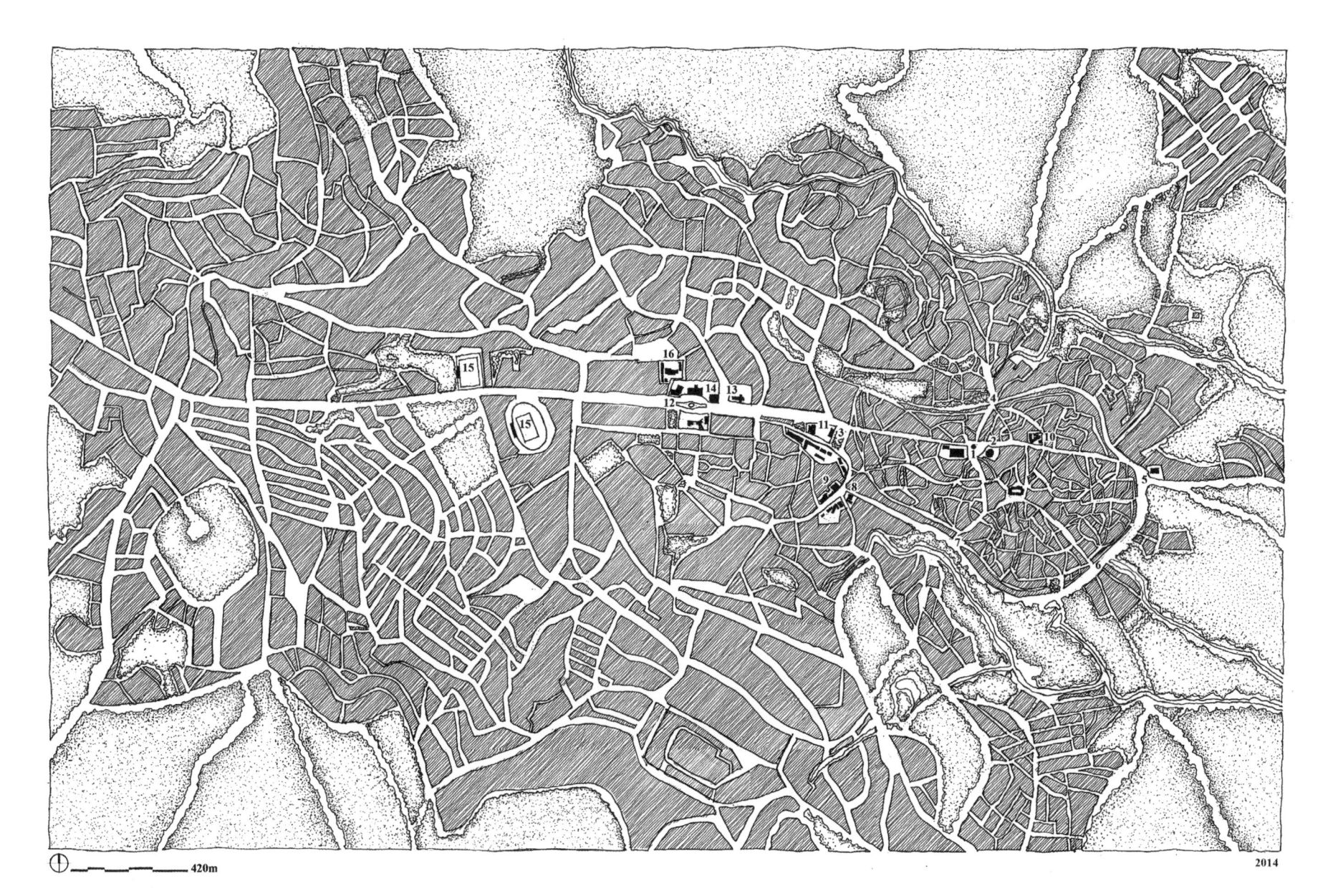

420m

2014

MOMBASA, KENYA

FOUNDED: 900 BC
URBAN AREA: 297.7 km²
POPULATION (2014): 1,200,000
URBAN AREA DENSITY: 5,224/km²
GPS: 4° 3'47.11"S, 39° 40'39.84"E
4° 3'42.70"S, 39° 40'46.14"E

By sea, air or land, Mombasa is the threshold to Africa for many coastal tourists, with a large international airport and also the largest seaport in East Africa. It is Kenya's second largest city, extending from Mombasa Island to the mainland, which is separated from another by two creeks. Given its low elevation above sea level at only 50 m, and relatively flat topography, the city is particularly vulnerable to climate change and also has a history of disasters related to climate extremes such as flooding.

The city structure of Mombasa is the reflection of a unique set of circumstances, including its geography that restricts urban expansion, and a series of historical influences ranging from the British regulatory stimulus to Islamic cultural laws.

For centuries, sailing ships such as Arabian dhows have used monsoon winds to facilitate movement between the East African coast and Asia. Historically, Mombasa has therefore been a mixture of cultures, which is reflected in the city: it hosted the settlement of Arabs, Turks, Persians, Indians, Chinese, Portuguese, and the British. However, Islamic influence prevails in the city, characterised also by Swahili-type houses, and narrow streets in the old town with multi-storeyed buildings and ornate arches. Originally, the settlement centred around the north-eastern edge of the island, where a protective bay provided shelter for its visiting ships. The narrow streets of the old town were the result of its modes of transport on foot and by donkey-cart. While its earliest settlement was focused along the bay, substantial changes were brought about subsequent to the construction of a railway line by the British early in the previous century. The interface between the Arab-Swahili and the British resulted in changes to land tenure which in turn shaped the city. To manage the growth of the city, the British developed a form of a master plan based on a grid street pattern, introduced in 1926. The master plan largely ignored the old town. A system was developed whereby landowners pooled land together, had it planned in an orderly manner and subsequently subdivided the land and returned it to its previous owners.

Over time, the island has faced ever increasing transport, industrial and commercial challenges, while the mainland has accommodated sprawl along road and rail which, according to King'Oriah, has resulted in the emergence of broad concentric patterns of land uses.

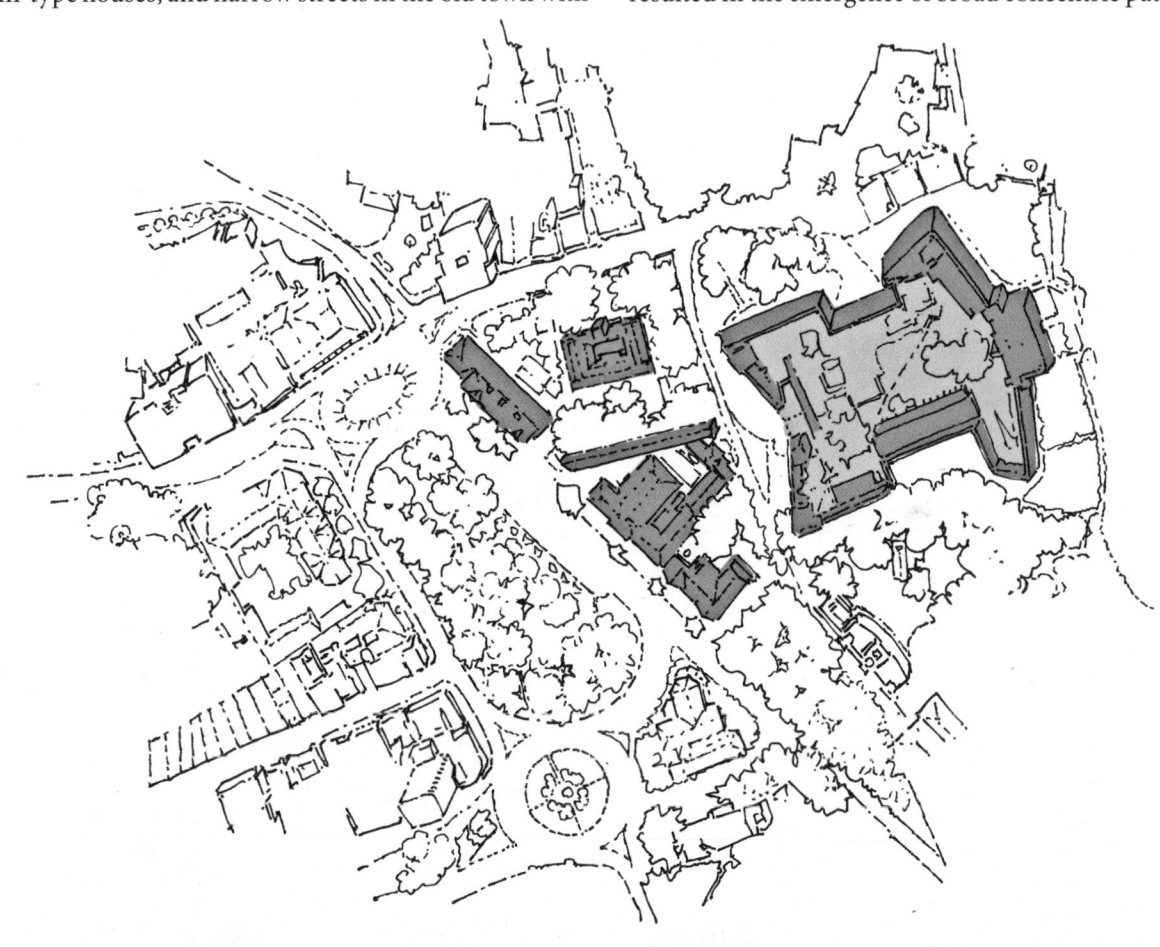

EASTERN AFRICA **57**

1 Makadara Old Town
2 Central Station & Jubilee Square
3 Jamhuri Park
4 Fort Jesus Museum
5 Town Hall & Treasury Square
6 Mombasa Sports Club
7 Port
8 Coast General Hospital
9 Sports Centre
10 Makupa Causeway Bridge
11 New Nyali Bridge
12 Fort St Joseph
13 Holy Ghost Cathedral
14 Uhuru Gardens
15 Sikh Temple
16 Cemetery

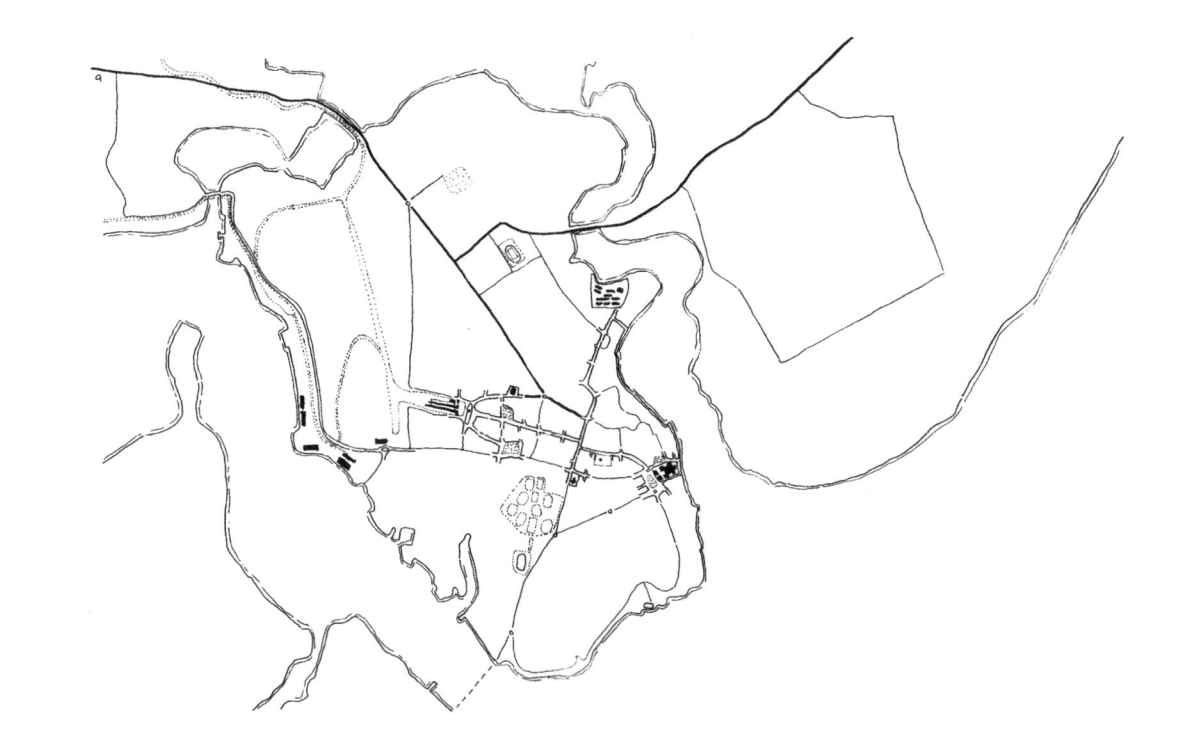

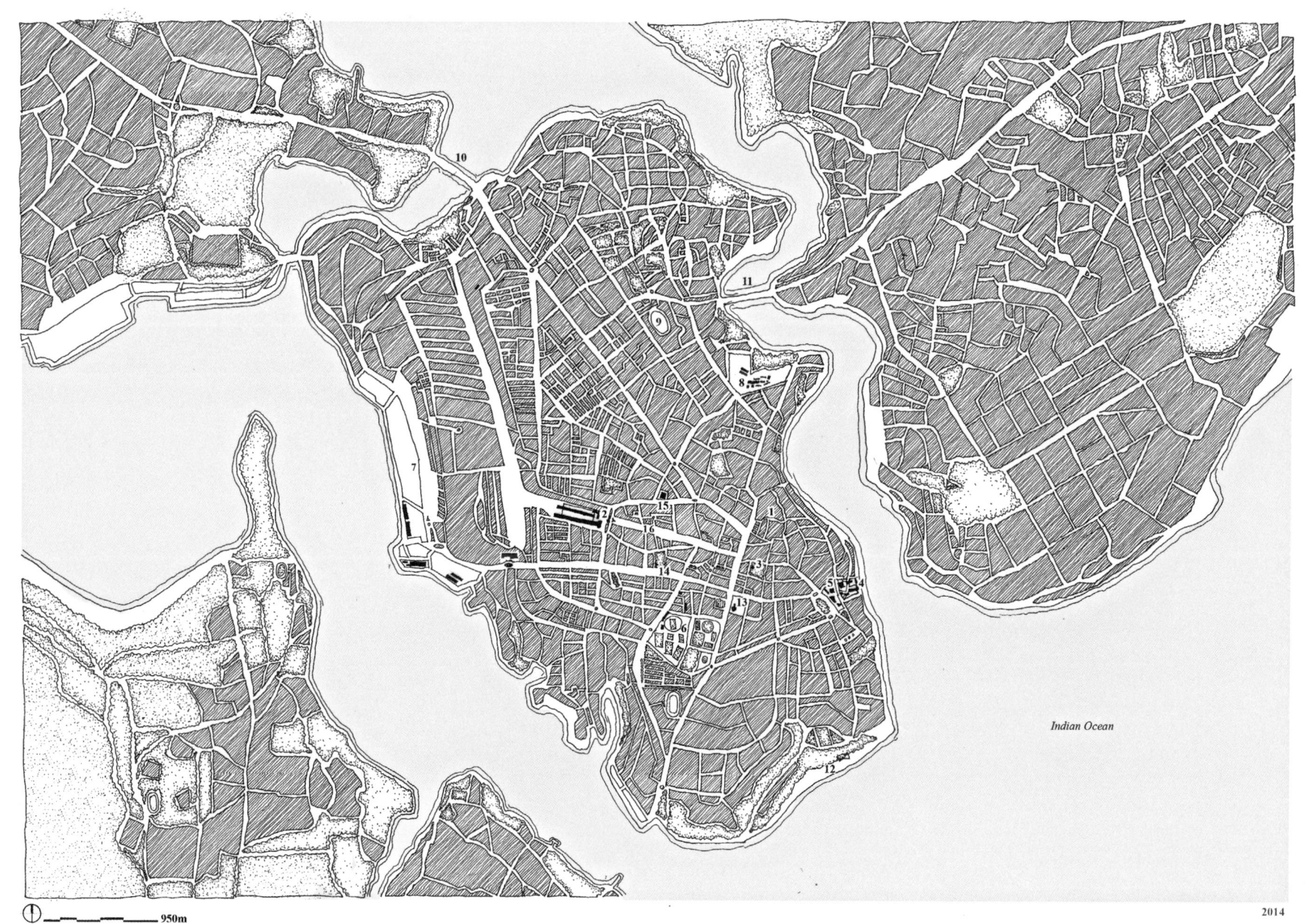

950m

Indian Ocean

2014

NAIROBI, KENYA

FOUNDED: 1899
URBAN AREA: 696 km²
POPULATION: 3,375,000 (2009 census)
URBAN AREA DENSITY: 4,850/km²
GPS: 1° 17'14.55"S, 36° 49'21.02"E

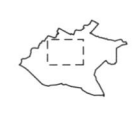

Nairobi, the capital and largest city of Kenya, lies on the Nairobi River and is located at the southern end of the agricultural nucleus of Kenya. It is one of the largest urban centres in Africa, and developed as an important trade post – even during the pre-mercantile period when it was located along a caravan route which linked the interior to the Indian Ocean. Up to the present day, investment flows into Africa are intimately tied to former colonial relations, and intra-African city connections are also important. Mogadishu, for example, is heavily dependent on the decisions made by Somali traders in Nairobi (UN-Habitat, 2014).

Nairobi, founded as a railway town by the British in 1899, was the main headquarters of Kenya Railways. Today, this is still situated at Nairobi railway station, located near the city centre. The town grew rapidly to become the capital of British East Africa in 1907, and eventually the capital of the newly independent Kenyan republic in 1963.

It was originally designed by railway engineers, but was firmly born within a political framework of imperial expansion. Spatial patterns were based on the 1898 designs for a Railway Town and the 1899 Plan for Railway Staff Quarters. This design laid the foundations for the physical appearance of Nairobi as it still is today, and provided the basis for the segregation of the town's functions, as well as its segregation by class and race (Emig & Ismail 1980). Using the concept of functionalism, the plan created a modern national city to cater for industrial expansion and the growing numbers of African wage earners working in the industries. The plan also used the garden city concept to divide residential areas into neighbourhood units. Like others before, this plan was to some extent responsible for the current layout of the built-up area of Nairobi.

The City Square in the Central Business District forms the heart of the city, surrounded by the Kenyan Parliament buildings, the Holy Family Cathedral, Nairobi City Hall, Nairobi Law Courts, and the Kenyatta Conference Centre. Nairobi has grown around its central business district. It takes a rectangular shape around the Uhuru Highway, Haille Selassie Avenue, Moi Avenue, and University Way. Since its independence, Nairobi has experienced rapid growth with a resultant pressure on the city's infrastructure. Congestion has also become a fact of life for the city today.

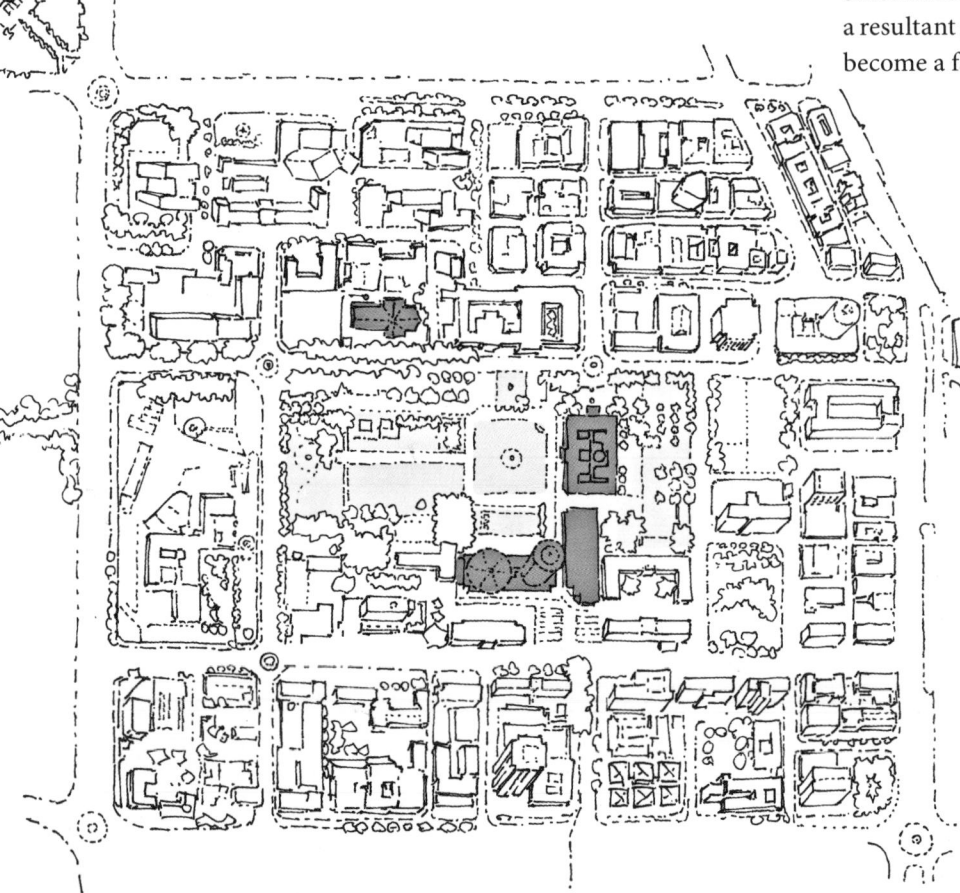

EASTERN AFRICA **59**

1 Uhuru Park
2 Parliament
3 City Square & Supreme Court
4 Nairobi Central Station
5 University of Nairobi
6 Central Park
7 Hospital
8 Nairobi Public Service Club
9 National Stadium
10 Kenya National Art Gallery and Archives
11 City Park
12 Nairobi Arboretum Park
13 National Museum
14 City Stadium

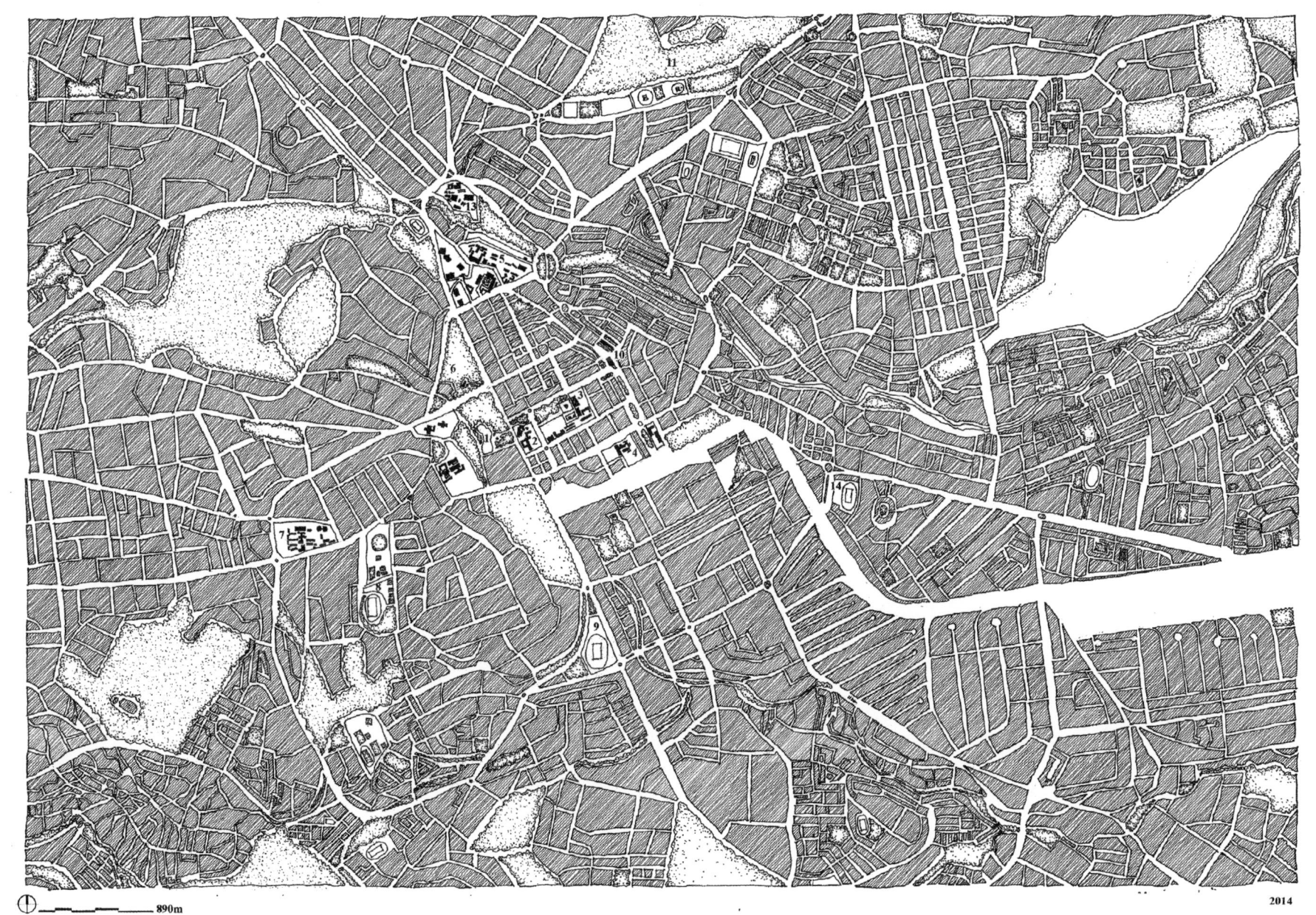

890m

2014

ANTANANARIVO, MADAGASCAR

FOUNDED: circa 1625
URBAN AREA: 88 km²
POPULATION: 1,613,375 (2005)
URBAN AREA DENSITY: unknown
GPS: 18° 55'6.88"S, 47° 31'55.66"E
18° 54'34.45"S, 47° 31'31.23"E
18° 54'20.54"S, 47° 31'24.59"E

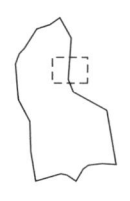

The capital city of Antananarivo, or Tana for short, is a tropical mountain city situated in the centre of the island of Madagascar. It occupies a commanding position on the summit of a long and narrow rocky ridge so that the city adopts a Y-shape. Unlike most capital cities in Africa, Antananarivo was already a major city before colonisation took place.

While European contact began as early as the 1500s, it was only in the late seventeenth century that the French established trading posts along the east coast. In 1793, Antananarivo was made the capital of the Merina kings – their palace still overlooks the city from the top of the ridge.

The city was captured by the French in 1895 who incorporated it into their Madagascar protectorate, which was followed by major infrastructure upgrades. This included the area around the central space called Andohalo. Lake Anosy was created to provide hydraulic power to industrial factories. During French rule, the population increased steadily with this trend accelerating after independence in 1960. The military seized power in the early 1970s and set up a socialist state. The economy went into decline and by 1982, the authorities were forced to adopt a programme imposed by the International Monetary Fund.

Freeman (2010) from Andrianaivoarivony (1998) maintains that the urban structure reflects a spatial distinction that has its origins in the principles of arrangement employed by the monarchs who settled the site originally.

The king occupied the hill, while his subordinates occupied space in close proximity. Further down the hill were commoners of lower status, and lowest of all were the slaves of the royal household and rice fields. Alongside this "altitudinal mapping of hierarchy there operated a cosmological division of lived space which associated the cardinal points with certain positive and negative values. For example, the eastern quarters of the capital were associated with the sacred power of the royal ancestors, while the west was considered impure and profane. In many ways this hierarchical arrangement of urban space is still relevant today as the distinction between *haute ville* and *basse ville* maps differences in social class, wealth, infrastructural provision and political influence".

The *haute ville* includes the quarters lying along the ridge that forms the Y-shaped backbone of the city, including the Royal Palace. In these upper districts are the original residential quarters of the Merina bourgeoisie.

By contrast, the *basse ville* is the area of the new, expanded and overcrowded city where the majority of the urban population live below the poverty line.

1 Lake Anosy & Aux Morts Monument
2 Presidential Palace
3 Place l'Independence
4 Place de 13 Mai
5 Central Train Station
6 Ambohijatovo Park
7 Andohalo Square
8 Andafivaratra Museum & Palace of the Premier Minister
9 The Rova
10 Andohalo Cathedral
11 Anglican Cathedral
12 Mahamasina Municipal Stadium
13 Analakely Market
14 Joseph Ravoahangy Andrianavalona Hospital
15 Supreme Court
16 Archeological Museum
17 Palace of Justice
18 Fort-Voyron
19 Ankadilalana Park & Zoo
20 Lake Bohoririka
21 Stadium
22 Andravoahangy Market
23 University of Antananarivo

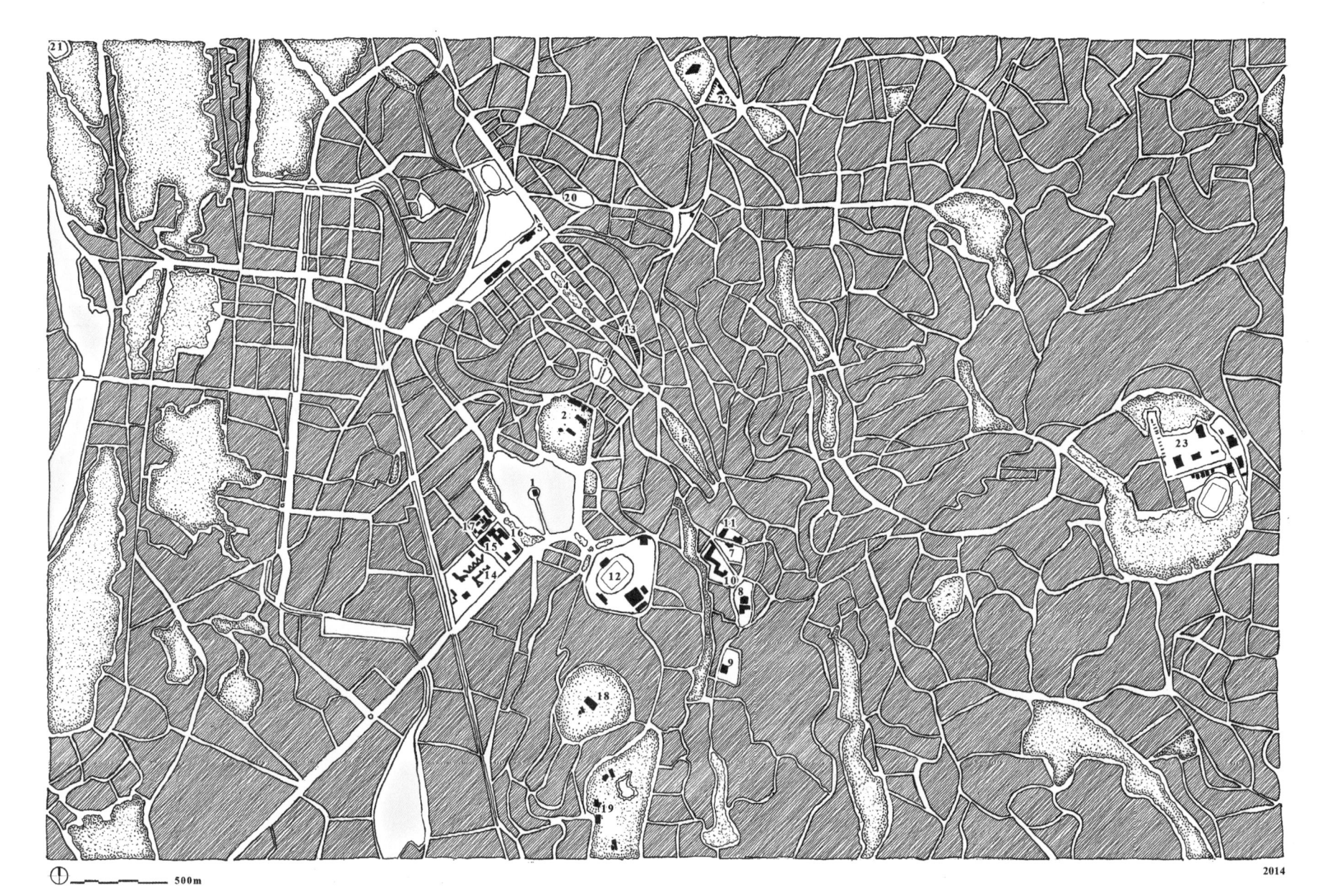

ANTSIRANANA, MADAGASCAR

FOUNDED: 1885
URBAN AREA: unknown
POPULATION: 73,491 (2001)
URBAN AREA DENSITY: unknown
GPS: 12° 16'56.84"S, 49° 17'33.83"E
12° 16'39.42"S, 49° 17'28.60"E

Antsiranana, formerly known as Diego-Suarez (named after the Portuguese navigators Diego Diaz and Fernando Suarez who visited the bay in 1543), is a city situated on the northern tip of Madagascar. The town, still called Diego by the locals, is the capital of Madagascar's northernmost province. Located on a peninsula at the south end of a bay, it was developed primarily as a military base by the French navy in 1885 and then became the capital of the French colony. The city was used as one of their military and naval bases until the socialist revolution of 1973.

Antsiranana's natural deep water harbour is one of the largest and most beautiful in the Indian Ocean with the picturesque Sugarloaf Mountain in the background. The harbour is shaped like a four-petalled flower with a narrow mouth at its eastern tip, which opens into the Indian Ocean. Although development of the harbour is hampered by its remote location, the local economy is still largely dependent on the naval yards and the transhipment of cargoes between coasters and larger vessels. The town's main industry is ship construction and repair.

The Commonwealth War Graves Commission maintains the cemetery [5] in the centre of town with its rows of white gravestones where British soldiers who fell in the Battle of Madagascar are buried. The town's layout is predominantly influenced by the natural boundary of the ocean. Place of Independence [3], a roundabout, is located at the centre of the radial street layout which forms part of the formal grid in the central area, resembling classic French urban planning.

The town is characterised by the decaying colonial architecture which includes the old covered market [4] and the former Hôtel de la Marine for seafarers. The old military quarter north of Place Foch [1], occupies a peninsula and overlooks the port [10].

The colonial architecture is most prevalent on Rue Colbert with the string of colonnades all the way down to Rue Richelieu. The brick buildings with street arcades topped by upper-storey verandas from the colonial era are scattered throughout the town. Development becomes denser towards the ocean along the east and west coasts. There are signs of urban sprawl towards the interior as the southern region is dominated by the forested Tsaratanana Massif, which includes the highest mountain in the country, Maromokotra Peak at 2,876 m. The Ankara caves south of Antsiranana are a notable feature of the region.

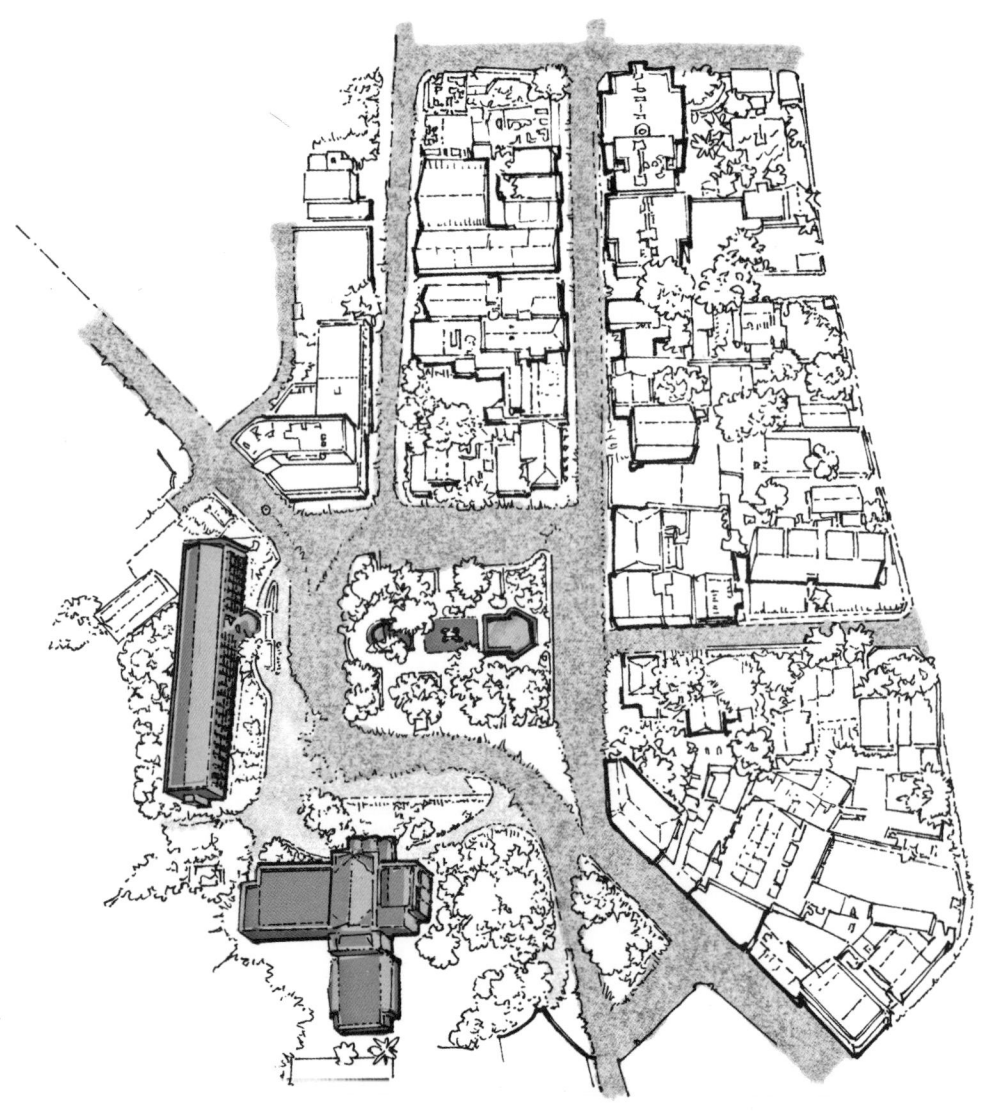

EASTERN AFRICA **63**

1 Place Foch
2 Town Hall
3 Place of Independence
4 Central Market
5 French War Cemetery
6 Municipal Stadium
7 Market & Clinic
8 Regional Mayor Residence
9 Nosy Be's Hospital
10 Port
11 Place Kabary
12 Higher Institute of Technology Antsiranana
13 Institutional Complex
14 Harbour & Pontoon

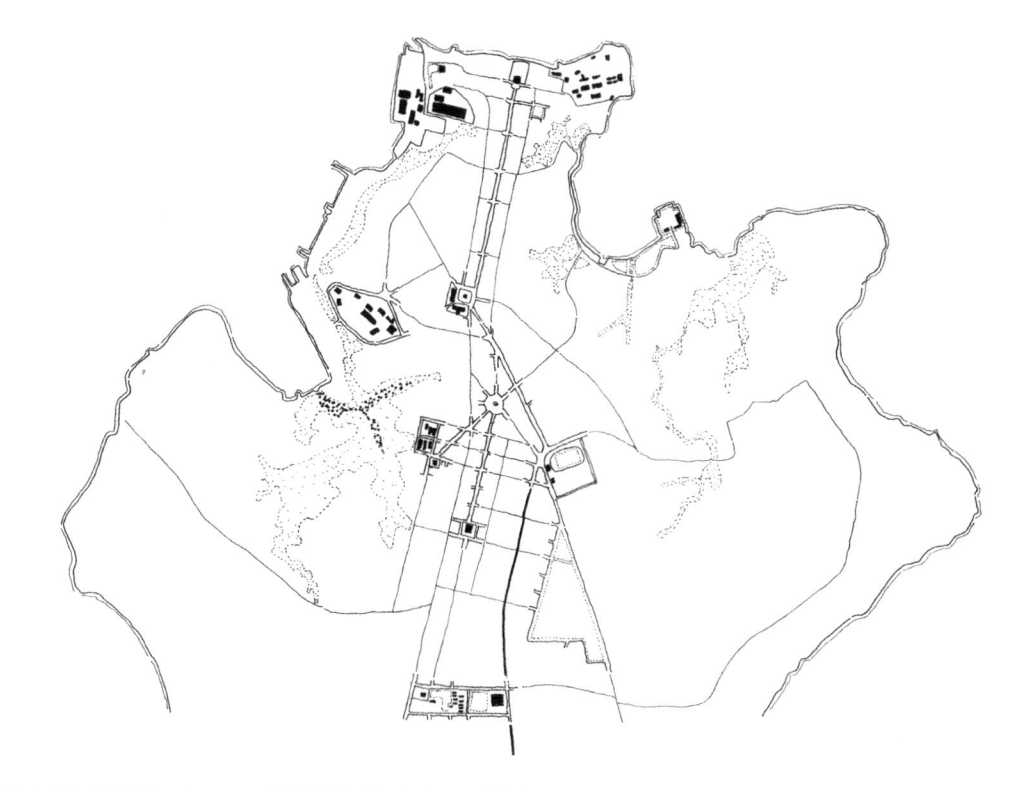

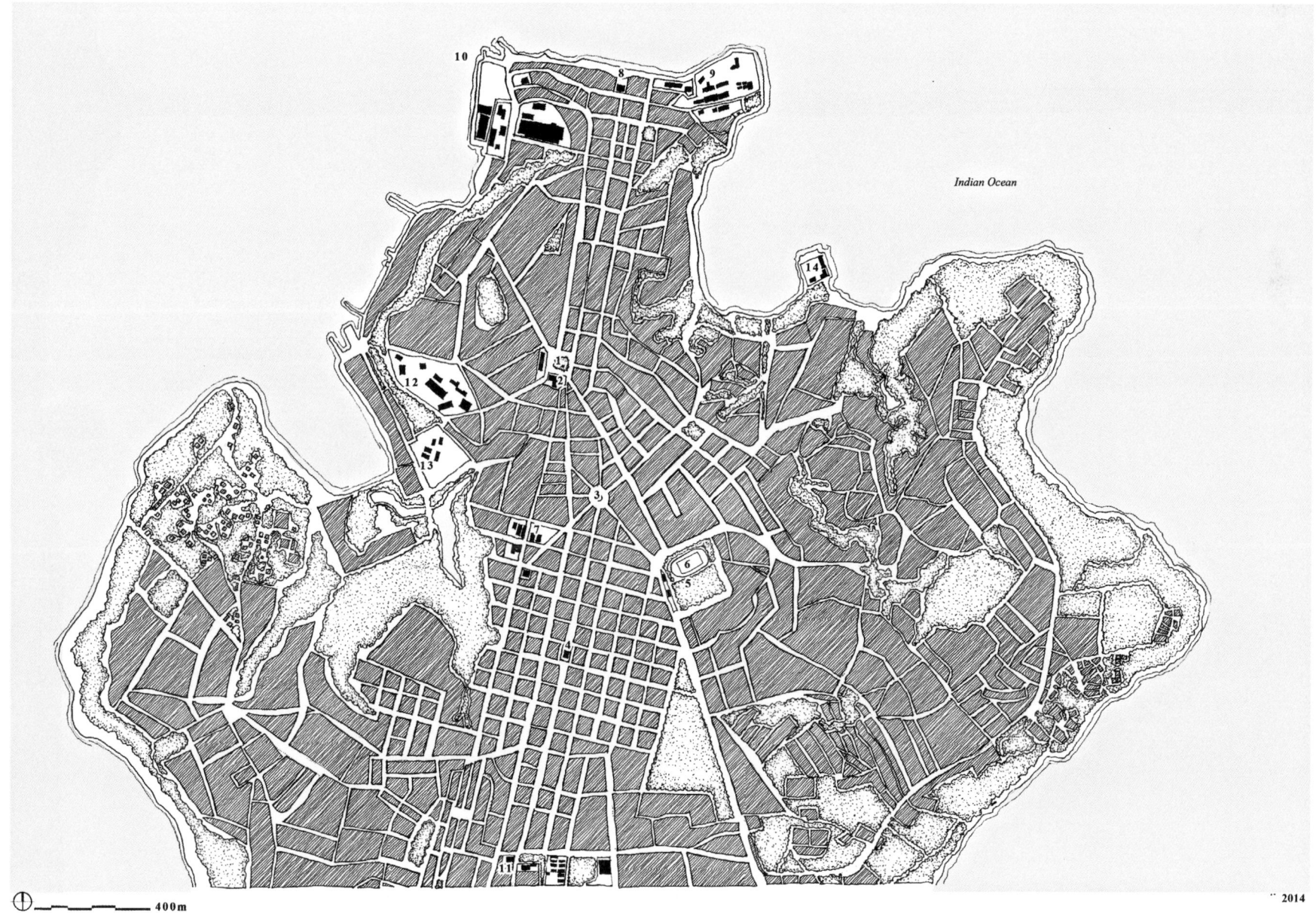

TOAMASINA, MADAGASCAR

FOUNDED: unknown
URBAN AREA: unknown
POPULATION: 179,045 (2001)
URBAN AREA DENSITY: unknown
GPS: 18° 9'15.18"S, 49° 25'0.57"E

Toamasina, also known as Tamatave, is the capital of the Atsinanana region on the east coast of Madagascar on the Indian Ocean. The city is the primary and largest seaport of the country, serving as the commercial hub of Madagascar. The coral reef forms a spacious and fairly extensive harbour with two openings. The city centre is built on a sandy peninsula. Historically, as a prominent commercial port and slaving centre, it was one of the first major targets of the European colonial powers, resulting in a structured urban layout with tree-lined avenues for the colonial capital city.

Central Toamasina has a rectangular grid system. Boulevard Augagneur and Boulevard Joffre are the main thoroughfares in Toamasina city and all the major commercial activities such as banks, car rentals and restaurants are located in these north-south boundary streets. The waterfront road, Boulevard Ratsimilaho, runs parallel to them. The tree-lined Araben'ny Fahaleovantena (or Ave Poincare or l'Avenue de l'Independance) was the structuring element for the modern city centre after most of the town was destroyed by a hurricane in 1927. It is also the main east-west thoroughfare connecting the waterfront with the trainstation and the city's widest street. All major administrative buildings are located near the l'Avenue de l'Independance.

There are various stories related to where the name Toamasina came from. Some say that it was derived from the Portuguese name São Tornás (St Thomas), while others believe it is derived from King Radama I's first visit to the seaside in 1817; it is said that the king knelt to taste the water and said, "Toamasina" ("It is salty").

The colonial origins of the city are prevalent in the wide boulevards lined with palm trees and ancient colonnaded buildings. Bazary Be is a famous colourful street market, specialising in exotic spices and locally made handicrafts. The central market [5] is located in the heart of the city and is one of Toamasina's most popular sites.

The University of Toamasina is located in the city and is part of Madagascar's public university system. The town is the railhead for the line to the capital (Antananarivo) with the central train station at the end of l'Avenue de l'Independance. Toamasina is the northern end of the Canal des Pangalanes, one of the longest canals in the world.

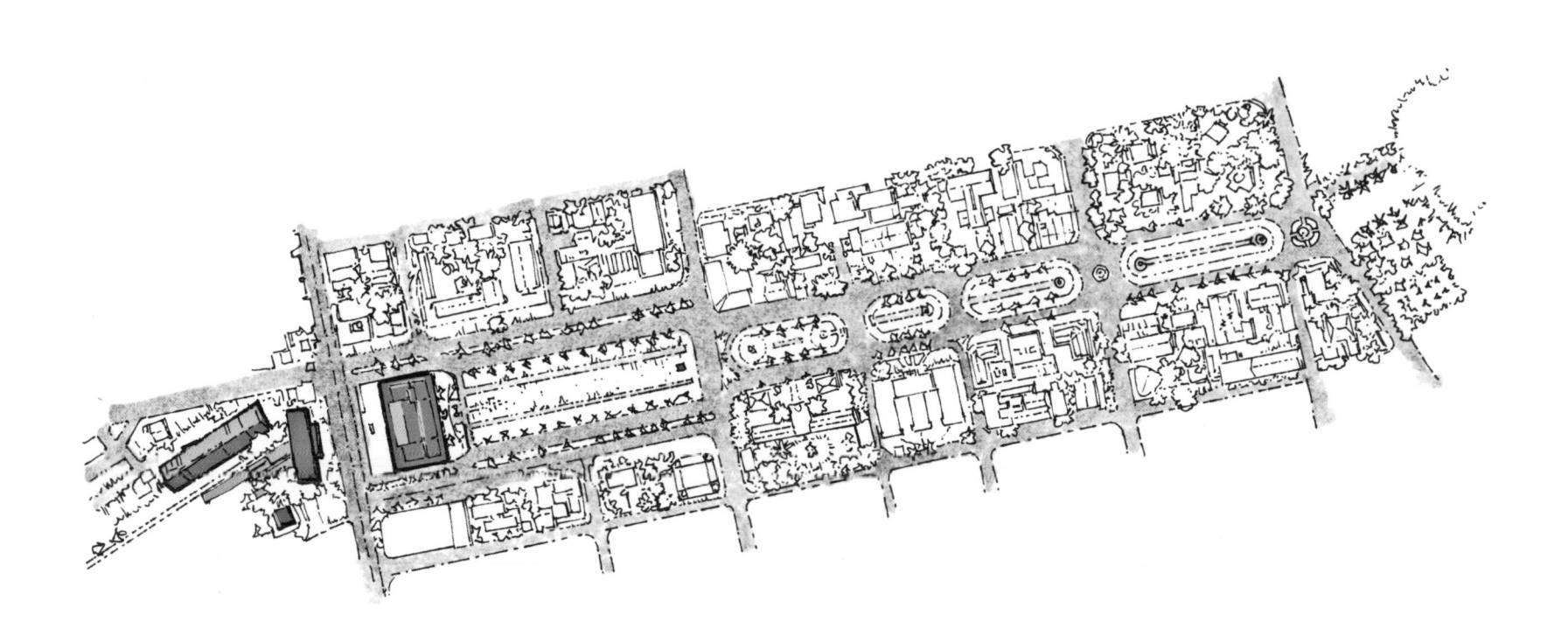

1 Central Toamasina Hotel & Place de la République
2 Central Station
3 Beach & Indian Ocean
4 Fiangonana Notre Dam de Loures
5 Market
6 Municipal Stadium
7 Port
8 Regional Sports Centre
9 Canal des Pangalanes
10 Cemetery
11 Cemetery
12 School
13 Hospital

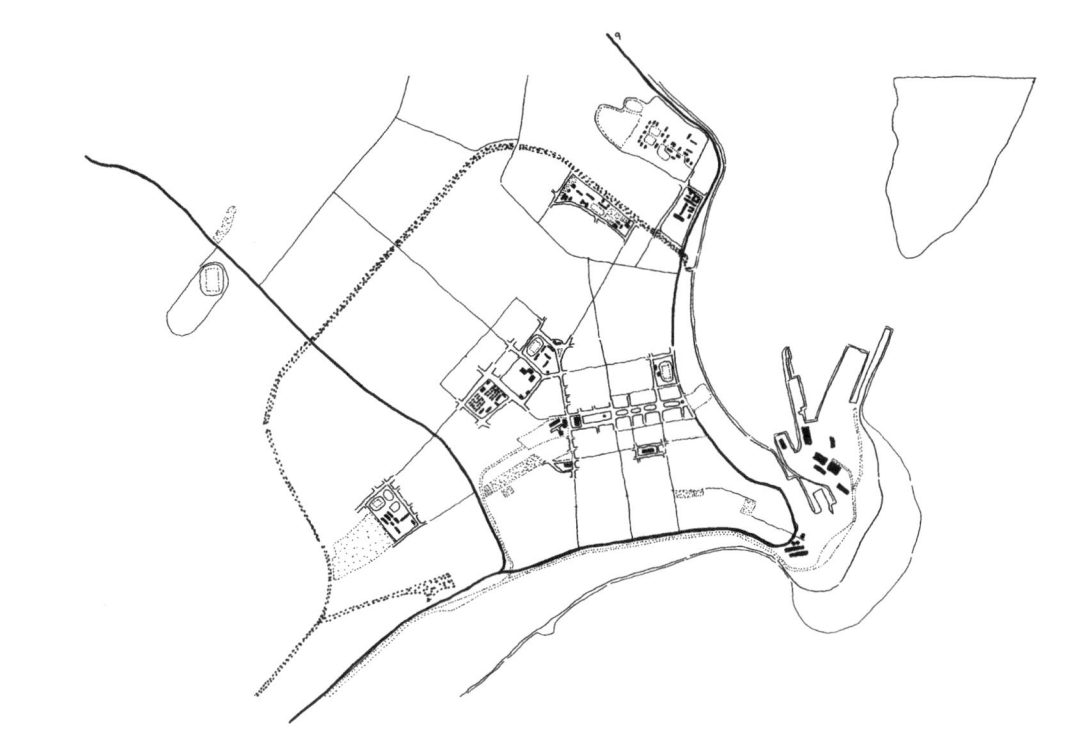

LILONGWE, MALAWI

FOUNDED: unknown
URBAN AREA: unknown
POPULATION: 978,800 (2014)
URBAN AREA DENSITY: unknown
GPS: 13° 57'18.17"S, 33° 47'19.87"E

Lilongwe, originally a small district administrative centre, was established in 1904 by the British administration of the colony, then known as Nyasaland. The city replaced the southern city of Zomba as the new capital of Malawi in 1965, when Hastings Banda announced that the capital should be centrally located where all Malawians could reach it.

The city of Lilongwe is divided into two parts: the Old Town, located at the intersection of the major highways of the central region, and the New Town (City Centre), situated north of the Old Town. The City Centre is a well-laid-out grid of streets that contains the government, banking and commerce buildings. The area to the northside of the City Centre is home to the ex-patriot community as well as the more well-to-do of Malawi culture.

The Old City's streets resemble an old African market. The Lilongwe Nature Sanctuary is situated between the old and new towns and includes a "People and Wildlife" animal rescue and education facility.

Lilongwe's planned city structure, resembling colonial planning forms, is attributed to "white South Africans from a private Johannesburg firm at the height of apartheid". Banda created the Capital Cities Development Corporation (CCDC) with a loan from the apartheid regime (Myers 2003: 139). The CCDC's plan of the city replicated most of the ideological goals of the colonial city, where zones of residential density, starkly set off from one another by physical and natural boundaries, separated who belonged where by class (Mjojo 1989). What the geographer Deborah Potts (1986: 26) referred to as a "virtually clinical degree of orderliness" was meant to segregate functions in the city in a direct continuation of colonial policies.

The "Lilongwe Master Plan", which provided the architectural, social, economic and political outline of the city, was based on a strict land-use zoning scheme (Gerke & Viljoen 1968) that divided the city into functionally differentiated zones assigned to specific politico-administrative, industrial, commercial, cultural and leisure purposes.

Today, the majority of Lilongwe's population live outside the regulated formal city in informal settlements which have developed around the edges of the original planning area of the capital. Similar to other Eastern African cities, it suffers from inefficient infrastructure, poor service provision and lacks proper formal institutions.

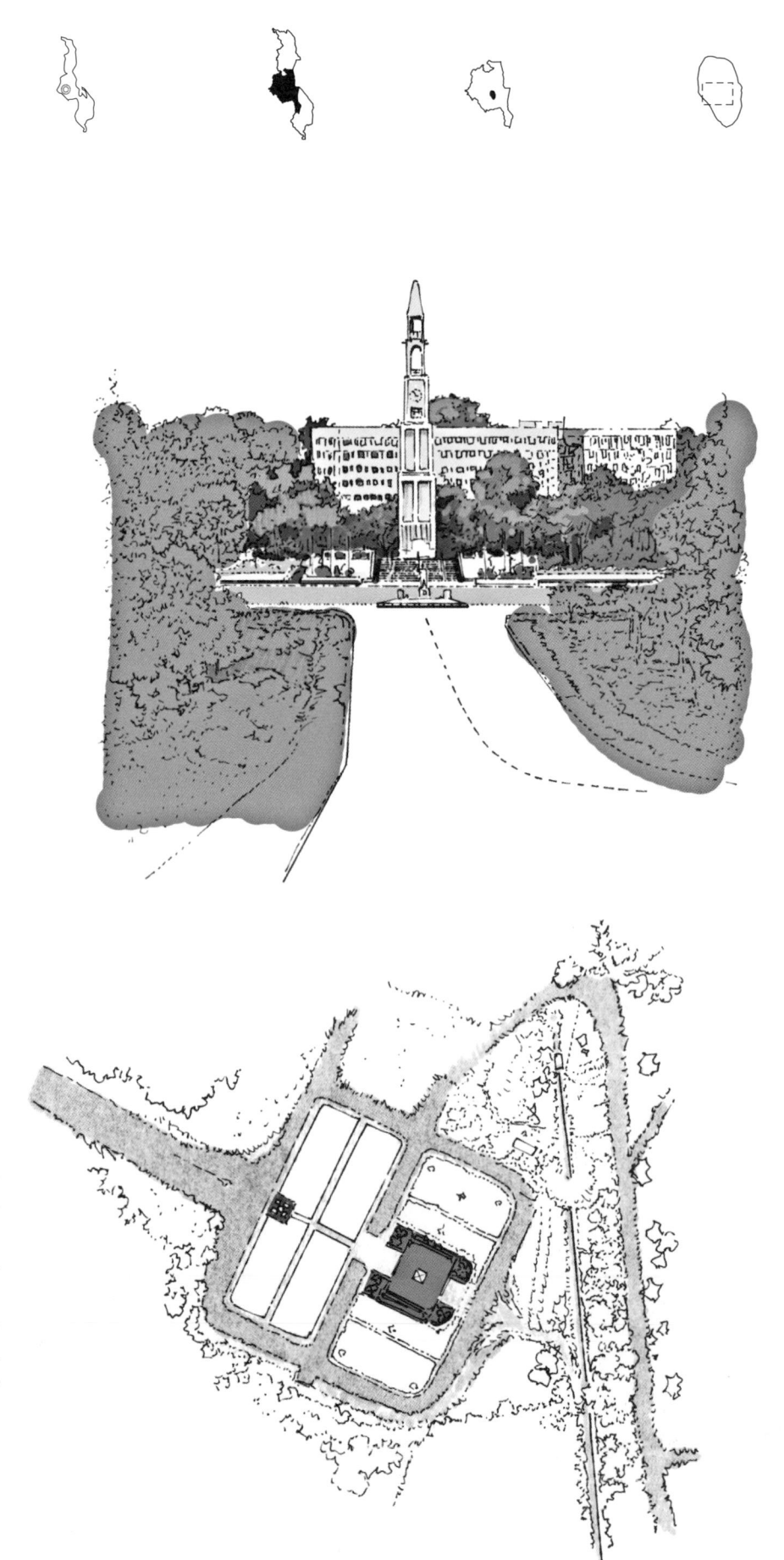

EASTERN AFRICA **67**

1 Capital Hill
2 Parliament
3 Kamuzu Mausoleum
4 Dr Banda Memorial
5 Lilongwe Nature Sanctuary & Wildlife Centre
6 Kamuzu Central Hospital
7 Town Hall
8 Civo Stadium
9 Al-Falaah Masjid Mosque
10 Mosque
11 Market & Central Bus Station
12 Muslim Sports Club

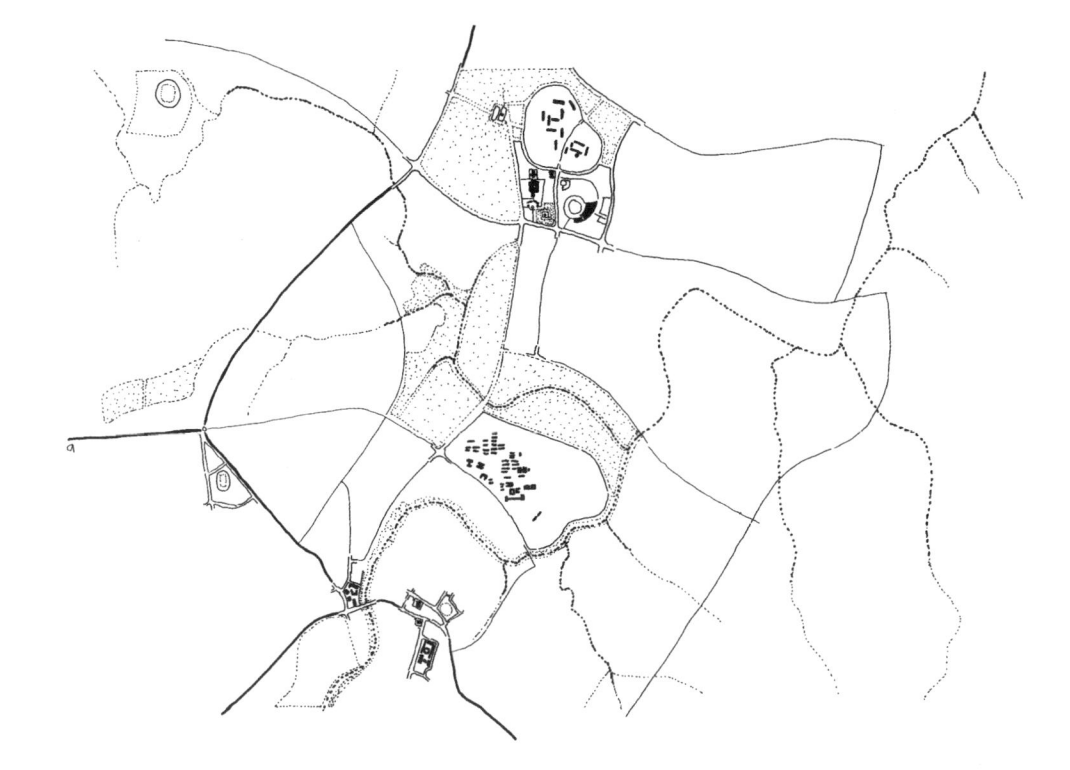

PORT LOUIS, MAURITIUS

FOUNDED: 1735
URBAN AREA: 42.7 km²
POPULATION: 148,416
URBAN AREA DENSITY: 3,000/km²
GPS: 20° 9'54.46"S, 57° 30'21.63"E
20° 9'38.45"S, 57° 29'54.10"E

Port Louis, the capital and largest city of Mauritius, is the country's main port on the Indian Ocean. Located in the north-west, the city links the south of the island to the north. This small but vibrant city is positioned between the sea and mountains. The port is strategically located between Africa and Asia and was used as a halfway stop for provisions by French ships sailing around the stormy Cape of Good Hope. The city is surrounded by the Port Louis Moka mountain range.

Although the Dutch originally settled in the city, the French took possession of Mauritius at the beginning of the eighteenth century. Governor Mahé de Labourdonnais envisioned the city as the main harbour and an administrative hub. He thus commissioned schools, hospitals, public and military buildings as well as streets and an aqueduct to be constructed. As the capital of "Isle de France", it soon became the most important stopover on the route to India and therefore the most important city of the Indian Ocean.

The city was named in honour of King Louis XV. Governor Labourdonnais is commemorated with a statue at the quayside end of Place d'Armes [1], the square that marks the city centre and the city's most prominent boulevard, lined with royal palms and leading up to the French Colonial structure, Government House [2], dating from 1738.

Port-Louis is composed of a multicultural population consisting of Indians, Chinese people, Africans and Europeans. The city's various districts, including Port-Louis's own Chinatown, reflect the cultural diversity. These areas include Plaine Verte [10], the Muslim district where some of the oldest mosques on the island, the Jummah Mosque and Al-Aqsa Mosque can be found. The many religions share space since many of the worshipping places (churches, mosques, the cathedral [4], Hindu temples and pagodas) are located within close proximity to one another. One of Port Louis's many historic and colonial buildings is a fortification named Fort Adelaide [6], or La Citadelle, which was built by the British in 1835. This was due to the fear of a civil war with the remaining French settlers on the island, and also for the purpose of guarding the harbour against enemy attacks. Slightly elevated on one of the city's largest hills, most of the city and its harbour can be viewed from La Citadelle. The Champ-de-Mars [5] was designed under the French colonisation in 1740 for their military drills and has been used as a racecourse since 1812. The colourful central market [8], located between Farquar and Queen Streets, was built in 1828 and is known as the "Bazaar".

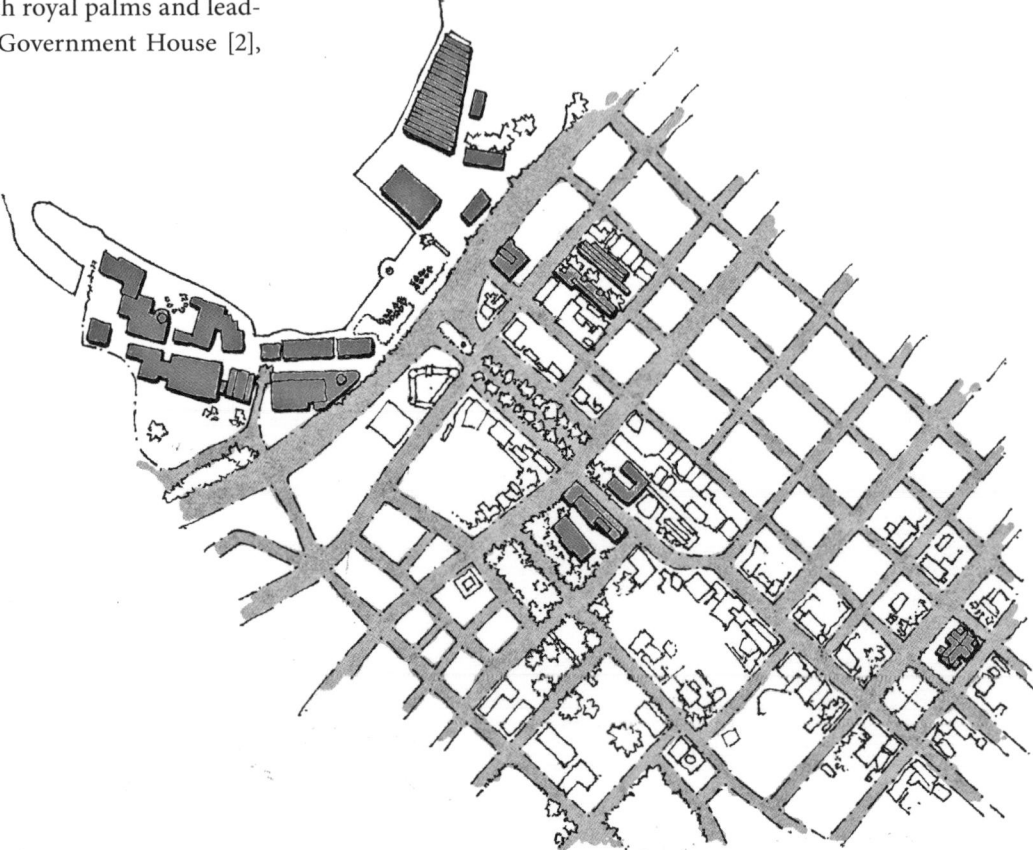

EASTERN AFRICA **69**

1 Place d'Arms
2 Government House
3 Natural History Museum & Company Gardens
4 St Louis Cathedral & Cathedral Square
5 Champ de Mars Racecourse
6 Fort Adelaide
7 Les Casernes & Central Police
8 Central Market
9 Dr Jeetoo Hospital
10 Plaine Verde Gardens
11 St Francois Stadium
12 Port
13 Postal Museum
14 Commercial Centre
15 SSR Memorial Centre for Culture
16 St Francois Evangelist Church

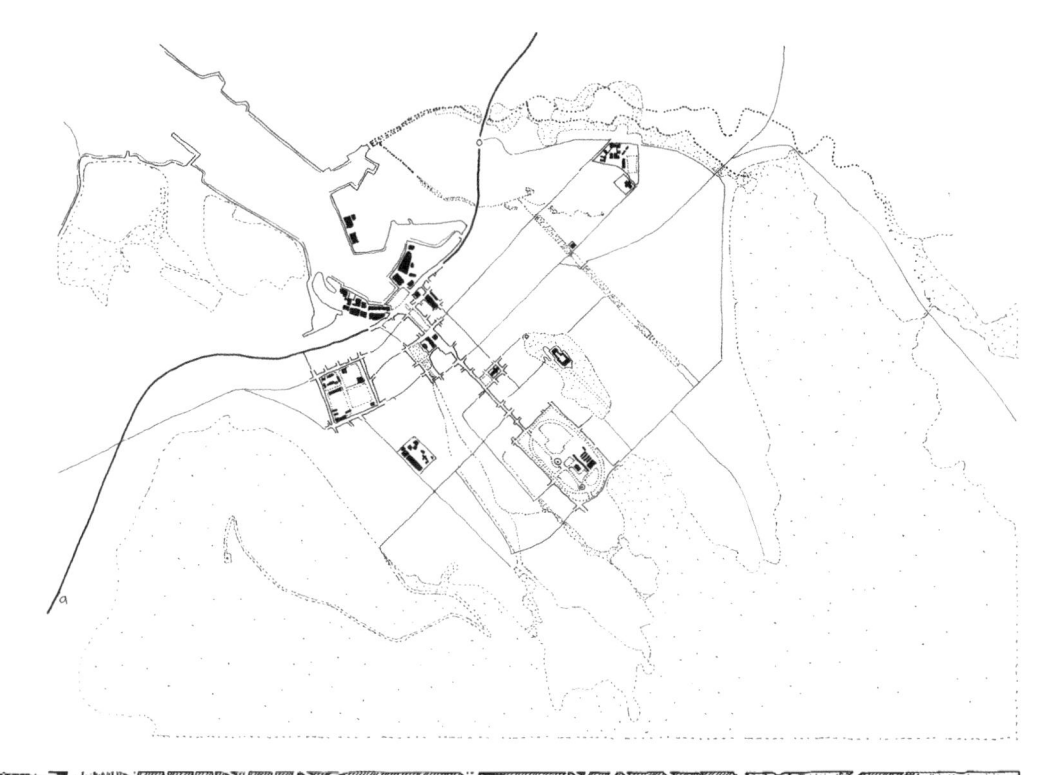

BEIRA, MOZAMBIQUE

FOUNDED: 1887
URBAN AREA: 633 km²
POPULATION: 436,240 (2007)
URBAN AREA DENSITY: 690/km²
GPS: 19° 50'2.38"S, 34° 50'8.88"E
19° 49'54.32"S, 34° 50'6.34"E

Beira is Mozambique's second largest city and is located in the central region of the country in the Sofala Province, where the Pungue River meets the Indian Ocean. The Port of Beira was a significant, well-equipped seaport as a gateway (for tourism, fishing and trade) for the central interior portion of the country, as well as the land-locked nations of Zimbabwe, Zambia and Malawi.

Beira, also informally known as "Zinc City", acquired its nickname from the first buildings which were built from zinc. The city was initially built for military purposes during the colonial period and regarded as a temporary settlement. However, the development of the port and "Beira Corridor" – a road and railway line constructed from the coast eastwards, connecting Zimbabwe with its main outlet to the sea – has secured the city of Beira on the African map.

The sprawling city is built on swampy ground at the mouth of the Pungwe River. The city developed as Portuguese families settled in the area as a result of the development of the port and "Beira Corridor". After independence from Portugal in 1975, the city was ravaged by the civil war (1977–1992) leading to many white ethnic Portuguese deserting the city. Beira was further devastated by floods in 2000, leaving millions homeless as well as having detrimental effects on the local economy.

The cathedral, located south-east of the city centre and once gleaming white, was built in 1925 with imported Portuguese stone. This was used for the sixteenth century Fort of San Caetano in Sofala, the first Portuguese fort in Mozambique (which has since disappeared under the sea). The town can be divided into three main areas: the compact city centre developed around the Praça do Municipo and Praça do Metical which marks the heart of the city. The area hosts most of the shops, businesses and restaurants and is dominated by medium-rise buildings. On the south-east side of the square is the marble municipal building that has a tile mural of the historical Sofala Castle in its entrance hall. The second area is the old town with its wide, tree-lined avenues and old Portuguese villas, located between Avenida Samora Machel and the Praça da Independência. The third and more modern residential sector is located between the lighthouse [26] and the Praça. After years of neglect and abuse, the buildings still have a certain charm, while the infrastructure of the city is slowly being re-established.

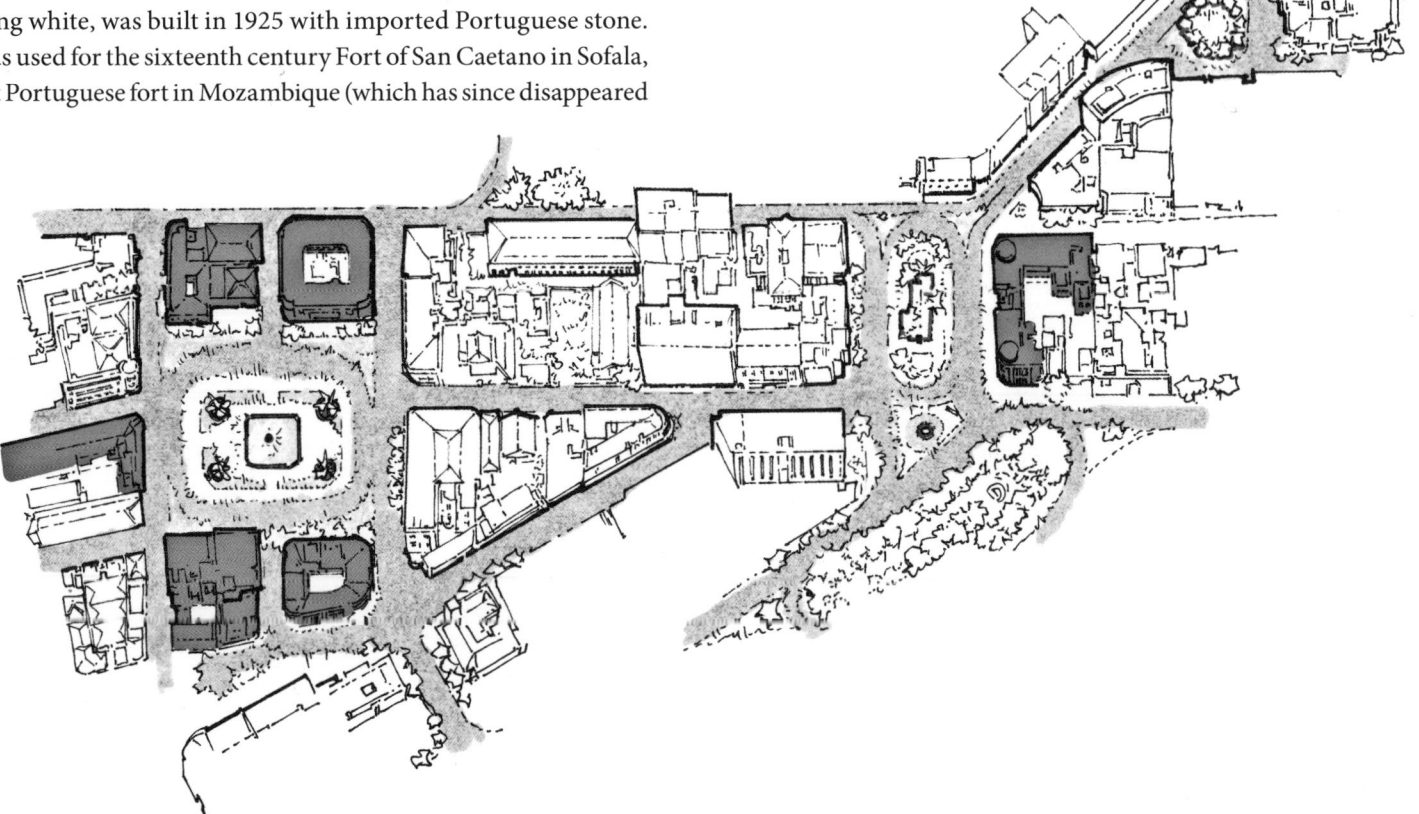

EASTERN AFRICA 71

1 Central Train Station
2 Manuel Antonio de Sousa Park
3 Port
4 Courthouse Beira
5 Praça do Metical
6 Bank National
7 Praça do Municipio
8 Town Hall
9 Chamber of Commerce
10 Beira Cathedral
11 Praça Almirante Reis
12 Cinema São Jorge
13 Our Lady of Angels College
14 Meteorological Observatory & Telegraph Office
15 Praça da India
16 Park
17 Praça Arthur Brandão
18 Beira Club
19 Sports Field
20 Geographical Information Centre
21 Pêro de Anaia Secondary School
22 Santa Isabel Cemetery
23 Our Lady of Fatima Church
24 Macuti Hospital
25 Afonse de Albuquerque Place
26 Lighthouse

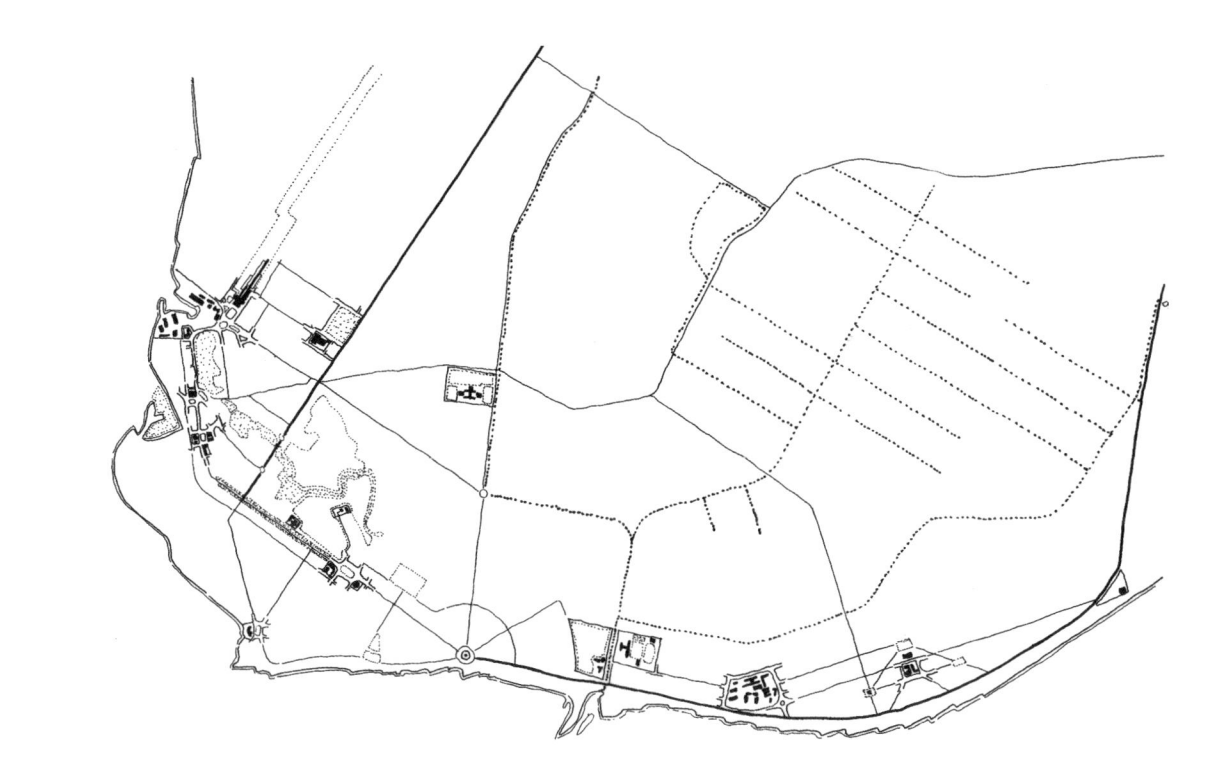

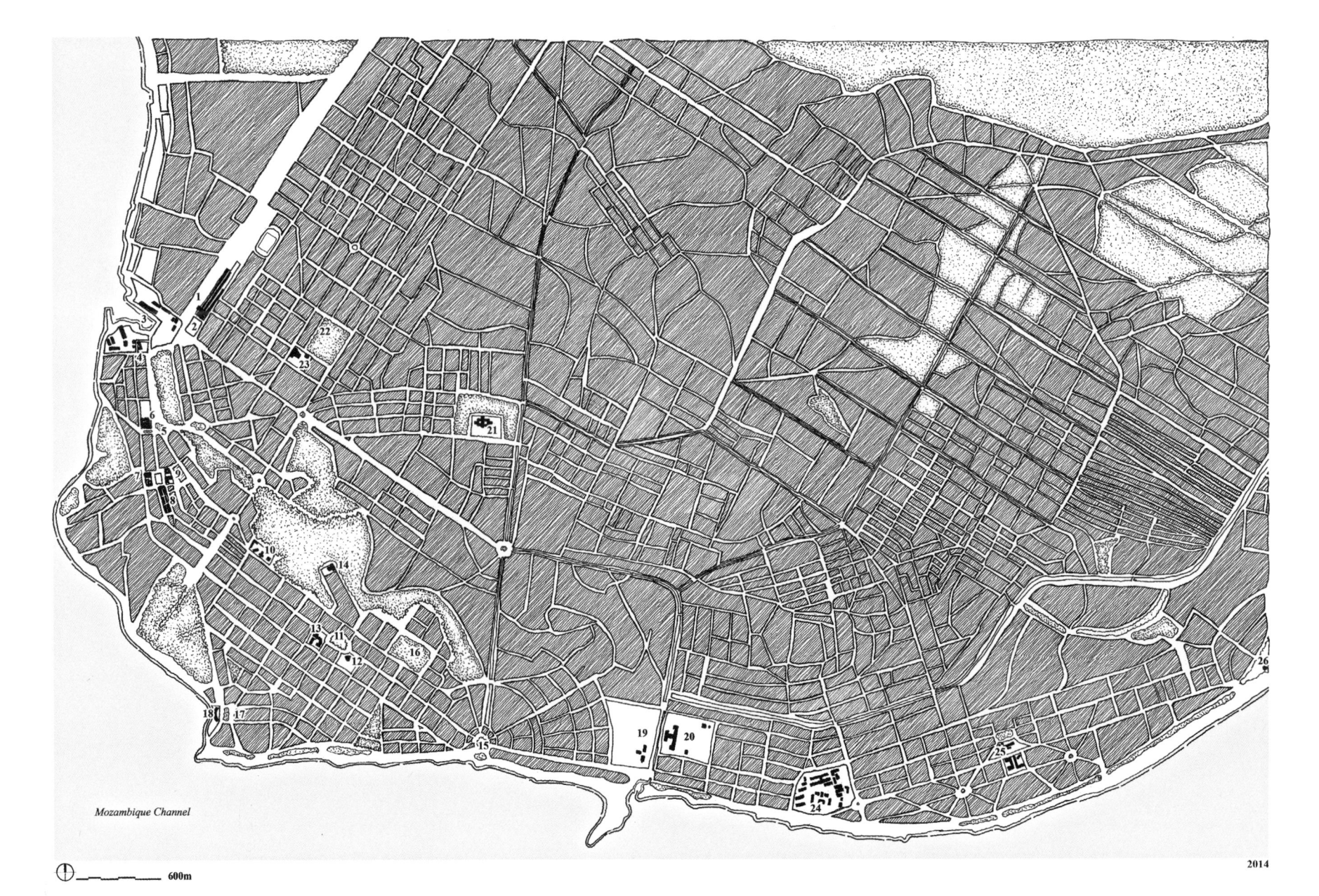

Mozambique Channel

600m

2014

ILHA, MOZAMBIQUE

FOUNDED: unknown
URBAN AREA: unknown
POPULATION: approximately 14,000
URBAN AREA DENSITY: unknown
GPS: 15° 2'0.05"S, 40° 44'6.48"E
15° 1'52.39"S, 40° 44'13.57"E

The small island Ilha de Moçambique, located along the coast of the Indian Ocean, was once the capital of Portuguese East Africa. It was strategically located as a major trading post in intercontinental maritime trade. The island was declared a UNESCO World Heritage site owing to the unique richness of its architecture and cultural history. The island has been referred to as "a long slim ribbon of gold floating in a sea of emerald". A narrow concrete bridge constructed during the 1960s connects the island with the Nampula mainland.

The island city, approximately 3 km long and 500 m wide, is divided into two parts: the colonial settlement, known as Stone Town with its colonial Portuguese stone-built, lime-washed architecture, founded by the Portuguese enroute to India, and the southern part, only inhabited during the second half of the nineteenth century as a bairro indígena or "the Macuti town" – native quarters for freed slaves and other local people. The Macuti town with its Swahili-inspired buildings was laid out in a grid with regulated building lines, heights and entrances, reflecting the desire for structure and order, characteristic of colonial planning. The urban pattern is tight in many areas with narrow alleys and small backyards. The streets serve as public places and the openness of the houses is in keeping with the idea of the public living room. The original layout of the town provided larger open areas with towering trees surrounding water points and offering shade as part of the public space. However, these public spaces have been compromised by uncontrolled building after independence, and restrict the areas previously planned for natural water drainage.

The Chapel of Nossa Senhora de Baluarte [1] dates back to 1522 and is believed by some to be the oldest standing building in the Southern Hemisphere. The Fort of San Sebastião [2] was built by the Portuguese during the late 1500s to early 1600s and is located at the northern end of the island, built around a spring – the only reliable source of drinking water on the island. The Palace and Chapel of São Paulo, dating to the 1700s, is located in the heart of Stone Town and was built as the former governor's residence with direct access for him to receive mass. The Old Hospital [12] was constructed in 1877 and for many years considered to be the biggest hospital south of the Sahara. The Church of Santo Antonio [15] is located on a headland at the southern end of the island.

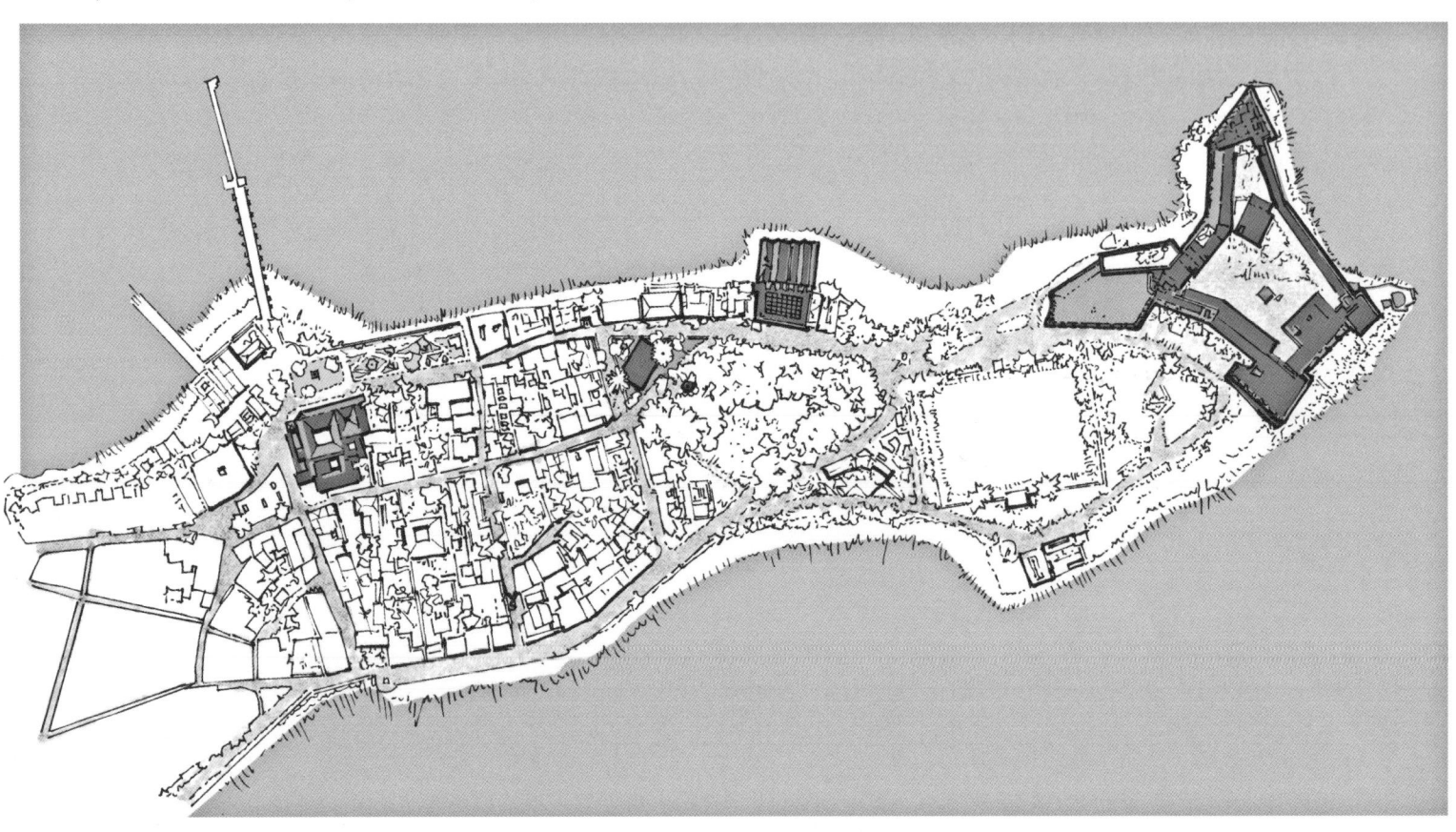

EASTERN AFRICA

1 Chapel of Our Lady of the Bulwark
2 St Sebastian Fort
3 Park
4 Old Mosque
5 Statue of Vasco de Gama & Park
6 Governor's House
7 Luis de Camoes Statue
8 Ancient harbour & harbour entrance
9 Park
10 Municipal Market
11 Park
12 Old Hospital
13 Church of Health
14 Mosque
15 Church & Fort of St Antonio
16 Market
17 Cemetery
18 Chapel of St Francis Xavier
19 Bridge towards mainland

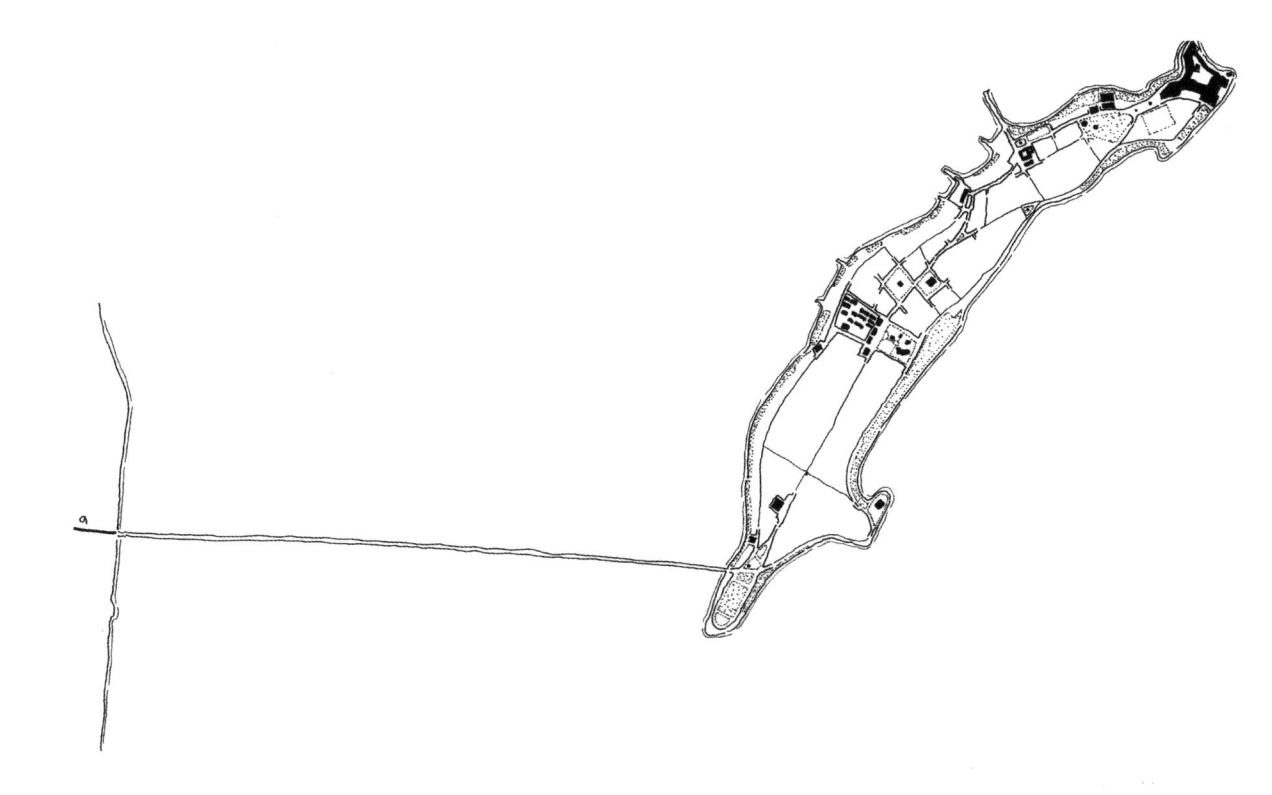

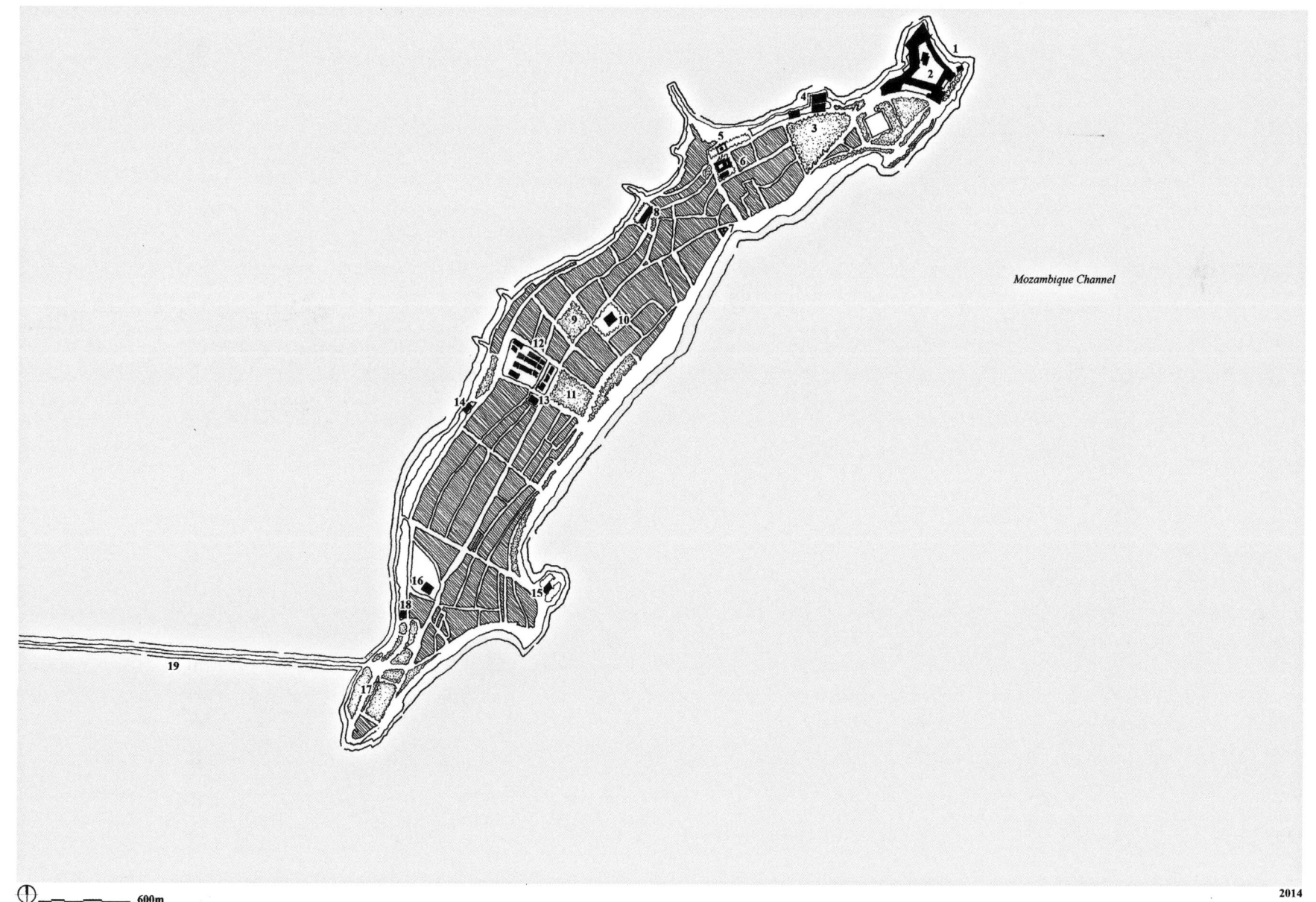

Mozambique Channel

MAPUTO, MOZAMBIQUE

FOUNDED: 1782
URBAN AREA: 347 km²
POPULATION: 1,766,184
URBAN AREA DENSITY: 5,100/km²
GPS: 25° 58'8.23"S, 32° 34'24.53"E
25° 58'17.55"S 32° 33'55.02"E

Maputo, the capital of Mozambique and the area previously known as Lourenço Marques, was formerly established as a settlement by the Portuguese, circa 1780. Despite evidence of early human settlement since 100 BC, historical records indicate that the bay was only discovered by Portuguese navigators in the mid-sixteenth century. The port was mainly used as a trading station for ivory. This Indian Ocean port city originally developed around the Portuguese fortress [1], while the economy is currently centred around the harbour.

Maputo is located on the western side of the Maputo Bay, in close proximity to the Estuário do Espírito Santo where the Tembe, Umbeluzi, Matola and Infulene rivers drain into the Indian Ocean. The bay is 95 km long and 30 km wide.

Although the central area of Maputo can be mistaken for a planned city with square blocks and wide avenues, the city's layout informally developed around the public gathering space – a central square (*praça*) with clear sightlines from the fortress [1]. The approved master plan of 1972 was only implemented partially — urban land layouts and construction were left half finished. The inner city boasts architecture by masters of the trade such as Gustav Eiffel, Pancho Guedes, Herbert Baker and Thomas Honney.

The Praça de Independência is a focal point in the city with a statue of the country's first president, Samora Machel, surrounded by the luminous white Roman Catholic cathedral, the neoclassical City Hall and the French-Mozambican cultural centre, a grand restored old colonial building. The informal market is Maputo's largest employer (household food purchases are nearly 100 percent from informal markets) and the long-established fish market [30] in Maputo has become a normative feature of the city's urban fabric.

The informal settlements on the other hand developed in the peri-urban rural low-lying coastal wetland and estuarine zones and flood plains, threatening the city's capacity to sustain crucial and ecosystem-dependent industries such as fishing and tourism, as well as posing threats to the habitants as these areas are prone to flooding. Mozambique is one of the poorest and most aid-dependent countries in the world, yet the city has recently been experiencing construction booms linked to foreign investment and increased trade.

The significant trans-boundary Maputo Development Corridor connects Maputo to the Witwatersrand. The historic railway route, built in 1895, is being redeveloped as a joint Special Development Initiative between South Africa and Mozambique.

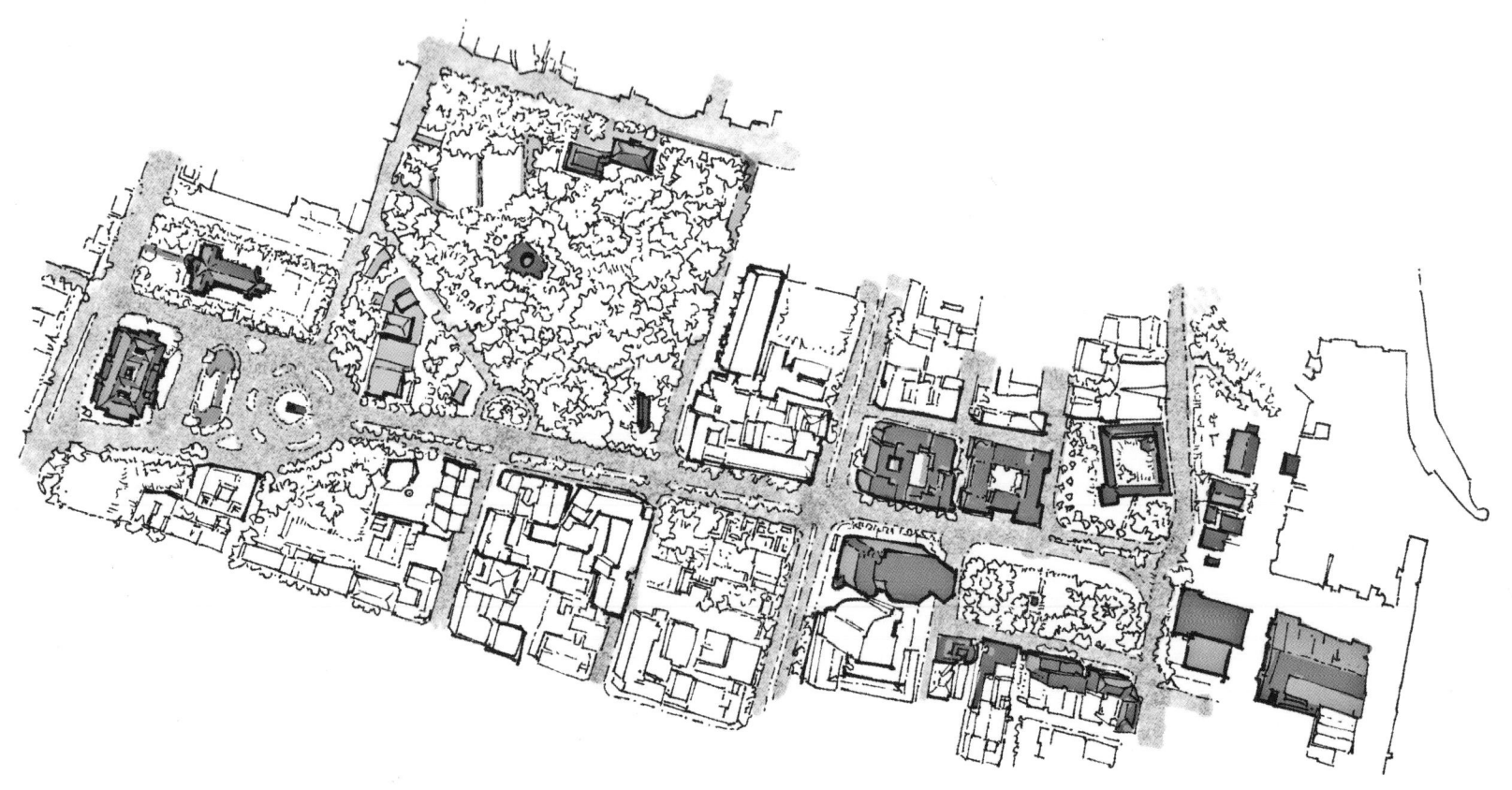

1 Maputo Fort	19 Garden Valentine, Jardim dos Namorados
2 25th June Square	20 Assembly of the Republic & Hall of the 4th Congress
3 Maputo Central Train Station	21 Red Star Secondary School
4 Tunduru Botanical Gardens	22 September 7th Felipe Samuel Magaia Primary School
5 Independence Square	23 Church of Our Lady of Victories
6 Maputo City Hall	24 Followers Park, Parque dos Continuadores
7 Cathedral of Our Lady of Conception	25 Military Installations
8 Maputo Central Hospital	26 Military Hospital
9 St Francis Xavier Cemetery	27 Peace Gardens, Square of Peace & Bull Fight Arena
10 National Art Museum	28 General Hospital of Chamanculo
11 Museum of the Revolution	29 Botanical Nursery
12 28th May Garden	30 Fish Market
13 Agha Khan Building	31 Park
14 Josina Machel Secondary School	
15 Natural History Museum	
16 Garden of Professors	
17 Municipal Market	
18 Sports Pavilion	

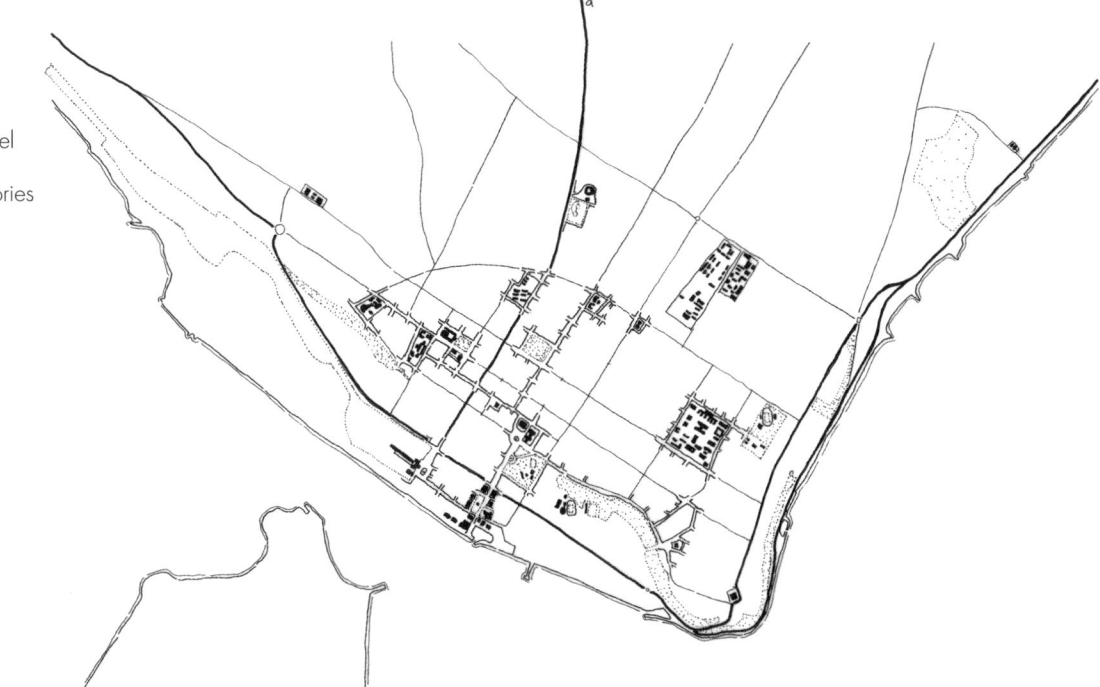

Mozambique Channel

KIGALI, RWANDA

FOUNDED: 1907
URBAN AREA: unknown
POPULATION: 1,135,428 (2012)
URBAN AREA DENSITY: 1,600/km²
GPS: 1° 56'39.46"S, 30° 3'42.67"E

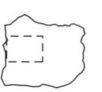

Kigali is Rwanda's capital and largest city. Located in proximity to the geographic centre of the country, the city has been the economic, cultural, and transport hub of Rwanda since independence in 1962. Established in 1907 under German colonial rule, Kigali only became the capital in 1962 with Rwandan independence.

The undulating hilly landscape exposes the city's built form, sprawling across the four ridges and valleys in-between. One ridge top is home to the city centre, with the main government area situated on another. The ridge tops are generally inhabited with larger houses and office buildings, while the poorer people – around 80 percent of the population – live in informal neighbourhoods in the valleys. The city is predominantly surrounded by higher hills, with a suburban sprawl rising up these.

As seen in most African cities, rapid urbanisation resulted in unplanned and squalid settlements, urban sprawl, and increasing urban poverty (Niyonsenga, 2012). The infrastructure is under increased pressure as the system was designed to provide for 450,000 people, with a population currently exceeding 1,000,000 (The World Bank, 2011). This predominantly informal city has a historical background of urban planning from as early as 1964, when a Conceptual Master Plan was developed for Kigali with the assistance of the French Ministry of Cooperation. The plan was partially implemented in 1969 with the delimitation of the area around Nyarugenge hill for the extension of Kigali, and the structuring of the hills of Nyarugenge.

The genocide of 1994 resulted in a massive population loss and devastation of the built environment. With a growth rate of around 8 percent, the urban population of Kigali exceeded its pre-genocide level in 1999 while the built environment of Kigali has remained relatively unchanged.

The rapid urban growth is predominantly informal with limited access to basic infrastructures. The government's relentless determination to improve the city and its living conditions has been remarkable, earning the city a UN-Habitat Scroll of Honour Award in 2008. The city has been praised by the media as the future "Singapore of Africa" due to measures taken to improve the plight of slum dwellers; improved waste management; as well as the banning of plastic bags and smoking in public spaces. Tough zoning and permit laws are followed to the letter, with poor and rich held to equal standards, while city authorities are easily able to clear squatters off public land slated for approved projects.

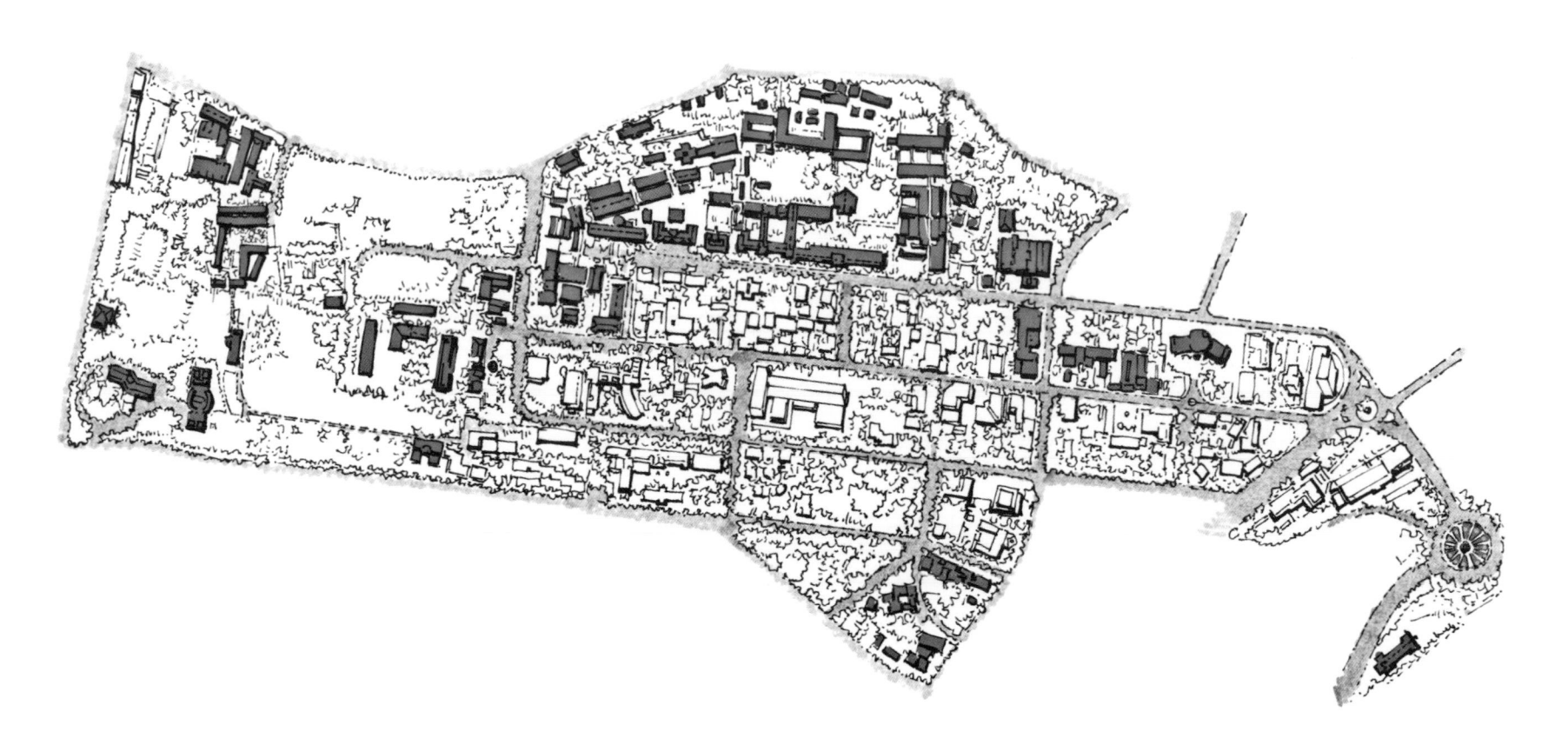

EASTERN AFRICA **77**

1 Place de l'Unite
2 St Familli Church
3 Place de la Constitution
4 Kigale City Council
5 Ministry of Finance
6 St Michel Church
7 Radio Rwanda
8 Central Hospital & Kigale University Hospital
9 Belgium Memorial Site
10 Kigale Institute of Science and Technology
11 Presidential Residence
12 School for Finance and Banking
13 Kigale Centenary Park
14 Office of the Prime Minister
15 Ministry of Defence
16 Parliament
17 Amahoro Stadium
18 Ministry of Infrastructure
19 Ministry of Education
20 US Embassy
21 Rwanda Police Headquarters
22 Police Hospital
23 Kigale Genocide Memorial Centre

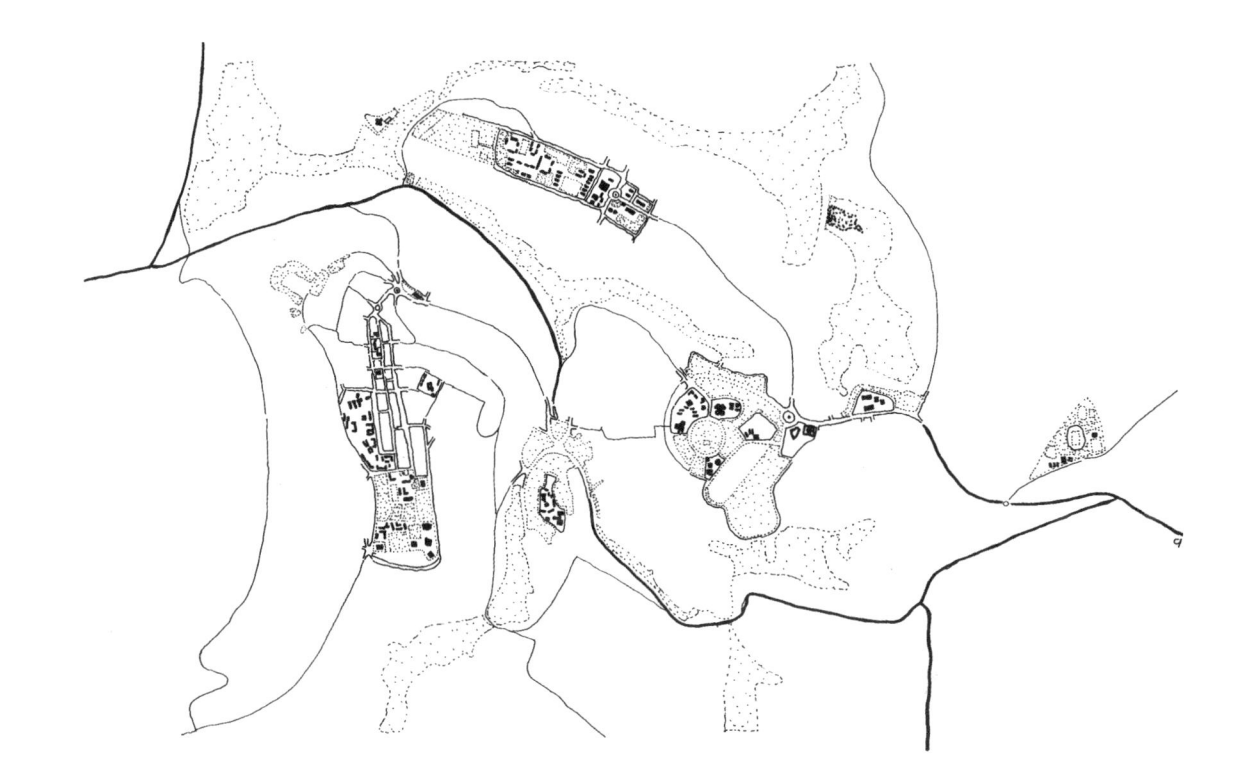

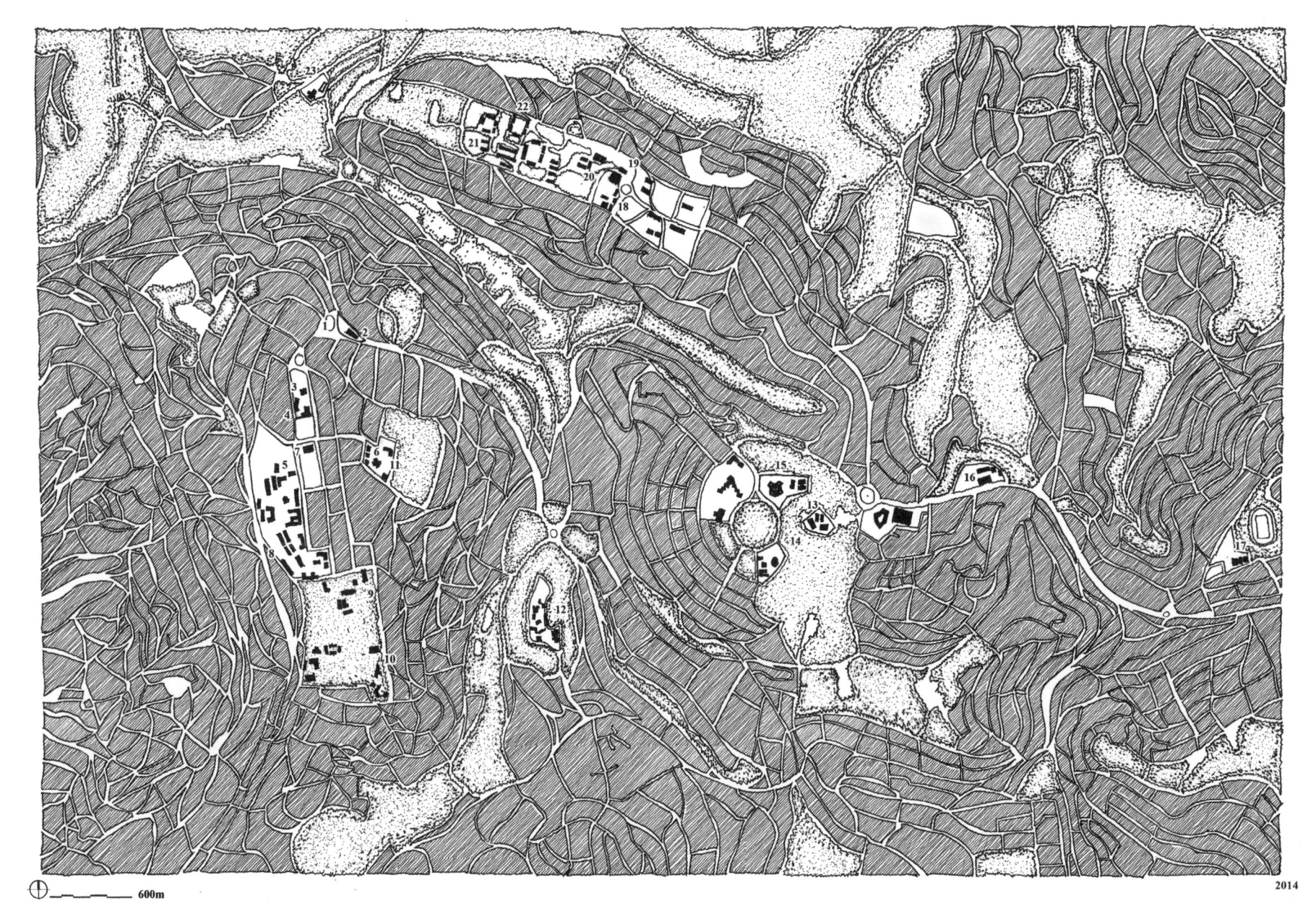

600m

2014

VICTORIA, SEYCHELLES

FOUNDED: unknown
URBAN AREA: unknown
POPULATION: 25,000 (2002)
URBAN AREA DENSITY: unknown
GPS: 4° 37'23.55"S, 55° 27'8.47"E

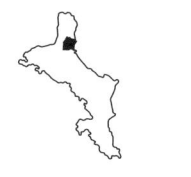

Victoria, named after Queen Victoria of England – also referred to as Port Victoria – is the capital of Seychelles and one of the smallest capital cities in the world. The city is located on the north-eastern side of Mahé island, the archipelago's main island, and developed in response to the location of the island's natural harbour and the country's single major port. The inner harbour shapes the eastern boundary of the town.

It is said that the French first settled in this area around 1778 until the British took ownership in 1811 under the Treaty of Paris. The country became a crown colony and Victoria was established as the capital of Seychelles in 1903. Seychelles remained a British colony until independence in 1976.

This vibrant city is home to around a third of the country's population and is a melting pot of cultures with a mixture of French, British colonial and modern styles and an added infusion of Chinese and Indian cultures. The small city, bound by the sea on the one side and the hilly topography on the other, limits the areas for development. This resulted in a form of urban sprawl emerging along the narrow belt of the coastal plain as commerce, services and institutional facilities are concentrated in the central area of the city. The road infrastructure dates back to the colonial period and has limited capacity to cater for the increased demand. Francis Rachel Street is the main direct arterial into the CBD and approach into Victoria from the airport.

The UN-Habitat report identifies Victoria as a city vulnerable to sea-level rise. In 2004 the Indian Ocean earthquake and tsunami caused a lot of damage to the city, including the collapse of one of its largest bridges.

This tiny capital scattered with colonial buildings is easily covered on foot. St Paul's Cathedral was built on the site of the first Seychelles church. The Sir Selwyn Selwyn-Clarke Market Place originated in 1840 and is a focal point for both locals and visitors. The famous Victoria Clock Tower [3] in the heart of the city was erected as a memorial to Queen Victoria. The tower was built in 1903 and modelled after that of Vauxhall Clock Tower in London. The town centre is home to the courthouse [4] and post office [5], both still virtually unchanged since colonial times.

Other significant places include the Cathedral of the Immaculate Conception [10] the Victoria Botanical Gardens [8], the Victoria National Museum of History, the Victoria Natural History Museum and the Victoria Market. The national stadium [19] is also situated in the city.

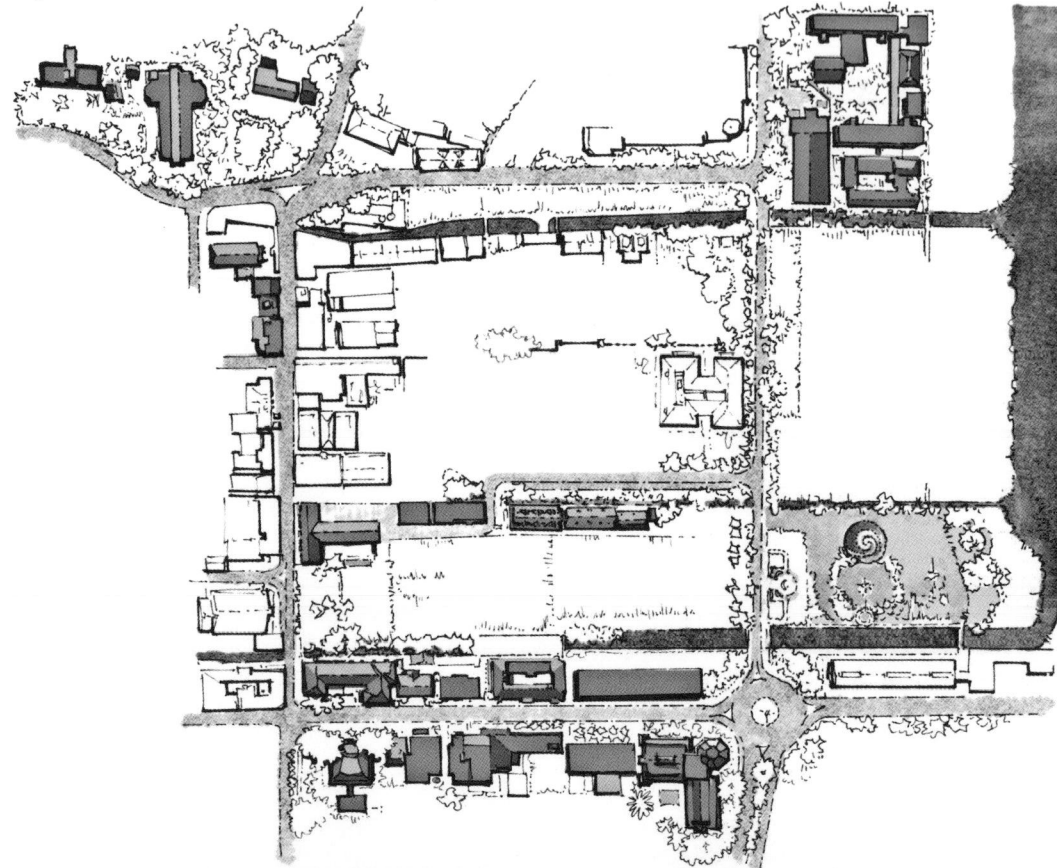

1 State House
2 Victoria House
3 Victoria Clock Tower
4 Supreme Court/Old Courthouse
5 Liberty House & Post Office
6 Independence House
7 Fishing Port
8 Botanical Garden
9 Victoria Hospital
10 Cathedral of the Immaculate Conception
11 Market
12 Freedom Square
13 Belonie Secondary & Primary Schools
14 English River School
15 Anglican Church
16 Kanti House
17 Sheikh Mohamed Khalifa Mosque
18 Graveyard
19 Unity Stadium & Sports Complex

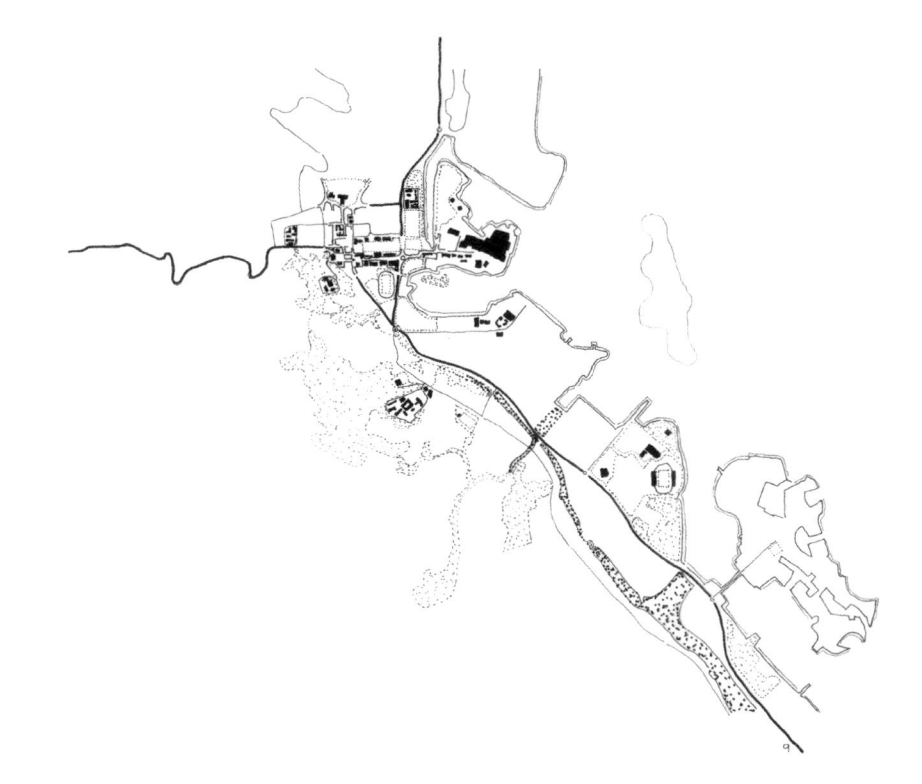

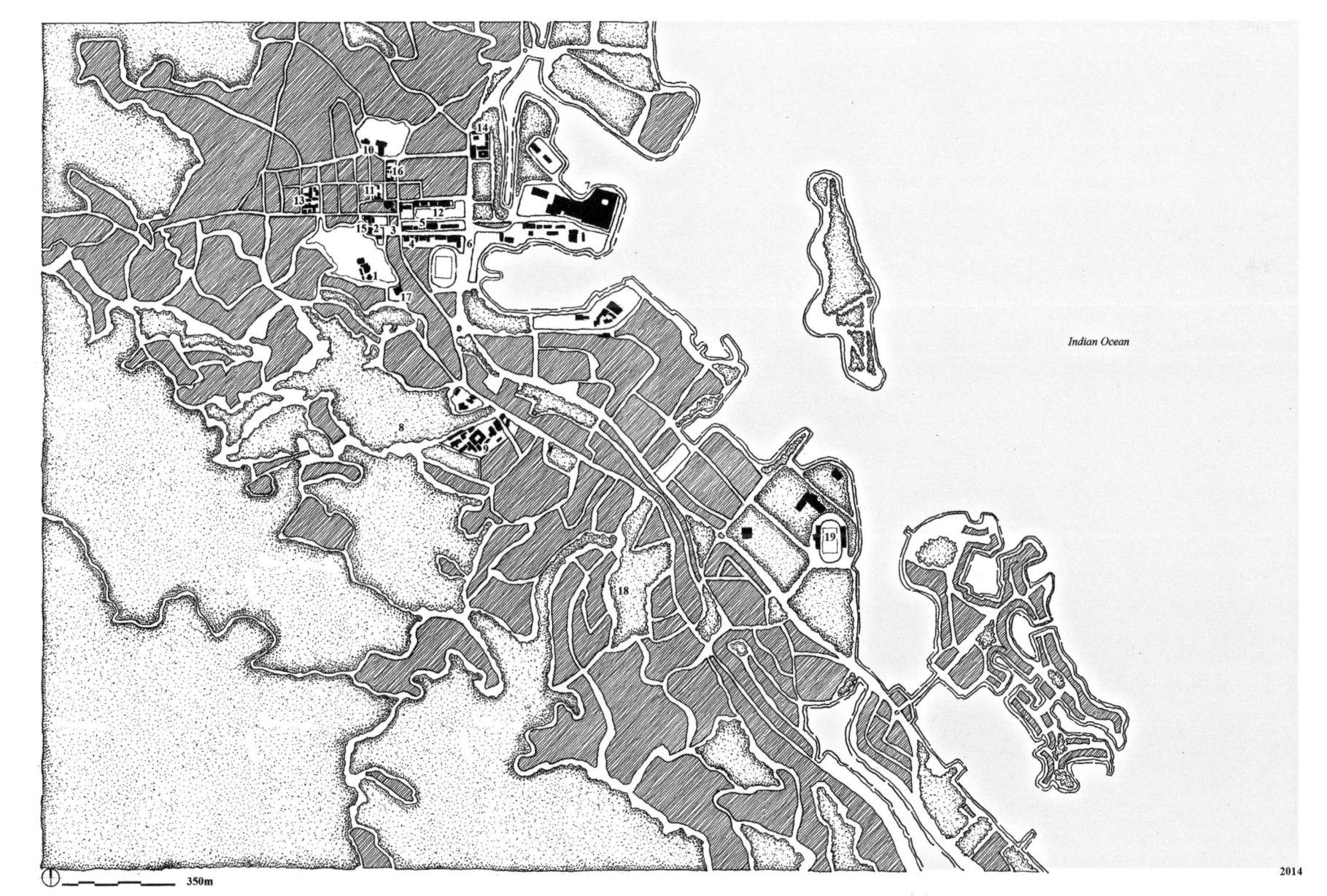

MOGADISHU, SOMALIA

FOUNDED: at pinnacle of prosperity by the year 1331
URBAN AREA: 1,657 km²
POPULATION (2009): 1,353,000
URBAN AREA DENSITY: 817/km²
GPS: 2° 2'5.58"N, 45° 20'33.55"E
2° 1'55.84"N, 45° 20'31.71"E

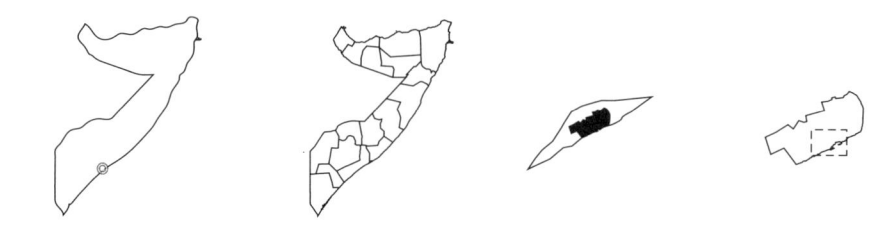

Twenty years of civil war saw much of the city of Mogadishu – once described as the "White Pearl of the Indian Ocean" – destroyed. Located along the Indian Ocean, Arabs, Persians, Indian merchants, and later European settlers, came into contact with this Somali trade city. Its modern history began when the Italians took control in 1889 and purchased the port of Benadir. In 1908, Mogadishu was officially made the capital of the new colony of Southern Somalia. The built form pre-dating this period was of a compact walled city with an Arab-style old centre. The transformation of the old city began under Italian rule and radically altered the character of the old city.

Under the 1912 master plan for the city, the walls of the old Arab centre were destroyed and two new native suburbs were constructed to its east and west. According to Ali (2014), in contrast to other colonial planning models – such as the one for Asmara where the colonial city developed next to the existing indigenous city – in Mogadishu the buildings of the occupying power were literally inserted into its old centre. By 1928, a second master plan followed the first, which adapted caravan routes and was shaped by the coastal outline connected by a series of roads. The Italians left an indelible mark on the city, recognisable today in the grid-block street plan and also in the architectural heritage.

Much of the character of Mogadishu in the first half of the previous century tended to be a mixture of Islamic, colonial, and indigenous vernacular and later modernist influences. However, according to Ali, it was modernist buildings that were to have an enduring influence on post-independence architecture, since this was largely seen as a way for the country to assert its identity through new architectural forms. Examples include the National Theatre and the National Assembly that were completed between 1969 and 1974.

Following independence, the history of the country was marked by conflict and authorities that became increasingly totalitarian. By the early 1990s, the Battles of Magadishu had started that would span a period of twenty years. Despite its conflict-ridden past, the city's demographic pressures are exceptionally high with a projected average annual growth rate of almost 9 percent, according to the 2014 UN-Habitat report.

1 Old Mogadishu
2 National Government Ministries Building
3 Park & Arch
4 Mogadishu Cathedral
5 Old Parliament Building
6 Monument/Dhagaxtuur
7 Somali National Museum & National Library
8 National Theatre Mogadishu
9 Masaajidka Isbahaysigga Mosque
10 Sayyid Muhammed Abdille Hassan Statue
11 Villa Somalia
12 Mogadishu New Port
13 Mogadishu International Airport
14 Beerta Nasashada Park
15 Mogadishu Old Port

JUBA, SOUTH SUDAN

FOUNDED: 1922
URBAN AREA: 52 km²
POPULATION (2011): 372,410
URBAN AREA DENSITY: unknown
GPS: 4° 51'1.52"N, 31° 34'59.48"E

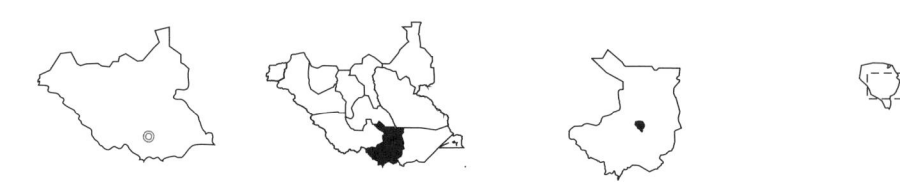

Juba, capital of South Sudan, was established in 1922 along the Nile River as a small town of Greek traders who contributed to what are visible structures in the urban fabric to this day (such as Juba Market and the so-called Greek Quarters, a small suburb which today is called Hai Jalaba).

South Sudan gained independence in 2011 and according to the UN-Habitat report (2014), 75 percent of Sudan's oil now falls inside the new landlocked republic. This, and the failure of Juba and Khartoum to reach agreement on a number of outstanding issues – including the shipment of landlocked South Sudan's oil through Port Sudan on the Red Sea – has resulted in an economic catastrophe for both countries

On a regional level, Juba is considered a crossroads of activity due to its location on the Nile River. Its proximity to neighbouring countries such as Uganda and Kenya also enhance trade activity at the regional and international levels. Juba is strategically placed within an important geographic triangle made up of Wau, Malakal and Juba. These three locations each have modernised airports and active river ports. Such linkages are critical for the movement of goods and people throughout Southern Sudan and greatly increase their propensity as key locations for trade.

Although Juba is currently the capital of South Sudan, with a population that doubled to nearly 400,000 since the civil war ended in 2005, the authorities are set on relocating the capital to Ramciel, which is a site more centrally located than Juba.

As surrounding areas of Juba are swallowed up by settlements, space for agriculture has become largely unavailable. Insecurity in peri-urban areas has increased significantly compared to during the war years when the Sudanese armed forces were in firm control. As there has been no proper urban framework in place, the expansion of the town is largely unmanaged. Rapid urbanisation is also having profound effects on the forest environment around Juba.

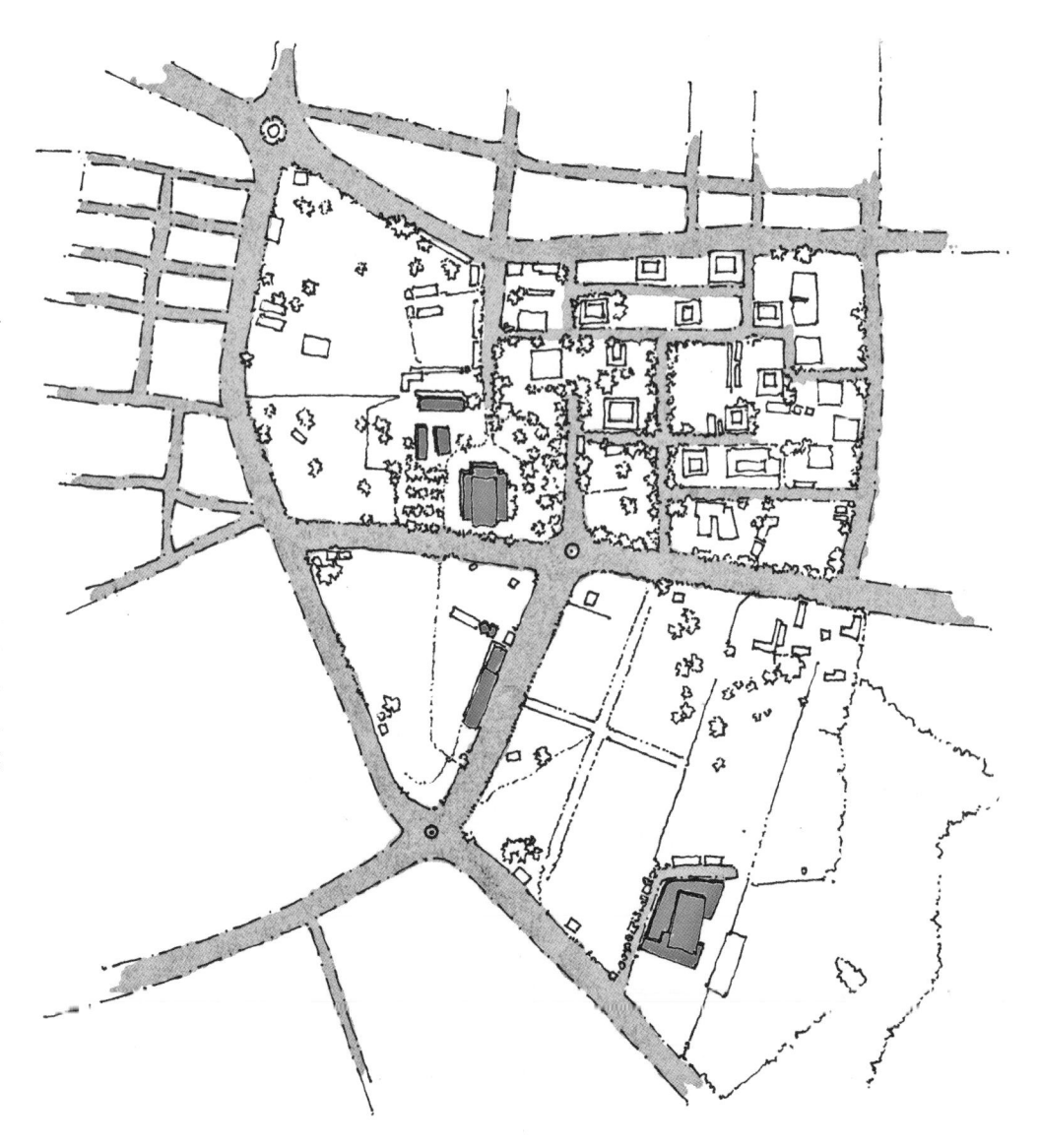

EASTERN AFRICA **83**

1 John Garang Memorial Site
2 South Sudan Parliament
3 Freedom Hall
4 Public Square Celebration
5 South Sudan Police Hospital
6 Juba International Airport
7 South Sudan Military Hospital
8 Stadium
9 Market
10 Church

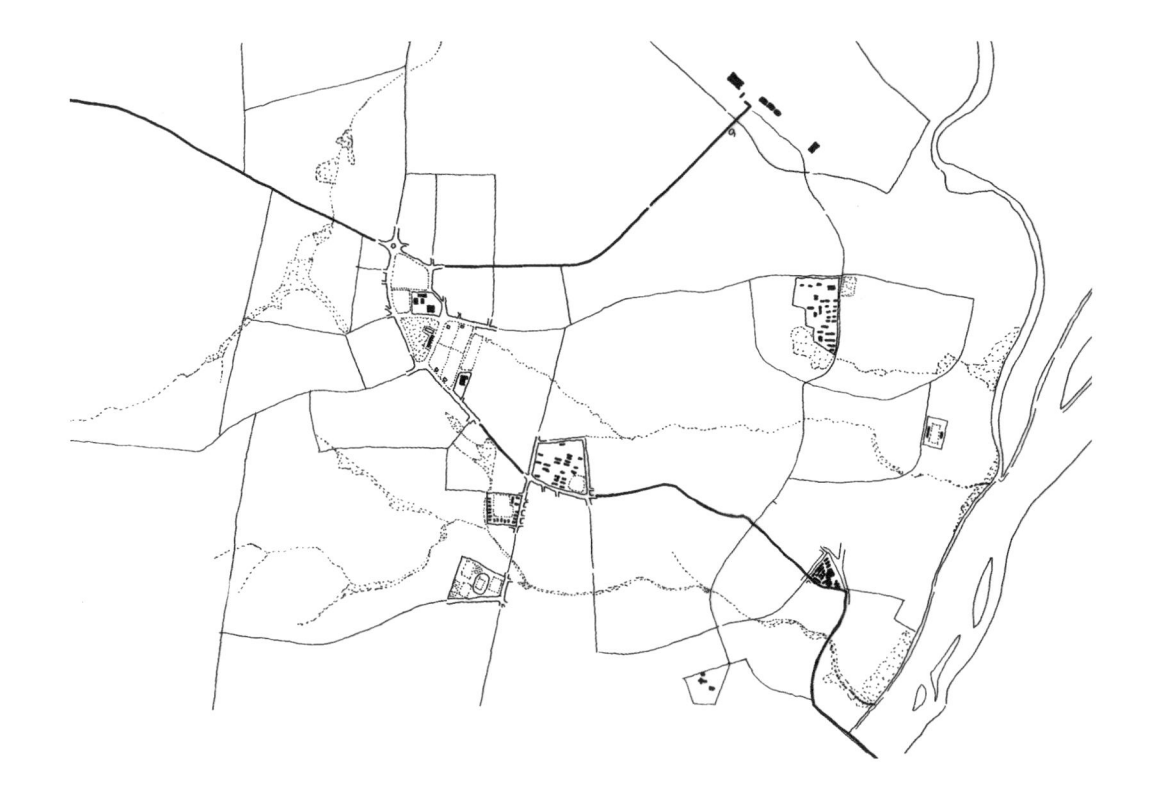

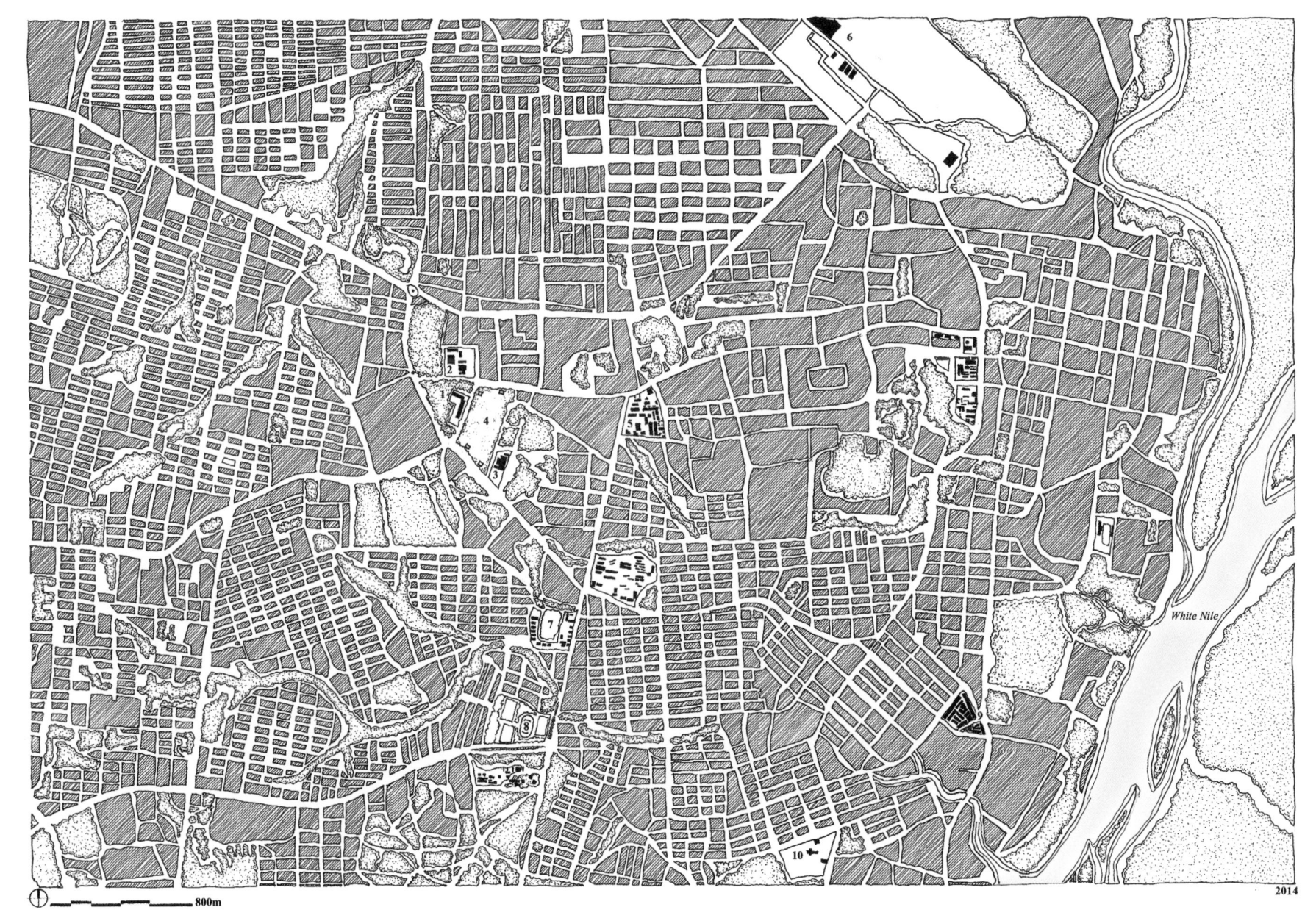

800m

2014

White Nile

DAR ES SALAAM, TANZANIA

FOUNDED: 1857 or 1865
URBAN AREA: 1,590 km²
POPULATION (2012): 4,364,541
URBAN AREA DENSITY: 1,787/km²
GPS: 6° 49'5.39"S, 39° 17'24.98"E
6° 45'8.80"S, 39° 16'20.10"E

The Tanzanian port city Dar es Salaam, – meaning "House of Peace" – is one of sub-Saharan Africa's most important and fastest growing urban centres. In fact, it has overtaken Nairobi as Eastern Africa's largest city and is likely to reach megacity status within a generation, if current growth trends persist (UN-Habitat, 2014).

Historically, the site around the area of modern Dar es Salaam was of commercial importance because of its location on the shipping route between the Middle East and Mozambique. Owing to the city's role in international trade, the urban area grew and consumed regional settlements, which are today constituencies within the present-day city. While the British government historically financed the construction of a road from the coast to the interior, the city's growth was especially facilitated by the establishment of the German East Africa Company for which the city served as a colonial administrative and commercial centre. Industrial expansion resulted from the construction of the Central Railway Line during the early 1900s. Under German rule, the urban centre of the city developed systematically along a grid-block system. German historical influences from the 1800s are still visible in the city today, for example in the Lutheran churches, German Hospital and St Joseph's Cathedral.

The British seized German East Africa during the First World War and renamed it Tanganyika. During this time, the city's economy experienced great growth paralleled by urban migration. In 1961, Tanganyika declared independence from the British Crown and merged with Zanzibar to form Tanzania.

In 1996, Dar es Salaam lost its status as capital city and the capital was moved to Dodoma. Despite this reclassification, the city remained Tanzania's economic centre. Since 1980, the population of the city has quadrupled to reach over four million by 2012. The city's planning agencies have been unable to keep up with the rapid expansion of the city and as a result, an estimated 70 percent of Dar es Salaam's population lived in poor, unplanned settlements by 2002 (World Bank, 2002). Today, these communities still face many challenges, which, paired with heavy rainfall and flooding, result in turbulent urban circumstances such as transportation constraints, insecure housing, problems in accessing clean water, unhygienic sanitation provisions and hardship.

Despite these challenges, Dar es Salaam is widely regarded by the youth of Tanzania as a fantastic place of opportunity and is commonly referred to as *Bongoland*, meaning "brainland" (UN-Habitat, 2014).

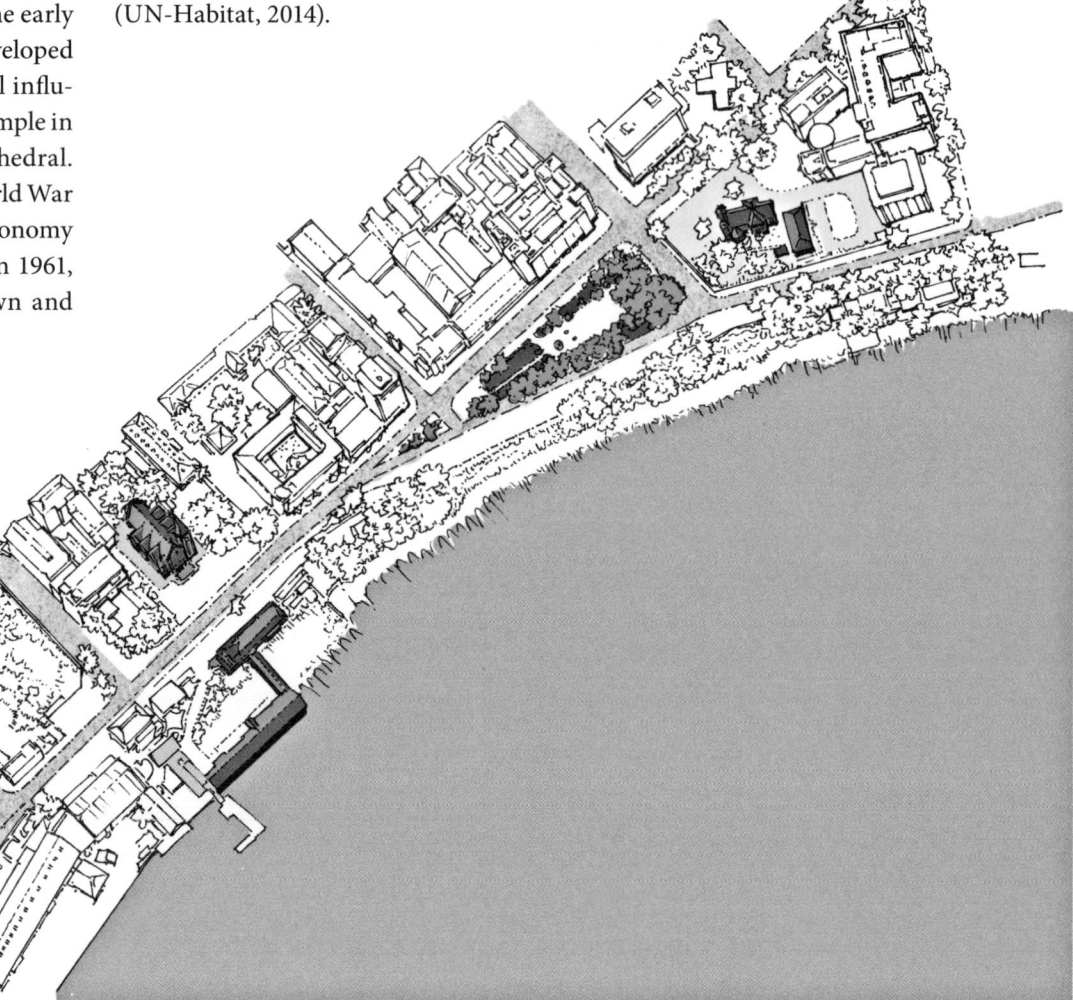

EASTERN AFRICA 85

1 Ocean Road Cancer Institute
2 National Institute for Medical Research
3 Botanical Garden
4 Karimjee Hall
5 State House
6 Parliament
7 Mzizima Fish Market & Harbour
8 Dar es Salaam Club
9 Bustani ya Posta Park
10 Azania Front Lutheran Church
11 Tanganyika National Library
12 St Alban's Anglican Church
13 City Hall
14 St Joseph's Cathedral
15 Zanzibar Ferry Terminal
16 Mtendeni Primary School
17 Mnazi Mmoja Primary & Secondary Schools
18 Mnazi Mmoja Park & Memorial
19 Mnazi Mmoja Hospital
20 Uhuru Monument
21 Central Train Station
22 Jangwani Playing Fields
23 Jangwani Girls Secondary School
24 Karume Memorial Stadium
25 Ilala Park
26 Kigamboni Ferry Terminal

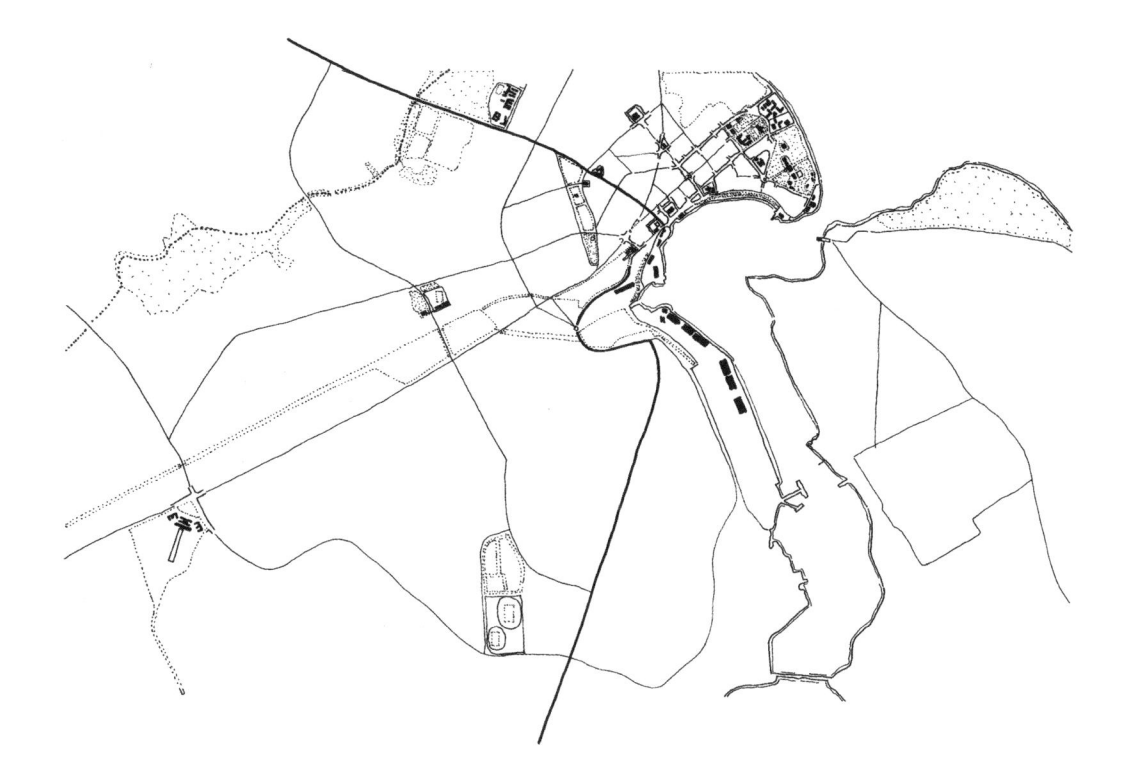

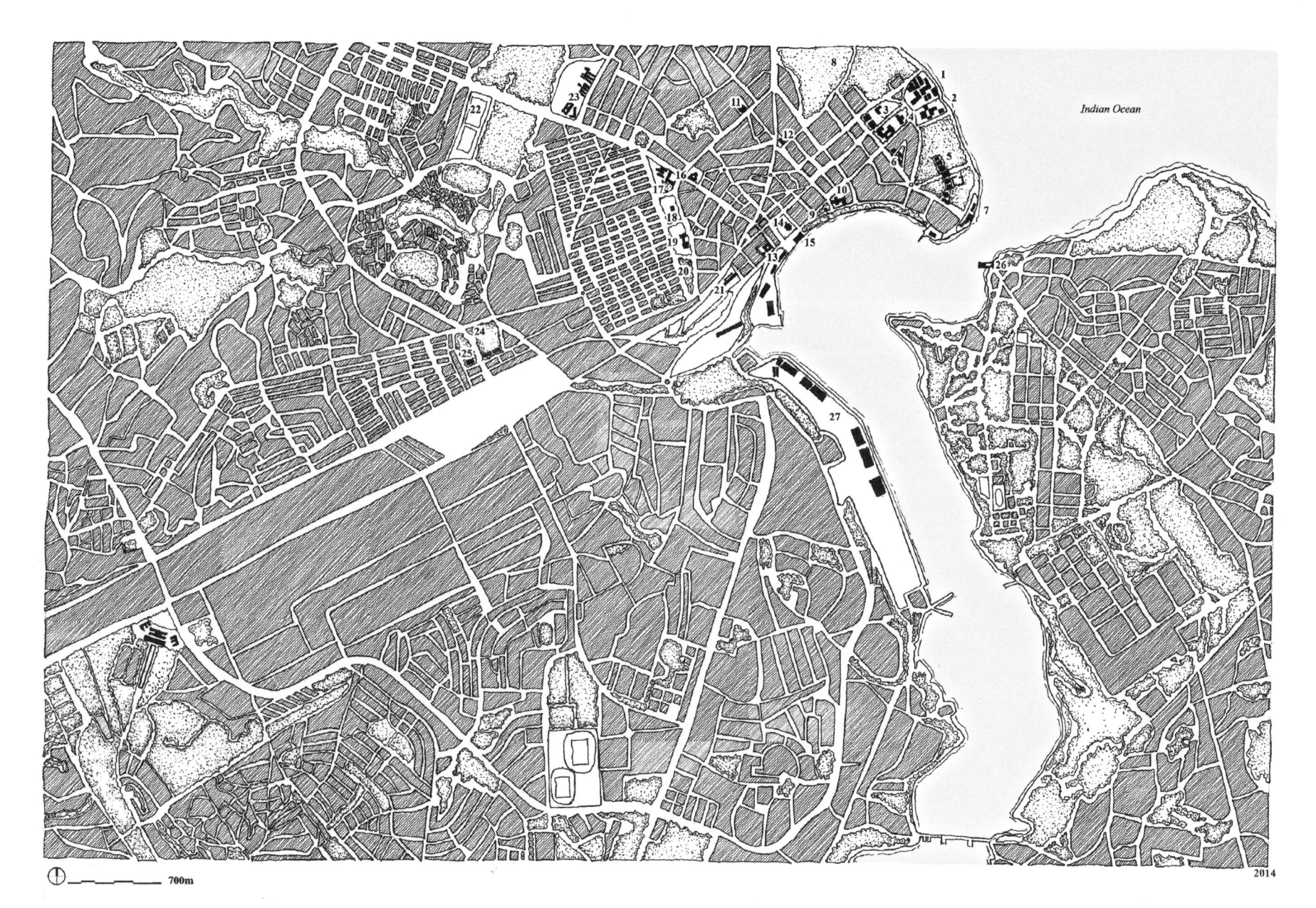

700m

2014

DODOMA, TANZANIA

FOUNDED: 1907
URBAN AREA: 625 km²
POPULATION (2012): 410,956
URBAN AREA DENSITY: unknown
GPS: 6° 10'44.56"S, 35° 44'50.14"E

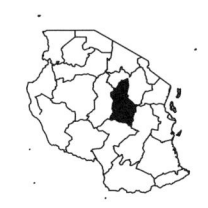

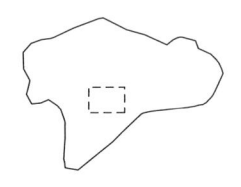

In 1973, a public referendum in Tanzania approved that the capital be moved from Dar es Salaam to the inland location of Dodoma. Some of the most important reasons for the transfer of the capital included the desire to reduce pressure on the old capital and to increase economic opportunity in central Tanzania. According to Abubakar and Doan (2012), in the African context, new town strategies were adopted as part of national planning policies after independence and these strategies were the basis for establishing new capital cities such as Dodoma. These new capitals were often established based on the garden city model that was intended to essentially wipe away the colonial imprints on existing cities.

Dodoma was a small settlement by the 1890's before the German colonists officially founded it in 1907 during the construction of the Tanzanian central railway. When Dodoma was selected to be the new centrally located capital, it was an already established town at a major crossroads. Situated on the eastern edge of the southern highlands, the city is surrounded by agricultural land. It is served by an international airport and the Central Railway Line, which connects it over a distance of 465 km with Dar es Salaam along the coast.

According to Abubakar and Doan, by 1976 a master plan had been prepared by Canadian planning consultants, which was subsequently revised during the late 1980s. A Capital Development Authority and a supervisory ministry were set up to coordinate and administer the new capital city. The Dodoma master plan drew heavily on international models, focusing on the aforementioned British garden city concept, western architectural ideals and rationalised urban form, despite its original intentions to be non-monumental and embody the local culture.

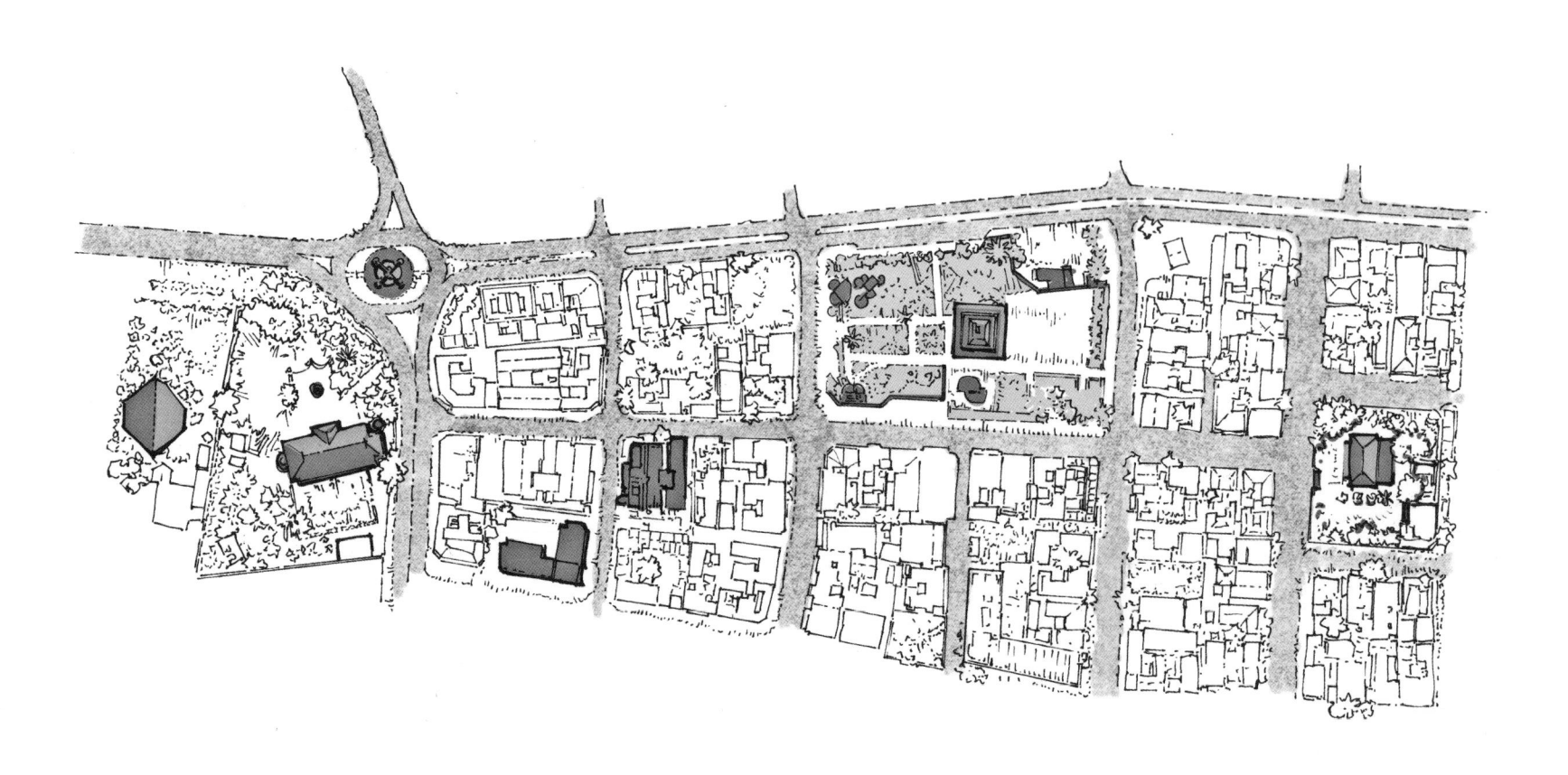

EASTERN AFRICA **87**

1 Central Train Station
2 Ismaili Mosque
3 Lutheran Cathedral
4 Jamatini Bus Station
5 Prime Minister's Office,
    Regional and Local Administration Office
6 Nyerere Square
7 Anglican Church
8 Dodoma International Airport
9 Jamhuri Stadium
10 Gaddafi Mosque
11 Parliament
12 Dodoma & Viwandani Secondary Schools
13 Catholic Cathedral
14 Cemetery
15 Museum of Geoscience

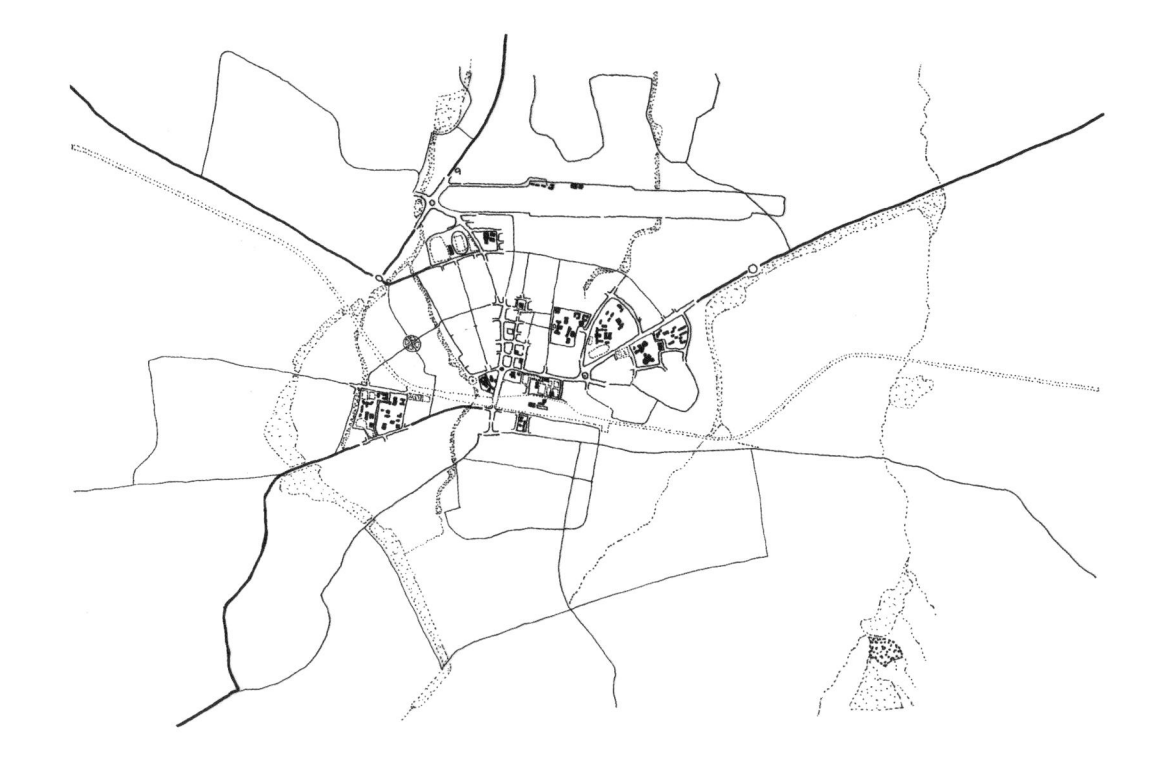

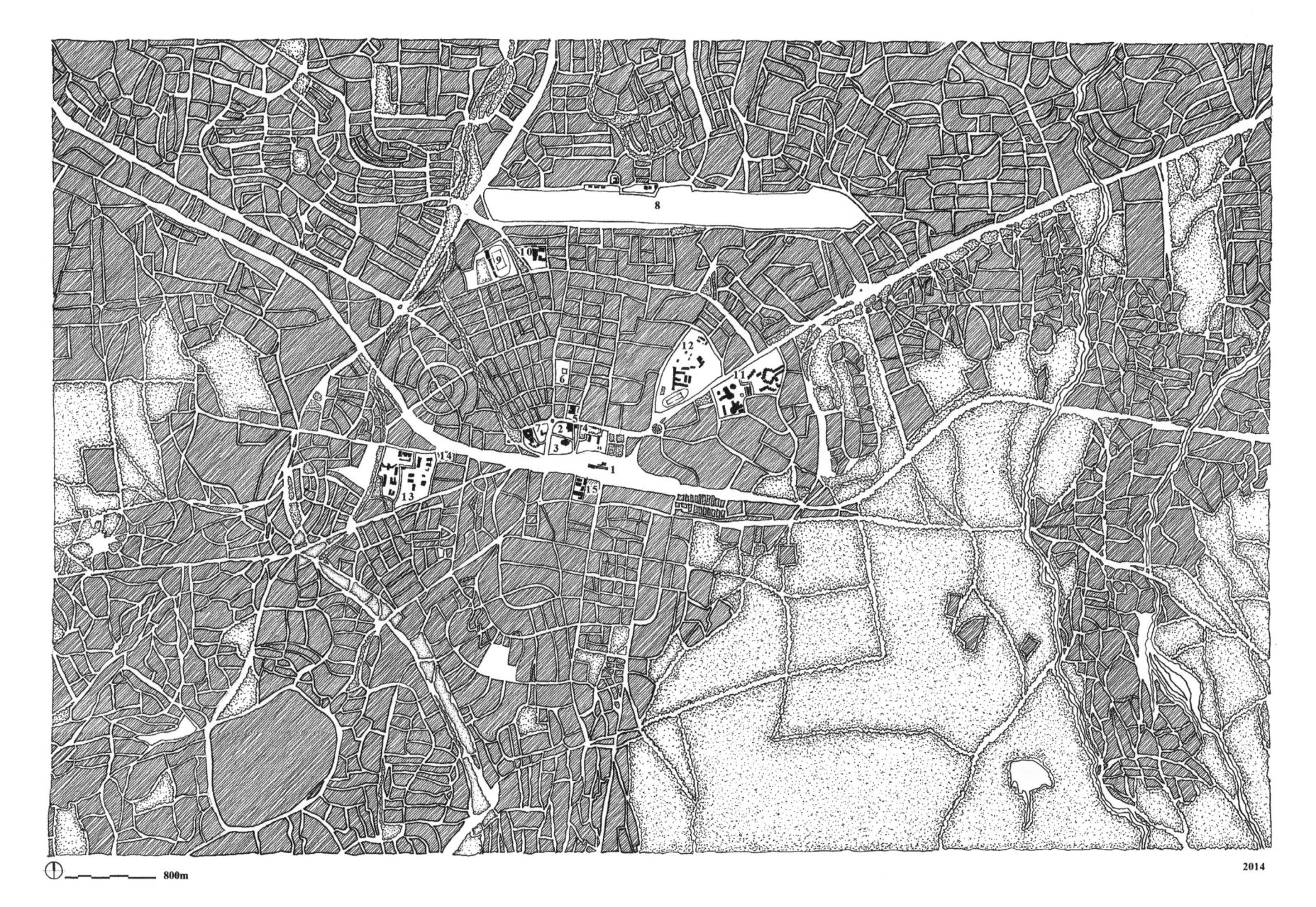

800m

2014

ZANZIBAR, TANZANIA

FOUNDED: capital of the Sultanate of Muscat and Oman in 1832
URBAN AREA: 62 km²
POPULATION: 220,000
URBAN AREA DENSITY: 3,548/km²
GPS: 6° 9'38.73"S, 39° 11'19.90"E

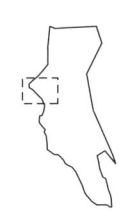

Zanzibar consists of a few islands in the Indian Ocean, off the coast of Tanzania. The capital of Zanzibar is Zanzibar City, which reflects its divided history as a dual urban space. Race and class literally shaped its urban structure. The colonial regime created a split between a centre (Stone Town, a World Heritage Site) of imposing stone structures occupied by the elite (mostly Indians, Arabs and Europeans) along the western coastline, separated by a creek from the unplanned inland periphery or Ng'ambo, meaning "the other side" of the city where poorer Africans were consigned to live.

Until the 1950s, the creek separated the historic core of the city from the Ng'ambo. As a result of the 1923 British Lancaster master plan, the creek was filled and drained with the addition of two major routes in the city. This crossroad became the major economic and transit node for the city, which evolved into the city's market area. Flanked to the west by the well-defined historic Stone Town, the space leaks out to the east into a series of informal single-use residential neighbourhoods, characterised by 1960s East German "Plattenbauten". This term denotes a series of five-storeyed linear apartment blocks, in this case set along the road to the interior of the island in a cross formation. Following the revolution of 1964 and the overthrow of the colonial powers, the old centre was appropriated by the State. All land was nationalised while landmark structures were changed into government offices or social centres. The new regime was unable to provide an economic base for its redistributive policies so that by the 1980s, socialism was seen as a failure and blamed for the urban decline. The historic core showed decay with buildings starting to collapse. Seeking to reverse the situation, the government pursued policies of liberation. At the same time, external investors were relied upon to leverage tourism – which included a UN-sponsored conservation programme and master plans to guide interventions. A boom of building restoration followed, with resultant souring property values for the core of town. Since 1985, a newly created agency, the Stone Town Conservation and Development Authority, has assumed overall responsibility for carrying out conservation policies.

Stone Town is typical of the Swahili coastal trading towns of East Africa. Owing to the implementation of conservation policing, its urban fabric and townscape have been retained and left virtually intact and buildings of historical architectural value have been preserved. Stone Town embodies the disparate elements of the cultures of Africa, the Arab region, India and Europe over more than a millennium.

EASTERN AFRICA **89**

1 Arab Fort
2 Forodhani Gardens
3 House of Wonders
4 Sultan's Palace Museum
5 The Customs House
6 Zanzibar Ferry Terminal & Port
7 Shangani Square
8 Old Slave Market
9 Darajani Market
10 Dala-Dala Terminus
11 Malindi Grounds
12 Jamhuri Gardens
13 Mnazi Mmoja Gardens
14 Peace Memorial Museum
15 Victoria Hall & Gardens
16 Mnazi Mmoja Hospital
17 State House
18 High Court
19 Blue Mosque
20 Maktaba Kuu Library
21 Zanzibar National Museum of Natural History & Culture
22 Lumumba Secondary School
23 Amaani Stadium
24 Kidongo Chekundu Hospital

Indian Ocean

1000m

2014

KAMPALA, UGANDA

FOUNDED: 1902 (establishment of township)
URBAN AREA: 189 km^2
POPULATION (2011): 1,659,600
URBAN AREA DENSITY: 9,429/km^2
GPS: 0° 18'54.28"N, 32° 34'43.94"E

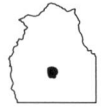

According to O'Connor (1983), the most interesting African cities are those that combine elements of two or more types of origin clearly distinguishable in its urban fabric. In Kampala, for instance, the colonial element became dominant, while the city took on a more hybrid character after the establishment of a single authority in 1966.

Kampala is the capital of Uganda and evolved from a small town to become one of the fastest-growing cities in Africa. The city derived its name from "Hill of Impala" (antelope) that roamed the area before it was urbanised. Its history can be traced back to the traditionally "mobile" headquarters of the Buganda Kingdom, a monarchy that dates back 800 years. Today it occupies more than twenty-five hills that include Makerere Hill on which the city's oldest university is located. The hills shaped its urban morphology, with steep slopes separated by wide valleys.

Like many other major urban centres in Uganda, it owes its growth to colonial presence since the 1890s. Kampala became the British colonial administrative headquarters next to Mengo, the indigenous capital or Kibuga, set on the hill of the main palace of the Kabaka (King) of the Buganda Kingdom. The pre-colonial African city, or Kibuga, was an urban unit or centre of governance and acted as a cultural transmitter. The first colonial urban planning scheme for Kampala was undertaken in 1912, covering amongst others Old Kampala Hill where modern Kampala had begun its evolution after the establishment of a fort on the site in 1896. Several planning schemes followed from 1919 to 1994. The colonial influence is traceable where a fine grid is constrained by the topography, conflicting with the organic layout of the traditional city, which followed the natural contours.

Today, like other Eastern African primate cities, continued growth has resulted in acute housing shortages, traffic congestion, pollution and uncontrolled peri-urban sprawl. Slum proportions in Kampala have reached 85 percent (UN-Habitat, 2014). In addition, the city experiences increased rainfall, making it vulnerable to flooding, pollution and health risks, especially affecting the urban poor.

By contrast, Kampala is also one of Africa's "greenest" cities with parks, gardens and even golf courses in the city centre. The city established priorities for green growth, but is grappling with the challenge of how to prioritise pressing developmental needs with making choices that will ensure sustainability. Many green projects are underway in the city, such as the Kasubi-Kawala neighbourhood that entered into a partnership to recycle neighbourhood waste – of which 75 percent is organic – into animal feed, compost and alternative fuel (UN-Habitat, 2014).

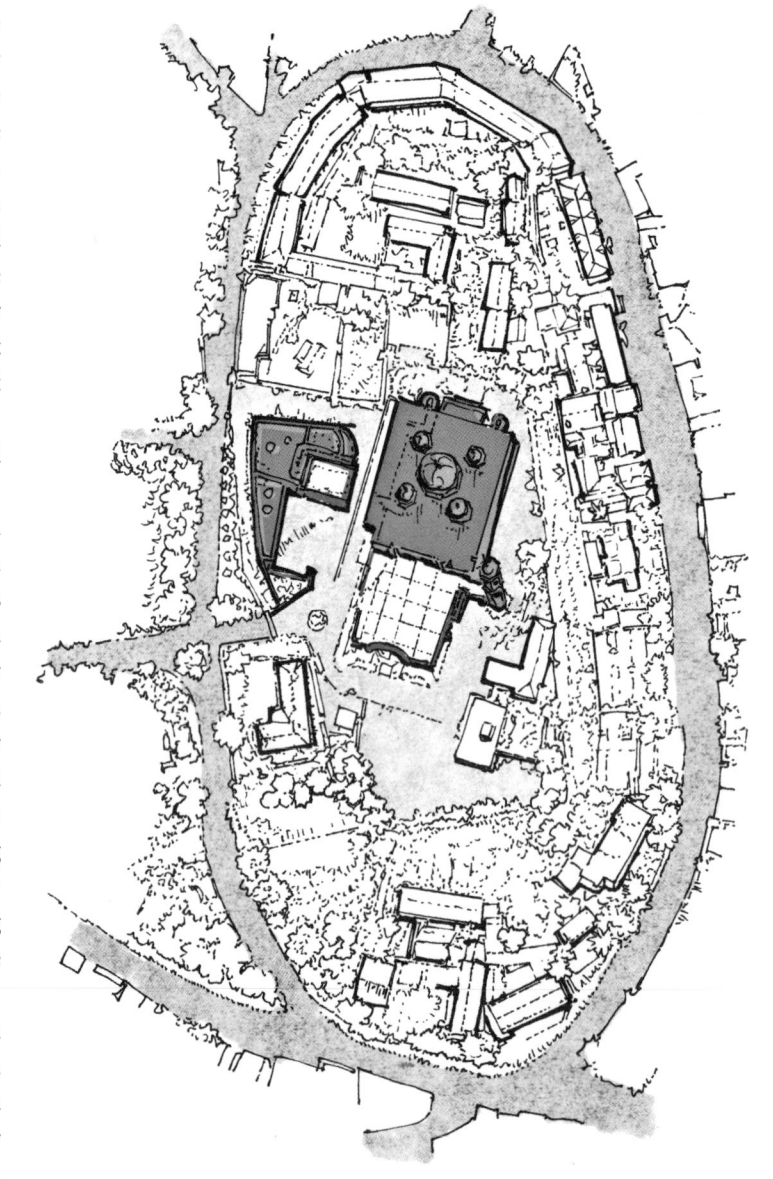

1 Kasubi Hill, Kasubi Tombs & Kabaka's Palace
2 Kampala Hill, Gaddafi Mosque & Fort Lugard
3 Kibuli Hill & Kibuli Mosque
4 Namirembe Hill & Namirembe Anglican Cathedral
5 Lubaga Hill & Rubaga Catholic Cathedral
6 Nsambya Hill & Nsambya Hospital
7 Pan African Freedom Square
8 Constitutional Square
9 High Court
10 Nakivubo Stadium
11 Buganda Cultural & Development Foundation
12 National Water Reservoir
13 Sheraton Gardens
14 Uganda National Museum
15 Nakasero Hill & Nakasero Old Fort
16 Kabaka's Lake
17 Kampala Railway Station

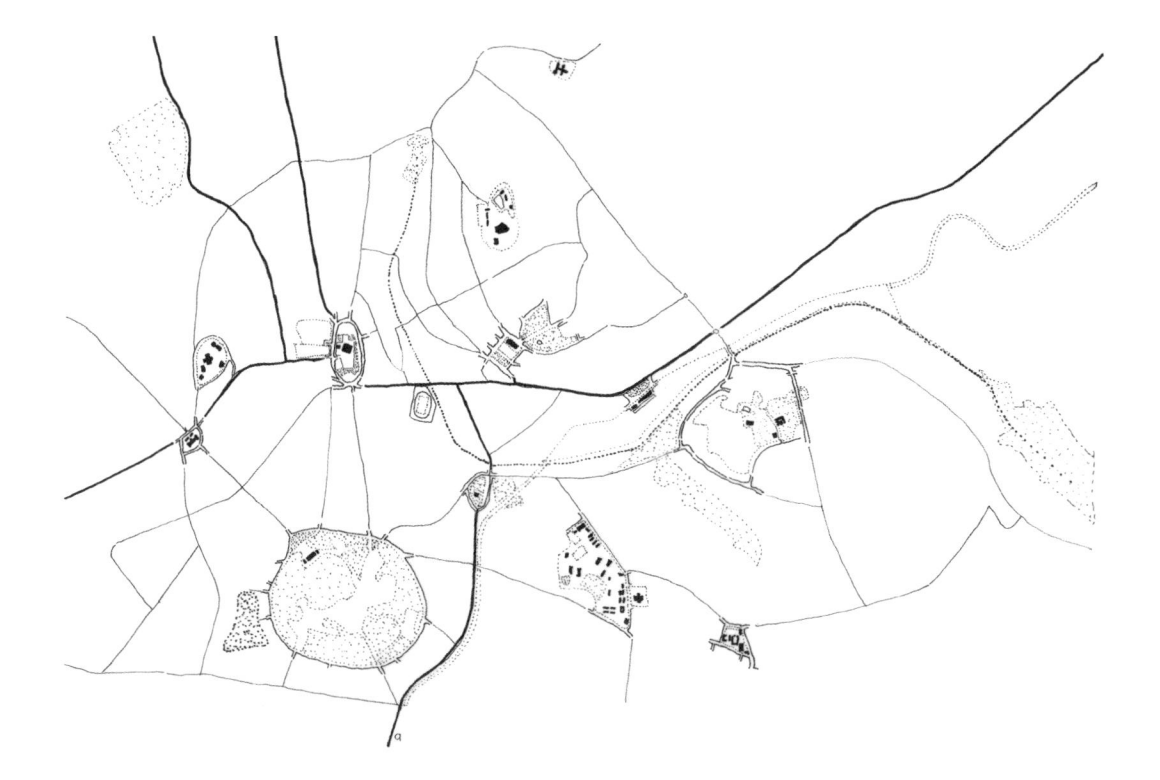

LUSAKA, ZAMBIA

FOUNDED: 1905
URBAN AREA: 360 km²
POPULATION: 3,100,000 (2009)
URBAN AREA DENSITY: unknown
GPS: 15° 25'23.66"S, 28° 17'25.51"E
15° 25'20.00"S, 28° 18'32.34"E

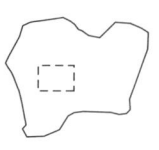

Lusaka, the capital and largest city of Zambia and also one of the fastest-developing cities in southern Africa, is located in the southern part of the central plateau.

The city originally developed as a railway siding in 1905 when the railway line, constructed primarily to transport copper from the present-day Democratic Republic of the Congo to the seaports of South Africa, reached Lusaka. White settler farmers moved to the area soon after. Lusaka started out as a narrow 5 km long, 1.5 km wide strip of land developed along the railway line under the jurisdiction of the Lusaka Village Management Board (Williams, 1984). Lusaka's rapid growth began in 1931 when it was designated as the new capital and principal administrative centre of Northern Rhodesia (Zambia today).

Lusaka's position as the centre of development was reinforced by its central location. It was also within easy reach of the country's economic heartland, the copper belt, and was located on the main north-south axis of the railway line, as well as at the intersection between the main roads to the north and south, and east and west. Lusaka was primarily planned as an administrative centre only, making provision for government administration, domestic and menial services, but overlooking all industrial activities as well as the needs of the large population. During the implementation of the plan, it was revised to make provision for light and heavy industrial areas.

Light industrial activities were designated to the area between Church Road, the railway line and the Great East Road, with heavy industrial industries allocated to the immediate western side of the commercial area, which had emerged to the west of the railway line. The commercial shopping area was planned on the hilly and more charming, well-drained land on the Ridgeway, south-east of the railway line.

Lusaka, as the fastest growing city in the post-independence period, was never intended to be a large city. It expanded from a mere 2.6 km² to 18 km² in 1931, and today covers an area of 360 km². The significant population increase in the city has led to land shortages. The development of the Integrated Development Plan for the city was completed in the year 2000, which includes a proposed extension of the city boundary to include additional land around Lusaka within its boundaries.

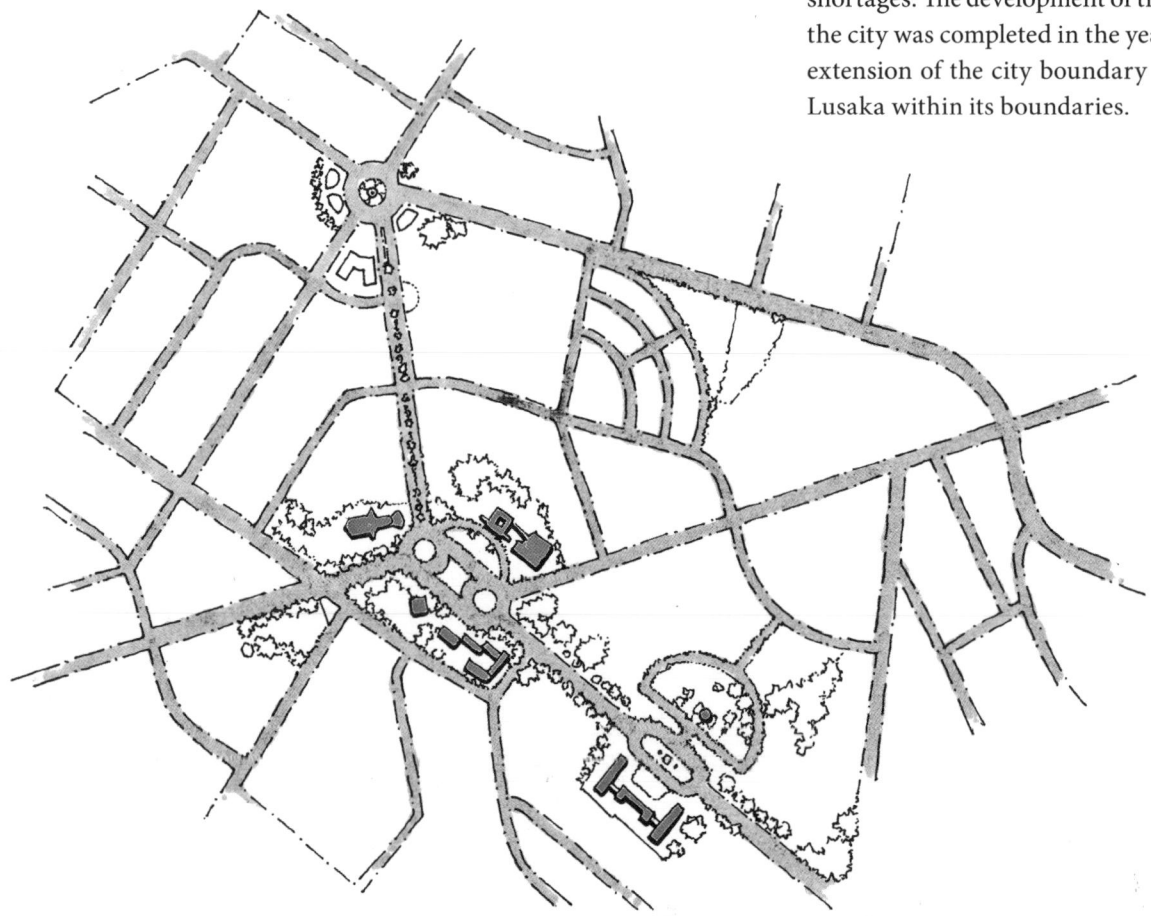

1 Central Station
2 Mukuba Pension House
3 Lusaka National Museum
4 Freedom Square
5 Jame Mosque
6 Lusaka Central SDA Church
7 Anglican Cathedral of the Holy Cross
8 High Court of Zambia
9 Ministry of Finance Headquarters
10 Cabinet Offices
11 Dr Ley Patrick Mwanawasa Memorial Grave
12 Embassy Park
13 Lusaka International Airport
14 Town Centre Market
15 Soweto Market
16 State House
17 National Assembly

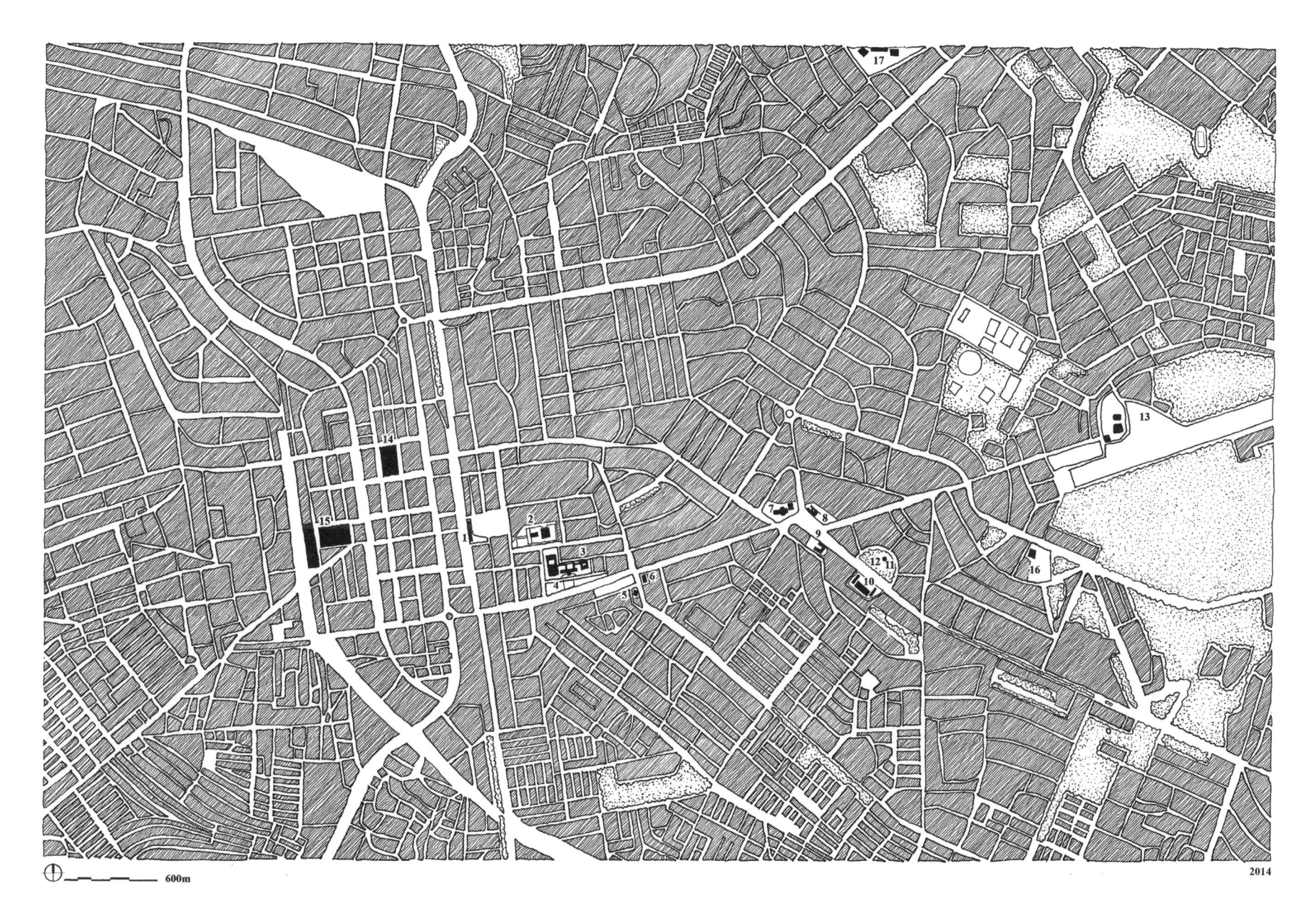

HARARE, ZIMBABWE

FOUNDED: 1890
URBAN AREA: 960 km²
POPULATION: 1,606,000 (2009)
URBAN AREA DENSITY: 2,540/km²
GPS: 17° 49'46.00"S, 31° 3'7.37"E
18° 20'8.64"S, 29° 54'48.38"E

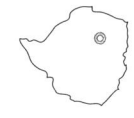

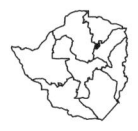

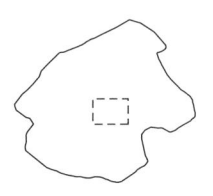

Harare – officially called Salisbury until 1982 – is the capital and largest city of Zimbabwe. Harare developed as a colonial urban settlement and was used as a military fort. It was established along the route of entry followed by an expeditionary force called the pioneer column under the British South Africa Company. Harare was a resting point on the route followed by the expedition. During the first years of settlement the focus was on the exploration and mining of the various mineral wealth, gold in particular.

Harare's urban layout was primarily shaped by the colonial political economy, which focused on a racial division of society between Europeans and Africans. The structural layout was designed to control and regulate land-use activity and ensure adequate provision of social and physical infrastructure.

O'Connor classifies Harare as a European city in his typology of African cities, as the planning and design was determined by, and for, the incoming settler needs. He explains that "such urban areas were set up by Europeans as places for Europeans to live in and some reflected European town planning ideas more clearly than many towns in Europe."

Captain Thomas Ross planned the first version of Harare's rectangular grid pattern, with a grid of streets aligned to the north. The city was designed with large open spaces, such as the National Botanic Garden. Racial segregation was implemented early on when the sanitary board promulgated regulations in 1892 to establish a "separate native location which was later developed on a 25 hectare site approximately 4 km from the centre". The city was therefore reserved for the development of a wealthy settler community with the native Africans providing migrant labour and maintaining a "two-legged" existence in both rural and urban areas. This dual urban environment has become significant of the colonial era.

The original township of Salisbury (Harare) was established from 1891 to 1984 and consisted of 2,548 stands, varying between 400 m² in the south to 592 m² in the centre and up to 892 m² in the east. The residential neighbourhood in the north had plots that ranged from 2,000 m² to 4,000 m² (Wekwete, 1988). Today, Harare is a city of modern buildings, wide streets, and several parks and gardens. The city can be viewed from the Kopje, a granite hill rising above the south-west corner of central Harare.

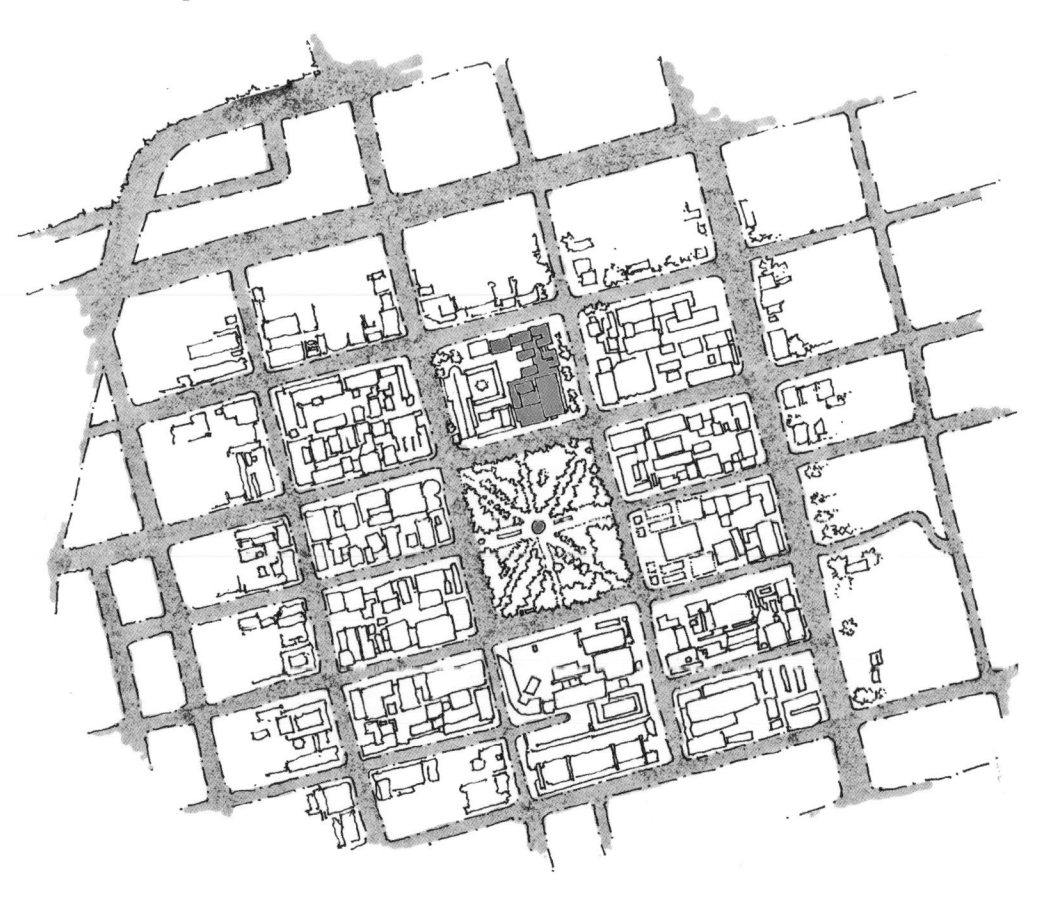

1 African Unity Square
2 Parliament
3 Telecommunications Office
4 Harare Gardens
5 Harare City Centre Seventh Day Adventist Church
6 Dominican Convent School
7 The Cathedral
8 Geological Museum
9 David Livingstone Primary School
10 Greenwood Park
11 The President's Residence
12 Harare Sports Club & Alexandra Park
13 Market
14 Harare Central Station
15 Harare City Library
16 Rainbow Towers & Conference Centre
17 Raylton Sports Club
18 Girls' High School
19 Queen Elizabeth School
20 Park
21 Harare Polytechnic
22 Prince Edward School
23 Allan Wilson School
24 National Gallery of Zimbabwe

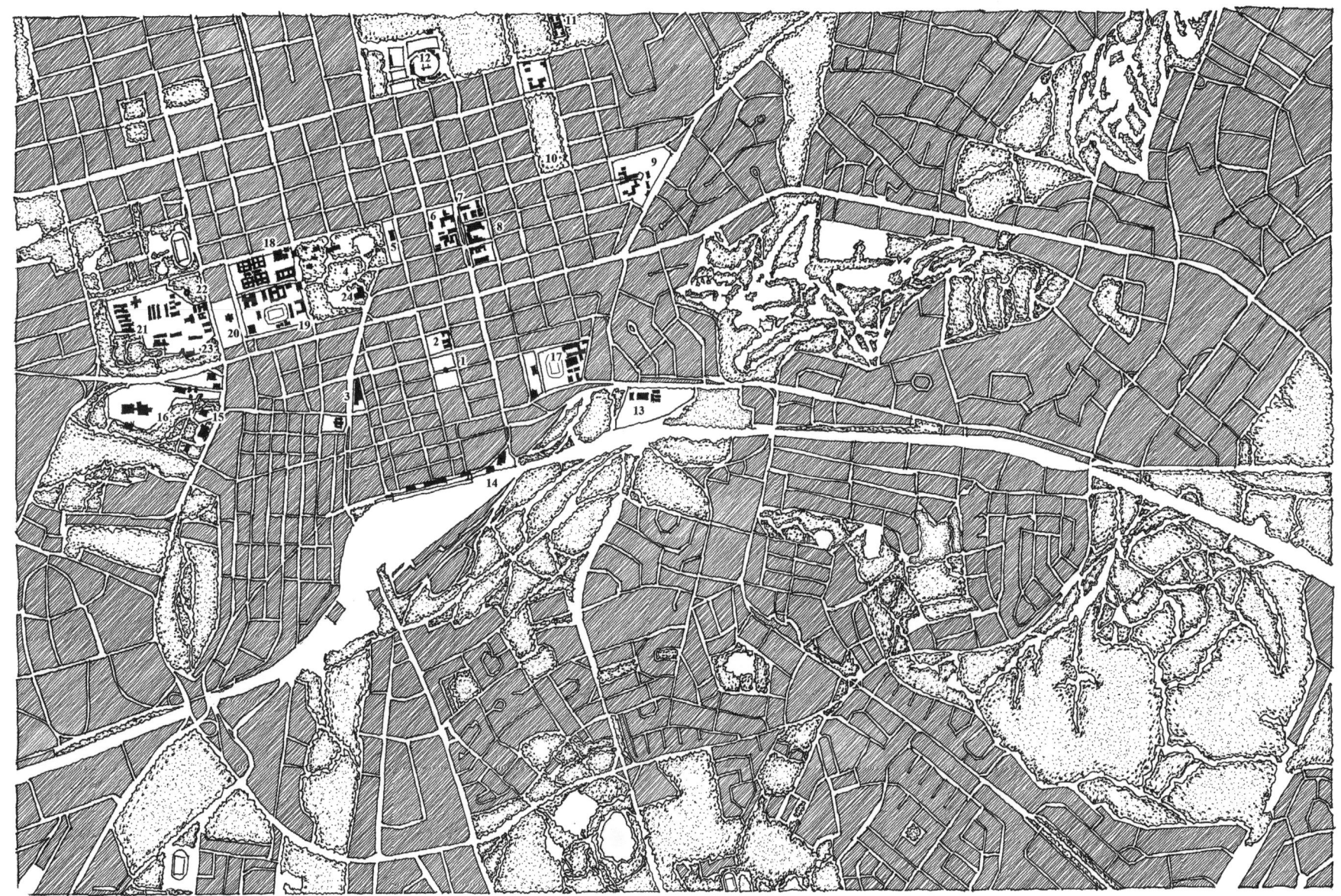

ALGIERS, ALGERIA

RE-FOUNDED: 944
URBAN AREA: 363 km²
POPULATION: 2,916,000 (2011)
URBAN AREA DENSITY: 9,400/km²
GPS: 36° 46'51.44"N, 3° 3'40.30"E
36° 46'34.67"N, 3° 3'30.11"E
36° 46'20.97"N, 3° 3'34.14"E

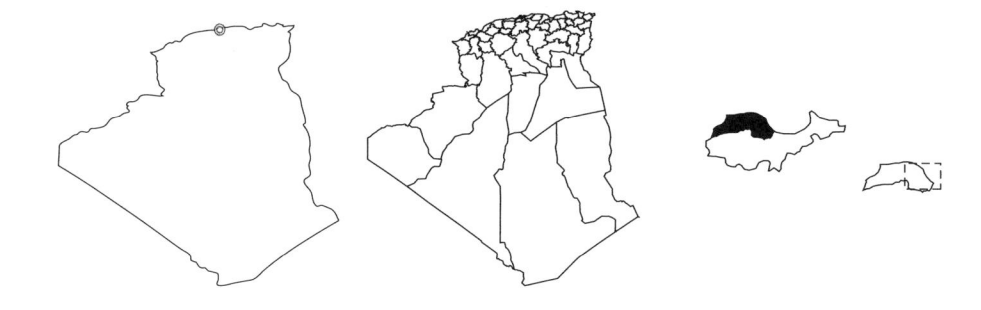

Algiers, located on the west side of a bay of the Mediterranean Sea is the capital and largest city of Algeria. The city's form has been influenced by the topography of the site. Steep hills are separated by valleys behind a flat band along the water. The organic expansion of the lower city was linear as it developed along the coastline.

The original city (old city), crowned by the casbah or citadel, is built on the steep slopes of the hill, with the modern part of the city on the lower lying areas in the coastal plain. The French invaded Algiers and initially focused the city's structuring efforts on militaristic and practical objectives which were limited to the opening of the Place du Gouvernement and the widening of the main arteries, Rue Bab el-Oued and Rue Bab Azzoun. Emphasis was put on defence with the construction of new fortifications.

As a Muslim North African city, the town was structured around the main mosque, the al-Jami' al-Jadid Mosque, which was surrounded by souks in the form of a market and commercial streets. The residential quarters were grouped according to ethnic origin, economic, social or professional status. The street network was organised into three main arteries. The Bab al-Jazeera Road led traffic to the port. The Bab Azzoun Road connected with the southern gate towards the southern rural fields and the Bab el-Oued Road connected the northern gate. The citadel was fortified with strong walls, measuring 2,500 m long, and ramparts which were between 11 and 13 m high and 1.5 and 14.5 m wide. It also featured five gates and was isolated on the highest point in the city.

In 1962, Algeria gained its independence from France, with Algiers as its capital. The city has expanded rapidly ever since. Significant buildings in the city include: the Great Mosque, which is the oldest mosque in Algiers, initially constructed by Yusuf ibn Tashfin; the New Mosque, dating from the seventeenth century; the church of the Holy Trinity (built in 1870) at the southern end of the rue d'Isly; the Ketchaoua Mosque; and the cathedral of St Philippe that dates back before independence in 1962, located at the foot of the casbah. The Notre Dame d'Afrique, a church built from 1858 to 1872, displays a mixture of the Roman and Byzantine styles and is one of the city's most exceptional monuments.

As car ownership increases, the city expands in a sprawling manner with richer residents migrating to the periphery. Most other Algerian economic activities are in Algiers and there are regional development plans to promote growth outside the city to reduce pressure on the Algerian capital.

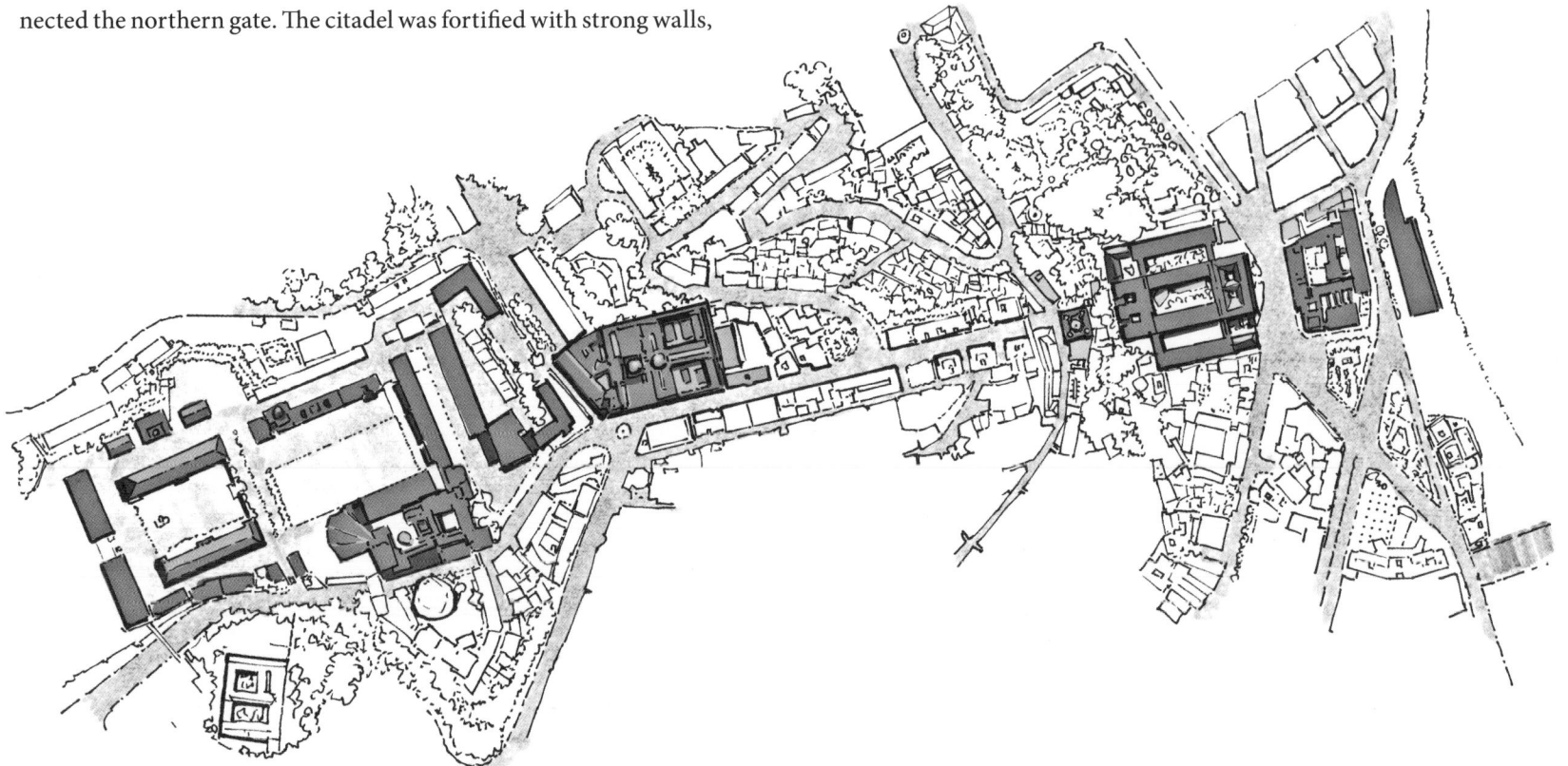

NORTHERN AFRICA 97

1	Place El-Kettani & Old Fort Wall	21	National Library
2	Place Wiaam Beo & Old Fort Wall	22	Djemaa el-Kebir
3	Park, Jardin Taleb Abderrahamane	23	Djemaa el-Djedid or Pcherie Mosque
4	Park, Jardin de Prague	24	Djemma Ali Bitchine or perviously Notre Dame des Victoires
5	School Emir Abdelkader		
6	Palais des Raïs	25	National Museum of Antiquities
7	Casbah	26	Parc de la Liberté
8	Place des Martyrs	27	Hospital Mustapha Pacha
9	Bab Azzoune et Square or Square Port Said	28	Bordo National Museum of Prehistory and Ethnography
10	Place de l'Émir Abdelkader	29	People Palace
11	Grande Poste Square	30	Zoo
12	Park, Jardin Sofia	31	Makam Echahid/ Martyrs' Monument
13	Algerian National Theatre		
14	National Assembly	32	Hospital El Kettar & Cemetery
15	Palace of Justice	33	Market
16	Government Palace	34	National Library
17	Fort of the Casbah	35	Stadium 20th Aug 1955
18	Museum	36	University of Algiers
19	Palace du Dey	37	Port
20	Ministry of National Defense		

1500m

2014

ANNABA, ALGERIA

FOUNDED: circa twelfth century BC
AREA: 49 km²
POPULATION (2008): 257,359
DENSITY: 5,300/km²
GPS: 36° 53'45.04"N, 7° 45'20.54"E
36° 53'58.08"N, 7° 45'44.07"E

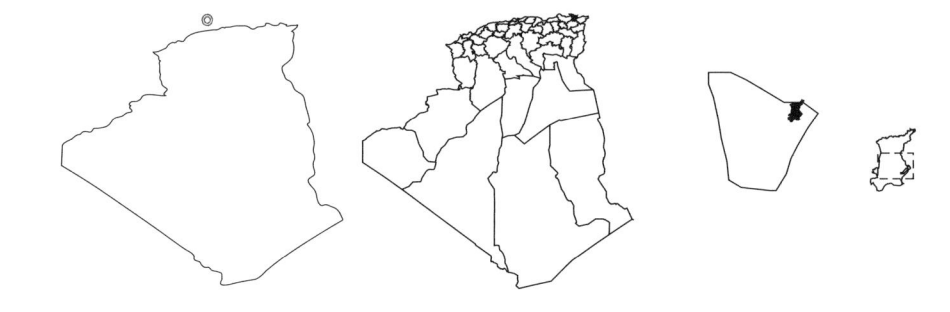

Known in ancient times as Hippo Regius – a Roman city – Annaba is a leading industrial and transport centre in modern-day north-eastern Algeria, which in recent years has undergone major expansion. Its metropolitan area has a higher population density than the other cities of the Algerian coastline.

From the shore, the city rises up slopes of local foothills covered with cork oak and has an excellent natural port. Its proximity to fresh water and fertile agricultural land initially attracted the Phoenicians and has ensured the city's continued prosperity. The old town with its narrow streets dominates the centre of the city and is grouped around the Place du 19-Août and its early French houses, along with the Mosque of Salah Bey (1787).

The new town, built since 1870 along both sides of the Cours de la Révolution road, holds the Cathedral (1850) and Basilica (1881) of St Augustine, schools, public buildings, the Hippo Museum and public gardens. On the outskirts lies the ruins of the ancient city of Hippo Regius, also known as Hippone, which are among the most evocative in Algeria, stretching across a rolling site overlooked by the imposing Basilica of St Augustine.

Typical of ancient Roman colonial towns, a *cardo* was a north-south axis translated into a street. The *cardo* was lined with shops and vendors and served as a hub of economic life. The main *cardo* was called *cardo maximus*. Most Roman cities also had a *Decumanus Maximus*, which was an east-west oriented street that served as a secondary main street. The forum was normally located at the intersection of the *Decumanus* and the *Cardo*.

Roads or rail lines to several other cities of north-eastern Algeria connect Annaba. The city saw little of the violence that scarred other cities during the "black years" of the 1990s and many families moved here from elsewhere in Algeria.

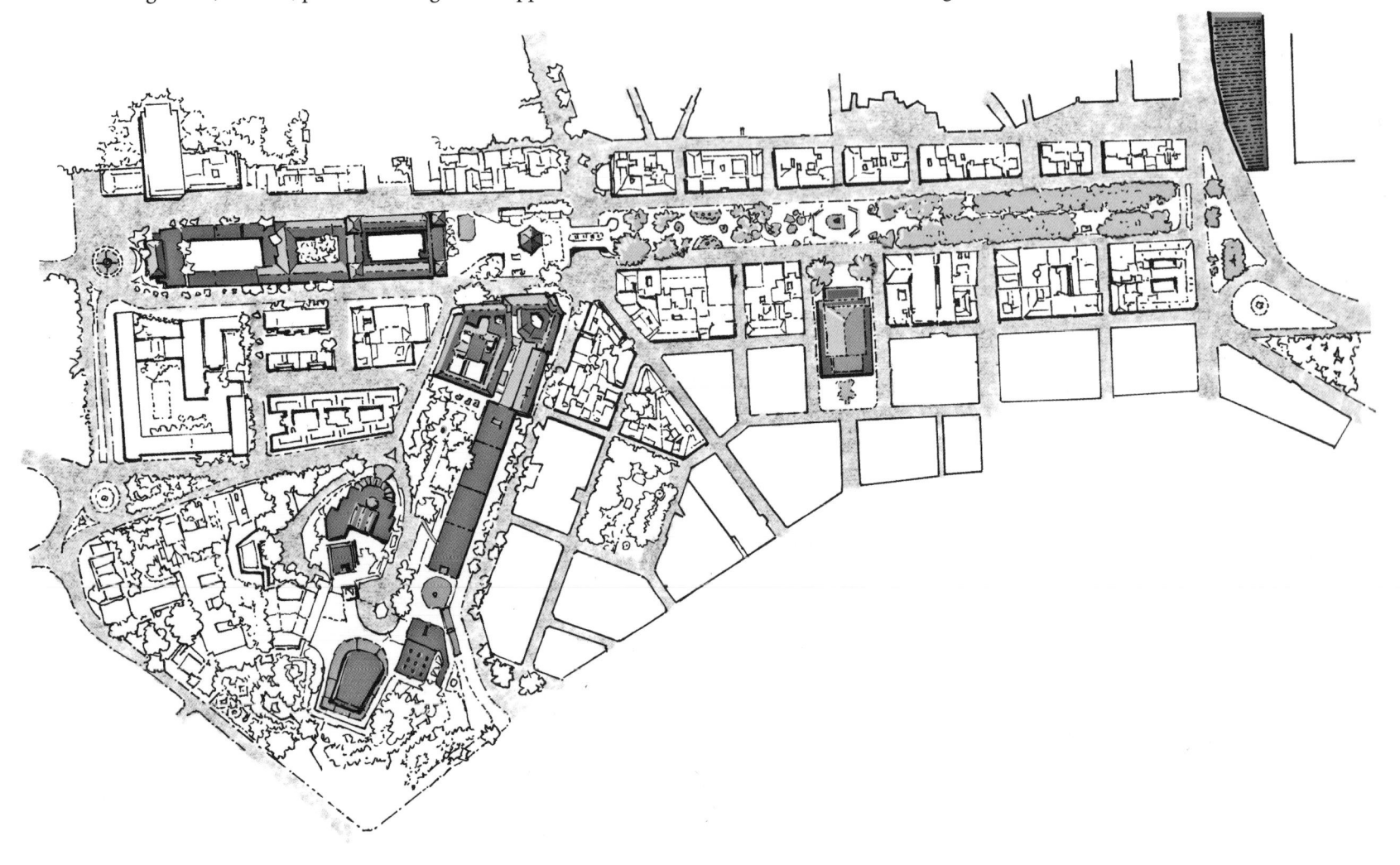

1 Place Nouri Hacene
2 Park & Gendarmerie Nationale
3 El-Houria Square
4 Palace of Justice
5 Central Train Station & Park
6 Park
7 Preparatory School of Economic Sciences and Management Sciences
8 Mohamed Boudiaf Palace of Culture
9 Square August 19, 1956 or Place du 19 Aout 1956
10 Mosque & School of Sidi Brahim
11 Basilica St Augustin
12 Colonel Chabou Municipal Stadium
13 Edough (North) Square
14 Cemetery
15 Hippo Regius Ruins
16 Football Fields

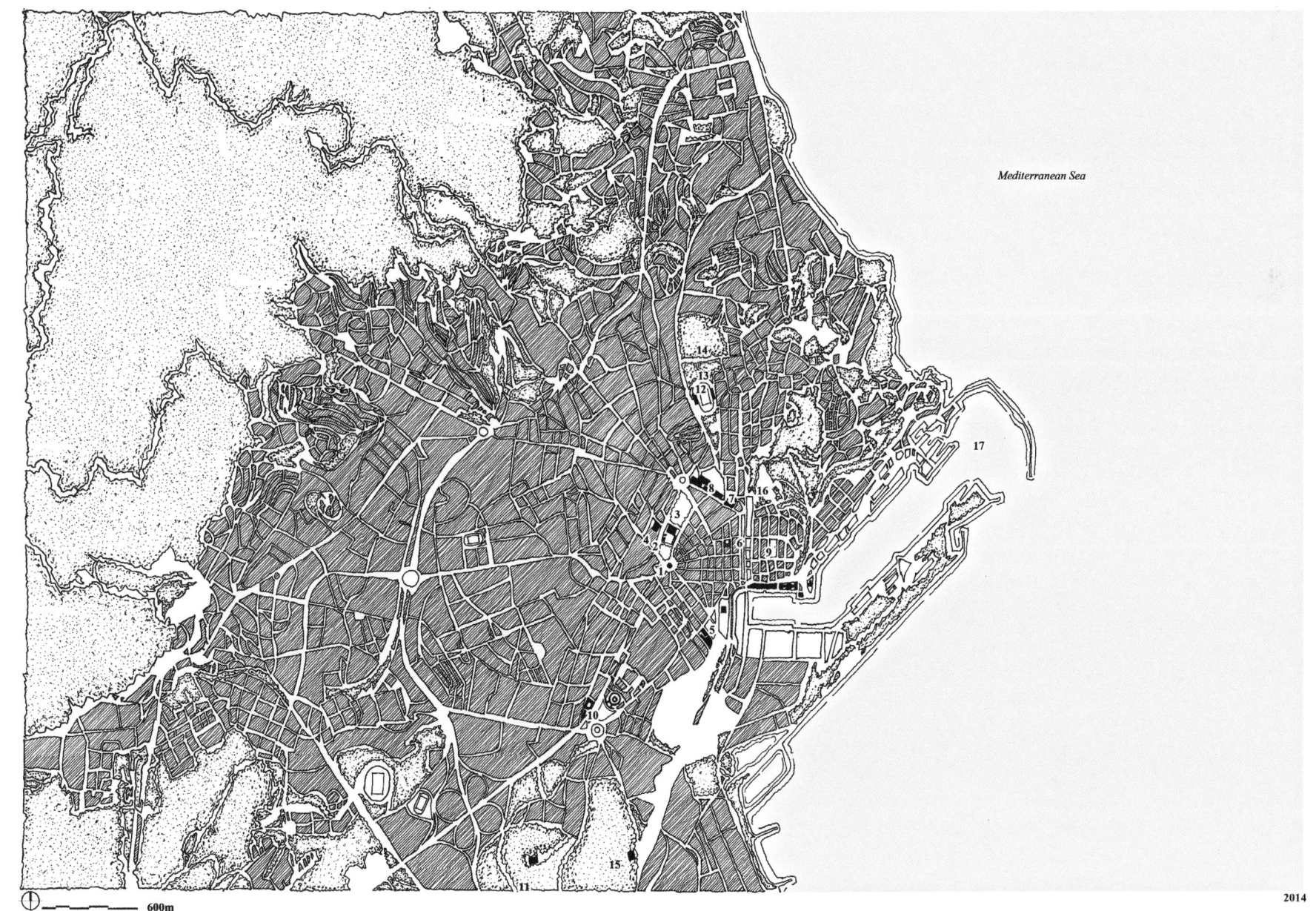

CONSTANTINE, ALGERIA

FOUNDED: unknown
URBAN AREA: 232 km²
POPULATION: 448,374
URBAN AREA DENSITY: 1,936/km²
GPS: 36° 21'55.65"N, 6° 36'35.87"E

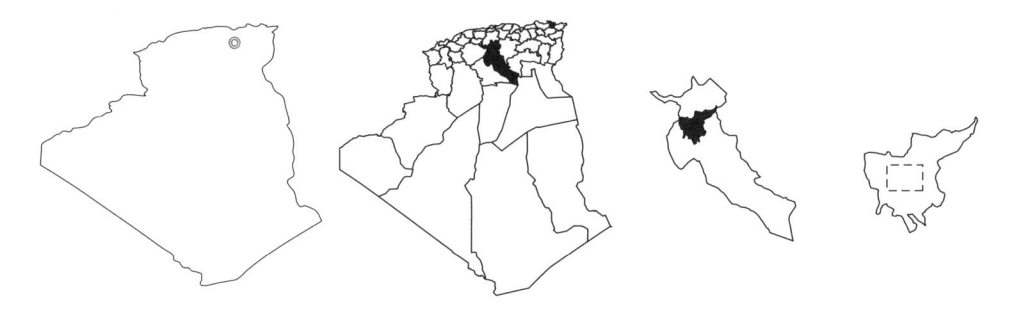

Constantine, named after Emperor Constantine the Great, is Algeria's third largest city, located on the gorge of the Rhumel River. The city is often referred to as the "City of Bridges" due to its unique topography with the many picturesque bridges connecting the mountains upon which the city is built. Deep ravines surrounding these hills have inspired poets like Malek Haddad who wrote "You do not introduce Constantine. She introduces herself, and you salute her. She reveals herself and we discover each other."

This naturally fortified site can be accessed by the bridges of Sidi Rached, El Kantara, Sidi M'Cid, Ali Mellah the footbridge and the large square of Bab El Oued or "Breche" with the shortest one spanning 4.5 m and the longest one 365 m.

The city was historically located as an important commercial centre at the intersection of various major trade routes. During its history, the city has been the home and spatial outcome of many different rulers and civilisations, including Muslim Arab, Ottoman and the French, who have each contributed to the transformation and metamorphosis of the city. Constantine spatially consists of a collage of diverse entities, with the historic core or medina, the colonial fabric, suburbs, large housing estates, informal settlements, self-built housing and slums.

The French had the largest influence on Constantine since they restructured the entire northern part of the town by demolishing a significant number of houses to construct European-inspired iconic buildings, symbolising colonial triumph over the natives. The layouts imposed social control and ideological representations of France as they performed their "duty to civilise" the "savage" societies. The Europeans flooded the city and established segregated residential neighbourhoods, separating them from the local Algerian population. As a result, the city expanded beyond the limits of its circular wall. A large number of local inhabitants lost their homes during this restructuring and the growth of early *gourbivilles* was initiated.

There are various museums and important historical sites around the city including the Palais du Bey, the Abd al-Hamid Ben Badis Mosque, the casbah, Emir Abd al-Qadir University and Mosque, the Soumma Mausoleum, Massinissa's Mausoleum, and the Ruins of the Antonian Roman aqueduct. The old city still displays features of Roman architecture today.

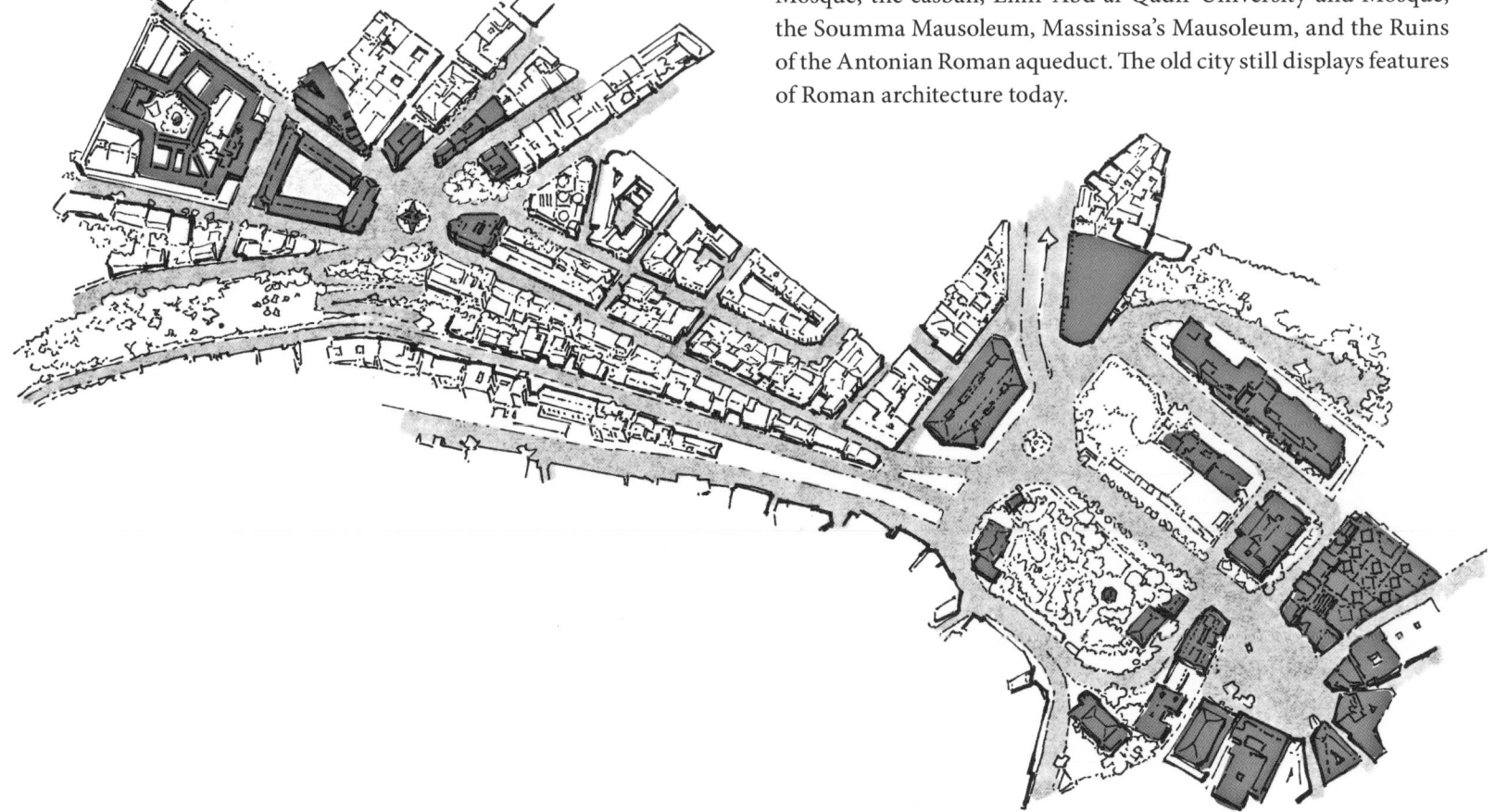

NORTHERN AFRICA **101**

1 Place des Martyres
2 Place 1st November
3 Bennacer Park
4 Courthouse
5 Museum Circa
6 El Houria School
7 Al-Istiklal Mosque
8 Historic Prison Coudiat
9 Place Benabdelmalek
10 Ben Abdelmalek Stadium
11 Ibn Badis Cemetery
12 Central Cemetery
13 Emir Abdelkader Mosque
14 Nabil Nahas City University
15 Great Mosque
16 Military Hospital
17 El-Kantara Park
18 Train Station
19 Fort Bellevue
20 Benbadis Central University Hospital
21 Sidi Meeid Fort & Israeli Cemetery
22 Old Grain Market
23 Old National Guard Building
24 Old Caserne Building
25 Old High School
26 Old Abattoir Building

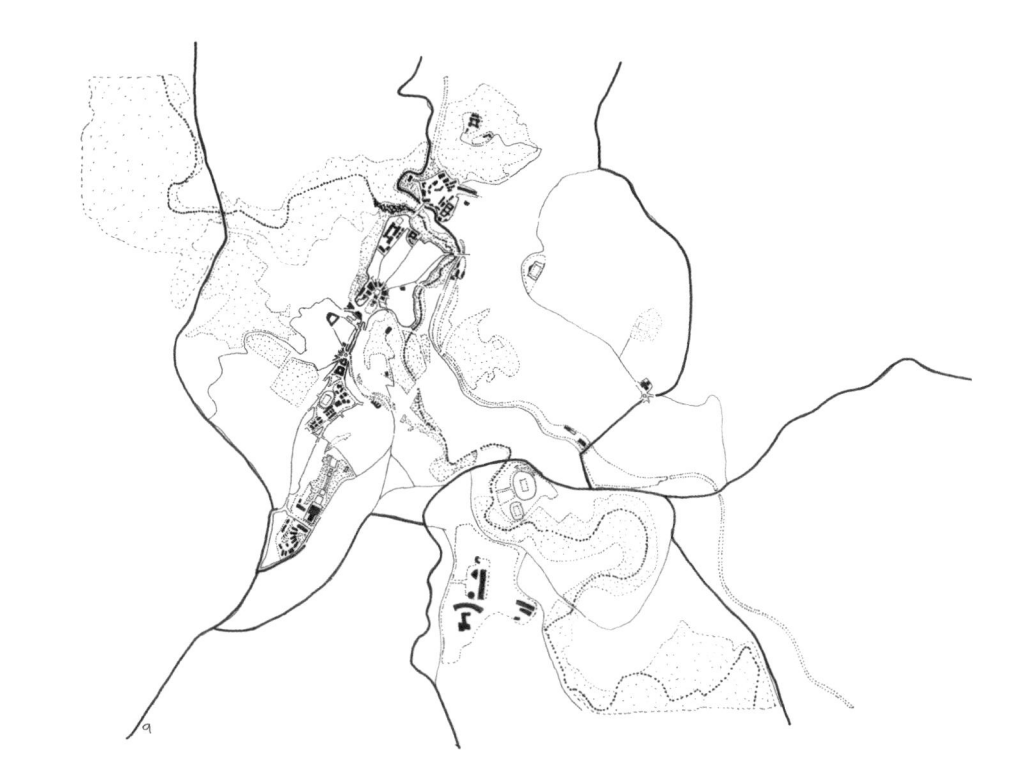

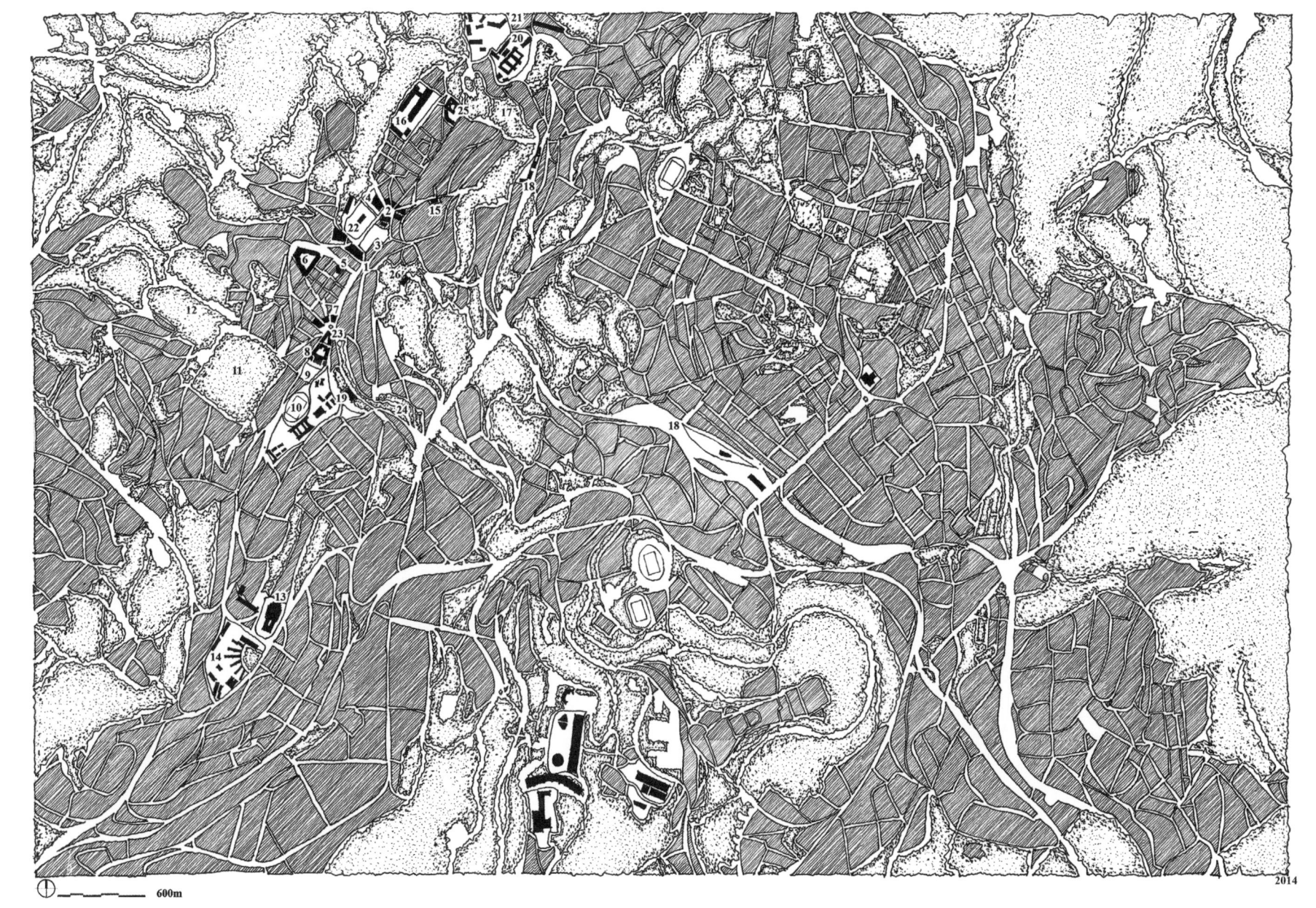

600m

2014

ORAN, ALGERIA

FOUNDED: 903
AREA: 2,121 km²
POPULATION (2008): 803,329
DENSITY: unknown
GPS: 35° 42'11.38"N, 0° 38'57.24"W
35° 42'7.87"N, 0° 38'43.72"W

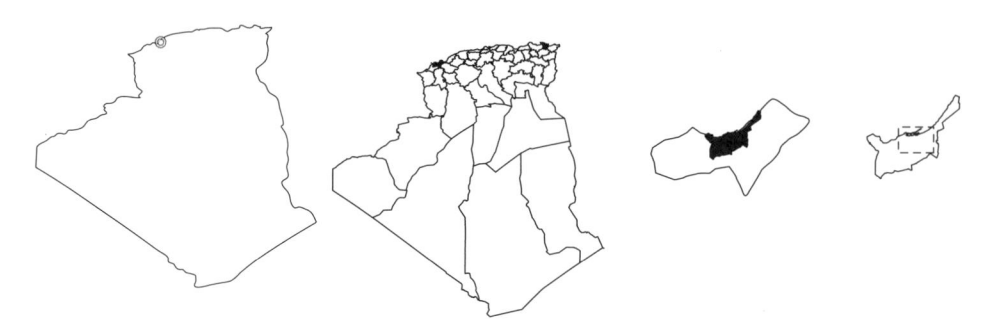

Oran, to the west of Algiers along the Mediterranean coast, provided the setting for the French Nobel Prize laureate Albert Camus's *The Plague* (published in 1947). It is the second-largest city in Algeria with a major port, protected by causeways, and an artificial harbour, and is the urban focus of north-western Algeria. Andalusian merchants founded the city at the beginning of the tenth century. A contested city, it was dominated by the Spanish for two centuries, from 1708 by the Turks, and later by the French. As a result, Oran reflects more European influence than any other city in Algeria, housing a large number of cathedrals and French colonial architecture so that the locals refer to it as the second Paris or Nice.

The city stands at the edge of a plateau, which is flanked by hills on the west, and has a salt lake at its edge. Typical of traditional Algerian cities, Oran's original walled citadel is called the *casbah* (Arabic for "fortress"). Outside of this relatively unchanged remnant of the old way of life, Algerian cities are a mixture of Western influence and Arabic tradition. The old Spanish-Arab-Turkish city, La Blanca, lies on a hill to the west of the gorge that originally divided the city geographically. La Blanca is crowned by the citadel of Santa Cruz that overlooks the city from its vantage point. The newer city, called La Ville Nouvelle, which was built by the French after 1831, occupies the terraces on the eastern bank of the gorge. The Spanish quarter, with its narrow streets, houses the former Cathedral of St Louis. The previous French sector now spreads across the ravine and far outside the second city wall that was built in 1866 and which has now largely been demolished.

The city has changed following independence in the year 1962. The cancellation of the first national elections thirty years later saw the return to *de facto* military rule. In the struggle between the military and Islamists during the 1990s, Oran experienced less violence and terrorism in comparison to Algiers; yet the paralysis on the city was severe.

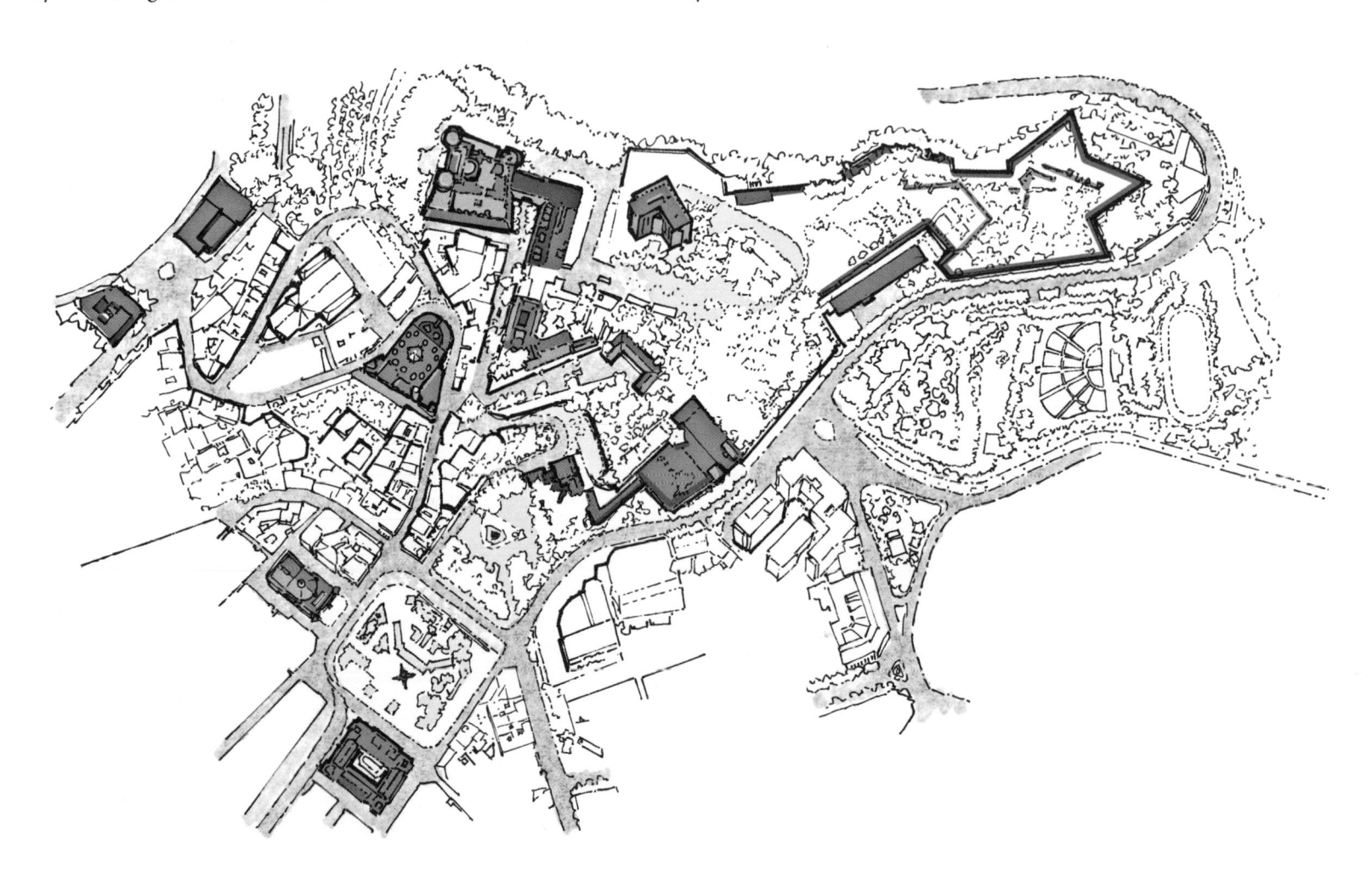

1 Chateau Neuf
2 Place Premier 1st November 1954
3 Theatre of Oran
4 Place Kleber
5 Mosque Pacha
6 Military Hospital
7 Old Fort St Philippe & Stadium Magenta
8 Old Military Barracks
9 Cemetery
10 Oran Zoo & Park
11 Place Sebastopol
12 Palace of Culture and Arts
13 Regional Library of Oran
14 Maitre Thuveny Square
15 Abdellah Ben Salem Mosque
16 Town Hall
17 Central University Hospital of Oran
18 Central Station
19 Cemetery
20 Wilaya d'Oran
21 Old Post Office & Park
22 Old Artillery Quarters
23 Pasteur High School & French Consulate
24 Fatmi El-Houari School & Sports Ground
25 Old Military Barracks
26 Fort Lamoune & Port

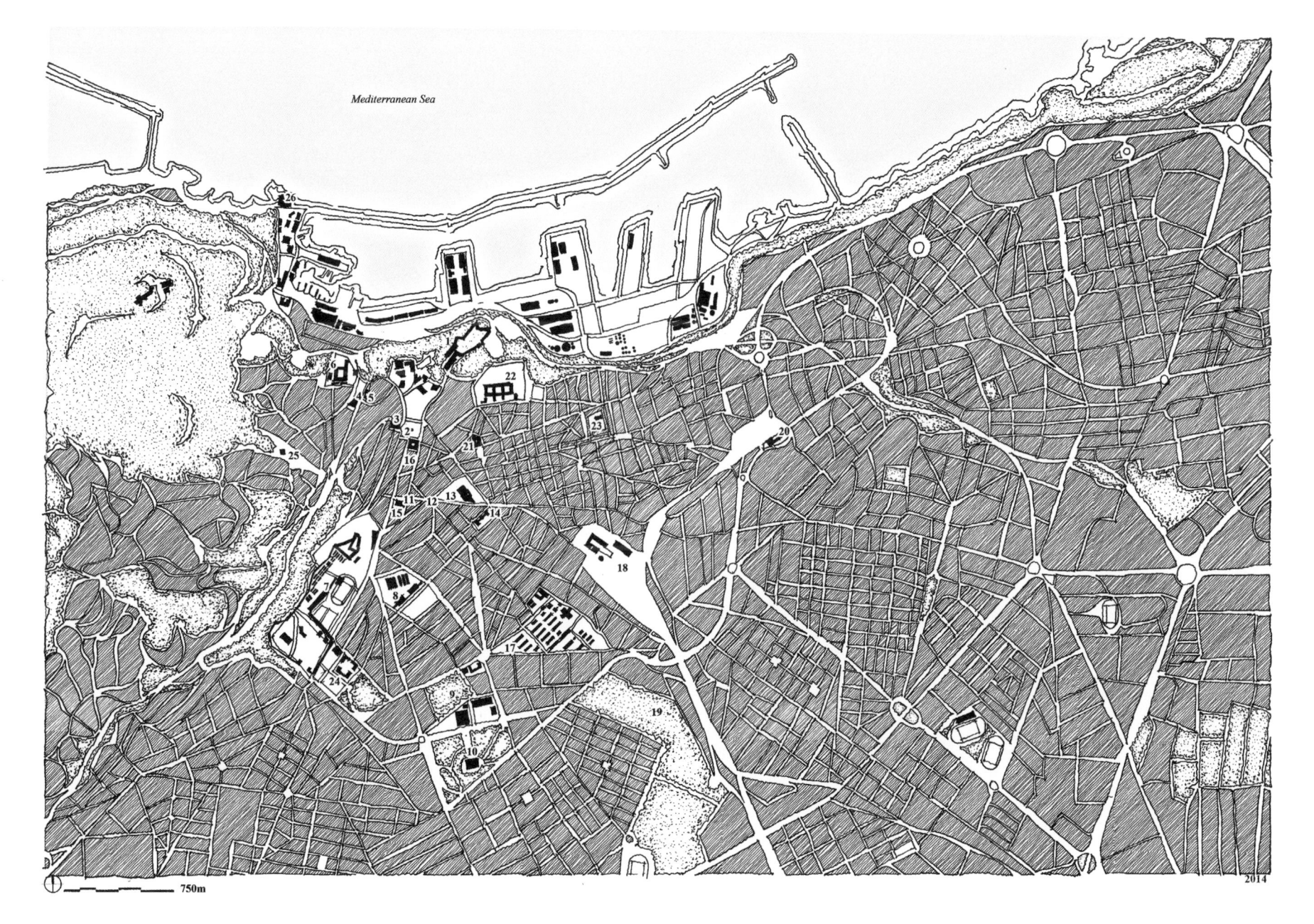

ALEXANDRIA, EGYPT

FOUNDED: 331 BC
AREA: 2,679 km²
POPULATION (2013): 4,546,231
DENSITY: 1,700/km²
GPS: 31° 11'34.36"N, 29° 54'12.81"E
      31° 10'45.18"N, 29° 54'25.51"E
      31° 12'3.65"N, 29° 53'57.55"E

Like Cairo, Alexandria is a city of contrasts, religious dogma, party politics and recently of upheaval. According to the 2014 UN-Habitat report, Alexandria could soon qualify as a *de facto* megacity. By 2030 it is anticipated that its population will have increased to reach 6.8 million. It is the second largest city in Egypt, an important industrial centre and is Egypt's largest seaport, serving approximately 80 percent of imports and exports. Given its rich historical layering, it is also an important tourist destination.

Alexander the Great founded the city in 331 BC as a hub of Greek culture and commerce. Designed on a massive scale as the early Ptolemaic capital of Egypt, it was a splendid city by the third century BC. At its eastern end was the Great Lighthouse, one of the Seven Wonders of the World. The magnificent Temple of Serapis, the royal palace, the largest library of the ancient world, the museum and the Sema, or tomb, of Alexander made up some of the landmarks of its historical fabric. Today, the contemporary Bibliotheca Alexandrina – conceived as a revival of the ancient library and the result of an international architectural competition in 1989 – is built on a magnificent site alongside Alexandria's ancient harbour in the historic centre. Along the Canopic Road of the ancient city, from east to west, were colonnades and prominent buildings – so that it formed the longitudinal focus of the urban layout. The gate on the eastern side was the Gate of the Sun and the one to the west, the Gate of the Moon. Conversely, the east held the Eleusis and the west the Necropolis, or city of the dead. The city was divided into five quarters enclosed by a wall. The island of Pharos, situated opposite the western portion, was connected to the mainland via a causeway. An elaborate system of underground canals supplied water. The city was designed on a grid-block principle – the orthogonal grid being a Greek ordering device or neutral framework. Greek cities were also built as examples of an ideal balanced world in harmony with nature.

Today a dusty seaport city, Alexandria's immediate hinterland consists of low-lying areas, lakes and wetlands. Much of it is below sea level and subject to flooding. As the city and its slums expand, careful urban planning will hopefully reduce the impact of disasters, guided by the 2030 Greater Alexandria Master Plan (UN-Habitat, 2014).

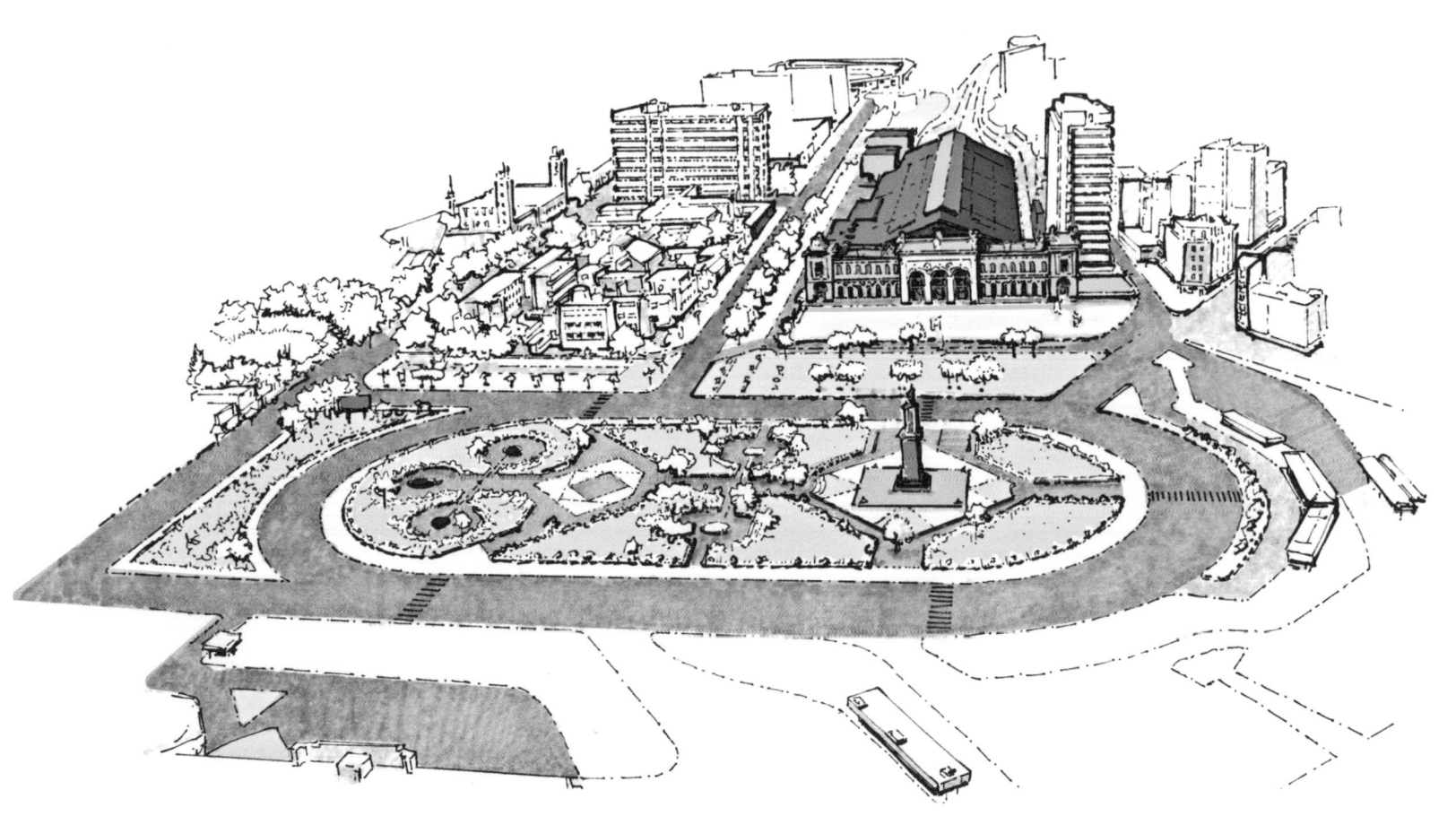

1   Saad Zaghloul Square
2   Al-Shohaba Square
3   Misr Railway Station
4   Roman Amphitheatre
5   Pompey's Pillar
6   Cemetery
7   Catacombs of Kom el-Shukafa
8   St Catherine's Cathedral
9   El-Nadwa Old Lighthouse & Fort
10 Fort / Citadel of Qaitbay
11 Fort El-Ada or Fort Kadah
12 Al-Anfoushi Tombs
13 Ras Elteen Palace
14 Old Arsenal Buildings
15 Bibliotheca Alexandria
16 Sea Bridge Statue & East Fort Qaitbay
17 El-Shalalat Park
18 El-Khandek El-Qably Park
19 Cemetery
20 Alexandria National Museum
21 Patriarchal Saint Mark
22 Eliyahu Hanavi Synagogue
23 Port

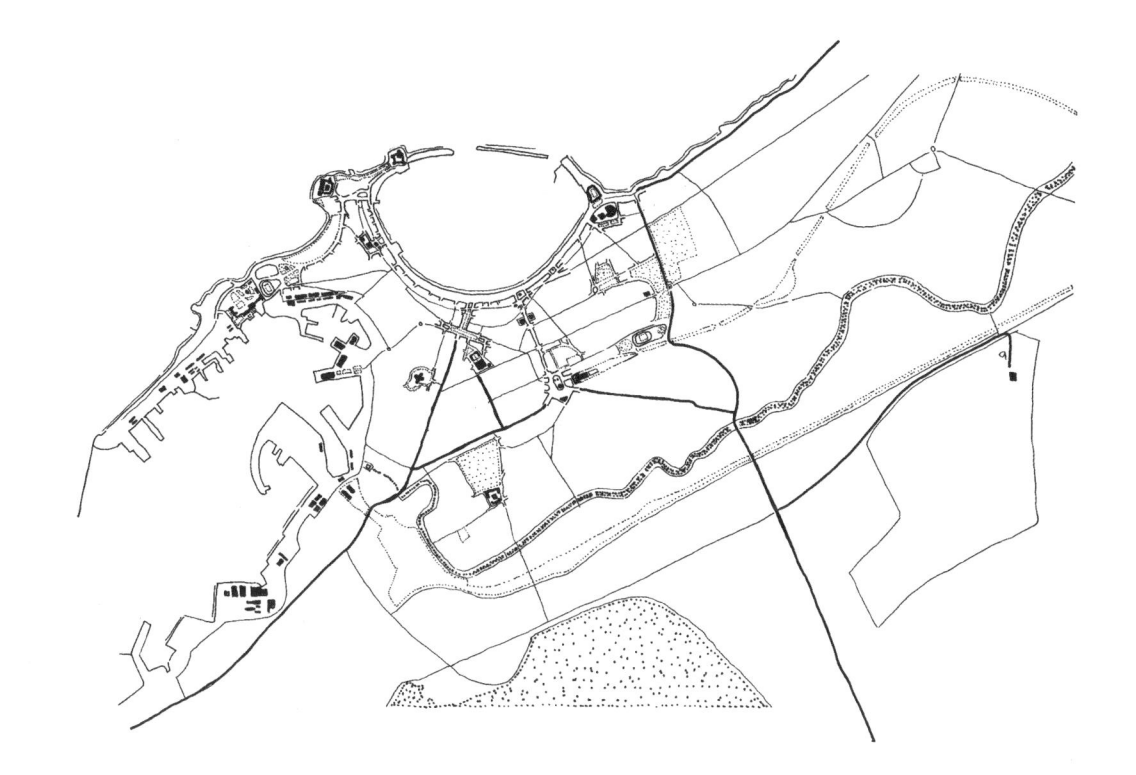

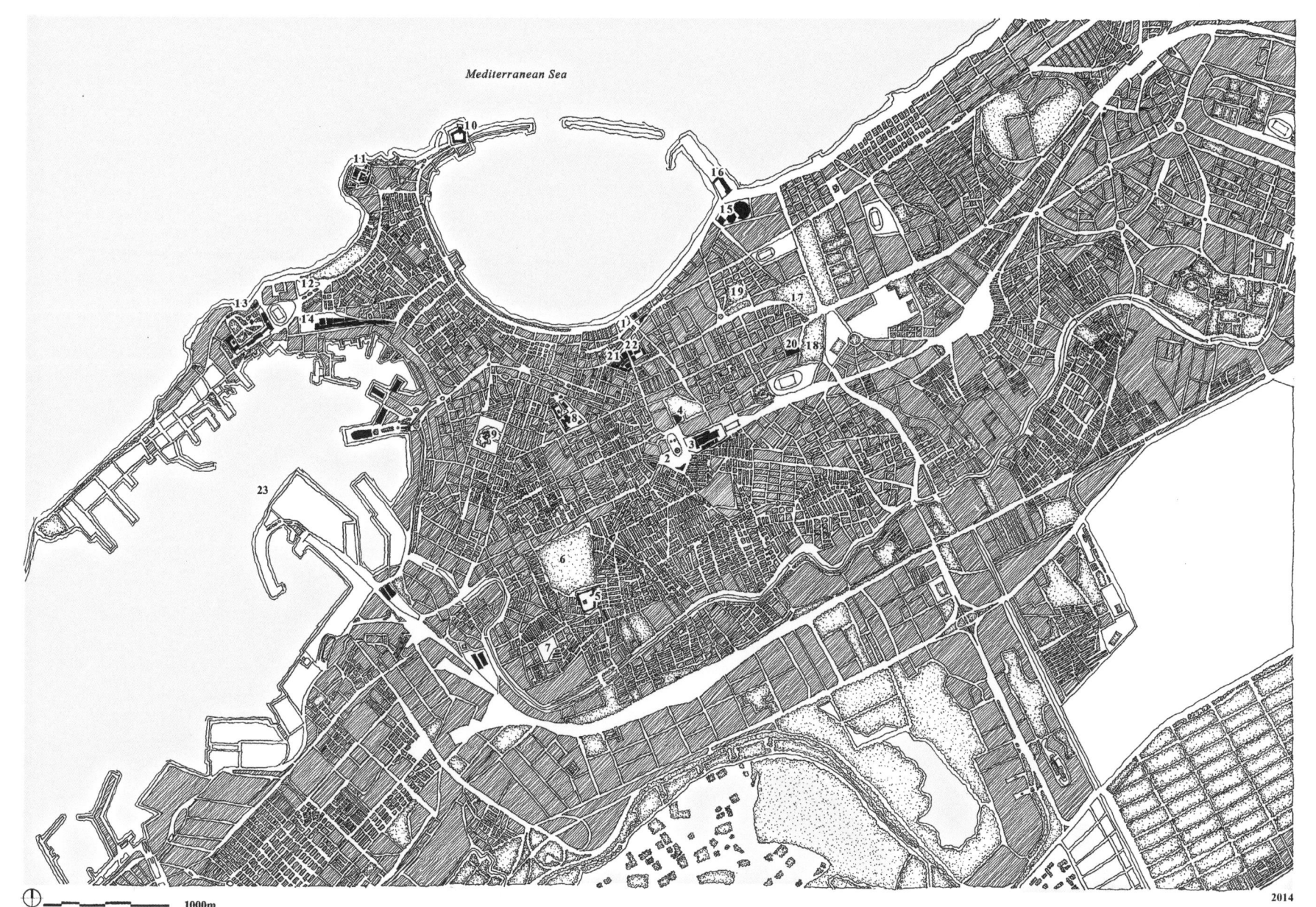

CAIRO, EGYPT

FOUNDED: 969 BC
AREA: 528 km²
POPULATION (2011): 11,169,000
DENSITY: 19,376/km²
GPS: 30° 2'39.29"N, 31° 14'7.76"E
30° 3'2.90"N, 31° 14'49.58"E
30° 3'44.00"N, 31° 14'48.32"E
30° 2'51.18"N, 31° 14'18.56"E

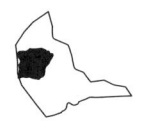

Cairo, in Arabic "al Qahira", meaning the victorious, was established in 969 BC by military forces of the Fatimid dynasty. Today a megacity, it is projected to grow at an annual rate of at least 2 percent until 2020 (UN-Habitat, 2014).

Stewart (1999) simplifies the history of Cairo into roughly four consecutive eras that each contributed to the development of the city: the Islamic, Imperialist, Arab Socialist and Transitory periods.

Since its founding, Cairo was a contested arena for successive Islamic dynasties. Initially, the main focus of the city was around military and religious constructs. Features from its earliest period include new walls around the city, an open parade ground, the Azhar Mosque and various markets. Under the Ayyubids (1171–1250), the city flowered into a classical Arab capital and a global economic force. Egypt's strong economy was based on control of the Red Sea, establishing many of the famous markets in the city. The Ayyubids created new city walls for the expanding city, along with the Bulaq port. Al Qahira entered into an era of decline due to various complex internal and external factors during the Ottoman period (1517–1882), so that the arrival of the French by the end of the eighteenth century set the stage for European Imperialism.

Although brief, French occupation had a profound effect on re-awakening linkages between Europe and "the Orient". Political power was transferred from the Islamic Citadel to the European Abdeen Palace, resulting in a shift of the city's centre westwards. A wide boulevard was constructed, literally cutting through the Fatimid city so that the city became divided into two realms: east (traditional) and west (modern).

Following independence in 1952, urban policy experienced a fundamental shift towards large-scale urban projects, designed to cope with the rapidly expanding Cairo. The cornerstone of the new socialist government presence was the Mugamma, a huge central administrative complex. Nasser City housed new governmental agencies and large-scale public recreation facilities, along with high-rise apartment blocks for the civil servants. A plan was formed to create four new satellite cities in the desert around Cairo to support the increasing population.

Since slowly opening to capitalism from 1973 onwards, marking the transitory period, evidence of integration into the world system can be found especially through private initiative. Exacerbated by its recent political instability, Cairo is faced with many challenges. As one of the world's most densely populated cities, it has one of the lowest provisions of road space per capita.

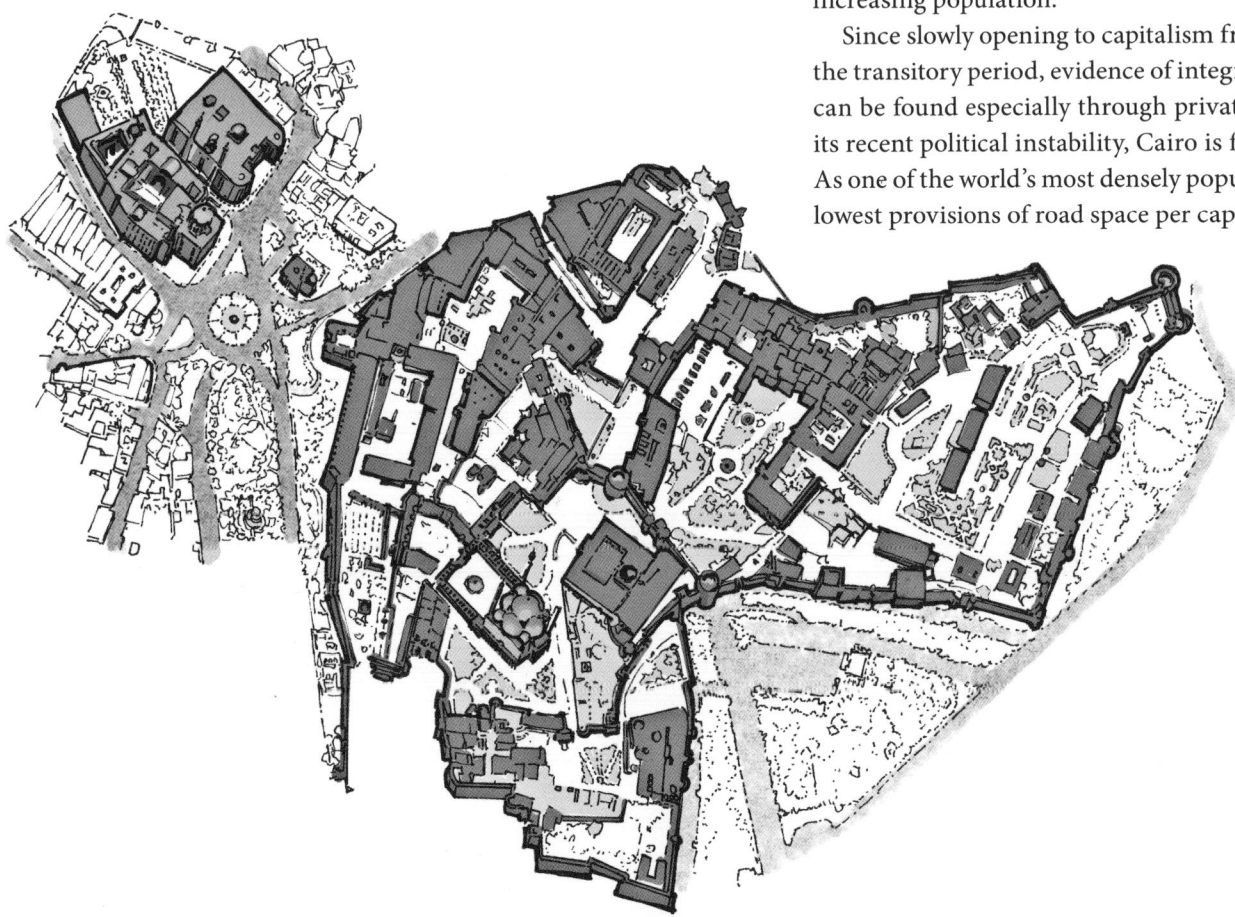

1 Old Cairo
2 Manisterli Palace & Nilometer
3 Amr Ibn el-As Mosque
4 Remains of Fustat
5 Zoo & Botanical Gardens
6 Manyal Palace
7 Ibn Tulun Mosque
8 Cairo Citadel
9 Fort Mohammed Ali
10 Sultan Hasan & El-Rifai Mosques
11 Ezbekiya Gerdens & Opera, Opera Square
12 Abdin Palace
13 El-Tahrir Square
14 Talaat Square
15 Gezira Museum
16 Mukhtar Museum & El-Tahrir Gardens
17 Agricultural & Cotton Museums
18 Egyptian Museum
19 Mohammed Khalil Museum
20 St Joseph Church
21 Ramesses Square & Cairo Central Train Station
22 Al-Zahir Baybers Mosque
23 Al-Hakim Mosque
24 Bab el-Nasr Cemetery
25 Qaitbay Burial Mosque & Cemetery
26 Al-Azhar Park
27 Bab El-Wazir Cemetery

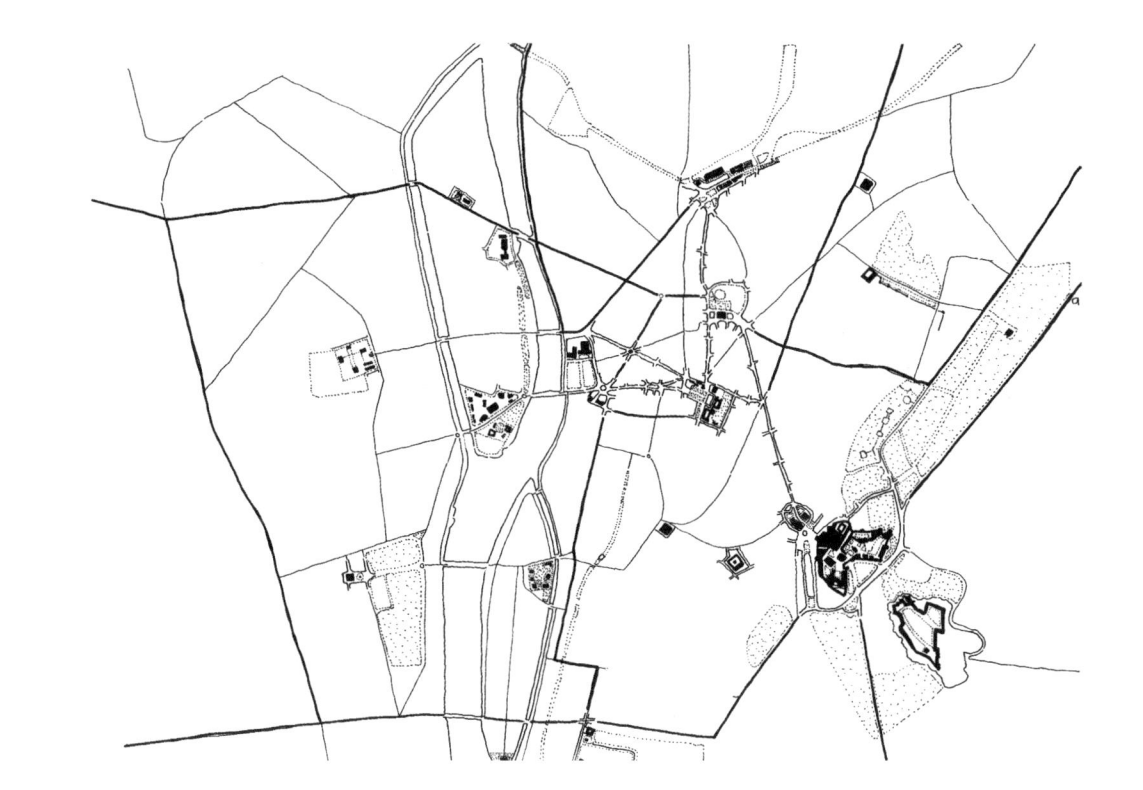

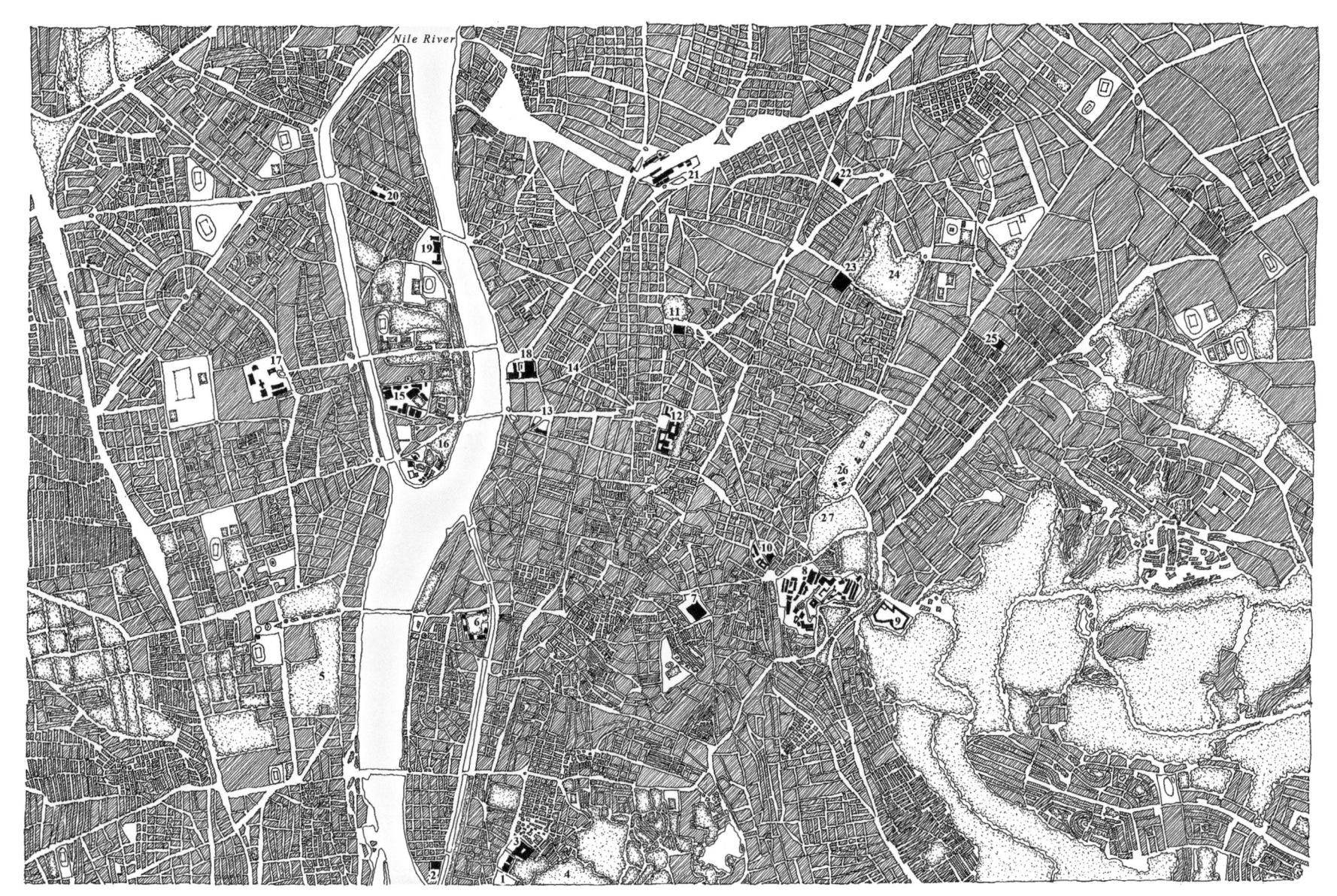

LUXOR, EGYPT

FOUNDED: 1400 BC
AREA: 416 km²
POPULATION (2012): 506,588
DENSITY: 1,200/km²
GPS: 25° 41'57.94"N, 32° 38'24.83"E

The longest river in the world, the Nile, measures 6,695 km from the source of one of its tributaries in Burundi to the Mediterranean. Though cities and other built-up areas comprise only 0.1 percent of the Nile basin's area, all are dependent on its waters for their livelihoods (UN-Habtitat, 2014). Set within the Nile Basin, and one of the first sites to be listed by UNESCO as a World Heritage Site (1979), is the ancient Pharonic settlement of Luxor (Thebes for the ancient Greeks), which owes much of its origin to the rich silt of the Nile River. It is a city that is highly dependent on the tourism market, which has plummeted in recent years due to political unrest and violence in Egypt.

Located in southern Egypt, Luxor is home to a treasure of world-renowned monuments. Ruins of magnificent temple complexes from the ancient world stand within the modern city, which symbolically nestles close to the eastern banks of the Nile River. Across the river are the monuments, temples and tombs on the West Bank, symbolising the Necropolis or city of death, which include the Valley of the Kings and Valley of the Queens.

The Luxor Temple in the east is parallel with the riverbank. The Avenue of Sphinxes was the site of ceremonial processions and originally connected the temples of Luxor and Karnak. Highly visible in the urban fabric, it stretched 2.7 km and would once have had 1,350 sphinxes lining its sides. A strong north-south axis parallel to the Avenue of the Sphinxes axis was also established stretching north-south, re-enforced by the railway. Urban growth had always been contained by the River Nile on the west and the railroad tracks on the east. Luxor Bridge and Luxor Airport – south and east of the city – have dramatically influenced the growth of the city in their directions. However, while the city has been expanding in the eastern direction, arable land has been lost. Encroachment of settlements on the sites surrounding the Karnak Temple and the adjacent arable lands is a major threat to the livelihood of the city.

A twenty-year development plan was created as a framework to attract and guide development of the city in a sustainable manner, while addressing the deterioration of monuments and controlling new settlements in order to direct urban growth away from existing resources. The investment project focuses on the renovation of the Avenue of the Sphinxes to improve the touristic experience, increase the vitality of the city centre, and form the centrepiece of an Open Museum.

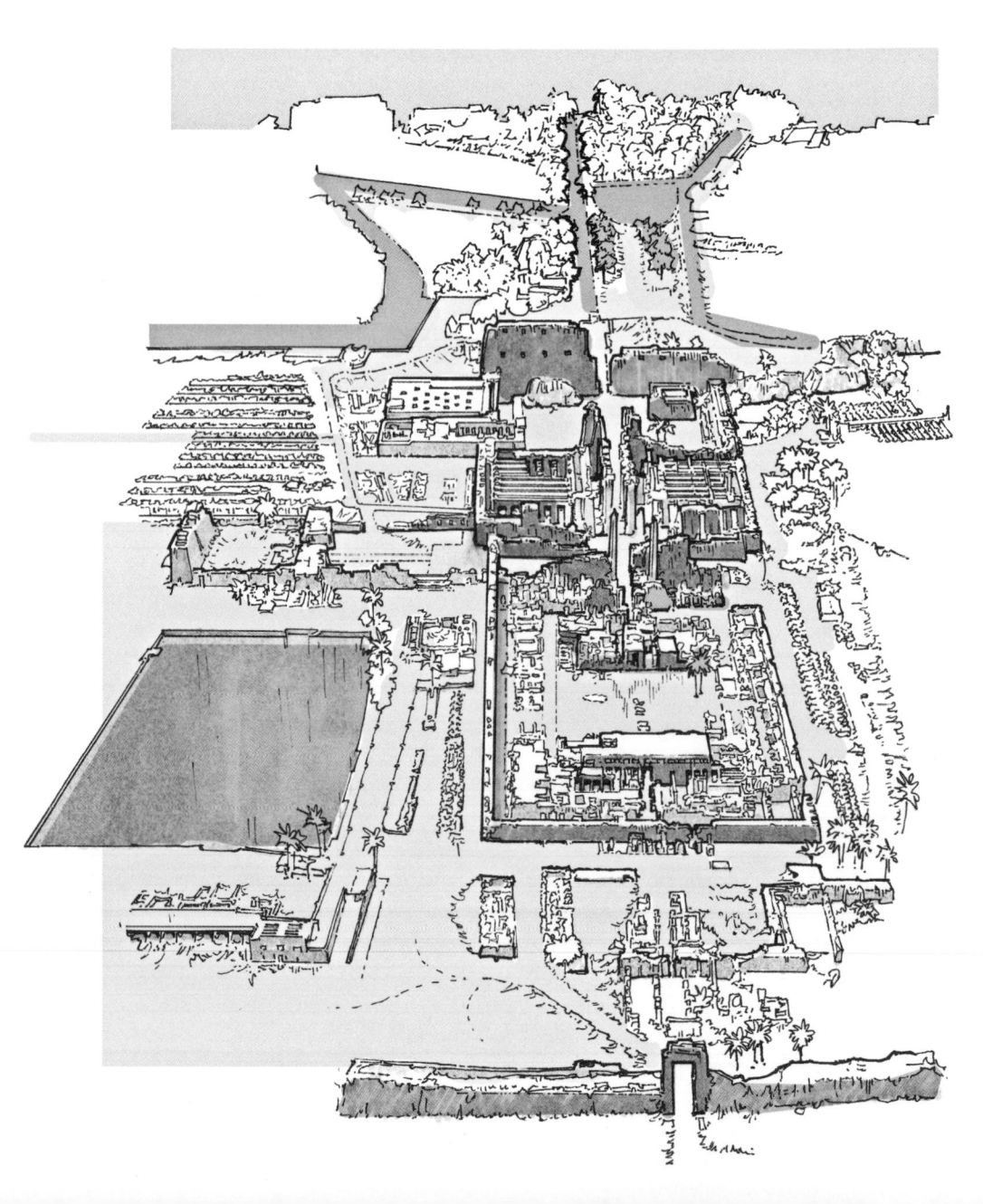

1 Luxor Temple and Luxor Museum
2 Luxor Train Station
3 Karnak
4 Colossi of Memnon
5 The Ramesseum
6 Valley of the Queens
7 Ruins of Deir el-Medina
8 Valley of the Kings
9 Medinat Habu
10 Temple of Seti I

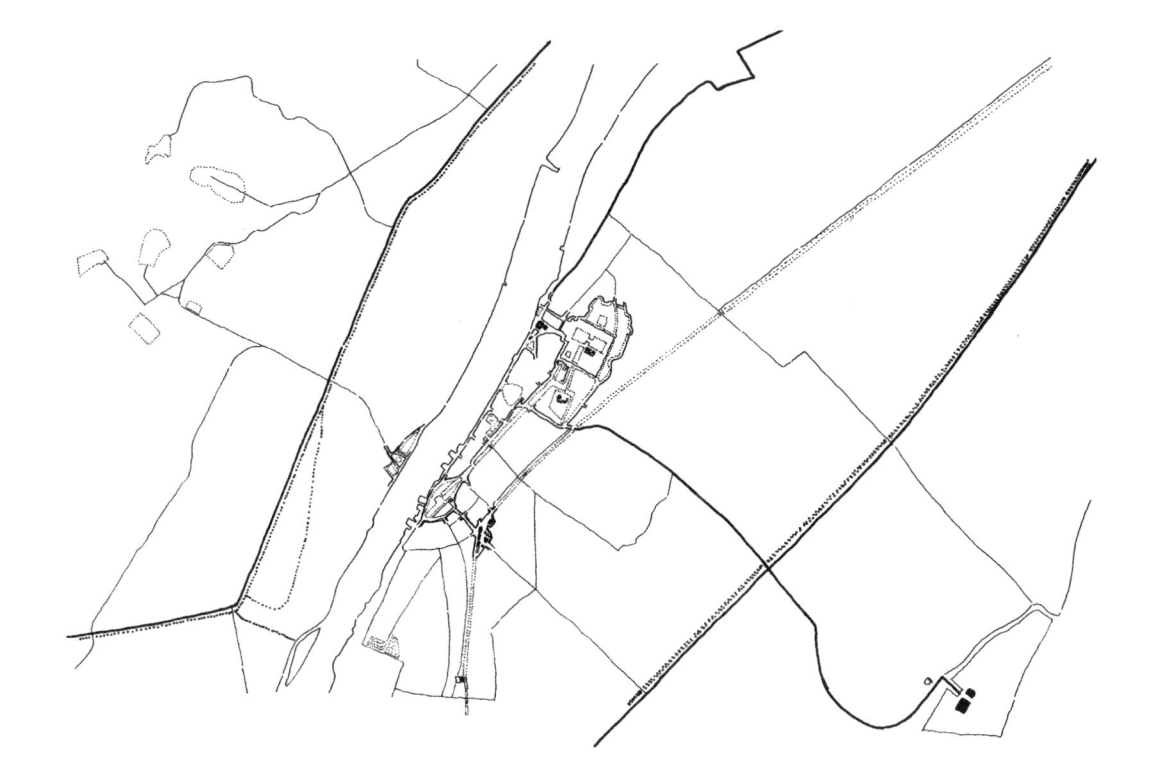

PORT SAID, EGYPT

FOUNDED: 1859
AREA: 1,351 km²
POPULATION (2010): 603,787
DENSITY: 450/km²
GPS: 31° 16'4.00"N, 32° 18'13.43"E

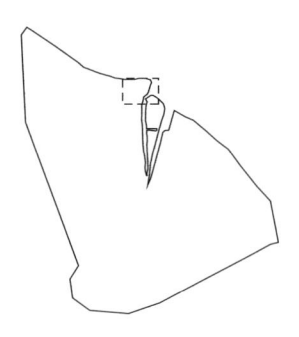

Situated largely on man-made land, the city of Port Said was founded in 1859 on a low sandy strip as a new cultural hub at the crossroads of the ancient continents and trading routes. Consisting initially of a grid-pattern European quarter and a native Egyptian sector, the town had a cosmopolitan character from the outset. By the late nineteenth century, Port Said was the world's largest coal-bunkering station, catering to Suez Canal traffic. After the railway was completed in 1904, it became Egypt's chief port after Alexandria. Given its prominent location, Port Said was severely damaged during the 1956 Sinai War. In the Six-Day War of June 1967, Israeli forces occupied the eastern bank of the canal, which then remained closed until 1975.

The city was restored after the "Open Door" policy of the 1970s, with new housing and a tax-free industrial zone. There are also port and shipyard facilities and in 1980 a bypass north of the city on the Suez Canal opened.

The city has a rich and unique architectural heritage. While its built heritage has a recent history compared to other Egyptian cities, conservationists are concerned about the future of the historic urban fabric due to rapid development and pressure on land.

Megahed (2014) divides the historic urban fabric into three broad categories, according to the typology and usage of buildings: the European quarter, the Arab quarter, and the garden city of Port Fouad. The roughly triangular European quarter (Al-Sharq) is easily recognised in the urban fabric to the north and further south along the western bank of the Canal as an ordered grid-block layout, combining European city planning and architectural styles.

The Old Lighthouse and Suez Canal Authority Building in an Islamic architectural style are situated in this area. The Arab quarter (Al-Arab), located immediately along the west of the European quarter, also has a regular layout and is famous for its old nineteenth and early twentieth-century timber buildings. The 1926 garden city of Port Fouad is located on the Asian bank across the canal in the East. It was planned with a radial layout; its buildings were designed according to European styles for the employees of the Suez Canal administration. Megahed (2014) further maintains that the city later witnessed a construction boom that gave birth to a unique architectural hybrid, merging European city planning with Arab and Islamic influences.

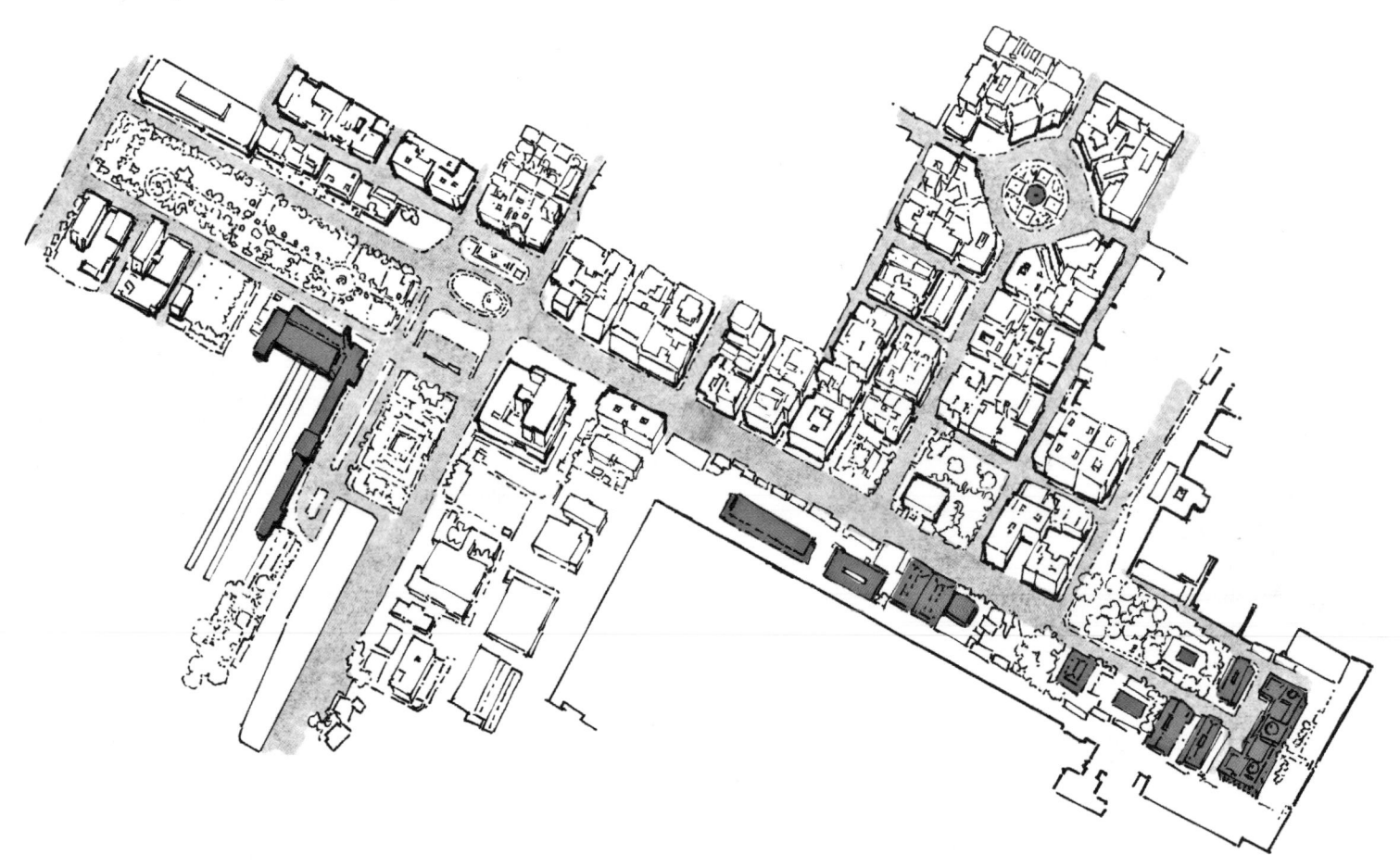

1 Suez Canal House
2 Suez Canal
3 Central Train Station & Farma Park
4 Obelisk Park
5 Military Museum
6 Primary Court Port Said
7 Government Office
8 Ferial Park
9 History Park
10 Saad Zaghloul Park
11 Al-Shatee Park
12 Port Said Stadium
13 Al-Sulaiman Hospital
14 Port Fouad Grant Mosque
15 Port Fouad Court
16 Genena Montazah Park
17 Port Fouad Grant Mosque
18 Qebaa Mosque
19 Port

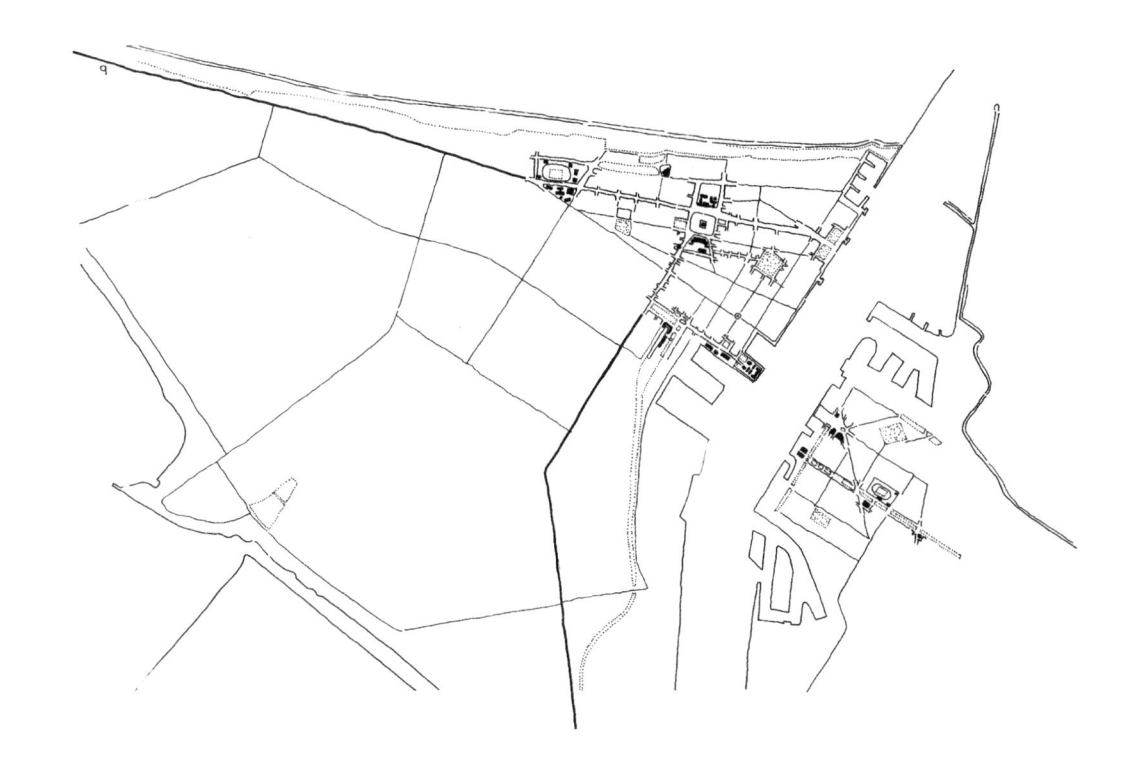

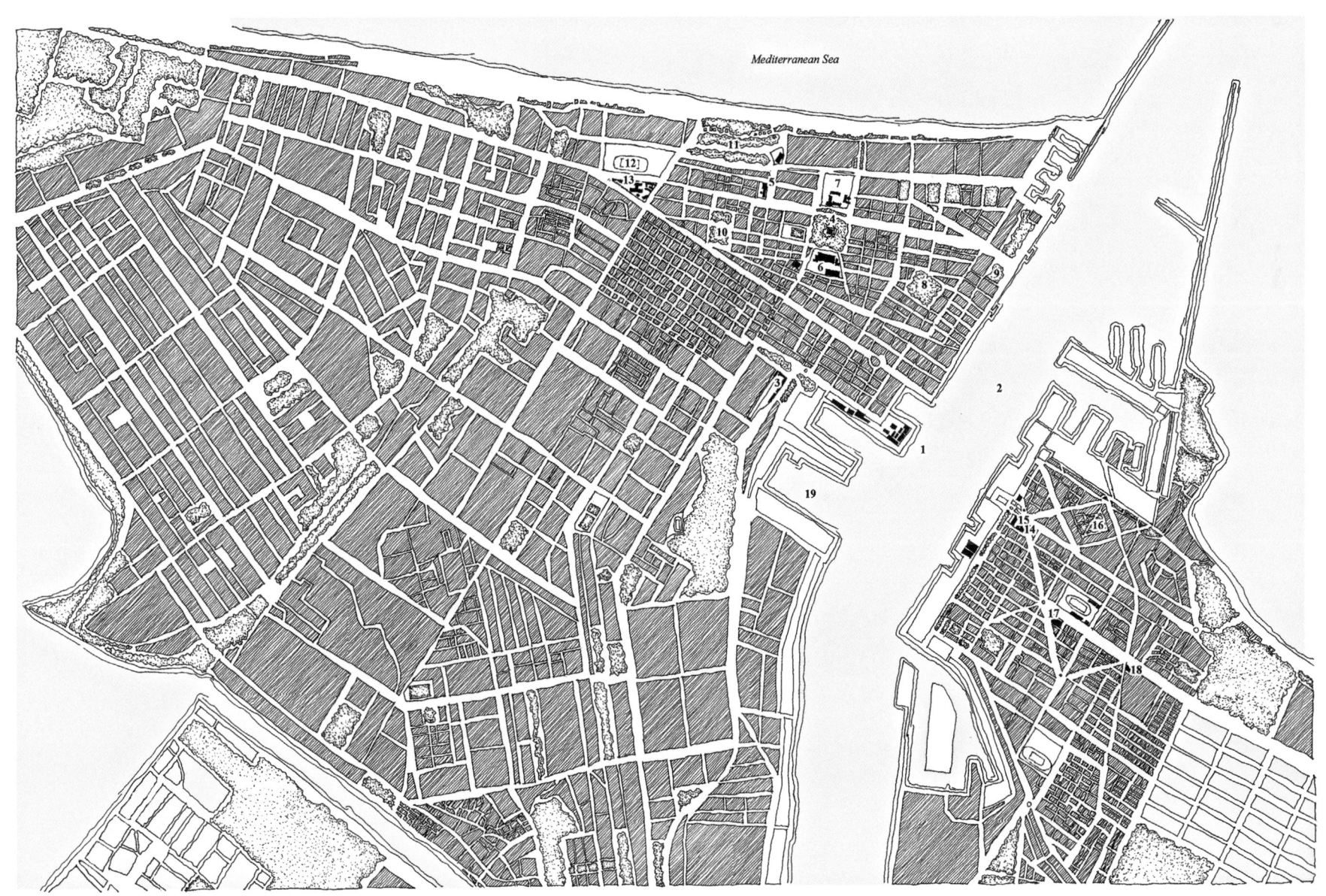

TRIPOLI, LIBYA

FOUNDED: seventh century BC
URBAN AREA: 400 km²
POPULATION: 127,000 (2011)
URBAN AREA DENSITY: 4,500/km²
GPS: 32° 53'40.51"N, 13° 10'50.77"E

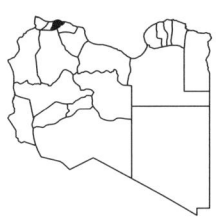

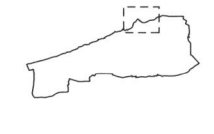

Tripoli, the capital and largest city of Libya – strategically located on the north-western Mediterranean coast of Libya – is also known as Tripoli-of-the-West (to distinguish it from its older Phoenician sister city Tripoli in Lebanon). It is nicknamed "Mermaid of the Mediterranean" by some, alluding to its turquoise waters and whitewashed buildings.

The city is home to the main Port of Tripoli and is the country's largest commercial and manufacturing centre. The vast Bab al-Azizia barracks holds the former family estate of Muammar Gaddafi from where he essentially ruled the country.

The city's long history, rich heritage and cross-cultural references are duly reflected in the urban fabric with various archaeological significant sites throughout the city. The Old City's (the medina) dense fabric appears to have formed organically over time, bearing resemblances to old North African and Middle Eastern cities in hot climates with secluded courtyards and lively markets.

Numerous buildings constructed by the Italian colonial rulers were later demolished under Gaddafi. Tripoli's urban and architectural forms dating from Italian colonial rule are still visible today despite Gaddafi's efforts to "de-Italianise" the country. Mussolini's spatial imprint on Tripoli included stately boulevards, centralised green space and extensive highway systems that represent the power of state authority. This layout led to much social isolation in contemporary Tripoli.

David Rifkind, Associate Professor at Florida International University's College of Art and Architecture, notes how "the Italians saw the importance of also building mosques in the cities they colonised. It was an important gesture of benevolence on their end to establish good will within the colony".

Significant places in the city include the Red Castle Museum (Al-saraya al-Hamra), a substantial palace complex with several courtyards located on the fringes of the medina that dominates the city vista. The Arch of Marcus Aurelius, the only surviving feature of the Roman town of Oea, dates back to the second century. The Gurgi Mosque with its distinctive octagonal minaret is comparatively small with a more intricate design. This was completed in 1833.

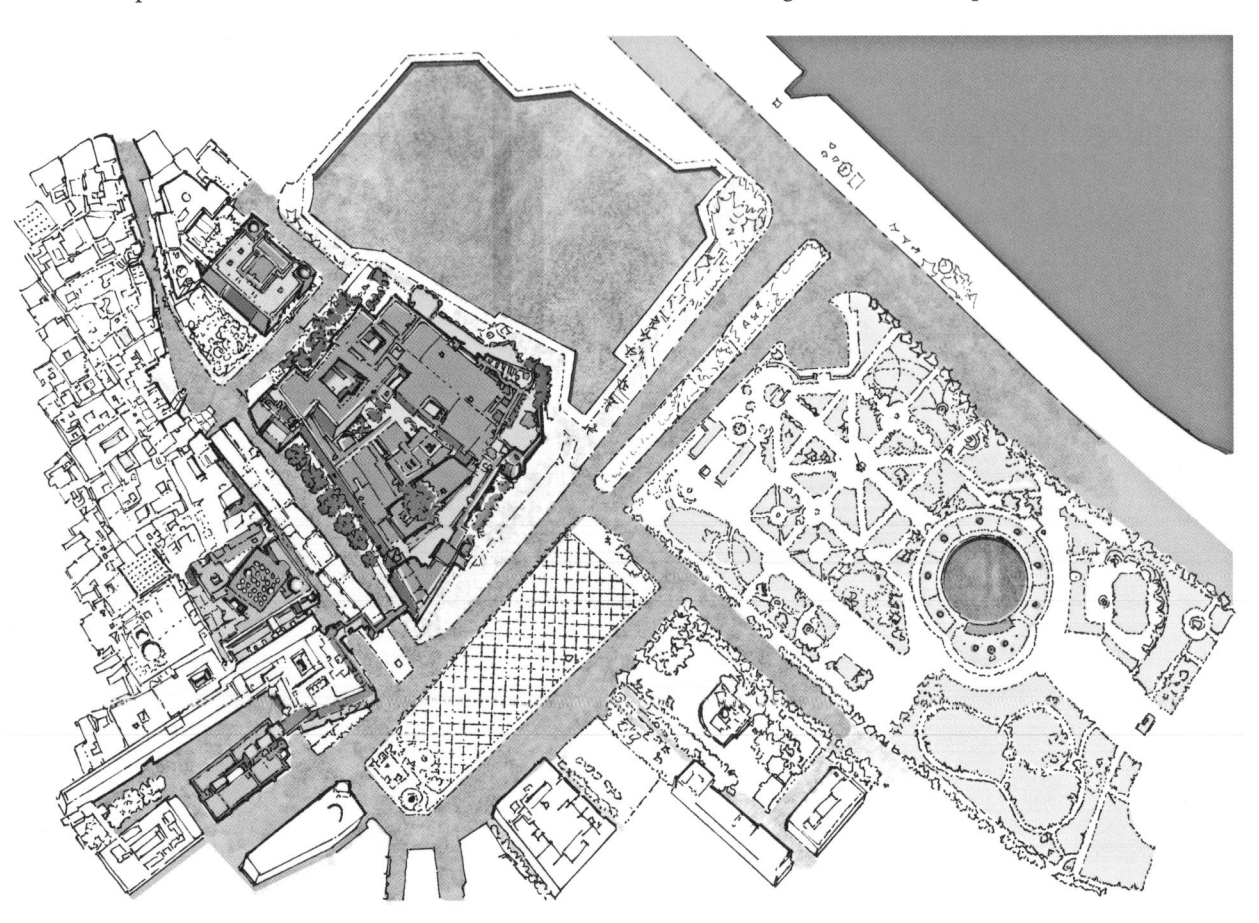

1 Martyrs' Square
2 Al-Saraya al-Hamra or Red Castle and Jamahiriya Museum
3 Old Tripoli City
4 Green Square & Park
5 Park
6 The Museum of Libya
7 Maqbarah Sayyidi Munaydar al-Islamiyyah Cemetery
8 Jnan El-Nawwar Park
9 Central Park & Al-Markazia School
10 Tuesday Major Market Park
11 Piazza Del Aurora
12 Madrassat al-Founoun Wasana'a al-Islamiya or Arts and Crafts School
13 Bab al-Azizia Military Compound
14 Zaweit Eddahmany Health Centre
15 Road Shat Park
16 Al-Quds Mosque
17 Azzawiya Central Hospital
18 Maqbarah Cemetery
19 Masjid Jamal Abdel Nasser Mosque
20 San Francisco Church
21 Port
22 Gurgi Mosque
23 Arch of Marcus Aurelius
24 Bab al-Azizia barracks

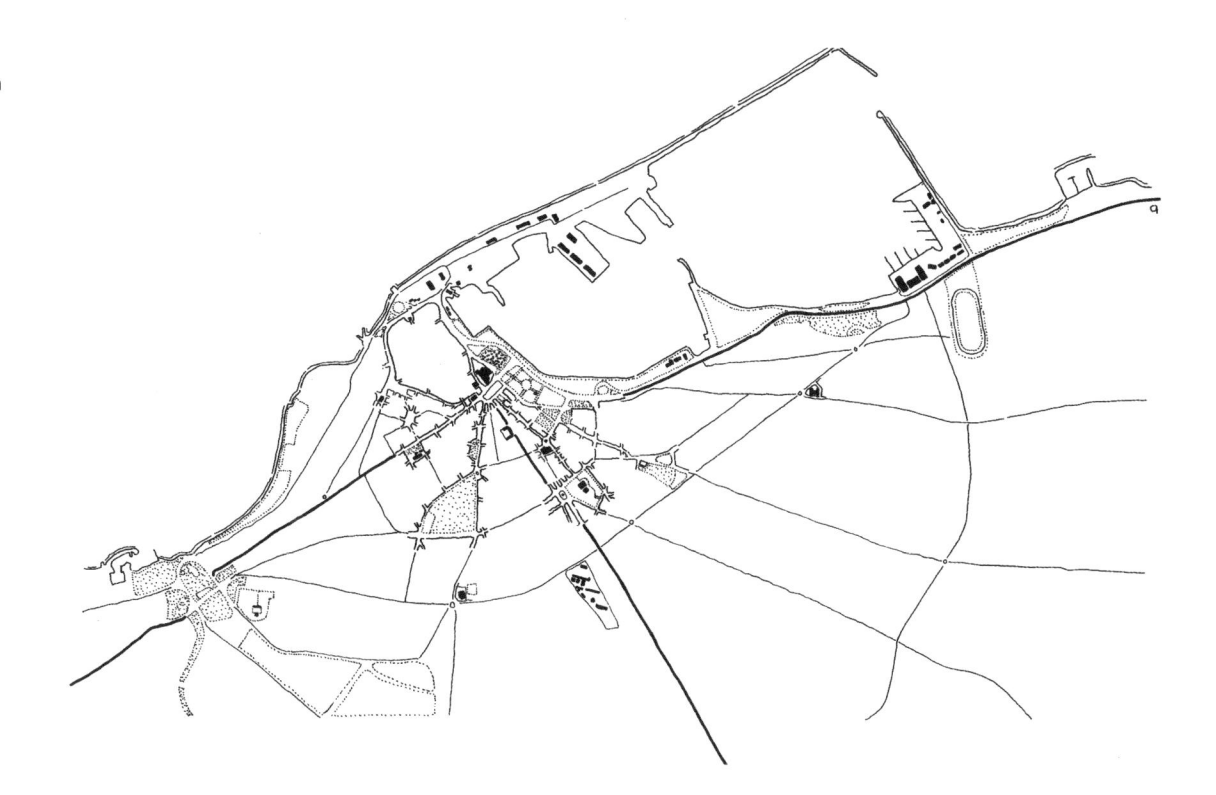

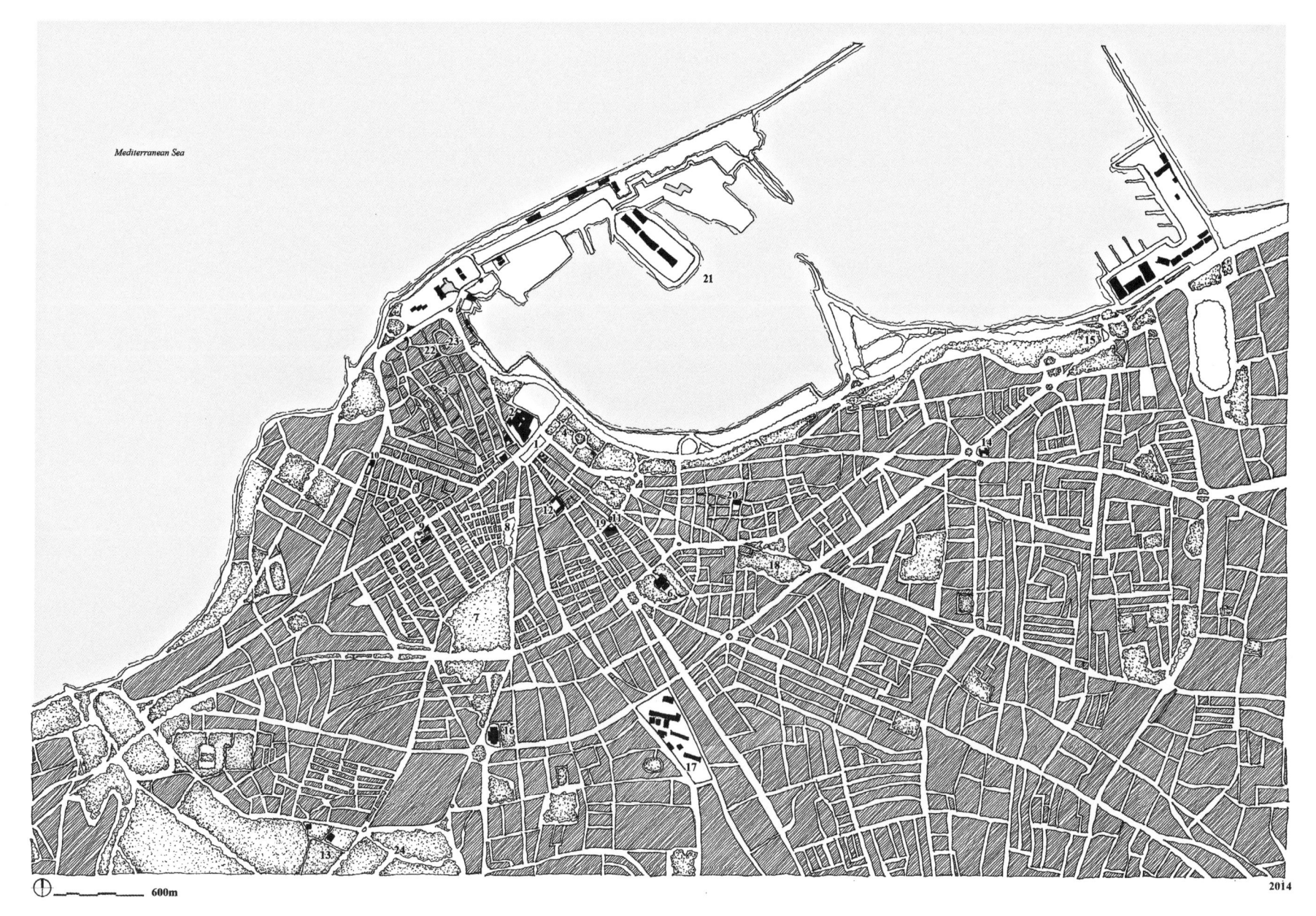

CASABLANCA, MOROCCO

FOUNDED: seventh century BC
URBAN AREA: 386 km^2
POPULATION: 4,150,000 (2013)
URBAN AREA DENSITY: unknown
GPS: 33° 36'22.24"N, 7° 37'54.46"W
33° 35'28.69"N, 7° 37'8.55"W

Casablanca, meaning "White House", is the largest city of Morocco, located in the western part of the country on the Atlantic Ocean. It is also the largest city in the Maghreb (the five countries that make up North Africa: Morocco, Algeria, Tunisia, Libya, and Mauritania), as well as one of the most important cities in Africa, both economically and demographically.

Casablanca is Morocco's economic, business and industrial centre and chief port. It is also one of the largest artificial ports in the world and the largest port in North Africa.

Casablanca is a city characterised by disparities with a traffic-congested *ville nouvelle*, simmering social problems and sprawling slums in contrast to wide boulevards, well-kept public parks, fountains and striking colonial architecture. The French word *bidonville* for slum or shantytown appears first to have been used in Casablanca when the rapid population growth in 1921 gave rise to the development of these squatter settlements, which were constructed out of flattened tin drums (*bidons*) still prevalent on the city's edge today.

Casablanca, originally founded by Berbers in the seventh century BC, had several settlers including the Phoenicians and later the Romans who used it as a port. The Portuguese-controlled town was abandoned in 1755 when an earthquake destroyed most of it. Sultan Mohammed ben Abdallah (1756–1790) reconstructed the town after that.

The French colonial control of Casablanca was formalised by 1910, and the Ville Nouvelle (New Town) of Casablanca was designed by the French architect Henri Prost with the main streets running south and east from Place des Nations Unies. One of the most significant places in Casablanca is the remarkable Hassan II Mosque, designed by the French architect Michel Pinseau. It is the largest mosque in Morocco and the third largest in the world. The minaret is the tallest in the world reaching 210 m. The mosque can accommodate 25,000 worshippers inside, with a further 80,000 in the courtyard.

Old Medina is the small walled-in traditional old town located north of the Place des Nations Unies. Cathédrale Sacré-Coeur (Sacred Heart Cathedral), located in Centre Ville (Downtown) was built in 1930 under Casablanca's French rule. The towers present an impressive view of the city. The Place Mohammed V (Mohammed V Square) is surrounded by beautiful public buildings such as the Hôtel de Ville (City Hall) established in 1918. The Marché Central (Central Market) is located in the central area of the downtown area.

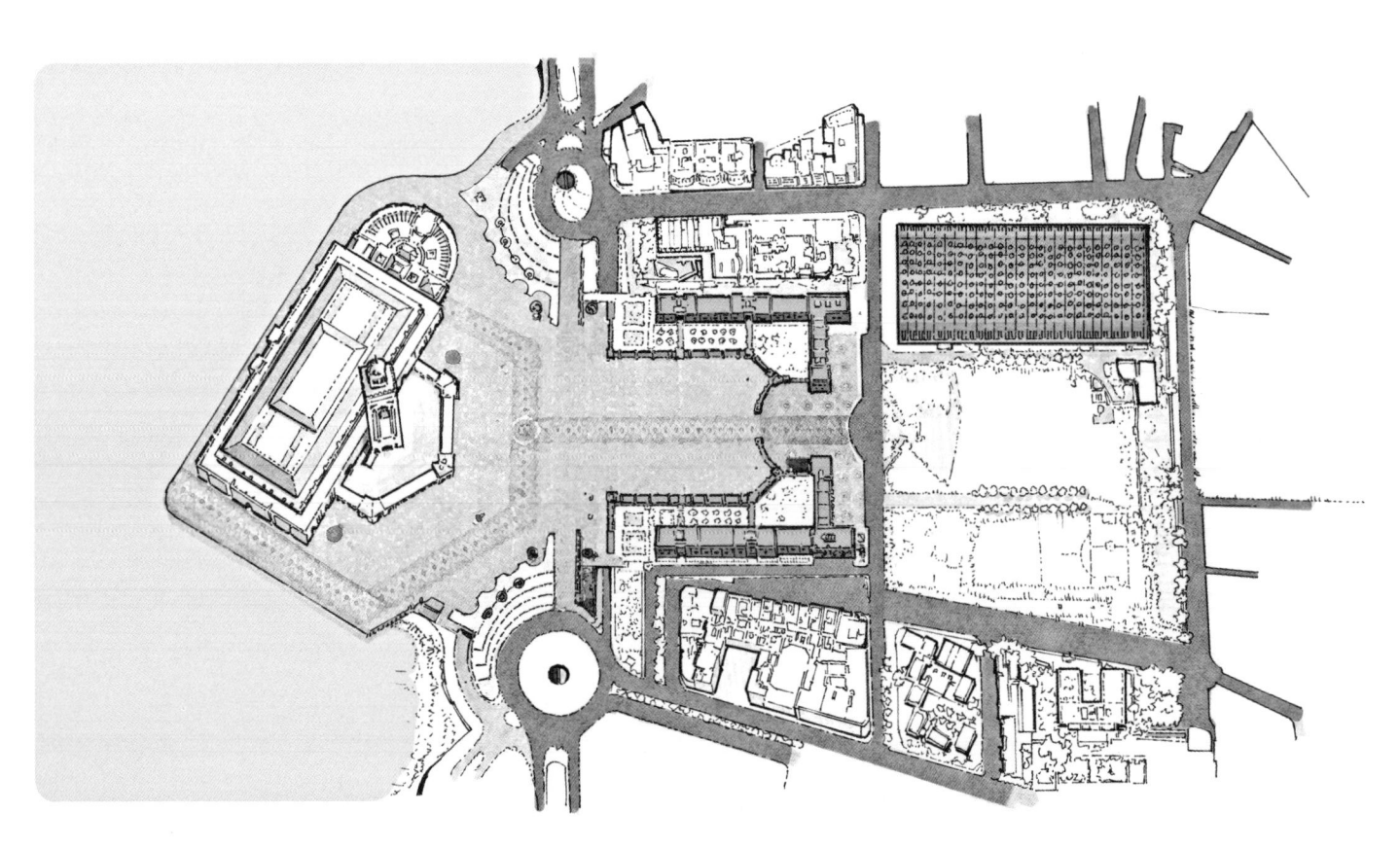

NORTHERN AFRICA **115**

1 Casablanca Old City
2 Place des National Unies
3 Place Mohamed V
4 Palace of Justice
5 Yasmina Park
6 Central Train Station
7 Hassan II Mosque & Museum
8 Weld Alhambra Mosque
9 Casablanca International Fair
10 Mohamed V Stadium
11 Place Sidi Mohammed
12 Train Station
13 Place Al Yassir
14 Church of Our Lady Of Lour
15 Place le Maigre du Breuil
16 Khnata Bent Bakkar School
17 Royal Palace Casablanca
18 Children's Hospital Ibnou Rochd
19 El-Hank Cemetery
20 Lyauté School & Sports Complex
21 Port
22 Cathédrale Sacré Couer
23 Marché Central
24 Hotel de Ville

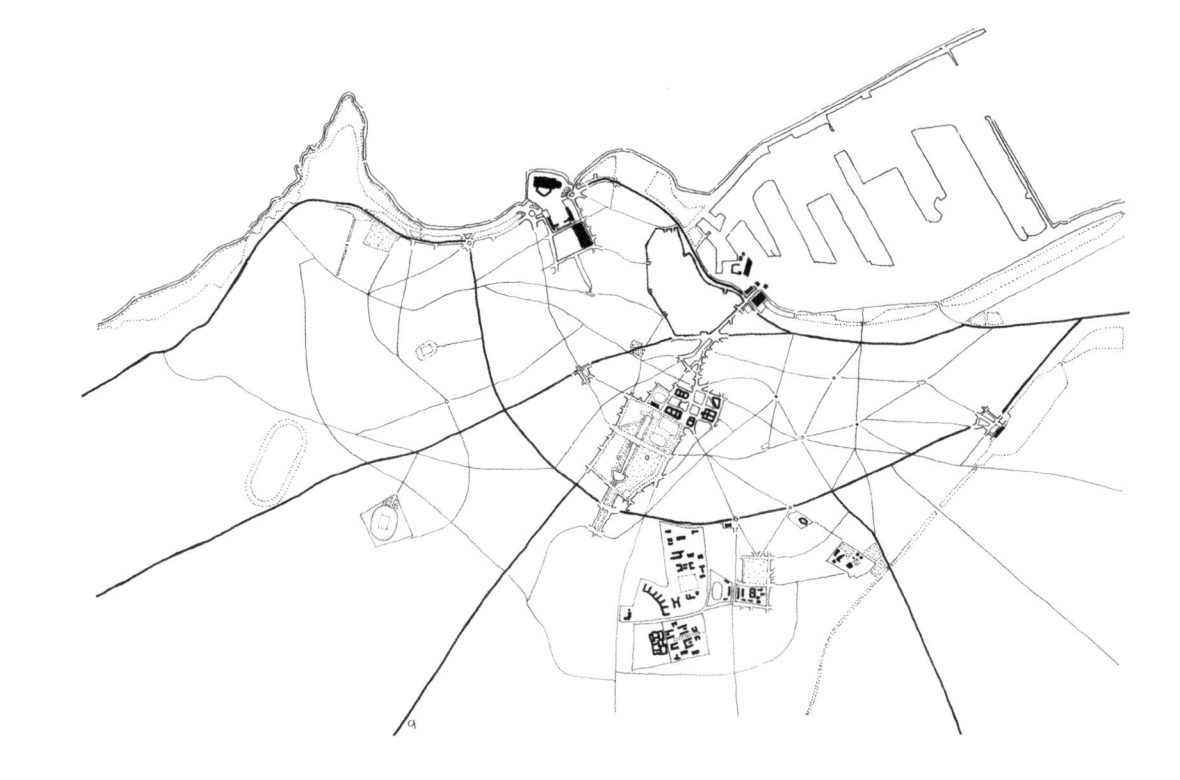

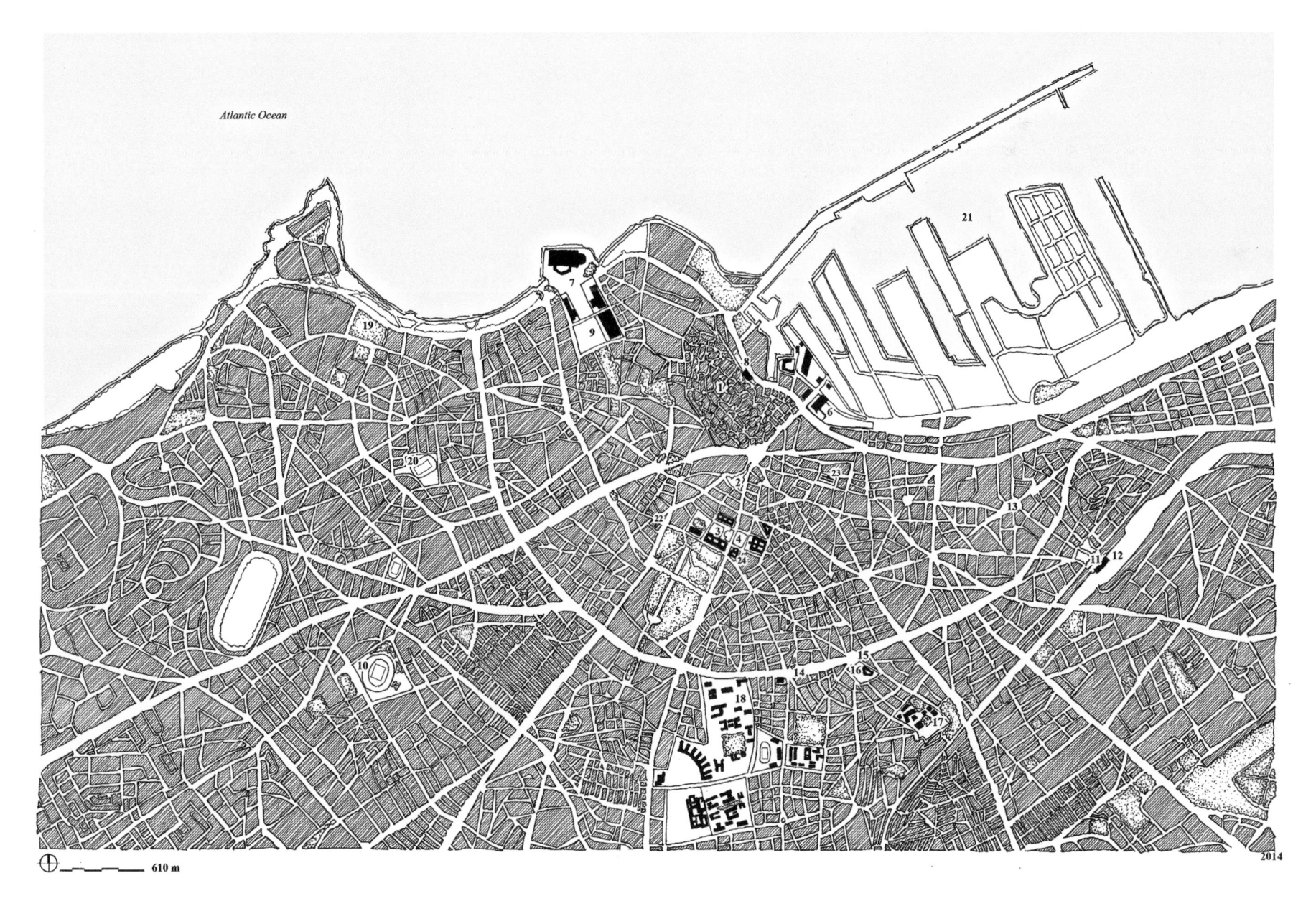

FES (FEZ), MOROCCO

FOUNDED: 789
URBAN AREA: unknown
POPULATION: 1,088,000 (2011)
URBAN AREA DENSITY: unknown
GPS: 34° 3'34.55"N, 4° 59'31.17"W
   34° 2'31.79"N, 5° 0'0.09"W

Fes (Fez) is the third largest city of Morocco and has been referred to as the "Mecca of the West" and the "Athens of Africa". Regarded as one of the best preserved medieval Islamic cities in the world, the urban structure of medieval Fes is described as "epitomising the almost sacred requirement of Islamic urbanism to ensure a secure and inviolable private space for its citizens".

Founded on a bank of the Jawhar River and known to have been the largest city in the world between 1170 and 1180, Fes is also home to the oldest university in the world. The urban fabric and the key monuments in the medina – which include madrasas, fondouks, palaces, residences, mosques and fountains – date from the period between the thirteenth to fourteenth centuries when Fez reached its peak. Up until today, Fes is still recognised as the country's cultural and spiritual centre. The original town consisted of two large fortified quarters separated by the *Fez wadi*: the banks of the Andalous and those of the Kaïrouanais. During the eleventh century, the Almoravids reunited the town within a single fortified wall under the dynasty of the Almohads.

The Medina of Fez is considered "one of the most extensive and best conserved historic towns of the Arab-Muslim world", declared a UNESCO World Heritage Site and believed to be one of the world's largest car-free urban areas. In contrast with the traditional Roman layout of cities, the "Moslem cities in North Africa were not laid out according to street plans; the location of the streets was determined by the arrangement of the buildings". The streets became an extension of the private domain. The area is vulnerable due to pressure from uncontrolled urban development. Fez Jedid (the new town), was founded (in 1276) to the west of the ancient one built outside the walls of the old city. The urban layout was based on the city of Marrakech's structure. Ville Nouvelle, approximately 2 km to the west, was built by the French in line with the colonial planning principle of preserving the old cities for the local population and of building separate *villes nouvelles* for the Europeans. The new city is in stark contrast to the narrow, uneven and non-rectilinear alleys of the medina. The area is recognised by its wide boulevards, lined with modern shops and continuous traffic congestion.

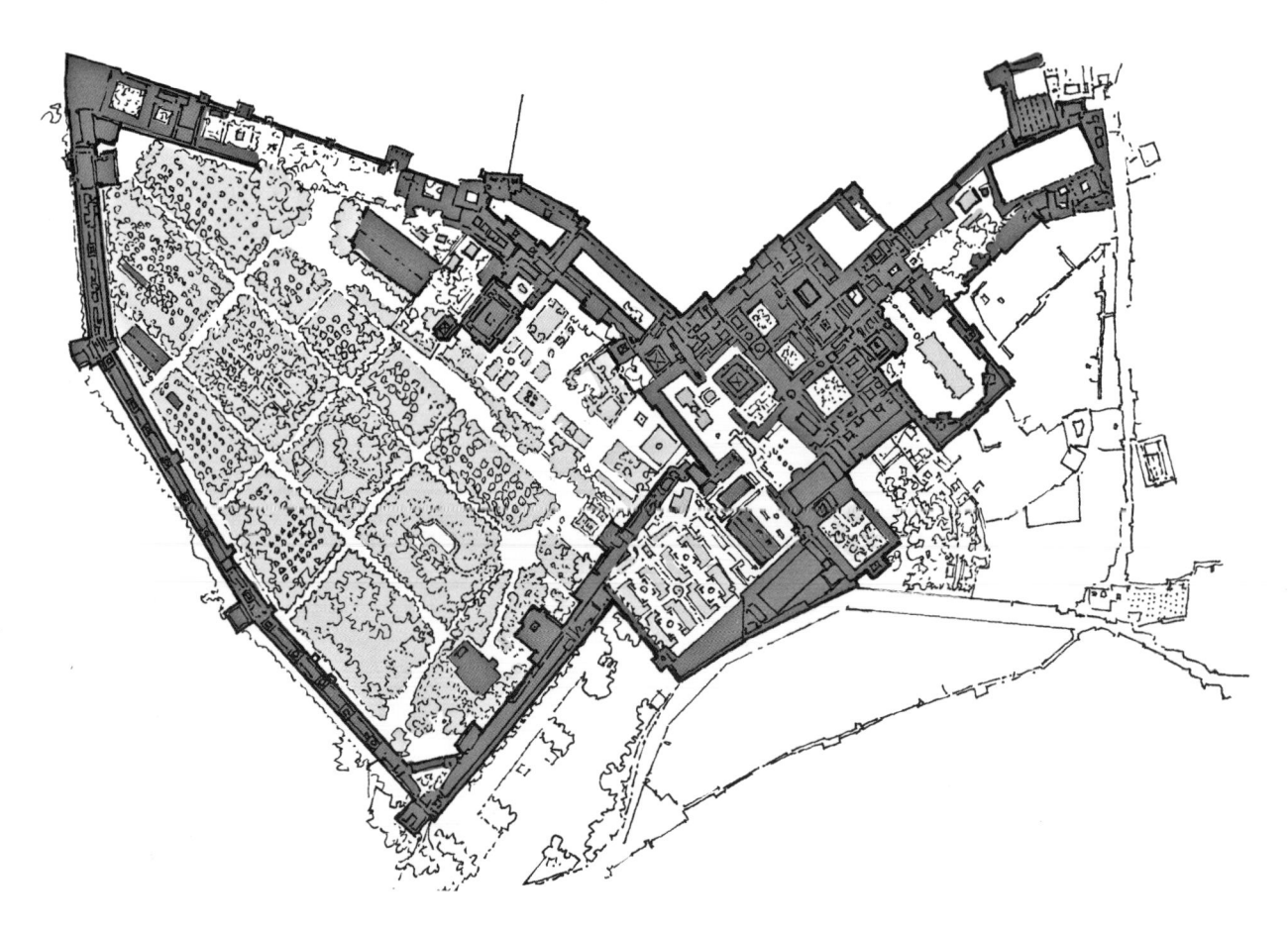

1 Fez Old City
2 Bab Makina Plaza
3 Dar el-Makhzen Royal Palace
4 Place de Florence
5 Place of Resistance
6 Place Ahmed El-Mansour
7 Place Roi Faycal
8 Fez Central Train Station
9 Piscine Municipality & Sports Ground
10 Lalla Amina Park & Place 20th August
11 Place Allal Al-Fassi
12 Hospital Ghassani
13 Royal Palace
14 Méchouar Park
15 City Park
16 Batha Museum
17 Bab Mahrouk Cemetery
18 Place Boujloud
19 Park Jnan Sbil
20 Bab Boujloud or Main Gate
21 Bab Lahdid Gate
22 Bab Ziat Gate
23 Bab Semmarin Gate
24 Bab Schorfa Gate
25 Bab Segma Gate
26 Place Alawites

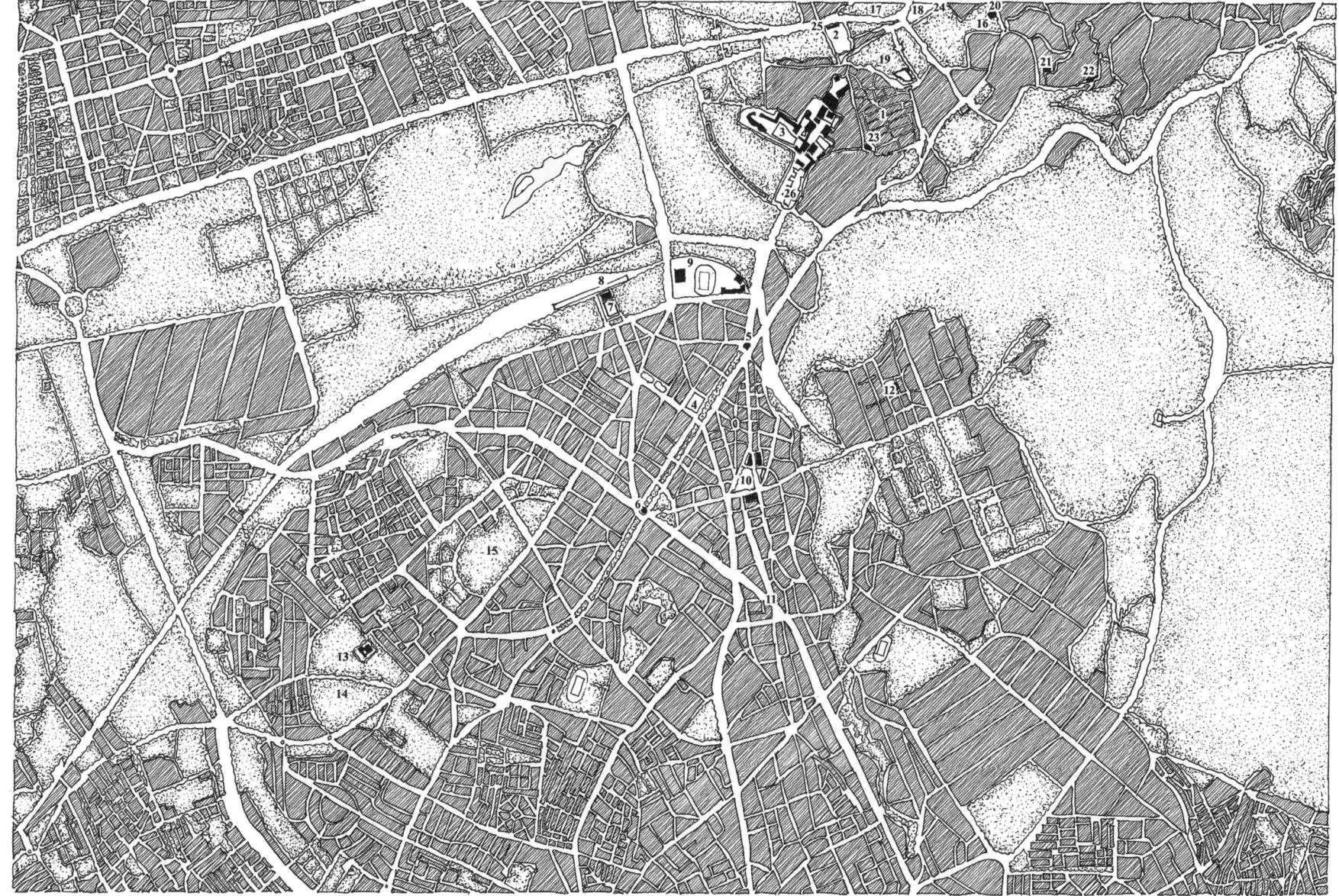

MARRAKECH, MOROCCO

FOUNDED: 1062
URBAN AREA: unknown
POPULATION: 939,000 (2011)
URBAN AREA DENSITY: unknown
GPS: 31° 37'27.97"N, 7° 59'34.47"W
31° 37'12.20"N, 7° 59'5.94"W
31° 37'34.09"N, 7° 59'16.33"W

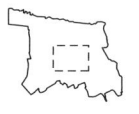

Marrakesh or Marrakech, nicknamed the "Red City", is a major city of Morocco. The city is set against the backdrop of the snow-capped Atlas Mountain foothills. Globally accessible via the Ménara International Airport and the Marrakesh railway station, which connects the city to Casablanca and northern Morocco, the city has become a popular tourist destination.

Marrakesh, similar to many other Moroccan cities, is made up of an old fortified city, which includes the medina, and is bordered by the new town with modern neighbourhoods. One of the great citadels of the Muslim world, the medina ("old town area") was declared a UNESCO World Heritage Site in 1985, raising international awareness of the cultural heritage of the city. Medieval urban development was significantly influenced by this capital of the Almoravids and the Almohads, as Fès Jedid – an integral part of the medina of the city Fez (listed on UNESCO's World Heritage list in 1981) – was based on the earlier urban model of Marrakesh. The city was founded by the Almoravids in 1070–1072. Up until today, it is a prominent economic centre and one of the busiest cities in Africa.

Several notable buildings and monuments throughout the city include the Koutoubiya Mosque, the casbah, the battlements, distinct monumental doors, the Bandiâ Palace, the Ben Youssef Madrasa, the Saadian Tombs, several great residences and Place Jamaâ El Fna, a veritable open-air theatre, the Jemaa el-Fnaa Square, listed on the UNESCO World Heritage list, and one of the best known squares in Africa. Marrakesh is also famous for its traditional Berber market, closely associated with its souks, cited by Paul Sullivan as the principal shopping attraction in the city: "A honeycomb of intricately connected alleyways, this fundamental section of the old city is a micro-medina in itself, comprising a dizzying number of stalls and shops that range from tiny kiosks no bigger than an elf's wardrobe to scruffy storefronts that morph into glittering Aladdin's Caves once you're inside."

The distinctive red clay fortification walls, stretching for approximately 19 km around the medina, were built by the Almoravids in the twelfth century. The Menara Gardens, built around 1130, are located to the west of the city, at the gates of the Atlas Mountains.

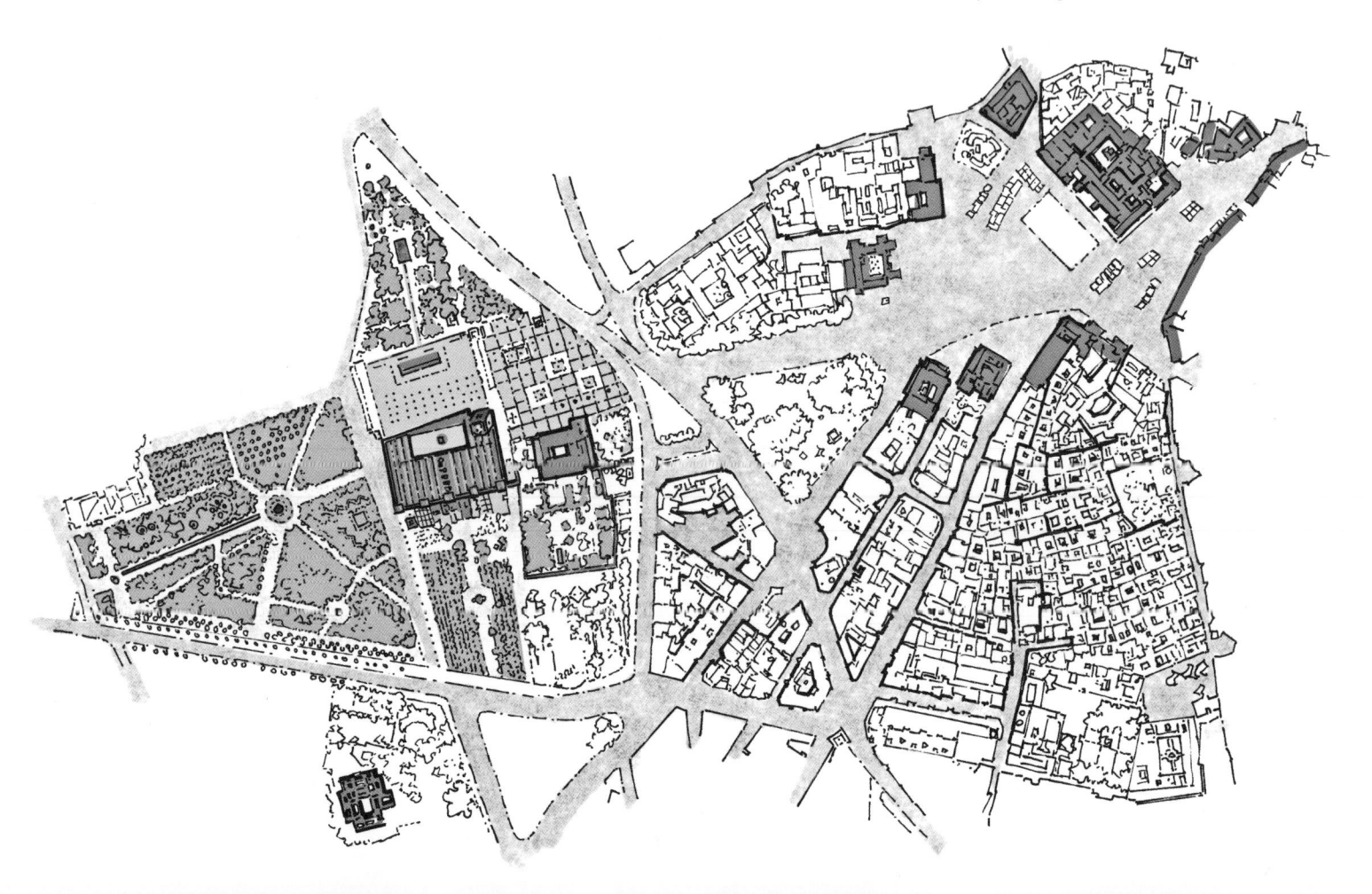

1 Old Marrakech City	17 Badi Palace
2 Place Jemaa El-Fnaa	18 Marrakech Museum, Almoravid Koubba, Dar Bellarj & Ben Youssef Mosque
3 Place Foucauit	
4 Koutoubia Mosque	
5 Koutoubia Park	19 Bab Agnaou
6 Lalla Hasna Park	20 Place Liberty
7 Sidi Ahmed El-Kamel Park	21 Park Bab El-Khmiss
8 Place Ferblantiers	22 Place Bab Doukkala
9 Mosque Berrima	23 Cemetery Bab Doukkala
10 Agdal Gardens	24 Cheikh Daoud El-Antaki Hospital
11 Majorelle Park	
12 Bab Ghmat Cemetery	25 Mouloudia Football Field Marrakech
13 Bahia Palace	
14 Dar Si Said	26 Ben Youssef Madrasa
15 Rosier Park	27 Kasbah
16 El-Mansour Mosque & Saadian Tombs	28 Menara Gardens

600 m

2014

MEKNES, MOROCCO

FOUNDED: eleventh century
URBAN AREA: unknown
POPULATION: unknown
URBAN AREA DENSITY: unknown
GPS: 33° 53'34.43"N, 5° 33'47.72"W
33° 53'35.27"N, 5° 33'56.88"W
33° 53'49.75"N, 5° 33'1.89"W

Meknes, surrounded by the fertile plains below the Middle Atlas Mountains, is renowned for its impressive architecture, medieval ramparts and beautiful gates. The city was founded in the early eleventh century by the Almoravids as a military settlement, and became a capital under the rule of Sultan Moulay Ismaïl (1672–1727), founder of the Alawite dynasty. The city was transformed under the rule of the sultan who created vast gardens, numerous edifices, mosques and monuments as well as 40 km of sturdy walls and monumental gates lining the city.

In 1755, an earthquake destroyed parts of the city. Historical monuments, many dating back to the reign of the sultan (seventh century) can be seen throughout the city. Significant places include the Great Mosque, the Great Mosque Tower, the Royal Palace and the Moulay Ismaïl Mausoleum.

The city is divided in two – typical of a North African City – with the new town (Ville Nouvelle) on the one side, and the medina as part of the old city on the other, connected by a bridge over the dry Oued Boufekrane (river). The old city is fortified with exceptionally high walls (15 m) and contains several remarkable gates, the Bab el-Mansour gate being the largest and most impressive. The medina is a network of alleyways with no particular geometric layout: significant of historical Muslim areas where the orientation and socio-spatial structure of the building precedes the layout of the street network. The new city is in contrast to the historical area with its orderly and spacious layout. The casbah, in contrast, has vast open areas. The well-preserved, remarkable blending of the Islamic and European architecture and town planning of the seventeenth century contributes to the significance of Meknes. UNESCO listed Meknes as a World Heritage Site in 1996, giving credit to its extraordinary design including "elements of Islamic and European design and planning in a harmonious fashion". The designation inspired many significant renovation projects with a raised awareness to help preserve these remarkable monuments for the future.

The Medinas 2030 Initiative was launched by the European Investment Bank in cooperation with international organisations, city associations and various experts to document and possibly protect the medinas identified in several countries. Meknes was selected as the focus of the pilot project.

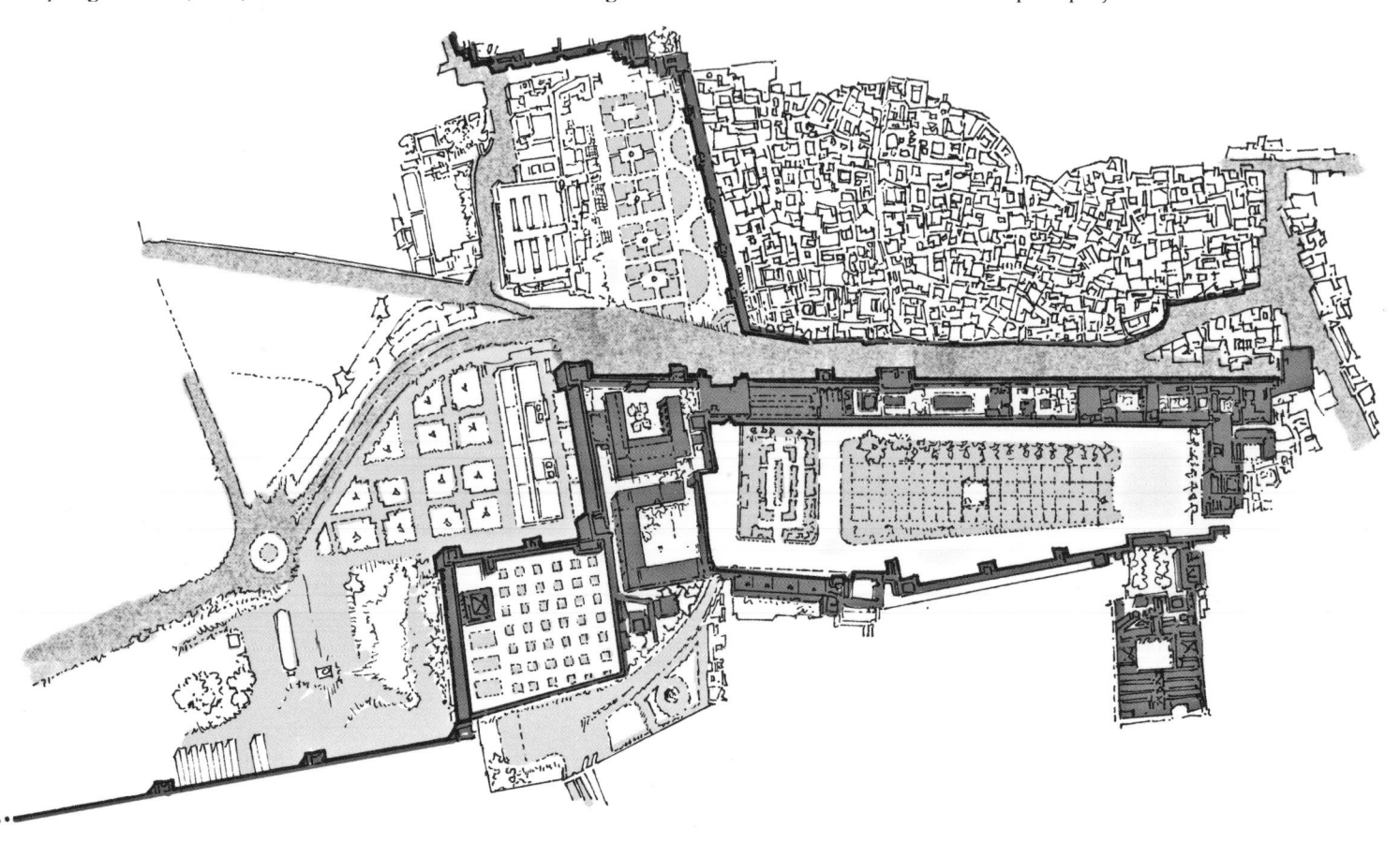

1 Old Meknes City
2 Place Lahdim
3 Dar Jamaï Museum
4 Lalla Aouda Square
5 Court House
6 School of Imam Bukhari
7 Koubbat as-Sufara
8 Park
9 Muslim Cemetery
10 Park Lahboul
11 Heri es-Souani & Agdal Basin
12 Grand Mosque
13 Medersa Bou Inania
14 Muslim Cemetery & Mausoleum of Sidi ben Aïssa
15 Mausoleum of Moulay Ismail
16 Bab el-Mansour Gate
17 Central Train Station
18 Meknès Park
19 School
20 Stadium 20th August
21 Al-Quds College High School
22 Christian Cemetery
23 Library
24 Place Abdelkrim Al-Khatib
25 Lalla Amina High School
26 Place Abdelaziz Ben Idriss
27 College Moulay Hafid
28 Royal Palace

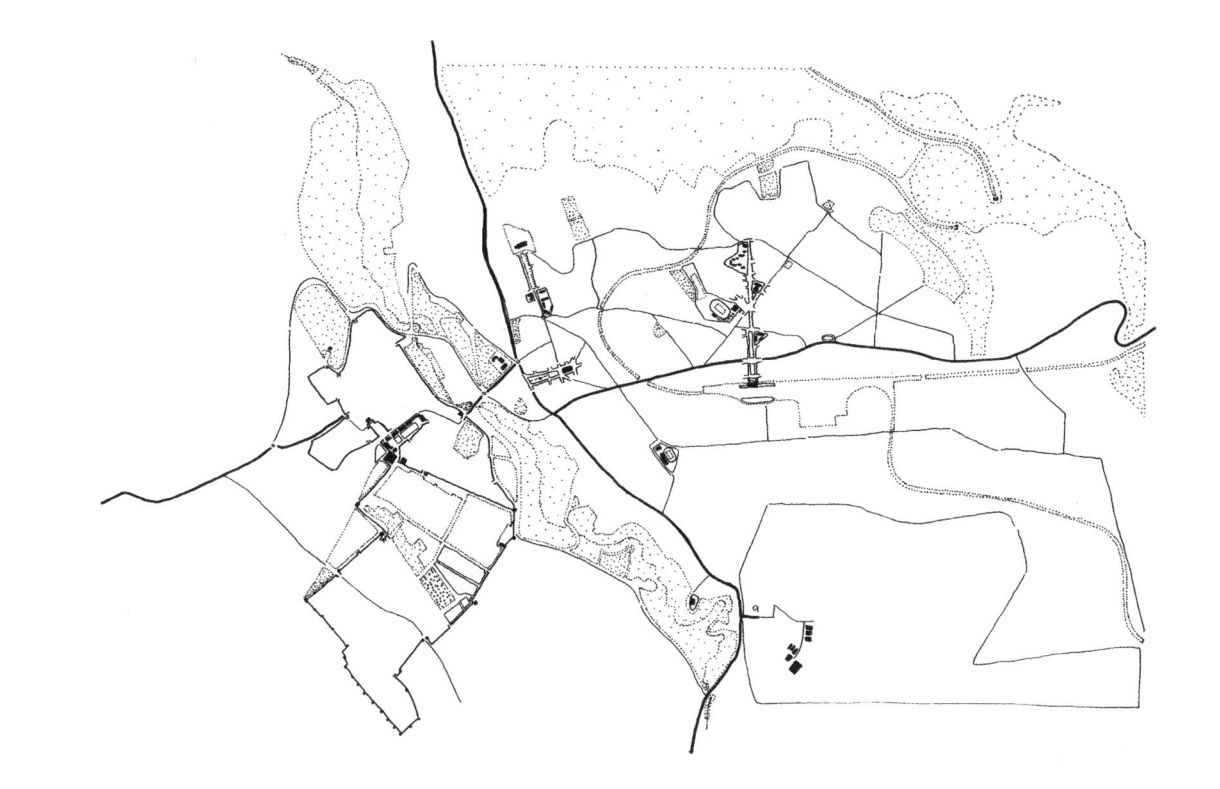

RABAT, MOROCCO

FOUNDED: 1146
URBAN AREA: 117 km²
POPULATION: 1,843,000 (2011)
URBAN AREA DENSITY: 5,300/km²
GPS: 34° 1'23.27"N, 6° 49'22.38"W
  34° 1'5.42"N, 6° 49'50.97"W
  34° 1'18.81"N, 6° 50'26.80"W

Rabat, meaning "Fortified Place", is the capital and second largest city of Morocco. It is located in the north-west of the country on the Atlantic coast, at the mouth of the Bou Regreg River. The city initially developed as a military base, giving rise to its name derived from the term "stronghold of victory." Even though the city is a relatively new capital (established as the capital by the French in 1912), it has a rich history.

As is the case with most Moroccan cities, the city is divided into two with the new town (Ville Nouvelle) built by the French, and the medina ("old-walled city") dating back to the twelfth century.

The medina was a fortified area protected by the Andalusian ramparts and divided by dedicated market areas called souks. These were laid out in a grid pattern – in contrast to the traditional mazes of streets found in the older parts of cities throughout Morocco. The older parts include the Hassan Mosque (built in 1184) and the Almohad fortifications and gates, the sole surviving parts of the project for a distinguished capital city of the Almohad caliphate, as well as remains from the Moorish, or Andalusian, principality of the seventeenth century.

Henri Prost was appointed in 1913 to design the Ville Nouvelle (Rabat's modern quarter) as an administrative sector. The city has been hailed modern with its rationally and geometrically designed quarters and buildings, wide boulevards, and clearly defined and separated neighbourhoods. Ville Nouvelle is regarded as one of the largest and most ambitious modern urban projects built in Africa during the twentieth century due to its modernist town planning and architectural manifestations, interweaved with the older city's historic components. The royal and administrative areas, residential and commercial developments and the Jardins d'Essais botanical and pleasure gardens are all located in the new town.

The city is said to visibly celebrate a heritage shared by several major cultures of human history: ancient, Islamic, Hispano-Maghrebian and European. Significant landmarks in the city include the Royal Palace, the unfinished mosque with its striking Hassan Tower, the necropolis at Chellah and the grand Mausoleum of the Kings (Mohammed V and Hassan II). The Moroccan government also plans to connect Rabat to Casablanca and Tangiers with a high-speed train railway system.

NORTHERN AFRICA

1. Old Rabat City
2. Grande Mosque
3. Ash-Shuhada Cemetery
4. Nouzhat Hassan Park
5. Mohammed V School
6. Place Bab el-Had & fountain
7. Bab El-Alou Gate
8. Place des Oudaias
9. Casbah des Oudaias
10. Museum des Oudaias
11. Andalusian Park
12. Place 16th November
13. Tour Hassan Mosque & Park, Mausoleum of Mohammed V
14. Bab Mellah
15. Moulina Mosque
16. Justice Ministry
17. Church of Saint Francis
18. Moroccan Parliament
19. Sports Park
20. National Museum of Postal Services and Telecommunication
21. Assounna Mosque
22. Archeological Museum
23. Place Al-Joulane & Church
24. Mohammed V National Theatre & Ministry of Culture
25. House of Culture & Place Golan
26. Chellah Cemetery
27. Old Roman City of Chellah
28. Mechouar Park
29. Al-Fes Mosque
30. Botanical Garden
31. Old Sale City
32. Place Bab Lekhmiss & Park
33. Place Bab Khebaz & Park
34. Sidi Benachir Cemetery
35. Port
36. Royal Palace

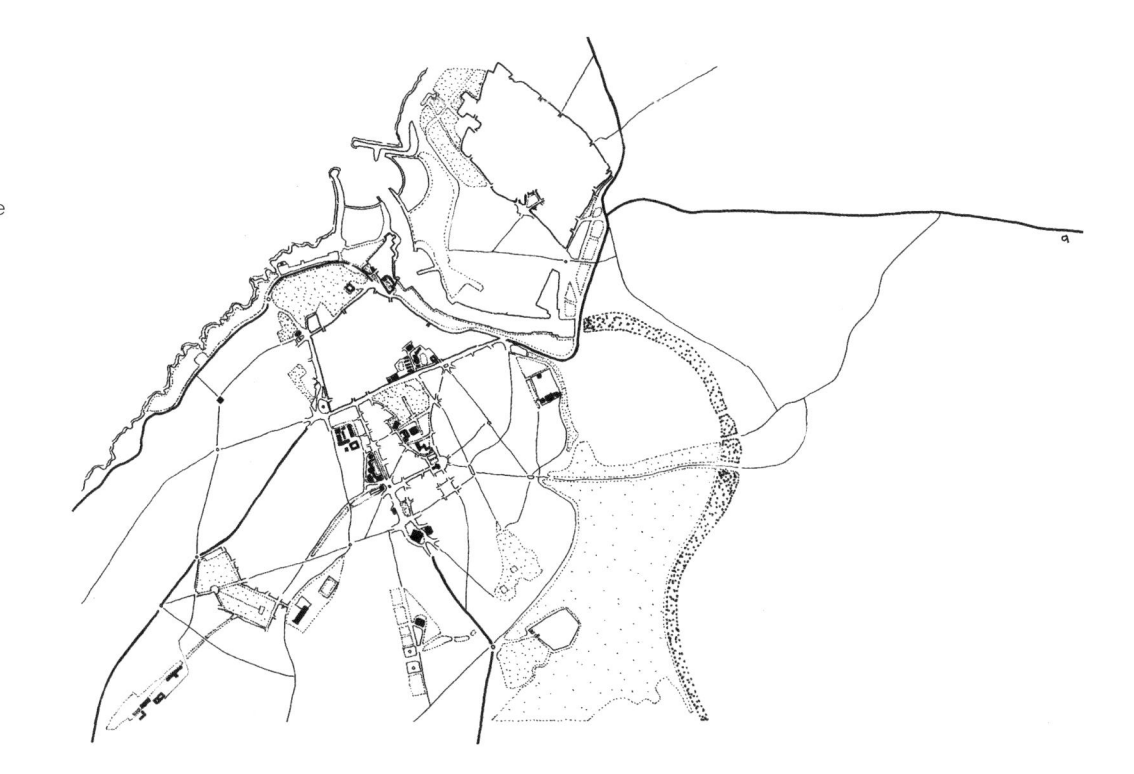

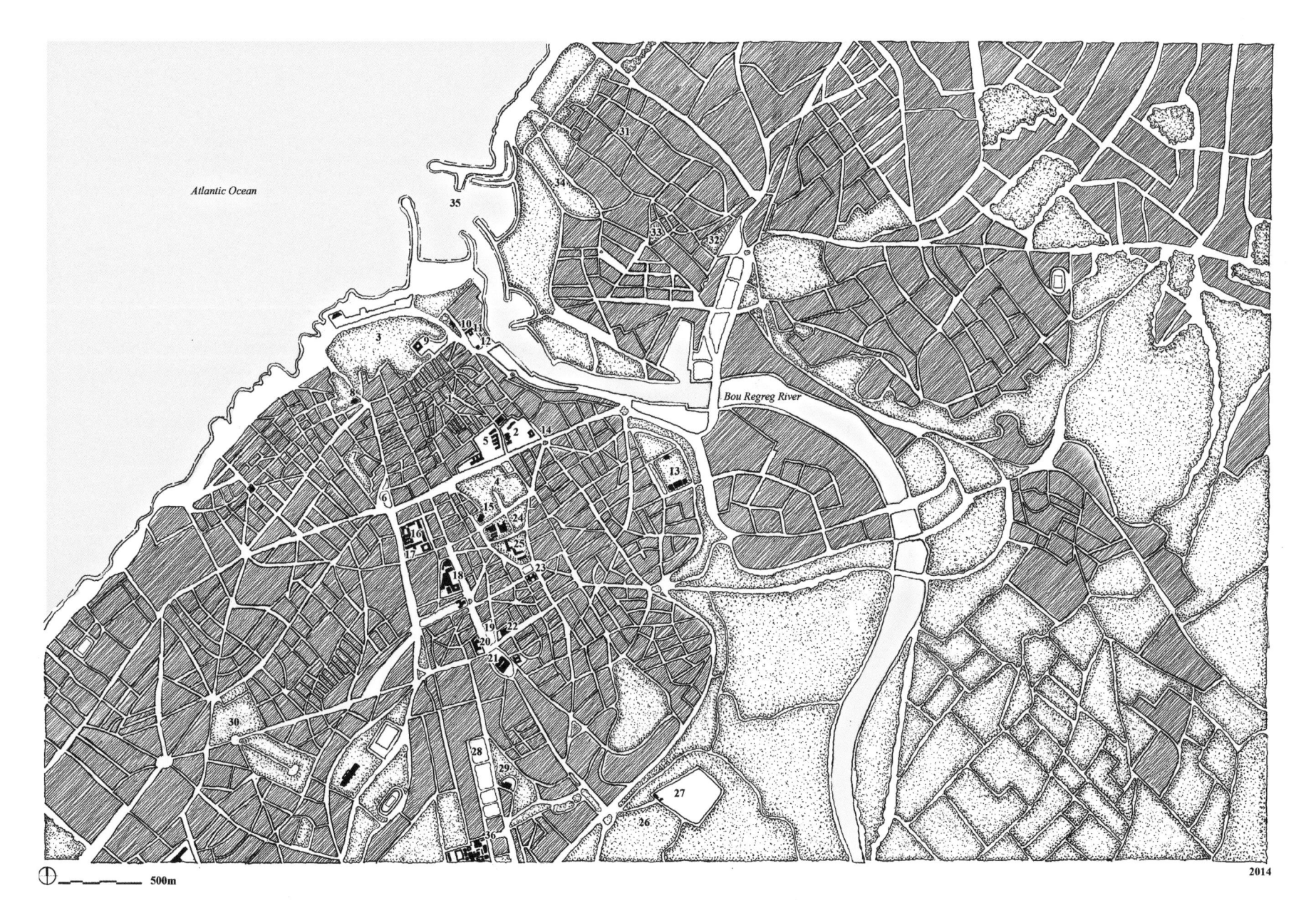

KHARTOUM, SUDAN

FOUNDED: 1821
AREA: unknown
POPULATION (2011): 4,632,000
DENSITY: unknown
GPS: 15° 36'25.36"N, 32° 31'39.40"E

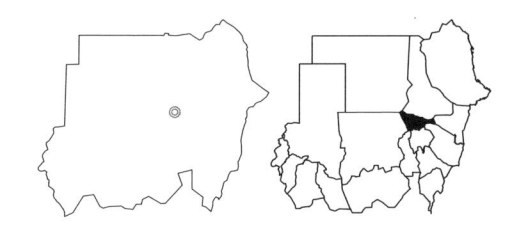

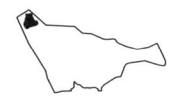

Well-known architectural historian Christian Norberg-Schulz once described the city of Khartoum, set within a cosmic desert landscape, as offering the feeling of an infinite setting, defined by the movement of the sun and the Nile River.

Khartoum, capital of Sudan, is literally bisected by the Nile River, historically forming three towns that create a triangle with Tuti Island at its centre and is separated by the White, Blue and Main Niles. Omdurman (not depicted on the next page) to the west of the White Nile is known for its traditional and political history as the old Mahdist (1885–1898) capital. Khartoum, south of the Blue Nile, is considered the commercial hub with the Khartoum Airport to its south. Khartoum North (Bahri) on the northern bank is considered the industrial centre. Tuti Island (upper left-hand corner of the map) is regarded as the origin of Greater Khartoum with traditional mud-brick buildings and agricultural land. Until recently, Khartoum's downtown centre, characterised by colonial architecture and colonial wide streets, was the commercial heart of the city. However, the relocation of the central bus station and associated markets further out has diminished its importance. Khartoum city was the British colonial town designed to be the centre of government and education. Its centre was along the Nile River where the palace, government offices and university are located (depicted in the vignette). The old capital, Omdurman, is an indigenous city with a UNESCO World Heritage Site marketplace at its centre. It has retained its traditional character, with narrower streets and houses built around courtyards.

Pantuliano et al (2011) describes Khartoum as a "… patchwork of wealth and poverty, demographic density and sprawl and robust and atrophied infrastructure. It is, in short, a microcosm of the contradictions that mark Sudan as a whole".

According to Pantuliano et al (2011) there has been increasing gentrification in some neighbourhoods of the city. Recent waves of Gulf-based real-estate investment has resulted in the city being nicknamed the "Dubai on the Nile" with sun-reflective high-rise towers coupled with the emergence of gated properties and Sudan's first golf course. By contrast, the urban poor of Khartoum, which a recent study led by UN-Habitat puts at approximately 60 percent of the total population, is scattered in and around the city in low-density squatter areas.

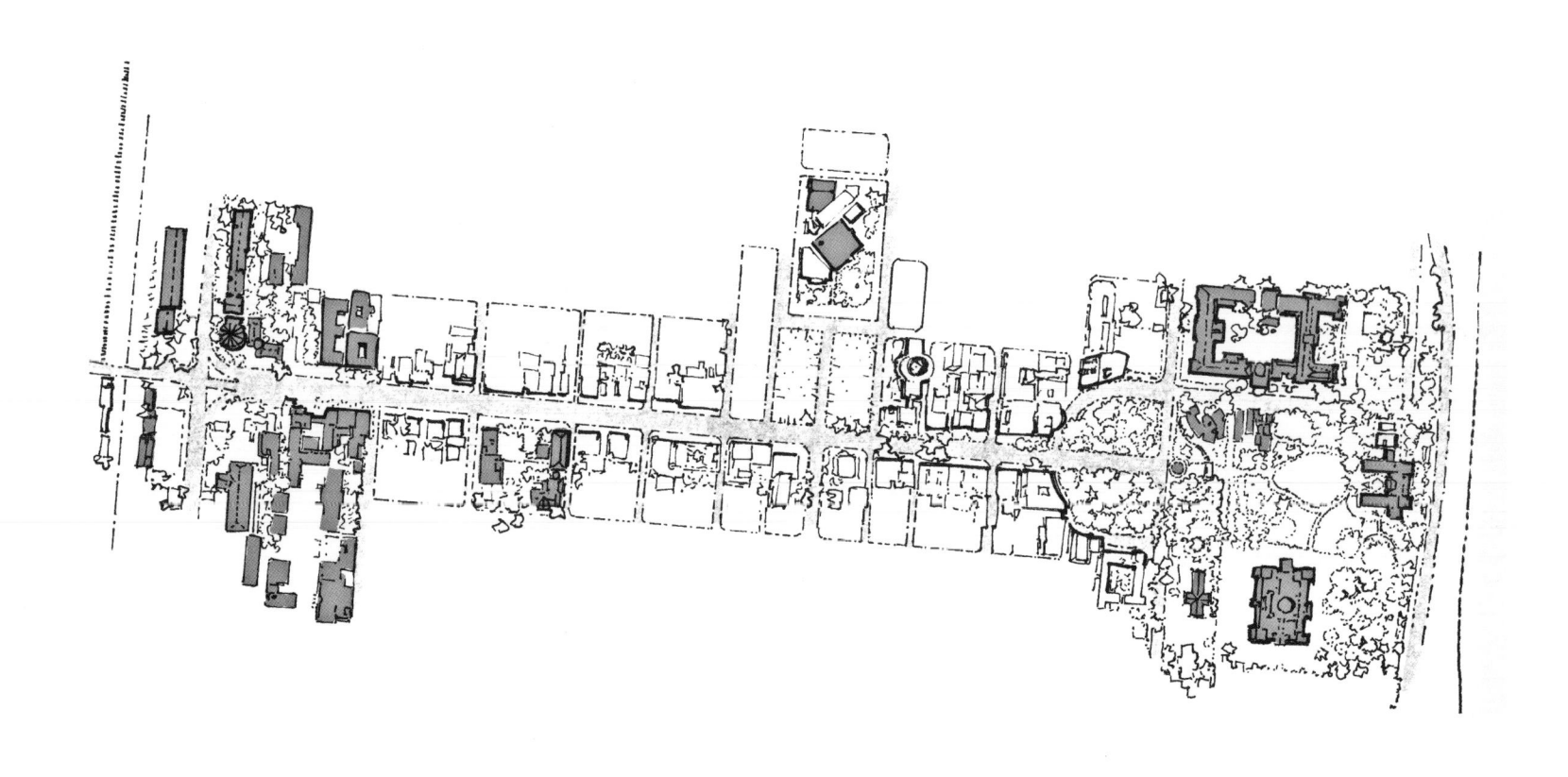

NORTHERN AFRICA **125**

1 Sudan National Museum & Fellowship Hall
2 6th of April Gardens
3 Khartoum Botanical Garden
4 Blue Nile
5 White Nile
6 Coptic Church
7 Republican Palace & Museum
8 Al-Shuhada Park
9 Al-Kabir Mosque
10 Southern Private Hospital
11 Faculty of Medicine & Pharmacy, University of Khartoum
12 Khartoum Central Train & Bus Station
13 Commonwealth War Cemetery
14 Roman Catholic Church & Farouq Mosque
15 University of Khartoum
16 Al-Salaam Gardens & Burri Cemetery
17 Khartoum International Airport
18 El-Qurashi Gardens
19 Abdul Moneim Square
20 Farouq Cemetery
21 Mosque

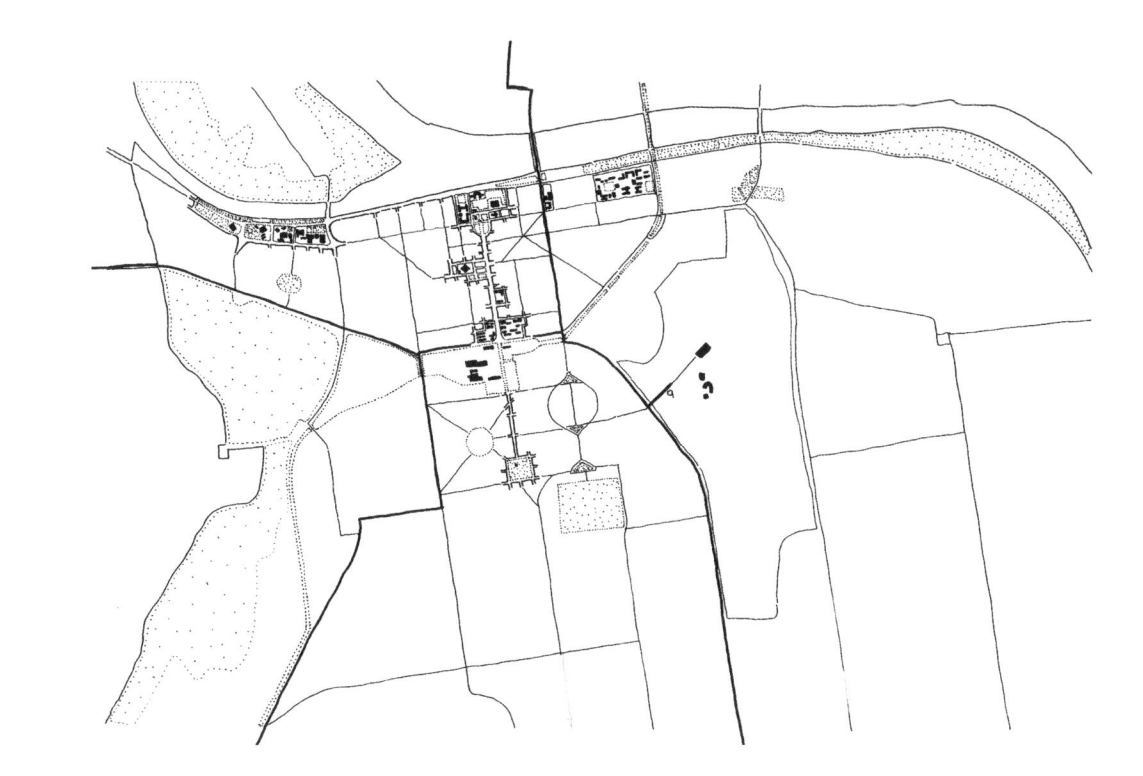

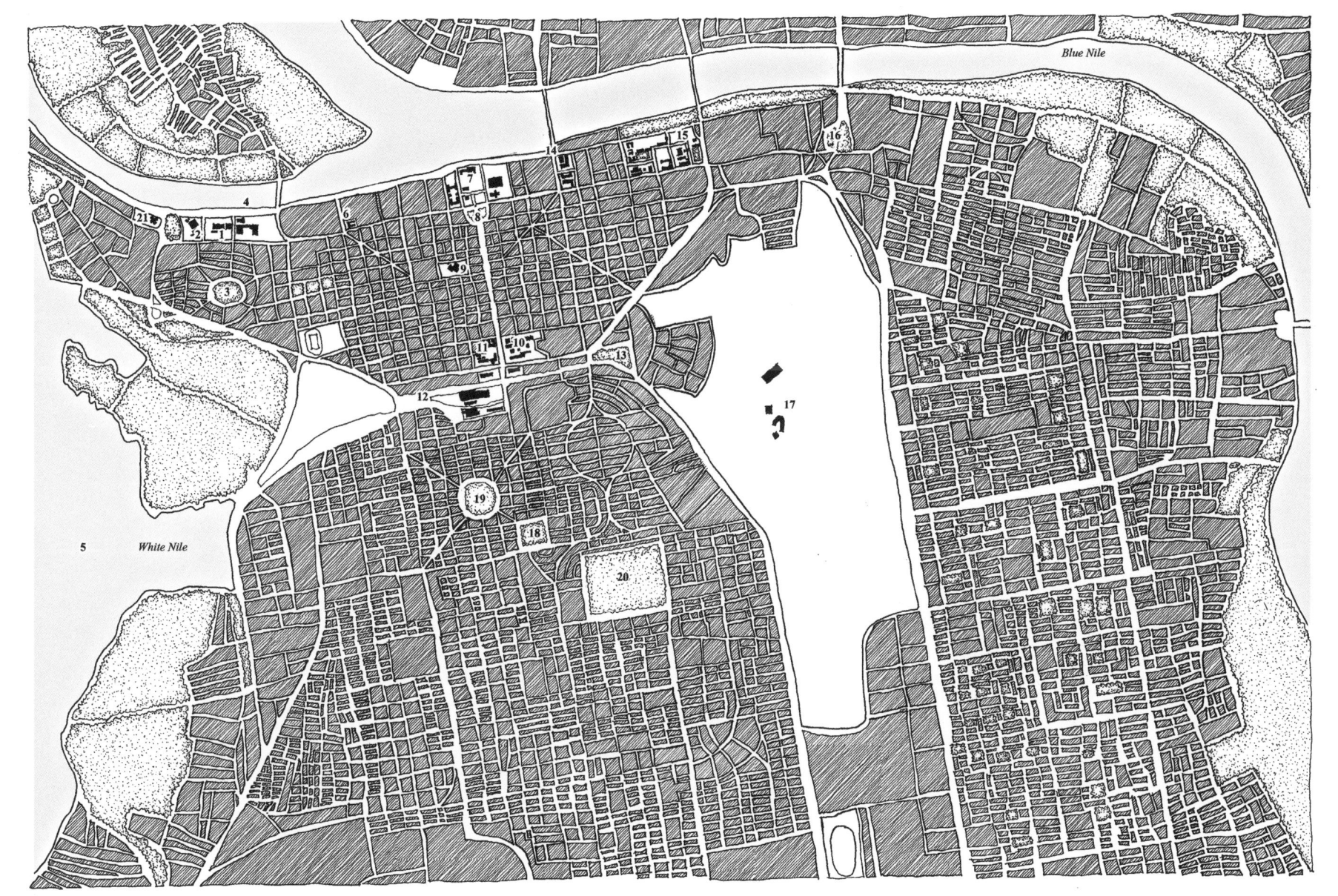

KAIROUAN, TUNISIA

FOUNDED: circa 670
AREA: approximately 70 ha
POPULATION (2003): 150,000
DENSITY: unknown
GPS: 35° 40'39.84"N, 10° 6'6.81"E
35° 40'27.62"N, 10° 6'3.54"E
35° 40'55.85"N, 10° 6'9.83"E

Kairouan is an inland city in Tunisia, referred to as the Islamic Cultural Capital, and is a UNESCO World Heritage Site. Arabs founded the city circa 670 and it became a prominent centre for Islamic learning. Its Great Mosque, rebuilt in the ninth century, is a universal architectural masterpiece.

The medina – the old walled part of a North African town – and its outskirts represent all the components of an Arab-Muslim town. Kairouan Medina is a trapezoid-shaped urban site measuring 52 ha, with a north-south structuring axis, called the Rue du 7 Novembre, prominently off-centre towards the west. It links the two main gates of the walled city while giving access to the souks at the heart of the urban fabric.

Openings in the fabric consist of the courtyards of houses, narrow streets, dead ends and squares. Squares are concentrated on the fringes of the urban fabric, in the north and east of the city and around the Great Mosque. The Place Jraba, which forms an integral part of the souks, stands out as the most prominent square. The streets of the medina are between 3 and 5 m wide and the buildings alongside them are no higher than one storey. The streets are marked with architectural landmarks that often announce the transition between different types of streets and squares. Dead ends represent the transition between the street and private space and are considered to be the immediate extension of the Driba or Skifa (entrance hall). The most prominent house would be located at the end of a dead-end street, with more modest homes in front. The methodical establishment of large houses along the main streets is characteristic of the Kairouan Medina. Running perpendicular to the main artery of Rue du 7 Novembre and in the heart of the medina, the souks form the largest mass of urban fabric.

The Kairouan Medina is a unique living museum of Arab-Muslim art and architecture owing to its monuments, souks, houses and streets which are still powerful witnesses to its past.

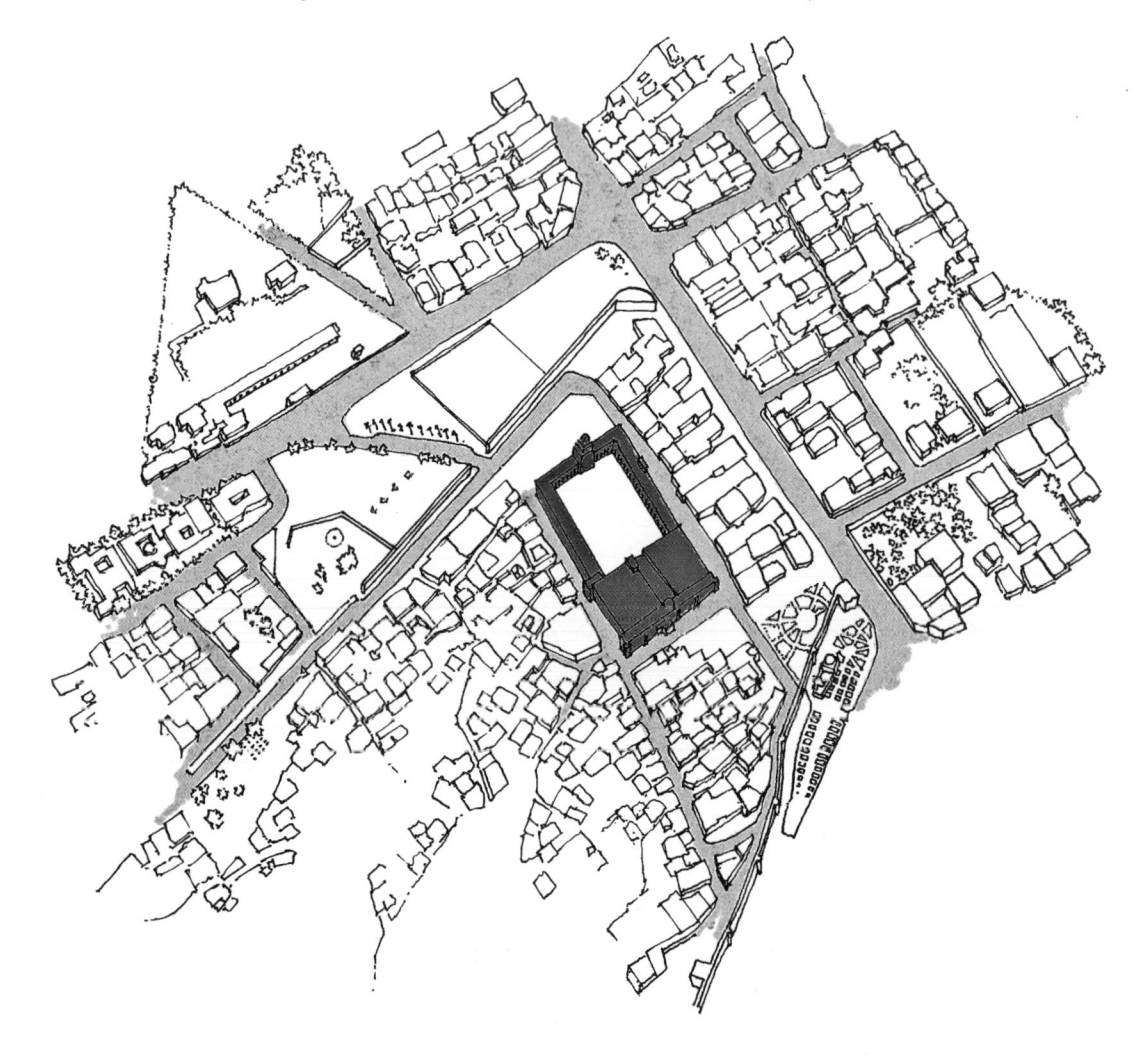

1 Place Martyrs
2 Old City of Kairouan
3 Cultural Centre & Negra Mosque
4 Great Mosque
5 Cemetery
6 Aghlabid Pools
7 Zaouia Sidi Sahab Cemetery
8 Koraïch Cemetery
9 Sidi Afra Tomb & Cemetery
10 Victory Square
11 Mosque of Three Doors

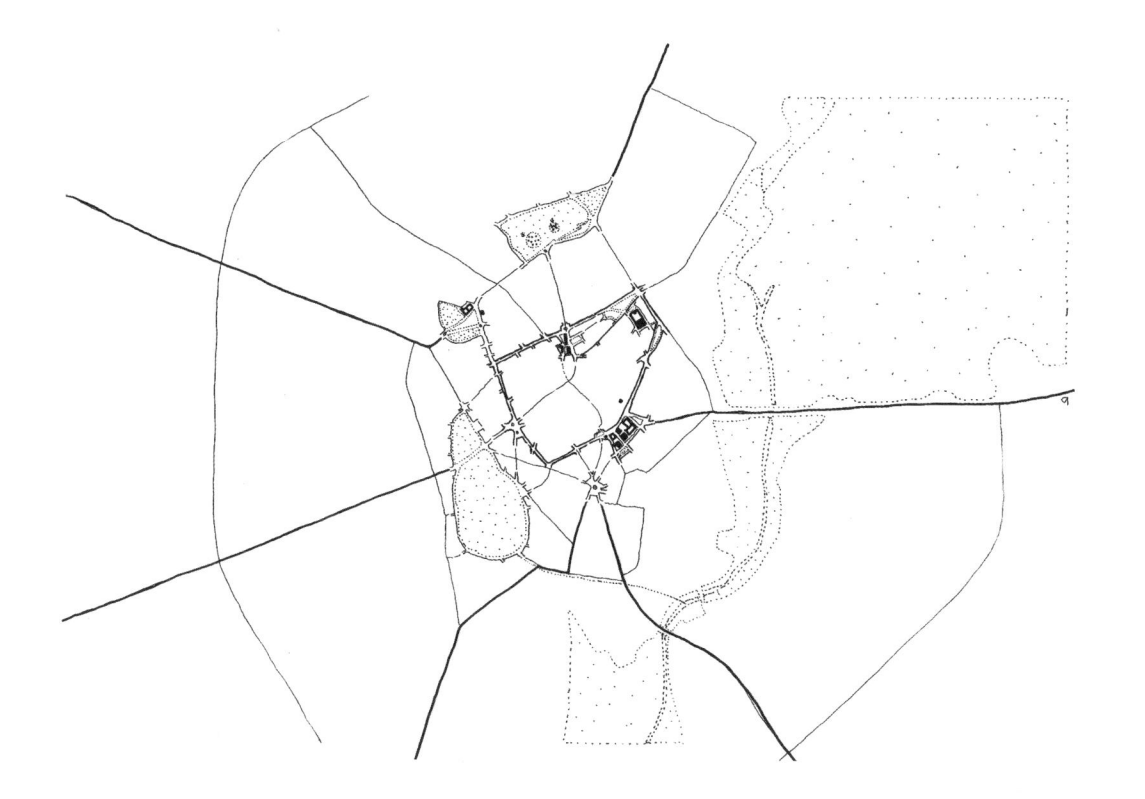

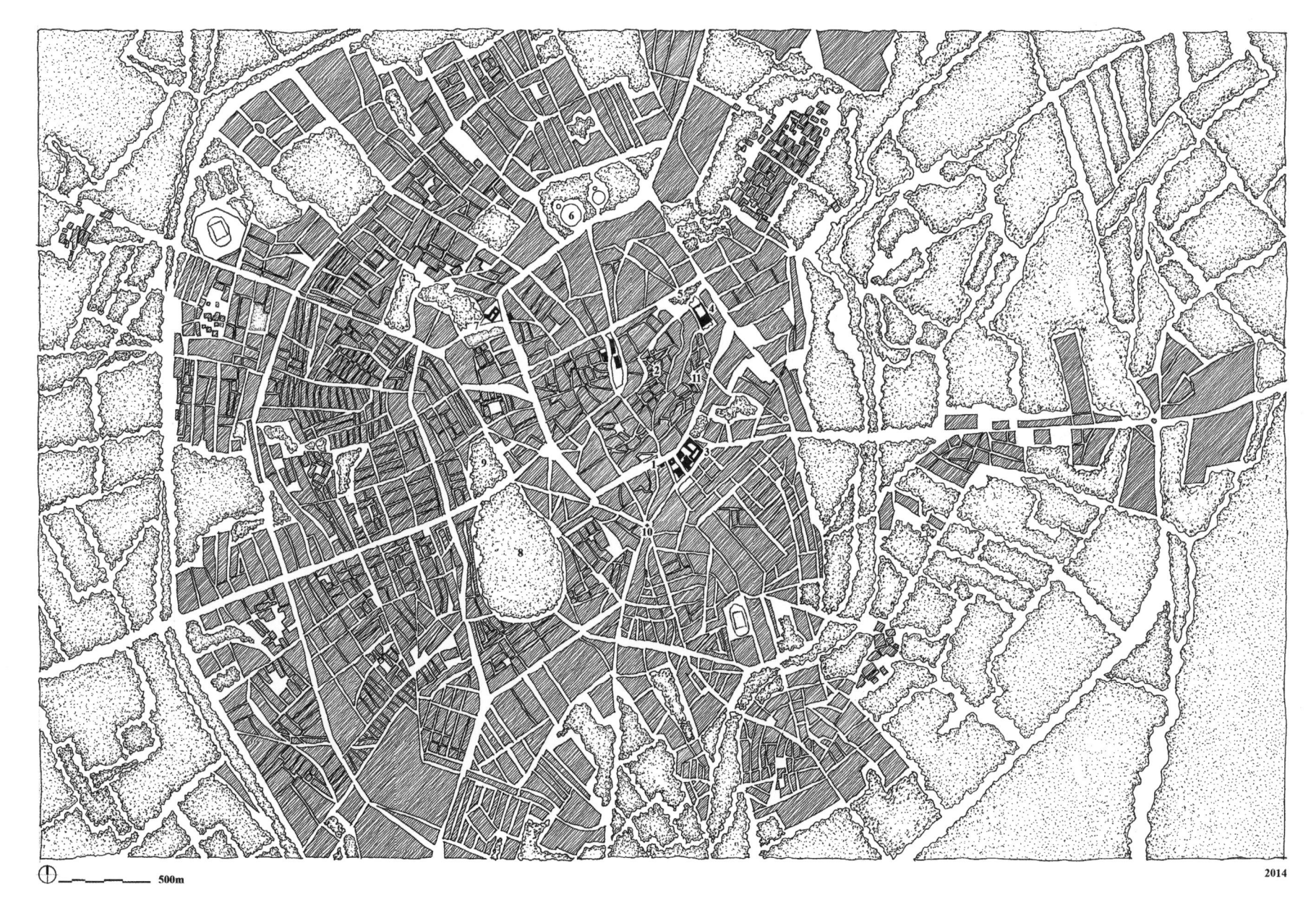

SFAX, TUNISIA

FOUNDED: 849
AREA: unknown
POPULATION (2005): 340,000
DENSITY: unknown
GPS: 34° 44'0.22"N, 10° 45'51.59"E
    34° 43'58.70"N, 10° 45'48.04"E

Sfax is Tunisia's second-largest city after its capital Tunis and is a major port, market, and transportation hub. It is also Tunisia's commercial centre. Ferries to the Kerkennah Islands leave from Sfax, and the nearby airport handles international flights. Industrial stagnation and escalating unemployment challenges faced the city during the late 1990s to early 2000s and impacted its growth trajectory. Plans were developed by the local authority to revitalise the area and its economy.

Built on the site of two small settlements of antiquity, the city of Sfax grew as an early Islamic trading centre. The old walled city, namely the medina quarter, is highly visible in the urban fabric. The Sfax Medina holds the city's tenth-century Great Mosque – built after the Great Mosque of Kairouan – at its centre and the casbah (or "citadel") is surrounded by the original ramparts built during the ninth century.

According to Salat (2010), the Friday Mosque is usually at the centre of the classical medina with souks that closely encircle the mosque. This is in such a way that the shops mask the presence of the mosque completely. Thus, the mosque literally disappears from view, and only the minaret is there to hint at its presence. Salat describes the Friday Mosque as the invisible heart of the medina.

Salat further explains that the opposition between "a single centre and a linear perimeter forms the basis of the medina's primary structure: the relationship between the centre and the periphery regulates the city's internal functions and determines the positioning of the different economic and cultural agents within it. At some distance from the central souks, the residential quarters form a homogeneous continuous fabric within the medina. The housing blocks of the medina are formed by a gradual and homogeneous additive process based on a single type: the courtyard house. The houses are situated as far as possible from the centres of public and commercial activity, at the heart of the blocks located at the ends of cul-de-sacs".

The Sfax Medina reflects the dramatic change in street patterns and in the urban grid size between the historic Arabic city and the current road system. While the medina was earlier a walkable city, it is now surrounded by a sprawling car city.

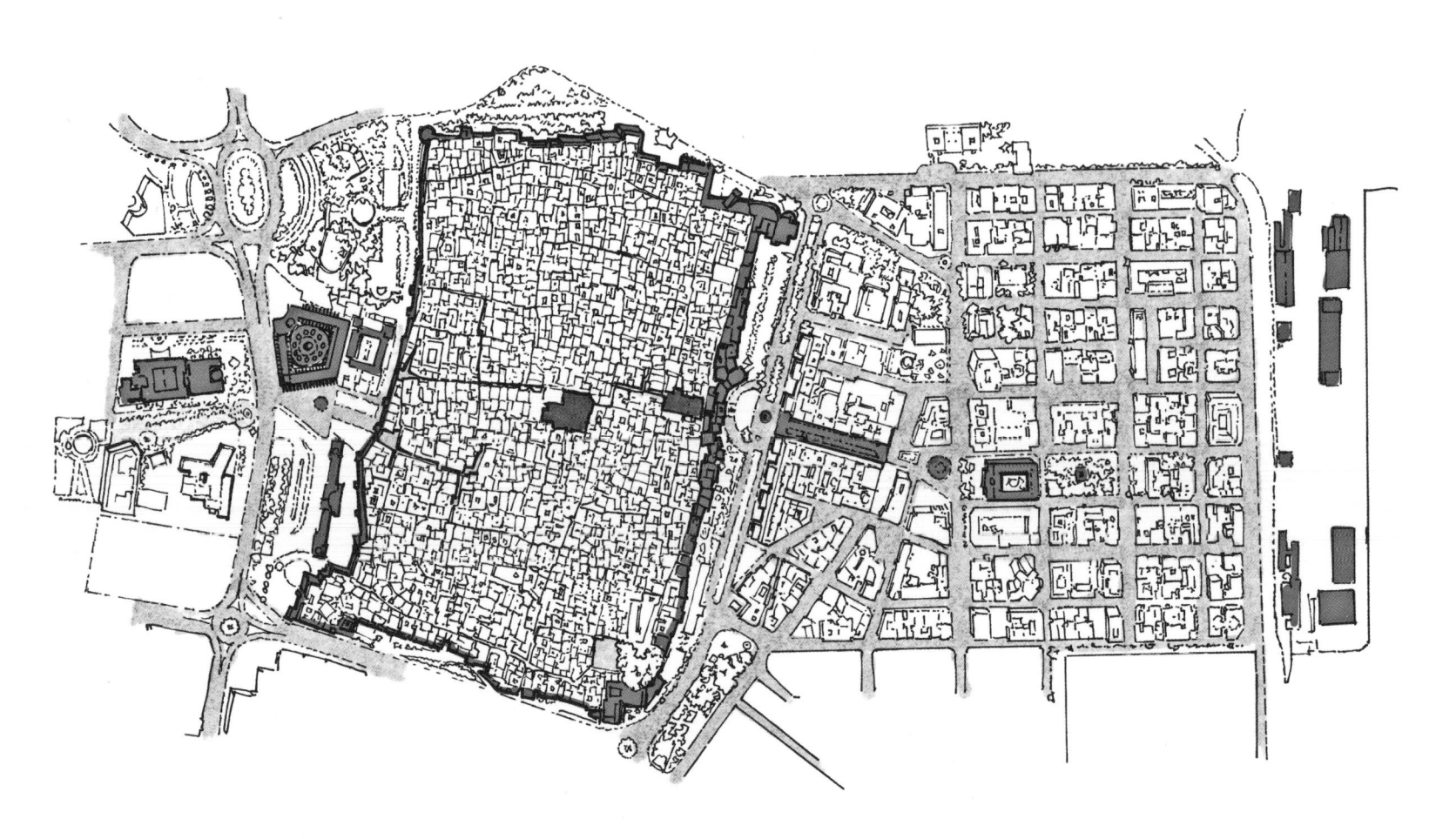

NORTHERN AFRICA

1 Old City of Sfax & Dar Jallouli Museum
2 Great Mosque
3 Bab Diwan Gate
4 Fish Market
5 New Mosque
6 Gardens for Mother & Child
7 Republic Square
8 Sfax Municipality
9 Municipal Park
10 Commercial Port of Sfax
11 Central Train Station
12 Central Market
13 Finance Building
14 Park Dakar
15 Technical School April 9, 1938
16 Palace of Justice
17 Borj Ennar Fort
18 Nasria School
19 Hedi Chaker & Habib Bourguiba Hospitals
20 Faculty of Medicine of Sfax
21 Taïeb Mhiri Stadium
22 Zoo Touta
23 Hedi Chaker School

TUNIS, TUNISIA

FOUNDED: unknown
URBAN AREA: 212 km²
POPULATION: 790,000 (2011)
URBAN AREA DENSITY: 9,406/km²
GPS: 36° 48'27.51"N, 10° 11'8.88"E
  36° 47'48.10"N, 10° 10'49.28"E
  36° 47'43.44"N, 10° 10'45.74"E

Tunis, capital and largest city of Tunisia, is located in the northeastern part of the country on Lake Tunis. It is thus connected to the Mediterranean Sea's Gulf of Tunis by a canal which terminates at the port of La Goulette/Halq al Wadi.

The city, built on a hill, slopes down towards Lake Tunis where it stretches along the coastal plain and the hills that surround it. It is located at the crossroads of a narrow strip of land between Lake Tunis and Séjoumi – the isthmus between them, called the "Tunis dome" (hills of limestone and sediments) by geologists, forms a natural bridge and links Tunis with several major roads.

As typically seen in North African cities, the medina is the historical heart of the city. The medina, a UNESCO World Heritage Site since 1979, contains roughly 700 monuments, including palaces, mosques, mausoleums, madrasas and fountains dating from the Almohad and the Hafsid periods. These include: The Great Mosque (with the Muslim University and library) Aghlabid Ez-Zitouna Mosque ("Mosque of the Olive") built in 723 by Obeid Allah Ibn-al-Habhab to celebrate the new capital, the Dar-al-Bey, or Bey's Palace, as well as the tenth-century palace of Ziadib-Allah II al Aghlab. The medina, as seen with other Moslem cities in North Africa, were not laid out according to a strict grid or geometric street plans. The buildings were arranged based on a socio-cultural code, according to the types of complex human relations. The street therefore became an extension of the private domain, shaped by the built form. The new city was gradually developed east of the original city centre by the French at the end of the nineteenth century. The new city is structured around the axis of the tree-lined Avenue Habib Bourguiba (designed to be the Tunisian form of the Champs-Élysées) where colonial-era buildings are in clear contrast to smaller, older structures. The city expanded with residential and business districts in the northern end, while the south developed into industrial districts and accommodates the lower-income population.

Although population growth is not as severe as in other northern African countries, it nevertheless will result in a gradually changing landscape of urban sprawl with associated social challenges brought about by rapid modernisation.

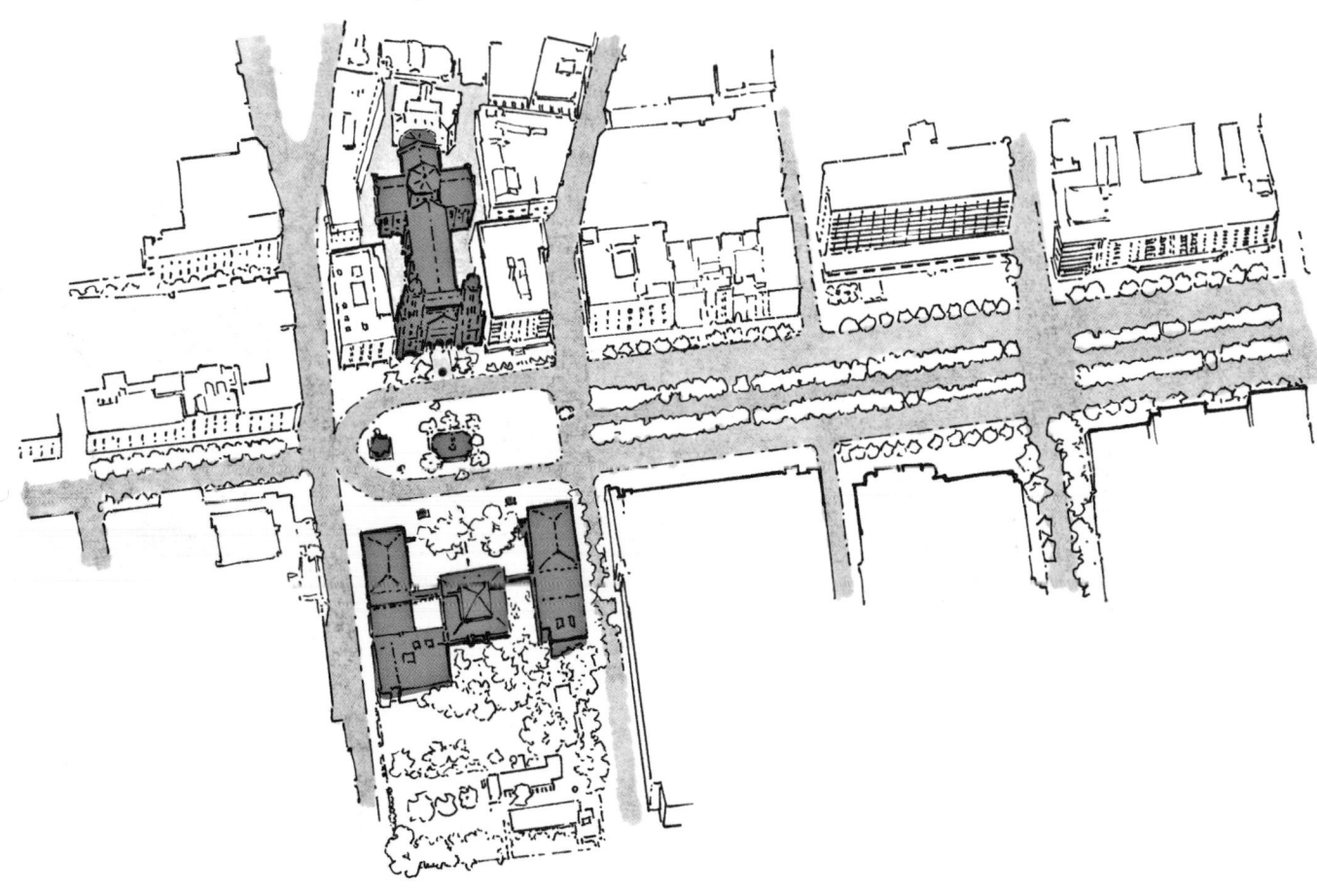

NORTHERN AFRICA **131**

1 Old Tunis
2 Victory Square
3 Government Square
4 Dar el-Bey & Government Palace
5 Tunis Hotel
6 Hammouda Pacha Mosque & Mausoleum
7 Dar El-Haddad & Mosque El-Kssar
8 Mohammed Bey & Zaouia Sidi Mehrez Mosques
9 Dar Lasram & Palais Kheïreddin
10 St George's Anglican Church
11 Independence Square
12 Cathedral of St Vincent de Paul
13 Municipal Theatre of Tunis
14 14th January 2011 Square
15 Barcelona Square
16 Central Train Station
17 Habib Thameur Park
18 Human Rights Square
19 National Congress
20 Artisan Palace
21 City of Culture
22 Belvedere Park & Zoo
23 Al-Jallaz Cemetery
24 Courthouse
25 Charles Nicolle Hospital & Emergency
26 Central Market
27 Port

LAÂYOUNE (EL AAIÚN), WESTERN SAHARA

FOUNDED: 1938
CITY AREA: unknown
CITY POPULATION (2010): 196,331
CITY DENSITY: unknown
GPS: 27° 9'48.73"N, 13° 12'17.95"W
27° 9'27.64"N, 13° 12'26.30"W

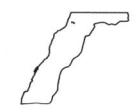

A former Spanish colony, Western Sahara is Africa's last "open file" at the United Nations Decolonisation Committee as a non-self-governing territory. Its only major populated city, Laayoune (also El-Aaiun, El-Ayoun, al-Ayun) is a city created *ex nihilo* on the edge of the desert with seemingly nothing else around it.

Laayoune is the largest city in Western Sahara and the capital of one of the three provinces that Morocco established in the territory, served by the Hassan I Airport. Located 13 km inland from the Atlantic Ocean, it lies in an artificial oasis where crops are grown through irrigation. The discovery of drinking water at the site resulted in the establishment of a Spanish military garrison in 1938, marking the beginning of the town with its barracks established along the northern banks of the dry river of Saguia el Hamra that divides the settlement into two. In 1958, the town was made the capital of Spain's new Sahara province. It was also the administrative and military centre. The Spanish authorities subsequently established a port on the Atlantic coast 30 km from the town, along with facilities for the export of newly discovered valuable phosphates. The Spanish constructed their colonial town along the southern banks of the dry river. A cathedral from that era is still used today. Behind the cathedral, the Moroccans constructed the Place Mechouar, which hosts four Moroccan-inspired towers and the Palais de Justice in the centre. As an Islamic centre and in a typical Northern African tradition, buildings have flat roofs, small apertures, and many courtyards that characterise the horizontal city. A very unusual feature of the city, to the south-west of the library, is the 1967-Aaiún Hexagons mass-housing development for locals.

According to the 2014 UN-Habitat report, Morocco laid claim to the 266,000 km² phosphate-rich territory of Western Sahara over the objections of the armed liberation movement Polisario Front, a local Saharawi rebel group – which proclaimed the territory's independence as the Sahrawi Arab Democratic Republic (SADR). The SADR is currently recognised by 50 states and by the African Union, leading to Morocco's withdrawal from that organisation. Negotiations about a referendum to decide the territory's future are currently frozen, and Polisario has threatened to resume its liberation struggle.

Morocco has sought to consolidate its control of the region by implementing large-scale infrastructure projects in addition to hospitals, schools, a football stadium and the expansion of drinking water facilities.

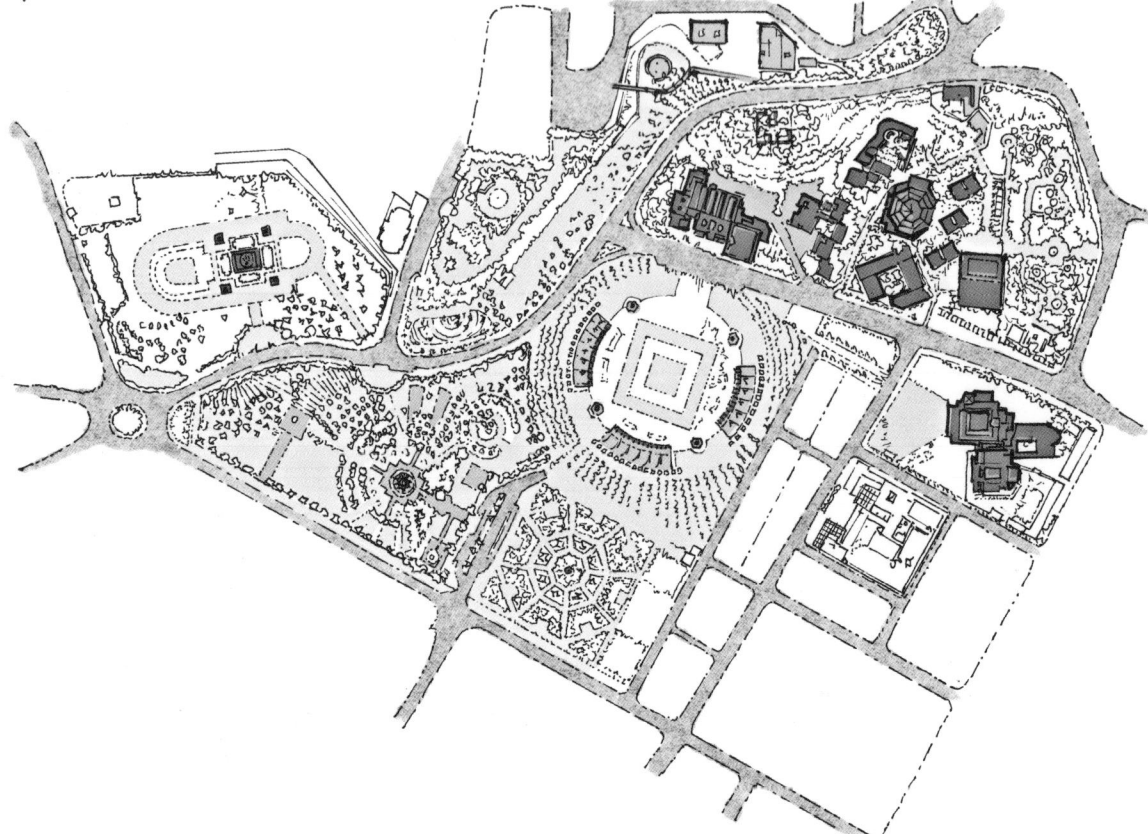

1 Place El-Mchawar
2 National Congress
3 Moulay Abdel Aziz Mosque
4 Birds Garden
5 Municipal Park
6 Spanish Cathedral
7 Municipal Office
8 Souk Lamkhakh
9 Mosque
10 Institute for Management & Information
11 Lissan Eddine & Hassan II Schools
12 Great Library
13 Military Hospital
14 Military Zone
15 Moulay Hassan Ibn al-Mahdi Hospital
16 Sheikh Mohammed Laghdaf Stadium
17 Hassan Airport
18 Old Legion Barracks
19 Place of Resistance
20 Hassan I College
21 Mosque
22 Ibno Khaldun School
23 Miftah al-Hamd Mosque
24 Auxiliary Forces

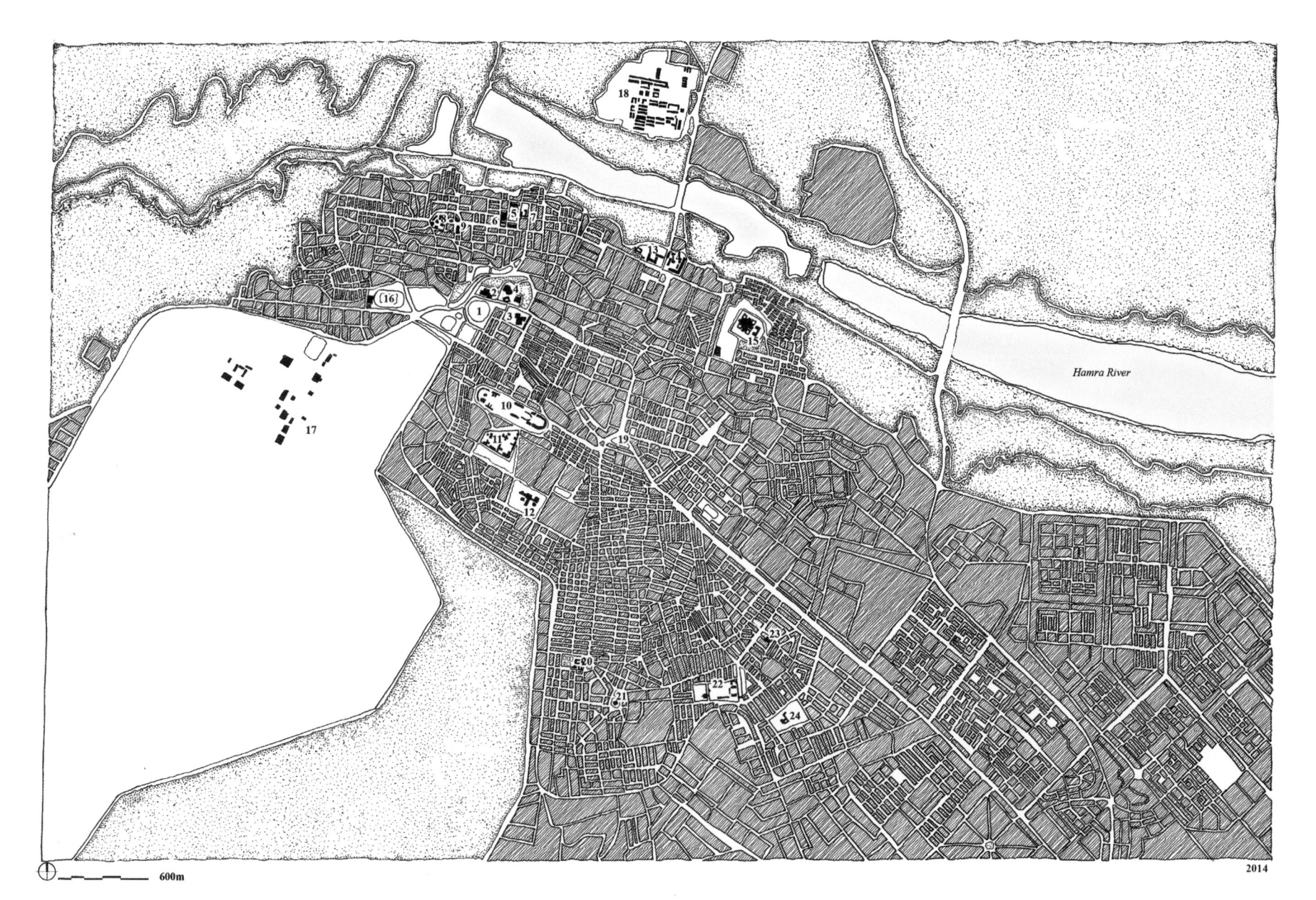

GABARONE, BOTSWANA

FOUNDED: 1964
URBAN AREA: 169 km²
POPULATION: 231,626 (2011)
URBAN AREA DENSITY: 1,400/km²
GPS: 24° 39'29.38"S, 25° 54'42.31"E

Gaborone, capital and largest city of Botswana, is located between Kgale and Oodi Hills on the Notwane River in the south-eastern corner of the country.

The city was originally designed with pedestrian walkways and large open spaces, based on the garden city principles. The city centre is structured along a central axis bordered by commercial businesses, referred to as "the Mall". The government offices are located in the semicircle-shaped area at one end of the axis, west of the Mall, while the eastern end is home to the Gaborone City Council, the Civic Centre and the Pula Arch that commemorates Botswana's independence. Geoffrey Cornish famously likened the layout of the CBD to the shape of a "brandy glass".

The greater part of the city was constructed within three years. The rapid construction of the city resulted in a substantial influx of labourers who built illegal settlements on the new city's southern industrial development zone, which was later rezoned to a low-income housing area. As one of the fastest-growing cities in Africa, Gaborone is experiencing increased pressure. Originally planned for 20,000 inhabitants, rural-urban migration has led to the development of a sprawling city where land acquisition is now sought from the surrounding commercial farms and tribal areas. The city was originally developed along the railway line which still remains an important link today, cutting across the city in a north-south direction. The railway station is located just south of the Parliament House.

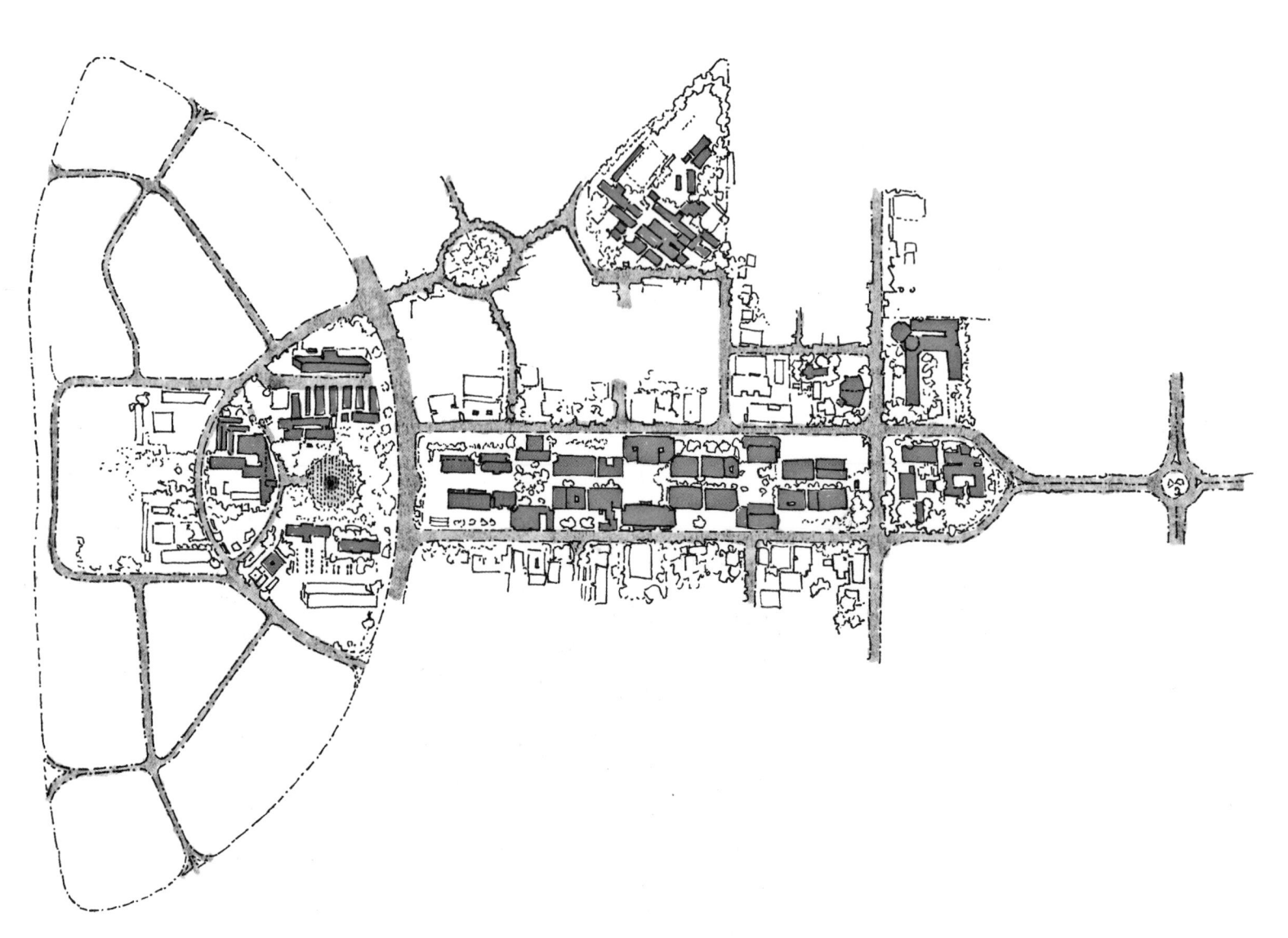

1 National Assembly
2 Park & Sir Seretse Khama Statue
3 Department of Education
4 Department of Home Affairs
5 British Council & Debswana House
6 Gaborone City Council
7 National Museum and Art Gallery
8 National Stadium
9 Princess Marine Hospital
10 University Of Botswana
11 University Of Botswana Stadium
12 University Of Botswana Teaching Hospital
13 Gaborone Central Train Station
14 Ben Thema Primary School, Ext 2 Clinic & Gaborone Seventh-day Adventists Church
15 Thornhill School
16 Three Dikgosi Monument
17 Botswana High Court
18 Department of Youth, Sports & Culture
19 Faculty of Engineering & Technology East Campus
20 Bostwana Polytechnic College
21 Bostwana National Productivity Centre
22 University of Botswana Village
23 Gaborone Nature Reserve & Visitors Centre
24 Botswana Examinations Council

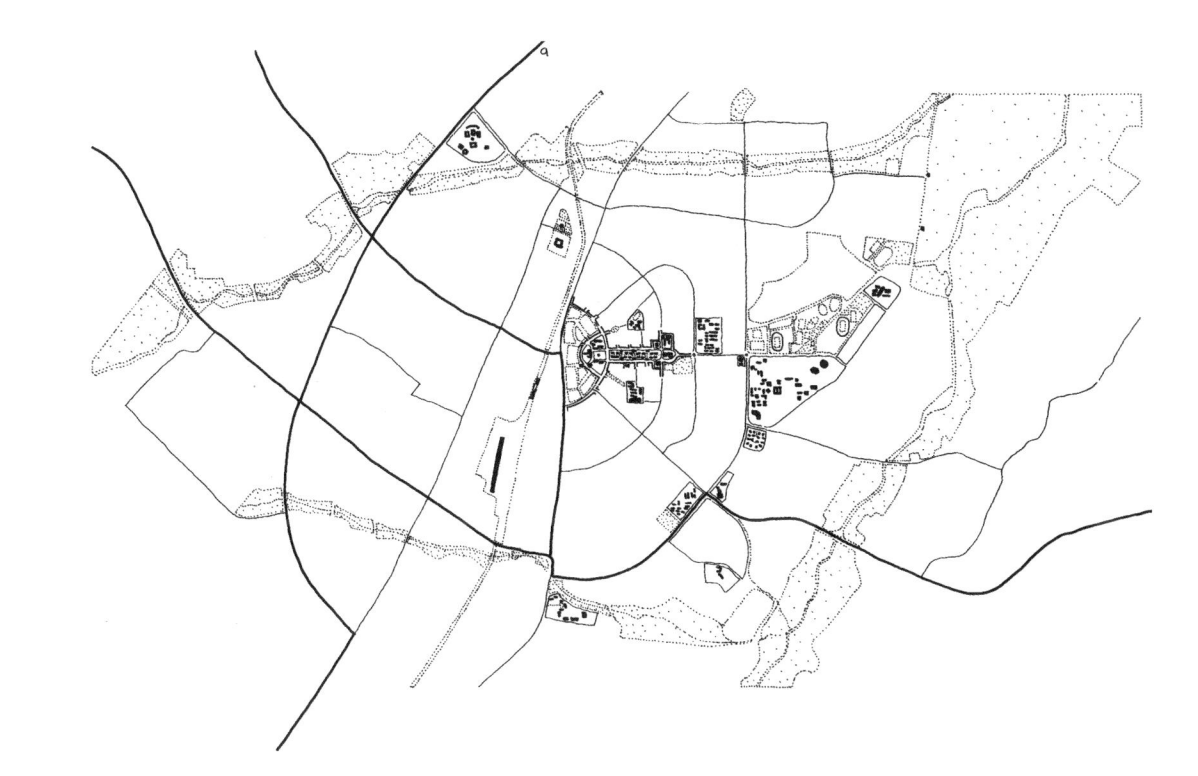

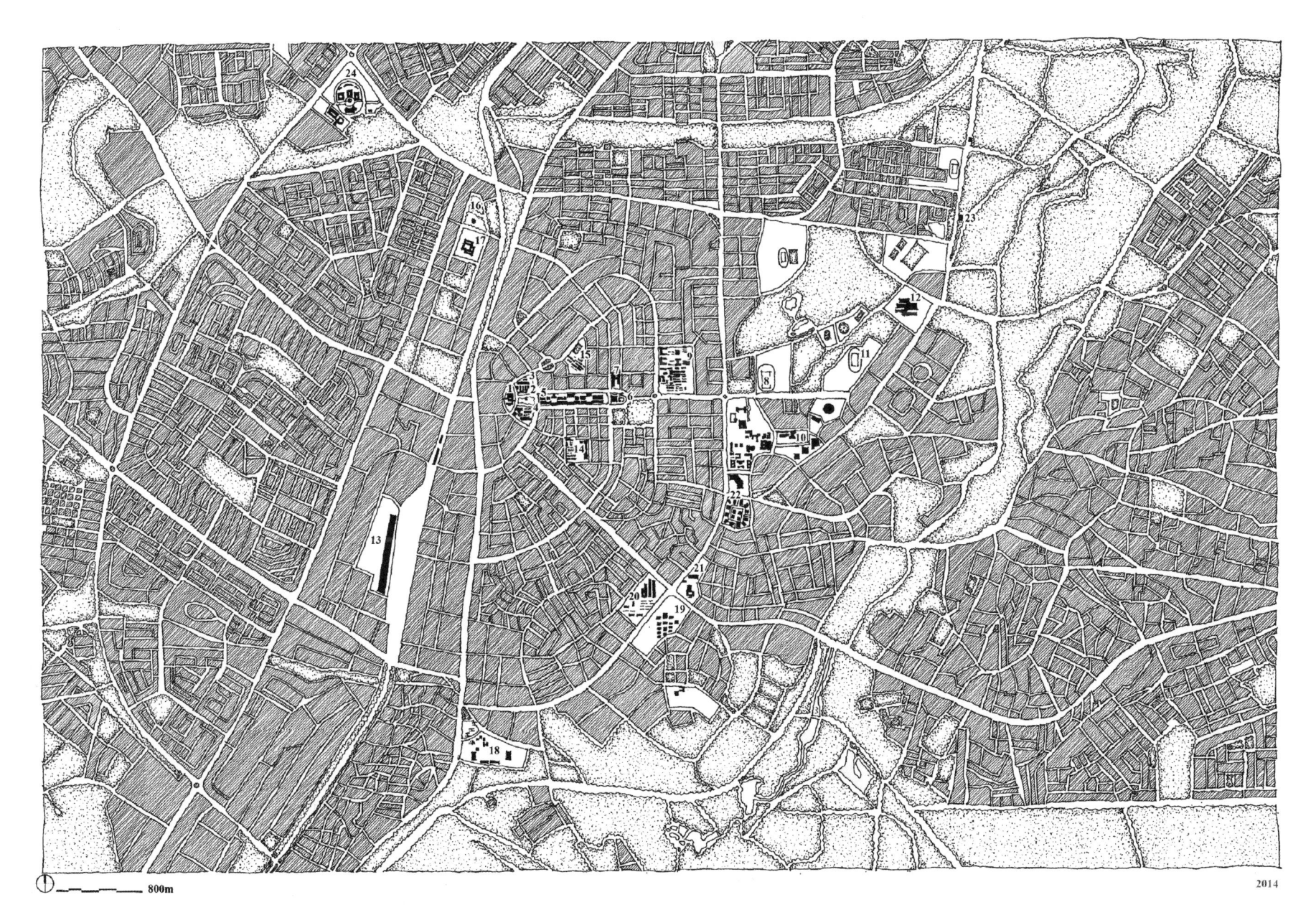

WINDHOEK, NAMIBIA

FOUNDED: 1890
URBAN AREA: 5,133 km²
POPULATION: 268,132
URBAN AREA DENSITY: 63 km²
GPS: 22° 34'2.35"S, 17° 5'15.28"E

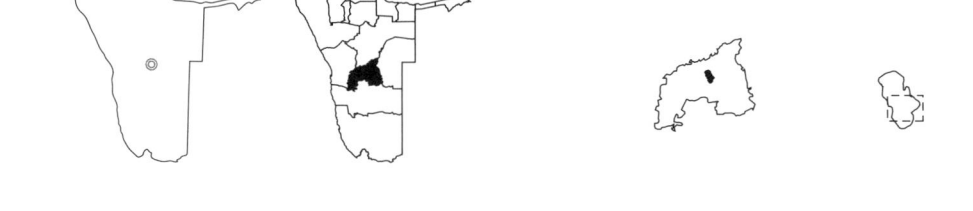

Windhoek, capital and largest city of the Republic of Namibia, is located in central Namibia in the Khomas Highland plateau area on a sloping plain. Windhoek is the social, economic and cultural centre of Namibia. The town was initially established when Jonker Afrikaner built a stone church for his community close to a permanent spring in the area. The original town was unfortunately destroyed during rivalry struggles, with nothing remaining but neglected fruit trees.

The town was re-established in 1890 when the remains of the stone fort (Old Fortress) was fixed up by Von Francois. The town rapidly expanded from 1907 as rural-urban migration saw an influx of people moving to Windhoek. Large commercial buildings and the three castles (Heinitzburg, Sanderburg, and Schwerinsburg) were constructed during this period.

The development of Windhoek slowly waned, only picking up again in 1955 when large buildings such as schools and hospitals were built and major roads were tarred.

Windhoek's expansion is hampered by the area's topography, the rocky mountainous landscape surrounding the city, and the natural springs towards the south. The Brakwater area in the north remains the only area suitable for future growth. Windhoek's city boundaries were nonetheless extended in 2012, with the city now encompassing a total of 5,133 km², making it the third-largest city in the world, but with a very low population density of a mere 63 people per km².

Significant landmarks in the city include the Alte Feste (Old Fortress), Christuskirche (a Lutheran church dating back to 1910), the historic centre of Windhoek, Parliament Gardens, Tintenpalast, the Heroes' Acre, the National Library of Namibia, St Marien Kathedrale and the historic Turnhalle building dating back to 1909. The three castles of Windhoek are reminders of early German colonisation.

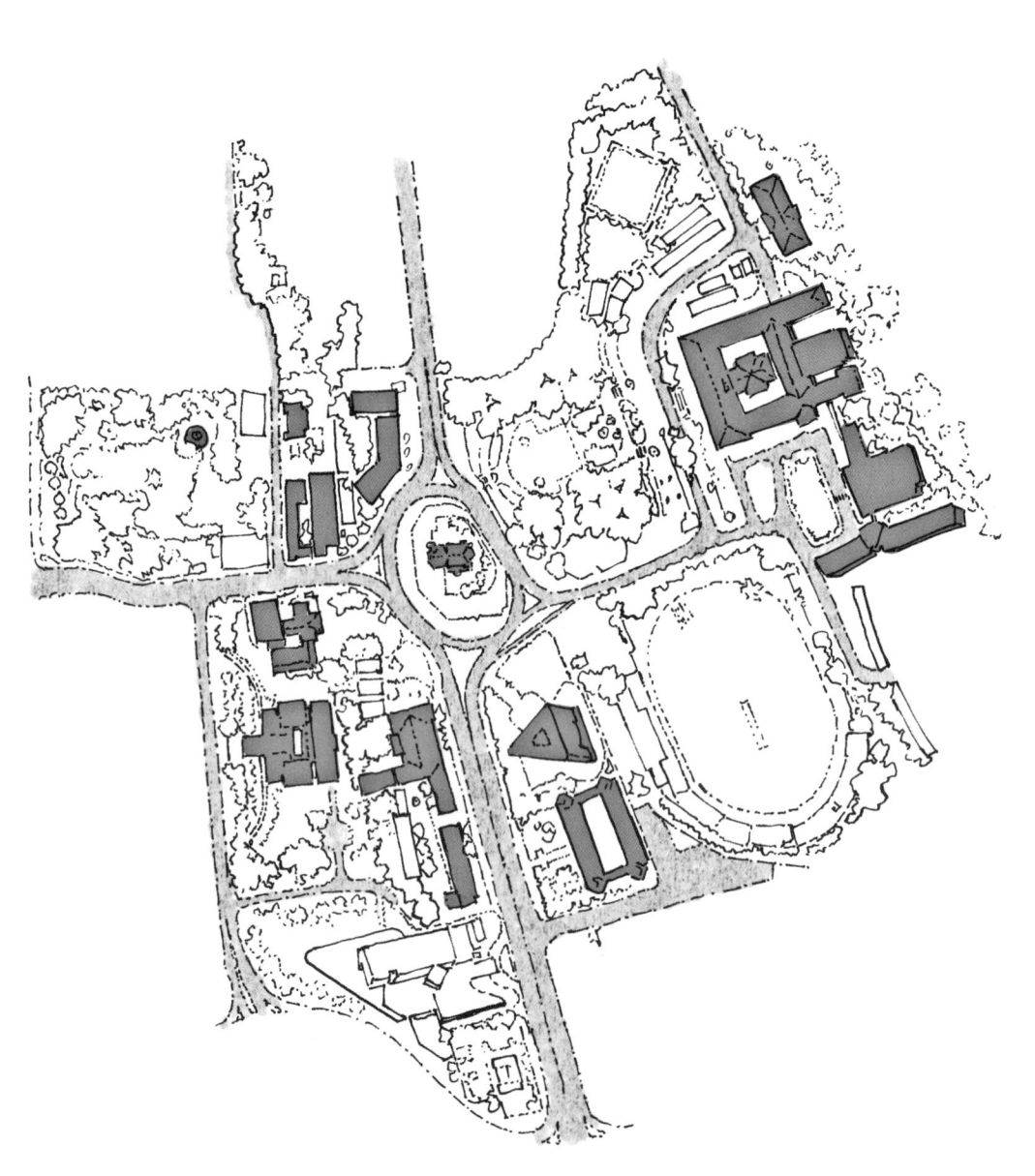

SOUTHERN AFRICA **137**

1. Parliament Gardens
2. Lutheran Church
3. Tintenpalast
4. Department of Foreign Affairs
5. Windhoek High School, Alte Feste National Museum and Stadi
6. Zoo Park, War Memorial & Old German Lutheran Church
7. Supreme Court of Namibia
8. Curt von Francois Monument
9. Park or Old Ausspannplatz
10. Church
11. Angola Embassy
12. Heinitzburg
13. Botanical Garden
14. Garden of Remembrance
15. Trans-Namib Transport Museum Central Train Station
16. Cemetery
17. Roman Catholic Church
18. German Cemetery
19. Government Office Park
20. Voortrekker Monument
21. Rider Memorial
22. Old Magistrates' Court
23. National Theatre
24. Turnhalle
25. Werth Lookout Point
26. Monument

MASERU, LESOTHO

FOUNDED: 1869
URBAN AREA: 138 km²
POPULATION: 227,880 (2006)
URBAN AREA DENSITY: 1,651/km²
GPS: 29° 18'49.75"S, 27° 28'58.82"E

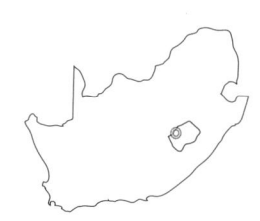

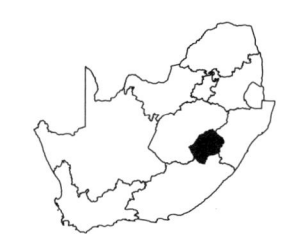

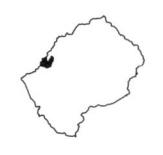

Maseru, capital of Lesotho, located on the Caledon River, was originally established as a police camp. It was named the capital in 1869 after the country became a British outpost. The city retained its status as capital after the country achieved independence in 1966. The name of the city means "place of the red sandstone" in Sesotho.

Maseru was relatively small before Lesotho's independence, enclosed within well-defined colonial boundaries with limited room for expansion. The town was used as a small police camp, explaining the limited interest of the British in developing the city. The surrounding area soon developed into a bustling market town. After independence in 1966, Maseru was faced with rapid expansion as the area increased dramatically from a mere 20 km² to the current area of 138 km². The city's commercial district is centred around two neighbouring central business districts: the eastern business district – home to smaller businesses, markets and street vendors – and the western business district with its larger commercial buildings, department stores and banks. These districts are the key employment centres, developed around Kingsway road. Colonial buildings in the city include the Cathedral of Our Lady of Victories of the Roman Catholic Archdiocese of Maseru, and the Anglican St John's Church. Other significant buildings include the Royal Palace, the Parliament Building and the State House.

The development of Maseru in close proximity to the South African border is similar to other colonial towns which developed as ports elsewhere in Africa. According to Prof. Clement Resetselemang Leduka from the Institute of Southern African Studies, the peripheral location could be a result of factors such as the "security concerns of British colonial officers who were stationed in Lesotho (the peripheral location would have ensured quick exit in times of unrest) (Machobane, 1990); the facilitation of communication with the Cape Colony, then the headquarters of British colonial administration in Lesotho; the facilitation of import and export of goods and services; or the convenience of recruitment and transfer of migrant labourers to the South African mines."

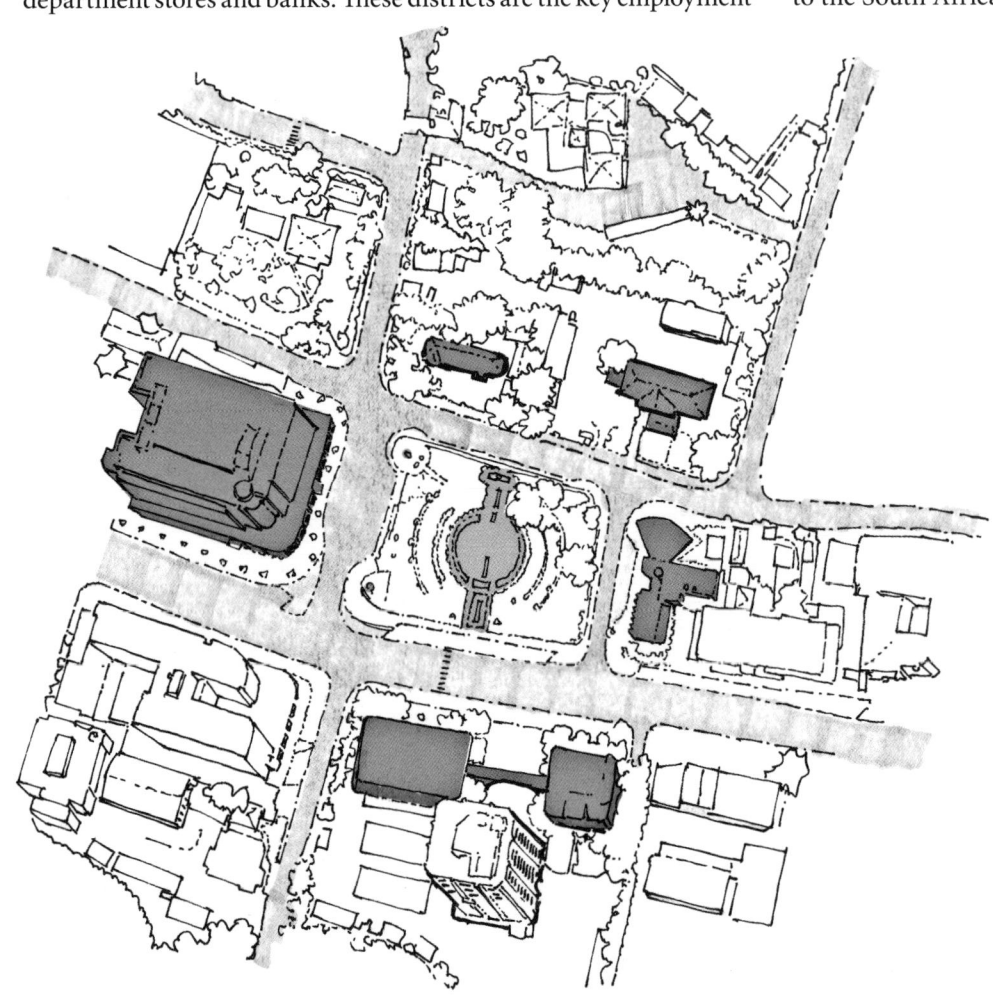

SOUTHERN AFRICA **139**

1 Makoanyane Square
2 Maseru Post Office
3 Maseru United Church
4 Our Lady of Victory Cathedral
5 Parliament Of Lesotho
6 Mathabiseng Convention Centre
7 St Joseph's High School
8 Finance House & Government Complex
9 Queen Elizabeth II Hospital
10 Setsoto Stadium
11 Mejametalana Airport
12 Republic of South Africa

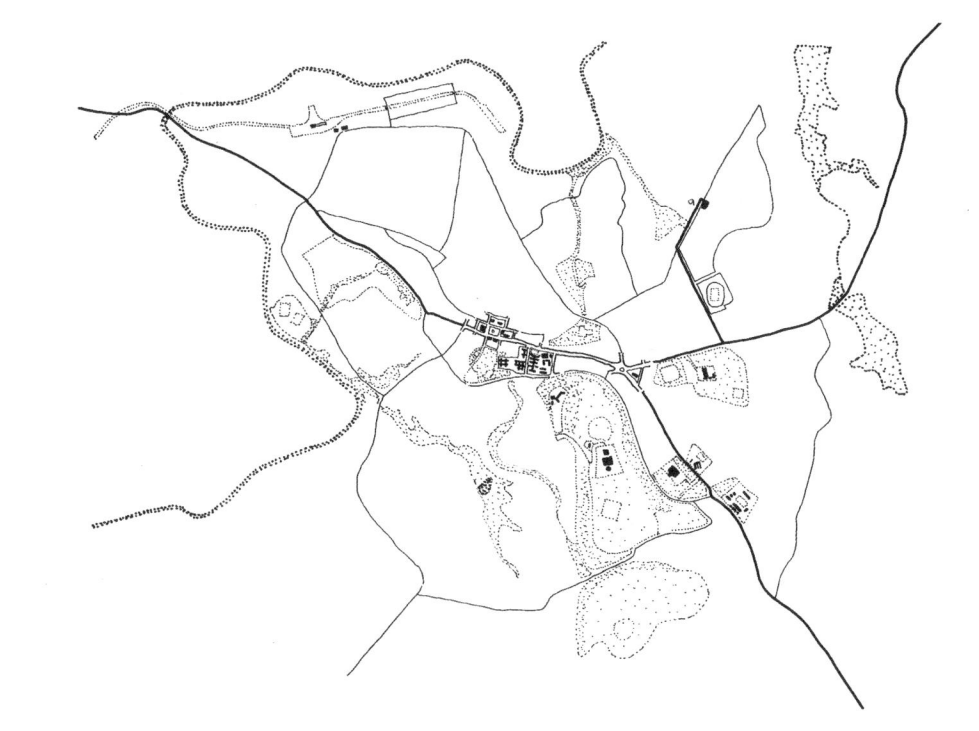

CAPE TOWN, SOUTH AFRICA

FOUNDED: 1652
METRO AREA: 2,445 km²
METRO POPULATION (2011): 3,740,026
METRO DENSITY: 1,500/km²
GPS: 33° 55'29.47"S, 18° 25'28.41"E
22° 34'2.35"S, 17° 5'15.28"E
33° 55'5.35"S, 18° 25'34.31"E
33° 55'9.93"S, 18° 25'26.13"E
34° 3'20.31"S, 18° 40'16.34"E

The city of Cape Town is considered to be one of the most beautiful cities in the world. Table Mountain, with its vertical cliffs and flat-topped summit, forms a dramatic backdrop to the central city bowl area. With rich, natural and cultural histories, tourist landmarks abound. The Castle of Good Hope is a case in point, and perhaps the most recognisable colonial inheritance in the urban fabric. Originally located on the coastline of Table Bay, the fort is now located inland following historical land reclamation. Another of many features of the city, in the heart of Cape Town's historical business district, is Greenmarket Square, originally a slave market. Today, the historical city centre is one of a multiple nodes of a polycentric metropolitan area, each playing different roles at different neighbourhood, regional and international levels. The original Dutch colonial settlement was laid out on a grid pattern, but subsequent British occupation saw the city growing organically. By the early twentieth century this had to be curbed with town planning schemes that reflected two different foreign influences: on the one hand the British garden city movement, and on the other the American idea of zoning according to use. Both of these concepts found expression in the urban form.

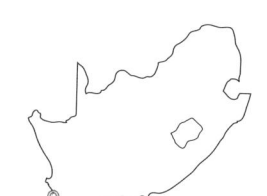

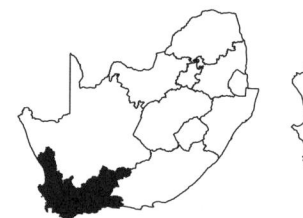

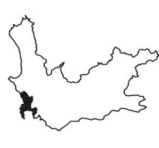

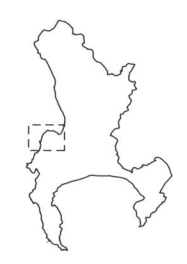

Similar to colonial cities planned elsewhere, the main objective of Cape Town's early planning was public health and the maintenance of social order, resulting in a racially segregated city expounded by the apartheid regime in subsequent decades. Freeways and the railway network were major structuring elements of the city, intentionally placed as barriers between communities. The post-apartheid city is therefore a fragmented manifestation of the hangover of spatial inequality. The poor of Cape Town continue to be housed in dormitory townships isolated from opportunities. Several newer parts of the city are located in climatically hostile areas such as the Cape Flats – an expansive, low-lying, flat area situated to the south-east of the CBD. Almost all of the communities of the Cape Flats remain poverty-stricken. In spite of progressive legislation and a huge investment in public housing and reconstruction programmes, the gap between rich and poor is ostensibly ever-increasing.

One of the more recent additions to the city's landmarks is the Cape Town Stadium, completed for the Fifa World Cup in 2010. Controversially located, the stadium is positioned on a prominent site between the sea and Signal Hill.

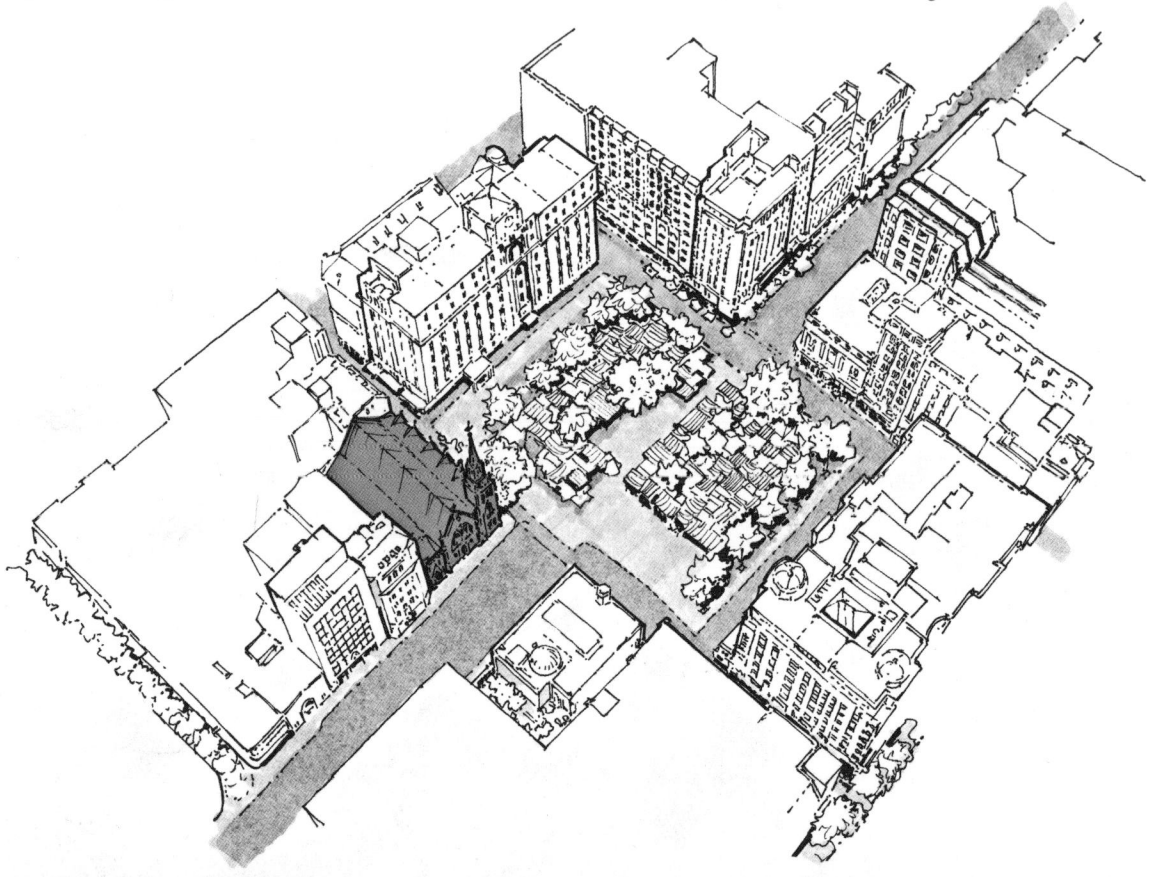

SOUTHERN AFRICA

1. The Grand Parade & Castle of Good Hope
2. City Hall
3. Cape Town Central Railway Station
4. Van Riebeeck Statue & Heerengracht
5. Bartholomew Dias Statue
6. Cape Town International Convention Centre
7. Civic Centre
8. Jetty Square
9. Thibault Square
10. Green Market Square
11. Central Methodist Church
12. St George's Cathedral
13. Library of Parliament & SA Museum Library
14. The Company Gardens
15. Slave Lodge & Cultural Historic Museum
16. House of Parliament
17. De Tuynhuys
18. Iziko South African Museum
19. Gardens Commercial High School
20. Cape Town Holocaust Centre
21. District Six Museum
22. Groote Kerk
23. Cape Peninsula University of Technology
24. Cape Town Stadium & Metropolitan Golf Course
25. Signal Hill
26. Table Mountain
27. Lions Head
28. Groote Schuur Hospital & Heart of Cape Town
29. Museum
30. District Six
31. Rhodes Memorial & University of Cape Town
32. V & A Waterfront, Market Square and Port
33. Fort Wynyard
34. Green Point Lighthouse
35. Park & Sports Fields
36. Sports Fields

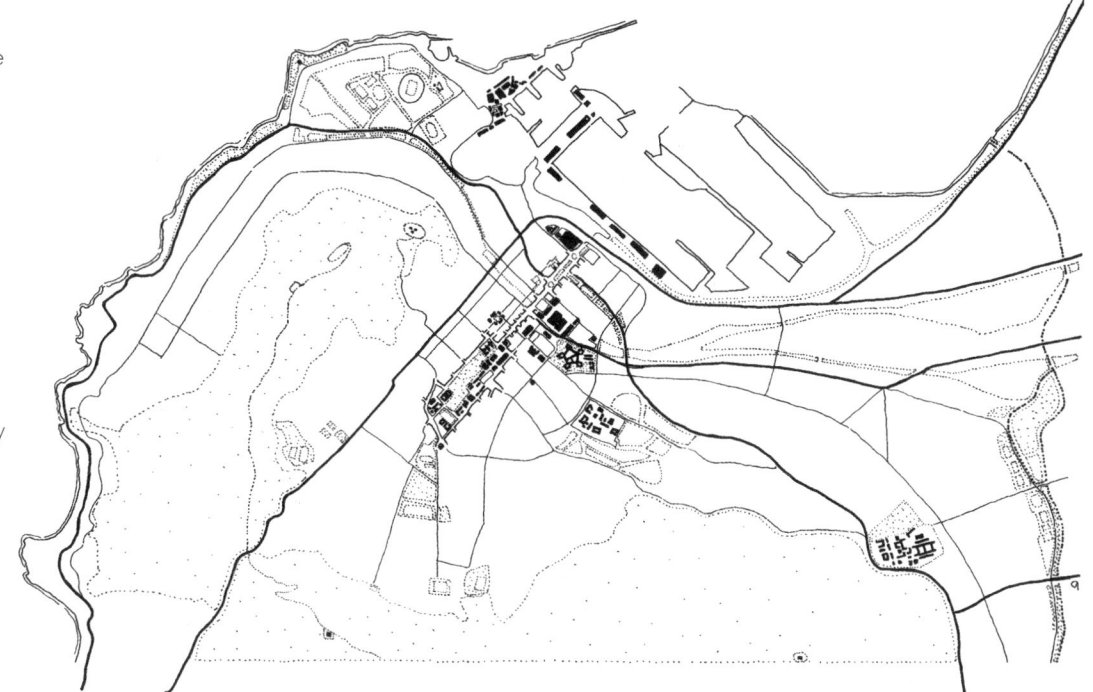

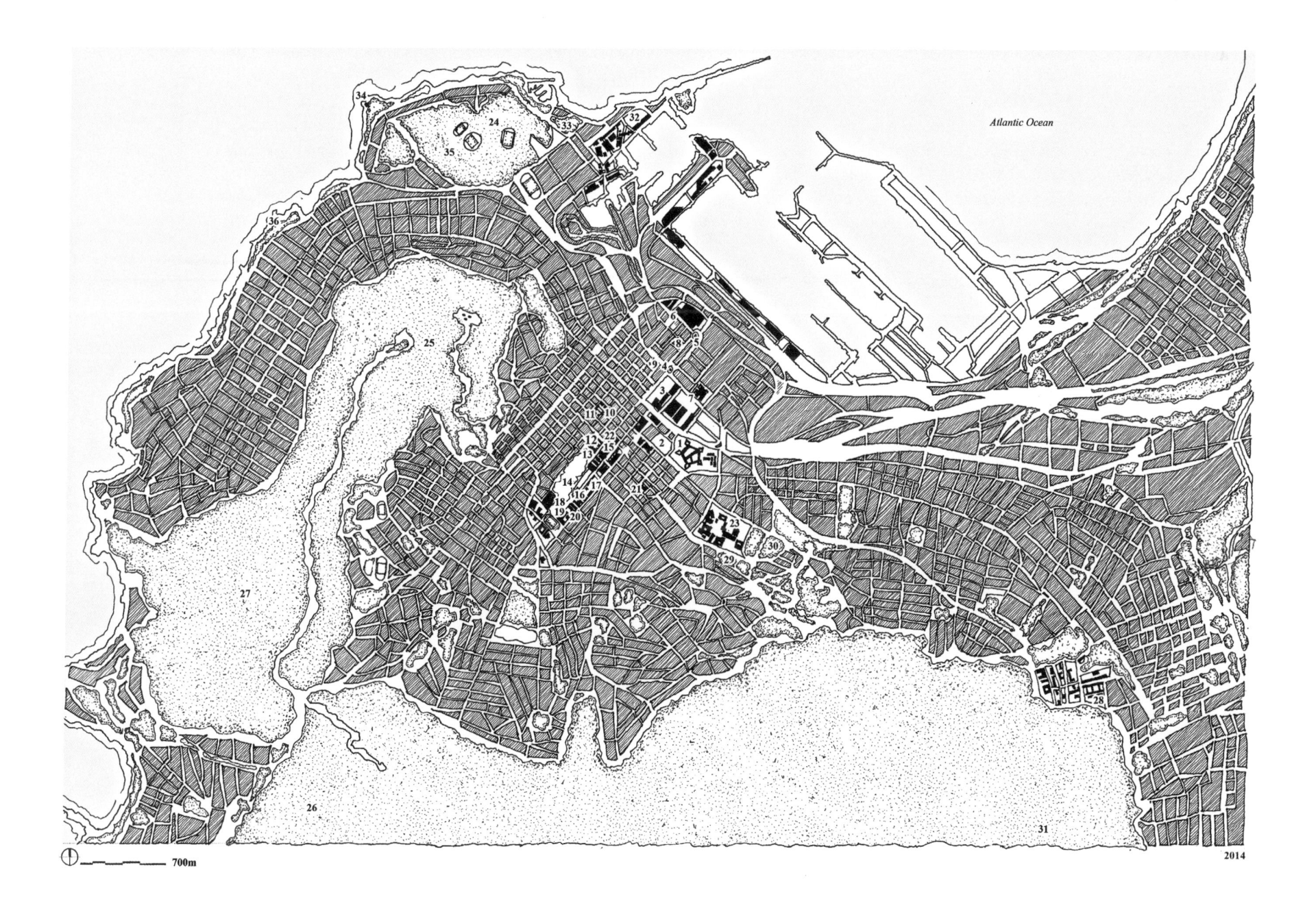

DURBAN, SOUTH AFRICA

FOUNDED: 1880
URBAN AREA: 2,292 km²
POPULATION: 2,954,000 (2010)
URBAN AREA DENSITY: 1,500/km²
GPS: 29° 51'31.34"S, 31° 1'30.99"E
29° 51'22.46"S, 31° 1'28.31"E

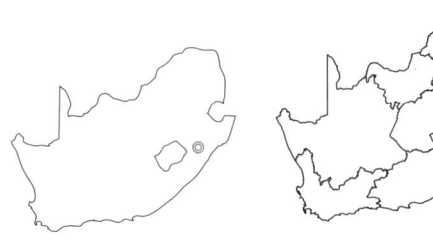

The city of Durban has a long history as a major port city. The city developed along the coast due to the busy harbour, with its suburbs developing on the surrounding hills. The city is also a popular tourist destination because of its warmer subtropical climate and long stretches of sandy beaches. The Golden Mile was developed as a tourist destination during the 1970s and was redeveloped and upgraded in 2009. The natural harbour, formerly known as the Port of Natal, is possibly the busiest container port in Africa.

Durban is strategically linked to Richards Bay and Maputo by regional development corridors towards the north, and Pietermaritzburg and Johannesburg towards the interior. The city is well connected regionally with national roads to Gauteng via the N3 highway, while the N2 Outer Ring Road links Durban with the Eastern Cape to the south, and Mpumalanga to the north. The Western Freeway is particularly important because freight is shipped by truck to and from the Witwatersrand for transfer to the port.

The Francis Farewell Square, located in the heart of the city, is the very location where the first settlement in the city was established as early as 1824 and from where the city consequently developed.

Numerous important buildings and monuments surround the square, providing insight into the history of this now bustling modern city. Adjacent to the square are the Durban City Hall and Old Court House. The massive cenotaph depicting a soldier's soul leaving his body, carried by two angels, is a memorial to soldiers who died in the First World War. There are also monuments dedicated to Queen Victoria, Louis Botha and Field Marshal, as well as a statue designed with scenes of the Anglo-Boer War at Ladysmith.

With the possible decentralisation of the inner city and major businesses and residents relocating to Umhlanga, the city has endeavoured to revitalise its inner city areas with the new Durban Point Waterfront development showcasing the uShaka Marine World and many new residential and leisure developments.

Significant landmarks in the city include the Golden Mile, Ushaka Marine World, the Moses Mabhida Stadium, The Victoria Embankment (also known as the Esplanade), Sahara Stadium Kingsmead, Kings Park Stadium, the Greyville Racecourse (home to the Durban July Handicap) and the Markets of Warwick – possibly the largest informal street market in South Africa.

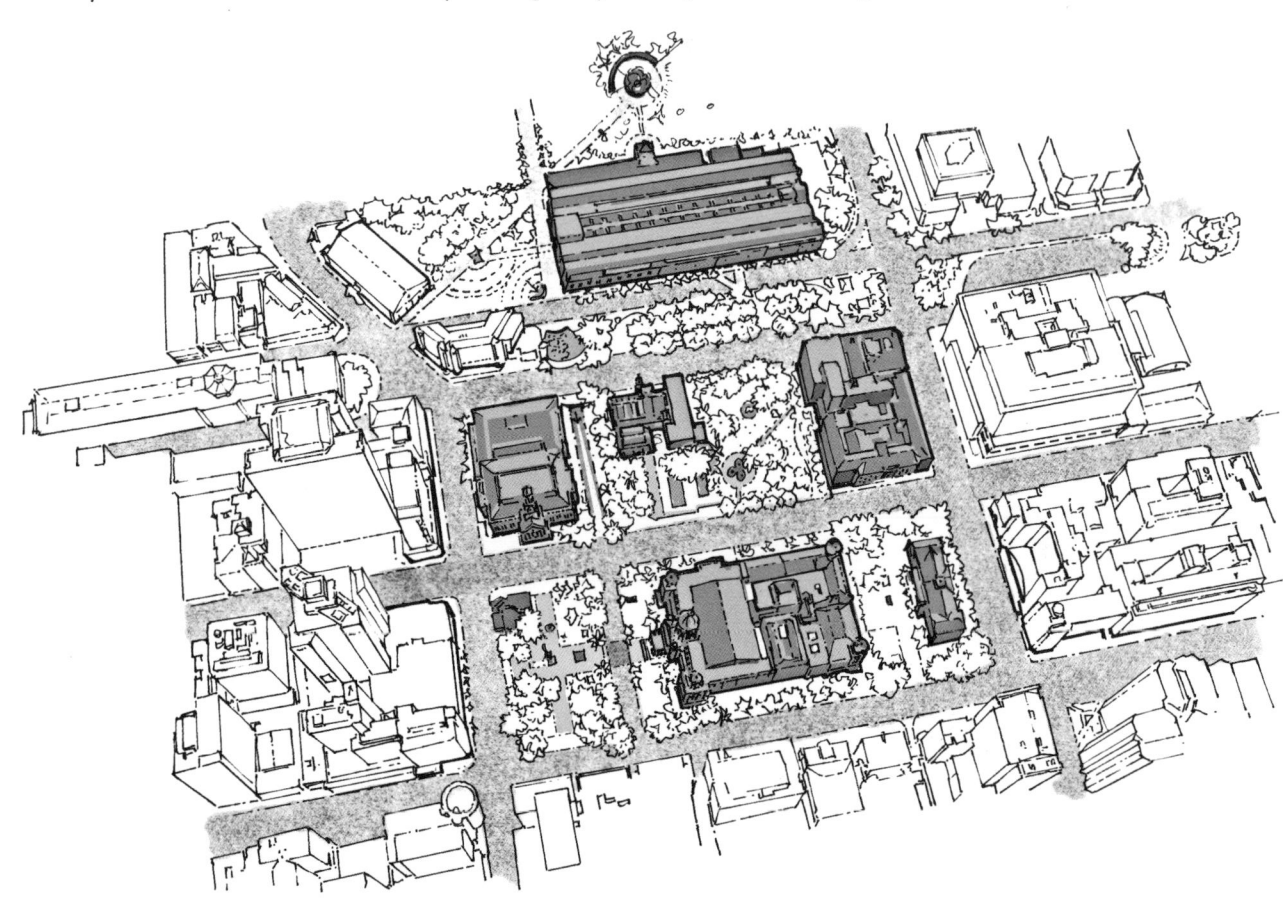

1 Market Square & The Workshop Centre
2 Central Park
3 Medwood Gardens & Kwazulu-Natal Tourism
4 Post Office
5 St Paul's Church
6 Natural Science Museum
7 Durban City Hall & Francis Farewell Square
8 Old Courthouse Museum
9 International Convention Centre
10 Victoria Park
11 Marine Parade
12 Maritime Museum & B.A.T Centre
13 Addington Hospital
14 uShaka Marine World
15 Albert Park & Clinic
16 Durban Central Train Station
17 Greyville Racecourse & Royal Durban Golf Club
18 Berea Road Train Station & West Street Cemetery
19 Durban Old Fort & Warrior Gate
20 Kingsmead Cricket Ground
21 Hoy Park
22 Amphitheatre Museum
23 Moses Mabhida Stadium
24 The ABSA Stadium
25 Botanical Garden & Municipal Sports Ground
26 Railway Goods Shed

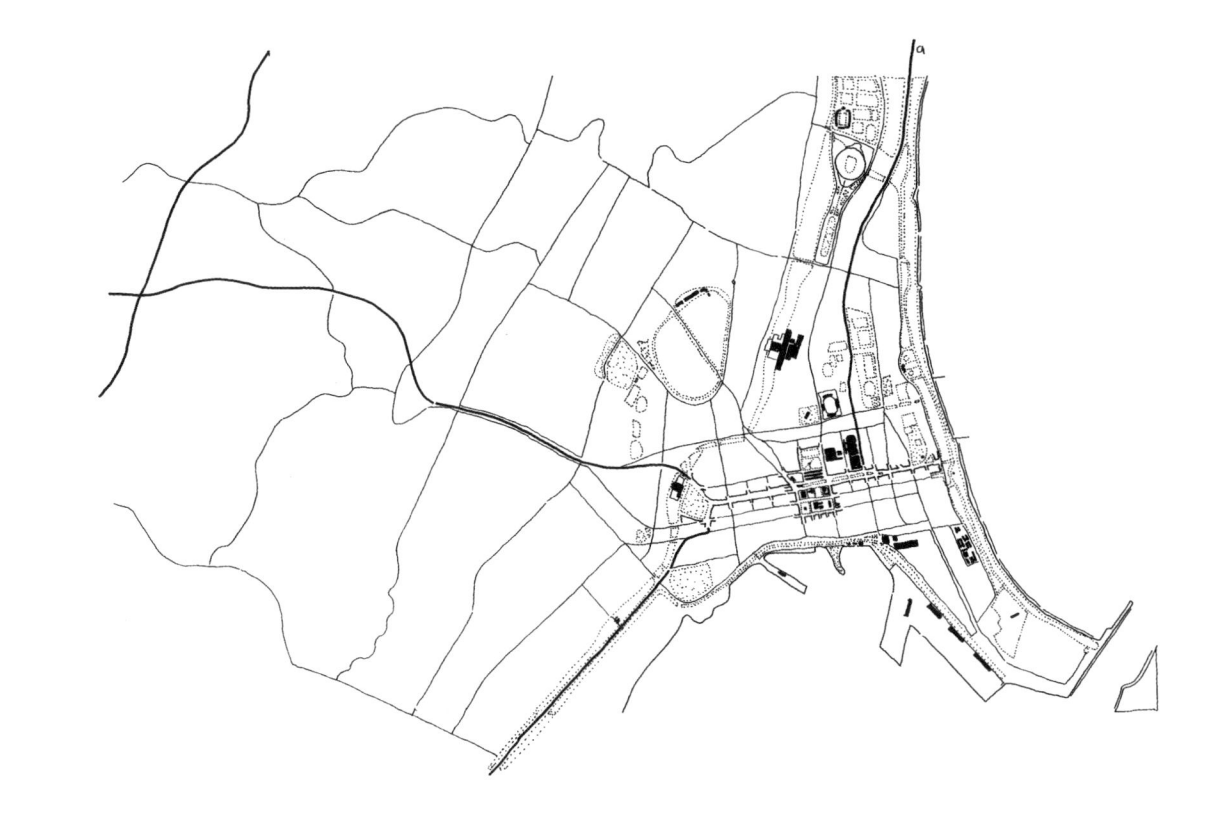

BLOEMFONTEIN, SOUTH AFRICA

FOUNDED: 1846
CITY AREA: 236 km²
CITY POPULATION (2011): 256,185
CITY DENSITY: 1,100/km²
GPS: 29° 7'5.33"S, 26° 13'17.74"E
29° 6'53.40"S, 26° 13'4.47"E

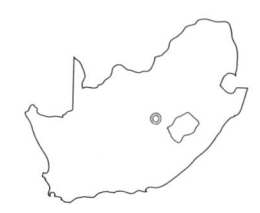

The city of Bloemfontein, centrally located in South Africa, was founded in 1846 as a British military base and has served as the Boer Republican capital, administrative headquarters and as the judicial capital since the founding of the Union of South Africa in 1910.

The topography and natural landscape features such as *spruite* ("streams") and hills became important reference points for the positioning of the first streets in colonial settlements. According to Van der Westhuizen (2011), during the formative years of the settlements, spaces were conceived in the context of the natural landscape. Connections to landscape features were critical for the survival of early settlers: protection of scarce water sources and hills for lookouts and defence. Architectural legibility in the urban fabric followed with new landmark buildings aligned with the axial demarcation of urban fabric.

According to Schoeman (1980), the first street (later called St George's Street) extended eastward along the east-west canal that connected with the military camp. The street was nestled between the canal to the north and a low hill to the south. The first few buildings in Bloemfontein were constructed along this dirt road. A north-south, east-west grid town plan was soon laid out by the land surveyor Andrew Bain. Following the discovery of diamonds in 1870 in the northern Cape, transportation routes were directed through Bloemfontein. As the town grew in stature, a site at the western end of Maitland Street was allocated for new government buildings. The erection of the Bloemfontein train station terminated the east end of this urban axis. After the Anglo-Boer War, the city core was enlarged by the expansion of the city grid in all major directions. Larger land uses such as Grey College and the University of the Orange Free State could be accommodated within the urban grid. In 1910, the city was formally elected as the judicial capital of South Africa – aligned with the completion of the High Court (1909) and Appeals Court (1910). President Brand Street became a major public space in the town, housing prominent architectural landmarks (Schoeman, 1980).

The outward growth of Bloemfontein after the 1940s increased the spatial integration of the central city street grid. Connecting corridors would later become the main thoroughfares of Bloemfontein, generating the significant expansion of the CBD in a westerly direction where the airport was later constructed.

SOUTHERN AFRICA **145**

1 Hoffman Square or Old Market Square
2 Bloemfontein Post Office
3 Bloemfontein Central Train Station
4 National Afrikaans Literary Museum and Research Centre, Lebohang Building
5 Fourth Raadsaal
6 National Museum Bloemfontein
7 Hertzog Memorial Garden
8 Bloemfontein City Hall
9 Dutch Reformed Church
10 Old Supreme Court Building
11 Fire Station
12 Old Presidency
13 Central University of Technology
14 President Brand Cemetery
15 Queens Fort & Military Museum
16 Anglican Church
17 Ramblers Club
18 Free State Stadium
19 Loch Logan & Zoo
20 University of the Free State
21 Joubert Park
22 Naval Hill
23 National Women's Monument & War Memorial
24 Signal Hill, Grants Hill & Oliewenhuis Art Museum
25 Grey College
26 Eunice Primary School

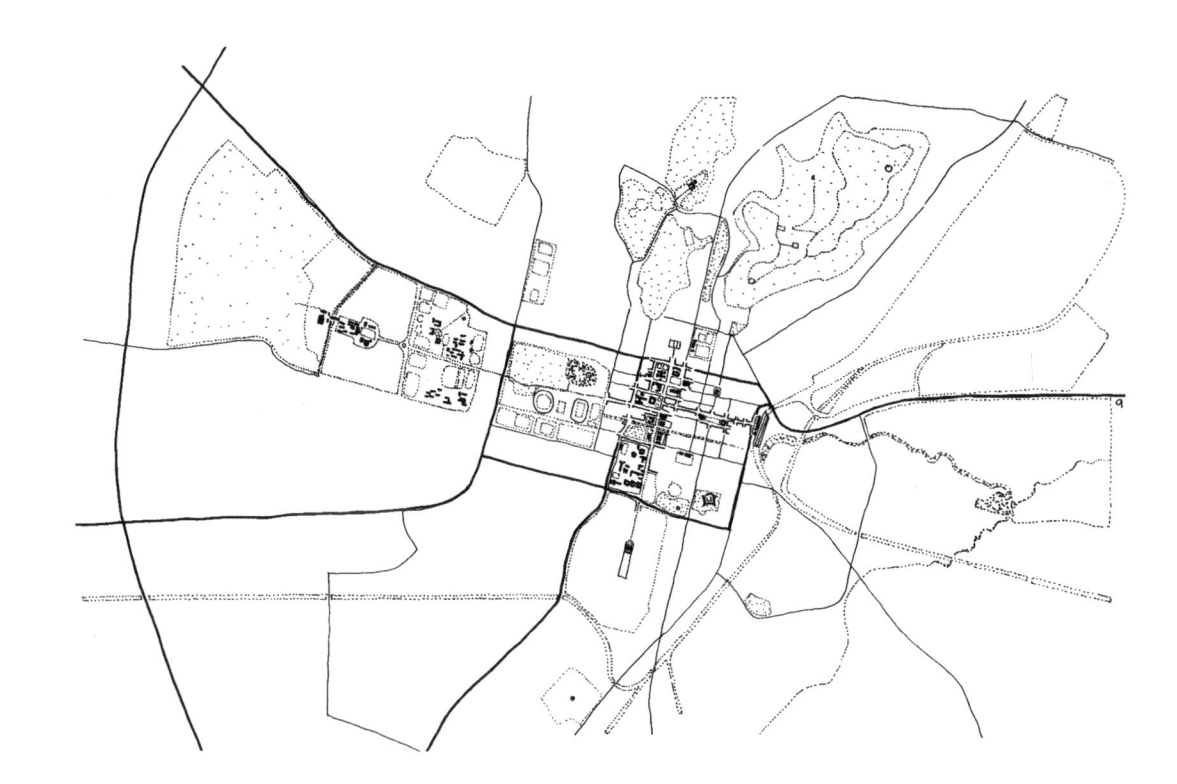

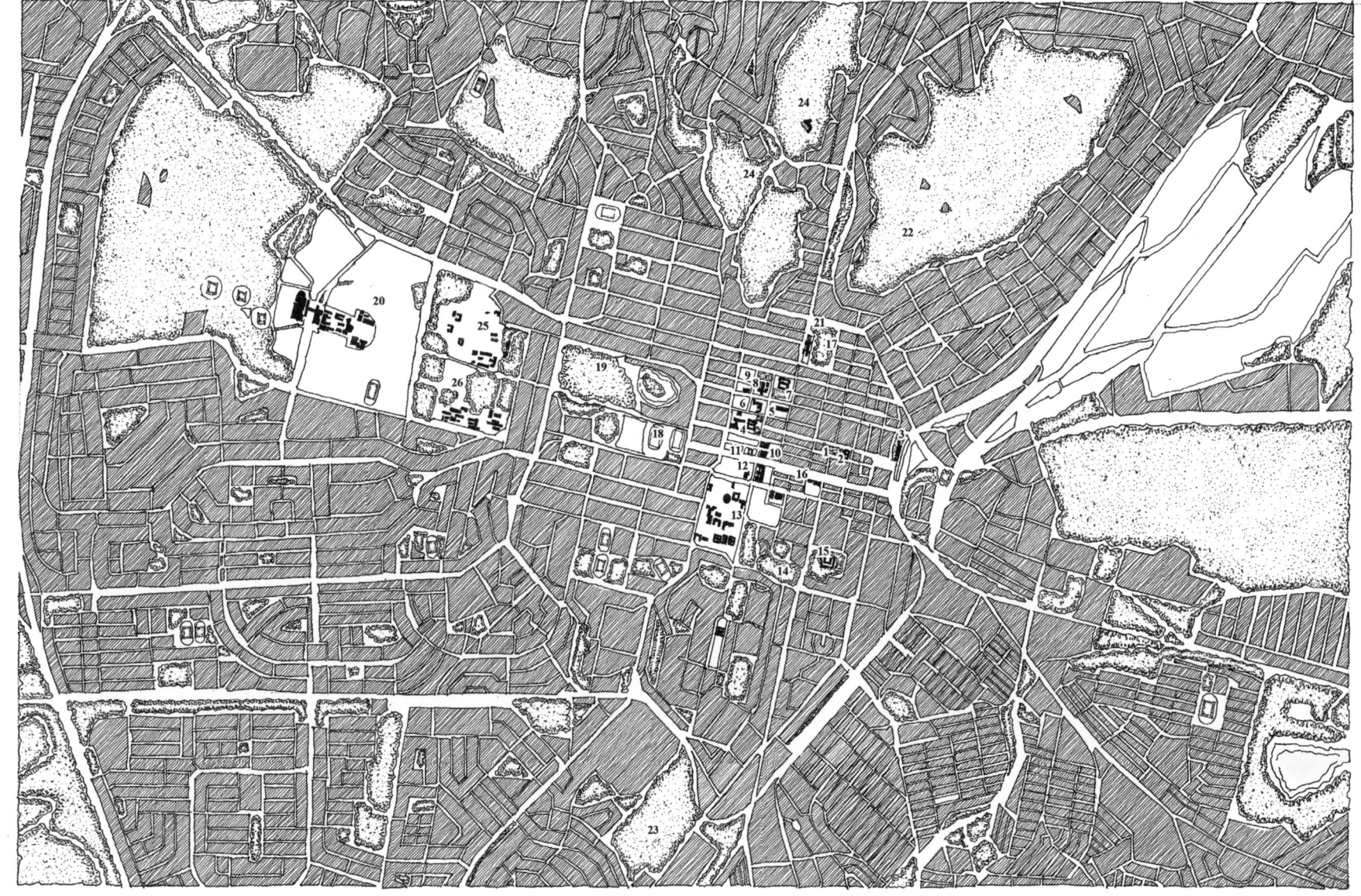

JOHANNESBURG, SOUTH AFRICA

FOUNDED: 1886
CITY AREA: 335 km²
CITY POPULATION (2011): 957,441 (Metro: 4,434,827)
CITY DENSITY: 2,900/km²
GPS: 26° 16'39.93"S, 27° 53'16.36"E
26° 12'24.02"S, 28° 2'36.14"E
26° 12'9.30"S, 28° 1'51.47"E
26° 6'26.68"S, 28° 3'17.02"E

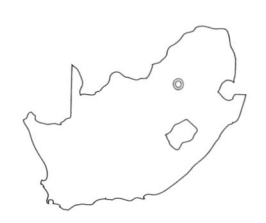

Johannesburg is the heartbeat of the wealthiest province in South Africa and source of large-scale gold mining that is also its *raison d'être*. In 1886, gold was discovered along the Witwatersrand ridge that soon led to a vast cosmopolitan mining encampment on a triangular *uitvalgrond* ("surplus ground"). The triangular form is still visible in the urban street grid.

The central triangular *uitvalgrond* was where southerly trade routes diverged to cross the east-west horizon of the gold-bearing conglomerate reef. Two strong directional influences were accommodated inside the grid plan and are still reflected in the major transit networks that dissect the city: the north-south passage determined by political economy, and the east-west route responding to geology. Since the mid–1990s, the north-south Johannesburg-Pretoria corridor (along with the highway to Johannesburg International Airport) has been the fastest-growing development area in South Africa.

As Johannesburg sprung up around the mining belt, all development historically took place to the north and south of the triangular core. The city's setting within the natural ridges of the landscape, called the *witwatersrand* ("white waters ridge") – a series of hills that form the continental watershed – brought about undulating street patterns to the north of the rigid core. Along the south, mining dumps – now fast disappearing – made up an artificial landscape that also separated the city along racial lines under apartheid, including the black suburb Soweto to its south-west (South Western Townships). Urban segregation came to be implemented over several decades under a wide range of legislative measures.

After the transition to democracy of the early 1990s, South Africa underwent profound transformation that included political, socio-economic and spatial changes reflected in the urban landscape. Perhaps one of the most dominant characteristics of the post-apartheid city is the random distribution of informal settlements across the urban landscape. Juxtaposed to these are an increasing number of fortified, hermetic enclaves, typically for middle and high-income groups regardless of race. Simultaneously, there are several ongoing attempts to lessen, if not eradicate, the legacy of exclusionary planning. In recent years, the topography of the city has changed to the extent that it has become a city region, a new urban form characterised by a diversity of worlds that overlap in various ways. By contrast, gentrification of inner-city regions has resulted in renewed energy of its core. Johannesburg is an incredibly vibrant city, with a mixture of people from all over Africa and the world calling the city their home.

1 Old Market Square	22 Egoli Gasworks, Keystone Film Productions & 44 Stanley
2 Johannesburg City Library	
3 Johannesburg City Hall	23 SABC, South African Broadcast Corporation
4 Rissik Street Post Office	
5 Park & Old Goods Station	24 University of Johannesburg, Auckland Park Campus
6 Museum Africa & Market Theatre	
	25 University of Johannesburg, Kingsway Campus
7 Mary Fitzgerald Square	
8 Workers Museum	26 Helen Joseph Hospital
9 Johannesburg Magistrates Court	27 University of the Witwatersrand [Medical Campus] & Linder Auditorium
10 Anglo Ashanti Ltd & Old Gas Works / Turbine Hall	
	28 Charlotte Maxeke Johannesburg Academic Hospital
11 Ferreira Town & Westgate Station	
	29 The Wilds Park
12 Ghandi Square	30 Brenthurst Library and Press
13 Arts on Main & Maboneng Precinct	31 Park
	32 Origins Centre
14 Ellis Park Stadium, Johannesburg Stadium & Standard Bank Arena	33 Park & Primrose Terrace
	34 Melville Koppies
	35 Johannesburg Zoo
15 Joubert Park & Johannesburg Art Gallery	36 Fordsburg, Oriental Plaza & Hamidia Masjid Mosque
16 Johannesburg Civic Centre	37 Main Reef
17 Constitutional Hill	38 Nelson Mandela Bridge
18 University of the Witwatersrand [East & West Campuses]	39 Mandela & Tambo Law Office
	40 Old Milner Park Hotel & The HUB Johannesburg
19 Braamfontein Cemetery	
20 Brixton Cemetery	41 Park Station
21 Brixton Tower	

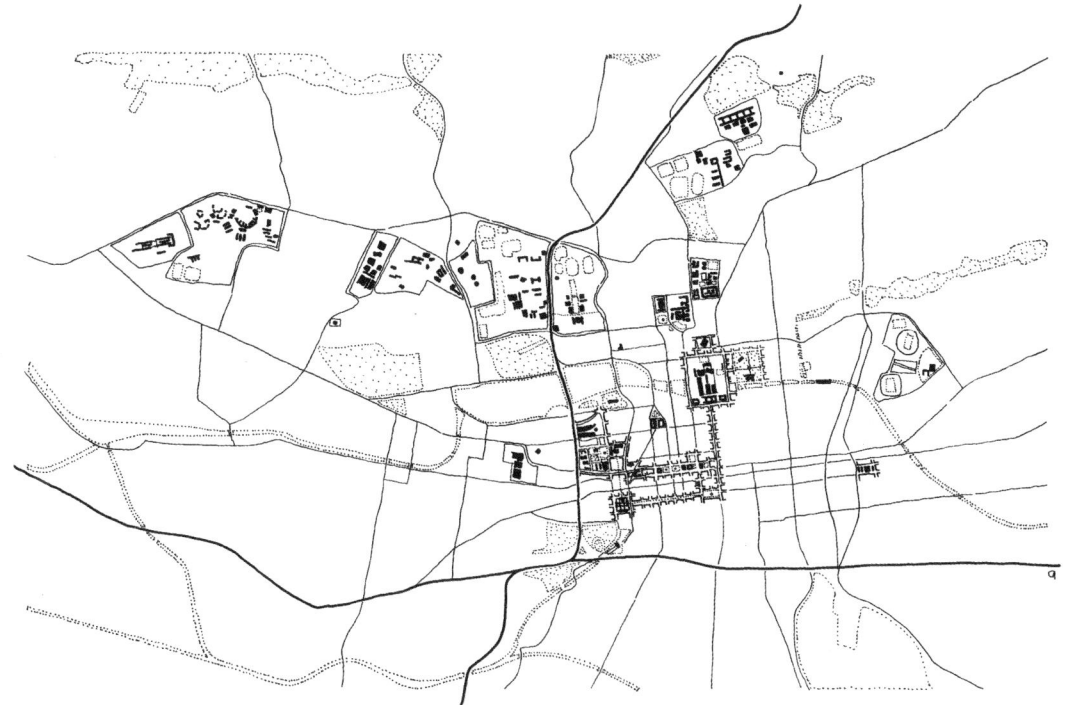

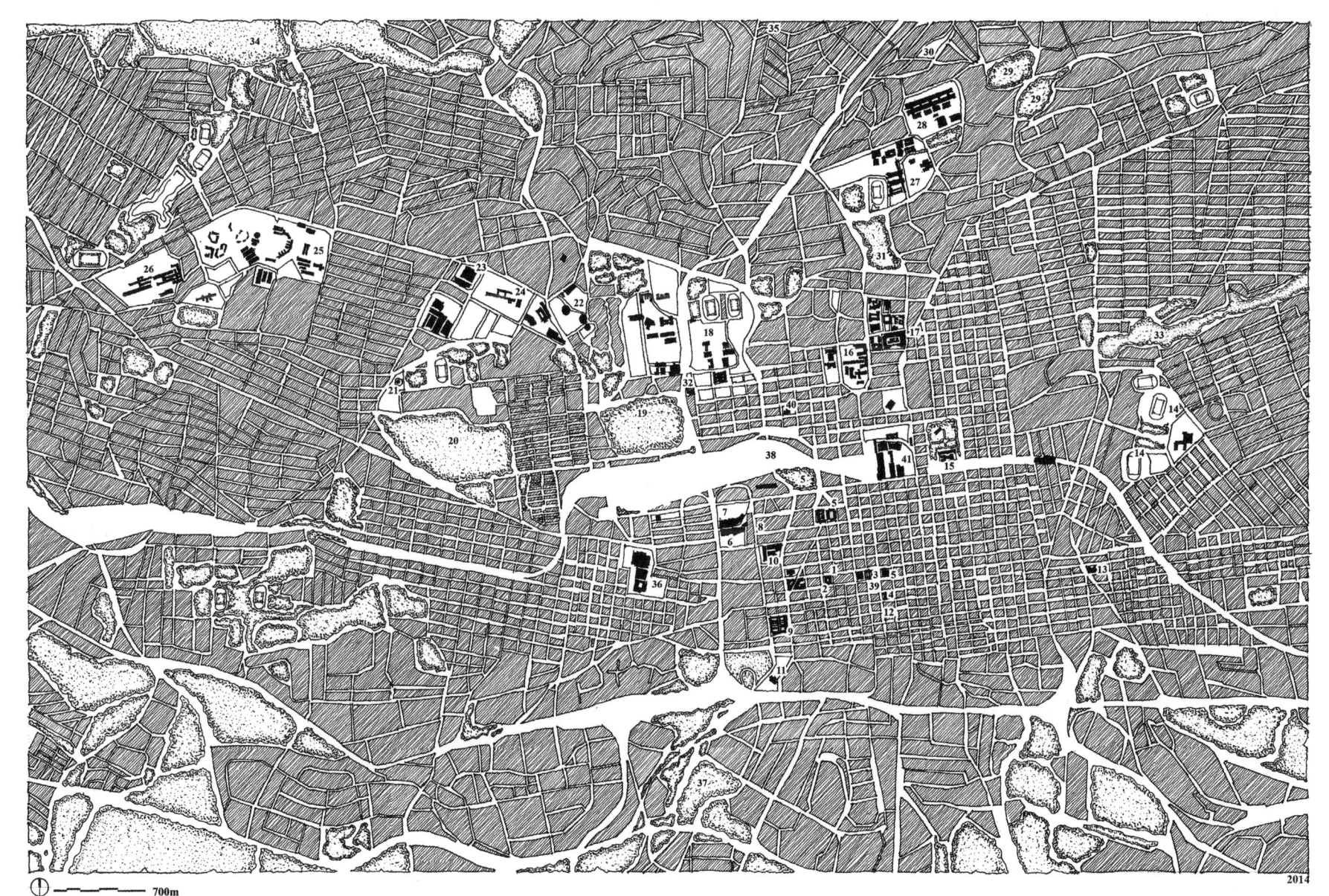

PORT ELIZABETH, SOUTH AFRICA

FOUNDED: 1820
CITY AREA: 251 km²
CITY POPULATION (2011): 312,392
CITY DENSITY: 1,200/km²
GPS: 23° 54'44.20"S, 29° 27'6.33"E
33° 53'53.90"S, 25° 36'20.70"E

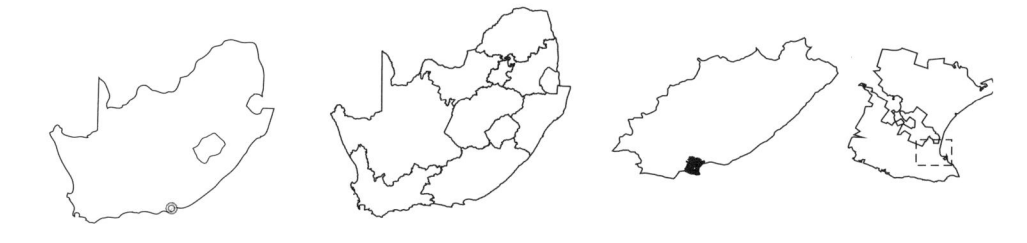

Laid out during 1815, the town of Port Elizabeth was only developed upon the arrival of British settlers in the Eastern Cape five years later. Port Elizabeth is one of the largest cities in South Africa, stretching for 16 km along Algoa Bay, and is one of the country's major seaports.

Port Elizabeth owes its form to a number of physical and historical constraints. Although initially serving the inland farming communities, a series of developments elsewhere in the southern African interior provided economic stimulus to the new town, and by the 1860s it had overtaken Cape Town as the Cape Colony's leading port. The European colonial port was the historic core of the city. Focused on the harbour and based on walking distances, the old city grew first on the narrow plateau along the shore north-west of the harbour and then expanded along the escarpment. Numerous manufacturing industries were established locally, creating extensive employment opportunities and resultant urban growth. During the colonial period, a pattern of residential segregation was developed based on perceived racial and economic differences. Since the early 1900s, colonial exclusionary planning and racial separation policies implemented after 1950 resulted in the city becoming a model "apartheid city". Buffer strips at least 100 m wide separated communities. These often concurred with existing physical barriers. According to Frescura, as a result industrial areas such as Struandale, and natural features such as the Swartkops River and its escarpment, and Parsonsvlei, were used to define the parameters of the city's suburbs. During the late 1980s, globalisation played a major role in the growth of the city, its economy and communities. Since this period, decentralising forces have dominated the complex sprawl of the city.

Despite the attempts of the post-apartheid regime to eradicate the effect of the Group Areas Act following the transition to democracy during the early 1990s, apartheid planning is permanently etched into the urban fabric of the city. Today, historical and cultural icons in Port Elizabeth include the Red Location Museum, a museum in New Brighton township that portrays the effects of institutionalised racism and the efforts of the anti-apartheid struggle.

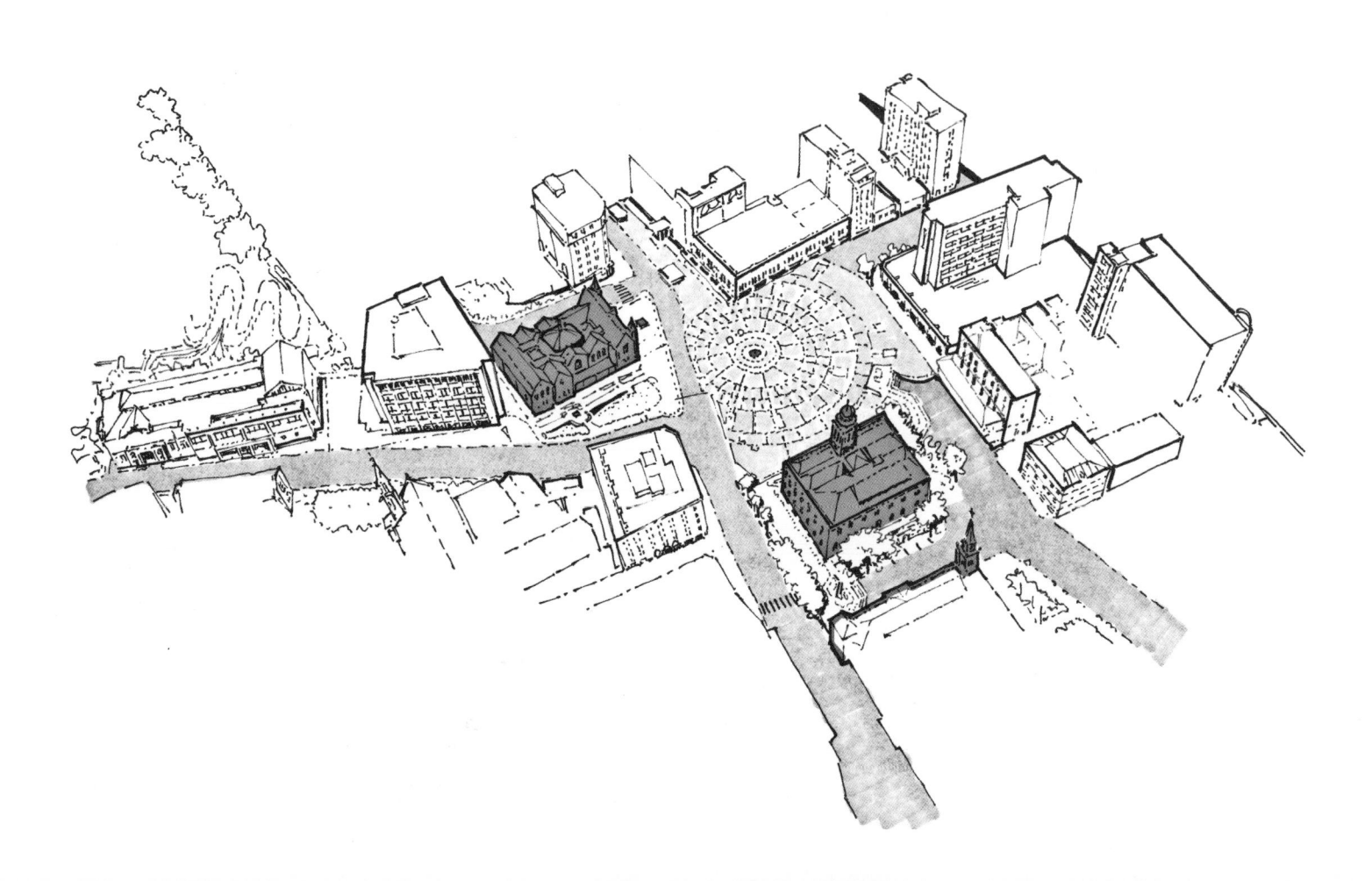

SOUTHERN AFRICA

1 Vuyisile Mini Square or Market Square
2 Main Library
3 Town Hall
4 The Campanile
5 Port Elizabeth Central Train Station
6 St Augustine's Cathedral
7 Donkin Reserve & Lighthouse
8 South End Museum
9 Nelson Mandela Metropolitan Art Museum
10 St George's Cricket Ground
11 Settlers Park Nature Reserve
12 Robert Searle Park
13 Nelson Mandela Bay Stadium & Holland Park
14 North End Cemetery
15 Kings Beach
16 Harbour

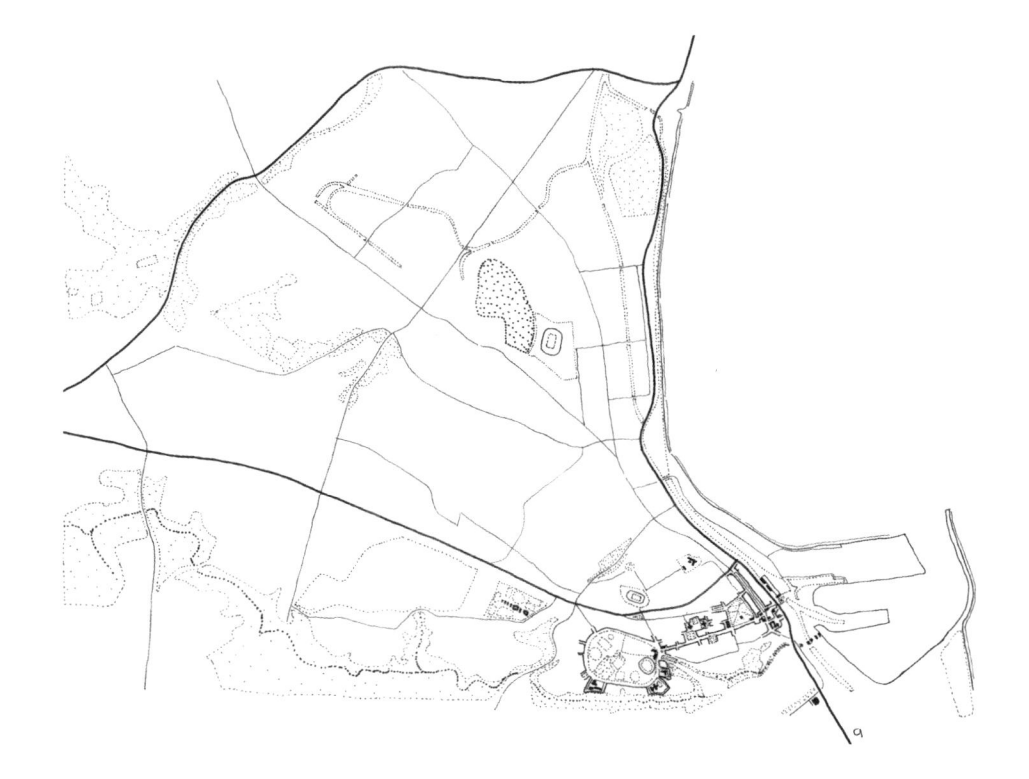

PRETORIA, SOUTH AFRICA

FOUNDED: 1855
CITY AREA: 687 km² (METRO: 6,298 km²)
CITY POPULATION (2011): 741,651 (METRO: 2.5 million)
CITY DENSITY: 1,100/km² (METRO: 460/km2)
GPS: 25° 44'47.17"S, 28° 11'17.10"E
25° 45'11.22"S, 28° 11'17.17"E
25° 45'26.41"S, 28° 11'20.28"E
25° 44'45.53"S, 28° 11'37.66"E

Pretoria is the historical core located within the City of Tshwane Metropolitan Municipality. It serves as the administrative and *de facto* national capital. Located at a short distance north of Johannesburg, it forms part of the economic heart of the country. Set in-between natural enclosures of repetitive rolling *koppies* and along the Apies River, place-making in Pretoria was considered under universal, cultural, and contextual aspects (Jordaan, 1989). The indigenous vegetation of the city varies as considerably as the topography, with the combined factors of north and south ridge faces.

The city was founded in 1855 as the capital of the Zuid-Afrikaansche Republiek (ZAR) in an uninhabited area with no existing territorially linked political power (Clarke & Corten, 2011). The new capital was set out as an orthogonal grid with Church Square located at the crossing of the main axes. The length and turning circles of oxen-wagons evidently determined the dimensions of streets forming the grid. Building lines of all new constructs were strictly regulated in order to keep the orthogonal grid. Citizens were instructed to plant trees in front of their property to provide shade in the streets. Fresh water was supplied along canals running along streets and were fed by the source of the Apies River, a fountain located at Elandspoort to the south of the settlement (Holm, 1998).

The discovery of gold in the Witwatersrand in 1886 had a major impact on the city, instigating an enormous influx of people. By the end of the 1880s, the City had expanded outside its central grid in an easterly direction. Pretoria was at the centre of the Second Anglo-Boer War (1899–1902), which brought the ZAR under British rule. In 1910, it became the administrative capital of the new Union of South Africa under British rule. Its importance as administrative centre grew along with industrialisation, causing further urbanisation and a building boom (Fisher, 1998).

During 1961, Pretoria became the capital city of the newly born Republic of South Africa. By then, apartheid politics were already reflected in the urban fabric. New townships, like Mamelodi to the east of the city centre, were constructed to house the non-white population.

Today the Union Buildings, the main architectural icon of the city, is the symbol of cultural diversity and reconciliation (Clarke & Corten, 2011).

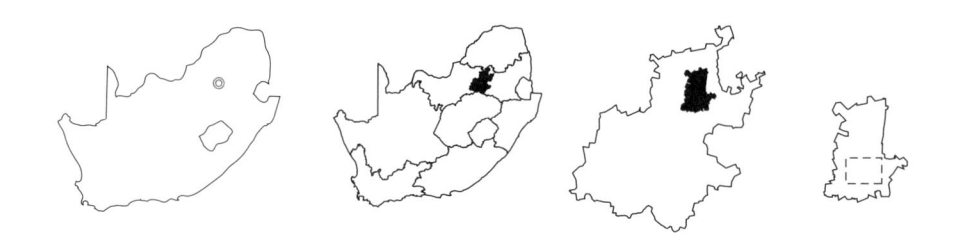

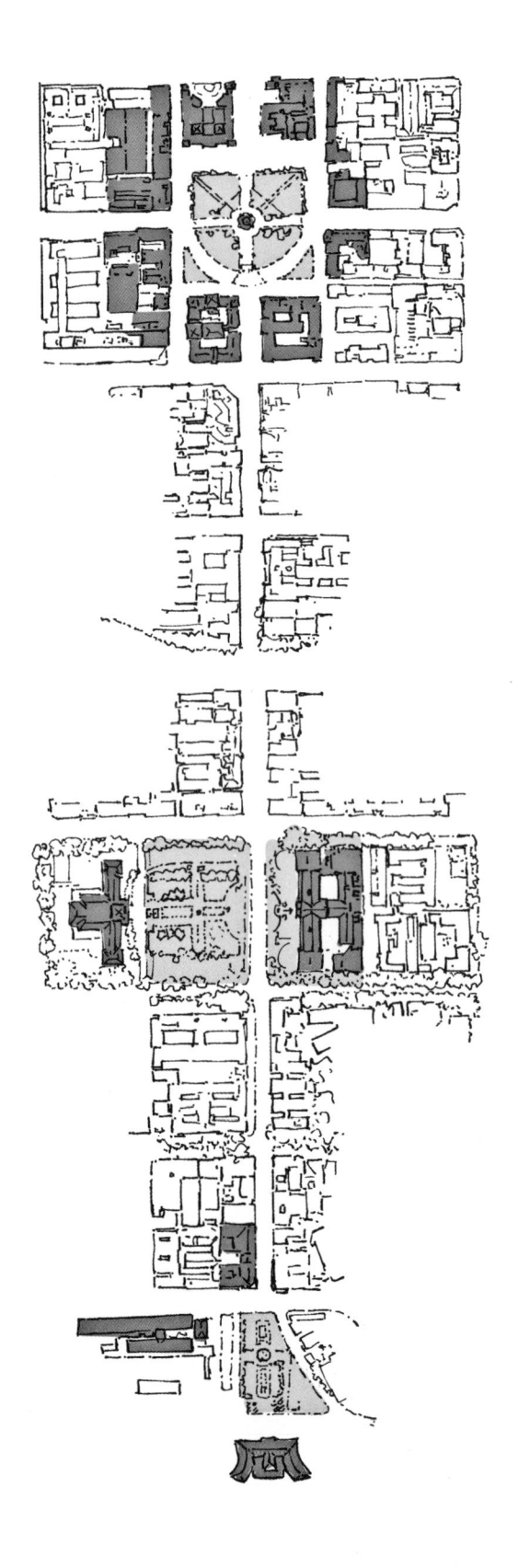

#		#	
1	Church Square with Café Riche, General Post Office, Palace of Justice, Ou Raadsaal Buildings	23	University of Pretoria Groenkloof Campus
2	Kruger House Museum	24	NRCS
3	Pretoria Reformed Church & Jakaranda Kindergarden	25	Telkom Lukasrand Tower
		26	Brookfield Park
4	Heroes' Acre Cemetery	27	Magnolia Dal
5	Prince's Park	28	Pretoria Boys' High School
6	Showgrounds & Pilditch Stadium	29	Afrikaans Hoër Seunskool
7	Old Synagogue	30	Afrikaans Hoër Meisieskool
8	Pretoria Zoo	31	Dutch Reformed Church / Petrakerk
9	Old National Cultural History Museum	32	Loftus Versfeld Stadium & Pretoria High School for Girls
10	Belle Ombre Station	33	University of Pretoria Hatfield Campus
11	Fresh Produce Market	34	Hatfield Gautrain Station
12	Tshwane University of Technology	35	Springbok Park
13	Rebecca Cemetery	36	The Presidency
14	City Hall	37	Union Buildings & Meintjieskop
15	Ditsong National Museum of Natural History / Old Transvaal Museum	38	Venning Park
		39	Pretoria Art Museum
16	Burgers Park & Melrose House Museum	40	Caledonian Stadium
		41	Lion Bridge
17	Pretoria Station	42	Old Marylebone Cricket Club
18	Freedom Park	43	Weskoppies Psychiatric Hospital
19	Salvokop & Dequar Road National Defence Force Buildings	44	West Power Station
		45	1 Military Hospital & Old Iscor Building
20	Voortrekker Monument, Fort Skanskop & Skanskop	46	Rietondale Park
		47	Sammy Marks Square
21	Fort Klapperkop & Klapperkop	48	State Theatre
22	University of South African		

SOUTHERN AFRICA **151**

2014

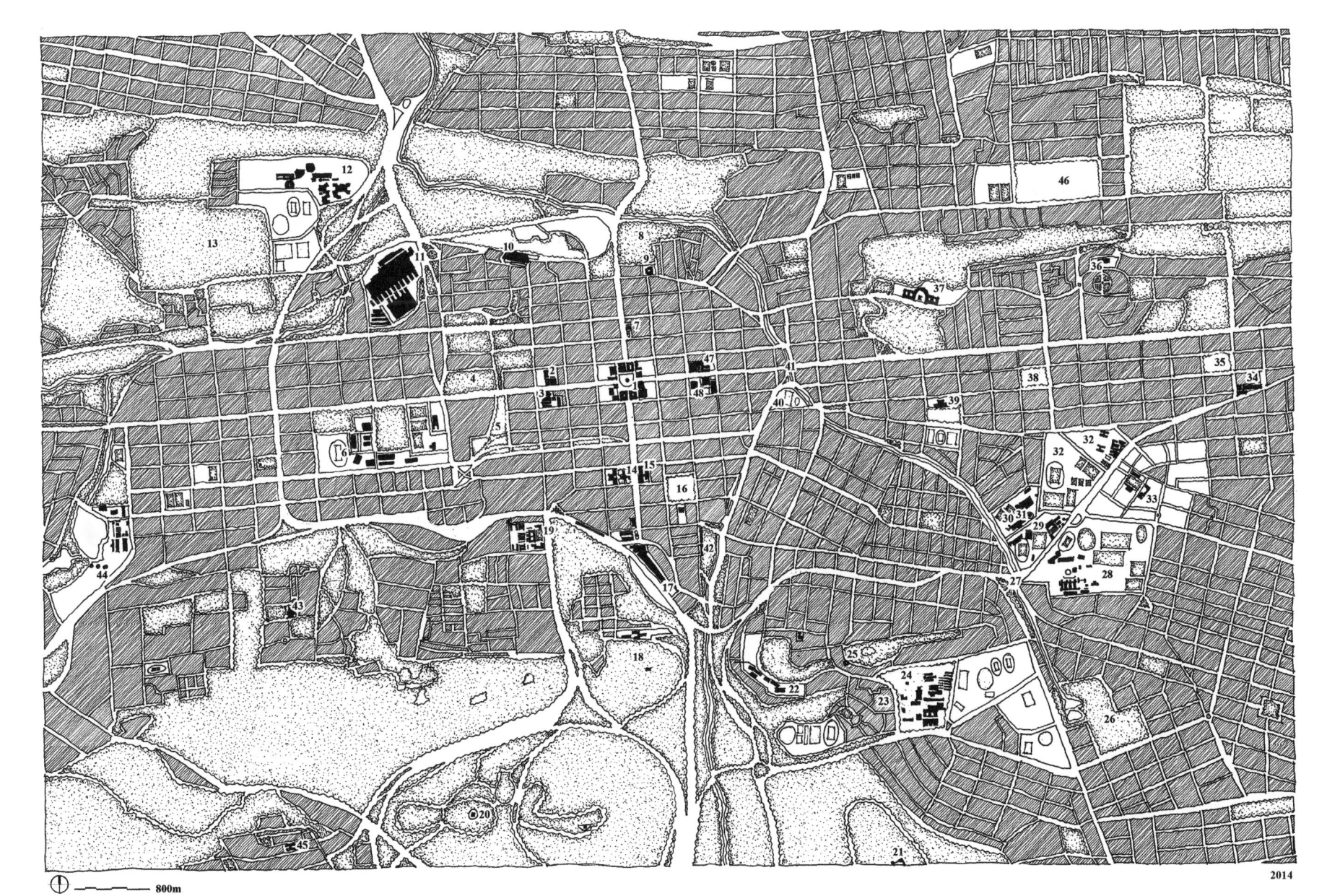

800m

MBABANE, SWAZILAND

FOUNDED: 1902
URBAN AREA: 150 km²
POPULATION: 94,874 (2010)
URBAN AREA DENSITY: 630/km²
GPS: 26° 19'35.92"S, 31° 8'39.09"E

Mbabane, capital and largest city in Swaziland, is located on the Mbabane River and its tributary, the Polinjane River, in the Mdzimba Mountains. The relatively small city is shaped by the hilly topography of the area, located in a valley and structured around the river. The town was only declared a city in 1992 by King Mswati III.

The city was planned with the major residential area within close proximity to the city centre, but has since sprawled over to the rolling hills and tree-lined expanses. Today, the city centre merely functions as a commercial and administrative centre, as residents no longer live in the inner city. Davidson and Acioly (1996) describe this trend as a case of "fluctuating densities" which left the city virtually dead at night with low-income housing sprawling on the city's periphery.

Street names are attributed to prominent people and other land surveyors who worked in the area. The city is home to several high-rise buildings such as that of the Central Bank of Swaziland, once the most prominent landmark. The Sidwashini Industrial Area, located west of the city, accommodates thriving light industries.

The tarred road in Mbabane which measured a length of 200 m in 1962 (along Allister Miller Street from what is now known as Standard Bank to the Gilfillan Street junction) has since been extended to approximately 91 km of tarred road and 51 km of gravel road.

Mbabane's close proximity to other major urban centres – both within and outside Swaziland with excellent transport networks – provides ample opportunities for companies involved in the distribution of goods. The nearest sea ports are Maputo in Mozambique and Richards Bay in South Africa, while the nearest railway station and international airport can be found at Matsapha, 30 km from the city.

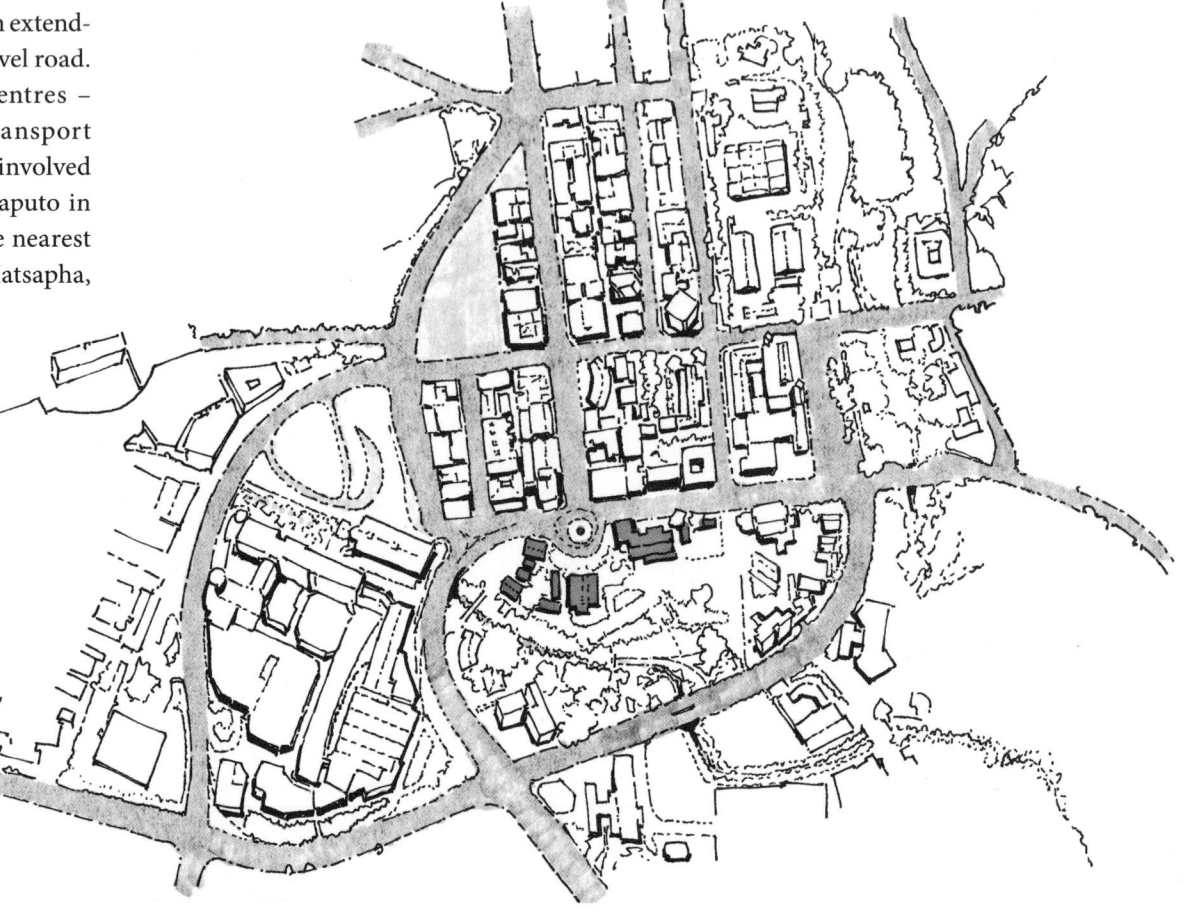

SOUTHERN AFRICA **153**

1 City Council
2 Coronation Park
3 Ezulwini Sun Hotel
4 Mbabane Hospital
5 Mbabane Bus Rank
6 Selection Park
7 West Ridge Park
8 Sifundzani High School

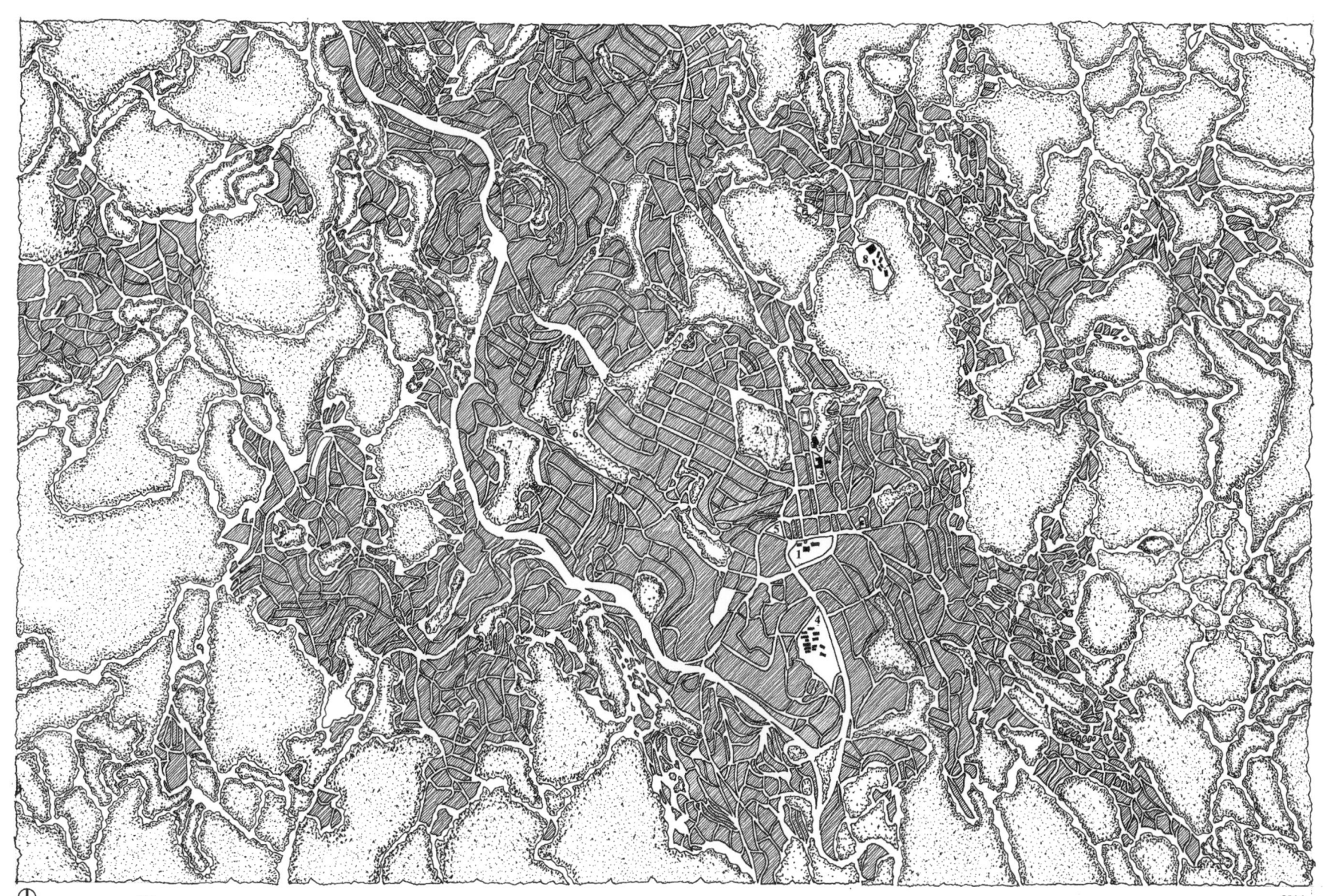

700m

2014

COTONOU, BENIN

FOUNDED: 1851
AREA: 79 km²
POPULATION (2012): 779,314
DENSITY: 9,900/km²
GPS: 6° 22'16.93"N, 2° 24'35.21"E

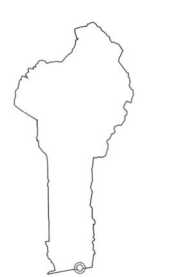

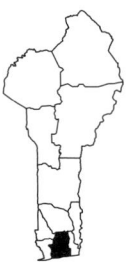

Cotonou had its origins as a small fishing village at the beginning of the nineteenth century. Today, the city is the largest city and economic centre of Benin. Set along the Gulf of Guinea – to the southeast of the country where the Oueme River flows into the Atlantic Ocean – the city has a major port and various other transport networks. The term *cotonou*, meaning "mouth of the river of death", is a reference to the city's demographic position in relation to the earlier slave trade. Lake Nokoué lies to the north of the city and the Atlantic Ocean to the south. Just across the lake, to the north-east, lies the capital, Porto-Novo. Both cities are situated very close to the border with Nigeria, so that Lagos is roughly 100 km to their east.

While the coastal location is important to Cotonou's subsistence, at 51 m above sea level the city is extremely vulnerable to sea-level rise with potentially catastrophic results. The erosion of the coast worsened in 1961 following the construction of the Nangbéto Dam and deep-water port. The Cotonou Canal, dug by the French in 1855, links the sea with Lake Nokoué, and divides the city into two unequal parts. Originally ruled by the Kingdom of Dahomey (1600s–1900s), the French made a treaty to establish a trading post at Cotonou in 1851. The territory was subsequently ceded to France until Benin's indepence in 1960.

Today, activities in the city are non-agricultural – apart from fisheries – with a primary focus on service-based and commercial undertakings facilitated by infrastructure, including the port of Cotonou and the Dantokpa international market, which constitutes a major landmark in the city fabric. Dantokpa Market is also the trading hub of West and Central African countries. Cotonou's self-governing port accounts for 90 percent of the country's customs receipts. In addition, service and craft production activities in the city, in addition to tourism, are a mainstay of Cotonou's economy. However, coastal fishing alone provides a livelihood for more than 15,000 people (Dossou & Gléhouenou-Dossou, 2007).

The city of Cotonou is laid out in a predictable grid pattern and is divided into various zones to accommodate residential areas, administrative and social facilities, as well as industrial/commercial activities. The city developed along an east-west oriented axis because of the natural constraints imposed by Lake Nokoué to the north and the Atlantic Ocean to the south. Running parallel to the east-west expansion is the railway line – a major urban structuring device. The bulk of the population is concentrated in the western part of the city, close to where the international airport is located at the centre's west.

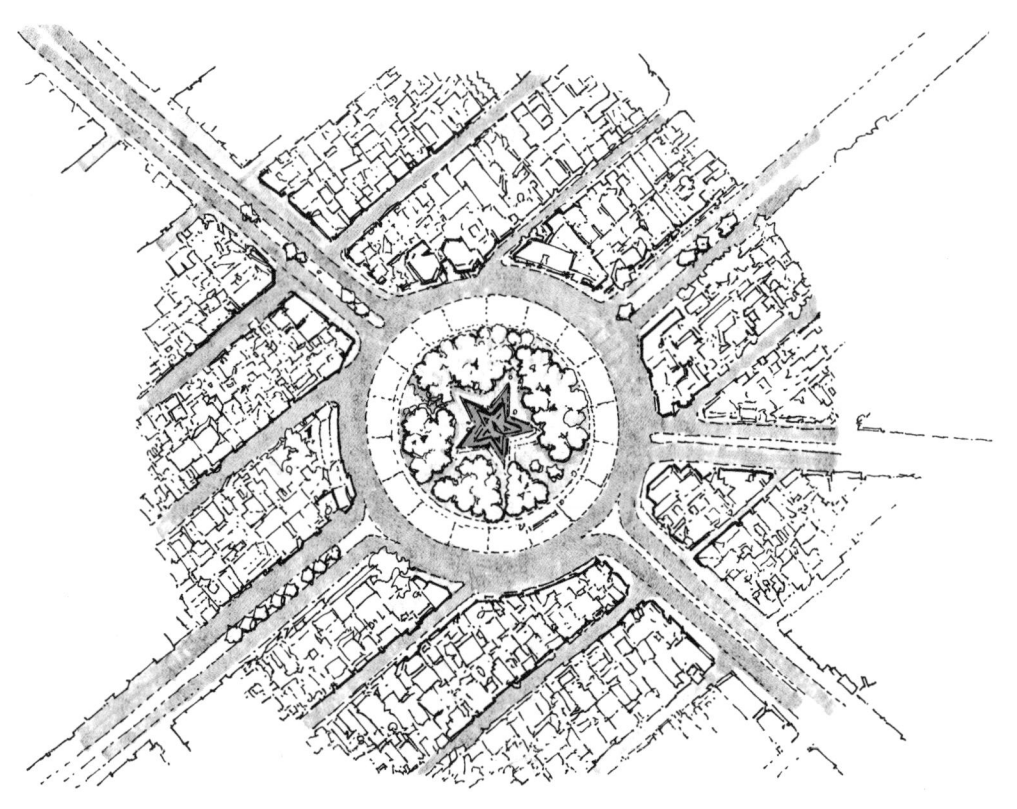

1	L'Etoile Red Square
2	Town Hall
3	Grand Market of Dantokpa
4	St Michel Church
5	Cotonou Central Train Station
6	Grand Zongo Mosque
7	Centre for the Promotion of Crafts
8	Arts Hall & Ministry of Youth Sports
9	Commissariat Central & Prison Civile, Central Office & Civil Prison
10	College of Our Lady of Apostles & The Neems Catholic Primary School
11	Collège d'Enseignement Général (CEG) Gbegamey & Bourse du Travail, College of General Education (CGE) Gbégamey & Labour Exchange
12	Place de Bulgarie, Square of Bulgaria
13	Mosquee du Rond-Point Gbegamey, Mosque of Gbégamey Roundabout
14	Guezo Camp
15	Centre National Hospitalier U'niversitaire, National Centre University Hospital
16	UAC Health Sciences Faculty
17	Courthouse
18	Secrétaire Général du Gouvernement, Secretary General of Government
19	Président de la République, President of the Republic
20	Cotonou International Airport
21	Maison du Peuple, House of the People
22	CEG Sainte-Rita
23	Martyr Square
24	Zinsou Foundation
25	Palais de Congrès, House of Congress
26	Port
27	Aidjeda Square
28	Old Bridge Cemetery
29	Sacred Heart Church
30	CED Akpakpa
31	Lenin Square
32	Akpakpa Centre General Education College
33	Akpakpa Celestial Church of Christ
34	René Pleven Stadium of Akpakpa
35	Town Hall & Centre de Perfectionnement du Personnel des Entreprises, Centre for Staff Development Business

2014

900m

PORTO-NOVO, BENIN

FOUNDED: seventeenth century
AREA: 110 km²
POPULATION (2009): 267,191
DENSITY: 410/km²
GPS: 6° 28'22.71"N, 2° 37'12.86"E

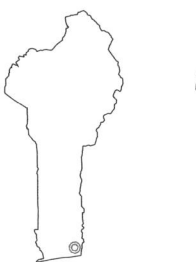

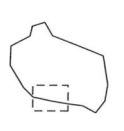

Porto-Novo – a city with its origins steeped in African myth – is the capital of Benin. To its south-west, across Lake Nokoué, lies the economic heartbeat of the country: the much younger city of Cotonou. The Porto-Novo Lagoon, forming the southerly boundary of the city, extends all the way to the Nigerian megacity, Lagos, about 100 km across the border to the east. The series of lagoons and wetlands cut off Porto-Novo from the coast. These lagoon plays an incredibly important role for the city as an ecological and socio-economic system.

Because of the natural barrier of the lagoon to the south, the city was forced to grow northwards. The city centre, situated immediately to the north of the lagoon, is bordered by a ring road (Boulevard Extérieur). Following the Second World War, the city began to expand beyond the ring road. The central axis of the city is formed by the Ballot Boulevard, forming a spinal system that connects east and west – including the Palace of King Toffa, the Great Market and Bayol Square while passing by the Governor's Palace.

Today, four major zones are recognised in the morphology of the city – namely the traditional city, the French colonial centre, the Afro-Brazilian centre, and to the north the newer, continuously expanding city. Some of the most important buildings of the old traditional part that make up the structure of the city are the Central Market, where slaves were sold centuries ago, and the series of royal palaces in the city centre.

The French colonial city grew close to the existing traditional city with little interference, so that Porto-Novo's structure reflects a dual urban system. The contact point between these two separate cities is Bayol Square in the city centre and a main structuring point of the principal structuring axis. The French created wide avenues bordered by trees to provide shade. To be able to build in this area, the trees belonging to the "sacred forest" of the King of Porto-Novo had to be cut down.

Oganla is where many Afro-Brazilians settled following their return to Africa after the emancipation of slaves in Brazil. This area houses interesting architectural hybrids displaying South American and local influences.

In their analysis of the city, Les Ateliers (2011) identified the area demarcated from the end of the bridge, the Bayol Square, the current National Assembly and the Botanical Garden ("old sacred forest"), and finally the Allée des Manguiers ("street with mango trees") which is the connection to the lagoon.

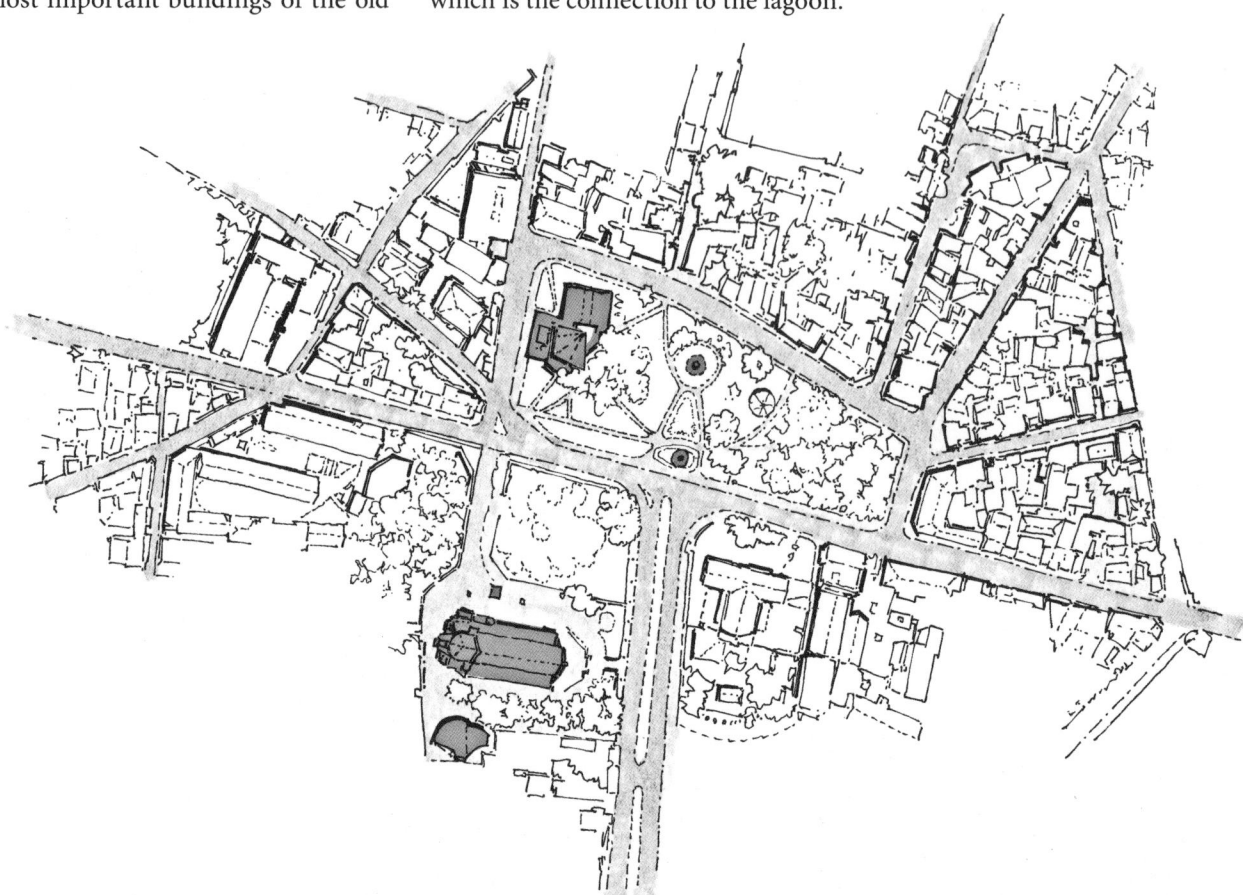

1 Bus Station
2 The Royal Palace - Honmé Museum
3 Ethnographic Museum of Porto-Novo
4 Bayol Square
5 Our lady of Porto-Novo Cathedral
6 National Assembly Square
7 Musée Da Silva, Da Silva Museum
8 Porto-Novo Market
9 Porto-Novo Great Mosque
10 Hospital
11 Cemetery
12 Charles de Gaulle Stadium

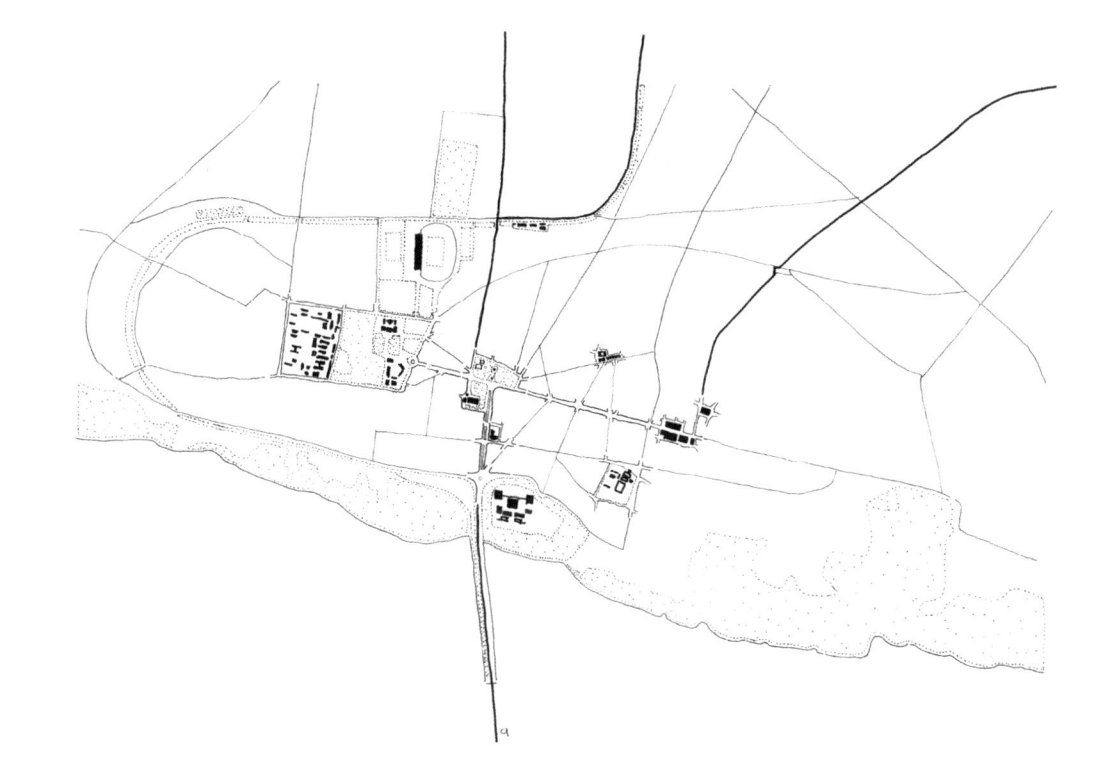

Lake Nokoué

900m

BOBO-DIOULASSO, BURKINA FASO

FOUNDED: fifteenth century
AREA: 137 km²
POPULATION (2012): 537,728
DENSITY: 3,900/km²
GPS: 11° 10'35.63"N, 4° 17'46.44"W
11° 10'35.63"N, 4° 17'46.44"W

Considered the economic centre of Burkina Faso, Bobo-Dioulasso is located 360 km south-west of the capital, Ouagadougou. Industrial activities in addition to commercial, craft and especially agro-pastoral drives make up its economic base – in fact, the city is the centre of the most agriculturally productive area in the country.

The local Bobo-speaking population refers to the city simply as "Sia". At the end of the nineteenth century, the area had two large villages, Tunuma and Sia proper, located a short distance from each other on a narrow strip of land confined by valleys on either side. These were carved by the We river to the east and by a tributary to the west. The French occupied the two villages during 1897 and created an administrative settlement near them, along the east side of the We river. A colonial military base was established in the southern sector of the city, adding to its growing importance.

Sia proper, which today is known as the Dioulasoba neighbourhood, dramatically changed in 1932 when a large roadway was built through it and its streets were widened in successive urban renewal projects. From 1926 to 1929, the French colonial government constructed a typical European grid pattern of new avenues and streets in the city, intersected by diagonals radiating from a centre, with square urban lots between them. A number of villages in the surroundings have been absorbed by the developing city and are now within its municipal boundaries, incorporated as part of the city. The Abidjan railway line reached Bobo-Diouolasso in 1934, increasing its access to markets, transportation and communications. The city is considered to house several examples of Sudano-Sahelian architecture – traditional mud buildings characteristic of this area – of which the Bobo Dioulasso Grand Mosque is arguably the best example.

Bobo-Dioulasso's economy has declined following decades of government policy favouring Ouagadougou. Since 2000, the city has engaged in a new growth spurt, gaining economic vitality following central government's re-investment in the city. Like Burkina Faso as a whole, the city is experiencing a range of climate change-related challenges that are becoming increasingly prevalent across the fragile Sahel region in which the city is situated. According to the 2014 UN-Habitat report, rainfall in Bobo-Dioulasso has been steadily decreasing. Lost vegetation cover exacerbates flooding when it does rain, which has also led to loss of harvests and dwellings. Various measures are being taken to curtail the effects of climate change.

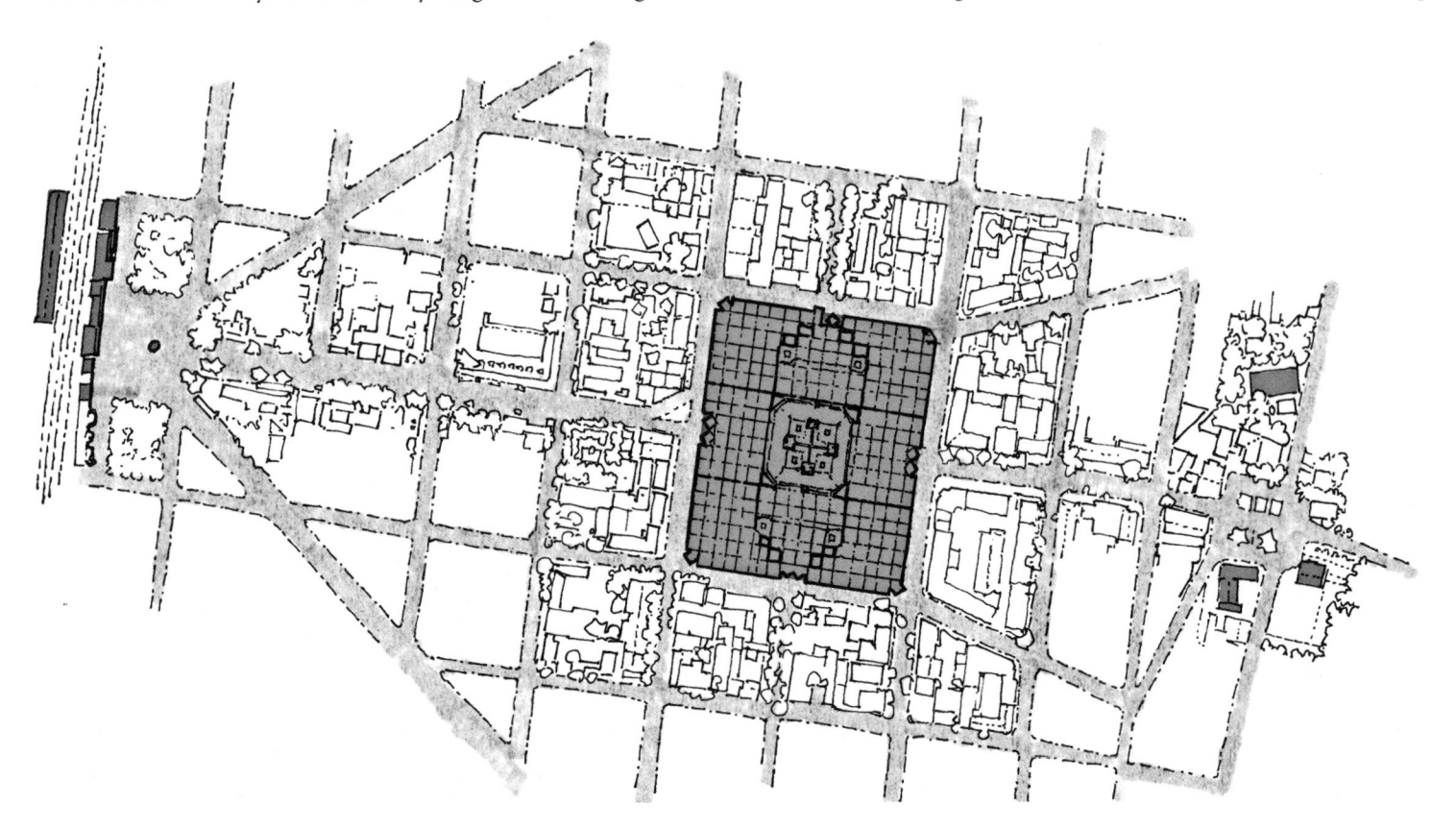

1 Bobo-Dioulasso Central Train Station & Tielo Amoro Square
2 Grand Marché de Bobo-Dioulasso, Great Market of Bobo Dioulasso
3 Revolution Square
4 Great Mosque of Dioulassoba
5 Hôtel de Ville de Sya, Sya City Hall
6 National Social Security Fund
7 Courthouse
8 Sourou Sanou Hospital
9 Treasury
10 Chamber of Commerce and Industry
11 Musée de Houet, Houet Museum
12 Stade Wobi, Wobi Stadium
13 Great Mosque of Geredougou
14 Hamdallaye School & Paré Issa Private College
15 Coulibaly High School
16 Kollo Sanou Municipal High School
17 Palais de la Culture, Cultural Centre
18 Mairie d'Arrondissement de Dafra, Borough Mayor Dafra
19 Sanou Mollo Provincial High School
20 Burkina Faso Jubilee Monument
21 Cemetery
22 Tounouma Primary and Secondary School
23 Tounouma Boys and Girls College
24 Tounouma Church
25 Omnisport Stadium
26 Bobo-Dioulasso Airport

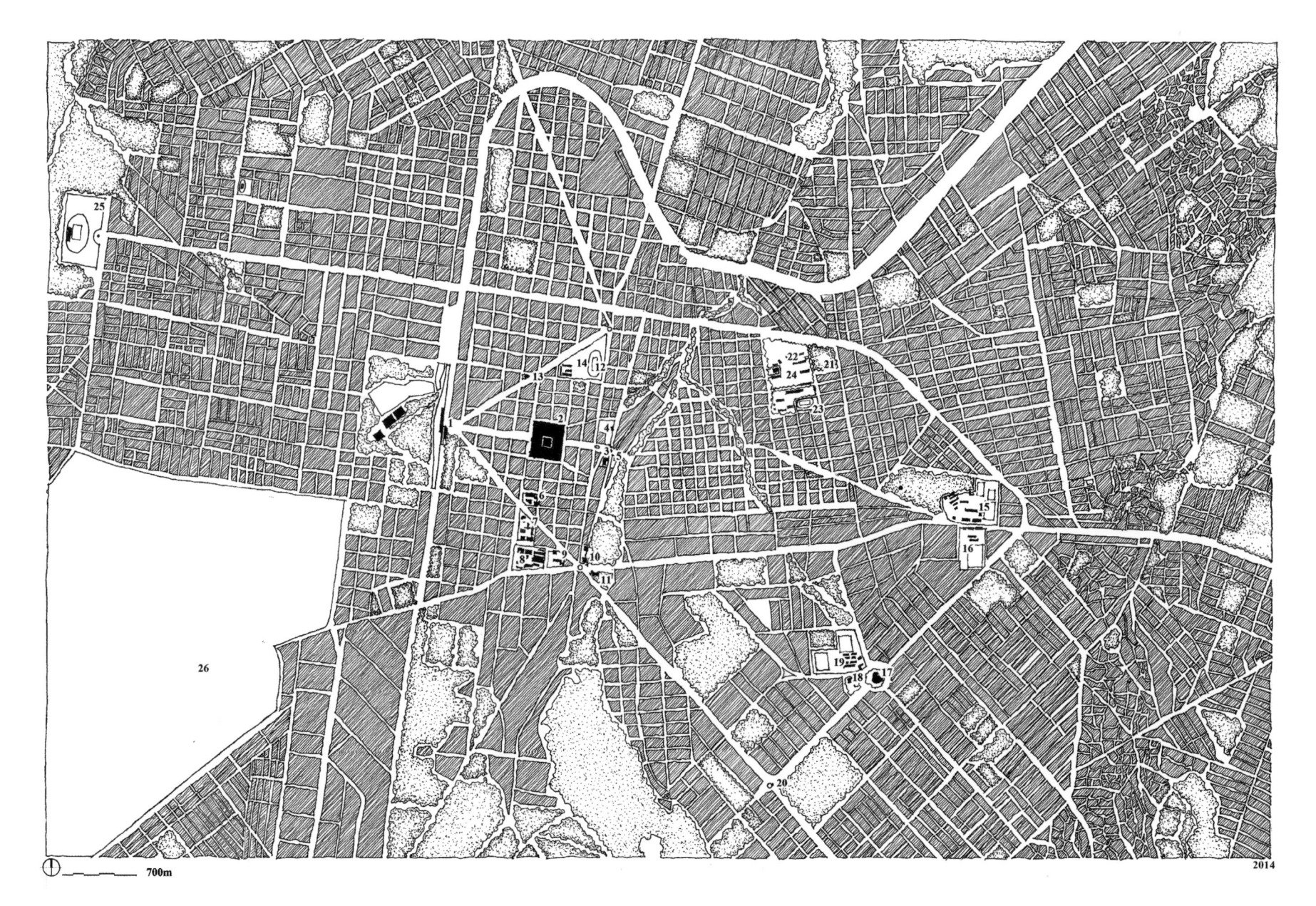

OUAGADOUGOU, BURKINA FASO

FOUNDED: fifteenth century
AREA: 217 km²
POPULATION (2011): 2,053,000
DENSITY: 6,727/km²
GPS: 12° 22'8.32"N, 1° 31'45.82"W

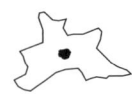

Ouagadougou, the capital of Burkina Faso, has an average annual growth rate of over 9 percent (UN-Habitat, 2014), making it one of the most rapidly growing cities in West Africa. It faces several attendant urban challenges; among them is poverty, with 50 percent of the population living in deprived conditions.

Ouagadougou's primary industries are food processing and textiles. It is served by an international airport and railway lines to Abidjan and the Ivory Coast. Landmarks in the city include the National Museum of Burkina Faso, the Moro-Naba Palace and several markets.

The city developed along a central plateau around the Imperial Palace of the King. Being an administrative centre of colonial rule, it became an important urban centre in the post-colonial era. Its morphology is roughly made up as follows (De Jong et al 2000): Pre-colonial quarters form the older parts of the inner city. These are densely populated and built-up, with traditional compounds with trees and narrow streets that have not been regulated. Growth of these quarters was restricted until independence in 1960. The old edge was developed from then onwards when Ouagadougou started to increase in size. During the early 1980s, the pace of growth was enormous. The morphology of the old periphery – a controlled grid urban pattern – results in a lower density than in the old centre. Three major industrial parks are located north-east of the old periphery, south of the airport and west of the city centre. When these industrial parks were constructed, they bordered onto the built-up area of the city. Not conducive to good place-making, high-rise buildings with large hard surfaces next to broad tarred roads – with little or no vegetation – make up the most recent additions to the city. A new periphery is constructed at the borders of the urban built-up area and comprises housing projects with green-belt development. By stark contrast, slum settlements make up the irregular, sprawling periphery of the city.

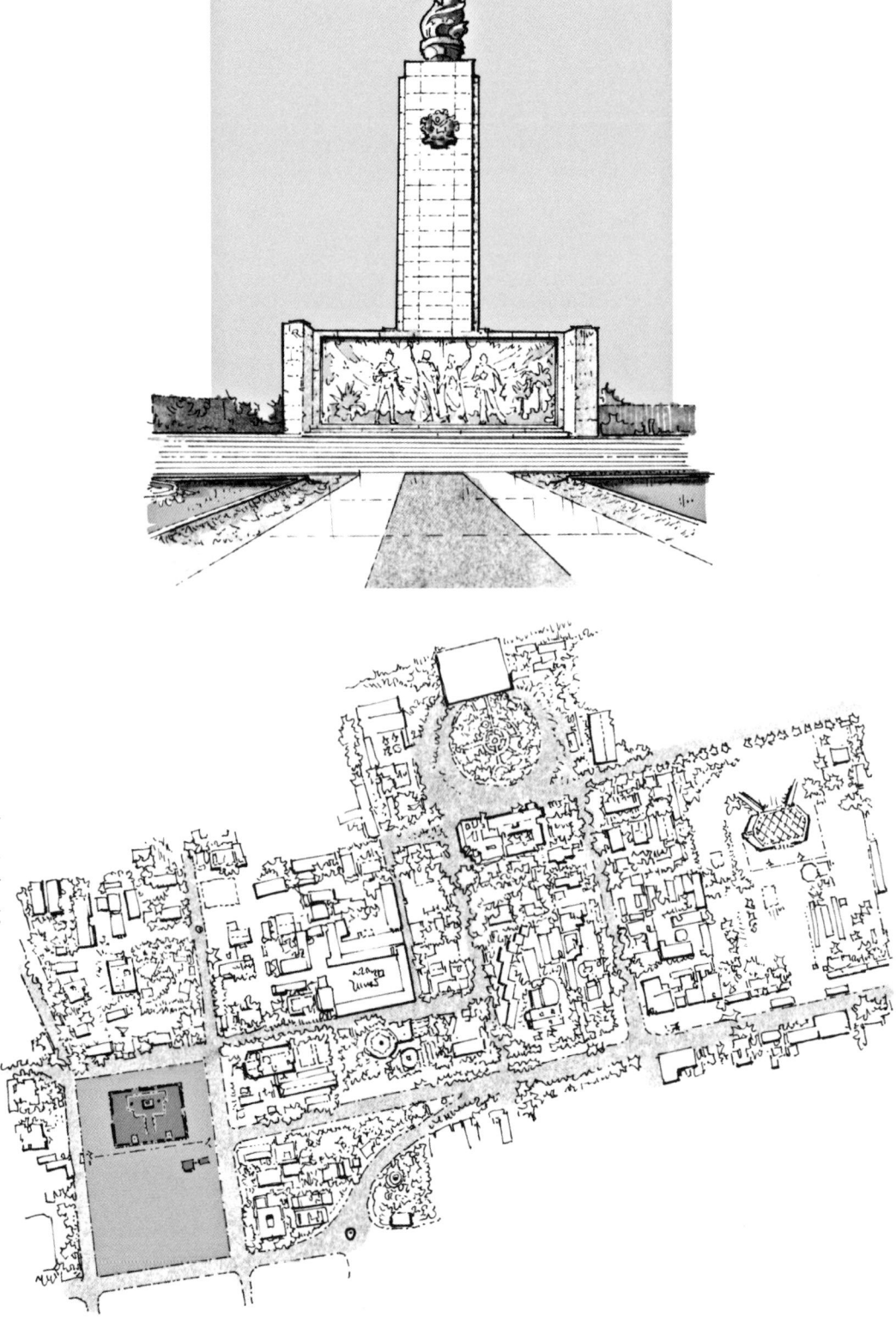

WESTERN AFRICA **161**

1 Nation Square
2 Mess des officier, Officers' Mess
3 Constitutional Council
4 Cinéastes Square
5 Jardin de la Mairie de Ouagadougou, Garden of the Mayor of Ouagadougou
6 Mairie de Ouagadougou, Mayor of Ouagadougou
7 Central Station
8 Naba Koom Garden
9 Municipal Cemetery
10 Bank of Africa
11 United Nations Roundabout
12 Garden on March 8
13 Municipal Stadium
14 Cathedral of Ouagadougou
15 Moro-Naba Palace
16 National Museum
17 Court of Justice
18 Prime Ministry
19 National Assembly of Burkina Faso
20 Ministry of Economy and Finance
21 Music Museum of Ouagadougou
22 Ministry of Labour, Employment and Youth

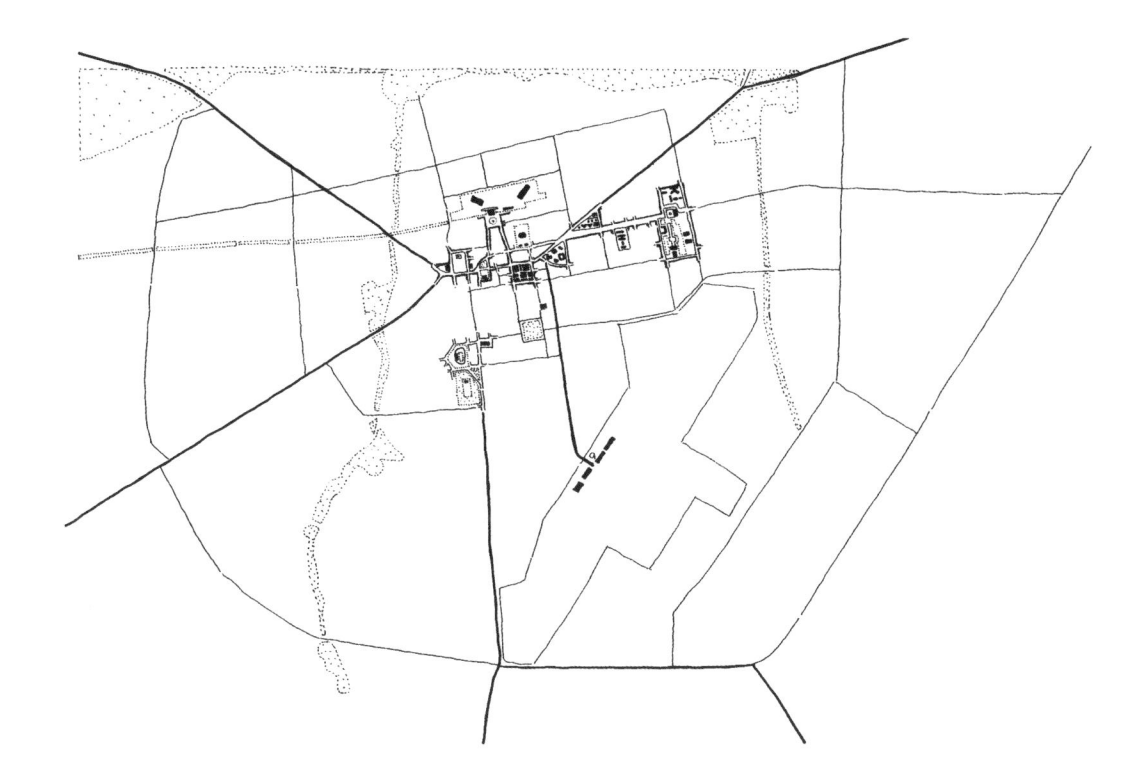

PRAIA, CAPE VERDE

FOUNDED: 1615
AREA: unknown
POPULATION (2010): 130,271
DENSITY: unknown
GPS: 14° 55'3.22"N, 23° 30'32.71"W
14° 55'10.31"N, 23° 30'26.35"W

Officially part of Africa, fifteen islands make up the Republic of Cape Verde located in the central Atlantic Ocean, 570 km off the coast of Western Africa. The series of islands were uninhabited when the Portuguese arrived in the mid-fifteenth century, soon incorporating them into the Portuguese empire. Positioned on the great trade routes between Africa, Europe, and the New World, the islands became a prosperous centre for the slave trade, but suffered economic decline after this practice was abolished in 1876. In the twentieth century, Cape Verde served as a shipping port. The islands became independent in 1975. Almost all the islands have a main or more important urban centre, along with smaller towns and villages. The most significant towns and cities have traditional Portuguese urban features, namely a coastal location, an organic street grid along the slopes, linkages between a fort and customs house, church and town hall – all characterised by a noble architectural heritage of formal simplicity (Heritage of Portuguese Influence – HPIP, 2014).

Praia is the capital and largest city of Cape Verde, located on the island Santiago (also see *São Filipe* and *Mindelo*). Geographically, Praia developed along a series of plateaus and valleys, reflected in its urban form. Given its short history, place-naming was a practical consideration for the Portuguese – Praia, meaning "beach", is the capital and largest city of Cape Verde. The city centre is known as *Platô* due to its location on a small plateau. The rest of the plateaus generally have the name *achada* (Achada de Santo António, Achada de São Filipe etc.) – *achada* being a Portuguese word meaning "volcanic plateau". *Platô* is one of the areas on UNESCO's "tentative list" to be declared a World Heritage Site (UNESCO, 2014).

Praia is the island's ferry port that ships coffee, sugar and fruit and is home to one of the nation's four airports. During the Portuguese administration, only the central plateau was considered to be the city proper. The remaining neighbourhoods developed in a more organic, chaotic way. It was only after independence that the neighbourhoods generally became accepted as part of the city with attendant infrastructure development. After independence, the city population increased rapidly as its population quadrupled in size. With recent rural urban migration on the rise, the pressure is increasing on existing water resources, sanitation and social services infrastructure like never before.

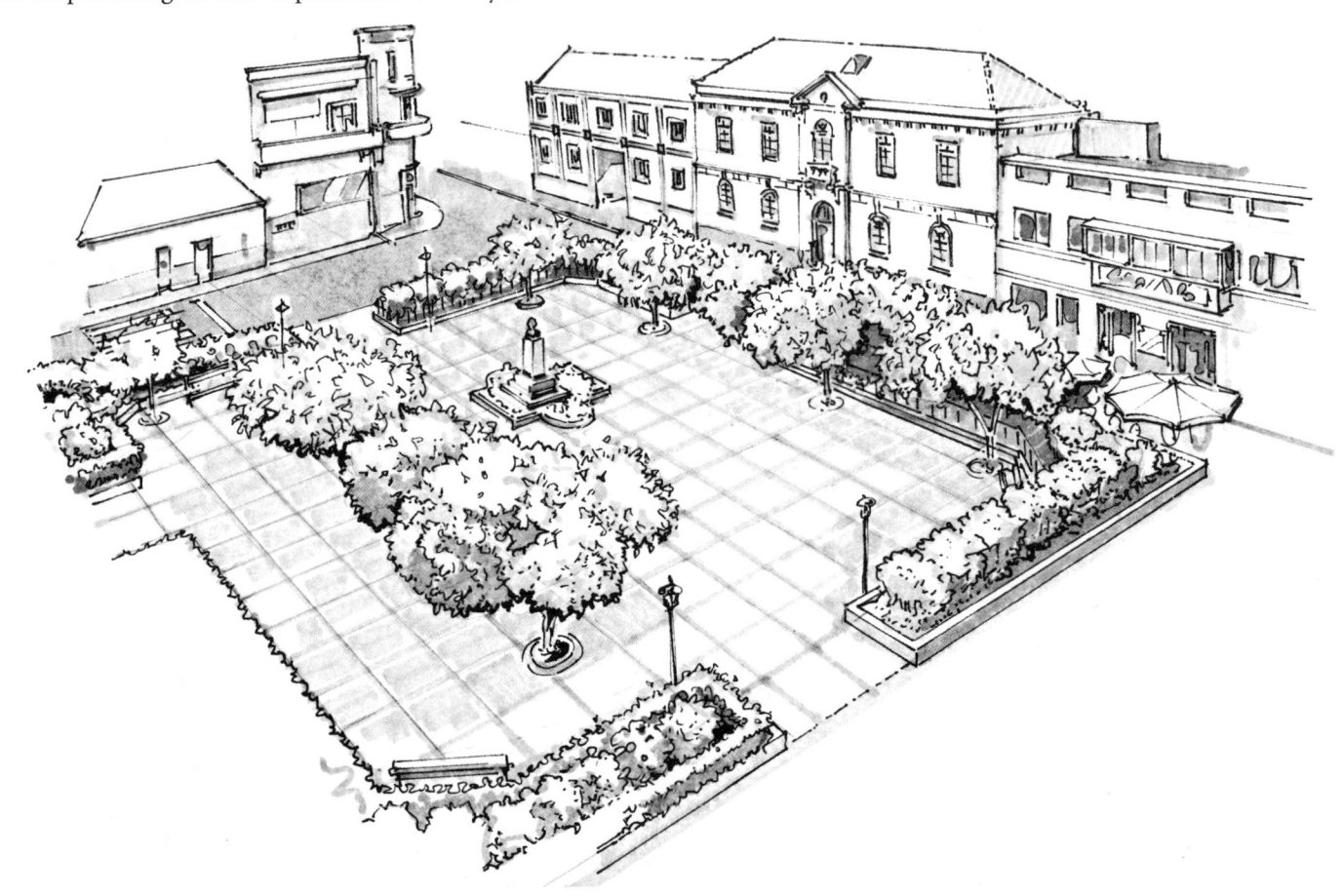

WESTERN AFRICA 163

1 Alexandre Albuquerque Square
2 Luís de Camões Square
3 Dominic Ramos Square
4 Church of Our Lady of Grace
5 Old City Hall
6 Presidential Palace
7 Jaime Mota Barracks
8 Municipal Market of Praia
9 Plateau 7th Day Adventist Church
10 Great School
11 Agostinho Neto Hospital
12 Music Yard & Ethnographic Museum Praia
13 Domingos Ramos School
14 July 5th Park
15 National Library
16 Estádio da Várzea & Núcleo Museológico da Praia, Praia Museum Centre
17 Palácio do Governo, Government Palace
18 Cemetery
19 Nelson Mandela International Airport
20 Port
21 National Assembly
22 Santa Maria Island

North Atlantic Ocean

2014

MINDELO, CAPE VERDE

FOUNDED: 1859
AREA: unknown
POPULATION (2005): 70,611
DENSITY: unknown
GPS: 16° 53'0.97"N, 24° 59'20.77"W
16° 53'22.99"N, 24° 59'16.67"W

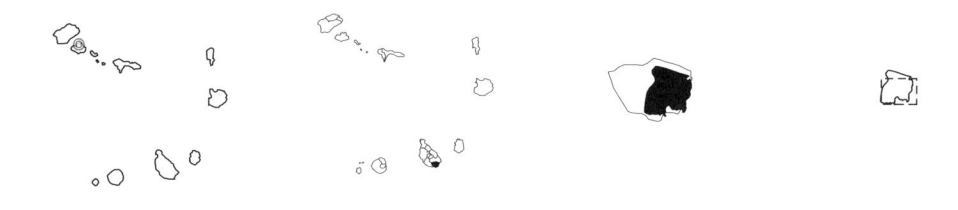

Mindelo is located on the island São Vicente – one of the islands making up the archipelago of Cape Verde (see *Praia* and *São Filipe*). Following its discovery, it remained practically uninhabited for more than 300 years and was used for cattle pasturage. After a few failed attempts at settlement (because, amongst other reasons, poor natural resources such as water) at the beginning of the nineteenth century, the British decided to establish a coal deposit in Porto Grande to supply ships on the Atlantic routes in 1838. The good port characteristics of the Bay of Mindelo – a natural harbour formed by a volcanic crater – transformed the island into an important trade post to supply ships that crossed the Atlantic.

In 1859, when the town was classified, it apparently had four streets, four cross-streets, two small squares and 170 houses, as well as being occupied by approximately 1,400 inhabitants who thrived on the establishment of several English coal companies. In 1875 it was considered to be the biggest coal port in the mid-Atlantic. Four years later, Mindelo was elevated to the category of city, with a population of 3,300 inhabitants.

The City of Mindelo is a structured city with well laid-out streets and architectural traits that show the early influence of the British, as well as monuments of heritage significance from earlier colonial times. The Main Square (Praça Nova) is a garden located in the heart of the city. The General Improvement Plan of Mindelo became a priority in 1927, which influenced the city's expansion until the mid-twentieth century. Planning studies were resumed in 1957. Some garden city models were proposed quite inappropriately given the water scarcity on the islands – the main goal being to modernise the islands and reorganise the two major port cities, Praia and Mindelo. The architectural heritage of the islands was also documented meticulously by the Portuguese architect Luis Benavente (1902–1993) (see *Praia* and HPIP, 2014). Today Mindelo is a tourist destination, described as the most picturesque city in Cape Verde. Enclosed between mountains and the ocean, the bay, Porto Grande, has been classified as one of the most beautiful in the world by UNESCO. The legendary singer Cesária Évora (1941–2011) hails from Mindelo, and the international airport was named after her.

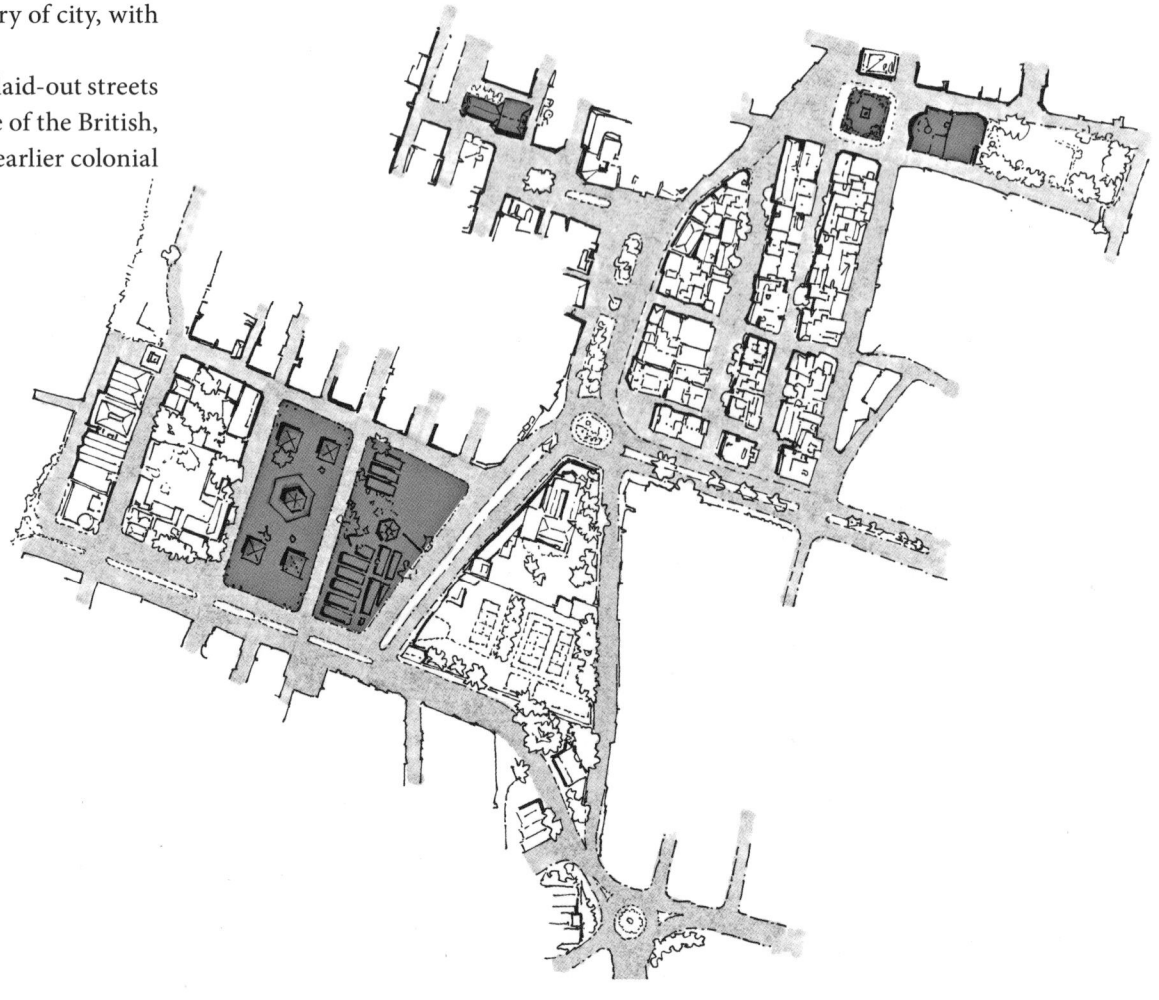

1 Star Square
2 Church Our Lady of Light
3 Municipality of São Vicente
4 Mindelo Marina & Pont d'Agua Leisure Complex
5 Presidential Palace
6 Amilcar Cabral Square
7 Nho Roque Park
8 The Church of Jesus Christ of Latter-day Saints
9 Municipal Market
10 Belem Tower
11 Post Office
12 Industrial and Commercial School of Mindelo
13 Courthouse
14 Baptista de Sousa Hospital & Old Hospital
15 Our Lady Help of Christians Church
16 Salesian College of Arts and Crafts
17 Aderito Sena Stadium
18 Port
19 Mindelo Cultural Centre

SÃO FILIPE, CAPE VERDE

FOUNDED: sixteenth century
AREA: unknown
POPULATION (2010): 22,227
DENSITY: 97/km²
GPS: 14° 53'39.52"N, 24° 29'58.16"W
14° 53'44.13"N, 24° 30'1.54"W

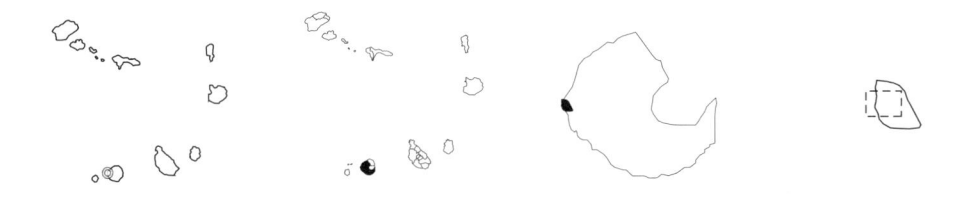

The archipelago of Cape Verde (see *Praia* and *Mindelo* respectively for an introduction and overview) was formed by magma rivers with steep ravines and blackish-brown rocky soil. According to the 2014 UN-Habitat report, temperatures have risen by between 0.5 °C and 1 °C in parts of Cape Verde. For its cities, the urban heat-island effect – as well as increased vulnerability to air and land pollution – are of critical concern. According to the World Bank, the islands fall within the Sahelian climate, with prolonged periods of drought, a marked shortage of fresh water, and a 2.7 percent population growth rate that will exert intolerable pressure on the fragile agriculture base.

Poor natural resources and the underdeveloped, narrow economic base are the main causes of poverty in Cape Verde. According to the World Bank, in the past, high mortality rates, famines, and emigration balanced population and poor domestic resources. As a result of falling mortality rates, coupled with stable fertility rates and declining opportunities for emigration, the pressure on the poor domestic resources is again increasing.

Against this backdrop, tourism plays a vital role for the livelihood of the inhabitants of Cape Verde. Amongst its tourist sites is the largest city of Fogo Island, São Filipe. Fogo Island has the largest mountain on the islands – an active volcano, the Pico do Fogo. With just over 20,000 inhabitants, it is the fourth-largest city of Cape Verde following Praia, Mindelo and Assomada. This is also the site of the island airport, which offers connections from and to the other islands.

Set amidst black lava beaches, this picturesque little city rises approximately 100 m above the high, steep coast. Alto San Pedro, a long plaza, separates the lower city (Vila Baixo) from the upper city (Vila Riba). The town hall is located in the lower city – one of the most representative vernacular buildings which was built in 1928. Similar to other settlements on the islands, the church is the main centre of the small city. The church of Nossa Senhora de Conceição is situated below Alto San Pedro Plaza, surrounded by colourful vernacular dwellings. These typically exemplify "unsophisticated constructions that simplified erudite themes in a standardised manner" (HPIP, 2014), particularly during the nineteenth century. São Filipe is on the "tentative list" of World Heritage Sites because of its historic colonial buildings.

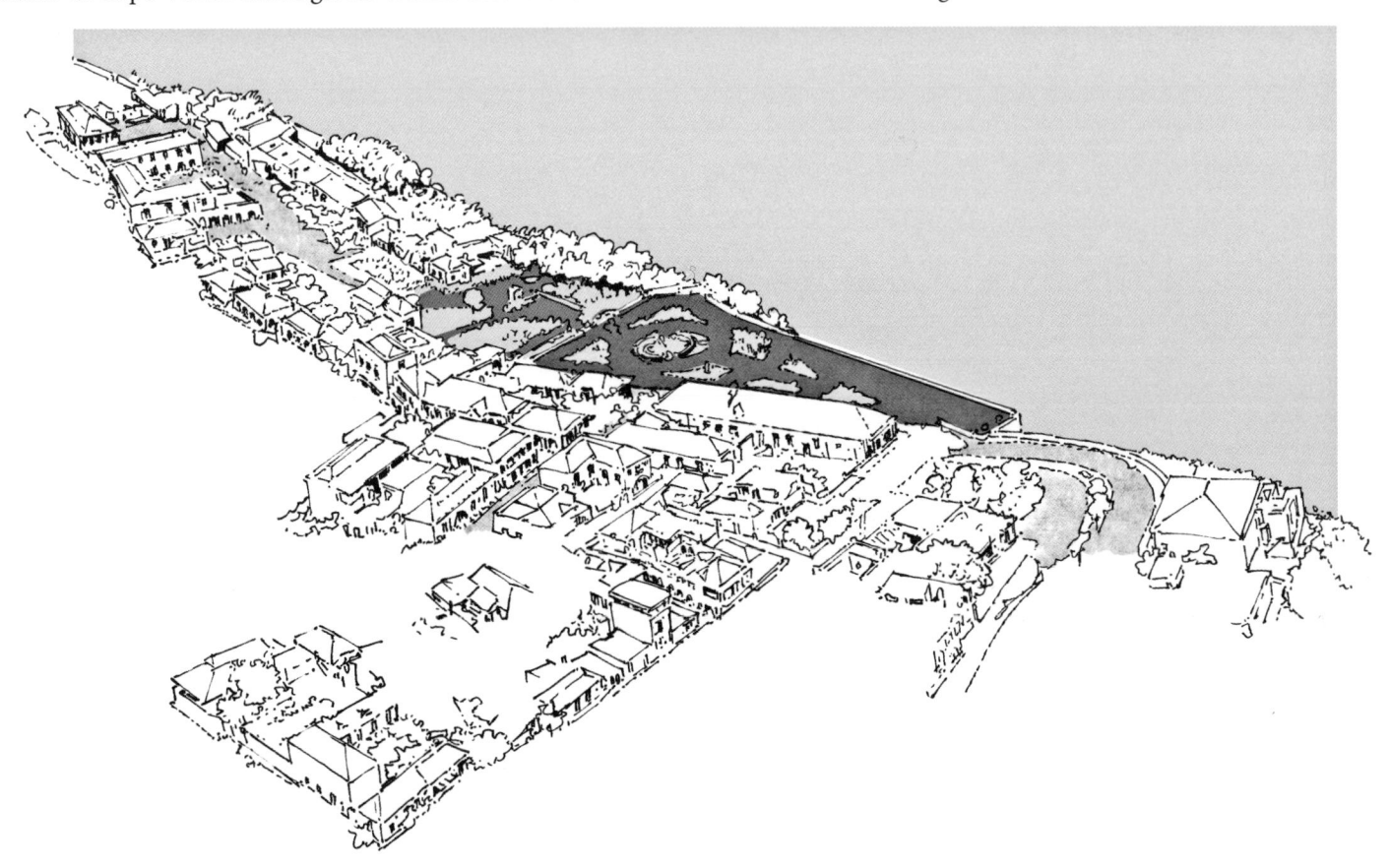

1	12th September Square
2	Town Hall
3	Fortress Square
4	Church Of Our Lady Of Conception
5	Old Cemetery & Beach
6	Chapel on Alberto da Silva Square
7	Carlota Fortress
8	Alberto da Silva Square
9	Municipal Museum
10	Stadium
11	São Filipe Airport

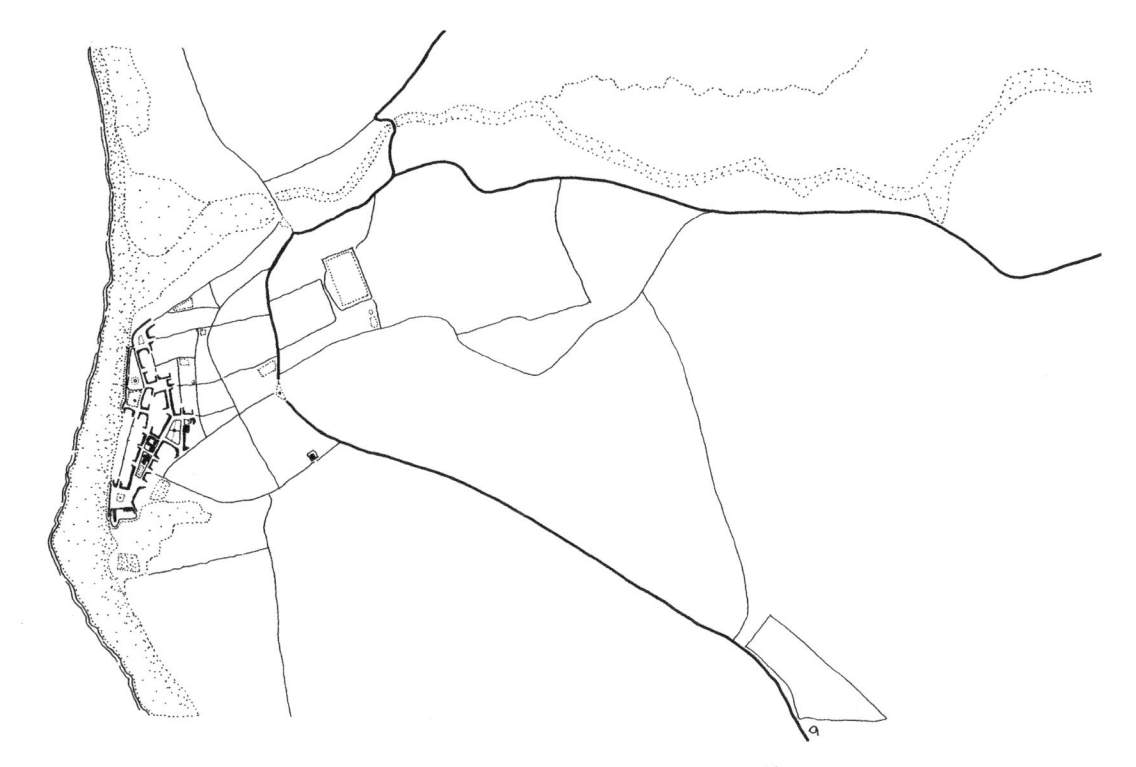

ABIDJAN, CÔTE D'IVOIRE

FOUNDED: 1903
AREA: 577 km²
POPULATION (2012): 4,476,397
DENSITY: 2,100/km²
GPS: 5° 19'17.18"N, 4° 1'9.24"W
5° 19'0.37"N, 4° 1'10.56"W

Originally a coastal fishing village, the tropical city of Abidjan was founded by the French at the turn of the previous century. By 1934 it was the capital of the Côte d'Ivoire. In 1983, the rapid growth of the city led to the decision to relocate the capital of Côte d'Ivoire to Yamoussoukro.

The site of the city comprises distinct topographic elements: the coastal cordon, the island of Petit Bassam, the Ebrié Lagoon that stretches northwards from the coast, and the plateau that stretches towards the sea. The lagoon divides the city into northern and southern sections.

According to Appessika (2003), the first stage of the development of the city was the colonial period, when its expansion was closely linked to the railway. From 1930 to the post-war period, the then town of Abidjan only consisted of three districts with Le Plateau – the administrative centre and European Quarter – separated from the two African districts of Treichville and Adjamé. According to Appessika (2003), the current physical appearance of the town was sketched in the Badani Plan of 1948 that introduced its planning and restructuring, as well as marked the passage from administrative centre to port.

The second stage of the city's development commenced with the completion of the Vridi Canal in 1951. The city was connected to the Atlantic Ocean – thus securing its status as a trading centre. The headquarters and warehouses of large import-export firms were set up in the town. The railway line to Ouagadougou and vast road network converging towards the harbour boosted the city to a hub for foreign trade. Extensive urban development and the cumulative impact of the growth of services contributed to a dramatic expansion of the city (Appessika 2003). It was during this stage that the modernist architect Henri Chomette was commissioned to design the Abidjan City Hall and the Société Générale Bank – both landmarks of the Modern Movement in the tropics and completed in the mid-1950s.

The new urban perimeter of the city, which marks the third stage according to Appessika, is the product of sustained demographic growth, which, from the 1970s, gave birth to districts that were more or less planned. A series of environmental problems are linked to its rapid urbanisation. According to the 2014 UN-Habitat report, Abidjan will likely be affected by sea-level rise and saline intrusion into coastal aquifers and agricultural areas. In addition, Ebrié Lagoon is becoming increasingly polluted due to discharge of industrial effluents and the pumping of organic sewage.

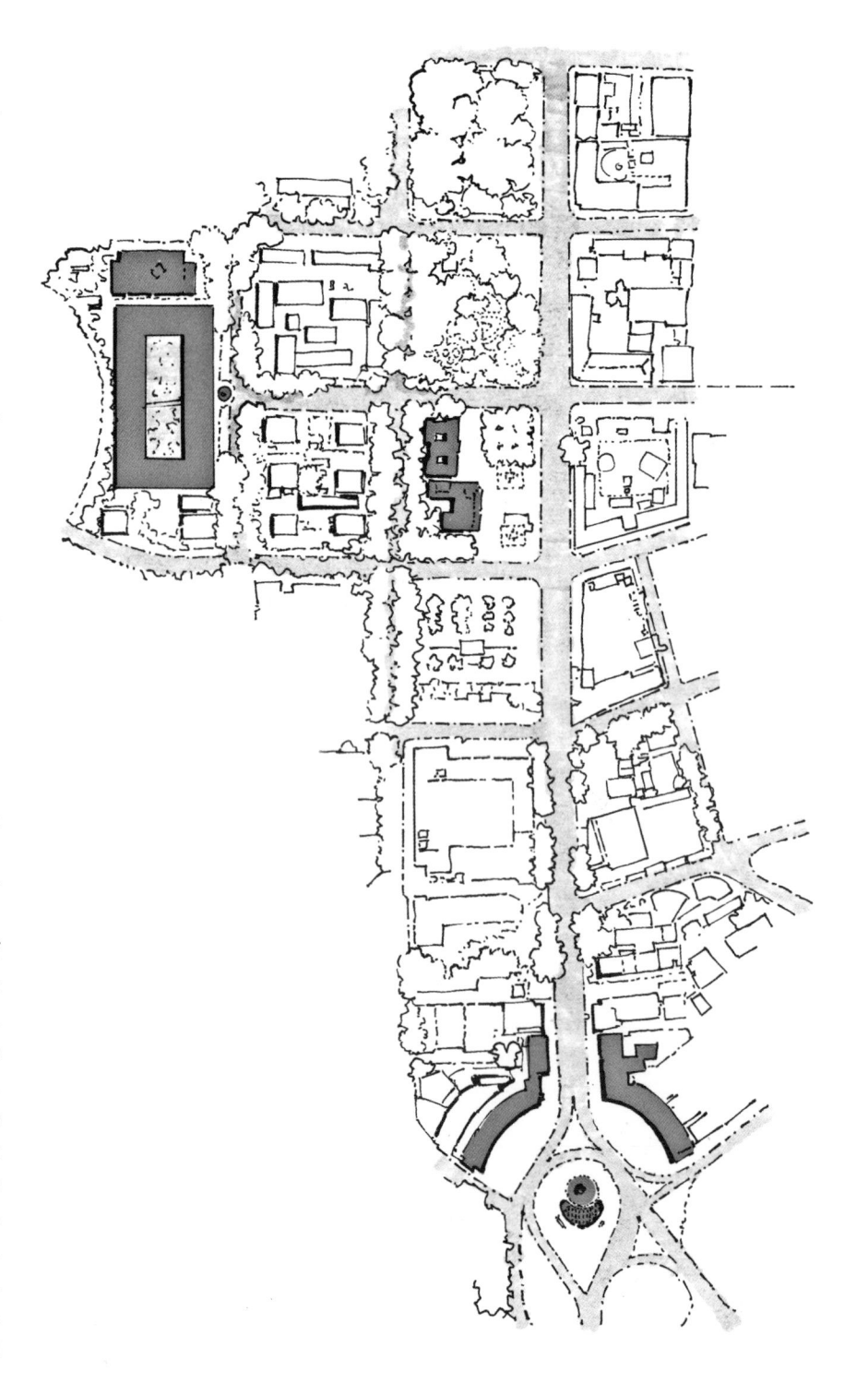

1 Republic Square
2 Train Station
3 Post Office
4 Presidential Palace
5 Ministères, Ministries
6 Public Park
7 Former Plateau Market
8 Great Mosque
9 F. Houphouët Boigny Stadium
10 National Assembly
11 Courthouse
12 St Paul's Cathedral
13 National Museum
14 Municipal Stadium
15 Palais de la Culture, Cultural Centre
16 Treichville Market
17 Banco Forest
18 Technical School
19 St Jean Church
20 Hôtel Sofitel Abidjan Hôtel Ivoire, Sofitel Abidjan Hotel Ivoire
21 Sainte-Marie School
22 Catholic University of West Africa
23 Universal Church
24 Pyramid Building
25 Port

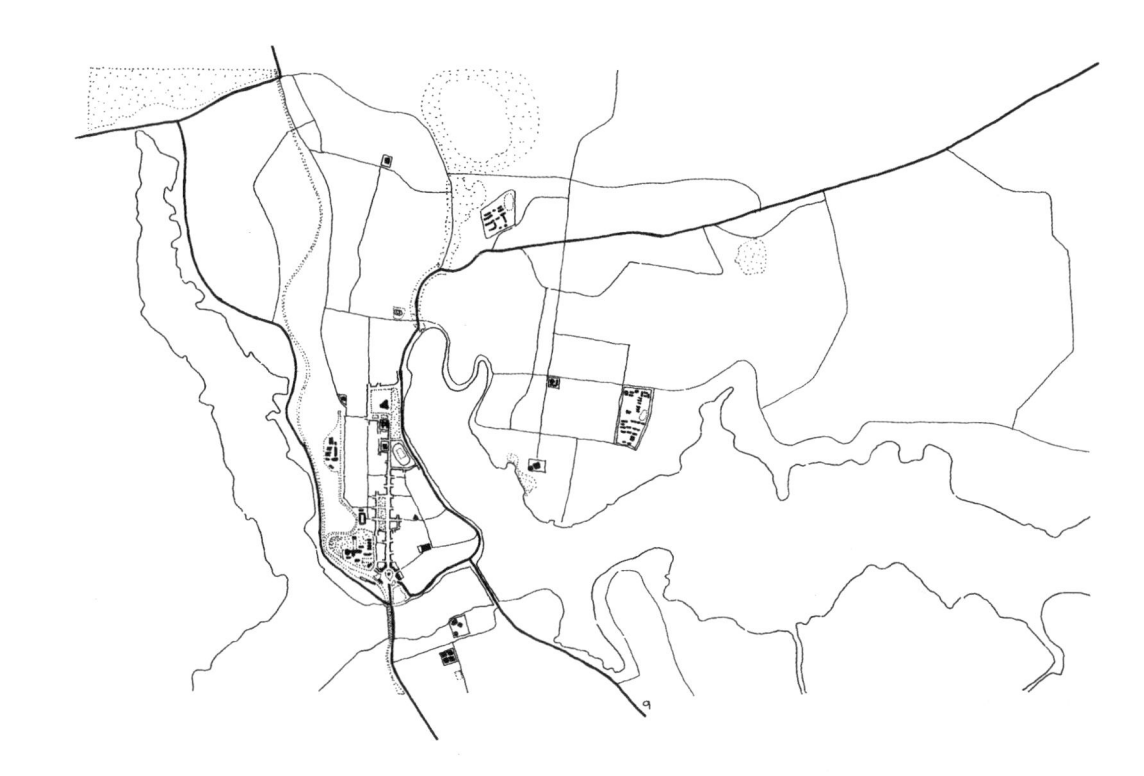

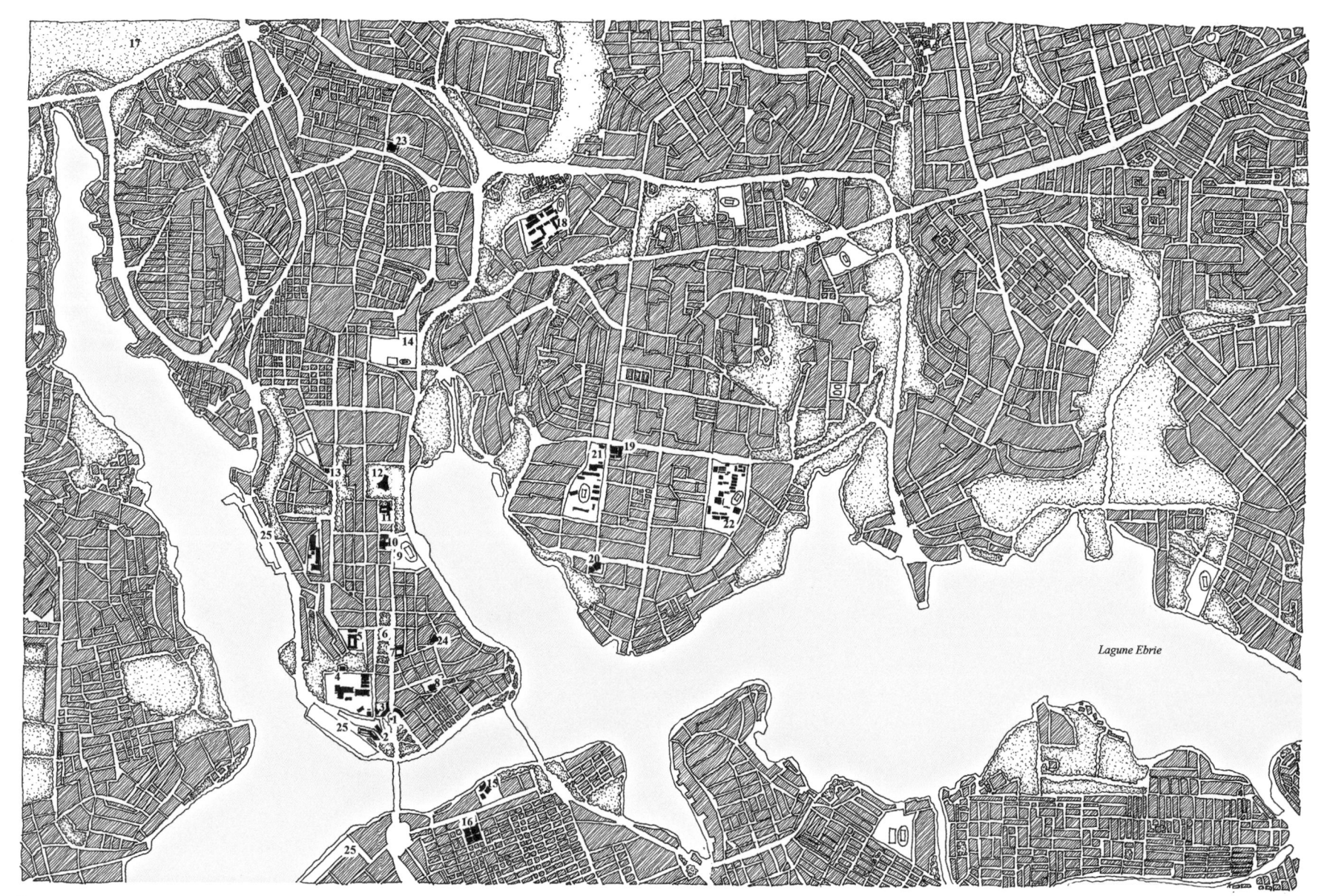

YAMOUSSOUKRO, CÔTE D'IVOIRE

FOUNDED: unknown
AREA: unknown
CITY POPULATION (2011): 966,000
DENSITY: unknown
GPS: 5° 25'14.80"N, 4° 1'4.69"W

A small village in 1901, Yamoussoukro became the political capital of Côte d'Ivoire in 1983, while Abidjan remained the country's economic capital. Elleh (2002) describes Yamoussoukro as a "twentieth-century Versailles in Africa". Usually, the idea behind the relocation of a coastal capital to an inland location (such as in the case of Lagos to Abuja) is to develop and unify the country while forming a new national identity free from the former colonies. The primary reason, however, for the relocation of the capital of Côte d'Ivoire from Abidjan to Yamoussoukro was nepotistic since Yamoussoukro was the then head of State's birth hometown.

The master plan for the new city was prepared by the Tunisian-born architect Olivier-Clément Cacoub during the 1970s to early 1980s. It was an attempt to harmonise a great city and a village in the form of a new town made up of a collection of modern villas.

The Yamoussoukro master plan has one major landmark – an island wedged between two branches of an artificial lake. From the island, the town spreads out in all directions. The city contains 169 villages and hamlets with the road that crosses the island forming the major axis. Elleh maintains that the town has no major vocal point since it was intended to be a village made up of a collection of villas. These are separated by broad streets that respond to the major buildings in the town. Buildings are therefore isolated from another.

The massive Our Lady of Peace Basilica (1985) – said to be the largest Christian place of worship on Earth – is situated in the south-west corner of the town. It is purposefully designed to be isolated from the centre of the town and from all major objects in Yamoussoukro (Elleh, 2002). At 149 m high, this building dwarfs the surrounding urban landscape.

WESTERN AFRICA **171**

1 Basilica of Our Lady of Peace of Yamoussoukro
2 Palace of the President
3 Crocodile Lake
4 Market
5 Park
6 Great Mosque
7 Church of St. Augustine
8 Mamie Adjoua Secondary School
9 City Hall
10 Félix Houphouët Biogny Foundation
11 Palace of Congress
12 Hotel President
13 Park
14 Tourism Office
15 House of Deputies
16 Scientific Secondary School

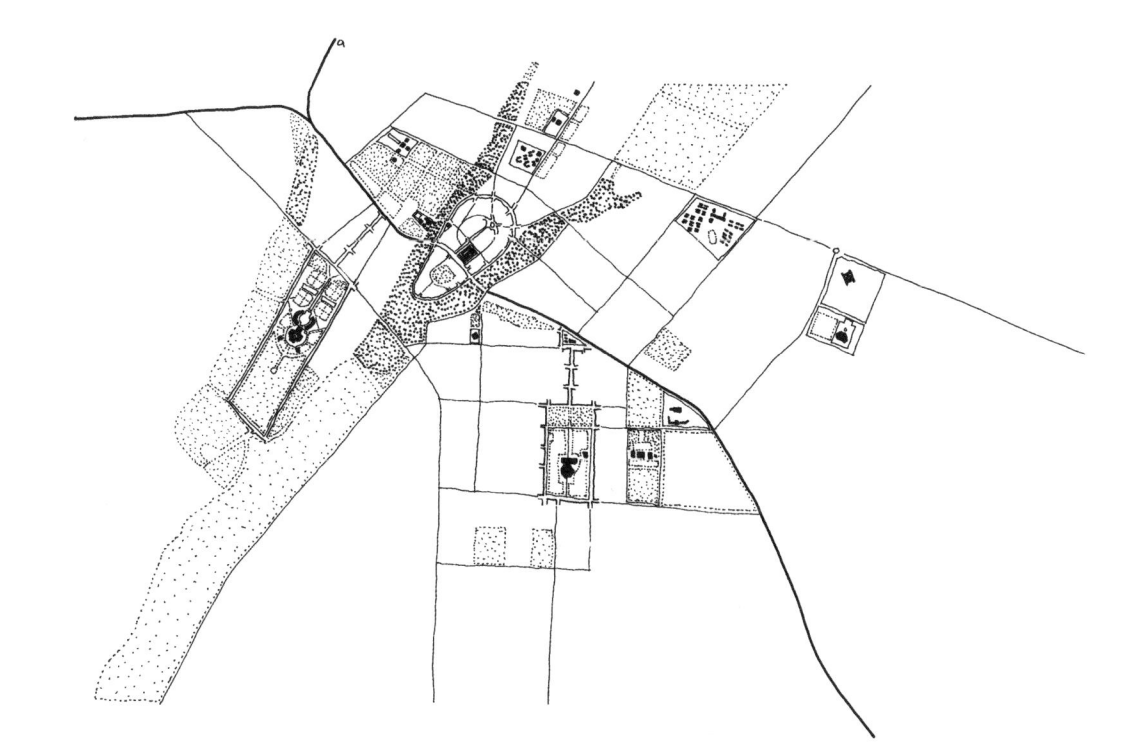

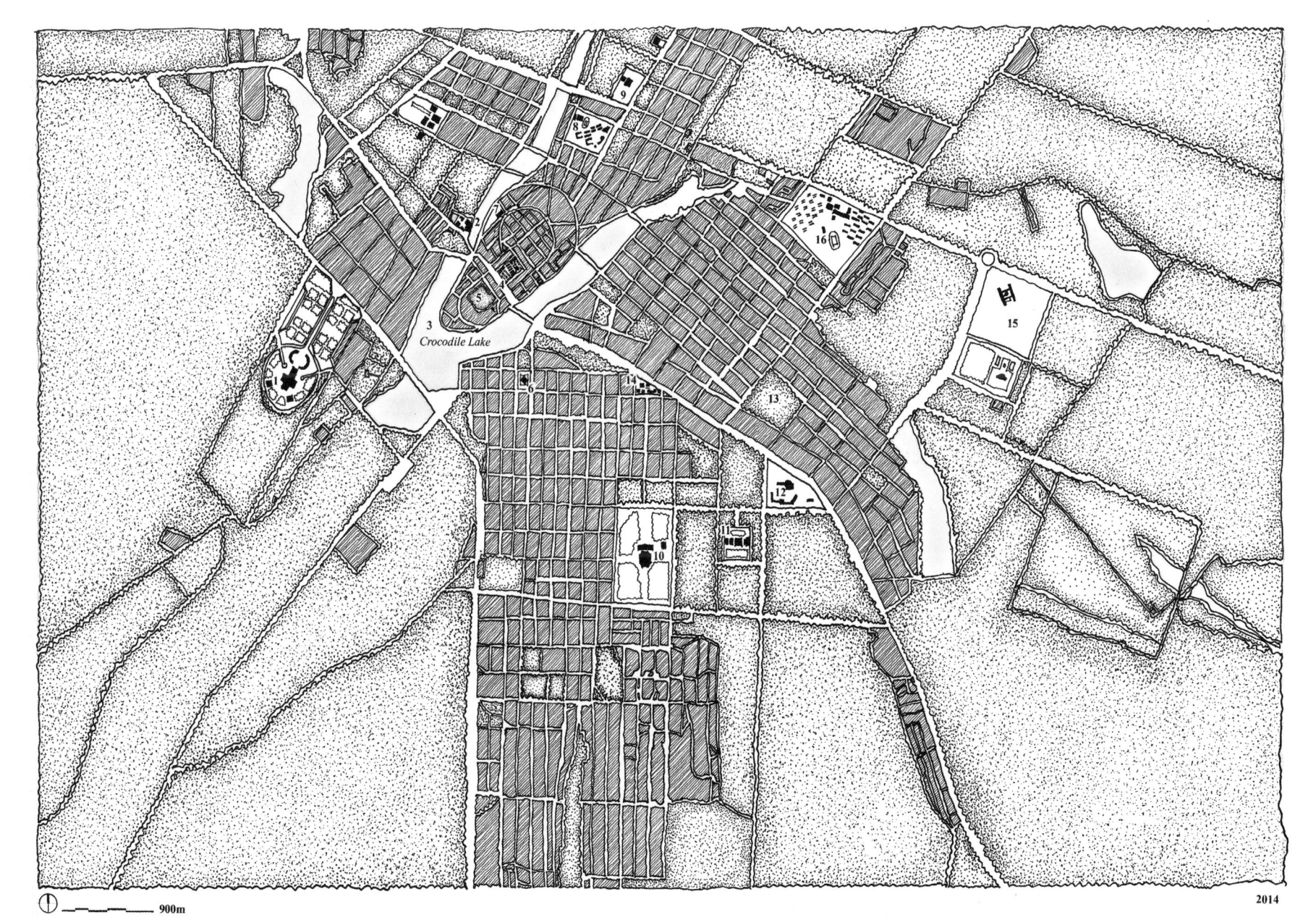

2014

BANJUL, THE GAMBIA

FOUNDED: 1816
URBAN AREA: 93 km²
POPULATION: 357,238
URBAN AREA DENSITY: 3,800/km²
GPS: 13° 27'36.69"N, 16° 34'56.27"W
13° 27'13.15"N, 16° 34'28.35"W

Banjul, formerly known as Bathurst, is a relatively small African city and capital of the Gambia. The city is situated on St Mary's Island (Banjul Island), where the Gambia River flows into the Atlantic Ocean. The island is connected to the mainland by the singular access point of the Denton Bridge. Banjul can also be accessed by ferries which link Banjul to the mainland opposite the river. The development of the city has been inhibited by its location on an island and is threatened by rising sea levels. This small pedestrian-friendly port city has a structured and ordered layout. The city is also home to the bustling Albert Market. Significant landmarks in the city include: the Gambian National Museum, Albert Market, Banjul State House (one of Banjul's most impressive buildings and still used as the presidential office), Banjul Court House, as well as two cathedrals and several mosques. Arch 22 was built as a commemorative monument in 1996, and is located at the gateway entrance to the capital. The structure rises to a height of 35 m and stands at the centre of an open square. The War Memorial & Fountain erected to celebrate the coronation of Britain's King George VI in 1937 is located near MacCarthy Square. MacCarthy Square has a colonial atmosphere with pleasant nineteenth-century architecture.

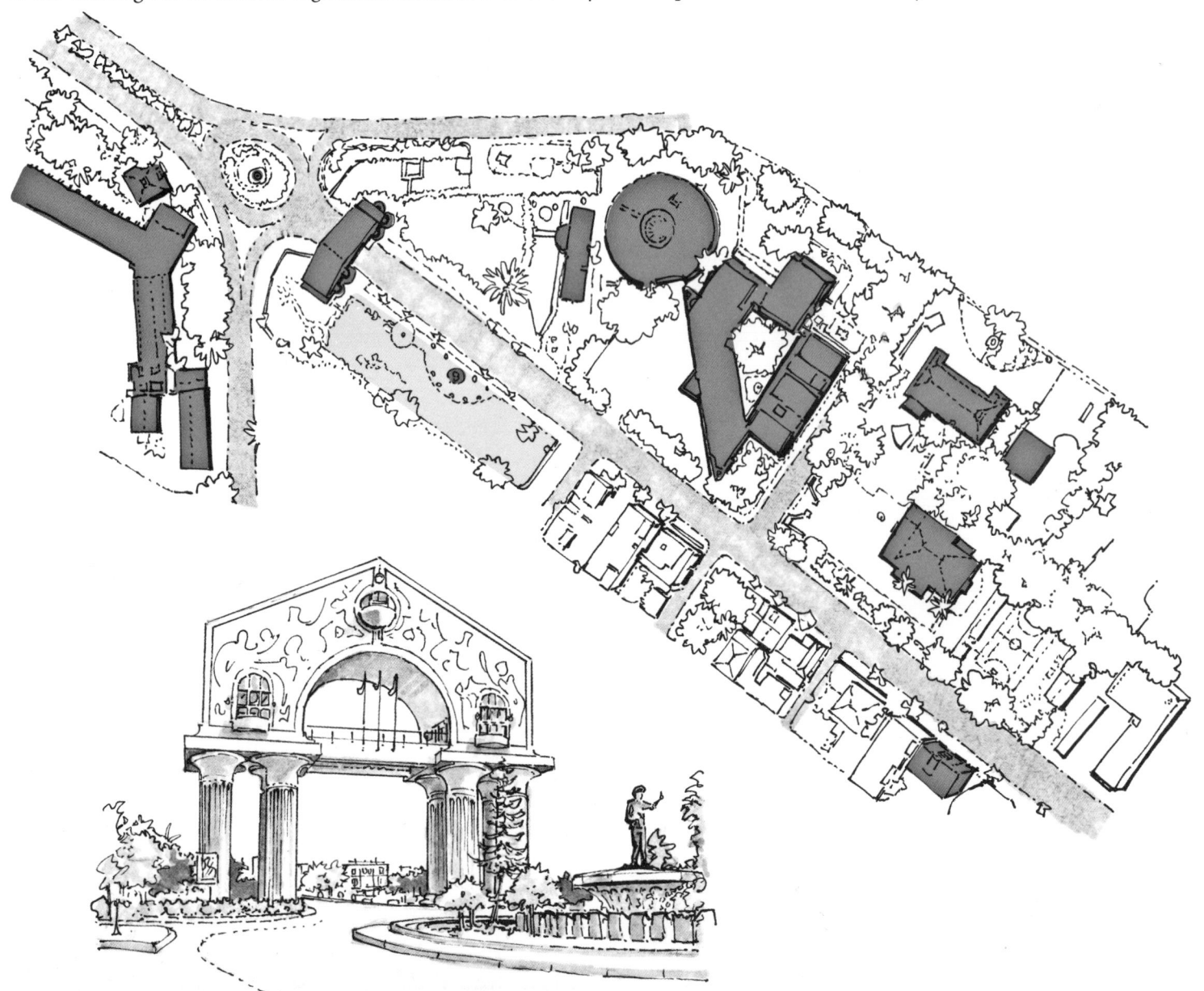

1 July 22th Square
2 Statue of the Unknown Soldier
3 Arch 22
4 National Centre for Arts and Culture
5 Supreme Court
6 National Assembly
7 Banjul Mosque
8 Banjul City Council
9 Royal Victoria Teaching Hospital
10 National Museum
11 New National Assembly
12 Ecole Sénégalaise de Banjul, School Senegalese Banjul
13 National Library
14 Christian Cemetery
15 Muslim Cemetery
16 King Fahad Mosque
17 St Augustine Senior Secondary School
18 Crab Island Upper Basic School
19 King George V Stadium
20 Muslim Senior Secondary School
21 Banjul Port
22 Post Office
23 Market
24 State House
25 Six Gun Battery
26 Banjul Ferry Terminal

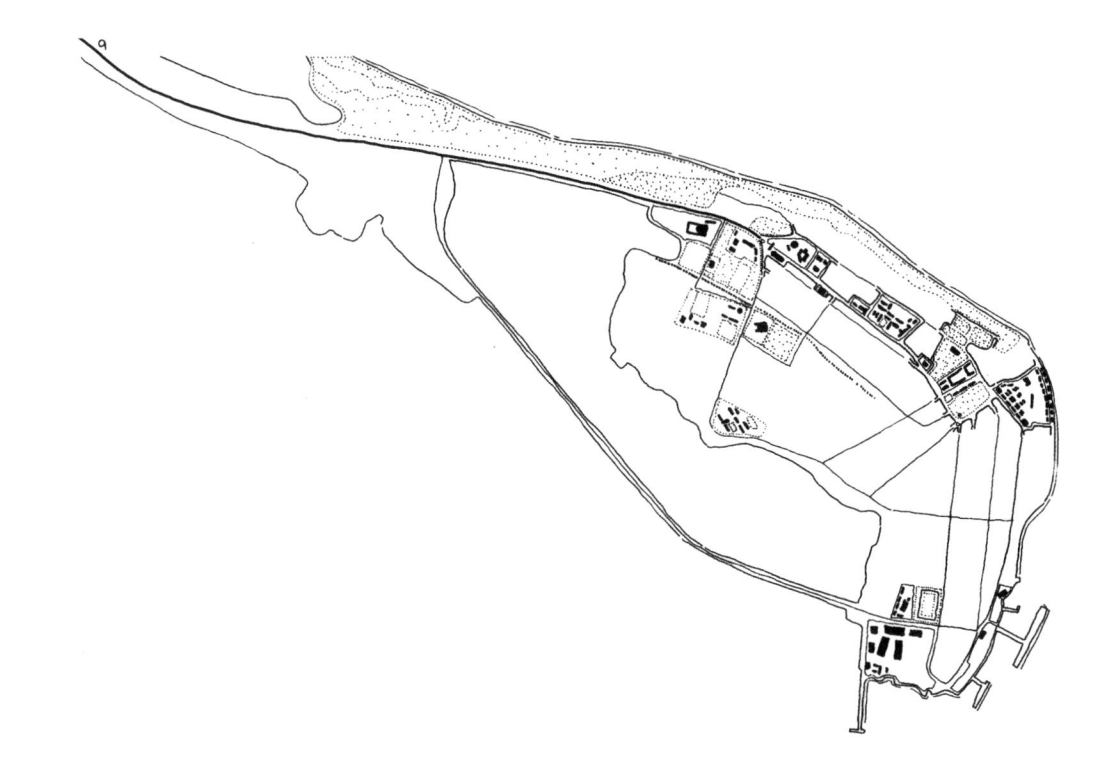

ACCRA, GHANA

FOUNDED: unknown
URBAN AREA: 173 km²
POPULATION: 2,291,352
URBAN AREA DENSITY: 9,590/km²
GPS: 5° 32'50.97"N, 0° 11'33.56"W
5° 34'43.45"N, 0° 11'11.98"W

Accra, capital city and one of the largest cities in Ghana, was originally established as a group of fishing villages during the sixteenth century. The city, located along the Ghanaian Atlantic coast, initially developed around the port and served as the capital of the British Gold Coast between 1877 and 1957. What started out as a fishing village developed into a modern metropolis. This is reflected in the city's architecture which includes everything from historical buildings, such as the Cathedral of the Holy Spirit (the seat of the Roman Catholic Archdiocese of Accra), to modern skyscrapers and apartment blocks.

The city did not develop as one centralised urban core, but from scattered settlements connected by footpaths (Grant, 2009). The downtown streets were not organised in a structured grid, but rather developed as needed. Therefore, the spatial structure seems unplanned and is characterised by overcrowding, substandard housing and inadequate sanitation.

The earthquake of 1862 destroyed significant portions of Accra and presented the colonial rulers with an opportunity to plan and rebuild the city according to their needs. The year 1877 marks the development of Accra as an urban centre when the forts were changed to administration centres. As in most colonial cities, European neighbourhoods and commercial areas were deliberately separated from the commercial and residential areas of the local population. Accra's current spatial pattern reveals a historically rooted central urban core, which has retained some remnants of its British Town Planning design, albeit blended with a more recent Ghanaian influence. The relatively dense inner core of the city contains the commercial centre and administrative core. The urban periphery is characterised by organic and uncontrolled sprawling development, gradually replacing agricultural and forest lands with low-density single-family housing, and a variety of local commercial uses (World Bank, 2008).

Accra is divided into various areas. Accra central consists of the CBD and the oldest historic districts of the city, separated from the outlying suburbs by the Ring Road. The area's main attractions include the Kwame Nkrumah Mausoleum, the National Museum, Independence Square, the National Theatre and Ohene Djan Stadium. In contrast to the relatively unplanned central Accra, the more recent neighbourhoods follow a regular grid system. Northern and Western Accra are residential and business districts while Eastern Accra is largely residential. The Jamestown area, claimed to be the city's principal historical site, includes the Ussher Fort and James Fort, as well as Osu Castle (also known as Christiansborg), built by Danish settlers in the seventeenth century.

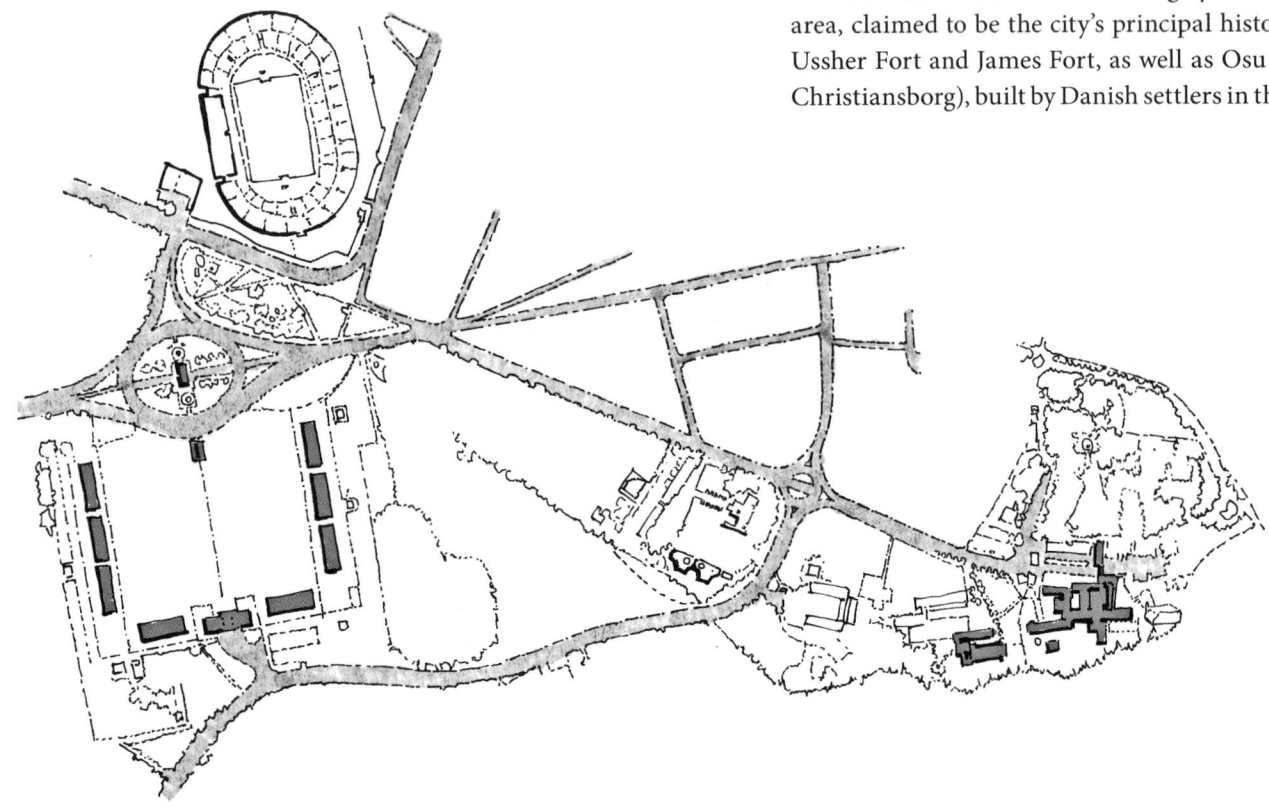

1 Fort James
2 Jamestown Lighthouse
3 Fort Ussher
4 Holy Trinity Cathedral
5 Kwame Nkrumah Memorial Park
6 Independence Square
7 Accra Central Train Station
8 Community Courts
9 Accra Sports Stadium
10 Military & Osu Cemeteries
11 Parliament House Ghana & State House
12 Accra International Conference Centre
13 Kinbu Gardens & The Octagon
14 Efua Sutherland Children's Park
15 The National Theatre of Ghana
16 National Museum
17 Revolution Square
18 Christ the King Parish
19 Presidential Palace Multi-Complex
20 Osu Castle
21 Ridge Hospital
22 Holy Spirit Cathedral

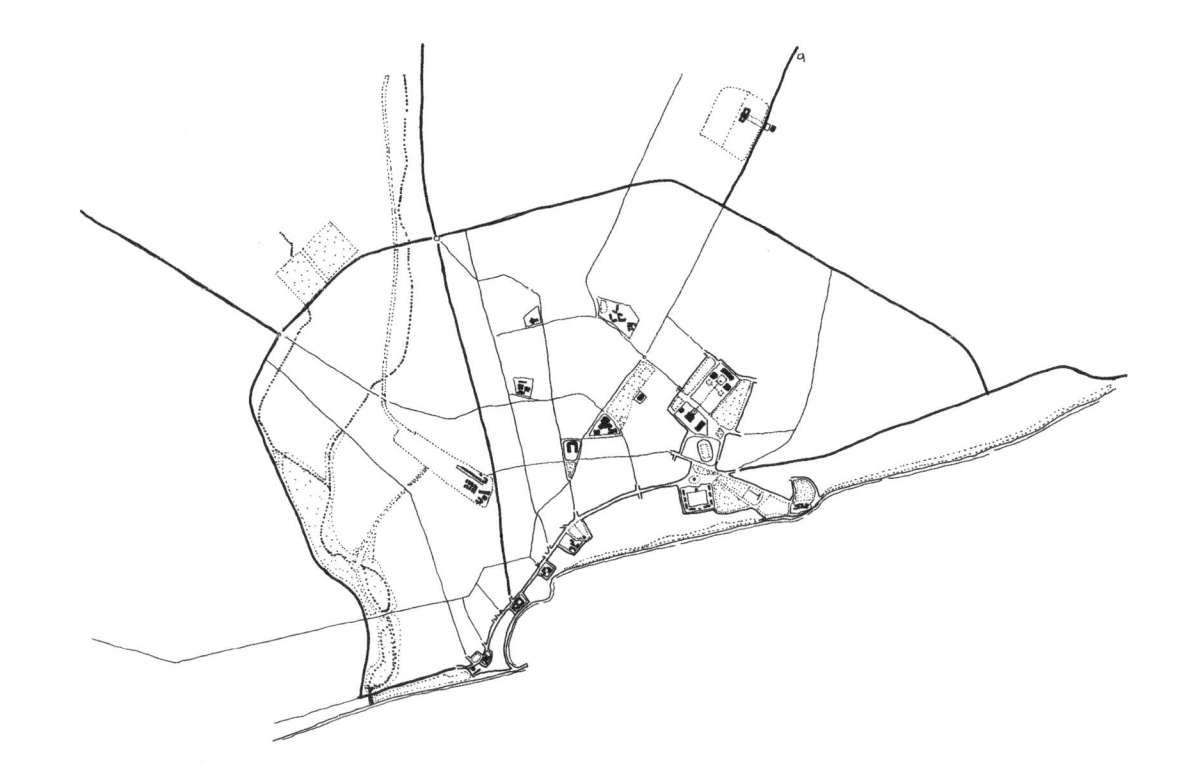

KUMASI, GHANA

FOUNDED: 1680
URBAN AREA: 254 km²
POPULATION: 2,069,350
URBAN AREA DENSITY: 8,100/km²
GPS: 6° 41'39.10"N, 1° 37'24.07"W

Kumasi, capital city of the Ashanti Region of Southern Ghana, is among the largest metropolitan areas of the country. The city is recognised as a significant and historical centre for Ghana since this ancient capital of the Ashanti kingdom is the site of West Africa's largest cultural centre, the palace of the Ashanti king. The city is located in the rainforest region near Lake Bosumtwi, surrounded by rolling green hills.

Owing to the meeting point of various routes, the centre of Kumasi has an organic radial structure. Historically, the intersection of various significant trade routes gave rise to the richness of the Asante Empire. The city itself served as a political and economic centre for the chiefdoms/nuclei around it. The city is home to a palace complex and has a large vibrant market in the city centre as found in so many other African cities. However, the majority of the population lives "outside" of the city in various neighbourhoods arranged as nuclei.

The urban grid is patterned by the primary radial urban road network, which developed as a consequence of the crossing of the various historic trade routes, while the street network in the surrounding neighbourhoods developed in response (as a secondary element) to the forms of the nuclei. The city did not grow from its centre, but rather progressed spontaneously as more of these nuclei neighbourhoods developed around the central city, creating an urban condition of various centralities. The nuclei initially developed as various separate small towns with a rural economy, dispersed throughout the forest.

Significant landmarks throughout the city include Fort Kumasi (built in 1896 to replace an Asante fort and which now functions as a museum) and the Kumasi Hat Museum. Royal Asante attractions include the Kumasi National Cultural Centre, the Asantehene Palace (built in 1972), and the Manhyia Palace, dating from 1925, now a museum located in the northern part of the city. Kumasi is also home to the St Peter's Cathedral Basilica which is the seat of the Roman Catholic Archdiocese of Kumasi.

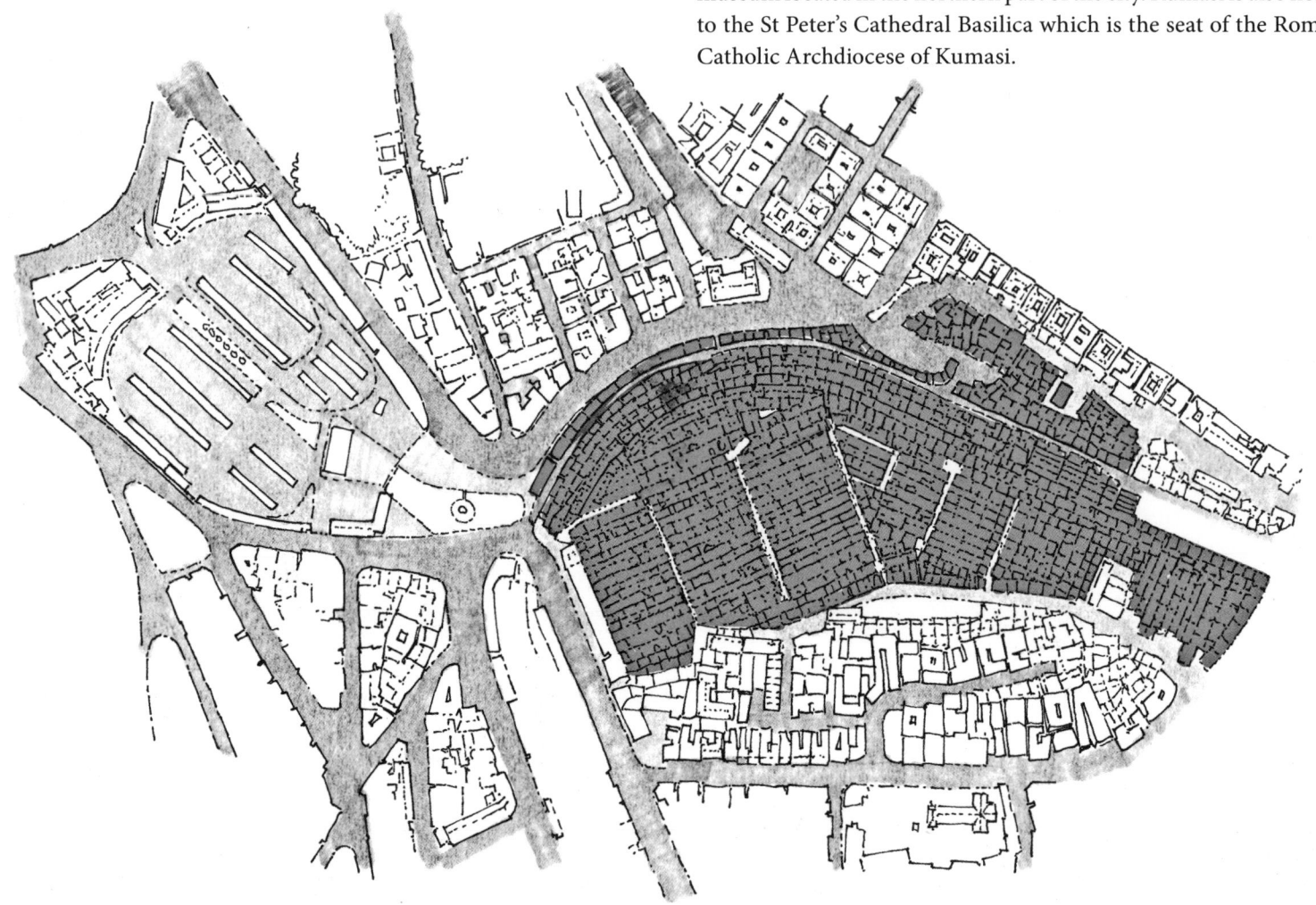

1 Central Market
2 Kumasie Circle & Ashanti Monument
3 St Peter's Basilica
4 Komfo Anokye Teaching Hospital
5 Bantama Taxi Station
6 National Zoological Garden
7 Former Train Station
8 Prempeh Assembly Hall
9 Kumasi Ghana @ 50 Jubilee Park
10 Prempeh II Jubilee Museum
11 Manhyia Palace Museum
12 National Cultural Centre
13 Stadium
14 Kumasi Airport
15 Kumasi Children's Park
16 Kumasi Technical Institute
17 Anglican Senior High School & Red Park
18 Kumasi Polytechnic
19 Wesley Methodist Cathedral

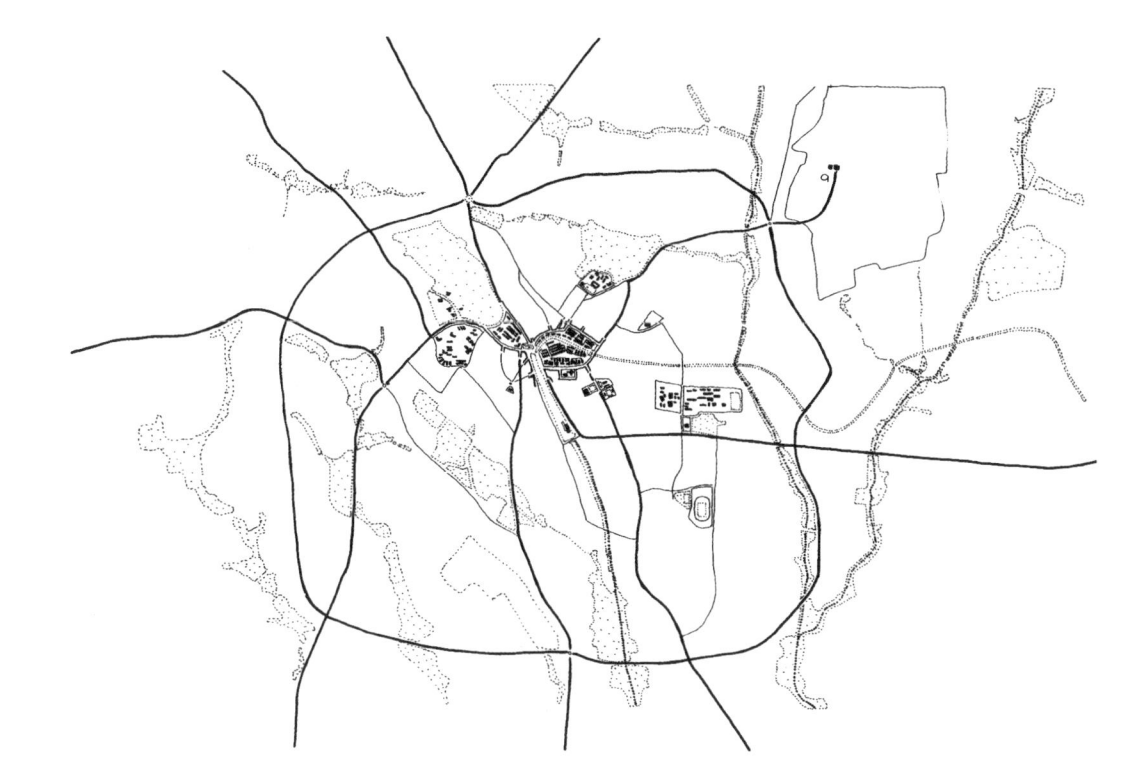

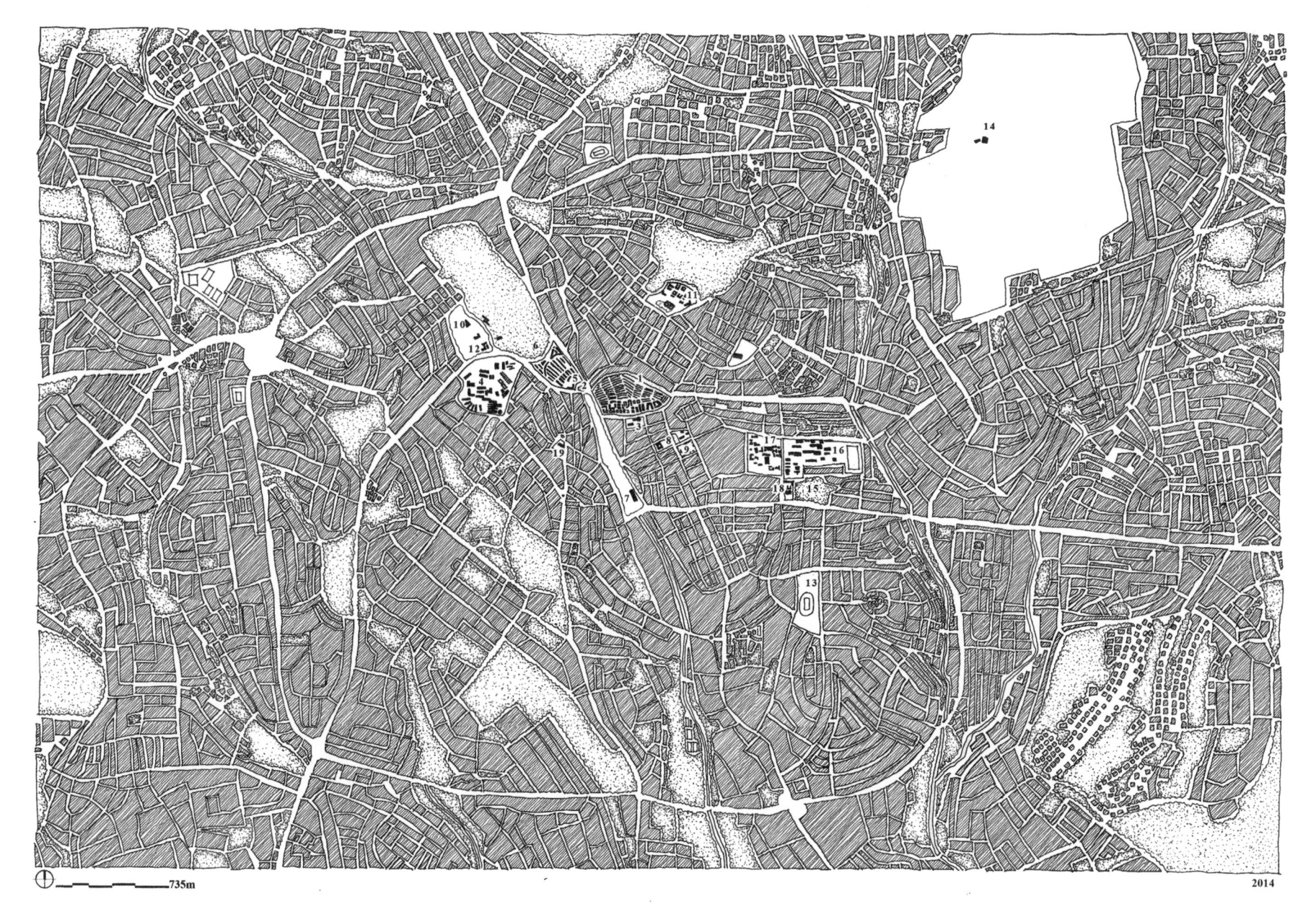

BISSAU, GUINEA-BISSAU

FOUNDED: 1687
URBAN AREA: unknown
POPULATION: 680,000 (2011)
URBAN AREA DENSITY: unknown
GPS: 11° 51'47.86"N, 15° 35'3.59"W
11° 51'36.22"N, 15° 35'0.99"W

Bissau is the capital and largest city of Guinea-Bissau. Located on the Geba River estuary, off the Atlantic Ocean, Bissau is the country's chief port, as well as administrative and military centre. Bissau is internationally accessible by the Osvaldo Vieira International Airport.

With Guinea-Bissau's GDP per capita being one of the lowest in the world, poverty and a lack of development are widespread. It was estimated that approximately 83 percent of the city's population was living in slums by 2005. The land surrounding Bissau is particularly low-lying and vulnerable to climate change and it will likely be affected by sea-level rise in the future.

Bissau, previously a Portuguese colony (until 1974) was elevated to town status in 1859 and city status in 1914. In 1919, the layout for the New City of Bissau designed by José Guedes Quinhones was implemented, resulting in a sprawling city beyond the original centre. In 1948, Governor Sarmento Rodrigues approved the *Plano Geral de Urbanização da Cidade de Bissau* (General Plan for the Urbanisation of the City of Bissau), which included the entire area within the urban perimeter. The city is surprisingly large and well aligned. The city centre is typical of a colonial plan, structured by an orthogonal layout formed by parallel and perpendicular streets. This neighbouring residential districts are all composed of geometric layouts that are connected to one another. The largest part of the city was constructed between the 1940s and 1960s.

The central area includes the main buildings in the city: the cathedral, town council, the commercial association, post office, civil registry, the public finances building, the courthouse, police station, and the bank (Banco Naçional Ultramarino). These buildings are all located along the Main Avenue, which stretches from the port to the governor's palace.

Significant landmarks include the Portuguese-built Fortaleza de São José da Amura barracks from the eighteenth century containing Amílcar Cabral's mausoleum, the Pidjiguiti Memorial dedicated to the many dockers killed in the Bissau dockers' strike on 3 August 1959, the Guinea-Bissau National Arts Institute, Bissau New Stadium and the local beaches. Many buildings in the city were destroyed during the Guinea-Bissau Civil War (1998–1999), including the Guinea-Bissau Presidential Palace and the Bissau French Cultural Centre (which has since been rebuilt).

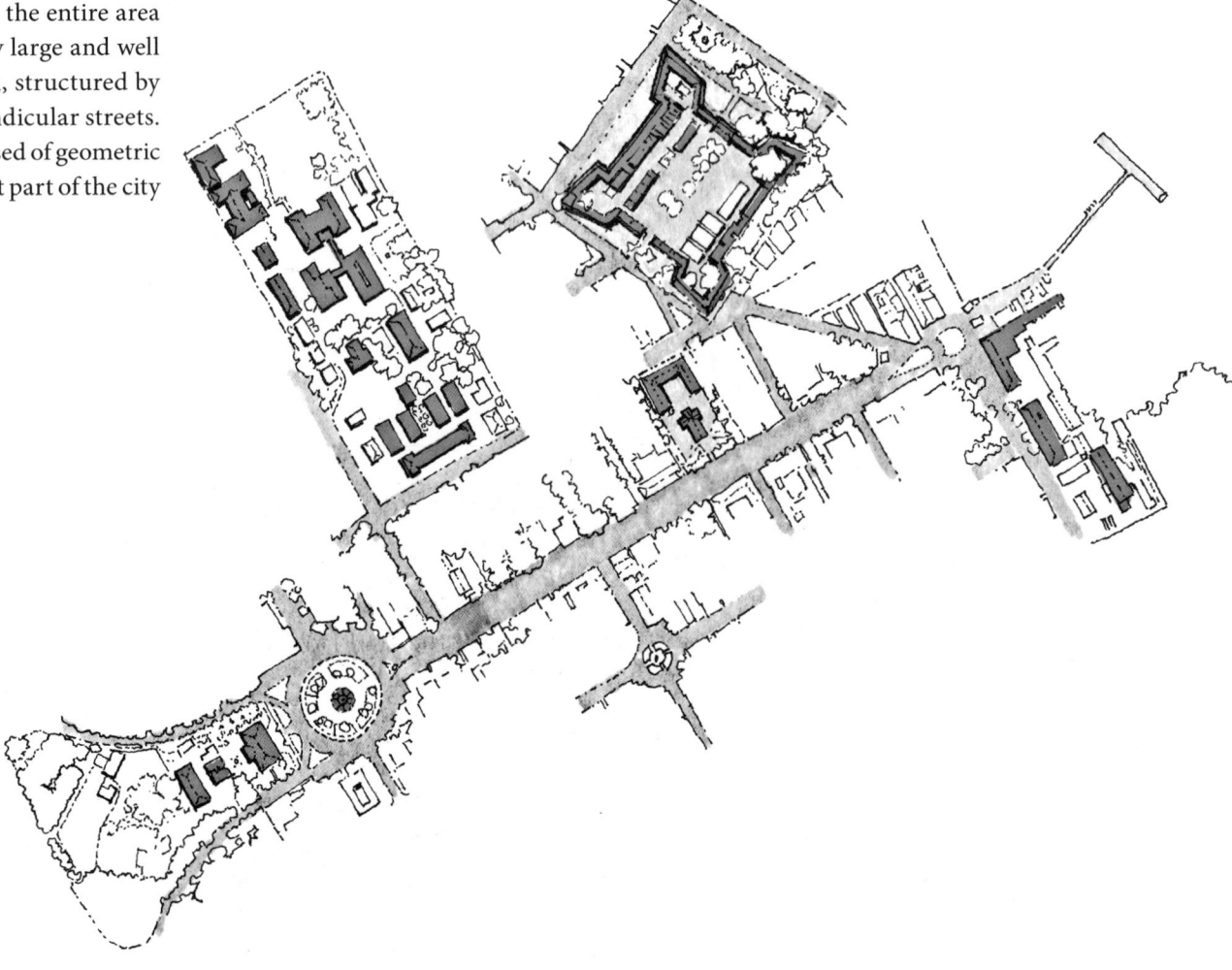

1 Fortaleza d'Amura, Fortress D'Amura
2 Catholic Church
3 National Heroes Square or Empire Square
4 Presidential Palace
5 Monument for Pidjiguiti Massacre
6 Fishing Harbour & Market
7 Bissau Parliament
8 Lino Correia Stadium
9 Che Guevara Square
10 Place of the Unknown Soldier
11 French Cultural Centre
12 Estádio 24 de Setembro, 24th September Stadium
13 Port
14 Simão Mendes National Hospital
15 Cemetery
16 Osvaldo Vieira Airport
17 Mosque
18 Lusophone University
19 Palácio do Governo, Government Palace

CONAKRY, GUINEA

FOUNDED: 1887
URBAN AREA: unknown
POPULATION: 1,786,000
URBAN AREA DENSITY: unknown
GPS: 9° 30'35.80"N, 13° 42'59.32"W

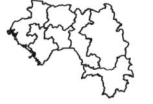

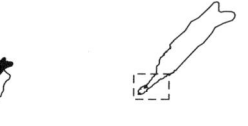

Conakry, a port city on the Atlantic Ocean, is the capital and largest city of Guinea. The city's harbour is central to its economy with modern cargo facilities. The resource-rich country is poorly developed with increased pressure being put on the limited infrastructure. The city was originally limited to the Tombo Island, one of the Îles de Los, but has since spread up the adjoining Kaloum peninsula where the colonial city developed on the 36-kilometre-long stretch of land (between 0.2 to 6 km wide). A 300-metre-long bridge links the island to the peninsula.

The city has a linear and ordered spatial structure while urban mobility is constrained by a poor and limited road network. The inadequate and disorganised public transport system contributes to this. Meanwhile, the colonial obsession with ordering and structuring the city for control is evident in the older sections of Conakry where a grid pattern is interspersed with boulevards. The assistance granted by the Soviet bloc is represented in newer buildings, such as the Palace of the People. The city developed along the peninsula with five main districts. Kaloum (the city centre) is situated on the tip in the south-west. This vulnerable low-lying coastal area is expected to be dramatically impacted by climate change with rising sea levels in the future. Owing to the relatively isolated location of the city from the mainland, the population growth has been significant since independence, coupled with lacking infrastructure.

Significant places in the city include Marché Madina and Marché du Niger. Palaces and museums include Casa de Belle Vue, the Center Culturel Franco Guineen, Conakry National Museum, Palais de Nations; the Presidential Palace, and Palais du Peuple. Parks and gardens include the Jardin 2 Octobre and Conakry Botanical Garden. Places of worship include Cathedrale Sainte-Marie and Paroisse Saint Michel Conakry Grand Mosque.

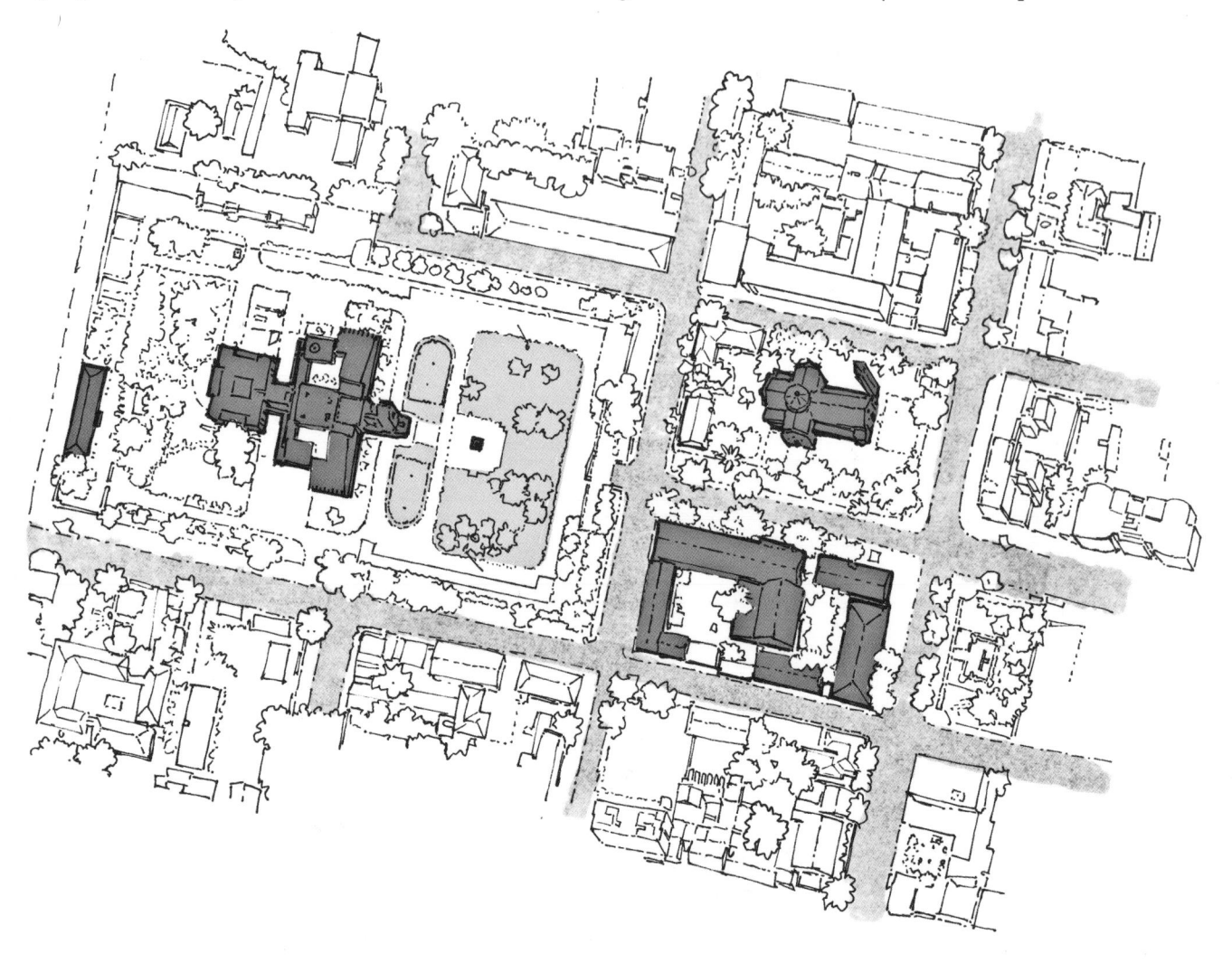

WESTERN AFRICA

1 Republic Square & Presidential Palace
2 St Mary's Cathedral
3 St Joseph of Cluny Schoo
4 Palais des Nations, Nations Palace
5 Ministère des Travaux Publics, Ministry of Public Works
6 Dean Igance Hospital
7 Port
8 Fishing Harbour
9 National Museum
10 Palais du Peuple, Parliament
11 Jardin 2 Octobre, October 2nd Garden
12 Botanical Garden
13 Great Mosque
14 Donka Hospital (CHU)
15 Coléah Market
16 Oppo Workshop
17 Gamal Abdel Nasser University of Conakry
18 Stade du 28 Septembre, Stadium on September 28
19 Madina Market

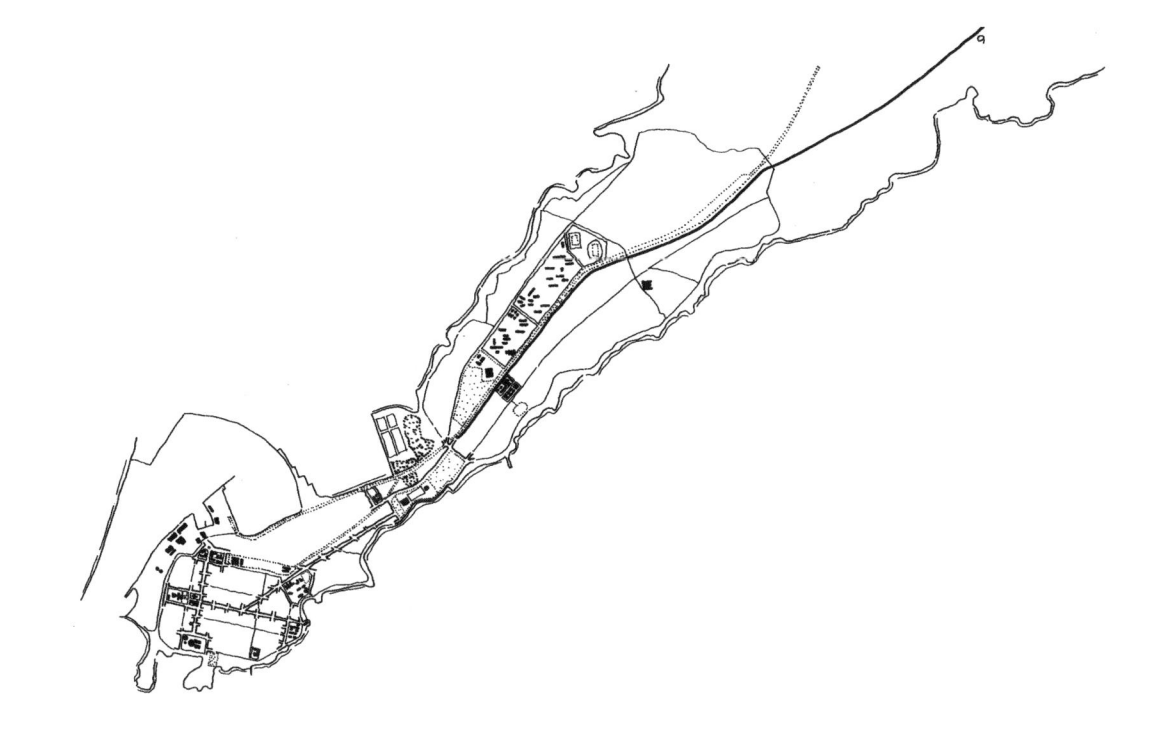

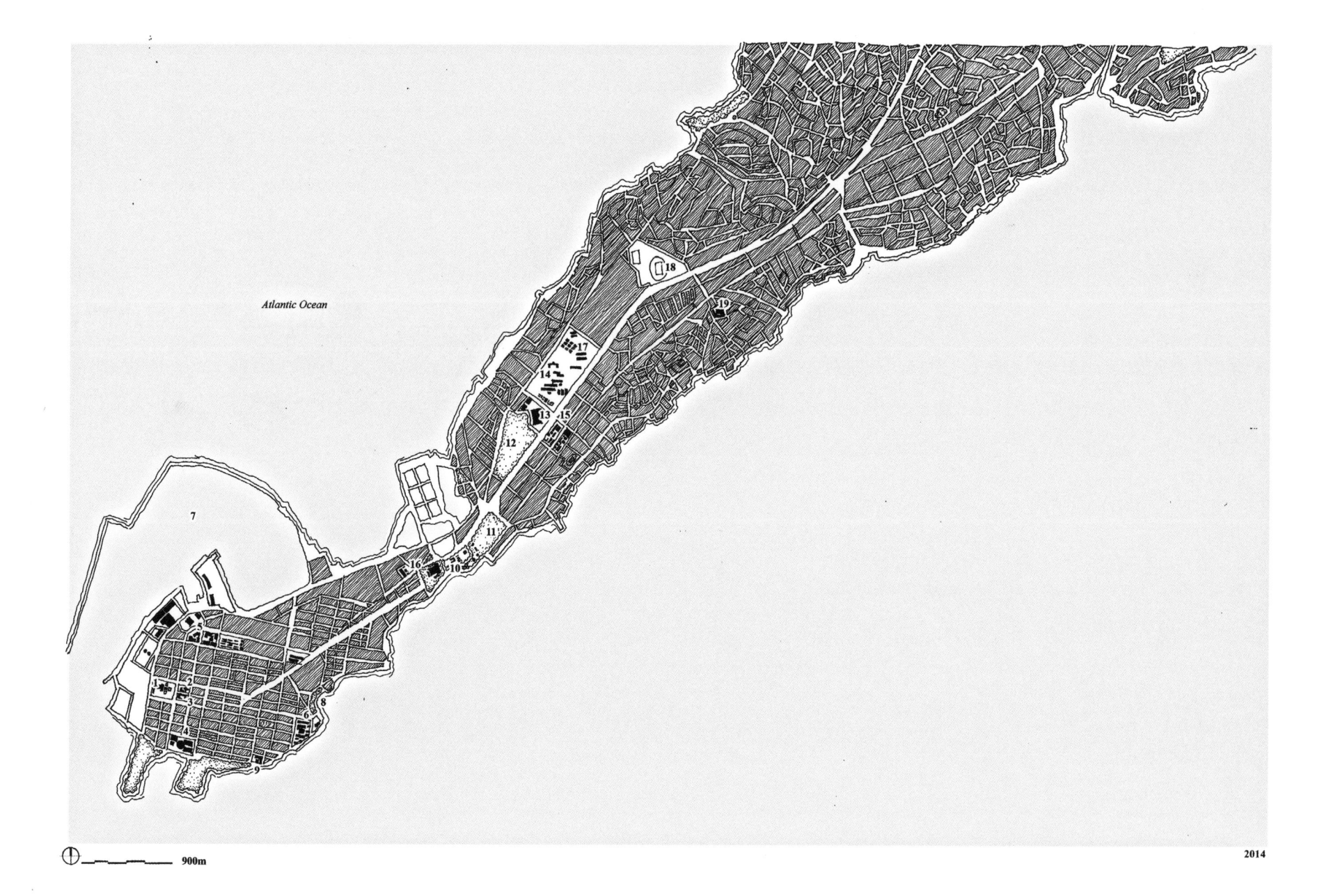

900m

2014

MONROVIA, LIBERIA

FOUNDED: 1822
URBAN AREA: 13 km²
POPULATION: 970,824 (2008)
URBAN AREA DENSITY: unknown
GPS: 6° 18'2.34"N, 10° 47'51.32"W

Monrovia, capital city of the West African country of Liberia is located along the Cape Mesurado peninsula, between the Atlantic Ocean and the Mesurado River. Monrovia is the African city geographically located closest to South America, approximately 3,029 km, or 1,634 nautical miles, across the Atlantic from Natal, Brazil. The city is internationally accessible through the Roberts International Airport – the largest international airport in Liberia, located 60 km from the city – and is regionally connected through a network of roads and railways. The World Bank has rebuilt several roads and streets in the city since 2005, inspiring the renovation of private and public infrastructures throughout the city.

Monrovia is Liberia's most densely inhabited city and is the cultural, political and economic core of the entire country. As with several other West African countries bordered by the Atlantic Ocean, the city's economy is dominated by its harbour.

Characteristic of most colonial settlements, Monrovia was divided into two separate areas at the beginning of the twentieth century. The first region, referred to as "Monrovia proper", was dedicated to the city's Americo-Liberian population with architecture resembling that of the southern United States, while Krutown was mainly inhabited by the ethnic Krus, Bassas, Grebos and other tribes. The rapid population growth was spurred by rural-urban migration which started in 1926.

The First and Second Liberian Civil Wars had detrimental effects on the city as nearly all buildings and infrastructure were destroyed. The historic downtown is centred around Broad Street at the end of the peninsula, with the market district, Waterside, to its immediate north, facing the city's large natural harbour.

Capitol Hill is situated south of the city centre, where the major institutions of national government, including the Temple of Justice and the Executive Mansion, are located. The original suburban residential district, today known as Sinkor, Monrovia's bustling midtown, is situated further east down the peninsula. This is the location of the Spriggs Payne Airport. Significant landmarks in Monrovia include the Liberian National Museum, the Masonic Temple, the Waterside Market, and several beaches.

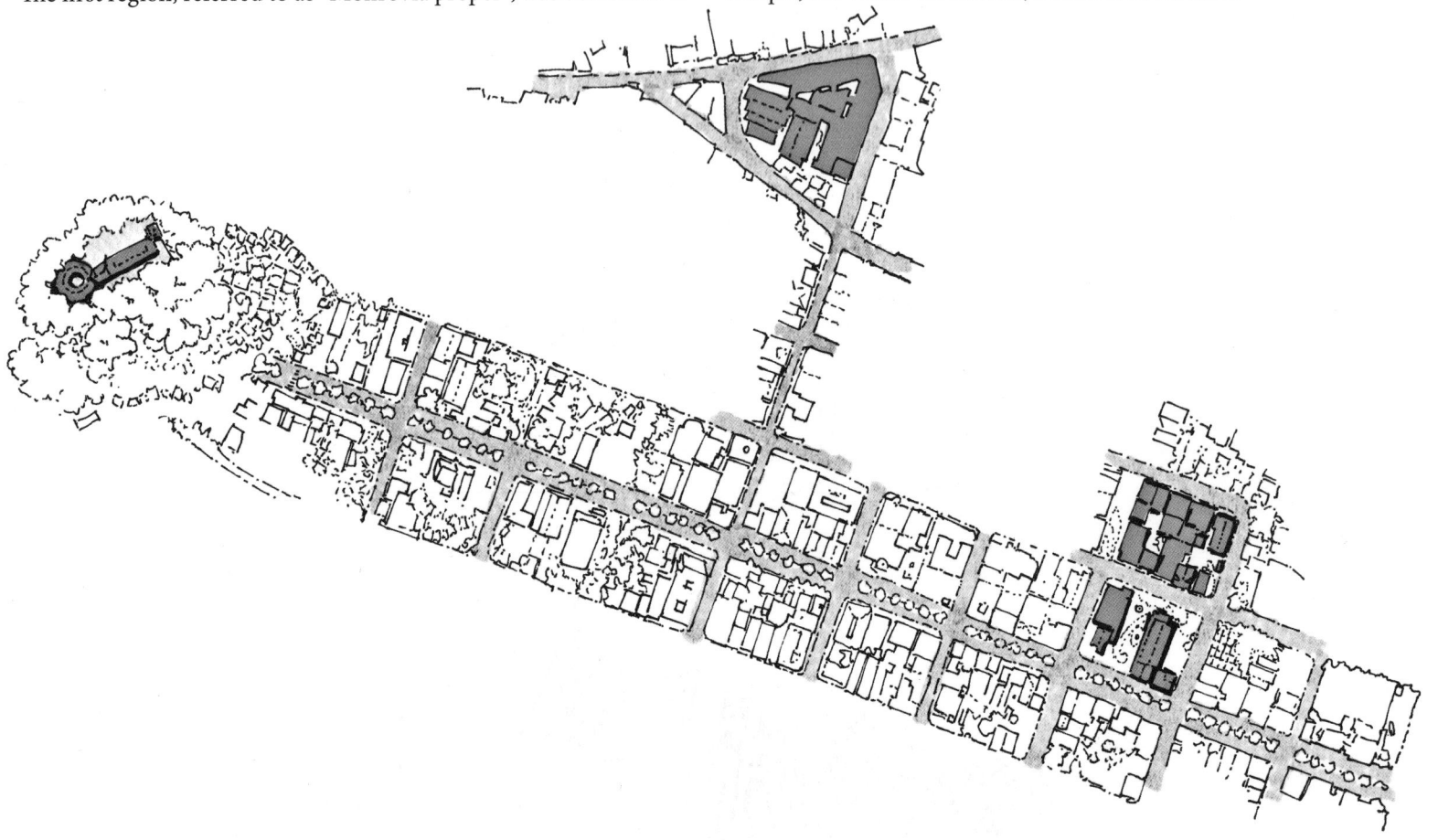

1 Liberia National Museum & Providence Baptist Church
2 Palm Grove Cemetery
3 Masonic Temple
4 Hotel Ducor
5 First United Methodist Church
6 EJ Roye Building
7 Secret Hart Cathedral
8 Rivoli Cinema
9 Legislature
10 Executive Mansion
11 Temple of Justice
12 Payne International Airport
13 University of Liberia
14 City Hall & United Nations Mission in Liberia
15 Monrovia City Hall
16 JFK Hospital
17 Centre for National Documents and Records
18 United Methodist Compound
19 Mesurado Bridge
20 Johnson Bridge
21 Providence Island
22 Attionnete Tubman Sports Stadium
23 Barclay Training Centre & Grey D Allison School

BAMAKO, MALI

FOUNDED: unknown
URBAN AREA: 245 km²
POPULATION: 2,037,000
URBAN AREA DENSITY: 7,384/km²
GPS: 12° 39'2.91"N, 7° 59'35.66"W
12° 38'46.42"N, 8° 0'5.01"W

Bamako, capital and largest city of Mali, was estimated to be the fastest-growing city in Africa and the sixth fastest-growing city in the world during 2006. The city is located in the Niger River valley. Bamako is the nation's administrative centre, and is the seventh-largest West African urban centre after Lagos, Abidjan, Kano, Ibadan, Dakar, and Accra.

The city's expansion is restricted by three important geographic entities: the Niger River, the hills on the North (Point G, the hill of the hope; and *Koulouba*, the "hill of power") and some reliefs on the southern bank (*Badalabougou*, the "hill of knowledge"). The city is built on the two opposing riverbanks, and is connected by three bridges: the Martyrs Bridge (1960); the Fahd Bridge (1992); and a third bridge completed in 2011.

The city was originally developed on the northern bank of the river between 1883 and 1960 – an area dating back to the colonial era – with the government and business districts as the historical centre. Owing to the rapid population growth after dependence, the river had to be crossed for further expansion which led to the development of mainly residential districts on both the shorelines of the riverbank, dating back to between 1960 and 1970, while the slums developed along the periphery.

The northern bank developed as a colonial city, with a geometrically planned urban structure featuring a coherent traffic network, public areas, a city centre and infrastructure including railways and a railway station. The area is still used as the commercial centre of the city. In contrast, the highly polluted and congested southern bank has developed without any clear plan. Nicknamed Bamako's *bedroom community*, it accommodates more than 50 percent of the population.

Significant landmarks include the National Library of Mali, the Bamako Grand Mosque, the central Market (Grand Marché), Bamako Cathedral, the BCEAO Tower, and the National Museum of Mali. Also of note is the Muso Kunda Museum, the Bamako Regional Museum, Bamako Zoo, the Bamako Botanical Gardens, the National Conference Centre Tower (NCC), the Souvenir Pyramid, the Independence Monument, Al-Quoods Monument, the triangular Monument de la Paix, the Hamdallaye Obelisk, the Modibo Keita Memorial, the Palais de la Culture Amadou Hampaté Ba and the Point G Hill.

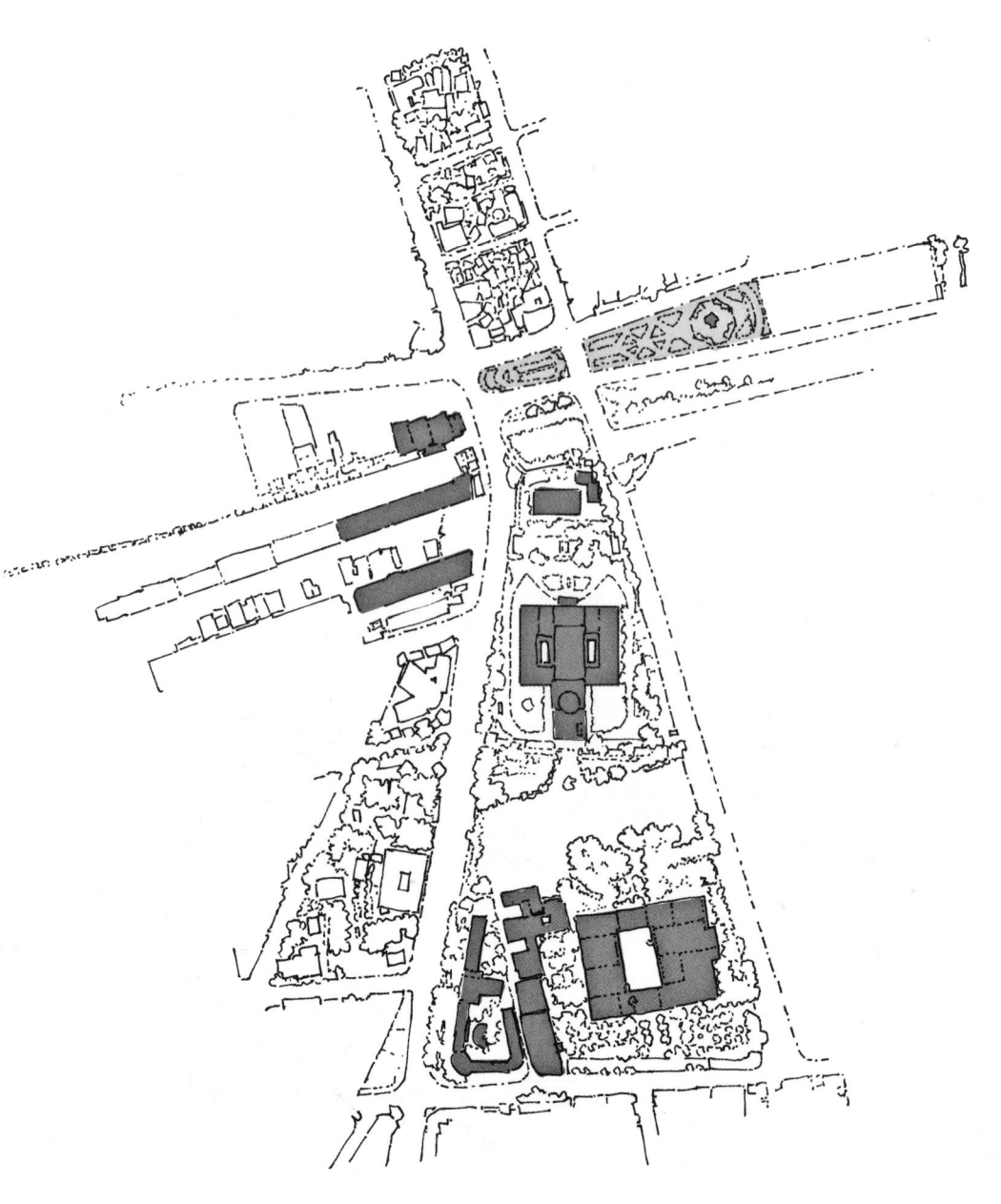

1 National Assembly
2 Great Mosque
3 Al-Quds Square
4 Freedom Square
5 Museum of Bamako
6 Bamako Railway Station
7 Great Market
8 Lumumba Square
9 Monument of the 26th March
10 Maison des Artisans & Echoppes Fétiche, Home of Artisans & Stalls Market
11 Botanical Garden & Office of the National Park of the Baoulé Loop
12 National Museum
13 Bamako City Administration
14 Modibo Keita Sports Stadium
15 Military Field Hospital
16 l'O.M.V.S Park
17 Independence Monument
18 Niarela Cemetery
19 Catholic Church of Bamako
20 Yacouba Guindo Mosque
21 Palais de la Culture, Cultural Centre
22 University of Bamako
23 Amadou BA Hampâté Cultural Centre
24 Primature, Prime Minister
25 Gabriel Toure University Hospital
26 Malian Office of Tourism and Hospitality

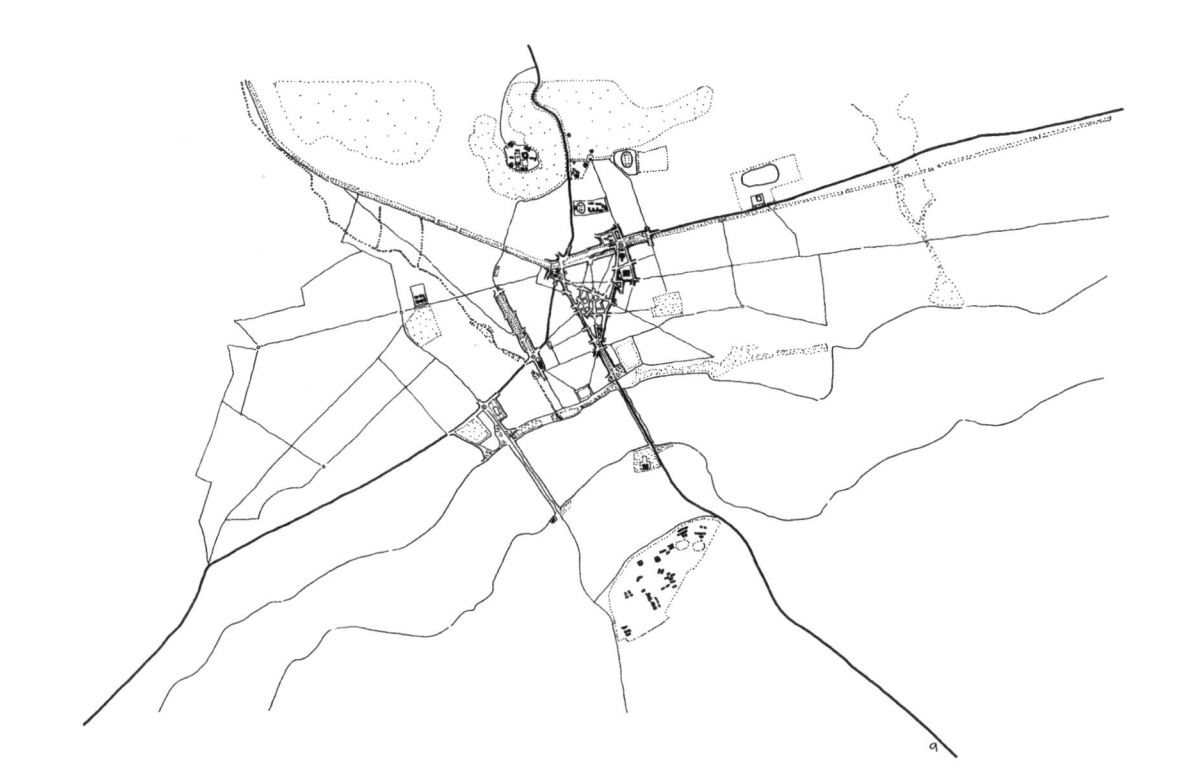

MOPTI, MALI

FOUNDED: unknown
URBAN AREA: 40 km²
POPULATION: 114,296 (2009)
URBAN AREA DENSITY: 2,900/km²
GPS: 14° 29'37.36"N, 4° 11'47.48"W

Mopti is a town and an urban commune in the inner Niger Delta region of Mali. The town is the capital of the Mopti Cercle and the Mopti Region. The town is loacted 460 km north-east of Bamako, at the confluence of the Niger and the Bani rivers and is linked by a bridge to the town of Sévaré. The urban area, including both the towns of Mopti and Sévaré, had a population of 114,296 during the 2009 census. From what was described in 1902 as a "miserable village with a few huts" by French colonial army officer, Capitaine Lucien Marc, this area has now developed into one of Mali's densest cities.

A 12-kilometre-long bridge was constructed between 1905 and 1912 by the French colonial forces which was to connect Mopti with Sévaré by road during the Niger's flood periods (between August and December). A commercial area developed during the 1930s as a response to the rapid expansion of the village in the first decade of the twentieth century.

The reconstruction of the great mosque, based on the Great Mosque of Djenné, was initiated by the French colonial administration. The Great Mosque (also known as the Komoguel Mosque) is an example of Sudano-Sahelian architecture. The UNESCO World Heritage Convention dates its origin between 1933 and 1935 while the Aga Khan Development Network estimated it was built slightly later, between 1936 to 1943. The mosque was added to the UNESCO Tentative List of World Heritage Sites in March 2009.

The relatively small islands were densely populated with numerous multi-storeyed buildings and narrow streets. The islands have gradually expanded over time as household trash has been compacted and used as infill around and between the natural islands.

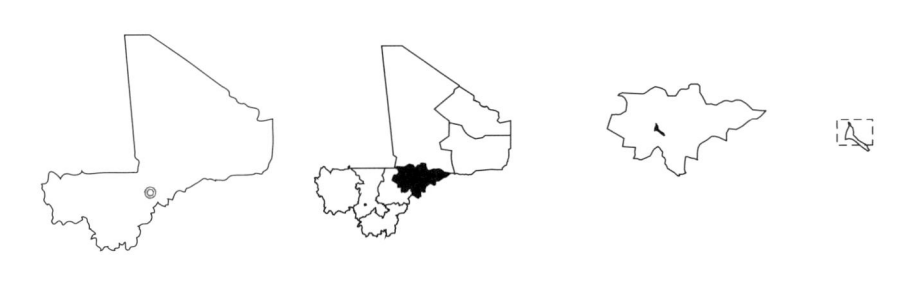

WESTERN AFRICA **187**

1 Misire Mosque
2 Souguni Market
3 Football Stadium
4 Barema Bocoum Stadium
5 Mosqué
6 Ottawa Market
7 Courthouse
8 Port
9 Ferry Port
10 Bus Station
11 Visitors' Centre
12 Hospital

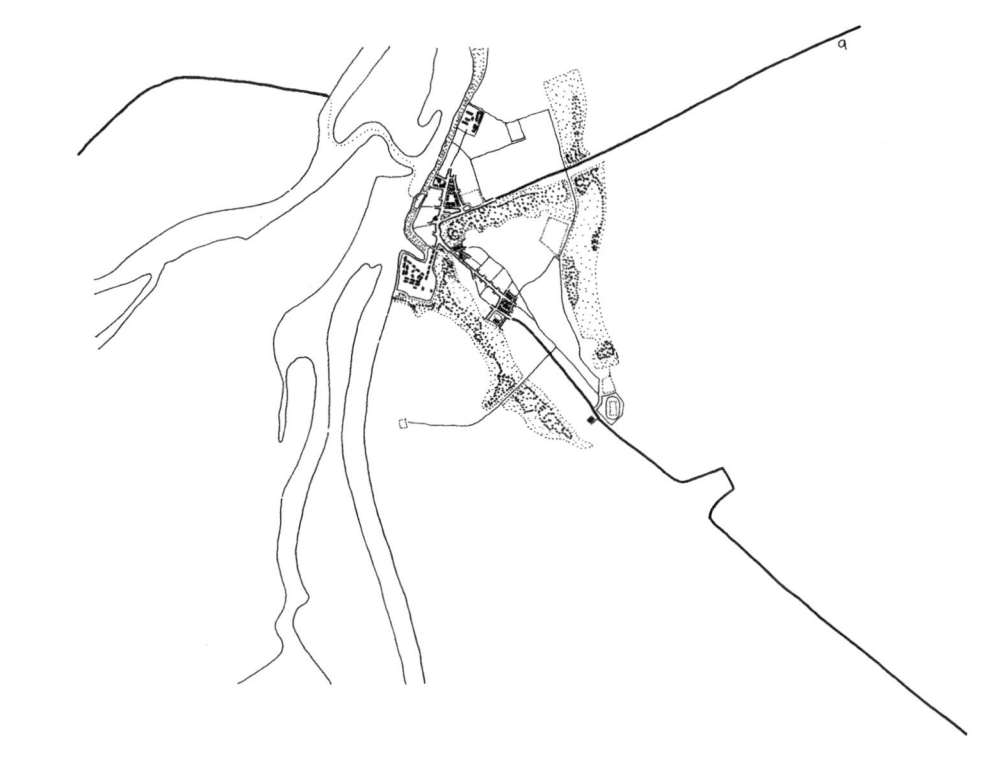

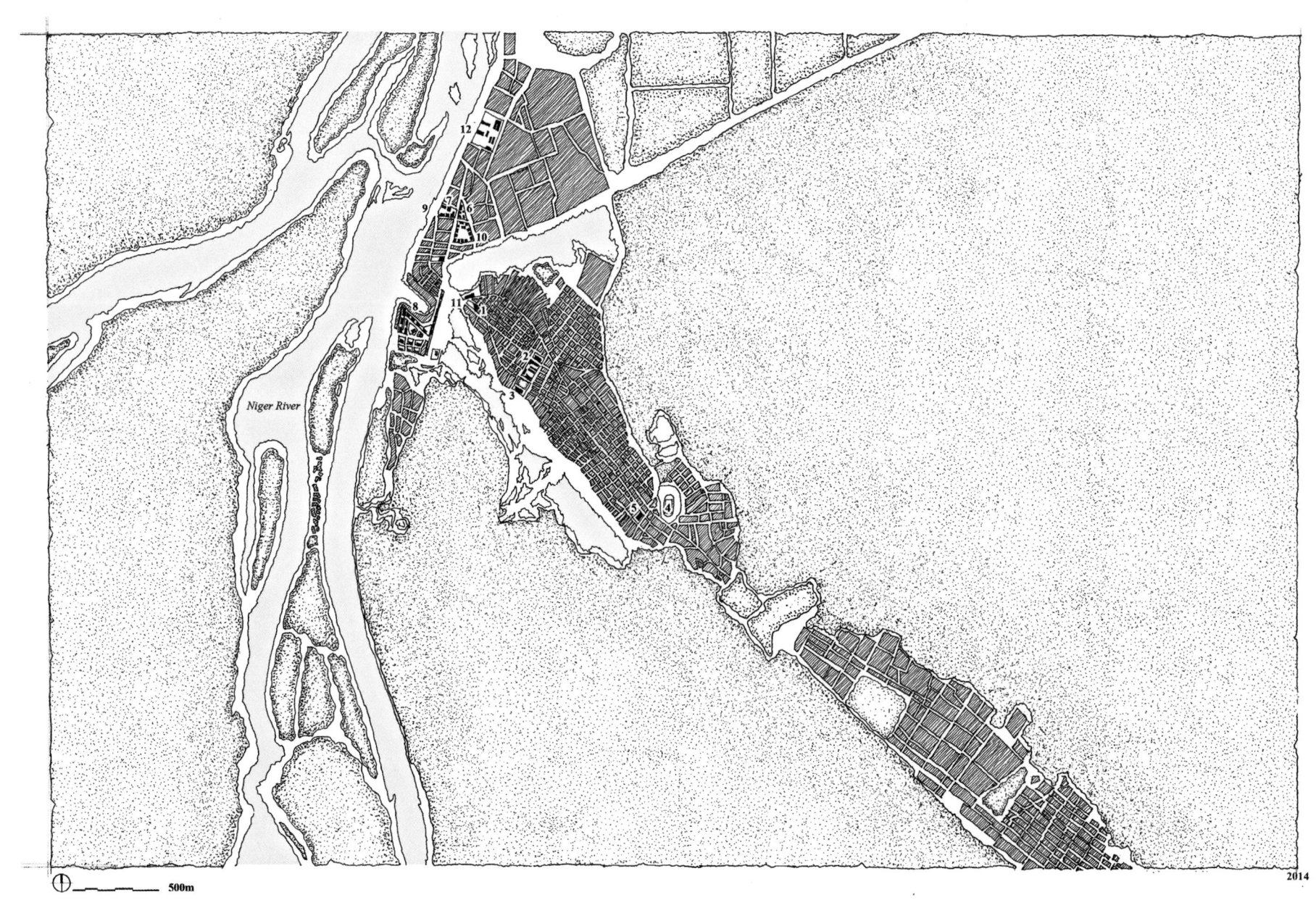

Niger River

500m

2014

TIMBUKTU, MALI

FOUNDED: fifth century
URBAN AREA: unknown
POPULATION: 54,453 (2009)
URBAN AREA DENSITY: unknown
GPS: 16° 46'29.33"N, 3° 0'26.11"W
16° 46'14.48"N, 3° 0'29.38"W
16° 46'33.95"N, 3° 0'18.44"W]

Timbuktu is an ancient city associated with a sense of mystery and, furthermore, is one of Africa's cities whose name is most profoundly associated with history. It is located in the West African nation of Mali at the gateway to the Sahara Desert, 20 km north of the River Niger. It was once a remarkable centre of learning and trade. Originally a seasonal settlement, the city of Timbuktu developed into a thriving trade centre due to its proximity to the Niger River, and its location on the long-established trade route across the Sahara. A shift in trading routes during the early twelfth century saw the city flourishing from the trade in salt, gold, ivory and slaves. During its Golden Age, the book trade established Timbuktu as a scholarly centre in Africa.

Today, the city is characterised by its mud buildings and narrow streets, juxtaposed with the intellectual treasures hidden behind these structures. The city is home to the prestigious Koranic Sankore University and other madrasas. Timbuktu was an intellectual and spiritual capital and a centre for the propagation of Islam throughout Africa. It reached its economic and cultural peak during the fifteenth and sixteenth centuries. Timbuktu's golden age is represented by its three great mosques, Djingareyber, Sankore and Sidi Yahia. These monuments are continuously restored, but are under threat from desertification. The city is recognised by UNESCO as a World Heritage Site: "The three mosques and mausoleums are outstanding witnesses to the urban establishment of Timbuktu, its important role of commercial, spiritual and cultural centre on the southern trans-Saharan trading route, and its traditional characteristic construction techniques" (UNESCO).

The city is constantly threatened by the surrounding sand dunes that cover the streets and buildings with sand, and also by vandalism of the World Heritage Sites from secular and Islamic rebel groups.

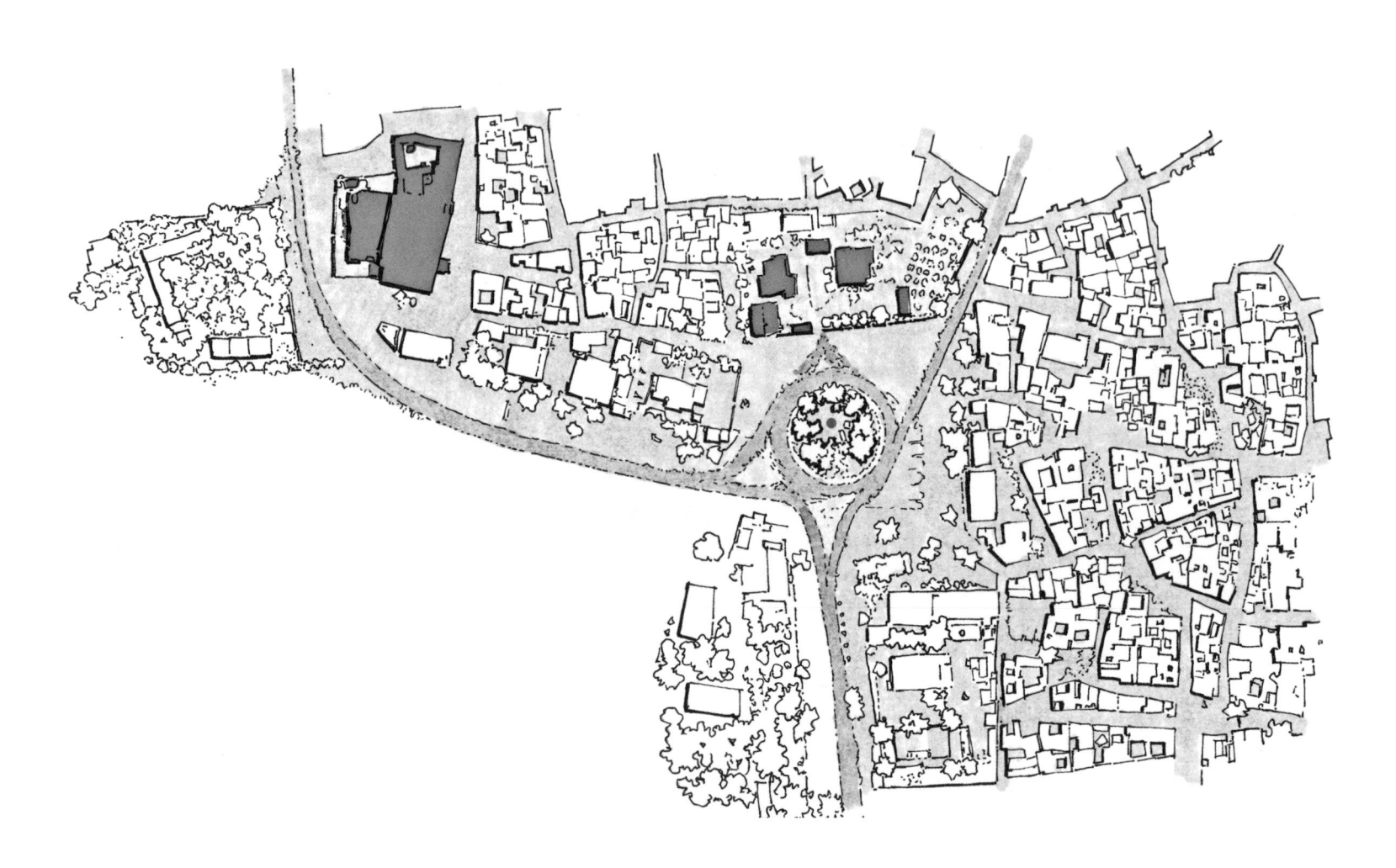

1 The Independence Square
2 Government Office
3 Military Fort
4 Djinguereber Mosque
5 Ahmed Baba Historical Research Centre
6 Jewish Cemetery
7 Courthouse
8 Sidi Yahiya Mosque
9 Large Market
10 Sankore Mosque
11 Heinrich Barth's House
12 Ethnological Museum
13 Stadium
14 Hospital
15 Cemetery

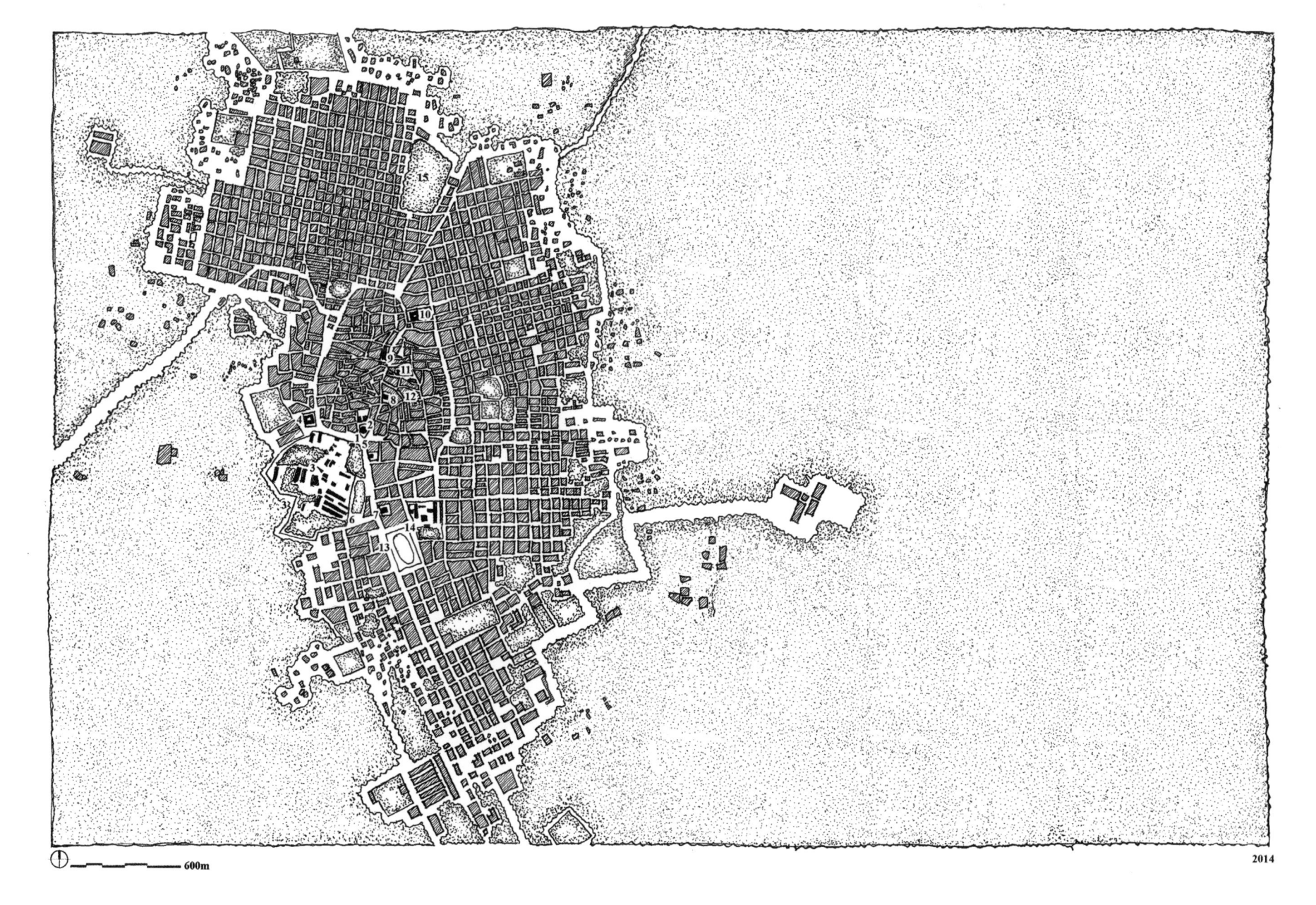

NOUAKCHOTT, MAURITANIA

FOUNDED: unknown
URBAN AREA: 1,000 km²
POPULATION: 881,000
URBAN AREA DENSITY: 881/km²
GPS: 18° 4'38.52"N, 15° 58'47.41"W

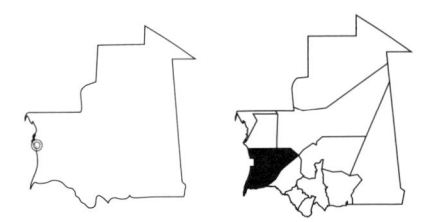

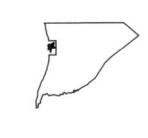

Nouakchott started out as a small fishing village with a mere 200 people. Since the city was declared the capital in 1957, Nouakchott has expanded to become the largest city in Mauritania (from less than 4 percent of the national population in 1962 to a current estimate of 62 percent) and one of the largest cities in the Sahara. Urban-rural migration has been spurred as a result of the North African drought since the 1970s and the urban primacy of the capital city. The city's deep-sea port opened in 1986 and is used mainly for imports.

The city is located on the Atlantic coast of the Sahara Desert and is globally accessible via Nouakchott International Airport. Development on the coast is limited to the Nouakchott Wharf and a deep-water port since there are areas of quicksand near the harbour and shifting sandbanks all along the coastline. The city is constantly faced with the sand dunes advancing from its eastern side, covering the city in sand. The UN-Habitat report classified Nouakchott as vulnerable to the impacts of desertification.

The city is essentially flat and buildings are generally limited to single-storeyed structures owing to the fragile and sandy terrain. Consequently, the city has spread out, and is still sprawling due to the low density nature of the built environment and the rapid uncontrolled urban growth. Squatter settlements take up more than 40 percent of the urban area.

The city developed around the large tree-lined street, Avenue Abdel Nasir, which runs north-east through the city centre from the airport. Apart from the mosques, the architecture in the city follows Western styles with a mixture of traditional French concrete buildings with Spanish and Asian influences.

1   Fishing Port
2   Great Mosque
3   Presidential Palace
4   Park
5   Urban Community of Nouakchott
6   Deydouh Park & Youth House
7   National Museum
8   Boys College & Girls College
9   Capital Stadium
10 Ibn Abbas Mosque or Friday Mosque
11 Moroccan Mosque
12 Marocaine Market
13 Cinquième Gardens, Fifth Gardens
14 Central Bank of Mauritania
15 Ministry of Foreign Affairs
16 National Guard
17 Nouakchott International Airport
18 French Embassy & French Cultural Centre
19 Olympic Stadium
20 Palais des Congrès, Palace Congress
21 Court
22 Boys High School
23 Ecole d'Application, Application School
24 SNDE Water Distribution Department

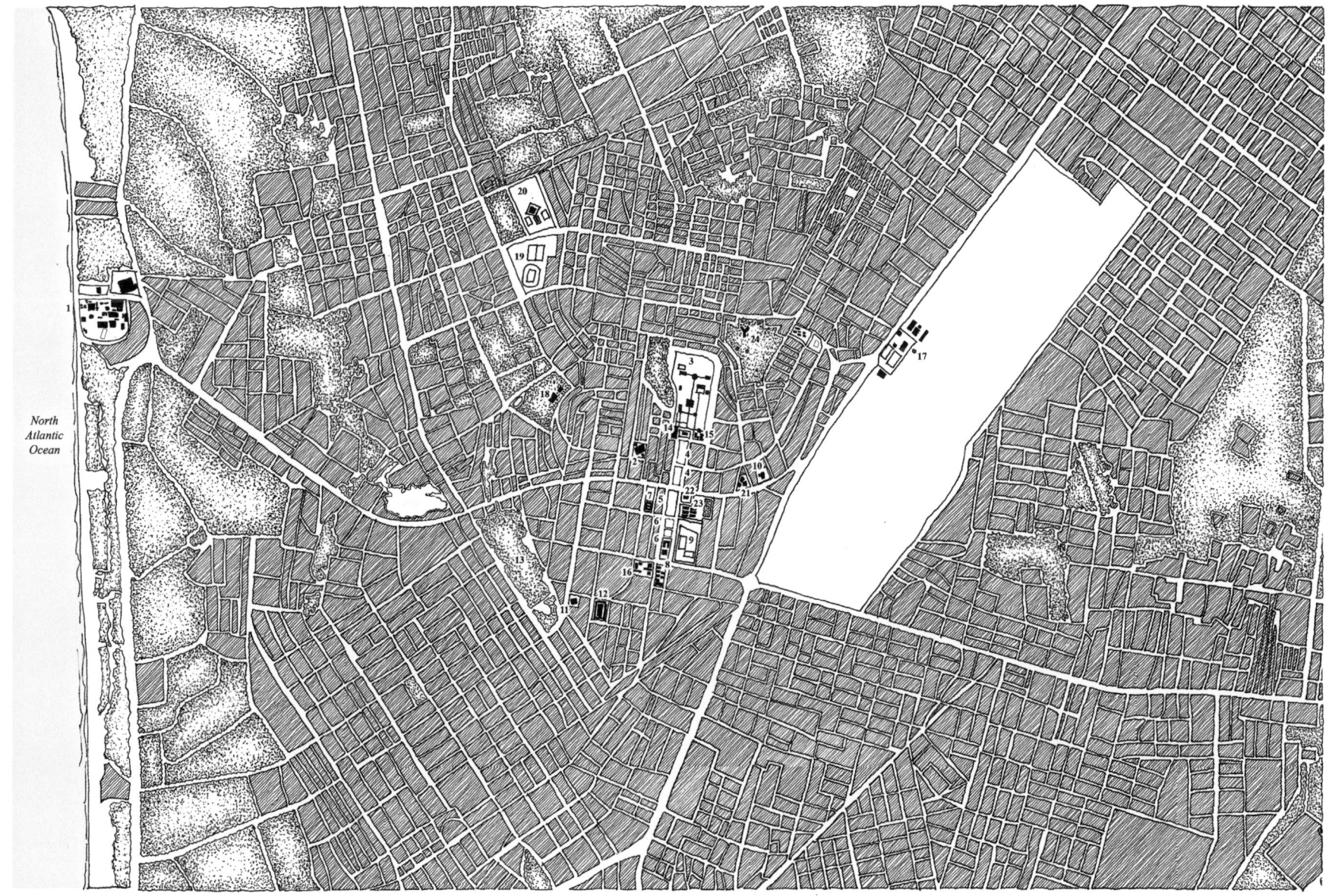

ROSSO, MAURITANIA

FOUNDED: unknown
URBAN AREA: unknown
POPULATION: 48,922 (2000)
URBAN AREA DENSITY: unknown
GPS: 16° 31'1.07"N, 15° 48'32.06"W

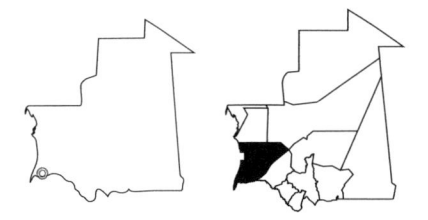

Rosso is the key city of south-western Mauritania and is the main town in the Trarza area. The city is located on the northern bank of the Senegal River and is situated 204 km south of the capital Nouakchott.

Rosso was once the capital of the Emirate of Trarza, a pre-colonial Sahrawi-dominated state. Before Mauritania's independence in 1960, Senegal and Mauritania were governed as a single entity under French colonial rule. Mauritania became its own entity with independence, and the small town of Rosso was consequently split into two with the Senegal River as the new frontier between the two countries.

Rosso is strategically located at the international ferry-crossing on the main road between Nouakchott and the Senegalese capital of Dakar. The town has been well known since ancient times when it was used as an Arabic trading post over the banks of the river. Since then, Rosso in Mauritania has been the commercial capital of the country. This market town serves the narrow strip of agricultural land stretching along the southern border of Mauritania.

The urban population has grown rapidly since independence, from a population of as little as 2,300 in 1960 to an estimated 48,922 inhabitants (according to the 2000 census). Over the past decade, the area has suffered severe natural disasters including drought, pests and floods.

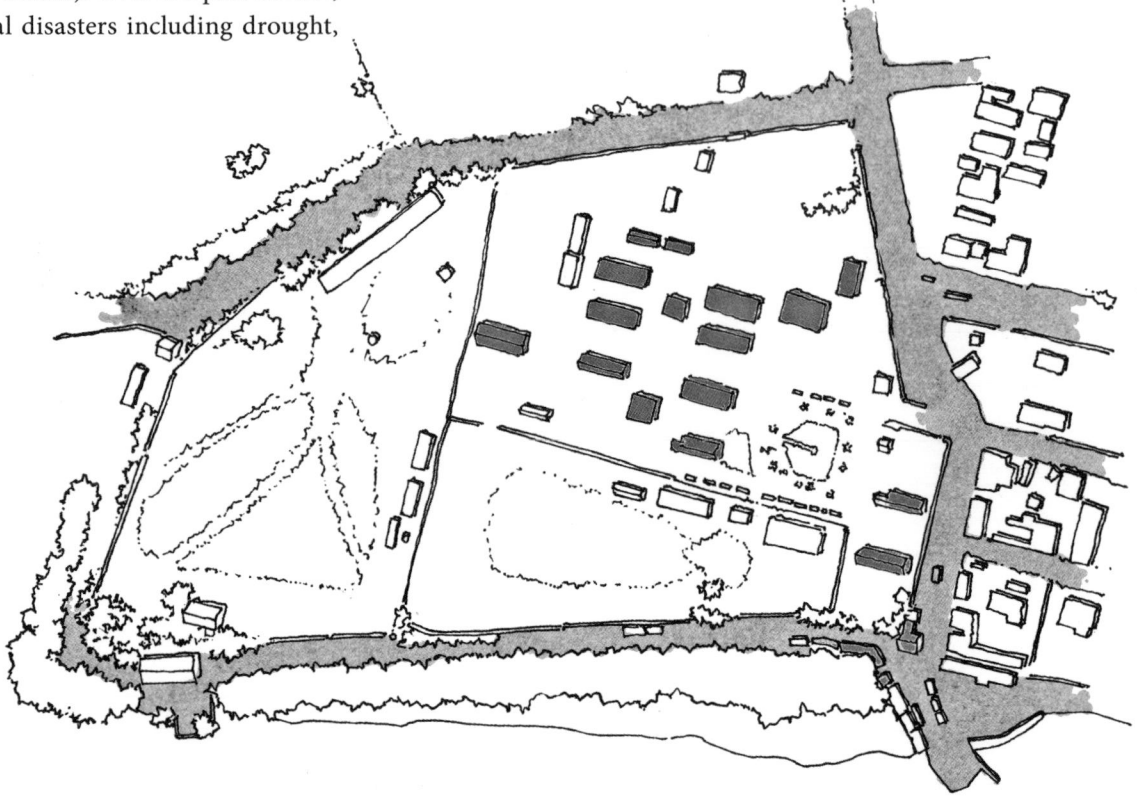

1 Ferry Port
2 Sahara Housing Project Market
3 Institutionnel, Institutional
4 Sports Field

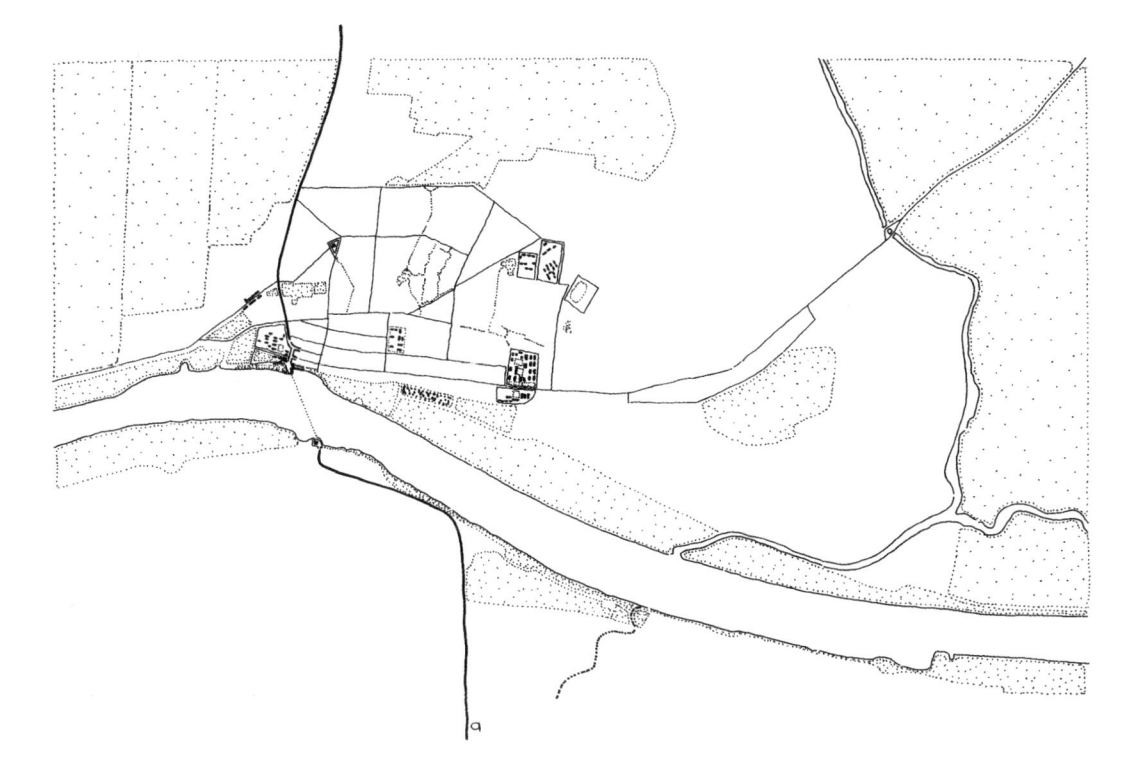

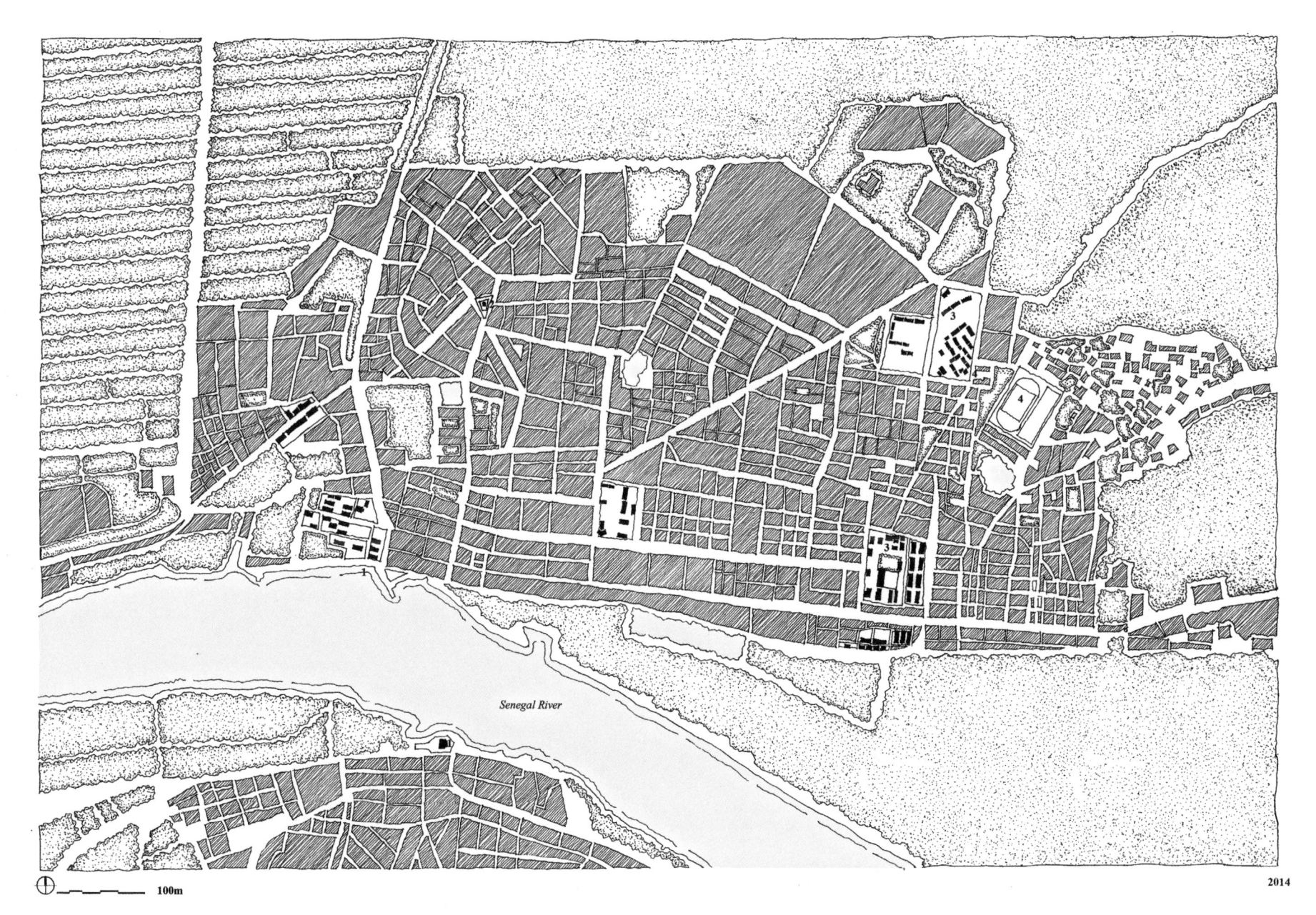

Senegal River

100m

2014

NIAMEY, NIGER

FOUNDED: unknown
URBAN AREA: 239 km²
POPULATION: 1,302,910
URBAN AREA DENSITY: 5 400/km²
GPS: 13° 30'41.72"N, 2° 6'49.90"E

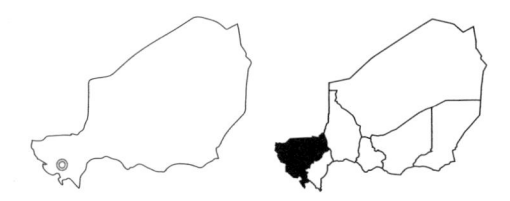

Niamey is the capital and largest city of the West African country of Niger. The city is situated on two plateaus with the Niger River in-between. The original city developed on the eastern side of the river. Niamey is the main hub for the trade and export of agricultural products as well as the political, and cultural centre of Niger.

Niamey, originally a small village, only became significant during the 1890s when the French developed a colonial post and the city grew into an important centre. The economic boom experienced between 1970 and 1988 – as a result of the revenue generated from the uranium mines at Arlit – saw Niamey's population growing from 108,000 to 398,365 inhabitants, reaching an estimated 1,302,910 nowadays. The city expanded from a mere 14 km² in 1970 to 44 km² by 1977 and currently covers approximately 239 km². The growth was accommodated by annexing neighbouring villages such as Lazaret.

The more recent excessive population growth has been assigned to rural-urban migration driven by the effects of droughts in the surrounding region and the urban primacy of the capital city. The city is vulnerable to the impacts of desertification and the intensity and severity of flooding which has increased over the past decade

A large part of the city is structured according to a geometric grid layout with wide streets and single-storeyed houses featuring central courtyards. The historic city centre's major commercial district is home to the traditional Niamey Market. The market was burnt down during the 1950s and rebuilt during the late 1980s. It is now strategically located at the intersection of the two major axes, the Avenue Ouezzin-Coulibaly, which runs from the river to the northern part of the city, and the Boulevard de la Liberté, which runs from east to west. The majority of the population lives in crowded areas alongside the Niger River and in large informal settlements on the outskirts of the city. The city is internationally accessible via a small international airport.

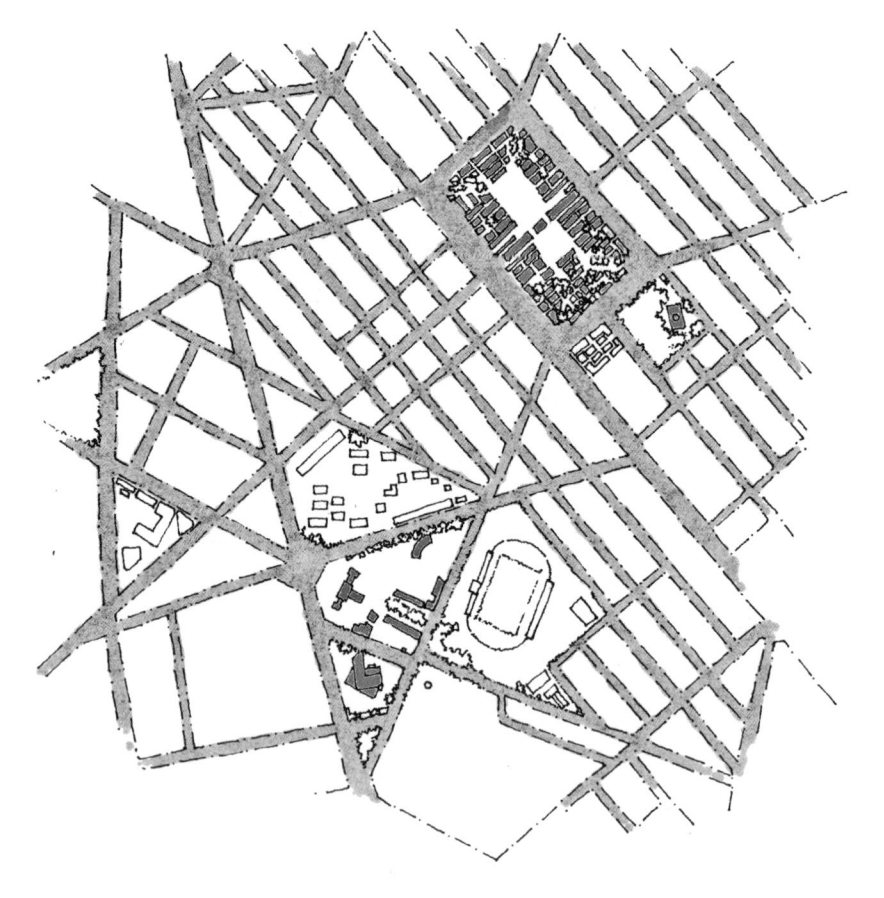

1 Niamey Grand Market
2 National Assembly of Niger
3 National Post
4 Municipal Stadium
5 Maourey Roundabout
6 Small Market
7 Town Hall of Niamey
8 Courthouse
9 Palais de Congrès, Congress Palace
10 General Hospital
11 Presidential Palace
12 National Museum
13 Nigerian Franco Cultural Centre
14 Cathedral
15 General Seyni Kountche Stadium & Sports Centre
16 Niamey High School
17 Mariana High School & Canada School
18 Muslim Cemetery
19 Military Zone
20 Racecourse
21 University of Niamey Abdou Moumouni
22 Christian Cemetery
23 National Guard
24 Great Mosque of Niameys

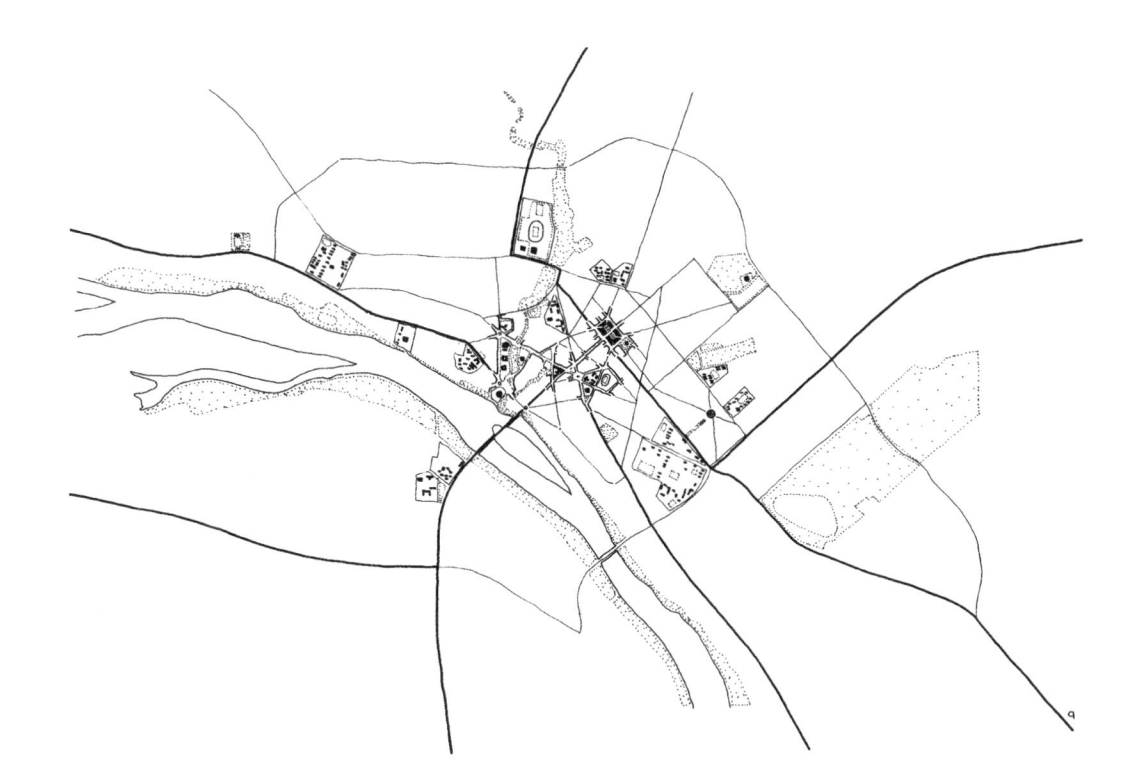

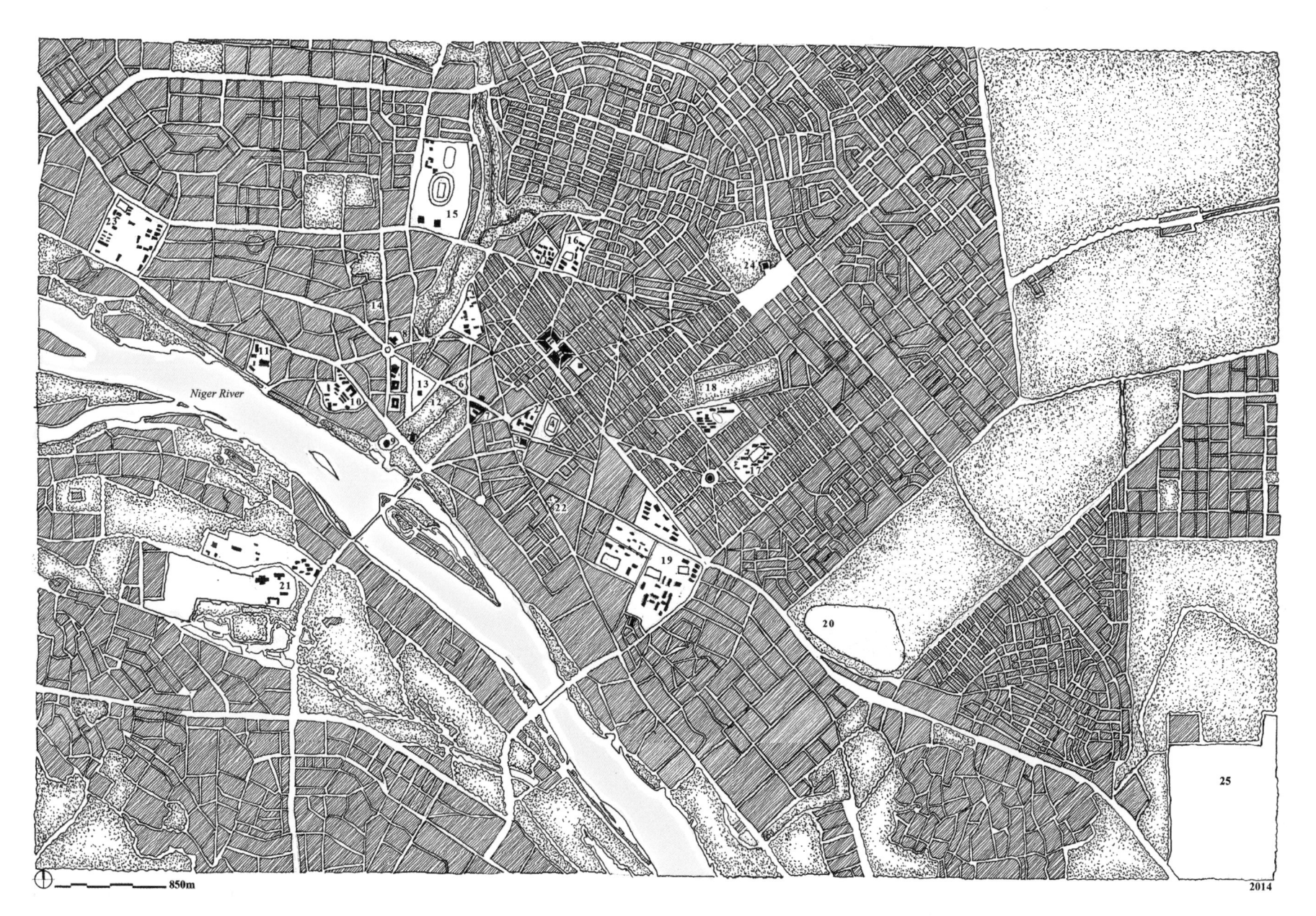

ABUJA, NIGERIA

FOUNDED: 1980s
AREA: 713 km²
LARGER MUNICIPAL POPULATION (2011): 2,153,000
CITY POPULATION (2006): 776,298
DENSITY: 1,088.8/km²
GPS: 6° 26'46.07"N, 3° 24'8.35"E
  6° 27'13.78"N, 3° 23'21.59"E

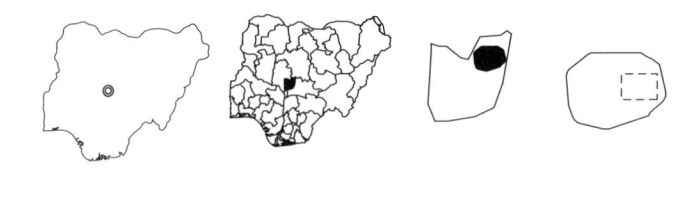

Abuja, a young, purpose-built city, was established by a military government decree in 1976 to replace Lagos as federal capital of Nigeria. A consortium of American consulting firms designed the 1979 master plan for the new city, which defined the general structure and major design elements of the city that are visible in its current form.

One of the many reasons for relocating the capital was to create a city that is more centrally located to serve the country and provide equal access to Nigeria's great diversity of cultural groups. Abuja is therefore located at the centre of Nigeria. The city was built mainly in the 1980s and officially became Nigeria's capital on 12 December 1991. Since then, the city has been experiencing population growth at an unprecedented rate. The site selected for the city is on a plain, marked by the most dominant topographical feature – the monumental Aso Rock. In developing a master plan, a study was apparently made to analyse the processes underlying the evolution of Nigerian cities. It emerged that the Nigerian urban tradition ostensibly supports the concept of a contiguous urban mass with a single core. The master plan proposed a crescent-shaped city that was defined as a centrally-oriented city, influenced by Brasília. The new city had to serve as a symbol of national integration and unity for the country. Aso Rock became the main topographical reference in the landscape from where the city was anchored in the landscape. The Presidential Complex, National Assembly and Supreme Court are strategically and axially arranged along the major structural alignment of the new city. Renowned Japanese architect Kenzo Tange came up with a more detailed design of the central areas of the capital, particularly its monumental core. It seems that "the garden city concept, orderly urban form and western architecture were given priority over human activities in the design of the new city" (Abubakar, Doan 2012). According to the 2014 UN-Habitat report, Abuja is currently increasing by more than 100,000 inhabitants annually.

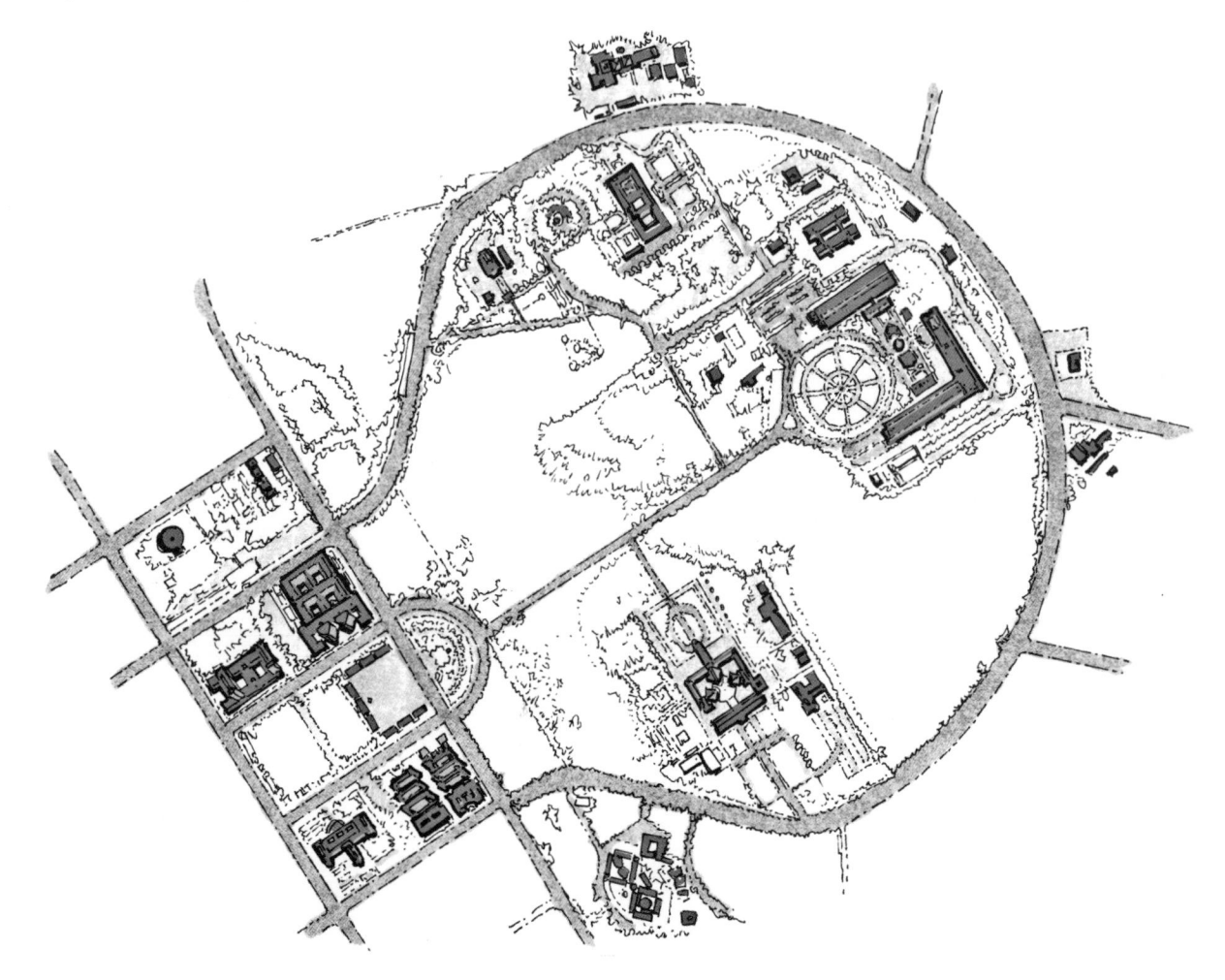

WESTERN AFRICA

1 National Assembly
2 National Arboretum Park
3 Secretariat Park
4 Eagle Square
5 Office of the Presidency
6 Supreme Court
7 Old Presidential Complex
8 Millennium Park
9 Federal Secretariat
10 Foreign Affairs
11 Lobito Cr Park
12 National Mosque
13 Church of Nigerian Anglican Commune
14 Durban St. Neighborhood Park
15 Abuja Park
16 National Hospital
17 Abuja National Stadium
18 Wonderland Park
19 National Children's Park & Zoo
20 Aso Rock

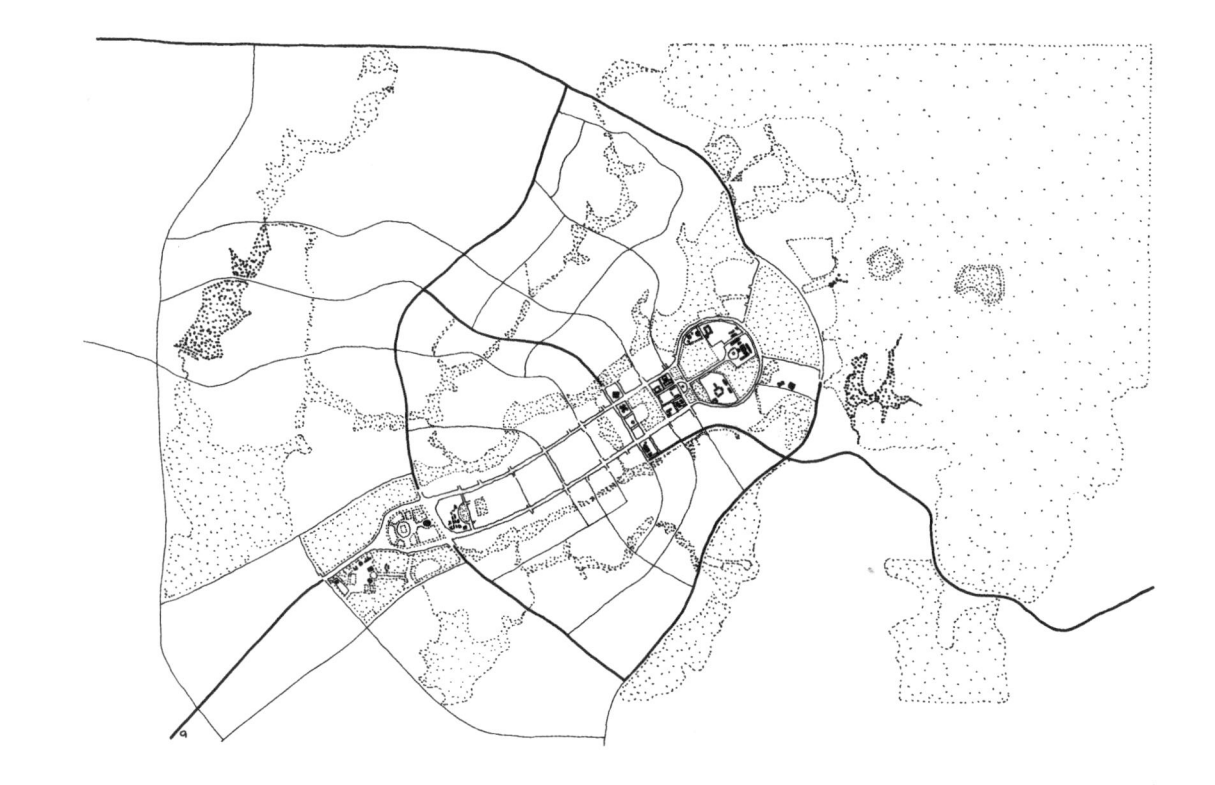

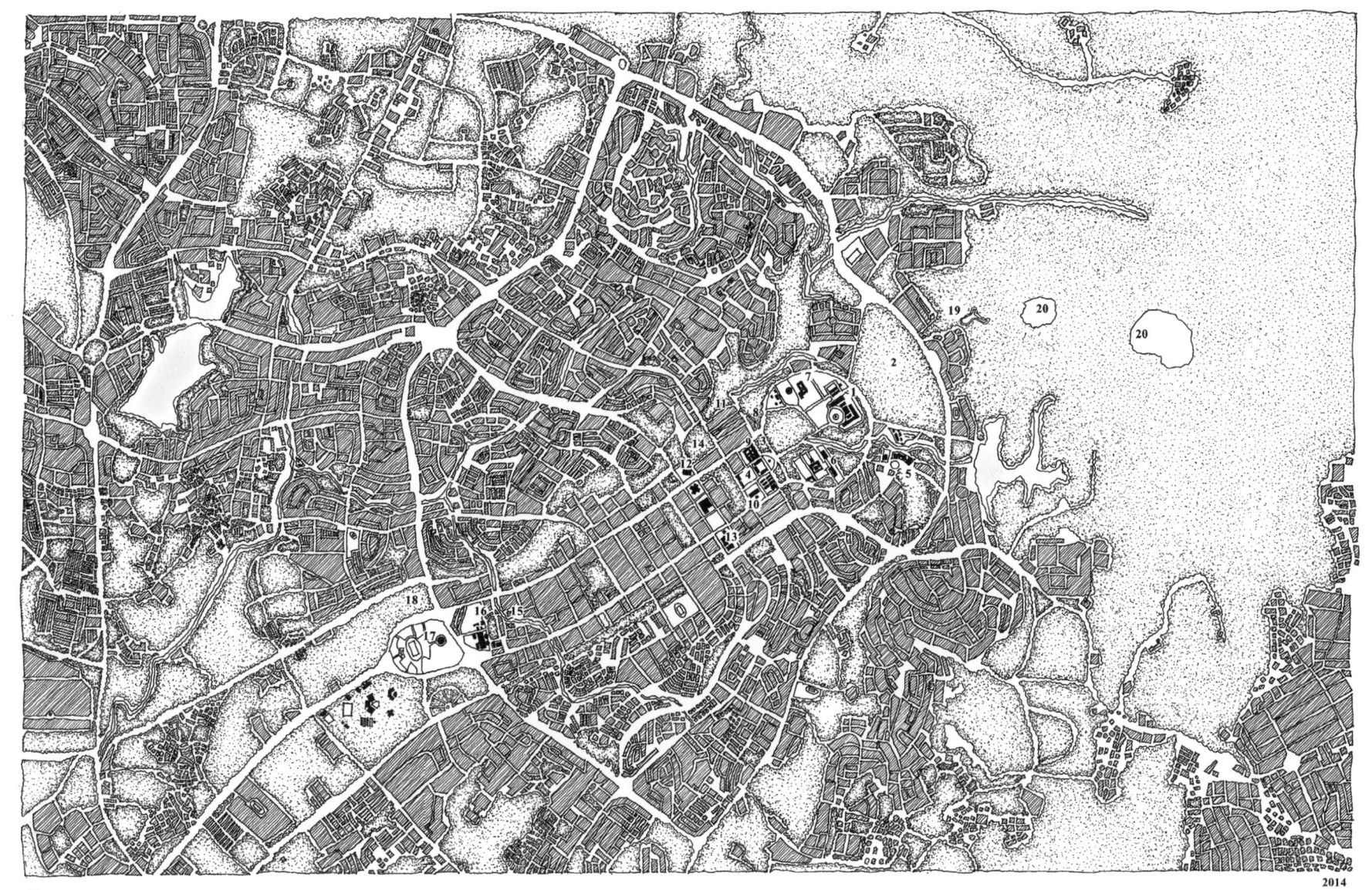

2000m

2014

IBADAN, NIGERIA

FOUNDED: unknown
URBAN AREA: 3,080 km²
POPULATION: 2,949,000 (2011)
URBAN AREA DENSITY: 828/km²
GPS: 7° 22'33.61"N, 3° 53'47.35"E

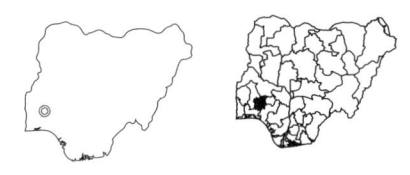

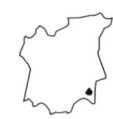

Ibadan – "the city at the edge of the savannah" – is the capital city of Oyo State and the third most populous. It is geographically the largest metropolitan area in Nigeria. This city, reputed to be the largest indigenous city in Africa south of the Sahara, is surrounded by seven hills.

The original city developed towards the end of the eighteenth century in response to its strategic location (then between forests and plains which have since been replaced by urban development) as the Yoruba settled in the area. By the end of 1829, the area thrived as a commercial, political and military centre.

The area became a British Protectorate in 1983, witnessing a population growth of up to 120,000. The colony was developed as an important trading hub, giving rise to the commercial centre we know today. The city has since been experiencing constant growth, significantly impacted by the construction of the Ibadan-Lagos highway during the 1980s, followed by the Eleiyele highway. The city has since spread further into the neighbouring areas.

Ibadan's long history is represented in the city's fabric and buildings that display both traditional and modern features. The old, indigenous core area is home to the king's palace and sections of the ancient city fortifications are still visible, dating back to the era of British colonial rule.

The city's structure, largely determined by the surrounding natural topographical features, consists of a range of winding roads criss-crossed with a predominantly organic street network. The city is a major transit point connecting the coastal region and the areas to the north. The city is served by the Ibadan Airport while the Ibadan Railway Station is part of the main railway line from Lagos to Kano

Significant landmarks include the Dugbe Market that acts as the core of Ibadan's transport and trading network. The Bower Memorial Tower can be seen from virtually any point in the city. Cocoa House was the first skyscraper in Africa. Mapo Hall, the colonial-style city hall, is perched on top of a hill.

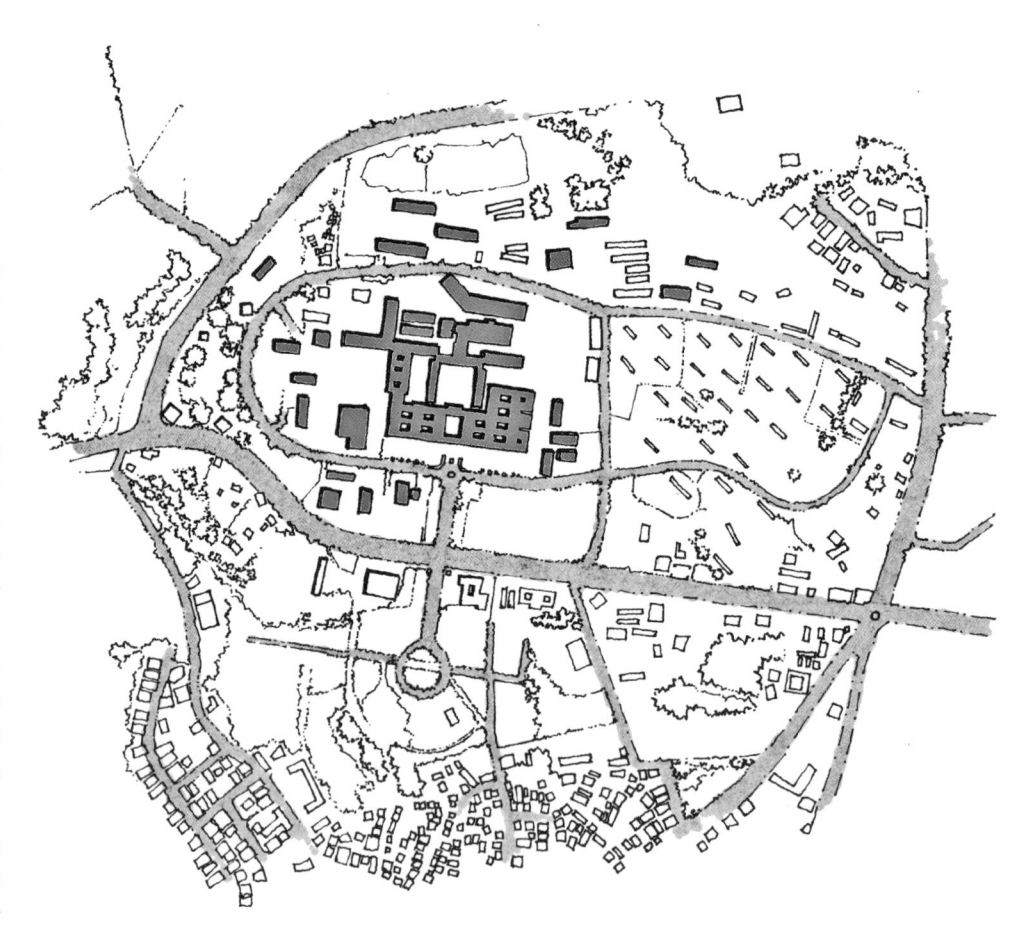

1 Agodi Gardens
2 University of Ibadan Teaching Hospital
3 Lekan Salami Stadium
4 Ibadan Central Train Station
5 Seminary of Saints Peter & Paul
6 Sango Cemetery
7 Mapo Hall
8 Adeoyo Hospital
9 Bower's Tower

LAGOS, NIGERIA

FOUNDED: fifteenth century
AREA: 999 km²
CITY POPULATION (2013): 10,788,000
METRO: 21 million
DENSITY: 20,000/km²
GPS: 6° 26'46.07"N, 3° 24'8.35"E
6° 27'13.78"N, 3° 23'21.59"E

Explosive growth – from 300,000 in 1950 to an estimated 21 million in the metro today – is a result of Nigeria's booming oil industry. While there are reports that Lagos is now officially the largest city in Africa, Cairo still remains the largest city on the continent (UN-Habitat, 2014). Lagos is the most important node for telecommunications and the most accessible city in Nigeria by land, air and sea. The string of lagoons along which it is set has prompted the Portuguese to call it "Lagos" or lagoon.

Lagos is made up of several islands which are connected to the mainland by a series of bridges. The city developed from Iddo Island to Lagos Island, its urban core, which had historically been positioned beneficially to commerce and trade. While the overall form is dictated by the major lagoon, smaller lagoon inlets determine the form of ports. The shape of the city becomes completely amorphous where swamps create deep nebulous inlets. Pressures on available land have resulted in floating slums that continuously blur the edge between land and water. A strong ordering axis in the city, which also dictated historical growth along its path, is the north-south railway that cuts through urban fabric and limits east-west movement. As it has grown, Lagos engulfed numerous Awori villages in the north, sometimes visible in the interruption in a "grid" street pattern (Peil, 1991).

While Lagos has a history of land reclamation, it has started to create artificial landforms similar to what is happening in Dubai. The new Eco Atlantic Island, currently being constructed, is purposefully positioned to save the coast from rising sea levels caused by global warming. An infrastructural nightmare, every inch of the city is inhabited, leaving little room for open space, which is often limited to space-left-over-after-planning. Residential density in central Lagos amounts to roughly 20,000 km², with over five persons per room. Market spaces essentially use all the "left-over" spaces, which is the way that public space is traditionally shaped in many African cities. Space is only filled as required and vacated after use, allowing traders to remain mobile and flexible. By contrast to Western public space, which is predominantly fixed in time and space, African public space is constantly in flux, reshaping itself.

On Lagos Island, dense informal trading energises various streets and bridges. Ebuto Ero Market – the city's first market – has been relocated but is still functioning between the bridges. Tafalawa Balewa Square is at the eastern end of the island. On the mainland, the National Theatre and Sports Stadium are major landmarks.

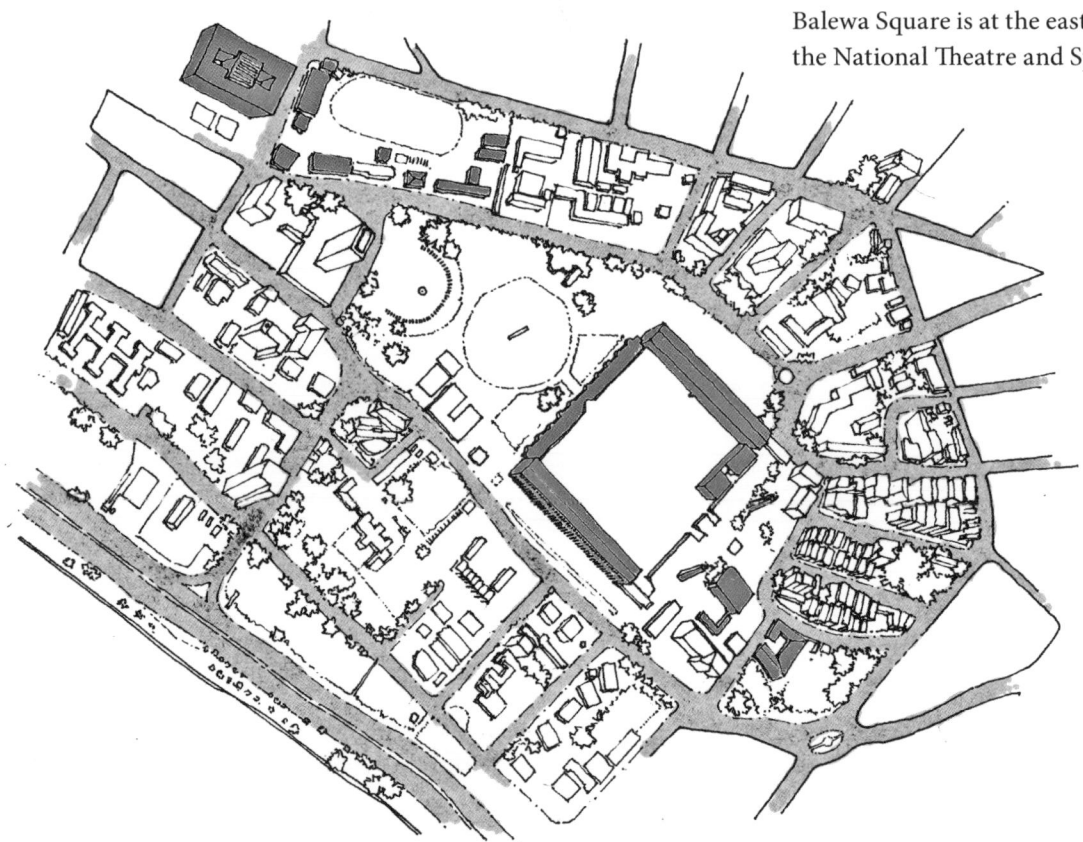

WESTERN AFRICA **201**

1 Tafawa Balewa Square
2 Place of Remembrance
3 Tinubu Square
4 National Museum
5 Freedom Park
6 Cathedral Church of Christ
7 Balogun Market
8 Lagos State Central Mosque
9 LSPDC House
10 Tom Jones Hall
11 Jankarta Market
12 The Entrance of King Ado High & Isale Eko Grammer Schools
13 Okesuna Cemetery
14 Cemetery
15 Lagos City Hall
16 Kings College Lagos
17 Onikan Stadium
18 National Theatre
19 National Library
20 Ikoyi Cemetery
21 Port
22 Muri Okunola Park
23 Civic Centre
24 Church of Assumption
25 National Open University
26 Nigerian Law School

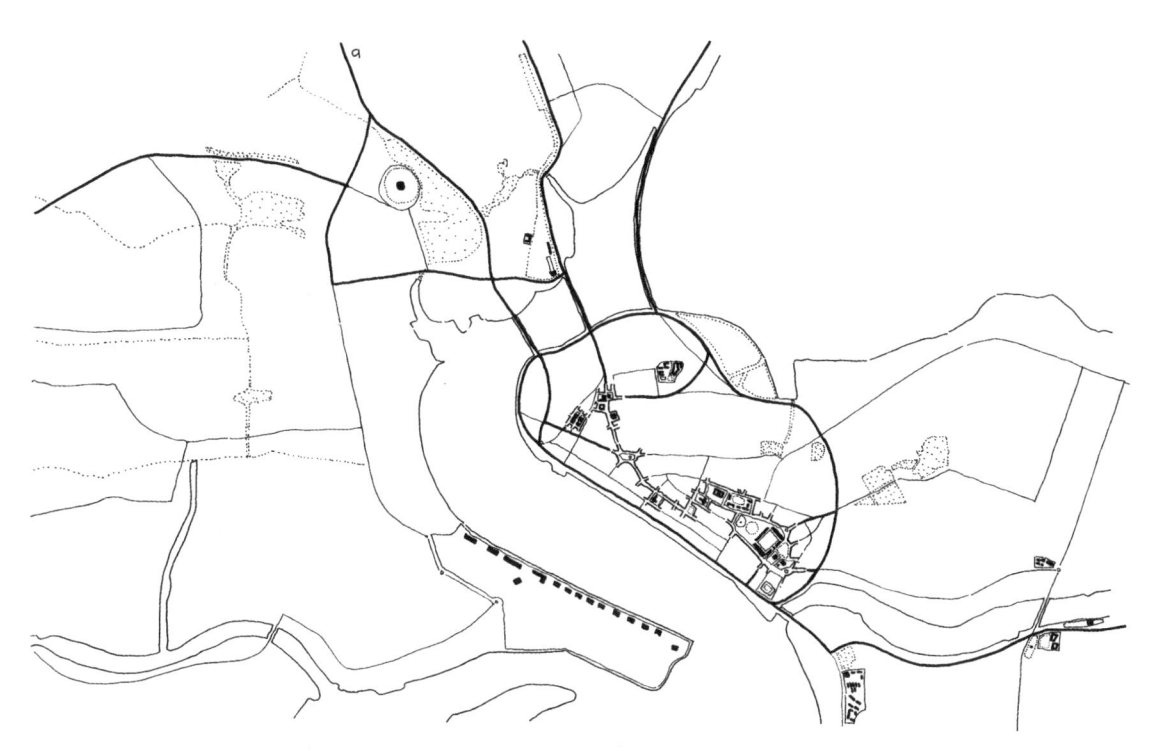

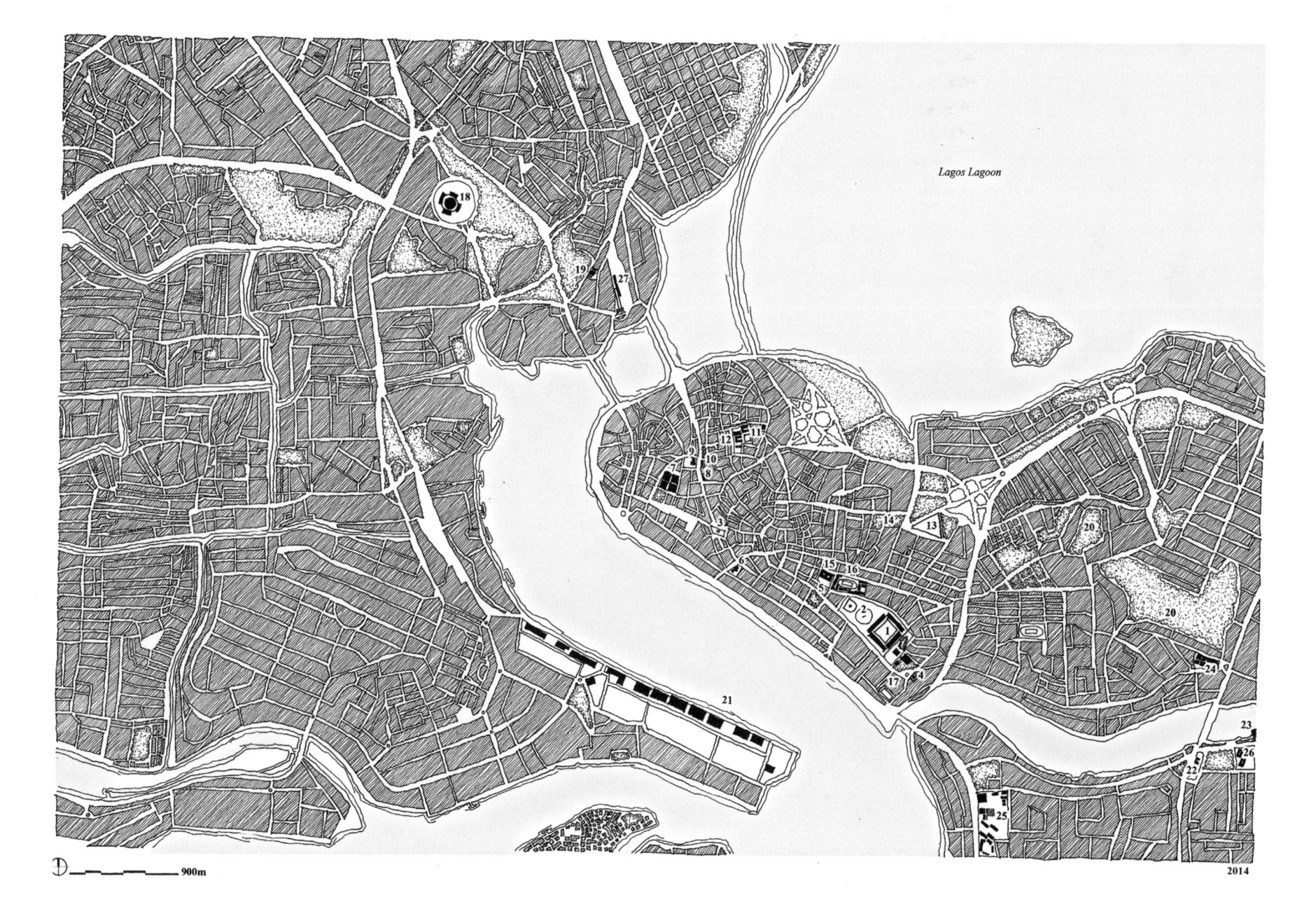

DAKAR, SENEGAL

FOUNDED: fifteenth century
AREA: 82 km² (METRO: 550 km²)
CITY POPULATION (2011): 2,396,800
DENSITY: 12,510/km²
GPS: 14° 40'48.23"N, 17° 26'36.64"W
14° 39'46.43"N, 17° 26'14.99"W
14° 40'10.19"N, 17° 25'54.99"W

Dakar, at the westernmost point on the continent, is the capital of Senegal. As an advantageous departure point for trans-Atlantic and European trade, it developed historically into a major port city successively occupied by various colonial powers. Gorée Island, a historical slave-trading station and UNESCO World Heritage Site, is located a short distance away from the port.

In the pre-colonial period, the Lébou community had settled in the region. Urbanisation accelerated in the nineteenth and twentieth centuries under French colonial rule. The area of the city is geographically funnel-shaped, and this in turn has shaped the urban structure. Three areas are generally recognisable in the urban form around the city's origins: the colonial Plateau to the south, the médina to its north and an industrial area that is stretched along the east of the north-south Autoroute and parallel railway line which both cut through the urban fabric. A French system of urban planning – such as the linear grid and series of urban axes – was imposed upon the existing coastal villages, most particularly in the area referred to as the Plateau, so that it still has a notably European character. In the orthogonal plan, Kermel's Square (today's Place de l'Indépendance) is clearly noticeable, breaking the iron-grid layout and is still a main urban market today.

The densely populated médina surrounding the Grande Mosquéé de Dakar, north of the Plateau, is the African quarter. It was established by the French colonial authorities, designated for the African population as an enforcement following an outbreak of the bubonic plague in 1914 – with wide cordons separating the settlements. Ironically, the name médina was evidently inspired by the French experience in North Africa (Bigon, 2012).

Various urban planning programmes were launched in Dakar between 1946 and 2001, especially to address the growth of the city following independence in 1960 and onwards. The monuments heralding the new post-independent nationalism are highly visible throughout Dakar's urban landscape.

Today the coastline between Douala and Dakar is highly vulnerable to the impacts of climate change. A projected sea-level rise of 0.5 m by 2100 will result in great losses of coastal land by erosion and submergence, and Dakar, like many other populous coastal cities of West Africa, is extremely vulnerable to projected sea-level rise impacts (UN-Habitat, 2014).

WESTERN AFRICA **203**

1 Independence Square
2 Hôtel de Ville, City Hall
3 Central Bank of the State of West Africa
4 Gouvernance
5 Chamber of Commerce
6 Presidential Palace
7 Soweto Square
8 National Assembly
9 Courthouse
10 Aristide Le Dantec University Hospital
11 Théodore Monod Museum or IFAN Museum
12 Cathedral
13 Sfax Square
14 Great Mosque of Dakar
15 Great National Theatre of Dakar
16 Train Station
17 Independence Monument
18 Kennedy High School
19 Zoological Gardens
20 Catholic Cemetery
21 Léopold Sédar Senghor International Airport
22 Muslim Cemetery
23 Old Bel Air Christian Cemetery
24 Place d'Arme 23ème Bima
25 Cheikh Anta Diop University

Atlantic Ocean

1000 m

2014

SAINT-LOUIS, SENEGAL

FOUNDED: 1659
AREA: unknown
CITY POPULATION (2005): 176,000
DENSITY: unknown
GPS: 16° 1'32.93"N, 16° 30'20.47"W
16° 1'34.19"N, 16° 30'29.88"W
16° 1'31.24"N, 16° 29'53.35"W
16° 1'57.28"N, 16° 30'29.76"W

Founded in 1659 as a French colonial settlement, the city of Saint-Louis was conceived in an exceptional landscape. The miniscule strip of land (about 2 km long and roughly 400 m wide) that forms the old colonial city is wedged between two arms of the mouth of the Senegal River. Besides its unique topography, Saint-Louis lies in the geographical location of the Sahel (the eco-climatic region of transition between the Sahara and the Sudanian Savanna). Lying north-south, the island is separated from the Atlantic Ocean to the west by a 300-metre-wide sand spit, the "Langue de Barbarie", which has also been urbanised. On the eastern mainland, surrounded by tidal marshes, lies the third section of the city, called Sor. Along with its regular town plan, structure of quays, and the characteristic colonial architecture, Saint-Louis has a distinctive character. The great architectural and urban quality of the site prompted UNESCO to include the island in the World Heritage list in 2000.

The North and South quarters and the Place Faidherbe – with the Government Palace situated in the centre – form the major zones on the Island. It is surrounded by a system of quays that serve as a reference for all the streets in the east-west direction. The little oceanic city was the political capital of the colony and French West Africa (FWA) up until 1902. It was also the capital of Senegal and Mauritania up until 1957, before falling into decline due to the transfer of the capital to Dakar. It has revived its economy based on fishing, agriculture and especially tourism – the latter resulting in the gentrification of the island. A new airport was recently inaugurated in Saint-Louis to facilitate access. The population has more than tripled in the last few decades. Sor is the only area of the city that can, to a degree, accommodate expansions and urban development. The existing urban area presents an incoherent and disjointed group since settlement was historically made without any spatial planning. Unfortunately, Saint-Louis is extremely vulnerable to sea-level rises in addition to higher water levels flowing out of the Senegal River, that now threaten the low-lying islands of the city. In 2008, Alioune Badiane of the United Nations' UN-Habitat agency designated Saint-Louis as "the city most threatened by rising sea levels in the whole of Africa".

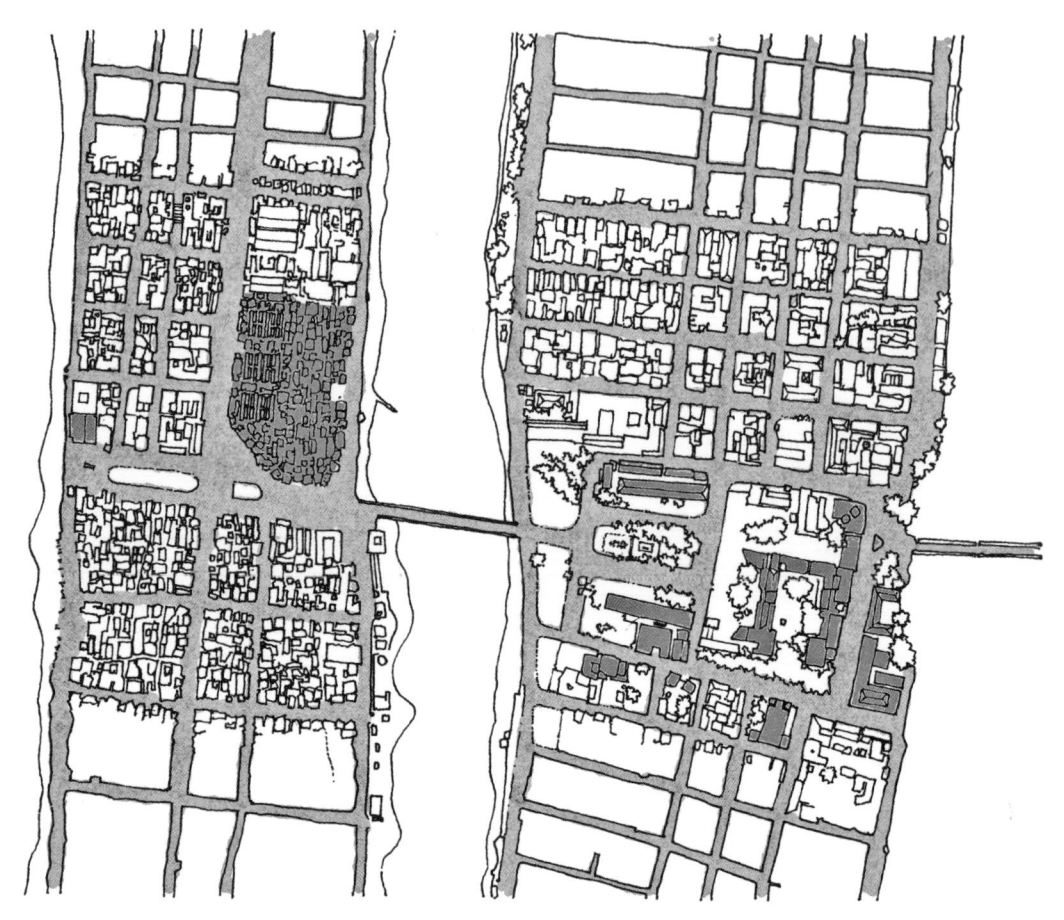

WESTERN AFRICA **205**

1 Monument for the Dead
2 Faidherbe Square
3 Market
4 Governor's Palace
5 Cathedral
6 Saint Joseph de Cluny
7 Faidherbe Bridge
8 Grand Mosque
9 Hospital
10 IFAN Museum
11 South Mosque
12 Rognat Barracks
13 Military Camp
14 Muslim Cemetery
15 Ablaye Wade Square or St Germain Square
16 Tendjiguen Market
17 Joseph Gaye Stadium
18 Sidy Tall Mosque
19 Idrissa Mbengue Mosque & Goxu Mbathie School
20 Railway Station
21 Bayal Mosque & Bayal Field
22 Maître Babacar Seye Stadium
23 Idy Diallo mosque
24 Cemetery
25 Park
26 Port

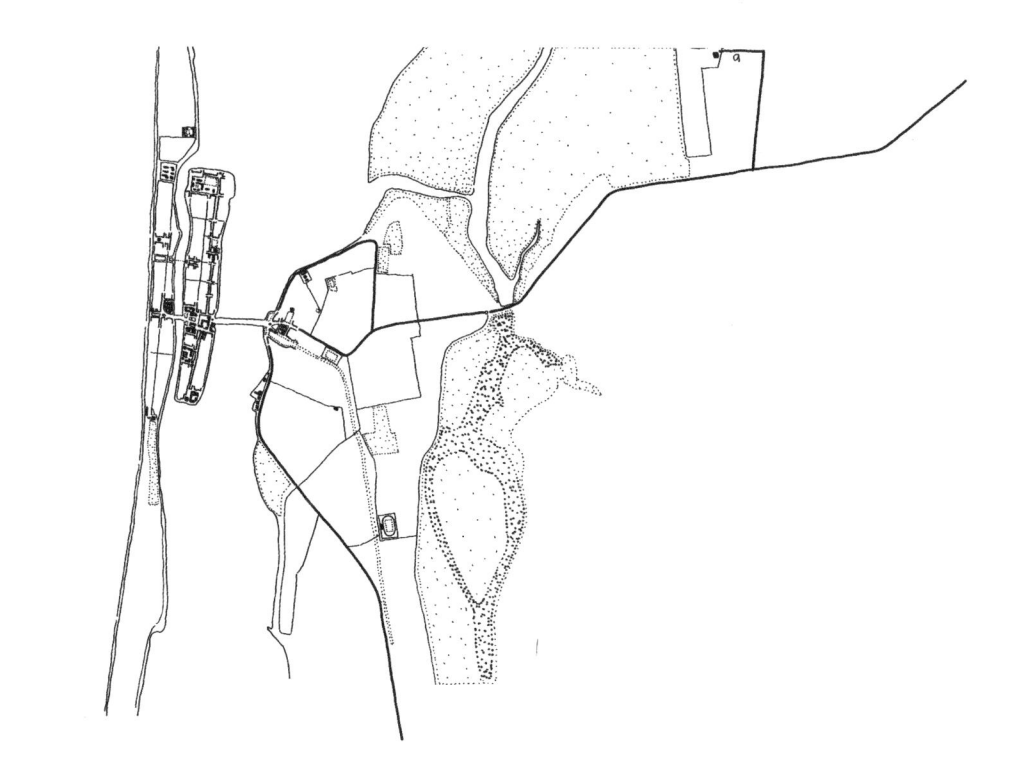

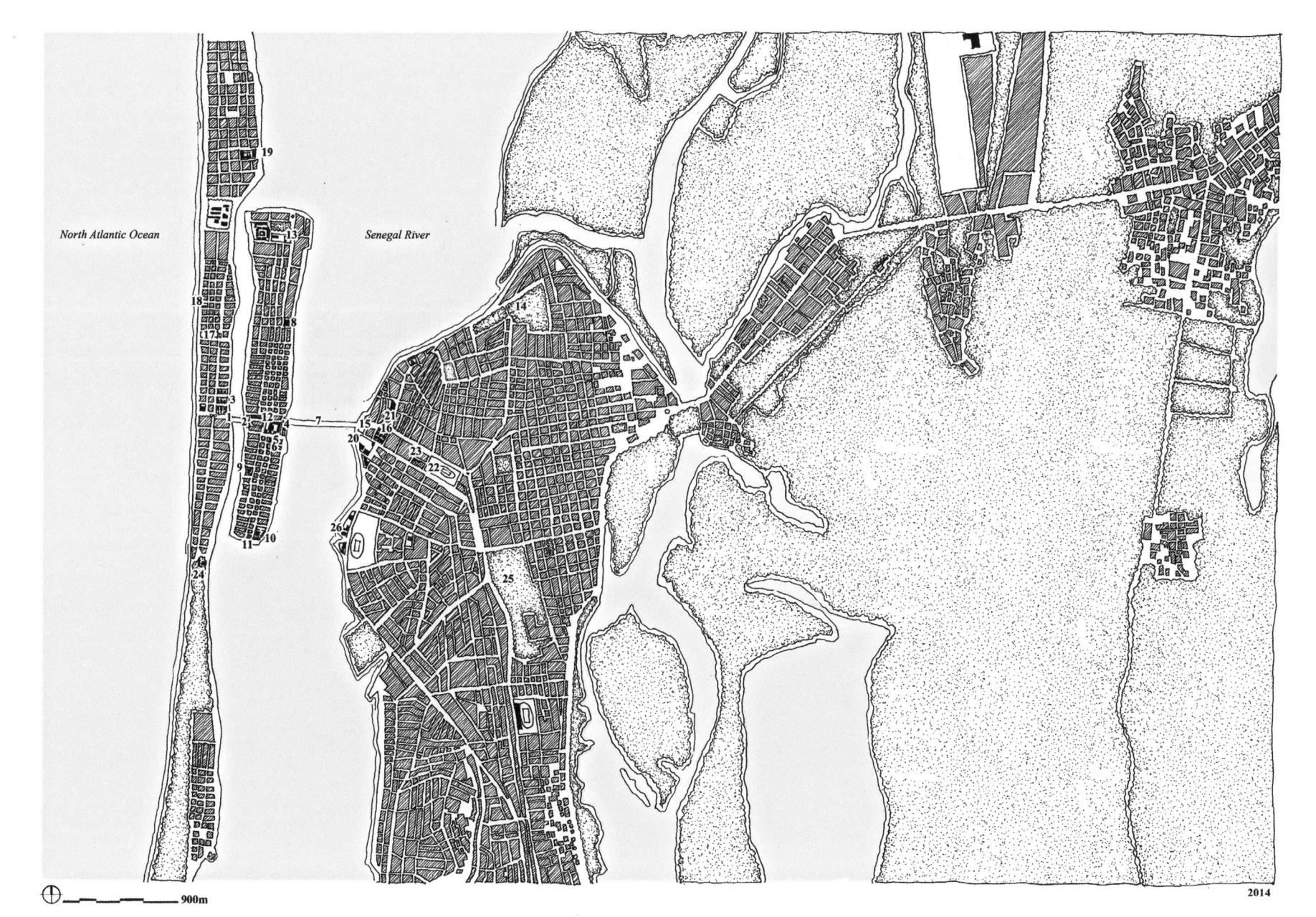

FREETOWN, SIERRA LEONE

FOUNDED: 1792
AREA: unknown
CITY POPULATION (2011): 941,000
DENSITY: unknown
GPS: 8° 29'12.63"N, 13° 13'57.06"W

Located on a peninsula on the southern bank of the estuary of the Sierra Leone River, Freetown is the capital and largest city of Sierra Leone. It is a major port city along the Atlantic Ocean. In fact, the economy revolves largely around the harbour which is one of the world's largest natural deep-water harbours. The city lies at the foot of the mountains along the peninsula.

By the mid-seventeenth century, the increased activity of British, French, Dutch, and Danish trading companies ended the limited degree of Portuguese control over the western coastline trade. The British selected the site in 1787 as a haven for African slaves, who were freed and left destitute in England. A massive Cotton Tree, which has stood in central Freetown for over 500 years, symbolically represents its history. The Cotton Tree gained importance in 1792 when a group of freed African-American slaves held a large gathering in its shade. In 1821, Freetown became the seat of government for all of Great Britain's West African colonies, a position it retained until 1874. Freetown became the country's capital in 1961 following independence.

Central Freetown is one of the oldest regions in this city that was planned in contrast to the rest of the city, which is in a sprawling, organic form. Several historical landmarks are recognisable in the urban fabric and connected to its African-American history of liberated slaves. The city is also home to the Fourah Bay College, which is the oldest university in West Africa, founded in 1827. There are also several mosques and churches, notably the Anglican St George's Cathedral (1852). The National Museum is housed in the former Cotton Tree Railroad Station.

Freetown, like the rest of Sierra Leone, has endured some challenging times during the recent civil war. Rebels occupied the city twice and the resident population and infrastructure suffered badly. Though the country has been peaceful since 2002, the population of the city is still much higher than it was before the war. This has put pressure on land and local services. Similar to many other African cities, parks and recreational gardens have been converted into waste dumps and increasing population density puts forests at a particular risk of biodiversity loss (UN-Habitat, 2014).

1 Cotton Tree
2 Sierra Leone National Museum
3 Ministry of Defence
4 State House
5 Victoria Park
6 Connaught Hospital & King's Yard Gate
7 St George's Cathedral
8 Kington Cemetery & St Edward's Secondary School
9 Orthodox Christian School & Cemetery
10 Siaka Stevens Stadium
11 Parliament
12 Circular Road Cemetery
13 National Railway Museum
14 Old Fourah Bay College
15 Old Boundary Cannons
16 Racecourse & Kissy Road Cemeteries
17 St John's Maroon Church
18 Old Wharf Steps
19 Law Courts
20 Police Clock Tower
21 Fourah Bay College
22 Pademba Road Prison

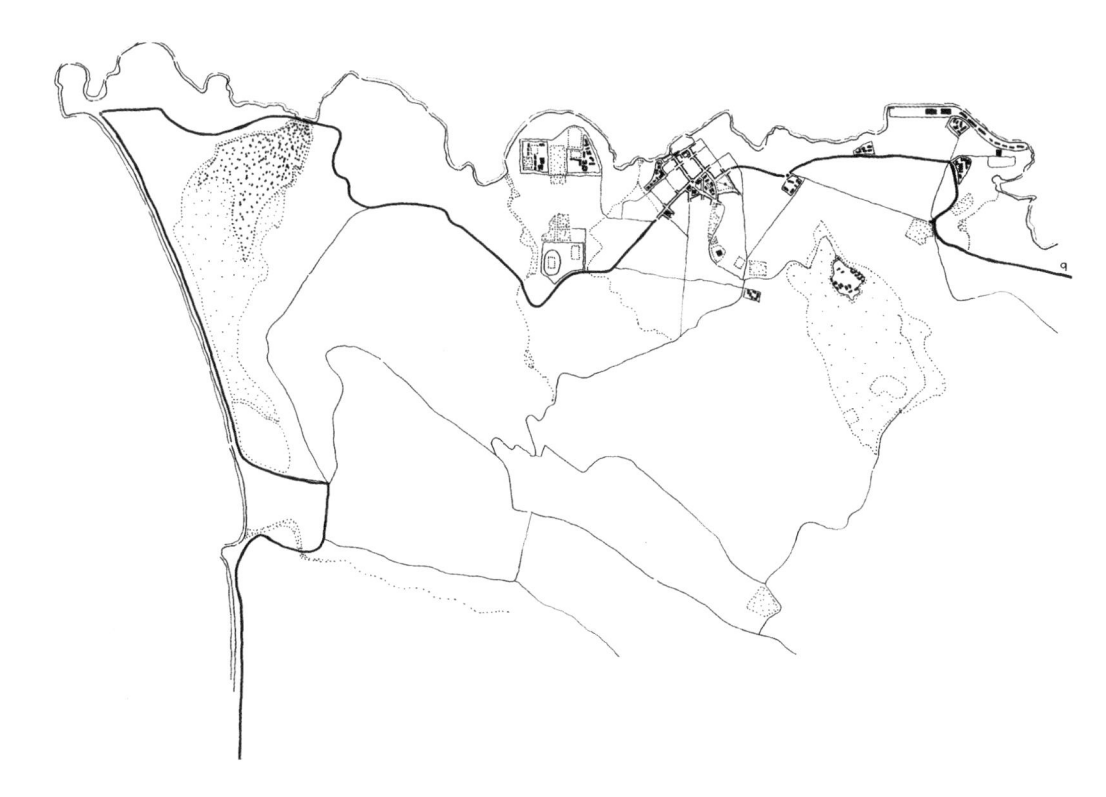

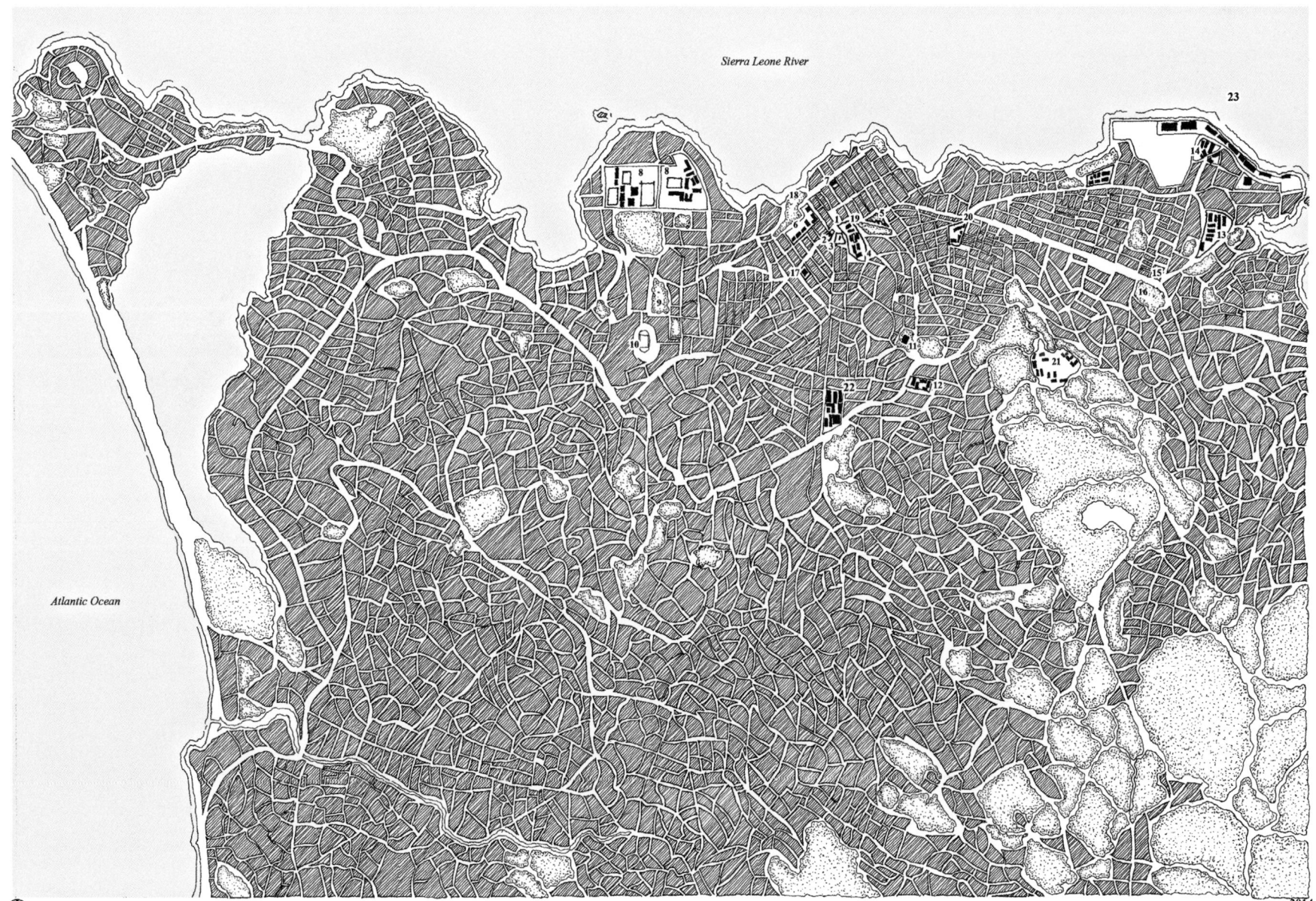

LOMÉ, TOGO

FOUNDED: 1880
AREA: 90 km²
CITY POPULATION (2010): 837,437
DENSITY: 9,305/km²
GPS: 6° 7′48.26″N, 1° 12′58.72″E]

Lomé is the largest city in Togo – a country that has been classified by the UN as being among the world's least advanced. Lomé's industrial and harbour free-zone was created in 1989, which has benefited from being at the crossroads between the maritime outlet of the landlocked states of West Africa and the coastal trade.

Lomé was founded by African, British and German traders. A lagoon to the north, where Éwé farming villages were already established when the Germans developed a large administrative centre next to them in the late 1890s, surrounds the city. The Germans established a protectorate in 1884, of which Lomé became the capital in 1897. Foreign traders were therefore the founders of the city, which is "neither an autochthonous [indigenous] city – old villages that would have grown – nor a colonial city created by making a clean sweep of the former rights" (Marguerat quoted by Gervais-Lambony, 2012). This original double city-centre core still exists today. According to Gervais-Lambony (2012), experiencing two colonial powers in succession is the main characteristic that distinguishes Lomé from other African capitals.

The 1920s were important in the history of Lomé. This period corresponded to an extensive development programme by the French, still visible in the urban fabric, including the completion of the Boulevard Circulaire. The French also constructed the law courts and the town hall, along with a new wharf in 1928.

Political landmarks in the urban landscape of Lomé represent the various political powers of the day: the colonial; the first Republic of Togo from the beginning of the 1960s (e.g. the Independence Monument); the authoritarian regime from 1967 to the beginning of the 1990s (e.g. the building of the *Rassemblement*); and finally, the drafting of a new symbolism since the beginning of the era of "democratisation". From 1990 to 2006, the struggle for control over public space was characterised by actions of demonstrators aiming to be as visible as possible in public spaces and to conquer symbolic places. The typical routes of the political demonstrations illustrate both the will to control public space and the actual symbolic sites of the city (Gervais-Lambony, 2012). Over time, the city saw disproportionate spatial expansion over a large area towards the north.

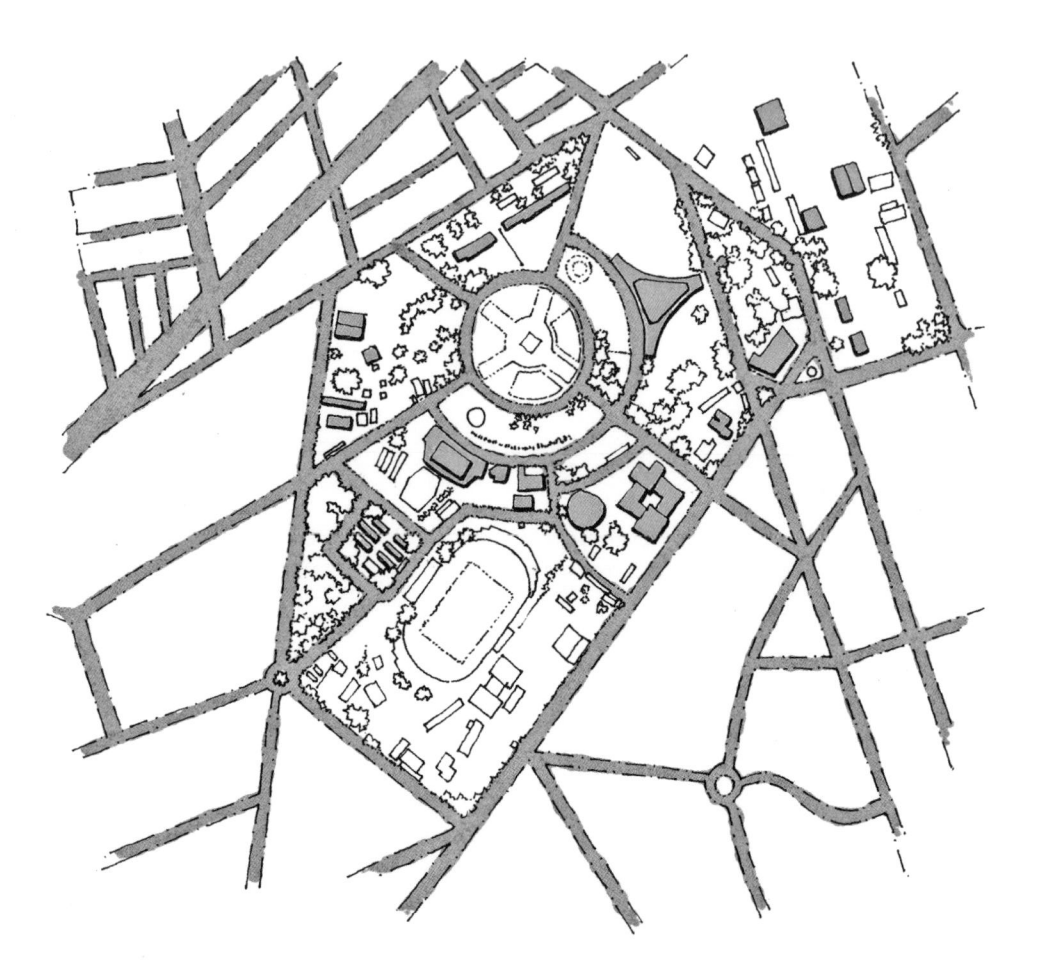

1 Monument of Independence
2 National Museum
3 Railway Station
4 Eyadema Omnisports Stadium
5 Presidential Palace
6 Large Market
7 Sacré Coeur Cathedral
8 French Cultural Center
9 Evangelical Presbyterian Church of Togo
10 Lomé-Tokoin Airport
11 West Lake
12 East Lake
13 Tokoin High School
14 Tokoin University Hospital
15 Port

Gulf of Guinea

RESOURCES

Research Reports, conference papers accessed on the web

Abubakar, I. and Doan, P. 2012. New towns in Africa: Are they close to achieving their objectives? Department of Urban and Regional Planning, Florida State University, Tallahassee, FL 32306 Paper. [O]. Available at http://www.researchgate.net/publication/259647235_New_towns_in_Africa_Modernity_andor_Decentralization (Accessed 11 March 2014)

Abu-Lughod, J.L. 1987. The Islamic City – Historic Myth, Islamic Essence, and Contemporary Relevance. International Journal of Middle East Studies, Vol. 19, No. 2 (May 1987), pp. 155–176. Cambridge University Press. [O]. Available at http://www.jstor.org (Accessed 11 June 2014)

Anon. 2007. Megacity Challenges. Research Report sponsored by Siemens and conducted by Globescan and MRC McLean Hazel. Germany: Siemens AG. [O]. Available at https://www.cee.siemens.com/web/ua/en/products_and_solutions/energy/Documents/MegaCity_Challenges_en.pdf (Accessed 8 May 2014)

Appessika. 2003. The Case of Abidjan, Ivory Coast. Understanding Slums: Case Studies for the Global Report on Human Settlements 2003. [O]. Available: http://www.ucl.ac.uk/dpu-projects/Global_Report/pdfs/Abidjan.pdf (Accessed 2 June 2014)

Azlitni, B.K.H. 2005. The Development of Physical and Urban Planning Systems in Libya Sustainability of Planning Projects. XXXIII IAHS World Congress on Housing, Transforming Housing Environments through Design, September 27-30, 2005, Pretoria, South Africa. [O]. Available at http://repository.up.ac.za (Accessed 22 May 2014)

Beeckmans, L. 2009. Agency in an African city. The various trajectories through time and space of the public market of Kinshasa. African Perspectives. [O]. Available: https://web.up.ac.za/sitefiles/file/44/1068/3229/9086/African%20Perspectives/PDF/Papers/Beekmans.pdf (Accessed 14 May 2014)

Berriane et al. 2010. New Mobilities around Morocco: A Case Study of the City of Fes. [O]. Available at http://www.imi.ox.ac.uk/pdfs/projects/aphm-pdfs/morocco-english-2011-report (Accessed 5 June 2014)

Bigon, L. 2012. A History of Urban Planning and Infectious Diseases: Colonial Senegal in the Early Twentieth Century. Urban Studies Research Volume 2012 (2012), Article ID 589758. [O]. Available: http://dx.doi.org/10.1155/2012/589758 (Accessed 1 June 2014)

Bisaillon, L. 2010. Harar, Ethiopia. Dualities, discursive meanings and designations. [O]. Available: urbanistica pvs, pp. 28-38. (Accessed 13 April 2014)

Bisaillon, L. and Mohammed, A. 2005. The two faces of the city Modern and Traditional Forms. [O]. Available: Academia.edu (Accessed 13 April 2014)

Bonine, M.E. 1990. The Sacred Direction and City Structure: A Preliminary Analysis of the Islamic Cities of Morocco. Muqarnas, Vol. 7, pp. 50-72. [O]. Available at http://www.jstor.org/discover/10.2307/1523121?uid=3739368&uid=2129&uid=2&uid=70&uid=4&sid=21104269411147 (Accessed 3 July 2014)

Byrnes, M. 2012. How Mussolini Influenced Qaddafi's Vision for Tripoli: City lab. [O]. Available at www.citylab.com/design/2012/01/how-mussolini-influenced-qaddafis-vision-tripoli/1086/

Clarke, N. and Corten, J-P. [sa]. Regenerating Pretoria's Historical Core. Presentation at Heritage as an Asset for Inner City Development, Theme 4 Session 3. [O]. Available at http://web.up.ac.za/research/2012/UP_Research_Publications-2012.pdf (Accessed 22 May 2014)

Cobbinah, P.B. and Amoako, C. 2014. Urban Sprawl and the Loss of Peri-Urban Land in Kumasi, Ghana. World Academy of Science, Engineering and Technology International Journal of Social, Management, Economics and Business Engineering Vol. 8, No. 1. [O]. Available at http://www.researchgate.net/publication/232957200 _Urban_Sprawl_and_the_Loss_of_Peri_Urban_Land_in_Kumasi_Ghana (Accessed 3 May 2014)

Coralli, M. 2011. The Future of Two Metropolises: Lomé and Cotonou Urban growth creates planning challenges in the Ibadan-Accra corridor. [O]. Available: http://thinkafricapress.com/population-matters/future-two-metropolis-lomé-and-cotonou (Accessed 31 May 2014)

Cybriwsky, R. A. 2013. Capital Cities around the World: An Encyclopedia of Geography, History, and Culture. [O]. Accessed as e-book at www.abc-clio.com.

De Jong, S. et al. 2000. Monitoring Trends in Urban Growth and Surveying City Quarters in Ouagadougou, Burkina Faso Using SPOT-XS. Geocarto International, Vol. 15, No. 2, June 2000. Hong Kong: Geocarto International Centre. [O]. Available at http://www.geocarto.com.hk/cgi-bin/pages1/june00/monitoring.pdf (Accessed 12 May 2014)

Dossou, K. and Gléhouenou-Dossou, B. 2007. The vulnerability to climate change of Cotonou (Benin): the rise in sea level. Environment and Urbanization 2007 19:65. DOI: 10.1177/0956247807 077149. [O]. Available: http://eau.sagepub.com/content/19/1/65 (Accessed 15 May 2014)

Duarte, J.P and Rocha, J. A. [sa]. Grammar for the Patio Houses of the Medina of Marrakech (eCAADe 24 – session 20: generative design systems). [O]. Available at http://cumincad.architexturez.net/system/files/pdf/2006_860.content.pdf (Accessed 4 April 2014)

Elwefati, N.A. 2007. Bio-Climatic Architecture in Libya: Case Studies From Three Climatic Regions (An unpublished thesis submitted to the Graduate School of Natural and Applied Sciences of Middle East Technical University). [O]. Available at http://etd.lib .metu.edu.tr/upload/12608674/index.pdf (Accessed 4 March 2014)

Fernandes, A.S., and Fernandes de Saì, M. [sa]. A bittersweet inheritance: the cocoa islands of Sao Tomé and Prìncipe from colonial hegemony to developing microstate. Research Centre on Architecture and Urbanism, Faculty of Architecture of the University of Porto. [O]. Available at http://repositorio-aberto.up.pt/bitstream/10216/63242/2/3563.1.pdf (Accessed 5 June 2014)

Freeman, L., Rasolofohery, S., and Randriantovomanana, B. 2010. Patterns, Features and Impacts of rural-urban Migration in Antananarivo, Madagascar. Urban Rural Migration Report. [O]. Available at http://www.hayzara.org/eng/Knowledge-bank/Cross-Cutting-Themes/Patterns-Features-and-Impacts-of-rural-urban-Migration-in-Antananarivo-Madagascar (Accessed 15 May 2014)

Frescura, F. [sa]. Port Elizabeth – An Abridged History of the Apartheid City. [O]. Available at http://www.francofrescura.co.za/urban-issues-PE.html (Accessed 11 March 2014)

Friedman, F. 2000. Deconstructing Windhoek: The Urban Morphology of a Post-Apartheid City. [O]. Available at https://www.bartlett.ucl.ac.uk/dpu/publications/latest/publications/dpu-working-papers/wp111.pdf (Accessed 21 March 2014)

Gaopotlake, E. 2001. The Place of Culture in a City Centre. [O]. Available at http://www.collectionscanada.gc.ca/obj/s4/f2/dsk3/ftp04/MQ63515.pdf (Accessed 13 April 2014)

IHS. [sa]. Urbanising Africa: The city centre revisited experiences with inner-city revitalisation from Johannesburg (South Africa), Mbabane (Swaziland), Lusaka (Zambia), Harare and Bulawayo (Zimbabwe). IHS Working Papers. [O]. Available at http://www.ihs.nl/fileadmin/ASSETS/ihs/IHS_Publication/IHS_Working_Paper/IHS_WP_026_Ahmad_Ayala_Chirisa_Geurts_Magwaro_Muchindu_Ndlela_Nkonge_Sachs_Urbanising_Africa_the_city_centre_revisite.pdf (Accessed 14 April 2014)

Institut d'amenagement et d'urbanisme. [sa]. Tripoli City Centre's Urban and Architectural Charter. [O]. Available at http://www.iau-idf.fr/en/detail/etude/tripoli-city-centres-urban-and-architectural-charter-2.html (Accessed 2 May 2014)

Isichei, U. 2002. From and for Lagos. Archis. [O]. Available at volumeproject.org.

Joseph, M.C. 2011. Beyond modernist planning: Understanding urban street vending in Botswana. [O]. Available at http://www.rc21.org/conferences/amsterdam2011/edocs2/Session%205/5-1-Molefe.pdf (Accessed 21 May 2014)

Khoza, B.M. [sa]. Towards Sustainable Human Settlements Development: The Incremental Upgrading of Urban Informal Settlements. [O]. Available at http://wiredspace.wits.ac.za/bitstream/handle/10539/11949/Corrected%20Final%20Report.pdf?sequence=2 (Accessed 12 May 2014)

Kilani, M. 2009. Religious act, public space: reflections on some Geertzian concepts. The Journal of North African Studies, Vol. 14, No. 3–4, pp. 359–368. [O]. Available at http://dx.doi.org/10.1080/13629380902924000 (Accessed 5 June 2014)

King'Oriah, G.K. 1990. Historical and cultural impacts on the city structure of Mombasa, Kenya. [O]. Available at http://iaps.architexturez.net/system/files/pdf/iaps_10_1990_1_081.content.pdf

Lagae, J. 2013. Kinshasa. Tales of the tangible city. ABE Journal, Vol. 3/2013. [O]. Available at http://dev.abejournal.eu/index.php?id=378 (Accessed 12 March 2014)

Lagae, J. 2005. Rewriting Congo's Colonial Past: History, Memory, and Colonial Built Heritage in Lubumbashi, Democratic Republic of the Congo. Repenser les limites: l'architecture à travers l'espace, le temps et les disciplines, Paris, INHA (Actes de colloques), 2005 [Enligne], mis en ligne le 23 juin 2009, consulté le 08 juin 2014. [O]. Available at http://inha.revues.org/499

Landman, K. and Ntombela, N. 2006. Opening up spaces for the poor in the urban form: trends, challenges and their implications for access to urban land. Urban Land Mark Position Paper 7. [O]. Available at www.urbanlandmark.org.za

Leduka, C.R. 2012. Lesotho Urban Land Market Scoping Study. Institute of South African Studies. [O]. Available at http://www.urbanlandmark.org.za/research/x59.php (Accessed 4 June 2014)

Les Ateliers. [sa]. Porto Novo 2011: A strategy and urban design for the city centre. [O]. Available at http://www.ateliers.org/IMG/pdf/2_analysis_file_en-2.pdf (Accessed 4 June 2014)

Lund, F. and Skinner, C. 2004. Integrating the informal economy in urban planning and governance: A case study of the process of policy development in Durban, South Africa.[O]. Available at http://liverpool.metapress.com/content/6055652532574441 (Accessed 4 June 2014)

Marx, C. and Charlton, S. 2003. Report on the Durban CBD: Understanding Slums: Case Studies for the Global Report 2003 Durban, South Africa. UN-Habitat. [O]. Available at http://www.ucl.ac.uk/dpu-projects/Global_Report/pdfs/Durban.pdf (Accessed 7 June 2014)

McGuinness, J. 2000. Neighbourhood notes: Texture and streetscape in the Médina of Tunis. The Journal of North African Studies, Vol. 5, No. 4, pp. 97 120. [O]. Available at http://www.tandfonline.com/doi/abs/10.1080/13629380008718414 (Accessed 5 June 2014)

Morange, M. et al. 2012. The Spread of a Transnational Model: 'Gated Communities' in Three Southern African Cities (Cape Town, Maputo and Windhoek) International Journal of Urban and Regional Research Volume 36, Issue 5, September 2012, pp. 890914. [O]. Available at http://www.ijurr.org.

Nascimento, A. [sa]. Poverty, of course we have it. Notes for the analysis of an institutional conscience about poverty and microviolence in Cape Verdean contexts, for the Instituto de Investigacao Cientìfica Tropical, Centro de Estudos Africanos ISCTE-IUL, Lisbon. [O]. Available at http://www.portaldoconhecimento.gov.cv/bitstream/10961/432/1/'Poverty…,%20of%20course%20we%20have%20it…'%20Notes%20for%20the%20analysis%20of%20an%20institutional.pdf (Accessed 3 June 2014)

Niyonsenga, D. 2013. Urban planning and social inclusion, a study of Kigali city, Rwanda. Annual World Bank Conference on Land and Poverty 2013. The World Bank. Washington DC, April 8–11, 2013. [O]. Available at http://www.urbanafrica.net/resources/urban-planning-and-social-inclusion-study-kigali-city-rwanda/ (Accessed 4 July 2014)

Pantuliano, S., Assal, M., Elnaiem, B.A., McElhinney, H. and Schwab, M., with Elzein, Y. and Ali, H.M.M. 2011. City limits: Urbanisation and vulnerability in Sudan. Khartoum case study by the Humanitarian Policy Group. [O]. http://www.odi.org/sites/odi.org.uk/files/odi-assets/publications-opinion-files/6520.pdf (Accessed 4 June 2014)

Planet Earth. 2005. Megacities our global urban future. Earth Sciences for Society. [O]. Available: www.yearofplanetearth.org (Accessed 24 May 2014)

Ryan, V. 2006. Morocco – The Medina in Fez. [O]. Available at http://www.technologystudent.com/culture1/fez1.htm (Accessed 12 June 2014)

Saho, B. & Roberts, B. [sa]. Walking Tour of Banjul – A History of Major Architectural Works. [O]. Available at http://www.smcm.edu/gambia/Publication/pdfs/2000/11_BanjulTour-Saho-Roberts.pdf (Accessed 23 June 2014)

Salama, A. 2002. Contemporary Cairo demystified. A critical voice on architecture and urbanism. [O]. Available at volumeproject.org (Accessed 13 June 2014)

Salat, S. 2010. Sustainable Arabic Urban Design at Neighborhood Scale, a Morphological Approach, Urban Morphology Lab, Sustainable Architecture and Urban Development, Amman. [O]. Available at http://urbanmorphologylab.com/proceedings/sustainable-arabic-urban-design-at-neighborhood-scale-a-morphological-approach-by-salat (Accessed 15 May 2014)

Schensul, D. & Heller, P. 2011. Legacies, Change and Transformation in the Post-Apartheid City: Towards an Urban Sociological Cartography. International Journal of Urban and Regional Research. Volume 35 Issue 1. [O]. Available online at http://www.ijurr.org

Stewart, D. 1999. Changing Cairo: The political economy of urban form. International Journal of Urban and Regional Research, Mar 1999, Vol. 23, No. 1, p. 128. [O]. Available at http://www.iupui.edu/~anthkb/a104/egypt/cairodevel.htm (Accessed 29 May 2014)

Temehu Tourism Services. [sa]. Tripoli: The Bride of the Mediterranean. [O]. Available at http://www.temehu.com/Cities_sites/Tripoli.htm

UN-HABITAT. 2000. The Gambia: National Urban Profile. International Journal of Urban and Regional Research. Vol. 24, 4 December 2000.

UNESCO CSI Pilot Project report, 2000 as accessed from www.unesco.org

UNESCO at http://whc.unesco.org/en/statesparties/CV/

UN Framework on Climate Change accessed at unfccc.int

UN-Habitat. 2014. The State of African Cities Report 2014: Re-imagining sustainable urban transitions. Kenya: United Nations Human Settlements Programme (UN-Habitat).

Van Oers, R. 2013. Swahili historic urban landscapes. Paris: United Nations Educational, Scientific and Cultural Organization (UNESCO). [O]. Available at http://unesdoc.unesco.org/images/0022/002228/222842e.pdf (Accessed 15 April 2014)

Windhoek Municipality. 1996. The Windhoek Structure Plan. [O]. Available at http://www.polytechnic.edu.na/academics/schools/engine_infotech/civil/lecturing/upd410s_module/(11.4)Windhoek%20Structure%20Plan%20Report.pdf (Accessed 17 May 2014)

Zychowska, M.J. [sa]. Saved Phenomenon (unpublished PhD thesis of Cracow University of Thechnology). [O]. Available at http://suw.biblos.pk.edu.pl/resources/i5/i5/i3/i1/r5531/ZychowskaM _Saved-Phenomenon.pdf (Accessed 12 April 2014)

Books, journals, research papers and encyclopedias

Abiodun O.J. 1997. The challenges of growth and development in metropolitan Lagos, in Rakodi, C. (ed.). The Urban Challenge in Africa. Growth and management of its large cities. Tokyo New York Paris: United Nations University Press.

Adebayo, A.A. 2002. The Streets of Africa: A search for identity and sustainability. Archis, Vol. 187: pp. 20-31.

Ahmad, A.M. 1992. The neighborhoods of Khartoum reflections on their functions, forms and future. Habitat Intl., Vol. 16, No. 4, pp. 27–45. Great Britain: Pergamon Press.

Akinyeye, O.et al. 1999. Eko, Landmarks of Lagos, Nigeria. Lagos: Mandilas Group.

Ambrose, D. 1993. Maseru: An illustrated history. Morija: Morija Museum & Archives.

Awosika, L.F.et al. 1993. Coastlines of western Africa. American Society of Civil Engineers.

Baumeister, J. and Knebel, K. 2009. The African Inner City: [Re]sourced. The Indigenous Urban Tissue of Addis Ababa – A City Model for the Future Growth of African Metropolis. African Perspectives 2009.

Bekker, S. and Therborn, G. (eds.). 2012. Power and Powerlessness: Capital Cities in Africa. Cape Town: HSRC and CODESRIA.

Bissell, W.C. 2000. Conservation & the colonial past – urban planning, space & power in Zanzibar in Anderson, D. and Rathbone, R. (eds.). Africa's Urban past. Oxford: James Currey.

Chattopadhyay, S. and White, J. (eds.). 2014. City Halls and Civic Materialism: Towards a Global History of Urban Public Space. London: Routledge.

Chipkin, C.1993. Johannesburg Style: Architecture and Society 1880s–1960s. Cape Town: David Phillip.

Chipkin, C. 2008. Johannesburg Transition. Architecture & Society from 1950. Johannesburg: STE Publishers.

Dewar, D. & Uytenbogaardt, R.S. 1991. South African Cities: A manifesto for change. Urban Problems Research Unit, University of Cape Town. Cape Town: s.n.

Dewar, Uytenbogaardt, Hutton-Squire, Levy & Menidis. [sa]. Housing –A comparative evaluation of urbanism in Cape Town. Cape Town: s.n.

Dichter, T. 2009. Are we there yet? Geertz, Morocco, and modernization. The Journal of North African Studies, Vol. 14, No. 3–4, pp. 543–557.

Djibril, K., Yun, Q., Ousmane, D. and Xiangrong, W. 2012. Processes and challenges of urban development in Côte d'Ivoire (Africa) with case study of Abidjan City. Journal of Geography and Regional Planning, Vol. 5, No. 13, pp. 353–361, 4 July, 2012.

Dubresson, A. 1997. Chapter 8 Abidjan: From the public making of a modern city to urban management of a metropolis in Rakodi, C. (ed.). 1997. The Urban Challenge in Africa: Growth and Management of its Large Cities. Tokyo, New York, Paris: United Nations University Press.

Elleh, N. 2002. Architecture and Power in Africa. United States of America: Praeger.

Fisher, R.C., Le Roux, S. and Maré, E. (eds.). 1998. Architecture of the Transvaal. Pretoria: UNISA.

Freund, B. 2001. Contrasts in Urban Segregation: A Tale of Two African Cities, Durban (South Africa) and Abidjan (Côte d'Ivoire). Journal of Southern African Studies, Vol. 27, No.3, September 2001.

Fuller, M. 2000. Preservation and self-absorption: Italian Colonisation and the Walled City of Tripoli, Libya. The Journal of North African Studies, Vol. 5, No. 4, pp. 121–154.

George, C. 2010. Challenges of Lagos as a mega-city. Daily Independent as published on 21 Feb 2010.

Gerke, W. J. C. and Viljoen, C. J., 1968. Master Plan for Lilongwe: the Capital City of Malawi. Johannesburg: Imex.

Gervais-Lambony, P. in Bekker, S. and Therborn,G. (eds.). 2012. Power and Powerlessness: Capital Cities in Africa. Cape Town: HSRC and CODESRIA.

Holm, D. 1998. Kerkplaats and Capitalist, in Fisher, R.C., Le Roux, S. and Maré, E. (eds.). 1998. Architecture of the Transvaal. Pretoria: UNISA.

Hudgens, J., Richard, T. 2003. A Rough Guide to West Africa. Edition: 4: 2003, pp. 1047–1048; Rough Guide.

Hull, R. 1976. African Cities and Towns before the European Conquest. New York: W.W. Norton.

Jordaan, G. 1989. Pretoria as 'Urbs Quadrata'. Architecture SA May/June 1989, pp. 26–29.

Le Roux, S. (ed.) and Botes, N. 1991. Plekke en Geboue van Pretoria. Vol. 2. Pretoria: Stadsraad van Pretoria.

Le Roux, S. (ed.) and Botes, N. 1993. Plekke en Geboue van Pretoria. Vol. 3. Pretoria: Stadsraad van Pretoria.

Machobane, L. B. B. J.1990. Government and Change in Lesotho, 1800–1966: A Study of Political Institutions. London: Macmillan.

Megahed, N. 2014. Heritage-based sustainability in Port Said: Classification of Styles and Future Development. International Journal of Architectural Research Archnet-IJAR, Vol. 8, No. 1, pp. 94–107.

Miller, S.G. 2009. Of time and the city: Clifford Geertz on urban history. The Journal of North African Studies, Vol. 14, No. 3–4, pp. 479–490.

Mjojo, B.1989. Urban Development: The Case of Lilongwe 1920–1964. University of Malawi Chancellor College History Department Seminar Series, Paper no. 12, Zomba.

Norberg-Schulz, C. 1980. Genius Loci. London: Academy Editions.

O'Connor, A. 1983. The African City. London: Hutchinson.

Peil, M. 1991. Lagos. The City is the People. London: Belhaven Press.

Phillipson, D. 1997. The Monuments of Aksum. Addis Ababa: Addis Ababa University Press.

Potts, D.1985. The Development of Malawi's New Capital at Lilongwe: a Comparison with Other New African Capitals, Comparative Urban Research, vol. 10, no. 2, pp. 42–56.

Potts, D.1986. Urbanization in Malawi with Special Reference to the New Capital City of Lilongwe, unpublished PhD thesis, University College London.

Raftani, K. and Radoine, H. The Architecture of the Hammams of Fez, Morocco. International Journal of Architectural Research Archnet-IJAR, Vol. 2, No. 3.

Rakodi, C. (ed.). 1997. The Urban Challenge in Africa: Growth and Management of its Large Cities. Tokyo, New York, Paris: United Nations University Press.

Rifkind, D. 2011. Gondar – Architecture and Urbanism for Italy's Fascist Empire. JSAH, Vol. 70, No. 4, pp. 492511.

Said, E. 2002. Access regulation in Islamic urbanism: The case of medieval Fès. The Journal of North African Studies, Vol. 7, No. 3, pp. 119–134.

Schoeman, K. 1980. Bloemfontein – die Ontstaan van 'n Stad 1846–1946. Cape Town: Human & Rousseau.

Sebego, R.J. and Gwebu, T.D. 2013. Patterns, determinants, impacts and policy implications of the spatial expansion of an African capital city: The Greater Gaborone example. International Journal of Sustainable Built Environment & The Unsustainable Urban Growth of Gaborone City, Botswana.

Seekings, J. and Freund, B. 2001. Introduction: Urban Studies in South Africa after Apartheid. Contrasts in Urban Segregation: A Tale of Two African Cities, Durban (South Africa) and Abidjan (Côte d'Ivoire). Journal of Southern African Studies (2001), Vol. 27, No.3, pp. 527–546.

Shetaway, A.A. and Dief-Allah, D.M.A. 2006. Restoration of the Avenue of the Sphinxes: Between Government Enforcement and Local Rejection in Luxor, Egypt. Journal of Al Azhar University Engineering Sector. Vol. 9, No.3, July 2006, pp. 887–901.

Songsore, J. [sa]. The Urban Transformation in Ghana: Urbanization, National Development and Poverty Reduction. Department of Geography and Resource Development, University of Ghana, Legon-Accra, Ghana.

Myers, G. 2011. African Cities – Alternative visions of urban theory and practice. London: Zed Books.

Stock, R. 2013. Africa South of the Sahara: A Geographical Interpretation. New York: The Guildford Press.

Van der Westhuizen, D. 2011. Colonial conceptions and space in the evolution of a city: evidence from the city of Bloemfontein, 1846–1946. SAJAH, Vol. 26, No. 3, pp. 90–103.

Wekwete, K.H.1988. Development of urban planning in Zimbabwe. Butterworth: Butterworth.

Zewde, B in Simone, A.M. and Abouhani, A (eds.). Urban Africa – Changing contours of Survival in the city, pp. 121–137. Dakar: Codesria Books.

Exhibitions

Ali, R. and Cross, A. 2014. Mogadishu – Lost Moderns. London: The Mosaic Rooms.

Additional websites accessed

http://www.urbanafrica.net
http://unu.edu
http://www.hpip.org
http://www.swazi.com/mbabane2000/development.html
http://www.capeverde.com/islands/fogo.html
http://lynnecooneydakarurbandevelopment.blogspot.com
http://www.omartake.com/images/nigeria.pdf
http://africanurbanism.net/2014/05/31/dakar-goree-tourism/
http://www.britannica.com/EBchecked/topic/218691/Freetown
http://www.rehabimed.net/Publicacions/Operacio_Kairouan/EN/02.The%20city%20of%20Kairouan.pdf
http://www.capetown.at/heritage/history/1910_dev_plan_art.htm
http://www.world-guides.com/africa/north-africa/libya/libya_attractions.html
http://en.wikipedia.org/wiki/Tripoli
http://www.tripadvisor.com/Travel-g293807-s201/Tripoli:Libya:Architecture.html
http://oubangui.blogspot.com
http://en.wikipedia.org/wiki/Casablanca
http://casablanca.cityseekr.com/cityguide/district-guide-1
http://en.wikipedia.org/wiki/Fes
http://www.insightguides.com/destinations/africa-middle-east/morocco/fez/overview
http://goafrica.about.com/od/moroccotopattractions/a/fesguide.htm
http://whc.unesco.org/en/list/170
http://en.wikipedia.org/wiki/Marrakesh
http://www.destination360.com/africa/morocco/marrakesh
http://whc.unesco.org/en/list/331 (Medina of Marrakesh)
http://whc.unesco.org/en/list/793
http://www.journeybeyondtravel.com/news/morocco-travel/meknes-morocco-travel.html
http://www.ovpm.org/en/morrocco/meknes
Morocco's Imperial Cities Revealed (http://www.journeybeyond travel.com/news/morocco-travel/morocco-imperial-cities.html)
http://en.wikipedia.org/wiki/Rabat
http://whc.unesco.org/en/list/1401
(http://www.boidus.co.uk/?p=1188)
http://en.wikipedia.org/wiki/Gaborone
http://boidus.co.bw/blog/?p=1738
http://en.wikipedia.org/wiki/History_of_Gaborone
http://www.cometotunisia.co.uk/regions-cities/tunis-around
http://en.wikipedia.org/wiki/Tunis
http://mmegiwritings.blogspot.com/2013/01/planning-history-of-gaborone-july-2012.html
http://en.wikipedia.org/wiki/Durban
http://www.southafrica.com/kwazulu-natal/durban/francis-farewell/
http://en.wikipedia.org/wiki/Maseru
http://www.golesotho.co.za/Other%20Pages/Maseru.html
http://en.wikipedia.org/wiki/Mbabane
http://en.wikipedia.org/wiki/Windhoek
http://www.namibia-travel.net/travelguide/central-namibia/windhoek.html
http://en.wikipedia.org/wiki/Abobo
http://www.akwaba-ci.net/index2.php?n=72&page=dos
http://www.rezoivoire.net/cotedivoire/ville/63/la-commune-d-abobo.html#.U60pBRblduY
http://en.wikipedia.org/wiki/Banjul
http://justgambia.com/excursions/banjul/
http://www.stephencodrington.com/TravelDiaries/West_Africa_2014_33.html
http://en.wikipedia.org/wiki/Accra
http://www.modernghana.com/news/469124/1/accra-airport-city-on-the-fast-lane.html
http://www.theguardian.com/cities/2014/mar/04/accra-stable-vibrant-optimistic
http://ww2.unhabitat.org/programmes/uef/cities/summary/accra.htm
http://www.worldbank.org/
http://www.geoatlas.com
http://www.lib.utexas.edu
google earth pro

Die *Deutsche Bibliothek* lists this publication in the *Deutsche Nationalbibliografie*; detailed bibliographic data is available on the internet at http://dnb.d-nb.de

ISBN 978-3-86922-423-7

© 2015 by DOM publishers, Berlin
www.dom-publishers.com

All rights reserved. No part of this book may be reproduced or transmitted in any form or by any electronic or mechanical means, including photocopying and recording, or by any other information storage or retrieval system, without written permission from the publisher.

Unless otherwise stated, area, population and density refer to the city area, not the metro area. Every effort has been made to ensure the accuracy of the information contained in this publication. The compilers welcome additional information or corrections.

Contributors
Gary White, Bouwer Serfontein, Marguerite Pienaar, Gerrit Jordaan, Claudia Filipe, Ilze Wessels, Anja Bredell-Olivier, Nicola Patrick, Craig Mitchell, Jacques Mouton, Ferdi Le Grange, Leone Pieters, Micheal Lotter, Nicci Labuschagne, Duard Burger, Tessa Dodds, Freddy Douglas, Dominique Peel

Proofreading
Danél Hanekom

Design
Hanli Deysel

Acknowledgements
University of Pretoria's Urban Research Group within the Department of Architecture

Printing
Tiger Printing (Hong Kong) Co., Ltd
www.tigerprinting.hk

Gary White, born 1966, architect and urban designer. Co-founder of South African-based Africa Drawn Project, which focuses on researching, visualising, and curating cities in Africa. Trained as an architect at the University of the Free State (BArch 1991) and as urban designer at the University of Cape Town (MCPUD 1993), he has worked in practice and academia for 23 years. Lives in Pretoria and works across Sub-Sahara Africa. Currently Director at GWA/HolmJordaan.

Marguerite Pienaar, born 1977, architect. Co-founder of MoMa Architects and senior researcher for South African-based Africa Drawn Project, which focuses on researching, visualising, and curating cities in Africa. Trained as an architect at the University of the Free State (BArch 2001) and Pretoria University (MArch 2013 Research), she has worked in practice and academia for 13 years. Lives in Pretoria and works across Sub-Sahara Africa. Currently Director at GWA/HolmJordaan.

Bouwer Serfontein, born 1977, architect. Co-founder of South African-based Africa Drawn Project, which focuses on researching, visualising, and curating cities in Africa. Trained as an architect at the Tshwane University of Technology (MTech Arch Prof 2006), he has worked in practice and academia for nine years. Lives in Johannesburg and Stuttgart, works in Europe and Sub-Sahara Africa. Currently Director at GWA/HolmJordaan.